Volume I The Pre-Marxist Period, 1912-1920

MAO'S ROAD TO POWER

Revolutionary Writings 1912·1949

This volume was prepared under the auspices of
the John King Fairbank Center for East Asian Research
Harvard University

The project for the translation of Mao Zedong's pre-1949 writings
has been supported by a grant from the National Endowment
for the Humanities, an independent federal agency.

The Cover

The calligraphy on the cover has been reproduced from the manuscript of Mao's foreword of 1917 to a volume by his friend Xiao Zisheng (Siao-yu), entitled *All in One* self-study notes. In this passage, he compares Chinese and Western approaches to learning. Our English translation can be found below, from "The defect of our country's ancient learning . . ." in the next-to-last line of p. 128, to ". . . will not be able to attain excellence," in line 11 of p. 129.

Volume I The Pre-Marxist Period, 1912-1920

MAO'S ROAD TO POWER

Revolutionary Writings 1912·1949

Stuart R. Schram, Editor

An East Gate Book

M.E. Sharpe

Armonk, New York
London, England

An East Gate Book

Library of Congress Cataloging-in-Publication Data

Mao, Tse-tung, 1893–1976.
[Selections. English. f1992]
Mao's road to power : revolutionary writings 1912–1949 / Stuart R. Schram, editor.
v. <1>
Vol. 1, translation of: Mao Tse-tung tsao ch'i wen kao, 1912.6–1920.11, and other Chinese sources
Includes bibliographical references and index.
Contents: v. 1. The pre-Marxist period, 1912–1920—
ISBN 1-56324-049-1 (v. 1); ISBN 1-56324-457-8 (p)
I. Schram, Stuart R. II. Title.
DS778.M3A25 1992
951.04—dc20
92-26783
CIP

Printed in the United States of America

The paper used in this publication meets the minimum requirements of American National Standard for Information Sciences— Permanence of Paper for Printed Library Materials, ANSI Z 39.48-1984.

∞

BB (c) 10 9 8 7 6 5 4 3 2
BB (p) 10 9 8 7 6 5 4 3 2 1

Contents

1919

Acknowledgments

Major funding for this project has been provided by the National Endowment for the Humanities, from which we have received two generous grants, one for the period from 1989 to 1991, and one for 1991–1993. Many individual and corporate donors, including the Harvard-Yenching Institute, James R. Houghton, James O. Welch, Jr., William S. Youngman, Dr. Park Un-Tae, Ambassador Yangsoo Yoo, and Robert H. Morehouse have also contributed substantially toward the required cost-sharing element of our budget. We also wish to thank the Committee on Scholarly Communication with the People's Republic of China, which provided the grant (paid by the U.S. Information Agency) for a visit to China in September–November 1991 by the editor of these volumes, Stuart Schram, to consult Chinese scholars and obtain information relevant to the work of the project.

Translations of the materials included in this volume have been drafted by many different hands. Bill Wycoff devoted himself to this work full time from 1989 to 1991. Other translators were, in alphabetical order, Hsuan Delorme, Li Jin, Li Yuwei, Lin Chun, Amy Mayer, Pei Minxin, Tian Dongdong, Wang Xisu, Ye Yang, Zhang Aiping, and Zheng Shiping. Bill Wycoff made a contribution to the editorial work on the volume. Sidney Tai provided expert and meticulous guidance regarding the rendering of early texts in the literary style. Michele Grant, Research Assistant in 1990–1991, drafted many of the notes, and also helped with the editing. Nancy Hodes, Research Assistant in 1991–1992, participated in textual revision and annotation. Her contribution to the checking of the final translations against the Chinese originals was of exceptional value. In a few cases, she also made translations, as did Stuart Schram. Final responsibility for accuracy and literary quality rests with him as editor.

This project was launched with the active participation of Roderick MacFarquhar, Director of the Fairbank Center until June 30, 1992. Without his organizing ability and continuing wholehearted support, it would never have come to fruition.

The general introduction to the series, and the introduction to Volume I, were written by Stuart Schram, who wishes to acknowledge his very great indebtedness to Benjamin Schwartz, a pioneer in the study of Mao Zedong's thought. Professor Schwartz read successive drafts of these two introductions, and on each occasion made stimulating and thoughtful comments which have greatly improved the final versions. For any remaining errors and inadequacies, the fault lies once again with the editor.

GENERAL INTRODUCTION

Mao Zedong and the Chinese Revolution, 1912–1949

Mao Zedong stands out as one of the dominant figures of the twentieth century. Guerrilla leader, strategist, conqueror, ruler, poet, and philosopher, he placed his imprint on China, and on the world. This edition of Mao's writings provides abundant documentation in his own words regarding both his life and his thought. Because of the central role of Mao's ideas and actions in the turbulent course of the Chinese revolution, it thus offers a rich body of historical data about China in the first half of the twentieth century.

The process of change and upheaval in China which Mao sought to master had been going on for roughly a century by the time he was born in 1893. Its origins lay in the incapacity of the old order to cope with the population explosion at the end of the eighteenth century, and with other economic and social problems, as well as in the shock administered by the Opium War of 1840 and further European aggression and expansion thereafter.

Mao's native Hunan Province was crucially involved both in the struggles of the Qing dynasty to maintain its authority, and in the radical ferment which led to successive challenges to the imperial system. Thus on the one hand, the Hunan Army of the great conservative viceroy Zeng Guofan was the main instrument for putting down the Taiping Rebellion and saving the dynasty in the middle of the nineteenth century. But on the other hand, the most radical of the late nineteenth-century reformers, and the only one to lay down his life in 1898, Tan Sitong, was also a Hunanese, as was Huang Xing, whose contribution to the revolution of 1911 was arguably as great as that of Sun Yatsen.[1] In his youth, Mao profoundly admired all three of these men, though they stood for very different things: Zeng for the empire and the Confucian values which sustained it, Tan for defying tradition and seeking inspiration in the West, Huang for Western-style constitutional democracy.

1. On Zeng, see the notes to Mao's "Classroom Notes" of 1913, and to his letter of August 23, 1917, to Li Jinxi. On Tan, see "Zhang Kundi's Record of Two Talks with Mao Zedong" of September 1917. On Huang, see the "Letter to Miyazaki Tōten" of March 1917. On Sun, see Mao's "Letter to Xiao Zisheng" of July 25, 1916. (All of these texts appear in Vol. I of this series.)

Apart from Mao's strong Hunanese patriotism, which inclined him to admire eminent figures from his own province, he undoubtedly saw these three as forceful and effective leaders who, each in his own way, fought to assure the future of China. Any sense that they were contradictory symbols would have been diminished by the fact that from an early age Mao never advocated exclusive reliance on either Chinese or Western values, but repeatedly sought a synthesis of the two. In August 1917, Mao Zedong expressed the view that despite the "antiquated" and otherwise undesirable traits of the Chinese mentality, "Western thought is not necessarily all correct either; very many parts of it should be transformed at the same time as Oriental thought."[2] In a sense, this sentence sums up the problem he sought to resolve throughout his whole career: How could China develop an advanced civilization, and become rich and powerful, while remaining Chinese?

As shown by the texts contained in Volume I, Mao's early exposure to "Westernizing" influences was not limited to Marxism. Other currents of European thought played a significant role in his development. Whether he was dealing with liberalism or Leninism, however, Mao tenaciously sought to adapt and transform these ideologies, even as he espoused them and learned from them.

Mao Zedong played an active and significant role in the movement for political and intellectual renewal which developed in the aftermath of the patriotic student demonstrations of May 4, 1919, against the transfer of German concessions in China to Japan. This "new thought tide," which had begun to manifest itself at least as early as 1915, dominated the scene from 1919 onward, and prepared the ground for the triumph of radicalism and the foundation of the Chinese Communist Party in 1921. But though Mao enthusiastically supported the call of Chen Duxiu, who later became the Party's first leader, for the Western values incarnated by "Mr. Science" and "Mr. Democracy," he never wholly endorsed the total negation of Chinese culture advocated by many people during the May Fourth period.[3] His condemnations of the old thought as backward and slavish are nearly always balanced by a call to learn from both Eastern and Western thought and to develop something new out of these twin sources.

In 1919 and 1920, Mao leaned toward anarchism rather than socialism. Only in January 1921 did he at last draw the explicit conclusion that anarchism would not work, and that Russia's proletarian dictatorship represented the model which must be followed. Half the remaining fifty-five years of his life were devoted to creating such a dictatorship, and the other half to deciding what to do with it, and how to overcome the defects which he perceived in it. From beginning to end of this process, Mao drew upon Chinese experience and Chinese civilization in revising and reforming this Western import.

2. Letter of August 23, 1917, to Li Jinxi, in Vol. I.

3. On Chen Duxiu and his role in the May Fourth movement, see "The Arrest and Rescue of Chen Duxiu," in Vol. I.

To the extent that, from the 1920s onward, Mao was a committed Leninist, his understanding of the doctrine shaped his vision of the world. But to the extent that, although he was a communist revolutionary, he always "planted his backside on the body of China,"[4] ideology alone did not exhaustively determine his outlook. One of Mao Zedong's most remarkable attributes was the extent to which he linked theory and practice. He was in some respects not a very good Marxist, but few men have ever applied so well Marx's dictum that the vocation of the philosopher is not merely to understand the world, but to change it.

It is reliably reported that Mao's close collaborators tried in vain, during the Yan'an period, to interest him in writings by Marx such as *The 18 Brumaire of Louis Bonaparte*. To such detailed historical analyses based on economic and social facts, he preferred *The Communist Manifesto*, of which he saw the message as "*Jieji douzheng, jieji douzheng, jieji douzheng*!" (Class struggle, class struggle, class struggle!) In other words, for Mao the essence of Marxism resided in the fundamental idea of the struggle between oppressor and oppressed as the motive force of history.

Such a perspective offered many advantages. It opened the door to the immediate pursuit of revolutionary goals, since even though China did not have a very large urban proletariat, there was no lack of oppressed people to be found there. It thus eliminated the need for the Chinese to feel inferior, or to await salvation from without, just because their country was still stuck in some precapitalist stage of development (whether "Asiatic" or "feudal"). And, by placing the polarity "oppressor/oppressed" at the heart of the revolutionary ideology itself, this approach pointed toward a conception in which landlord oppression, and the oppression of China by the imperialists, were perceived as the two key targets of the struggle.

Mao displayed, in any case, a remarkably acute perception of the realities of Chinese society, and consistently adapted his ideas to those realities, at least during the struggle for power. In the early years after its foundation in 1921, the Chinese Communist Party sought support primarily from the working class in the cities and adopted a strategy based on a "united front" or alliance with Sun Yatsen's Guomindang. Mao threw himself into this enterprise with enthusiasm and served first as a labor union organizer in Hunan in 1922, and then as a high official within the Guomindang organization in 1924. Soon, however, he moved away from this perspective, and even before urban-based revolution was put down in blood by Chiang Kaishek in 1927, he asserted that the real center of gravity of Chinese society was to be found in the countryside. From this fact, he drew the conclusion that the decisive blows against the existing reactionary order must be struck in the countryside by the peasants.

4. Mao Zedong, "Ruhe yanjiu Zhonggong dangshi" (How to study the history of the Chinese Communist Party), lecture of March 1942, published in *Dangshi yanjiu* (Research on Party History), No. 1, 1980, pp. 2–7.

By August 1927, Mao had concluded that mobilizing the peasant masses was not enough. A red army was also necessary to serve as the spearhead of revolution, and so he put forward the slogan: "Political power comes out of the barrel of a gun." In the mountain fastness of the Jinggangshan Base Area in Jiangxi Province, to which he retreated at the end of 1927 with the remnants of his forces, he began to elaborate a comprehensive strategy for rural revolution, combining land reform with the tactics of guerrilla warfare. In this he was aided by Zhu De, a professional soldier who had joined the Chinese Communist Party and soon became known as the "commander-in-chief." These tactics rapidly achieved a considerable measure of success. The "Chinese Soviet Republic," established in 1931 in a larger and more populous area of Jiangxi, survived for several years, though when Chiang Kaishek finally devised the right strategy and mobilized his crack troops against it, the Communists were defeated and forced to embark in 1934 on the Long March.

By this time, Mao Zedong had been reduced virtually to the position of a figurehead by the Moscow-trained members of the so-called "Internationalist" faction, who dominated the leadership of the Chinese Communist Party. At a conference held at Zunyi in January 1935, in the course of the Long March, Mao began his comeback. Soon he was once again in effective charge of military operations, though he became chairman of the Party only in 1943.

Mao's vision of the Chinese people as a whole as the victim of oppression now came decisively into play. Japanese aggression led in 1936 to the Xi'an Incident, in which Chiang Kaishek was kidnapped in order to force him to oppose the invader. This event was the catalyst which produced a second "united front" between the Communists and the Guomindang. Without it, Mao Zedong and the forces he led might well have remained a side current in the remote and backward region of Shaanxi, or even been exterminated altogether. As it was, the collaboration of 1937–1945, however perfunctory and opportunistic on both sides, gave Mao the occasion to establish himself as a patriotic national leader. Above all, the resulting context of guerrilla warfare behind the Japanese lines allowed the Communists to build a foundation of political and military power throughout wide areas of northern and central China.

During the years in Yan'an, from 1937 to 1946, Mao Zedong also finally consolidated his own dominant position in the Chinese Communist Party, and in particular his role as the ideological mentor of the Party. Beginning in November 1936, he seized the opportunity to read a number of writings by Chinese Marxists, and Soviet works in Chinese translation, which had been published while he was struggling for survival a few years earlier. These provided the stimulus for the elaboration of his own interpretation of Marxism-Leninism, and in particular for his theory of contradictions. Another of the main features of his thought, the emphasis on practice as the source of knowledge, had long been in evidence and had found expression in the sociological surveys in the countryside which he himself carried out beginning as early as 1926.

In 1938, Mao called for the "Sinification of Marxism," that is, the modification not only of its language but of its substance in order to adapt it to Chinese culture and Chinese realities. By 1941, he had begun to suggest that he himself had carried out this enterprise, and to attack those in the Party who preferred to translate ready-made formulas from the Soviet Union. The "Rectification Campaign" of 1942–43 was designed in large measure to change the thinking of such "Internationalists," or to eliminate them from positions of influence.

When Mao was elected chairman of the Politburo and of the Secretariat in March 1943, the terms of his appointment to this second post contained a curious provision: Mao alone, as chairman, could out-vote the other two members of the Secretariat in case of disagreement. This was the first step toward setting Mao above and apart from all other Party members and thereby opening the way to the subsequent cult. At the Seventh Party Congress in April 1945 came apotheosis: Mao Zedong's thought was written into the Party statutes as the guide to all work, and Mao was hailed as the greatest theoretical genius in China's history for his achievement in creating such a remarkable doctrine.

In 1939–1940, Mao had put forward the slogan "New Democracy" and defined it as a regime in which proletariat (read Communist Party) and bourgeoisie (read Guomindang) would jointly exercise dictatorship over reactionary and pro-Japanese elements in Chinese society. Moreover, as late as 1945, when the Communists were still in a weaker position than the Guomindang, Mao indicated that this form of rule would be based on free elections with universal suffrage. Later, when the Communist Party had military victory within its grasp and was in a position to do things entirely in its own way, Mao would state forthrightly, in "On People's Democratic Dictatorship," that such a dictatorship could in fact just as well be called a "People's Democratic Autocracy." In other words, it was to be democratic only in the sense that it served the people's interests; in form, it was to exercise its authority through a "powerful state apparatus."

In 1946, when the failure of General George Marshall's attempts at mediation led to renewed civil war, Mao and his comrades revived the policies of land reform which had been suspended during the alliance with the Guomindang, and thereby recreated a climate of agrarian revolution. Thus national and social revolution were interwoven in the strategy which ultimately brought final victory in 1949.

In March 1949, Mao declared that though the Chinese revolution had previously taken the path of surrounding the cities from the countryside, henceforth the building of socialism would take place in the orthodox way, with leadership and enlightenment radiating outward from the cities to the countryside. Looking at the twenty-seven years under Mao's leadership after 1949, however, the two most striking developments — the chiliastic hopes of instant plenty which characterized the Great Leap Forward of the late 1950s, and the anxiety about the corrupting effects of material progress, coupled with a nostalgia for "military communism," which underlay the Cultural Revolution — both bore the mark of rural utopianism. Thus Mao's road to power, though it led to total victory over the Nationalists, also cultivated in Mao himself, and in the Party, attitudes which would subsequently engender great problems.

Revolution in its Leninist guise has loomed large in the world for most of the twentieth century, and the Chinese revolution has been, with the Russian revolution, one of its two most important manifestations. The Bolshevik revolution set a pattern long regarded as the only standard of communist orthodoxy, but the revolutionary process in China was in some respects even more remarkable. Although communism is now widely seen as bankrupt throughout much of the world, the impact of Mao is still a living reality in China more than two decades after his death. Particularly since the Tiananmen events of June 1989, the continuing relevance of Mao's political and ideological heritage has been stressed ever more heavily by the Chinese leadership. Interest in Mao Zedong has been rekindled in some sectors of the population, and elements of a new Mao cult have even emerged.

Though the ultimate impact of these recent trends remains problematic, the problem of how to come to terms with the modern world, while retaining China's own identity, still represents perhaps the greatest challenge facing the Chinese. Mao did not solve it, but he boldly grappled with the political and intellectual challenge of the West as no Chinese ruler before him had done. If Lenin has suffered the ultimate insult of being replaced by Peter the Great as the symbol of Russian national identity, it could be argued that Mao cannot, like Lenin, be supplanted by a figure analogous to Peter because he himself played the role of China's first modernizing and Westernizing autocrat. However misguided many of Mao's ideas, and however flawed his performance, his efforts in this direction will remain a benchmark to a people still struggling to define their place in the community of nations.

INTRODUCTION

The Writings of Mao Zedong, 1912–1920

Mao Zedong was born in the village of Shaoshan, Hunan Province, on December 26, 1893. The first text included in this volume of our edition was therefore written at the age of eighteen, and the last text just before he turned twenty-seven.

Prior to 1912, Mao had undergone varied experiences, from working on the farm of his father, a relatively well-to-do but ill-educated peasant with little sympathy for his son's interest in learning, to half a year as a soldier in the revolutionary army, following the anti-Manchu uprising of October 10, 1911. He had also been able to study a little, first at the village school and then at a nearby higher primary school, but his education really began after his discharge from the army.

After trying police, soap-making, law, and commercial schools, Mao enrolled at First Provincial Middle School in Changsha, where he learned some traditional history (as evidenced by his class essay, discussed below, on Shang Yang). Half a year later, in a characteristic gesture, he withdrew from this school and spent six months reading independently in the provincial library, where he first encountered many Western writers in translation. In 1913, he entered Fourth Provincial Normal School, a teacher training institution at the secondary level. This merged in the spring of 1914 with First Provincial Normal School, from which Mao graduated in June 1918.

In many respects, "First Normal" shaped Mao's mind for life. There he acquired much of the learning he later possessed, both Chinese and Western, and also encountered several teachers whose ideas and ideals exerted a lasting influence on him. It was there, too, that he played a leading role in the foundation of the "New People's Study Society," a student organization which rapidly evolved toward the left and was to produce many future members of the Chinese Communist Party.

In the winter of 1918–19, after graduation, Mao visited the capital, Beijing, stopping off in Shanghai on the way back. Then, returning to Hunan, he participated actively in the "May Fourth" student movement, which constituted such a decisive watershed in Chinese political and cultural history.[1]

1. A brief characterization of the May Fourth movement can be found in the preceding General Introduction. See also Mao's article of July 1919, "The Arrest and Rescue of Chen Duxiu," and the notes thereto.

After a second visit to Beijing in the winter of 1919–1920, Mao made another more extended stay in Shanghai, where he discussed Marxism with Chen Duxiu, who became in the following year the first leader of the Chinese Communist Party. He then returned to Changsha to take up a position as principal of the primary school attached to First Normal School. Though in responding to a questionnaire as late as December 1921, he listed his proposed career as education, his life was in fact to be largely dominated by politics from 1920 on.

Mao's explicit commitment to Marxism and communism falls just after the date of the last text included in this volume.[2] Mao Zedong's thought during this pre-Marxist period had many facets, and underwent kaleidoscopic change. The 250,000 words of texts in this volume will, of course, admit of various interpretations, but their availability has moved the study of Mao Zedong's early thought once and for all from the realm of myth to the realm of history. From these richly textured materials, a few points emerge with particular clarity.

First of all, the dialectic between Chinese and Western ideas is not a theme invented by some foreign scholars; it was a problem of which Mao himself was acutely aware, and to which he returned again and again.

Second, despite his growing perception, beginning in 1919, of the people rather than the elites as the foundation of the state and the source of legitimacy, Mao never abandoned the belief in the central role of political power which he had early adopted as a student of traditional Chinese thought.

Third, for all the changes which Mao's ideas underwent during the decade after 1912, his personality (or cast of mind) remained strikingly consistent. In particular, the focus on the individual will or consciouness, and on the role of the hero, stands out in all of Mao's early writings, and indeed throughout his entire life. The emphasis on military heroism, and on the martial ethos, is also a recurrent trait, long antedating the beginning of his experience of guerrilla warfare in the countryside in 1927.

The first text in this volume, which constitutes the earliest written record of Mao Zedong's thought, is an essay on Shang Yang which he wrote in June 1912. It would be reading too much into a single document to conclude from

2. This volume of Mao Zedong's early writings comes to a close at the end of November 1920. Appended to this introduction is a brief chronology of Mao's life up to that time. We have chosen this cut-off date because that is when the editors of the new Chinese edition, which has been in preparation for several years, chose to make the break between the first volume, entitled *Mao Zedong zaoqi wengao* (The Early Writings of Mao Zedong), and the second volume, *Mao Zedong jiandang da geming shiqi de zhuzuo* (Mao Zedong's Writings of the Period of Setting up the Party and the Great Revolution [of 1924–27]). Since only the first volume is currently available, we prefer to adopt the same terminal date, in order to ensure that this volume of translations is entirely complete. (Regarding the history of this edition, and the prospects for the publication of other Mao writings in China, see the Note on Sources and Conventions which follows this Introduction.) Quite apart from the availability of sources, this division is also a logical one, since the present volume thus deals exclusively with Mao's pre-Marxist period.

this class essay that Mao was, as has often been argued by his critics since 1949, a "Legalist" from the beginning. It is none the less striking that the corpus of his writings should begin with a celebration of one of the principal founders of this authoritarian school of thought, with its emphasis on harsh punishments and strict state control of all social activity.[3]

"Shang Yang's laws," wrote Mao, "were good laws. If you have a look today at the four thousand-odd years for which our country's history has been recorded, and the great political leaders who have pursued the welfare of the country and the happiness of the people, is not Shang Yang one of the very first on the list?"[4] Mao wrote this piece at the age of eighteen, shortly after leaving the revolutionary army, in which he had enlisted in the autumn of 1911. He told Edgar Snow that he had asked to be discharged because he thought the revolution had already achieved its objectives. Certainly, Mao's castigation of the stupidity, ignorance, and darkness of the Chinese people does not suggest that he was at this time at all interested in political, let alone social, revolution. He aspired to radical reform, but believed it could only come from the top. Thus he wrote:

> Shang Yang sought to achieve victory over all the other states and unify the Central Plain, a difficult enterprise indeed. Then he published his reforming decrees, promulgating laws to punish the wicked and rebellious, in order to preserve the rights of the people. He stressed agriculture and weaving, in order to increase the wealth of the people, and forcefully pursued military success, in order to establish the prestige of the state. . . . This amounted to a great policy such as our country had never had before. How could the people fear and not trust him, so that he had to use the scheme of [moving] the pole to establish confidence? From this, we realize the wasted efforts of those who wield power. . . .

The themes enunciated here are so plainly and forcefully stated as scarcely to require comment. In Mao's view, there must be a strong state, and there must be unquestioning acceptance of its authority. It was the vocation of such a state to ensure the wealth of the people, as well as its own military power. Finally, the lot of the ruler was not an easy one, and entailed considerable "wasted effort" on the part of the person bearing responsibility for bold and enlightened policy choices which were not always understood by the people.

Early Encounters with Western Thought, 1912–1916

Two key points about China's relations with the outside world were adumbrated in Mao's essay on Shang Yang. "I particularly fear," he wrote in conclusion,

---

3. For a note on Shang Yang, see the text of Mao's 1912 essay, below, p. 5.

4. See below, p. 6, the "Essay on How Shang Yang Established Confidence by the Moving of the Pole."

"that if this story of establishing confidence by moving the pole should come to the attention of various civilized peoples of the East and the West, they will laugh uncontrollably so that they have to hold their stomachs, and make a derisive noise with their tongues. Alas, I had best say no more." Thus, on the one hand, Mao postulated that there were other peoples more civilized than the Chinese, who did not share the "ignorance and darkness" of the Chinese people "during the past several milennia," which had been manifested in their failure spontaneously to accord their confidence to so good a ruler as Shang Yang. And on the other, as made plain by the *cri de coeur* of his last sentence, he was profoundly ashamed at this situation, which had brought China "to the brink of destruction."

While the record of Mao's ideas is now so very much fuller than it was even in the recent past, there is no other text expressing his own ideas for nearly three years after this one. Apparently not a single writing of any kind is extant for the year 1914, and the only item from 1913 consists of the notes Mao took during lectures he attended on entering normal school in Changsha. These are, however, of remarkable interest, for they shed entirely new light on the intellectual influences to which he was exposed during his formative years.

How deeply these lectures to the "preparatory class" at Fourth Normal School, which Mao attended until it was combined with First Normal School in the spring of 1914, imprinted themselves on Mao's mind is shown by the fact that twenty-three years later, when he recounted his school days to Edgar Snow, it was precisely the two teachers concerned whom he singled out as the best and the most influential. Yang Changji, he said, had inspired his students with the aim of becoming just, moral men, useful to society. "Yuan the Big Beard," as Mao called Yuan Zhongqian, his teacher of the Chinese language and literature, had taught him to model his style on that of the Tang dynasty author Han Yu. As a result, Mao opined in 1936, he could still write a passable essay in *wenyan*, the old literary language.

The importance of these lectures for Mao's intellectual development is borne out by the quite remarkable direct influence which can be traced between the views of his two teachers, as recorded by Mao, and his own subsequent writings. The most striking instance of this is undoubtedly the passage in Yang Changji's lecture of November 1, 1913, on self-cultivation,[5] which contains in brief compass most of the key ideas Mao would later develop in his 1917 article "A Study of Physical Education," regarding the importance of physical strength and military force for national survival. Yang and Yuan likewise encouraged Mao in the admiration for the great conservative statesman Zeng Guofan, and for the early Qing patriotic or anti-Manchu philosophers Gu Yanwu and Wang Fuzhi. They also helped to make Zhuangzi Mao's favorite Daoist philosopher, whom he continued to cite frequently to the end of his life.

---

5. See below, p. 15.

Twelve of the twenty surviving texts from the years 1915 and 1916 are letters to Xiao Zisheng, also known as Xiao Xudong and Xiao Yu, who was one of Mao's two most intimate friends during his years at First Normal School.[6] There are also two very revealing letters to his former teacher Li Jinxi, who had moved to Beijing. Together, these materials give us a clear and vivid idea of the trend of Mao's thinking during this period.

Some themes represent Mao's response to the political circumstances of the time — for example, his strong reaction to Japanese bullying of China, as manifested in the Twenty-one Demands.[7] More broadly, he calls for exercising one's talents to the maximum, in order to revive the nation.[8]

Mao also displays, in these texts written at the age of twenty-one or twenty-two, a persistent sense of loneliness and insecurity, which finds its most striking expression in the "self-accusation" from his journal which he copied out for Xiao Zisheng. In this piece, he contrasted the bottle-gourd plant, which declines but leaves an end product, and the peony, which blooms showily but shrivels and leaves no fruit behind. "Your outside looks strong," he wrote, "but your inside is truly empty. Your ambitions for fame and fortune are not suppressed, and your sensual desires grow daily. . . . You always emulate what the peony does . . . , but deceive yourself by saying 'I emulate the gourd.' Is this not dishonesty? Having no answer, I shrank back, sweating profusely, morose and frustrated."[9]

In the first of his letters to Li Jinxi, dated November 1915, Mao declared that First Normal "was no place to study." "There is no freedom of will," he wrote, "the standards are too low, and the companions too evil. It is truly distressing to see my serviceable body and precious time dwindle away. . . ." He had never, he added, had "good teachers or friends" in his life.[10] These are surprising statements, in view of Mao's comments to Snow, and in other contexts, about the virtues of his teachers Yang Changji and Yuan Zhongqian, and his generally favorable assessment of the normal school as a whole.[11] No doubt Mao's nega-

---

6. Apart from their content, the sheer number of these letters confirms the closeness of Mao's relationship to Xiao at this time. After 1920, their paths diverged until they became bitter personal and political enemies. For Xiao's account of these years, see Siao-yu, *Mao Tse-tung and I Were Beggars* (Syracuse: Syracuse University Press, 1959). Mao's other intimate friend of this period, Cai Hesen, played on the contrary a considerable role in converting him to Marxism and to the Soviet model in 1920, as will be discussed below.

7. See his epigraph of summer 1915 to *Essays on the Sense of Shame*, calling for "revenge" (below, p. 66), and the anger expressed in his letter of July 25, 1916, to Xiao Zisheng that "our land, which stretches tens of thousands of *li* in all four directions, could submit to three islands" (below, p. 103).

8. Letter of July 1915 to Xiao Zisheng (below, pp. 67–68).

9. Letter of August 1915 to Xiao Zisheng (below, pp. 73–74).

10. See below, p. 84.

11. See Mao's autobiography, in Edgar Snow, *Red Star over China* (London: Victor Gollancz, 1937), pp. 142–43.

tive observations of 1915 reflected a mood, inspired by the frustration of his "fervent" desire to find friends, rather than a moment in his intellectual development. His letter of December 1916 to Li Jinxi consists in large part of a summary of arguments and examples from his article "A Study of Physical Education," which he was presumably engaged in writing at the time. It contains, however, one striking assertion: "Whether or not the soul remains immortal . . . does not depend on the length of life, but on the amount of one's achievement, which is really immortal."[12] There can be little doubt that Mao was then, and remained, concerned about his own immortality in this sense.

Intriguingly, in Mao's early encounters with Western thought, the problem of epistemology, to which he later attached his name with the essay "On Practice," looms large. Already in 1913, "Yuan the Big Beard" had taught him that, while there were merits in both Chinese and Western medicine, the contribution of Western medicine lay in its stress on experiments.[13] In 1915, however, Mao spoke rather of the importance of comprehensive knowledge, as opposed to narrow specialization. After reading Yan Fu's translation of Spencer's *Principles of Sociology*, Mao closed the book and exclaimed to himself: "Here lies the path to scholarship." Spencer, he adds, "wrote that specialized study often leads to blindness to universal laws." This might be seen as using a Western authority to support a deductive rather than empirical approach to knowledge, in harmony with the traditional Chinese perspective. Indeed, in the same letter, after urging his friend Xiao Zisheng to read Spencer's remarkable book, he went on to say that general knowledge of <u>Chinese</u> studies was "most crucial for our people."[14]

In Search of Wealth and Power: Mao's Thought in 1917

Mao Zedong's article, "A Study of Physical Education," published in April 1917, is one of only two major texts for the period prior to the foundation of the Chinese Communist Party that have long been available. It remains an important milestone in his development. In it, there is no explicit discussion of the relation between Chinese and Western culture, but many of the other themes evoked at the beginning of this introduction figure prominently: the central importance of the state, the role of the will, and of "conscious action," and the emphasis on military heroism.

Regarding the role of the state, Yang Changji had presented to Mao, in his lectures of 1913, an argument to the effect that because there was no relation between government and people in China except punishment and taxation, China had "freedom," whereas the Western countries had "despotism." As a result, he

12. See below, p. 107.

13. See below, "Classroom Notes," p. 33.

14. Letter to Xiao Zisheng dated September 6, 1915 (below, p. 79).

added, the Chinese people lacked the concepts of state and politics.[15] This particular teaching of Yang's does not appear to have had much influence on Mao, for we find him in 1915–17 still wedded to a view of the state analogous to that he had held five years earlier, placing primary emphasis on the wisdom and authority of those exercising political power. Perhaps the most striking illustration of this is the celebration of the virtues of Zeng Guofan which runs through all his writings of this period. Thus, in a letter of August 1917 to Li Jinxi, he ranked Kang Youwei above Yuan Shikai and Sun Yatsen, but added that only Zeng was really deserving of respect.[16]

"Self-cultivation" (*xiushen*) had been the title and main burden of Yang Changji's lectures of 1913, as recorded in Mao's notes. The cultivation and realization of the self of which he spoke was, however, in large measure the art of bringing the will into harmony with the decrees of Heaven and the teachings of the sages, in order that the scholar might play his role in maintaining the social order. Already by 1917, Mao was focusing more on another aspect of the matter, namely the intrinsic value of "consciousness" or "self-awareness" (*zi jue*). Thus, in his article of April 1917 he wrote:

> Strength comes from drill, and drill depends on self-awareness. . . . External forces are insufficient to move the heart. . . . If we want physical education to be effective, we must influence people's subjective attitudes and stimulate their awareness of physical education.[17]

The individual, in Mao's view of 1917, must not merely be conscious, and prepared to take the initiative; he must above all have a strong will, without which nothing could be achieved. "The will," wrote Mao, "is the antecedent of a man's career." It was precisely because a strong body was a prerequisite for a firm will that Mao recommended regular exercise to his fellow citizens.[18]

This point is directly linked, in "A Study of Physical Education," to that of the martial ethos:

> Physical education not only harmonizes the emotions, it also strengthens the will. The great utility of physical education lies precisely in this. The principal aim of physical education is military heroism. Such objects of military heroism as courage, dauntlessness, audacity, and perseverance are all matters of will.

---

15. Lecture of November 15, below, p. 22. This particular teaching is not typical of Yang, who had spent many years abroad, and admired many aspects of Western culture. On Yang Changji, see note 1 to the "Classroom Notes" of 1913, and the obituary of January 1920, of which Mao was a signatory.

16. Letter to Li Jinxi, August 23, 1917, p. 131. The four figures mentioned here are discussed in the General Introduction, and further details may be found in the notes to Mao's early writings.

17. Below, p. 113. Note also the reference to "individual initiative," p. 117.

18. See below, pp. 119–20.

The "individual" to whose will Mao attached such importance was obviously not the ordinary man. His concern, in the years prior to the May Fourth movement, was very much with the individuality of the hero or the sage. "Sages" and "superior men" alone, wrote Mao in his letter of August 1917 to Li Jinxi, could master basic principles and should do so in order to organize society to the benefit of the "little people." And he added:

> Those who turn their backs on the ultimate principles and yet regard themselves as instruments of rule can seldom avoid the fate of becoming laughingstocks of history who led a generation or a country to defeat. In their case, how can there be even the slightest modicum of wealth and power [*fuqiang*] or happiness to speak of?

Problems could be dealt with, he argued, and the state become "rich, powerful, and happy" if "all the hearts in the realm" were moved, but at the same time he made very plain that this unity around "ultimate principles" could be achieved only if there was an elite of "superior men" to "change fundamentally the thinking of the whole country."

Only an enlightened will, he added, was a true will, and in order to have such a will one must "first study philosophy and ethics." "Will," he argued, "is the truth which we perceive in the universe. Accordingly, it may be called that which determines the tendency of our minds. . . . If, for a decade, one does not obtain the truth, then for a decade one will be without a will. An entire life without truth is an entire life without a will."[19]

This view that only a will corresponding to "the truth about the universe" is a true will appears not unrelated to Wang Yangming's concept of innate or intuitive knowledge of the good (*liangzhi*) as a compass needle to point the way. In other words, at this time, Mao's conception of the will was still, like his thought in general, in large measure traditional.

From Traditionalism to Individualism, 1917–1918

It has long been known, from his article on physical education, that Mao Zedong remained until 1917 (when he was twenty-three years old) strongly marked by traditional ideas and values, though he was not unaware of the wider world. The evidence also showed that he leaned toward anarchism in the summer of 1919, and became a Marxist by the end of 1920, but the years from mid-1917 to mid-1919 were so ill-documented as to permit almost any speculation as to how he had moved from veneration for strong rulers and conservative statesmen of the Chinese past to admiration for Kropotkin, and then to the advocacy of Russia's proletarian dictatorship as the model which must be followed. On the basis of the fragmentary materials hitherto available, it could plausibly have been argued that though Mao was exposed to liberal or "bourgeois" ideas prior to the May Fourth period, such "Westernization" as he underwent was almost exclu-

19. Letter of August 23, 1917, to Li Jinxi, pp. 131–34 *passim*.

sively in Marxist or revolutionary terms. The new sources here translated entirely rule out such a view.

By the summer of 1917, his ideas had already undergone a significant change. In a foreword to a work by Xiao Zisheng, Mao praised the classifications employed in Western learning, "so clear that they sound like a waterfall dashing against the rocks beneath a cliff." Contrasting the "disorganized and unsystematic character" of ancient Chinese learning with the clear divisions between different fields in Western studies, he concluded that anyone who did not follow the Western example would "not be able to attain excellence."[20]

In a letter of August 1917 to Li Jinxi, Mao expressed the view that his countrymen had "accumulated many undesirable customs," and their mentality was "too antiquated." But at the same time, he declared that Fukuzawa Yukichi's position regarding the lack of correspondence between "Oriental thought" and "the reality of life," though well stated, was too one-sided. "In my opinion," he wrote, "Western thought is not necessarily all correct either; very many parts of it should be transformed at the same time as Oriental thought."[21]

This insight on Mao's part was soon overlaid, though perhaps not wholly superseded, by the views he formed during the winter of 1917–18 in his study of Paulsen's *System of Ethics*.[22] This crucially important document has previously been known only on the basis of fragmentary extracts taken out of context. In 1979, the Chinese published for internal circulation an ostensibly full text, subsequently reproduced in Volume 9 of the Tokyo edition of Mao's pre-1949 works, but this version was also seriously defective in two respects: the editors had left out long passages of Mao's often virtually illegible handwritten annotations and misread others; and they did not indicate clearly the passages of Cai Yuanpei's translation of Paulsen to which his comments referred. This situation has now been remedied by the appearance of the version translated below.

On the basis of this source, it is possible to state unequivocally that the winter

---

20. "Foreword" to Xiao Zisheng's *All in One* Self-Study Notes, below, pp. 128–29.

21. See below, p. 132.

22. Friedrich Paulsen was a minor German philospher, commonly classified as a neo-Kantian, who enjoyed a certain vogue around the turn of the twentieth century, and had no doubt attracted the attention of Mao's teacher Yang Changji when he studied in Berlin. Paulsen's book *System der Ethik* had been translated into English by the American Frank Thilly, who omitted the last of its four books, dealing with social and political issues. The Japanese version, by Kanie Yoshimaru and others, followed Thilly in this, and also omitted some sections which Kanie regarded as of little interest to non-European readers. In 1909, the leading educationalist Cai Yuanpei produced the Chinese version Mao studied in 1917–18, basing himself principally on the Japanese edition. From it, he translated only Book II, titling it (like Kanie's version of this portion of the work) *Lunlixue yuanli* (Principles of Ethics). Cai made further cuts in the portion he did translate, and condensed many passages, but at the same time he checked his version against the German original. The book thus conveyed the gist of Paulsen's interpretation of the various Western philosophers mentioned below.

of 1917–18 marked the high point both of Mao's absorption of Western thought and of his commitment to what would be called today in China "bourgeois liberalization." Among the authors to whom Mao was introduced were (in alphabetical order) Aristotle, Bentham, Fichte, Goethe, Hobbes, Kant, Leibnitz, Mill, Nietzsche, Plato, Schopenhauer, Spencer, and Spinoza. Though he knew about them in large part from the Chinese edition of Paulsen and from Yang Changji's lectures on it, Mao had already encountered some of these writers, both in the course of his independent reading in the library in Changsha a few years earlier, and subsequently, while a student at the normal school. That he thought seriously about the significance of the ideas of these foreign scholars is shown by the fact that in his marginal notes he expressed opinions about the views of nearly all those just mentioned, often at considerable length.

As can be deduced from the list of authors just mentioned, the Western influences to which Mao was exposed at this time cannot be characterized simply as "the liberal tradition." He was familiar, before turning to newer and more radical ideas beginning in 1919, with a broad spectrum of nineteenth-century European thought. None the less, the role of the individual, and the importance of the freedom of the will, is undoubtedly the most prominent single theme in Mao's annotations as a whole. Opposite Paulsen's statement that "the human will seeks the welfare of the individual and of others as its goal," he wrote: "Ultimately the individual comes first."[23]

It is assuredly no accident that the terms "individual" and "individualism" occur on nearly a third of the pages of the notes on Paulsen, as against less than 5 percent of the pages for 1912–18 and 1919–1920, and "the will" on a quarter of the pages, as compared to 2 or 3 percent for the earlier and later periods. Throughout his commentaries, Mao made over and over in different ways the basic point about the primacy of the individual vis-à-vis the group. Taking issue with Paulsen's criticism of Hobbes' view that every animal pursues self-preservation, Mao wrote: "I really feel that this explanation [of Paulsen's] is incomplete. Since human beings have an ego, for which the self is the center of all things and all thought, self-interest is primary for all persons. . . . Nothing in the world takes the other as its starting point. . . ."[24]

After asserting categorically that human beings seek to benefit others solely because in so doing they obtain pleasure or satisfaction for themselves, Mao wrote, opposite Paulsen's statement that in certain circumstances, when the interests of others were seen as most important, "I would have to distance myself from the core of my ego," the comment: "This is the Confucian righteousness (*yi*)."[25] More broadly speaking, the undeniable individualism of Mao's thought at this time is

---

23. See below, p. 201.
24. Below, p. 200.
25. Below, p. 290.

colored by a tendency to see the powerful or enlightened individual as a vehicle for causing the Way to reign in society, and is in that sense in harmony with traditional Chinese thought.

Mao's primary concern in 1918 was, however, with the self. Thus he wrote, "My desire to fulfill my nature and perfect my mind is the most precious of the moral laws." And again, "The value of the individual is greater than that of the universe. Thus there is no greater crime than to suppress the individual or to violate particularity." And again, ". . . the group in itself has no meaning, it only has meaning as a collectivity of individuals." And finally, "The only goal of human beings is to realize the self. Self-realization means to develop fully both our physical and spiritual capacities to the highest."[26]

Building on this position, Mao developed his conception of the hero:

> The truly great person develops the original nature with which Nature endowed him, and expands upon the best, the greatest of the capacities of his original nature. This is what makes him great. Everything that comes from outside his original nature, such as restraints and restrictions, is cast aside. . . . The great actions of the hero are his own, are the expression of his motive power, lofty and cleansing, relying on no precedent. His force is like that of a powerful wind arising from a deep gorge, like the irresistible sexual desire for one's lover. . . .[27]

Even though Mao claims that this priority to impulse rather than convention is in accord with the teachings of Mencius, who spoke of nourishing his "vast, flowing passion-nature,"[28] his view of the hero would appear to owe more to Nietzsche. In any case, Mao's study of Paulsen's *System of Ethics* marked a new phase in his search for a way of promoting the reciprocal transformation of Western and Oriental thought. While seeking for parallels with Mencius, Wang Yangming, and other Chinese philosophers, he was mainly concerned in 1918 with understanding and assimilating Western ideas. "All our nation's two thousand years of scholarship may be said to be unthinking learning," he remarks at one point.[29]

This comment relates to a passage in which Paulsen cites Nietzsche as a protagonist of the trend toward calling into question established ideas and customs:

> The contemporary age, whether in thought, or morality, or life styles, is rejecting all things old and seeking the new. . . . Their subjective ideas are breaking down the walls and escaping in all directions, in reaction to the old unthinking learning and the religions of unquestioning faith. These are the characteristics of the Enlightenment. . . . At first taking hold of the young people, today it is

26. See especially pp. 204–09.
27. Below, pp. 263–64.
28. Below, p. 264.
29. See below, p. 194.

> spreading among the common people. Those who have been oppressed by the . . . prescriptions on living of the past regard this as the blind leading the blind, and . . . want to do their own thinking and open up another world. Such is the right of freedom.

Opposite the words "At first taking hold of the young people . . . ," Mao has written: "This is the situation in our nation today."[30] Plainly, he was in tune with the ideas expressed by Chen Duxiu in his famous "Call to Youth" in 1915, which defined in so many respects the orientation of the New Culture movement.

The individual, argued Mao, came before the nation and was more important than the nation. Paulsen's contrary view, he wrote, "reflects the fact that he lived in Germany, which is highly nationalistic."[31] In his advocacy of individualism and independent thought, Mao went so far as to negate the state, and traditional morality. He wrote: "There is no greater crime than to suppress the individual or to violate particularity. Therefore our country's three bonds must go, and the churches, the capitalists, the monarchy, and the state constitute the four evil demons of the world."[32]

Three Stages in Mao's Political Thought, 1912–1920

While stigmatizing the immobility of Chinese culture and declaring bluntly that the "three bonds" of Confucian morality "must go" because they contributed to the great crime of the suppression of the individual, Mao at the same time expressed his confidence in the future of the Chinese state:

> I used to worry that our China would be destroyed, but now I know that this is not so. Through the establishment of a new political system, and a change in the national character, and a reforming of society, the German states became the German Reich. There is no need to worry. The only question is how the changes should be carried out. I believe that there must be a complete transformation, like matter that takes form after destruction, or like the infant born out of its mother's womb.[33]

From 1918 onward Mao Zedong devoted his entire life to resolving this question of how to carry out the "complete transformation" of Chinese society. Down to 1917, he had held, as already noted, that reform must take place from the top down, and must be the work of the "political leaders" such as Shang Yang whom he admired. In 1918, he turned sharply against these traditionalistic conceptions. But at the same time, he rapidly grasped that the reform of society

---

30. Below, p. 194.
31. See below, p. 281.
32. See below, p. 208.
33. See below, p. 250.

could not be carried out by the method of "everyone doing his own thing." Organization was needed, and the organization required for such a task was of a new type, which could be learned about from the West.

In broad outline, this aspect of Mao Zedong's thought passed through three stages in its development down to 1920: (1) supporting good rulers of a traditional type; (2) rebellion against this tradition, manifested in extreme individualism and exaltation of the hero; and (3) the search for a new, revolutionary political power. No such sudden and dramatic transformation can ever be total and irreversible, and the record of Mao's later years demonstrates that he had not wholly abandoned the ideal of a true and wise ruler. The changes in his outlook during the May Fourth period were, however, profound and far-reaching.

After the notes on Paulsen, there is a substantial blank in the documentation for more than a year. Apart from one brief letter to a friend and two family letters, the only significant item is a report on the work of the evening school at First Normal, which shows Mao focusing his mind on fund-raising. When Mao's thinking can once more be fully apprehended in July 1919, it is a very different Mao that we perceive.

Mao Zedong's Thought of the May Fourth Period

Because Mao's article of July–August 1919, "The Great Union of the Popular Masses," is (with that of 1917 on physical education) one of the two major texts for the period prior to 1921 which have long been available, the voluminous materials contained in this volume regarding the immediate post-May Fourth period contain no real surprises. The key points in his thinking, most cogently summed up in "The Great Union," include a shift from "the superior men" to "the popular masses" as the main artisans of historical change, and a call for "revolution," in order to achieve "liberation" from "oppression," and thereby to remedy "the decadence of the state, the sufferings of humanity, and the darkness of society." At the same time, he continued, in this different political framework, to stress the vital importance of mobilizing human capacities, and releasing human energies. "Aristocrats" and "capitalists" were now perceived as enemies, but Mao regarded Kropotkin as a better guide than Marx for dealing with them. In a word, Mao's recipe was something like "people power," and the "great union" he wanted to create was based on a broad coalition of workers, peasants, students, women, teachers, and even policemen.[34]

The first sentence of this, Mao's most important article of the May Fourth period, reads: "The decadence of the state, the sufferings of humanity, and the darkness of society have all reached an extreme." Thus the central importance of the state remained an axiom of his thinking. Nor had he entirely cut his ties to traditional Chinese conceptions of the state. In his account of the history and

34. See below, pp. 378–89 *passim*.

antecedents of the Hunan United Students' Association, Mao praised the School of Current Affairs, founded in the spring of 1898, on the eve of the Reform Movement, noting in its favor that the school "advocated revolutionary ideals" and also that students "all studied thoroughly what is called statecraft [*jingshi*]."[35] The statecraft school, with its emphasis on dealing efficiently with the concrete problems of the realm, might be seen as anticipating the emphasis on practice which Mao later depicted as one of the virtues of Western thought, but it had taken shape under the Ming and Qing and was assuredly very Chinese.

That being said, Mao's ideas regarding the nature and foundations of the state had undergone a profound change in directions basically inspired by Western thought and Western example. These new trends in his thought were reinforced by the situation during the years 1918–1919, when movements of all descriptions sprang into existence on every hand. Mao was, of course, not merely influenced by these developments; he was also a prime mover in setting up many such organizations.

The words "reform" and/or "revolution," which Mao used at this time in very similar senses, appear constantly in his writings of the period immediately following the May Fourth events. "Democracy, the great rebel," he wrote, "can be established."[36] The term, translated here as "rebel," *da ni bu dao*, designates someone in flagrant rebellion against lawful authority or against the whole Confucian moral code. Thus Mao was consciously advocating a sweeping repudiation of important aspects of the Chinese past. At the same time, he was not quite sure what he wanted to put in its place. All "oppressors" must, he wrote, "be overthrown under the great cry of democracy," but he hesitated between the "two views," anarchist and Marxist (which he also called "moderate" and "extreme"), as to how this should be accomplished.[37]

The new and much fuller record of Mao's thought for the latter half of 1919 does, however, fill out the picture in several important respects. First of all, one may note his frequent references both to Western history, including episodes such as the Renaissance and the Reformation, and to current developments throughout the world. Many of the articles on current events in the *Xiang River Review*, which Mao edited in July and August 1919, were written by him, including those on the waves of strikes in various countries, the Paris Peace Conference, and the views of Clemenceau, Wilson, and Smuts regarding the international situation.[38] These contained a few errors of fact, but also some keen insights. Thus, Mao recalled that the invasion of French territory in 1789–1790

35. See "An Overall Account of the Hunan United Students' Association," August 4, 1919, below, p. 399.

36. See "The Great Union," Part III, below, p. 385.

37. "Manifesto on the Founding of the *Xiang River Review*," below, pp. 318–20; "The Great Union of the Popular Masses," p. 380.

38. See below, in particular pp. 321–24, 338, 357–66, 367, 391.

by the armies of the Holy Alliance had brought about the rise of Napoleon, Napoleon's trampling over the German people had brought about the war of 1871, Wilhelm and Bismark's triumph on that occasion had brought about the First World War, and the Treaty of Versailles in turn contained within it the seeds of a new war. "I guarantee that in ten or twenty years, you Frenchmen will yet again have a splitting headache," he wrote. "Mark my words."[39] (The sympathy he displayed here, and in other writings of the May Fourth period, for Germany as an "oppressed nation," was then widespread in Chinese intellectual circles.)

In an article in praise of Chen Duxiu, Mao referred to the "total emptiness and rottenness of the mental universe of the entire Chinese people" as a greater danger than military weakness or domestic chaos. "Thought," he declared, "knows no boundaries." Therefore Chen was right to borrow "science" and "democracy" from the West.[40] "Scholarly research abhors most a deductive, arbitrary attitude," he wrote in another article. "We oppose Confucius for many other reasons as well, but for just this one reason alone, for his hegemony over China that has denied freedom to our intellectual world, that has kept us the slave of idols for two thousand years, we must oppose him."

At the same time, Mao stressed that if the new thought tide had not yet created a new climate in China, it was because this movement still did not have a "well-established central core of thought." To be sure, this central core should be created by the exercise of freedom of thought and freedom of speech, which were "mankind's most precious treasure," rather than by the hegemony of Confucius and of "the orthodox school." The idea of a "central core" as an axis for society none the less persisted in Mao's thought.[41] Plainly, a key role in the creation of this core would be played by students and intellectuals, whose role in the whole process of reform and renewal Mao saw as crucial.

A major theme of Mao's writings of late 1919 was the institution of marriage, and relations between the sexes. The broad outlines of his ideas on this topic, put forward with reference to the suicide of a young woman who had refused to accept a marriage arranged by her parents, have likewise long been known and have already been discussed in the literature. All such previous interpretations were, however, based on extracts from Mao's ten articles inspired by this incident. Apart from a more complete exposition of the central argument in favor of "freedom of the will" and the "freedom to love" versus the constraints of society and customs, and of equality between men and women, the full texts translated below contain an intriguing passage in which the domination of old men, who are interested only in eating and not in sex, is identified

39. "Joy and Suffering," below, p. 367.

40. See below "The Arrest and Rescue of Chen Duxiu," pp. 329–30.

41. See "The Founding and Progress of the 'Strengthen Learning Society,' " below, pp. 369–76.

with capitalism.[42] In fact, Mao's writings at least down to 1921, and to some degree even after, reflect only a vague grasp of what concepts such as "capitalism" were all about.

Pragmatism, Cosmopolitanism, and Revolution, 1919–1920

If Mao found Chinese learning and the morality of the Chinese people increasingly deficient, and was prepared to seek inspiration and guidance in the West as to how China could be transformed, he was, in the summer and autumn of 1919, far from having made up his mind as to *which* foreign ideas would be most useful for the purpose. A revealing text in this respect is the statutes of the "Problem Study Society," which Mao was instrumental in founding in September of that year. The name of the society clearly evokes the controversy launched in July 1919 by Hu Shi's article, "More Study of Problems, Less Talk about Isms." Hu's view was that the most important task of Chinese intellectuals was to study concrete problems. Li Dazhao and other future Communists argued that without theory or ideology it was impossible to understand problems. The long statutes Mao drafted pointed, like the name of the society, toward focusing on specific problems, and Mao was plainly closer to Hu Shi at this time than either of them were prepared to admit after 1949.

One of the problems to be studied, as listed in the statutes, was how to implement the educational doctrine of Hu Shi's teacher John Dewey, and it was Hu who, according to a letter dated March 1920, suggested the name of the "Self-Study University," which Mao was then planning to set up.[43] While in Shanghai in the spring of 1920, Mao consulted Hu about the problems of Hunan, and on July 9, 1920, two days after returning to Changsha, he wrote to Hu Shi in polite and deferential terms stating that in the future "there will be many points on which Hunan will need to ask your help once again."[44]

At the same time, however, Article III of the statutes of the Problem Study Society asserts that the study of problems should be solidly founded on academic principles. "Before studying the various problems, we should therefore study various 'isms.' "[45] From this relatively evenhanded attitude toward liberalism and socialism, Mao continued to evolve, as already noted, toward anarchism, and then communism. By June 1920, he had ceased to regard "reform" and "revolution" as interchangeable, and began calling for real, revolutionary change in China, instead of mere reformism.[46]

---

42. See "The Question of Love—Young People and Old People," below, pp. 439–41.

43. "Letter to Zhou Shizhao," March 14, 1920, below, p. 506.

44. "Letter to Hu Shi," July 9, 1920, below, p. 531. In this note, written on a postcard, Mao refers to a letter he had written to Hu while in Shanghai; this has apparently been lost.

45. "Statutes of the Problem Study Society," September 1, 1919, below, p. 412.

46. See his letter of June 7, 1920, to Li Jinxi, below, p. 519.

At the same time, however, Mao continued to reflect on the more general problem of the relation between Chinese and Western thought. Before his conversion to Marxism at the end of 1920, Mao's position on this issue can best be described as syncretistic. Perhaps the clearest and most detailed illustration is to be found in his letter of March 1920 to Zhou Shizhao. Noting that world civilization "can be divided into two currents, Eastern and Western," and adding, characteristically, "Eastern civilization can be said to be Chinese civilization," Mao admitted that he still did not have "a relatively clear concept of all the various ideologies and doctrines." He planned to form a "lucid concept" of each of them by "distilling the essence of theories, Chinese and foreign, ancient and modern." Since any contribution he might make to the world could not take place "outside this domain of 'China,'" and would require "on-site investigation and research on conditions in this domain," he proposed for the time being not to go abroad to study, but to remain in China and read about foreign cultures in translation. At the same time, he saw Russia as "the number one civilized country in the world," and hoped to organize a delegation to go there in two or three years.[47]

Increasingly, in any case, he tended to regard world culture as one. Thus, in July 1920 he wrote that not only China and Hunan, but "the whole world" did not yet have "the New Culture," though a tiny blossom was growing in Russia.[48] In November 1920, Mao praised the example of Li Shizeng and others in sending students to France to learn "cosmopolitanism." Cosmopolitanism, he wrote, "is an ism to benefit everyone." And he added: "With cosmopolitanism, there is no place that one does not feel at ease. . . ." But he likewise wrote: "Worldwide universal harmony needs to be built on the foundation of national self-determination."[49] This included self-determination for Hunan, so that the Hunanese could "embrace all the other peoples endowed with self-awareness in the world."[50]

Self-Government for Hunan, 1919–1920

A substantial proportion of Mao's writings from December 1919 to June 1920 deal with the movement to expel Zhang Jingyao, the particularly brutal military governor of Hunan, in which Mao was actively involved. These are on the whole of historical rather than intellectual interest. As the movement progressed, however, Mao began to raise also the question of Hunan's relationship to the rest of China, and of Hunanese autonomy. This latter topic occupied an even larger place in his thought and activity for a time, after Zhang was finally compelled to leave the province following a military defeat in mid-June 1920. Was Mao mainly concerned, during the crucial transitional year of 1920, with radical so-

47. Letter of March 14, 1920, below, pp. 505–6.
48. "The Founding of the Cultural Book Society," July 31, 1920, below, p. 534.
49. "Letter to Zhang Guoji," November 25, 1920, below, p. 604.
50. "Letter to Xiang Jingyu," November 25, 1920, below, p. 595.

cial revolution, or rather with the greatness of China, and of Hunan?

The problem of the relation between these two goals is squarely addressed in a letter of November 1920 to members of the "New People's Study Society":

> As I see it, last year's Movement to Expel Zhang, and this year's autonomy movement were not, from the perspective of our members, political movements we deliberately chose to carry out. . . . Both movements are only expedient measures in response to the current situation and definitely do not represent our basic views. Our proposals go way beyond these movements. . . . The movement to "expel Zhang," the autonomy movement, and so on are also means to achieve a fundamental transformation, means that are most economical and most effective in dealing with our "present circumstances." But this is true on one condition, namely that we always keep ourselves in a "supportive" role from beginning to end. . . . To put it bluntly, we must absolutely not jump on the political stage to grasp control.[51]

If Mao did not think it appropriate to grasp political control in Hunan, this was no doubt partly because the society he had helped to found, and in which he played a leading role, was a "study society" rather than a political party. But it was also because, prior to the end of 1920, he really was not sure how to go about carrying out "radical reform," or what shape it should ultimately take.

Must the strong, though revolutionary or democratic, state in which Mao profoundly believed be a unitary and centralizing state such as that which Shang Yang had helped to create? Mao's thirty-odd writings touching on the problem of Hunanese autonomy, from the end of 1919 to the end of 1920, throw significant light on this question. Taken as a whole, these pieces put forward an argument which can be summed up roughly as follows. Though China as a cultural and political reality is of fundamental importance, the existing Chinese state is a mere sham, not only repressive but ineffectual. Moreover, there is no way that a real and effective political entity embracing the whole of China can be created in the near or medium-term future. (In most instances, Mao says this cannot be done within twenty years.) The best course for the people of Hunan is therefore to establish a strong, democratic, and reformist or revolutionary political regime of their own, both so that they can enjoy the benefits of good government in the short term, and so that in the long run the unity of China can be rebuilt from the bottom up, with Hunan and all the other autonomous provinces as the building blocks. On several occasions, he likens these provincial regimes to the states which banded together to form the American Union, or the German Empire created by Bismarck.[52]

On a few occasions, Mao argued explicitly that Hunan should constitute not

51. See "Comments in Response to the Letter from Yi Lirong to Mao Zedong and Peng Huang," below, pp. 611–12.

52. See below, pp. 522–82 *passim*.

merely a fully autonomous political entity, but an independent state. Thus, on September 3, 1920, he wrote: "If the people of Hunan themselves lack the determination and courage to build Hunan into a country, then in the end there will be no hope for Hunan."[53] On November 25, 1920, he said he advocated that "Hunan set itself up as an independent country."[54] On one or two other occasions, he compared Hunan to Switzerland and Japan, asserting that geographically, Hunan was "in a much better position than Switzerland," which was "a glorious country."[55]

Most of Mao's writings on this theme, however, after recalling, significantly, the outstanding role played by Hunan and Hunanese in Chinese affairs, whether in the case of Zeng Guofan, Tan Sitong, or Huang Xing, stress that the ultimate goal is a new and revitalized greater China. Thus, on one occasion Mao wrote: "I would give my support if there were a thorough and general revolution in China, but this is not possible.... Therefore, in the case of China, we cannot start with the whole, but must start with its parts."[56] Or again: "Mr. Hu Shi has proposed not talking about politics for twenty years. Now I propose not talking about the politics of the central government for twenty years." At the same time, he criticized "the old Chinese malady of looking up and not down."[57]

Change and Continuity in Mao Zedong's Thought, 1920–1921

Although at the end of 1920 Mao Zedong regarded Russia as the "number one civilized country in the world," his thinking about the Russian revolution was rather complex. The problem of the social forces which had contributed to it, and might contribute to reform or revolution in China, is raised in interesting fashion in an appeal of October 1920, addressed to the citizens, or more literally the "townspeople" (*shimin*) of Changsha. This term was widely employed in Beijing in 1989, and has recently been interpreted to mean "civil society." Mao, however, placed it in a historical context which gave it a narrower and more concrete sense:

> The political and social reforms of the Western countries all started with movements of the citizens. Not only did the great transformations in Russia, Germany, and other countries which have shocked the world recently originate

53. "The Fundamental Issue in the Problem of Hunanese Reconstruction: The Republic of Hunan," September 3, 1920, below, p. 545.

54. "Letter to Xiang Jingyu," November 25, 1920, below, p. 595.

55. "Reply to Zeng Yi from the Association for Promoting Reform in Hunan," June 23, 1920, below, p. 529.

56. "Break Down the Foundationless Big China and Build Up Many Chinas Starting with Hunan," September 5, 1920, below, p. 547.

57. This article, with deliberate irony, was entitled "Opposing Unification," and dated October 10, 1920, the national day (the anniversary of the 1911 revolution). See below, p. 581.

> with the citizens, even in the Middle Ages it was the citizens of the free cities alone who wrested the status of "freemen" from the autocrats. The power of the citizens is truly great! The citizens are truly the proudest people under heaven![58]

Mao concluded, therefore, that only the three hundred thousand citizens of Changsha could lead the self-rule movement of the thirty million Hunanese, most of whom were "scattered" and "lacking in consciousness." This scattered and amorphous majority was, of course, made up of the peasants, on whom Mao was subsequently to rely so heavily for his rural revolution. As late as October 1920, however, he reasoned from a more Western-centered and urban-centered perspective.

Two other points can be made regarding this text. First of all, Mao placed Lenin's victorious Soviet revolution firmly in a European context. More broadly, he plainly saw himself as a citizen of the world, and of a world defined in many respects by Western history. In the manifesto for the first issue of the *Xiang River Review*, he had spoken of the liberating effects of the Renaissance and the Reformation. Now he placed the revolution to which he was about to commit himself in the succession from the "bourgeois" revolutionary struggles which had taken place in Europe from the dawn of the modern era.

Earlier, Mao had regarded himself as a member of the intellectual elite, with a responsibility to guide his less enlightened fellow citizens. Now he was beginning to see himself as a revolutionary leader, but always as a man with a special historical destiny. He wanted to be "one with the masses," but he never wanted simply to be one of them.

It was argued above that Mao's "Westernizing" phase did not, as widely believed hitherto, take place in large measure in Marxist or revolutionary terms, but involved deep and extensive interaction between his mind and the ideas of thinkers belonging rather to the Western liberal tradition. That does not mean, of course, that he thought like a young man who had grown up in the West. No Chinese of his generation, especially one from the Hunanese hinterland, could have cast aside his own heritage — nor, as we have seen, did Mao have any intention of doing so. He did, however, regard himself in 1919–1920 as a citizen of the world in a certain sense.

In his most celebrated article of the May Fourth period, "The Great Union of the Popular Masses," Mao proclaimed: "The world is ours, the state is ours, society is ours." In other words, he concluded, as he moved from his "liberal" to his "collectivist" period, that the liberation from the old society, the old culture, and the old morality to which he aspired could be attained only by the joint

---

58. "Appeal to the 300,000 Citizens of Changsha in Favor of Self-Rule for Hunan," October 7, 1920, below, p. 572.

efforts of all the victims of the existing order, and especially of the young.

But at the same time, the extraordinary emphasis in his thought on the role of the individual hero in shaping history was not inspired simply by Nietzsche or T. H. Green. It was also clearly rooted in the core Confucian belief that by cultivating himself and ordering his own family the sage would become capable of governing the state as well. It was, of course, Liu Shaoqi whose name was most closely identified with the idea of the "self-cultivation" of Communist Party members, but it is notable that Mao Zedong explicitly repudiated this term only in May 1967, nearly a year after he had launched the "Cultural Revolution" aimed at destroying Liu.[59] Thus ideas regarding the relation between self and society shaped by a multiplicity of influences in Mao's youth remained alive even when he grew old.

In his letter of December 1, 1920, to Xiao Xudong, Cai Hesen and others, Mao explicitly endorsed Cai's view that the only "method" by which it was possible to "transform China and the world" was a revolution on the Russian model. He suggested, however, that Lenin and his comrades had used such a "terrorist tactic" not because they wanted to do so, but because they had no alternative. At this time, Mao merely declared himself "skeptical" about anarchism. A month and a half later, in a letter of January 21, 1921, to Cai Hesen, he finally repudiated anarchism altogether, and accepted dialectical materialism as the Party's philosophical basis. Formerly, he wrote, he had not really studied the problem, but now he had concluded that the views of anarchism could not be substantiated.[60] The Marxist period, or rather the Marxist-Leninist period, in Mao's thought had begun.

The fact that Mao had thus espoused the cause of Communism did not mean that he had a clear understanding of Marxist theory, or of the road China should henceforth travel. How he began to acquire such a grasp of events will be the burden of the materials to be translated in our second volume.

---

59. Liu's work, commonly known in English as *How to Be a Good Communist*, is entitled literally *On the Self-Cultivation* [xiuyang] *of Communist Party Members*. This concept was echoed in the title, "Ideological Self-Cultivation," of Chapter 24 of the "Little Red Book," until it, and Mao's other writings, were "de-Liuized" in the spring of 1967.

60. These texts will appear in our next volume. For extracts and a more detailed summary, see S. Schram, *The Thought of Mao Tse-tung*, pp. 28–29.

A BRIEF CHRONOLOGY OF MAO ZEDONG'S LIFE TO 1920

Dec. 26, 1893	Born in Shaoshan, Hunan
1902–1907	Attends village school while working on father's farm
1910	Attends higher primary school
1911–12	Soldier in "New [modern-style] Army" in Hunan, in aftermath of the October 1911 revolution.
1913–18	Student in Fourth, then First Provincial Normal School in the provincial capital, Changsha, graduating in June 1918
April 1917	Publishes first article in *New Youth*
April 1918	Founds New People's Study Society
Aug. 1918–March 1919	Visits Beijing for the first time
March–April 1919	Visits Shanghai
July–Aug. 1919	Edits the *Xiang River Review*
Dec. 1919–June 1920	Participates in movement to expel the governor of Hunan, Zhang Jingyao
Dec. 1919–March 1920	Visits Beijing for the second time
April–July 1920	Visits Shanghai, discusses Marxism with Chen Duxiu
1920	Participates in movement for Hunanese autonomy
Sept. 1920	Appointed principal of primary school attached to First Normal
Oct.–Nov. 1920	Helps set up Socialist Youth League and Communist organizations in Hunan

Note on Sources and Conventions

This edition of Mao Zedong's writings in English translation aims to serve a dual audience, comprising not only China specialists, but those interested in Mao from other perspectives. In terms of content and presentation, we have done our best to make it useful and accessible to both these groups.

Scope. This is a complete edition, in the sense that it will include a translation of every item of which the Chinese text can be obtained. It cannot be absolutely complete, because some materials are still kept under tight control in the archives of the Chinese Communist Party. The situation has, however, changed dramatically in the decade and a half since Mao's death, as a result of the publication in China, either openly or for restricted circulation (*neibu*), of a large number of important texts. This process is reflected in the appearance of nine supplementary volumes to the Chinese-language edition of Mao's pre-1949 writings which had appeared in Tokyo in 1970–72, drawn almost entirely from the materials thus divulged in China. (The original ten volumes of the *Mao Zedong ji* [Collected Writings of Mao Zedong] were published by a small company called Hokubōsha; in 1983–86, these were reissued, with minor corrections, and the nine substantive volumes of the *Bujuan* [supplement] plus an index volume produced, by a new publishing house, Sōsōsha. Professor Takeuchi Minoru continued as chief editor of the whole series.)

Although the *Zhongyang wenxian yanjiushi* (Department for Research on Party Literature), which is the organ of the Central Committee of the Chinese Communist Party responsible for the publication of Mao's writings, has always disclaimed any intention of producing his complete pre-1949 works, it appeared in early 1989 that such an edition was in fact on the way, at least for a part of his early career. An advertising leaflet dated December 20, 1988, announced the appearance, in the spring of 1989, of two volumes, *Mao Zedong zaoqi zhuzuoji* (Collected Writings by Mao Zedong from the Early Period), and *Jiandang he da geming shiqi Mao Zedong zhuzuo ji* (Collected Writings by Mao Zedong during the Period of Establishing the Party and of the Great Revolution [of 1924–1927]), and invited advance orders for both volumes. The events of June 4, 1989, led first to the postponement of publication, and then to the decision to issue only the first of these volumes, for internal circulation, under the new title of *Mao Zedong zaoqi wengao* (Draft Writings by Mao Zedong for the Early Period). The publication of the second volume has been postponed indefinitely.

These two volumes were designed to be complete, with one minor qualification. Because this was an official edition, no text was included unless it could be attributed to Mao Zedong with virtual certainty. A strong probability that Mao was the author was not sufficient. Prior to June 1989, further volumes in the same format were in preparation, at least down to the early 1930s. These plans have now been set aside. A number of volumes of Mao's writings will, none the less, appear to mark the hundredth anniversary of his birth in 1993, including a six-volume edition of his military writings containing many texts never before published even for internal circulation.

In the light of these circumstances, we have decided to publish now, in the summer of 1992, only the first volume of our series of translations, which ends (like the *Wengao*) on November 30, 1920. Further volumes, already translated and edited, will be delayed until the relevant materials scheduled to appear in Chinese in 1993 can be incorporated into them, making each volume as complete as possible. Volumes 2 and 3 of our edition will appear in 1994, and two or three more will be published each year thereafter until the series, which will comprise up to ten volumes, is complete down to 1949.

As for our first volume, it is more comprehensive than the Chinese edition of Mao's writings from 1912 to 1920. Not being subject to the same constraints as the editors of the *Wengao*, we have chosen to translate items from the Tokyo edition which they have not included. In no case is there definite evidence that Mao did *not* write these texts, and in several instances it is very likely that he did. We have also included several couplets or *duilian* from a recent edition of Mao's poetry, *Mao Zedong shici duilian jizhu* (Annotated Edition of Mao Zedong's Poems and Couplets) (Changsha: Hunan wenyi chubanshe, 1991). These were omitted from the *Wengao* on the grounds that they had been dredged up from their memories decades later by Mao's contemporaries, who were then old men, and that there was no written evidence of their authenticity. Obviously they cannot be attributed to Mao with certainty, but two brief lines could well stick in the mind for a long time, and these items add their bit to the total picture of Mao's early years.

Because the range and nature of sources for successive volumes will vary, details for each volume are given separately at the end of this note.

Annotation. So that any attentive reader will be able to follow the details of Mao's argument in each case, we have assumed no knowledge at all of anything relating to China. Every person mentioned is briefly situated when his name first appears in the text, as are significant institutions, places, and events. To keep the resulting notes from occupying too much space, we have generally restricted those regarding Mao's contemporaries to their lives down to the period covered by each volume. We have also ruled out all annotations regarding people or events in the West, with rare exceptions for individuals whose significance for Mao or China needs to be explained.

In each biographical note, dates of birth and death, separated by a hyphen, are given immediately after the name. A blank following the hypehn should, in principle, signify that the person in question is still living. In the case of individuals born in the 1870s and 1880s, this is obviously unlikely, but in many instances even the editors of the *Wengao* have not been able to ascertain the facts. We have done our best to fill these gaps, but have not always succeeded. Sometimes a Chinese source ends with the word "deceased" (*yigu*), without giving the date of death. Here we have inserted a question mark after the hyphen, and have mentioned the fact in the note. It should not be assumed that all those born in the 1890s for whom no second date is given are already dead; some of them are in fact very much alive as of 1992.

The reader will soon discover that the personages who appear in these pages are as numerous as the characters in a traditional Chinese novel. To make it easier to locate information in the notes, frequent references have been inserted indicating where the first note about a given individual appears in the volume. In a few instances, notes about Mao's contemporaries have been split into two, so that the reader will not be confronted in reading a text of 1915 with information relating to 1919 or 1920.

The introductions, especially that to Volume I, should be considered in a very real sense as an extension of the notes. These texts will, we hope, help readers unfamiliar with Mao Zedong, or with early twentieth century China, find their *own* way through Mao's writings of the early period. Any controversial or provocative statements which they may contain are intended to stimulate reflection, not to impose a particular interpretation on the reader. This is a collection of historical source material, not a volume of interpretation.

Use of Chinese terms. On the whole, we have sought to render all Chinese expressions into accurate and readable English, but in a few cases it has seemed simpler and less ambiguous to use the Chinese word. These instances include, to begin with, *zi* (courtesy name) and *hao* (literary name). Because both Mao, and the authors he cited, frequently employ these alternative appellations instead of the *ming* or given name of the individual to whom they are referring, information regarding them is essential to the intelligence of the text. The English word "style" is sometimes used here, but because it may stand either for *zi* or for *hao*, it does not offer a satisfactory solution. The Chinese terms have, in any case, long been used in Western-language biographical dictionaries of China, as well as in Chinese works.

Similarly, in the case of second or provincial-level, and third or metropolitan-level graduates of the old examination system, we have chosen to use the Chinese terms, respectively *juren* and *jinshi*. The literal translations of "recommended man" and "presented scholar" would hardly have been suitable for expressions which recur constantly in Mao's writings; nor would Western parallels (such as "doctorate" for *jinshi*) have been adequate. We have also preferred *xian* to "county" for the administrative subdivision which constituted the lowest level of the imperial bureaucracy, and still exists in China today.

Apart from the Western connotations of "county," there is the problem that *xian* is also often translated "district" (as in the expression "district magistrate"), and "district" itself is ambiguous in the Chinese context. We have also preferred to use the Chinese word *li* rather than to translate "Chinese league" (or simply "league"), or to give the equivalent in miles or kilometers.

In one instance we have, on the contrary, used an English translation instead of a Chinese term. The main subdivisions in older writings, commonly referred to by their Chinese name of *juan*, are here called simply "volume" (abbreviated as "Vol."). Readers who consult the Chinese texts should have no difficulty in determining when this refers to the physically separate volumes of modern editions, and when it means *juan*.

Sources for Volume I

Because the *Wengao* is basically complete for the period June 1912–November 1920, and because it has been very carefully edited by scholars with access to the texts of Mao's writings and to much information about his life, we have taken this edition as the primary guide for our English edition. Whenever there are textual variants between it and the versions reproduced in the Tokyo edition, we have indicated them in the notes to the relevant item in this volume. We have not given the page references to the *Wengao* at the end of each of our texts, because any reader with a knowledge of Chinese can easily locate the original. The Chinese edition is divided into two parts: the first, totaling 579 pages, contains writings of which Mao is the sole author; the second, of 124 pages, contains items signed jointly with others, and unsigned texts drafted in whole or in part by Mao. We have put all of these in a single chronological sequence. In cases of joint authorship, the fact will be obvious from the signatures at the end. Information given by the *Wengao* editors regarding Mao's role in writing other texts is included in the notes to each item.

Everything in this volume is to be found in the *Wengao*, with the exceptions indicated below. *Writings*, followed by the volume number, stands for the *Mao Zedong ji* (Collected Writings of Mao Zedong); *Supplements* stands for the *Bujuan* (Supplements) thereto. *Couplets* stands for *Mao Zedong shici duilian jizhu* (Annotated Edition of Mao Zedong's Poems and Couplets).

Date	*Title*	*Source*
1917	On the Occasion of a Memorial Meeting for Students of First Normal School Who Died of Illness	*Couplets*, 153
1917	Mourning Couplet for a Student	*Couplets*, 154
1917	In Praise of Swimming	*Couplets*, 155
1917	In Answer to Mr. Xiao Mo'an	*Couplets*, 156
Dec. 24, 1919	Zhang Jingyao's Smuggling of Opium Seeds Uncovered	*Supplements* 9, 67–68

Jan. 4, 1920	Zhang Jingyao Smuggles Opium Seeds	*Supplements* 9, 69–71
Feb. 28, 1920	The New Campaign of Hunan Representatives to Expel Zhang	*Supplements* 9, 77
Apr. 27, 1920	The Hunan People Are Fighting Hard to Get Rid of Zhang Jingyao	*Supplements* 9, 85–87
June 5, 1920	The Hunan People Denounce Zhang Jingyao for Sabotaging the Peace	*Supplements* 9, 91
1920	Business Regulations	*Supplements* 1, 211–12
1920	General Regulations for Branch Offices	*Supplements* 1, 213–14
1920	For the Attention of Branch Offices	*Supplements* 1, 215
Sep. 23, 1920	Statutes of the Russia Studies Society	*Supplements* 9, 101–02
Oct. 8, 1920	Essentials of the Organic Law of the Hunan People's Constitutional Convention	*Supplements* 9, 105
Oct. 8, 1920	Essentials of the Electoral Law of the Hunan People's Constitutional Convention	*Supplements* 9, 104
Nov. 1, 1920	Notice from the Cultural Book Society	*Writings* 1, 73

Finally, some explanation should be offered here of the form in which the translation of Mao's marginal notes to Paulsen, and Paulsen's own text, are presented below. The extracts from Paulsen's book printed opposite the comments by Mao to which they refer are, with one exception (indicated in an endnote), those reproduced by the editors of the *Wengao.* As explained above, in a footnote to the Introduction, the Chinese translation which Mao read was made by Cai Yuanpei from the Japanese version, and then checked against the original German. Nevertheless, it may be convenient for readers wishing to place Mao's comments in the context of Paulsen's argument as a whole to have a guide as to where, in the English version, a given passage can be found. We have therefore used or adapted Thilly's English text, whenever its meaning was essentially the same as that of the Chinese. Where the sense of Cai Yuanpei's version is significantly different, the English text which appears in the right hand column has been translated directly from the Chinese. We have also added to the page numbers of the Chinese edition, which appear in this document as published in the *Wengao,* the corresponding pages from Thilly's translation.

Volume I The Pre-Marxist Period, 1912-1920

MAO'S ROAD TO POWER

Revolutionary Writings 1912-1949

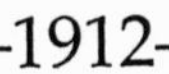

1912

Essay on How Shang Yang Established Confidence by the Moving of the Pole[1]

(June 1912)

When I read in the *Shi ji*[2] about the incident of how Shang Yang[3] established confidence by the moving of the pole,[4] I lament the foolishness of the people of our country, I lament the wasted efforts of the rulers of our country, and I lament the fact that for several thousand years the wisdom of the people has not been developed and the country has been teetering on the brink of a grievous disaster. If you don't believe me, please hear out what I have to say.

Laws and regulations are instruments for procuring happiness. If the laws and

---

1. This, Mao's earliest known writing, is an essay he wrote in June 1912 when, after leaving the army, he had enrolled as a first-year student at the middle school in Changsha. His teacher thought so highly of this effort that he marked it for circulation among all members of the class; he also singled out many passages with circles, indicating approval of Mao's style, and dots, registering appreciation of the content.

2. This work by Sima Qian (145–74? B.C.), *zi* Zichang, of which the title has been variously translated *Historical Records*, *Records of the Historian*, and *Records of the Grand Historian*, was the first major history of China from the earliest times down to the Han dynasty.

3. Shang Yang (c. 390–338 B.C.) was one of the founders of the "Legalist" school. His original name was Gongsun Yang; he was also called Wei Yang, because he was descended by a concubine from the royal house of Wei. He is most commonly known as Shang Yang because Duke Xiao of Qin, whom he served, enfeoffed him as Lord Shang. The earliest source on his life, to which Mao refers in this essay, was the biography included in the *Shi ji*. On Shang Yang, see the translation of the book which bears his name (but was probably not written by him) by J.J.L. Duyvendak, *The Book of Lord Shang* (London: Arthur Probsthain, 1928). A recent work, documenting the view of Shang Yang during the last years of Mao's life, is Li Yuning (ed.), *Shang Yang's Reforms and State Control in China* (White Plains, N.Y.: M.E. Sharpe, 1977).

4. The best translation of this passage is perhaps that of Creel:

> After the decree [incorporating his whole set of sweeping reforms] was drawn up Shang Yang did not at once publish it, fearing that the people did not have confidence in him. He therefore had a pole thirty feet long placed near the south gate of the capital. Assembling the people, he said that he would give ten measures of gold to anyone who could move it to the north gate. The people marvelled at this, but no one ventured to move it. Shang Yang then said, "I will give fifty measures of gold to anyone who can move it." One man then moved it, and Shang Yang immediately gave him fifty measures of gold, to demonstrate that he did not practice deception.
>
> — H.G. Creel, *Chinese Thought from Confucius to Mao Tse-tung* (London: Eyre and Spottiswoode, 1954), pp. 153–54.

regulations are good, the happiness of our people will certainly be great. Our people fear only that the laws and regulations will not be promulgated, or that, if promulgated, they will not be effective. It is essential that every effort be devoted to the task of guaranteeing and upholding such laws, never ceasing until the objective of perfection is attained. The government and the people are mutually dependent and interconnected, so how can there be any reason for distrust? On the other hand, if the laws and regulations are not good, then not only will there be no happiness to speak of, but there will also be a threat of harm, and our people should exert their utmost efforts to obstruct such laws and regulations. Even though you want us to have confidence, why should we have confidence? But how can one explain the fact that Shang Yang encountered the opposition of so large a proportion of the people of Qin?

Shang Yang's laws were good laws. If you have a look today at the four thousand-odd years for which our country's history has been recorded, and the great political leaders who have pursued the welfare of the country and the happiness of the people, is not Shang Yang one of the very first on the list? During the reign of Duke Xiao, the Central Plain was in great turmoil, with wars being constantly waged and the entire country exhausted beyond description. Therefore, Shang Yang sought to achieve victory over all the other states and unify the Central Plain, a difficult enterprise indeed. Then he published his reforming decrees, promulgating laws to punish the wicked and rebellious, in order to preserve the rights of the people. He stressed agriculture and weaving, in order to increase the wealth of the people, and forcefully pursued military success, in order to establish the prestige of the state. He made slaves of the indigent and idle, in order to put an end to waste. This amounted to a great policy such as our country had never had before. How could the people fear and not trust him, so that he had to use the scheme of setting up[5] the pole to establish confidence? From this, we realize the wasted efforts of those who wield power. From this, we can see the stupidity of the people of our country. From this, we can understand the origins of our people's ignorance and darkness during the past several milennia, a tragedy that has brought our country to the brink of destruction.

Nevertheless, at the beginning of anything out of the ordinary, the mass of the people [*limin*] always dislike it. The people being like this, and the law being like that,[6] what is there to marvel about? I particularly fear, however, that if this story of establishing confidence by moving the pole should come to the attention of various civilized peoples of the East and the West, they will laugh uncontrollably so that they have to hold their stomachs, and make a derisive noise with their tongues. Alas, I had best say no more.

---

5. Either deliberately, or by a slip of the pen, Mao here wrote *li* (establish, set up) instead of *xi* (move). His teacher replaced the first character by the second; the translation corresponds to Mao's wording.

6. I.e., the people clinging to their old ways, and the law being directed toward radical change, like Shang Yang's reforms.

1913

Classroom Notes[1]

(October–December 1913)

Baisha's[2] biography can be found in the *Ming Scholars' Academic Records.* As for the many scholars in the school of neo-Confucian[3] philosophy during the Song and Yuan dynasties, there is *The Song and Yuan Academic Records.*[4]

---

1. These notes were made by Mao when he was a student in the preparatory class at Fourth Normal School in Changsha in the fall of 1913, before that school was amalgamated in the spring of 1914 with First Normal School, where he continued his studies until graduation in 1918. The first eleven pages of the notebook Mao used contain his handwritten copy of the *Jiu ge* (Nine Odes), and Qu Yuan's *Li sao* (Song of Sorrow), two items from the *Chu ci* (Poems of Chu), a third century B.C. compilation which remained one of Mao's favorites to the end of his life. In the first two-thirds of the notes which follow, Mao's summaries of lectures by Yang Changji on self-cultivation *(xiushen)* alternate with notes on the lectures of Yuan Zhongqian regarding classical Chinese literature. The remaining third is devoted in large part to the author Yuan presented as a model of elegant and correct style, the Tang dynasty poet and essayist Han Yu (768–824), *zi* Tuizhi, *hao* Changli. These later notes contain so many lengthy and exact quotations from Han Yu's works that, as the editors of the *Wengao* surmise, they may well represent the fruit of Mao's own reading in the library. This change in character should not, however, be exaggerated; there are many direct quotations in Mao's earlier notes, and there are summaries, apparently from lectures, in the later portion. Mao remembered Yuan Jiliu (1868–1932), *hao* Zhongqian (known familiarly to his students as "Yuan the Big Beard") well in later years, and wrote an inscription for his tomb in 1952. Yang Changji (1871–1920), *zi* Huasheng, then Huaizhong, was, however, undoubtedly the teacher who influenced him the most during his period at First Normal. Yang, who had studied for a decade in Japan, the United Kingdom, and Germany, taught a moral philosophy which combined the emphasis of Western liberalism on self-reliance and individual responsibility with a strong sense of man's duty to society, rooted in neo-Confucianism. This dual inspiration is clearly conveyed by Mao's notes on these lectures. Yang's attachment to China is symbolized by the new *zi*, or style, he had taken during his long absence abroad, Huaizhong, literally "yearning for China." For further details on Yang see below the obituary notice mourning him dated January 22, 1920, of which Mao was a signatory.

2. Chen Xianzhang (1425–1500), *zi* Gongpu, *hao* Shizhai, was also known as Baisha xiansheng, after the district in Guangdong from which he hailed.

3. The term used here, *lixue*, sometimes loosely translated "idealist," is used both for the neo-Confucian thought of the Song and Ming dynasties in general, and for one of the two main divisions of that school, which stresses the primacy of *li* (objectively existing principle or reason) rather than of *xin* (the individual mind).

4. The *Mingru xue'an* (Ming Scholars' Academic Records) and *Sungyuan xue'an* (Song and Yuan Academic Records) are works by the celebrated late Ming and early Qing philosopher Huang Zongxi (1610–1695), *zi* Taichong, *hao* Nanlei. The first, completed by

Yubi,[5] a native of Anhui, was content to be poor but emphasized practice. His winnowing away the chaff was one example.

Disheng[6] said in his diaries that if a gentleman wants to transform the morals of the time, he must stress two principles: magnanimity and sincerity. To be magnanimous means not to be envious; to be sincere means not to boast, not to covet undeserved reputation, not to do overly impractical things, and not to talk about ideals too lofty. Do not do overly impractical things: Fukuzawa Yukichi[7] started Keiō University and considered education to be his vocation. He was not greedy, but was fair in dealing with money. Mr. Fukuzawa was learned in many different fields, and had the resolve to teach untiringly.

Do not talk about ideals too lofty: It is better to keep quiet if you know in your heart that something won't work but only sounds good.

When two armies come together face-to-face, the one that is at peace with itself will win, and the proud will lose.

If the teacher truly loves his pupils, even the obstinate will be moved.

True spirit: To do things honestly and to study with a true heart.

Ordinary people have much in common with one another, but have no spirit of independence.[8] Those who have a spirit of independence are heroes [*haojie*].

Gradual stroke: Gradual, the gradual permeation of water; stroke, the stroke of the hand.

The *hong* gate:[9] The college buildings.

Chinese Language

The character "shaan" in "Shaanxi" is composed of the radical for "big" and the radical for "enter"; the character "xia" in "xia'ai" is composed of the radical for "big" and the radical for "man."

Huang in 1676, was one of the earliest major histories of Chinese philosophy. The second, left unfinished at his death, was completed by his son, Huang Bojia, and others. Huang Zongxi, who belonged to the school of neo-Confucianism emphasizing mind rather than principle, was active in opposing the Manchu conquerors.

5. Wu Yubi (1391–1469), *zi* Zifu, *hao* Kangzhai, a Ming neo-Confucian philosopher.

6. Zeng Guofan (1811–1872). His original *zi* was Bohan; Disheng is the style (*gai hao*) he took at the age of twenty, and with which he signed many of his family letters. He is mentioned many times in these lecture notes, sometimes as Disheng or Zeng Guofan, sometimes by the title under which he was canonized after his death, Wenzheng. The views presented here by Yuan the Big Beard are a summary of ideas expressed in an entry in Zeng's diary dated the 24th day of the ninth month of the tenth year of the Xianfeng era (November 6, 1860), quoting directly some key phrases.

7. Fukuzawa Yukichi (1834–1901), the founder of Keiō University, was one of the leading advocates of modern and Western ideas during the Meiji Restoration in Japan.

8. A summary of Yang Changji's view; see *Yang Changji wenji* (Collected Writings of Yang Changji) (Changsha: Hunan Jiaoyu Chubanshe, 1983), p. 70.

9. The Chinese text here has "ku gate"; the editors of the *Wengao* suggest that *ku*, meaning "an urgent communication," is a slip of the pen for *hong*, an old word for school or college.

The nature of poetry is that it appeals to the sense of beauty.

When both true feeling and understanding are present, one can speak of poetry.

[Si]ma Qian[10] was a native of Longmen. Sometimes the prefectures and counties were not bounded by mountains and rivers.

A *jueshi*[11] has half the length of a *lüshi*.[12] It either leaves out the beginning and keeps the ending, or the other way around; therefore, a *jue* is based on a *lü*. Only those who have broad knowledge and a resolute character can compose it seamlessly.

Wang Youdan, *zi* Youhua, was a native of Heyang, Shaanxi. He was a *jinshi* in the early Qing dynasty and was good at poetry.

Wang Shizhen, *zi* Yishang, *hao* Ruanting, was a native of Xincheng, Shandong. His poetry set the standard of orthodoxy during a whole era in the early Qing period. Wu and Wang[13] shared renown at that time. The things of this world are constantly changing.

The Biographies of the Officials Who Served Two Consecutive Dynasties,[14] compiled by the Qing dynasty, was written to warn later generations. Who would anticipate that, during a time of political reforms, none was willing to die for the cause?

Zhenzhou: Yizheng county of Yangzhou. During the transition between the Ming and Qing dynasties, people enjoyed prosperity and affluence, civilization flourished, and scholars flocked there from all directions. It was indeed an historical site.

The carp of the north and the perch of the south: The most famous were from the Yellow River and the Song River.

An essay is judged outstanding on the basis of its arguments, a poem by the feelings it conveys.

One has to be touched before he can have feelings. When you have feelings and put them into poetry, only then is it both beautiful and elegant.

Chu Xiongwen, *zi* Siwen, was a native of Yixing, Jiangsu. He was a *jinshi* during the Kangxi period of the Qing dynasty. He was good at writing both poetry and essays.

The Chus[15] were all famous at the time, but the only one who was good at poetry was [Chu Xiong]wen.

Yangming[16] investigated things [*ge wu*]. He considered the principle of the bamboo tree.

---

10. On Sima Qian, see the note to Mao's essay of June 1912.

11. A stanza of four lines.

12. A stanza of eight lines.

13. Wu Weiye (see notes 20 and 93), and Wang Shizhen (1634–1711), on whom information is given in the two preceding sentences, and also in note 132.

14. *Er chen zhuan,* compiled in 1777 during the reign of the Qianlong Emperor.

15. The reference is to Chu Xin (1631–1706), *zi* Tongren, and to several of his sons and grandsons.

16. Wang Shouren (1472–1528), *zi* Boan, noted philosopher more often referred to, as Yuan does here, by his *hao*, Yangming, under which his collected works were published.

The more we use our spirits and minds, the sharper they become. As long as we apply our minds even to small things, we can learn great things.[17]

Whether it be poetry or prose, as long as it is well written, it is beautiful.

Anecdotes are used in three ways: (1) In *ci*,[18] such as fairies; (2) in essays, such as the "well-field" system, schools, and emperors; and (3) in science, i.e., physical reality.

Poetry needs to embody all three of them. Mysteries, stories, and reality should be written as appropriate according to the time and place.

Wang Lutai, Wang Gengyan, and Wang Yanke[19] were called the Three Wangs. Their paintings were treasured throughout the world.

To inscribe a title, the style of calligraphy is most important. (Poetry)

Titles should be succinct. Hence, you can tell a good poet simply by looking at the titles of his poems, without necessarily reading the poems themselves. They must be distinctive.

Protection by one's elders or ancestors was a system under the Tang, Song, Ming, and Qing dynasties. The descendants of high officials were able to be officials from generation to generation.

Wu Weiye's poems were much in vogue for a time.

Because he served the Qing dynasty, he always felt acutely ashamed in the face of Cangxue (Wang Gan).[20] This feeling can be found in the poems they exchanged. But Wu also suffered under various forms of pressure: one was his mother's aging, and another the severity of Qing laws. That's why he enjoyed Cangxue's companionship.

It is hard to compose good poems that are joyful, but easier to work on sorrowful ones. (This is an advantage for the poor and the sorrowful in writing poems.)

If the title looks mysterious, we need to enter into it with our spirit, and then the wondrous meaning will be revealed.

To jot down ideas at random, happily expressing what is on our minds, helps to maintain equilibrium (refers to travel diaries).

---

17. Above this passage Mao has written: "Words of Zeng," and it does indeed reflect ideas expressed by Zeng Guofan in his *Jiashu* (Family Letters). See especially the letters of the fourteenth day of the twelfth month of the seventh year of the Xianfeng era (January 28, 1858) and the ninth day of the fourth month of the eighth year of the Xianfeng era (May 21, 1858), both of which contain the words: "The more we use our minds, the more outstanding they become."

18. Poetry written to certain tunes with strict tonal patterns and rhyme schemes, in fixed numbers of lines and words, originating in the Tang dynasty (618–907) and fully developed in the Song dynasty (960–1279).

19. Wang Lutai was the *hao* of Wang Yuanqi, *zi* Maojing (1642–1715). Wang Gengyan was the *hao* of Wang Nian (1632–1717), *zi* Shigu. Yanke was the *hao* of Wang Shiming (1592–1680), *zi* Sunzhi. The first was the grandson of the third.

20. Cangxue, *zi* Duche, *hao* Nanlai, became a monk after the fall of the Ming. He died in 1656. Wu Weiye (1609–1672), *zi* Jungong, *hao* Meicun, was, in fact, a more complex character than suggested here. See below the discussion of his poem "Encountering a Hunt in the Snow" (note 93).

Yun Jing, *zi* Ziju, was a native of Yanghu, Jiangsu. He was a *juren* in the Qianlong period of the early Qing. He served as magistrate of Ruijin *xian* in Jiangxi. He wrote *Collected Writings from the Dayunshan Chamber*. His works have been identified with the Yanghu School.[21]

The Tongcheng[22] and Yanghu schools each had its merits. We can use one word to describe the essence of each school: Tongcheng was exuberant and Yanghu down-to-earth.

[Square] seals represent permanent officials; rectangular seals represent temporary officials.

The great reckoning [*daji*] meant the evaluation of whether an official was competent and virtuous or not so as to determine whether he should be dismissed or promoted.

Places of scenic beauty, historical ruins, dangerous passes, and popular customs, as well as coastal areas where commerce takes place — all these are things which ought to be noted in travel diaries.

Wei Xi went bankrupt and gave all he had, keeping nothing for his family. He behaved very much like Zhang Liang.[23]

A deft drummer hits the edges of the drum. (Those who handle the ladles understand this very well.)

When a sovereign knows men, he is wise, but this was difficult even for the emperor [Yao]![24]

A wise prime minister does not rely only on his own outstanding qualities, but gathers together all the talents in the world and makes use of them. Thus it is written: "Let me have but one resolute minister, plain and sincere, without other abilities, but having a simple complacent mind, and possessed of generosity, regarding the talents of others, as if he himself possessed them; and when he finds accomplished and sage-like men, loving them in his heart more than his mouth expresses. . . . "[25]

---

21. Yun Jing (1757–1817), *zi* Ziju, *hao* Jiantang, was a native of Wujin in Jiangsu, but chose to identify himself with neighboring Yanghu, and with the school named after it. The *Dayunshanshi wengao* (referred to by Mao as *Dayunshanshi ji*) was the principal edition of his works.

22. A school of essayists of the Qing period founded by Fang Bao (1668–1749), *zi* Fengjiu, *hao* Linggao, alternative *hao* Wangqi, of Tongcheng in Anhui, and continued by others from the same locality.

23. Wei Xi (1624–1681), *zi* Shuzi, alternative *zi* Bingshu, *hao* Suzhai, was a Ming loyalist writer who went bankrupt because he gave his family's fortune to an army resisting the Qing, and subsequently lived in retirement. Zhang Liang (d. 186 B.C.), *zi* Zifang, came from a family that had served the Kingdom of Wei for five generations. When Wei was destroyed by Qin, he used his family fortune in an effort to find someone who would cut down the King of Qin and avenge Wei.

24. This sentence is made up of two clauses from a passage in the *Shu jing*, also known as the *Shang shu*, translated by Legge as *The Book of Historical Documents*, II, III, I (Legge, Vol. III, p. 70). The chapter in question is that devoted to the counsels of Gao Yao, Emperor Yu's Minister of Crime.

25. This is a quotation from the *Book of Historical Documents* V, XXX, 6 (Legge,

Broad-mindedness means that a person with outstanding talents is on the throne. It does not mean to tolerate base things.

A spear kills, but a shield wards off enemies. Each has its own usage. This is called making tools serve men.

Those who are clothed in fur and ride on horses talk as if others are of no account.

When Liang and Le looked for good horses, they often went to areas foresaken by people.

First size up something before you measure it. Know people's personalities before you make friends with many people.

The great void means very empty. The way of ancient literature is terse and clear.

Treat an old acquaintance as if you were meeting for the first time, then you will not harbor resentment when you are old.

October 28

The ratio between the circumference and the diameter is 113:355 [*sic*].

The two most commonly used kinds of thermometers are Fahrenheit and Celsius. 32°F is the freezing point and 212°F is the boiling point. 0°C is the freezing point and 100°C is the boiling point. When computing, 5 degrees Celsius corresponds to 9 degrees Fahrenheit.

As regards the earth's longitude, for every fifteen degrees, there is one hour's difference because of the rotation of the earth around its own axis. (For every fifteen minutes of longitude, there is the time difference of one minute, and for every fifteen seconds of longitude, a time difference of one second.)

The reference line for longitude East or West is the Observatory of London, the capital of England.

The position of Beijing is longitude 116 degrees 30 minutes, and the position of Japan is longitude 139 degrees 40 minutes. Arithmetic.

November 1 Self-Cultivation

It is human nature to love comfort and fear hard work. Laziness is the breeding ground of all evil. If one is lazy, the farmer will waste his land, the worker will waste his tools, the merchant will waste his merchandise, and the scholar will waste his learning. When their calling is neglected, they have nothing to live on, and then destruction of self and family will follow. If a whole nation is lazy, at first, it will not progress, then it will retrogress, and subsequently it will grow weak and finally be destroyed. How fearful! That's why we say laziness is the breeding ground of all evil.

Struggle. If you seek to fight against an army of a hundred thousand soldiers

---

Vol. III, p. 629), with one or two verbal variations. Since these are very slight, we have used Legge's wording in the text.

with five thousand soldiers, or to mobilize exhausted soldiers and control newly tamed horses, and if you still want to survive, you will not be able to do so without struggle.

Vigor. Young people need to have vigor, or they will be overcome by lethargy. Lethargy enters through the breach of laziness. Therefore we say that idleness leads one to the tomb.[26]

The cure for bodily weakness. If many are frail, then a nation cannot be strong. This is the case of our nation now, and because of it, she cannot compete with the foreign countries. As for soldiers, their mission is to defend their country. If they are not valiant and strong, they cannot fulfill this task. Moreover, if they have little education, they cannot accomplish much. Since scholars in our country are so feeble, when soldiers are enlisted, many who fill the quota are scoundrels with little education. When driven to the battlefield, they will flee before they even encounter the enemy. Our nation has suffered greatly because of this for many years past. If you visited Japan, you would see a totally different picture. A leading educator said in a speech: "Japan is caught in the whirl of world competition; all the powers have come upon us with full force. What a dangerous situation! Without an army, we cannot stand. Therefore, it is an urgent task for us to temper our bodies, etc., etc." In Japan, schools attach the greatest importance to sports. There are various kinds of sports: Tennis,[27] baseball, soccer, archery, fencing, judo, rowing, swimming, hiking, and touring parties can be seen everywhere. It is the same with the Western countries. Take touring parties as an example. Periodically, the school has an outing. They first pick out a beautiful place as the destination. When they get there, speeches will be made in front of the crowd. Nobody dares not to continue to the destination. All these are ways to cure bodily frailty, and to encourage young people.[28]

Menial labor. The advantages of doing menial labor are to cure laziness and to remedy bodily weakness. Do not use brooms to sweep a room with wooden floors; otherwise, the dust will fill the room. Instead, you should wipe the floors with rags.[29]

Ni Kuan cooked for his pupils. Chen Gong did menial work for his disciples.[30]

---

26. At the beginning of this paragraph, Mao has once again written: "Words of Zeng." This plainly refers to Zeng Guofan, but the editors of the *Wengao* did not find the relevant passage, nor have we.

27. Yang, who had spent several years in Japan, here employs the characters used there, *tingqiu* (Japanese reading *teikyū*), meaning "court ball," rather than the Chinese term, *wangqiu*, "net ball."

28. This whole passage is derived from Chapter 13 of Yang Changji's "Jiaoyuxue jiangyi" (Lectures on Education), which is devoted to physical education. See *Yang Changji wenji*, pp. 191–192.

29. *Ibid.*, p. 196.

30. Ni Kuan, more commonly known as Er Kuan, was a scholar of the Western Han period. On cooking for his disciples, see the *Han shu* (History of the Han Dynasty), Vol. 58. Cheng Gong, *zi* Shaozi, lived under the Later Han; regarding this incident, see the *Hou Han Shu* (History of the Later Han Dynasty), Vol. 27.

Chinese (one o'clock)

To be discreet in what you say and what you do is to have gained learning. In ancient times, scholars emphasized action. Thus [Confucius] said: "When he has time and opportunity, after the performance of these things, he should employ them in polite studies."[31] Confucius praised Yan Hui for his love of learning, saying: "He did not transfer his anger; he did not repeat a fault."[32] Not to vent one's anger on others and not to repeat the same mistakes are the most difficult things to do. Though he had as many as three thousand disciples, Confucius singled out Yan Hui as "loving to learn." And when he praised Yan Hui, he only mentioned two things — not venting his anger on others and not repeating his mistakes. We may reflect on the reason for this.

All men seek to follow the examples set by the wise and virtuous in order to learn filial piety, righteousness, and a sense of honor and shame. Zeng Can was a filial son, but he did not understand the duty of [not] passively accepting minor punishment from his father, in order to avoid greater evil.[33] Shen Sheng was pious, but did not know how to prevent his father from committing an unrighteous act.[34] Chen Zhongzi was pure, yet he was mocked as too pretentious.[35] Ranzi loved righteousness, but did not understand that the way of the superior man is to help the distressed, but not to add to the wealth of the rich.[36] Yuanxian had a sense of shame, but declined the grain [offered to him by Confucius], not realizing he could give it away in the hamlets, towns, and villages.[37] Why? Their knowledge was insufficient.

Understanding the interrelationships of things. Understanding thing A might help us to understand thing B. Comprehension of one truth might lead to another.

---

31. Here Mao's notes reproduce verbatim the sentence in quotation marks from the *Lun yu* (Confucian Analects, hereafter *Analects*) I, VI (Legge, Vol. I, p. 140). The "things" referred to are filial conduct, truthfulness, benevolence, and the like.

32. *Analects* VI, II (Legge, Vol. I, p. 185). Yan Hui was Confucius' favorite disciple; his name occurs frequently in these lecture notes.

33. Zeng Can, *zi* Ziyu, 505–436 B.C., was one of the most famous disciples of Confucius. The story alluded to appears in the chapter "Jianzheng" of the *Xiao jing* (Classic of Filial Piety), authorship of which has been ascribed to Confucius. His father beat him so severely for a minor fault that he fainted; Confucius criticized Zeng for not getting out of the way, since by quietly submitting he might have caused his father to kill him, and no unfilial conduct could have been worse than that.

34. Shen Sheng was heir apparent to Duke Xian of Jin, who put him to death on the basis of a false charge by his favorite concubine.

35. Chen Zhongzi, or Tian Zhong, was a man of Qi of the Warring States period. For these conflicting judgments on him, see the *Mengzi* (The Works of Mencius, hereafter *Mencius*), III, II, X (Legge, Vol. II, pp. 284–287).

36. Ranzi, or Ran Qiu, *zi* Ziyou, was a man of Lu and a disciple of Confucius. The judgment referred to appears in the *Analects*, VI, III, 1–2 (Legge, Vol. I, pp. 185–86).

37. For this story regarding Yuan Xian, also known as Yuan Si, *zi* Zisi, one of Confucius' disciples, see the *Analects* VI, III, 3–4 (Legge, Vol. I, p. 186).

To expand this reasoning further: In the universe, so many interconnections have arisen among the myriad phenomena. This we call understanding the interrelationship of things.

If one learns behind closed doors, the learning is useless. If you want to learn about everything in all countries under the sun, you should not stop until you have traveled to the remotest places and all over the four quarters of the globe.

Traveling has many advantages! When you climb the peak of Zhurong, you see how small the other mountains and hills are; when you sail upon the Yellow Sea and the Gulf of Bohai, your eyes are opened and all the other rivers and lakes vanish into insignificance. [Si]ma Qian visited Xiaoxiang, rowed a boat on West Lake, climbed Mount Kunlun, and visited many famous mountains and great lakes. That is why he had such a broad mind!

When we read *The Travel Notes on the Five Surname Lake*,[38] we can see that the people mentioned in it were all renowned at the time. When I read about them, it seems that I know them as friends. Did the travelers only want to enjoy the scenery? They also got to know the distinguished, the giants, the wise, and the learned of the time. This is what is called befriending the eminent scholars of the world.

When we select literary works to read, it is best if we pick those with object lessons, which are appropriate for our times.

Letters to Weng Zhiyuan[39] warned against licentiousness. Licentiousness is the root of all evil. And licentious thoughts[40] are far more harmful than the real acts. We should be as careful as if we were in a deep gulf, or treading on thin ice.[41]

If you are not as capable as the men of today, you are not capable at all; if you cannot surpass the ancients in learning, you cannot be considered as learned.

There are none in the world who can be called truly capable, but some dominate an era and have no rivals in their day. If you want to speak of those who were a match for anyone, there are only Mengde, Zhongmou, and Zhuge.[42] Those who are criticized by others are also men of honor. Only the ordinary are

---

38. *You wuxinghu ji,* a work by Niu Yunzhen (1706–1758), *zi* Jieping, alternative *zi* Zhensu, *hao* Kongshan, of Shandong.

39. *Yu Weng Zhiyuan shu,* a work by Fang Bao. (See above, note 22.)

40. An allusion to the *Honglou meng* (Dream of the Red Chamber) by Cao Xueqin, Chapter 5. See David Hawkes' translation, under the alternative title *The Story of the Stone*, Vol. 1 (Penguin: Harmondsworth, 1973), especially p. 146, regarding "lust of the mind."

41. An allusion to a poem in the *Shi jing* (Book of Poetry), II, V, I, 6 (Legge, Vol. IV, p. 333). The text on which Yuan was drawing reads:

> "We should be apprehensive and careful,
> As if we were on the brink of a deep gulf,
> As if we were treading on thin ice."

42. Mengde was the *zi* of Cao Cao, Zhongmou was the *zi* of Sun Quan, and Zhuge refers to Zhuge Liang, *zi* Kongming. All were leading rulers and statesmen of the Three Kingdoms period and figure prominently in the *Sanguo yanyi* (Romance of the Three Kingdoms), which was one of Mao's favorite novels.

not controversial. Men of virtue are the targets of the multitude. Therefore, it has been said: "After something has been accomplished, there arise slanders; people of high moral character tend to attract condemnation."[43]

Chengzi[44] said, "If one cannot overcome these two temptations: money and sex, he is not worth anything."

Wicked deeds will eventually be revealed. Therefore, it is said, "If you do not want other people to find out, you'd better not commit any wrongdoing."

3rd day of the first decade of the 10th month,[45] Chinese

Yi Yin[46] was perfect in moral character, scholarship, economics, and practical achievements. We should follow his example. He was born in an era of despotism, but his heart was truly impartial. He had great insight and an imposing manner; therefore, he could break with the five- or six-hundred-year tradition regarding the relations between prince and minister, and was the first to advocate revolutionary change.

There are secrets to writing compositions. There have been two traditions from olden times, but one of them lacks vitality.

The *Book of Historical Documents* records the histories of Tang and Yu, and of the Xia, Shang, and Zhou dynasties.

Articles should store up forces within. Emerging from Longmen, the [Yellow] River rushes all the way down to Tongguan. As it turns eastward, it again rushes to Tongwa. Again it turns northeastward, and rushes to the sea. Once it comes out of hiding and changes its course, it goes for a thousand *li* without stopping. This is called a big turn. So it is with composition. When you write historical commentaries, you have to be certain of each word and sentence, such as the sentence, "emphasize self-cultivation and value selective friendship" in "On Fan Li"[47]; and the word "responsibility" in "On Yi Yin."[48]

---

43. The quoted sentence is from Han Yu's essay "Yuan hui" (Sources of Slander), *Changli Xiansheng ji* (Collected Works of Han Yu, hereafter *Collected Works*), Vol. 11.

44. Probably a misprint for Zhuzi, i.e., Zhu Xi, who made the same point in very similar language (*Zhuzi wenji* [Master Zhu's Literary Writings], Vol. 6, letter in answer to Wang Zihe). Zhu Xi (1130–1200), a partisan of the *li* or principle school of neo-Confucianism, cast that doctrine in terms which defined the standard of orthodoxy until the collapse of the imperial system.

45. This corresponds to October 31. At this time, and for a decade after, Mao wrote dates sometimes according to the Western calendar, and sometimes in the old style.

46. A leading statesman of the early Shang dynasty.

47. The essay "Fan Li lun" (On Fan Li) is by Yao Nai (1733–1815), *zi* Jichuan, a member of the Tongcheng school. The essay in question deals with how Fan Li came to grief in seeking to save his son, who had killed a man.

48. "Yi Yin lun" (On Yi Yin) was by Shen Jinsi (1671–1727). In it, he argued that Yi Yin's autocracy, and Emperor Tang's action in overthrowing the tyrant Jie, and thereby "changing the mandate" *(geming)* and founding a new dynasty, were aimed at assuming responsibility for the people's welfare.

When you set your heart on a certain goal and have penetrated the facts, nothing will be impossible to you.

Only after you have a clear understanding will you be able to make a sound decision. After it is clear and you have made a decision, nothing will be impossible. Yi Yin was this kind of person.

The human heart corresponds to the decree of Heaven. That is why it has been written: "Heaven sees as my people see."[49] What is the decree of Heaven? Principle [*li*]. If we succeed in following principle, then we do not violate human nature. If you have grasped the secrets of human nature, you know Heaven's will. Then there is nothing that cannot be done.

Composition and calligraphy. To compose well, we need to be skillful with transposition and rearrangement, hence the use of the word "do"; to write, we need to wield the brush furiously, hence the use of the word "sketch."[50] Popular sayings have been composed after much thought and hard work. Only after they have been proved logical and true can they go down through the generations and still stand firm after much battering.

November 15 Self-Cultivation

Wang Chuanshan[51]: "There have been heroes who were not sages, but there have never been sages who were not heroes."[52] Sages are those who are perfect both in virtue and in accomplishment; heroes lack virtue, but have great achievements and fame. Napoleon was a hero, but not a sage.[53]

Confucius once talked about the will, saying, "Let the will be set on the path of duty. Let every attainment in what is good be firmly grasped. Let perfect virtue be accorded with. Let righteousness be followed." He also said, "[My will

---

49. This is an often-cited quotation from the *Book of Historical Documents*, V, I, ii, 7 (Legge, Vol. III, p. 292).

50. To compose an essay is *zuo wen* (to do an article); the word for write, *xie*, also means sketch.

51. Wang Fuzhi (1619–1692), known as Wang Chuanshan after the name of the mountain where he retired after the fall of the Ming, was one of the most celebrated of the patriotic scholars of the Ming-Qing transition period. His influence was strong in his native province of Hunan at this time, and Mao attended meetings at the "Chuanshan xueshe," or Wang Chuanshan Study Society, in Changsha during and after his student days. The quotation is from Wang's essay "Si jie" (Unresolved Questions).

52. These two terms, *shengxian*, or sages, and *haojie*, or heroes, recur frequently not only in the classroom notes, but in Mao's other writings of this and later periods. Mao himself never claimed to be a sage, but during his years at First Normal, he and his two friends Cai Hesen and Xiao Zisheng called themselves *sange haojie*, or "the three heroes."

53. Yang Changji here calls Napoleon "old Mr. Na" *(Na weng)*. This is a respectful form of address, but does not convey a very dynamic image of a man for whom Mao later had great admiration.

is] in regard to the aged, to give them rest; in regard to the young, to treat them tenderly; in regard to friends, to show them sincerity." He also said, "There is no one whose mind is set on truth, and is yet ashamed of bad clothes and bad food."[54] Mencius once spoke of the will, saying, "The will is first and chief, and the passion-nature is subordinate to it. Therefore I say, 'Maintain firm the will, and do no violence to the passion-nature.' " He said, "But Heaven does not yet wish that the kingdom should enjoy tranquillity and good order. If it wished this, who is there besides me to bring it about?" He also said, "But what I wish to do is to learn to be like Confucius." Again he said, "I also wish to rectify men's hearts [*zheng xin*], and to put an end to those perverse doctrines, to oppose their one-sided actions and banish away their licentious expressions: — and thus to carry on the work of the three sages."[55]

Those whom Mencius called heroes were very close to sages. He said, "Chen Liang was a native of Chu. Pleased with the doctrines of the Duke of Zhou and of Confucius, he came northwards to the Middle Kingdom and studied them. Among the scholars of the northern regions, there was perhaps no one who excelled him. He was what you call a scholar of high and distinguished qualities."[56] He said, "The mass of men wait for a King Wen, and then they will receive a rousing impulse. Scholars distinguished from the mass, without a King Wen, rouse themselves."[57]

---

54. For these passages, see the *Analects* VII, VI, 1–4; V, XXV, 4; and IV, IX (Legge, Vol. I, pp. 196, 183, 168). There are several significant discrepancies between what Mao wrote down and the text of the *Analects*. In the first of these three quotations, the last sentence should read: "Let relaxation and enjoyment be found in the polite arts." Here in listening to Yang Changji he apparently mistook the character *yi* meaning art for its homonym meaning righteousness. In the second quotation, the order of the clauses relating to friends and to the young has been inverted. In the last quotation, the original reads: "A scholar, whose mind is set on truth, and who is ashamed of bad clothes and bad food, *is not fit to be discoursed with*." It is probably Yang rather than Mao who omitted the italicized words and thus modified the thrust of the sentence. In each case, Legge's translation has been used as the basis for our version here, but has been modified to correspond to the wording of Mao's notes.

55. *Mencius*, II, I, II, 9; II, II, XIII, 5; II, I, II, 22; III, II, IX, 13 (Legge, Vol. II, pp. 188, 232, 194, 284). There are minor verbal inaccuracies in Mao's transcription of these quotes, but they do not (as in the preceding references to Confucius) significantly affect the meaning. The "perverse doctrines" Mencius wished to oppose were in particular those of Yang Zhu and Mozi.

56. The words Legge translates here as "a scholar of high and distinguished qualities," and in the following quotation as "scholars distinguishing themselves from the mass," are simply *haojie zhi shi*, literally "scholars of heroic mold."

57. *Mencius*, III, I, IV, 12; VII, I, X (Legge, Vol. II, pp. 254, 454). King Wen, or Wen Wang (1231–1135 B.C.), was the father of King Wu, or Wu Wang, the founder of the Zhou dynasty. The Duke of Zhou, or Zhou Gong (d. 1105 B.C.) was King Wen's fourth son, who served as adviser to his brother, King Wu. Both have been commonly regarded in Chinese history as wise and virtuous men.

Let your ideals be lofty. (Once you have established an ideal, try to match it with your every word and deed.)

Ideal characters. An ideal is the mother of reality.[58]

A heart's desire is a goal. Old interpretation.

Chengzi said, "A petty man is not really small; his essence is not evil."[59]

"All things are nourished together without their injuring one another. The courses [*dao*] of the seasons are pursued without any collision among them."[60] This is ideal morality.

If I keep enlarging and enriching my own world, then the whole universe will be an extended self.

Mencius said, "Some parts of the body are noble, and some ignoble; some great, and some small. . . . He who nourishes the little belonging to him is a little man, and he who nourishes the great is a great man."[61] The individual self is the small self; the universal self is the great self. The individual self is the physical self; the universal self is the spiritual self.

Guanzi: "Do not waste an age. Human love is a constant element throughout the past, the present, and the future. It goes without saying that the people of the present age look for love. But so did the generation a millennium before us, and so will the generation a millennium after us. This is human nature. When we study history, we admire the loyal and the wise; when we buy properties, we go by a contract. Therefore we say there is no man who is not good."[62]

---

58. A quotation from Liang Qichao, *Guojia sixiang bianqian yitong lun* (On Similarity and Difference in Alterations in National Thought). Liang Qichao (1873–1929), *zi* Zhuoru, *hao* Rengong, alias Cangjiang, was born in Guangdong Province. A second-degree graduate of the Qing civil service examinations, he was, with his teacher Kang Youwei, one of the leading figures in the 1898 Reform movement, and in the intellectual ferment of the ensuing decade. He advocated constitutional monarchy, popular sovereignty, educational reform, and learning from the West. After the 1911 revolution, he opposed attempts at restoration, and engaged briefly in politics, before turning back to scholarship. He and Kang were Mao's models during primary school days, and Mao continued to venerate him until 1919 or 1920.

59. Chengzi refers to Cheng Yi, the younger and more celebrated of the two Cheng brothers Cheng Hao (1032–1085), *zi* Bochun, *hao* Mingdao, and Cheng Yi (1033–1107), *zi* Zhengshu, *hao* Yichuan. The "two Chengs" were tutors to Zhu Xi, and precursors in the development of neo-Confucianism. The sentence quoted by Mao differs slightly from Cheng's original statement, in *Henan Chengshi yishu* (Surviving works of the Messrs. Cheng of Henan), Vol. 6. It appears in this form in Yang Changji's "Dahuazhai riji" (Journal from the Studio of Progress in Transformation, hereafter "Journal"), in *Yang Changji wenji*, p. 26.

60. From the *Zhong yong* (The Doctrine of the Mean), XXX, 3 (Legge, Vol. I, p. 427).

61. *Mencius,* VI, I, XIV, 1 (Legge, Vol. II, p. 416).

62. The book called the *Guanzi* has been ascribed to Guan Zhong (d. 645 B.C.), but is probably not by him. This quotation, from the section "Mu min" (Shepherd the People), Part I, was frequently commented upon by Yang Changji. See *Yang Changji wenji*, pp. 26–27 and 73.

Someone said, "I see, in history, some great men did not regret even the sacrifice of their own lives and families." [The sages and worthies who wanted to save the world have acted thus, such as Confucius (at Chen and at Kuang), Jesus (who died on the cross), and Socrates (who took poison).][63]

A saying goes like this: "When a strong soldier's hand was bitten by a poisonous snake, he had to sever his wrist, not because he did not love his wrist, but because if he had not cut it off, he could not have saved his whole body. A benevolent man looks at the whole world and the whole of humanity as his body, and considers one individual and one family as his wrist. Because he loves the whole world so much, he dares not love himself and his family more. If he can save the whole world, even if it costs his own life and that of his family, he is at peace about it."[64] (A benevolent man seeks to remove the pain and suffering of all those living under heaven, so that they may be saved.)

Though China has freedom, the only relations between the government and the people are these two things: prosecution and imprisonment, and taxation. That is all. Therefore, it is said: "I start my work at sunrise and come home at sunset; I dig my own well and drink from it; I farm my own land and eat from it. What has the emperor to do with me?"[65] Just because of the lack of relationship, people lack the concepts of state and politics. China has freedom but the Western countries have despotism. China's politics and laws are simple and taxes are light, but the Western countries are just the opposite. (The Qing dynasty was not despotic.)

Nationalities occupied by foreign powers do not have freedom. Recent examples are Taiwan and Korea.

China was very generous toward its vassal nations; apart from their obligations to pay tributes and betrothal gifts, they were allowed to enjoy autonomy. Vietnam and Korea were two examples. After Vietnam came under French rule, people were forbidden to assemble for discussions in groups of more than five, or to hide weapons, and they were not allowed to close their doors at night in order to make it easier for the government to patrol. After Korea was ceded to Japan, she had to obey her rulers in everything. The people became as tame as sheep, and their sufferings were even worse than those of the Taiwanese.

November 23 Self-Cultivation

Zhangzi said, "Our goals are to establish a common mind for the whole world, to establish the way for the people, to restore and continue the teachings of the

---

63. A passage similar to this occurs in Yang Changji's "Journal," *Yang Changji wenji*, p. 27. For the two incidents involving Confucius, see the *Analects*, XV, I, and IX, V (Legge, Vol. I, pp. 294, 217). Paulsen's ethics textbook, which Mao was to read a few years later, discusses the cases of Jesus and Socrates; see below, Mao's marginal notes of 1918 on this book.

64. This is taken verbatim from Yang Changji's "Journal," as reproduced in *Yang Changji wenji*, p. 27. (This portion of Yang's diary had already been published in 1903.)

65. This quotation is from Huangfu Mi (215–282).

ancient sages, and to open the way to the great peace [*taiping*] for all future ages."[66] To point to the right way for the people is the way of mutual existence, mutual cultivation, mutual maintenance, and mutual governing; to usher in great peace for future generations is the goal and cause of great religious leaders.

There are administrators and there are teachers. The former were people like Zhuge Wu Hou and Fan Xiwen.[67] The latter were such as Confucius, Mencius, Zhu [Xi], Lu [Jiuyuan], and Wang Yangming.

In the Song dynasty, the names of Han and Fan were mentioned together, and during the Qing dynasty, Zuo and Zeng shared renown. But Han and Zuo were administrators, while Fan and Zeng were both administrators and teachers.[68]

Emperors are emperors for a generation, but sages and worthies are emperors for a hundred generations.[69] The rulers are mindful of political and religious affairs;[70] the masses are concerned with their daily living. Changes that are introduced by the rulers will have a more rapid impact, but will not necessarily last very long; changes that are brought about at the grass roots will take effect more slowly, but the effect may last longer. (Even though there have been sage emperors and wise prime ministers, the policies would disappear when these people died. Though their contribution might take effect more rapidly, it could also be easily changed.) Firmness is the foundation for establishing oneself. Those who are filled with desire cannot be strong willed. The reason why the dragon keeper could attract the dragons was that even though the dragons were as powerful as gods, they could not resist the temptation of delicious food.[71]

Only those who are content with poverty can achieve things. Therefore, it is

---

66. Zhangzi is Zhang Zai (1020–1077), *zi* Zihou, of Hengqu in Shaanxi, an uncle of Cheng Hao and Cheng Yi. For this quotation, see his "Yulu" (Recorded Sayings), in *Zhang Zai ji* (Collected Works of Zhang Zai), Vol. 10. What Mao copied down is virtually identical with the original; the only significant variant is that in the first clause, *zhi* (will) has been replaced by *xin* (mind or heart). On the concept of "great peace" see the note to Mao's letter of August 23, 1917, to Li Jinxi.

67. Zhuge Wu Hou is Zhuge Liang; Wu Hou is his posthumous title. Fan Xiwen is Fan Zhongyan (989–1052), *zi* Xiwen, an able administrator who served, in particular, as governor of Yan'an.

68. Han is Han Qi (1008–1075), *zi* Zhigui; Fan is Fan Zhongyan. Their names were linked because together they played a leading role in defeating a Tartar (Xixia or Tangut) uprising in Shaanxi and neighboring provinces. Zeng and Zuo are Zeng Guofan and Zuo Zongtang (1812–1885), *zi* Jigao, who was one of Zeng's leading subordinates in putting down the Taipings.

69. For an elaboration of these ideas, see *Yang Changji wenji*, p. 28, where Yang adds that sages are "kings without thrones."

70. An echo of the traditional principle of *zhengjiao heyi* (the union of politics and religion).

71. Regarding the dragon keeper, in the time of Emperor Shun, see the *Zuo zhuan* (Mr. Zuo's Commentary to the Spring and Autumn Annals), twenty-ninth year of Duke Zhao (Legge, Vol. V, p. 731). (Hereafter, to avoid this long and clumsy English description, the *Zuo zhuan* is referred to by its Chinese title.)

said, "If you can chew on vegetable roots, you can do all things."[72]

It is common that all men love gratification. Only the sages do not like physical gratification (i.e., worldly gratification), but love spiritual gratification. Therefore, it has been said: "With coarse rice to eat, with water to drink, and my bended arm for a pillow — I have still joy in the midst of these things. Riches and honors acquired by unrighteousness are to me as a floating cloud."[73]

Guangwu[74] had attended the Imperial College [*taixue*] and studied the *Book of Historical Documents.* The ancient Imperial College was divided into departments based on the [five] classics.

Yan Guang was a man of integrity of the Eastern Han dynasty. After Guangwu ascended the throne, he asked Yan Guang to serve him, but was turned down. The emperor went to visit him, arriving to greet him in a comfortable chariot.[75] The emperor sat on the soft seat [of the chariot] and asked him to come out. Guang, lying in bed, said, "When Yao and Shun were rulers, there was Chao You." When Guang came, the president of the Board of Revenue (i.e., the prime minister) Hou Ba (Guang's schoolmate) went to welcome him. Guang gave him a written statement: "His Majesty and you are in very high positions. This is very good. If you rule with benevolence and righteousness, then the people will be happy. It is necessary to resist flattery and complaisance." Hou showed this letter to the emperor. The emperor said, "It is the same old attitude this crazy slave had!" Later generations blamed Guang for not coming out to serve the emperor. But they did not know that Guang was the emperor's teacher. At the academy, Guangwu had already learned much from him. So when Guangwu emerged to take over state affairs, [Yan] Guang insisted on talking about integrity, rectifying customs, and passing on the teachings to future generations. Moreover, Guang did not give in to despotism. His integrity was so high that we cannot reach it.[76]

There are three stages in the development of Chinese learning: (1) A period of active development during the last years of the Zhou dynasty. (2) A period of passive development, when Buddhism flourished greatly, and the [Buddhist] scriptures were popular. Both the ruling class and the ruled sought after them, and they were in vogue for a time. This was during the Sui and Tang dynasties. (3) A period of both active and passive development, when Zhu, Cheng, Zhang,

---

72. The quotation is from Zhu Xi, *Xiaoxue* (Elementary Learning), Vol. 6, "Shanxing" (Virtuous Action).

73. Words attributed to Confucius in the *Analects*, VII, XV (Legge, Vol. I, p. 200).

74. Guangwu is Emperor Guangwu (6–57) (personal name Liu Xiu), the founder of the Later Han dynasty.

75. *An che,* a small one-horse chariot in which one traveled seated. According to the *Book of Rites*, I, I, I, 28–29, such a vehicle, and other privileges, should always be given by the prince to a high official if the sovereign refused to accept the latter's resignation when he offered it at the age of seventy. (See the French translation of S. Couvreur, *Mémoires sur les bienséances et les cérémonies* [Paris: Cathasia, 1950], pp. 9–10.)

76. For this anecdote, see the *History of the Later Han Dynasty*, Vol. 83.

Zhou, and others emerged, and the idealist school [*weilizhi xue*] enjoyed its day of glory. But it began with reverence for Buddhism and from there returned to the Six Classics. That is why it was a period of both active and passive development. This was during the Song and Yuan dynasties.[77]

November 29 Self-Cultivation

During the Five Dynasties, Buddhist priests flagrantly intervened in decision-making, and morals had fallen extremely low. Feng Dao[78] was representative of this. With the rise of the Song dynasty, things improved a little, but not completely. Only when Fan Wenzheng rose, and they encouraged each other to be honest and loyal, did the masses begin to keep the moral rules, not daring to violate them. At its apogee, Zhu Xi, the Cheng brothers, and the other men of propriety and righteousness emerged, and the morals of the empire rapidly improved to equal those of the magnificent Eastern Han dynasty.

Zeng Disheng's *Portraits of Sages and Philosophers* included thirty-two people:[79] Wen, Zhou, Kong, Meng; Ban, Ma, Zuo, Zhuang; Ge, Lu, Fan, Ma; Zhou, Cheng, Zhu, Zhang; Han, Liu, Ou, Zeng; Li, Du, Su, Huang; Xu, Zheng, Du, Ma; Gu, Qin, Yao, and Wang.

Fan Wenzheng was the son of an old and well-known family. He lost his father as a child and followed his mother, who remarried into the family of Zhu. Therefore, his name was Zhu Yue. At first, he did not know he was the son of the Fan family. When people told him about this, he was so moved that he broke into tears. He determined to study hard, and for three years he studied steadily without stopping. He once found money but did not take it for himself. He was a second Guan Ning. He was a native of Suzhou. His son, Yaofu, was like a

---

77. Yang had taken this tripartite division into periods of active, passive, and active-passive development from Wang Guowei (1877–1923), *zi* Wang Jing'an. See his essay of 1914 "Quan xue pian" (An Exhortation to Study) in *Yang Changji wenji*, p. 202. Zhu, Cheng, Zhang, and Zhou are Zhu Xi, the two Cheng brothers, Zhang Zai, and Zhou Dunyi (1017–1073), *zi* Maoshu, the teacher of the two Cheng brothers.

78. Feng Dao (881–954), *zi* Kedao, served ten sovereigns of four different houses, from the first emperor of the later Tang dynasty to the Liao, the later Han, and the later Zhou. He called himself Changle Lao, "The ever-happy old man." Giles (Herbert A. Giles, *A Chinese Biographical Dictionary*, various editions, entry no. 573) suggests very aptly that this finds its best equivalent in the "Vicar of Bray."

79. The subjects of the biographies in Zeng Guofan's *Shengzhe huaxiang ji* included Zhou Wenwang, Zhou Gongdan, Confucius, Mencius, Ban Gu, Sima Qian, Zuoqiu Ming (the author of the *Spring and Autumn Annals*), Zhuangzi, Zhuge Liang, Lu Zhi, Fan Zhongyan, Sima Guang, Zhou Dunyi, the Cheng brothers, Zhu Xi, Zhang Zai, Han Yu, Liu Zongyuan, Ouyang Xiu, Zeng Gong, Li Bo, Du Fu, Su Shi, Huang Tingjian, Xu Zhen, Zheng Xuan, Du Zuo, Ma Duanlin, Gu Yanwu, Qin Huitian, Yao Nai, and Wang Niansun. Because Cheng stands for the two Cheng brothers, there were actually thirty-three people included.

chivalrous knight errant. Once he came across an old friend on the way. When he found out that this friend was in dire need of money, he gave him a whole boatload of wheat.[80]

Lu Xiangshan said, "We should struggle fiercely, break through the nets, burn up the thorns and thistles, and clean up the filth and mire."[81] (This is nothing else but making our hearts clean.)

Lü Xinwu, named Kun,[82] of the Ming dynasty wrote *Moaning and Groaning Sayings*.

Zeng Wenzheng's eight fundamentals:[83] "When studying the classics, the fundamental thing is to write commentaries; when composing poems, the fundamental thing is the tones; in maintaining health, the fundamental thing is to lose one's temper only seldom; in serving one's parents, the fundamental thing is to please them; when residing at home, the fundamental thing is not to get up late; in establishing oneself, the fundamental thing is not to make reckless statements; in acting as an official, the fundamental thing is not to take bribes; when troops are on the march, the fundamental thing is not to disturb the civilians." Moses' ten commandments forbade men to bear false witness.

December 6 Self-Cultivation

Guo Yunxian[84] judged the prosperity or decline of each dynasty by whether people loved fame or monetary gain. Under the Han, they loved fame, and under the Wei dynasty, monetary gain; under the Jin, they loved fame, and under the Tang, monetary gain; the Song loved fame, and the Yuan, monetary gain; the

80. Fan Wenzheng is the name under which Fan Zhongyan (see note 67) was canonized posthumously. Guan Ning (158–241), *zi* You'an, was a figure of the Three Kingdoms period who refused office because of the disturbed state of the empire. Fan Dunren (1027–1101), *zi* Fan Yaofu, was Fan Zhongyan's younger son.

81. Xiangshan is the *hao* of Lu Jiuyuan (1140–1192), *zi* Zijing. For the passage alluded to here, see his "Yulu" (Recorded Sayings) in *Xiangshan xiansheng quanji* (Complete Works of Mr. Xiangshan), Vol. 35.

82. Kun was the *hao* of Lü Xinwu (1536–1618), *zi* Shujian.

83. Zeng Wenzheng is the name under which Zeng Guofan was canonized after his death. For Zeng's own formulation of these eight points, see his letter dated the 13th day of the third month of the eleventh year of the Xianfeng era (April 22, 1861), in his *Family Letters*. We have put this passage in quotation marks because Mao's version, translated above, differs only very slightly from Zeng Guofan's original text. Apart from the replacement of four characters by others which do not significantly affect the meaning, the only change is the inversion of points three and four and of points five and six.

84. Guo Songtao (1818–1891), *zi* Bochan, *hao* Yunxian, a Hunanese from Xiangyin *xian*, assisted Zeng Guofan in the suppression of the Taipings. Subsequently, he played an important role in foreign affairs and was sent in 1876 to open the Chinese Legation in London, becoming thus the first Chinese diplomat in modern times to be stationed in a Western country. For the passage cited here, see the entry for the 20th day of the seventh month of the eleventh year of the Xianfeng era (August 25, 1861) in *Guo Songtao riji* (Diary of Guo Songtao), Vol.1 (Changsha: Hunan Renmin Chubanshe, 1980), p. 471.

Ming loved fame, and the Qing, monetary gain.

Hou Chaozong[85] was born into an old and well-known family, and loved literature. Huang Lizhou said, "Young Master Hou could not endure loneliness."[86]

The actions of the sages are not understood by others. Their songs are too exalted and austere. People consistently slander them, and they are not in accord with the common people. But the way of the sages does not seek to be understood by others. Its spirit lies solely in inquiring of heaven and earth until no more doubts remain. It is universally applicable, it will never fail through a hundred generations, and it gives the sages themselves an easy conscience. Since they have no fear of slander, it has been said: "He refused . . . to be deterred though the whole world blamed him."[87] The more they are slandered, the more steadfast they will be. This is what is called "holding firm to the Way until death."[88]

"To stand tall and have no fear, and to escape from the world and not feel sorrowful."[89] The raging waves are surging but the pillar stays unmoved. Even though you are dreaming while drunk, your mind remains very clear.[90] Though Mount Tai were tumbling down in front of you, your face still would not change its color; though a fierce tiger were loitering behind you, you would still not be afraid. This is what we call standing tall and having no fear. If a country has no Way, it is a foolish country. If a country has no Way, then poverty and a mean condition are acceptable. "With a single bamboo dish of rice, a single gourd dish of drink, and living in his mean narrow lane, he did not allow his joy to be affected by it." This is what we call to escape from the world and not feel sorrowful.[91]

False fame cuts your blessings short.

---

85. Chaozong is the *zi* of Hou Fangyu (1618–1654), whose father and uncle, as members of the Donglin faction, were persecuted by the eunuch Wei Zhongxian during the declining years of the Ming dynasty. He made a name as a literary genius at an early age and revived the style of Han Yu in his essays.

86. Huang Lizhou is the studio name of Huang Zongxi, the celebrated Ming loyalist. (See above, note 4 to this text.) He made this observation because of Hou's addiction to banquets and courtesans even when his father was in prison.

87. The attitude of the philospher Song Rong, according to the *Zhuangzi*, I, 3. (We have taken this and other quotations from Zhuangzi from the authoritative translation of Angus Graham, *Chuang-tzu. The Seven Inner Chapters and Other Writings from the Book* Chuang-tzu [London: Allen & Unwin, 1981], whenever they are included in his selection. For this passage, see p. 44.)

88. The reference is to the *Analects*, VIII, XIII, 1 (Legge, Vol. I, p. 212).

89. The attitude of the superior man, according to the *Yi jing* (Book of Changes), Chapter "Da guo."

90. See Liang Qichao, *Xinmin shuo* (Discourse on the Renovation of the People), Chapter "Lun ziyou" (On Freedom).

91. See the *Analects*, VIII, XIII, 3, and VI, IX (Legge, Vol. I, pp. 212, 188). The first passage alluded to reads: "When a country is well-governed [*bang youdao*], poverty and a mean condition are things to be ashamed of. When a country is ill-governed, riches and honor are things to be ashamed of." The second passage is in praise of the virtue of Confucius' favorite disciple, Yan Hui.

Your old friend knows you, but you don't know him. Why? Yang Zhen.[92]
Stand firm. One single slip of the foot may cause you lasting regrets.

Chinese

"Encountering a Hunt in the Snow"[93]

gu:	sounds like "bone"; belongs to the family of eagles.
qu yu:	woolen blankets, padded saddle and the like.
qiu ling:	peacock plumes. Hat ornaments of the early Qing dynasty.
xi shu:	hats, i.e., sable hats.
tong jiu:	a fermented beverage. Mare's milk made into yoghurt after agitating.[94]

---

92. Allusion to a well-known anecdote about Yang Zhen (d. 124), *zi* Boqi. Having been appointed governor of Donglai in Shandong, he passed through a district where an old friend, Wang Mi, was then magistrate. When Wang called to present the usual gift of money to a superior, Yang Zhen rejected it, accusing him of forgetting their friendship.

93. This poem is by Wu Weiye, mentioned above (see note 20). A translation of the complete text, from *Meicun shiji* (Collected Poems of [Wu] Meicun), Vol. 6, kindly made by Tung Yuan-fang, a Ph.D. candidate at Harvard, follows:

> In the north wind snow flakes big as one's palm, The river bridge collapsed, road broken off, drifting ice sounds noisily.
> Utterances of sorrowful owls and hungry sparrows: chirping and twittering, Postures of robust hawks and remarkable eagles: powerful and vigorous.
> The general hunts at the corner south of the walls, Supple fur coat, quick horse with red saddle rug.
> Hung with peacock feathers, the sable hat keeps him warm, The emerald-studded brim adorned with bright pearls an inch in diameter.
> Golden geese on archers' attire: patterns of their robes seem wet, Attendants with mare's milk yoghurt and camel broth stand before his horse.
> In brocade boots, their faces white as jade, they pluck Qin zithers, Dotted with emeralds their multiple hair-coils are all in loveliness.
> As a lad he lived on Mount Helan, In the desert sand he went to capture creatures, and came right back in the night.
> As grasses grew desolate along the Iron Ridges, the beacon fire blazed, When ice filled up the Black River, he made his horse cross over.
> Deeds have been accomplished for ten years, since he passed Gaoliu, Having been the best hawk-shooter all his life, now he is left idle.
> Thousands of people casually sing the Chile Song, He alone pours a myriad measures of Tusu wine.
> This morning he feels as if he were again at Li Ling Terrace, The general is extremely delighted that the hunting field is open.
> When a roebuck suddenly passes by, he pursues and shoots at it with laughter, Fire seems to come out of his nose; he roars like thunder.
> When he returns, vermillion banners will fill the walls and the towers, And he won't believe that in the ditches lie the bones of the frozen dead.
> There are yet men on distant roads in far garrisons, And sad, sad troops at Yarkhoto ten thousand *li* away.
> He laughs at me — a man of learning in my short, not so warm commoner's robe, On a frail donkey I am passing by a village in a bamboo hat.
> Today there is no use for *fu* on Prince Liang's garden, Leaning on a staff I will go home and alone I will shut my gate.

94. There is a reference to this beverage as suitable for presenting to high officials in the *History of the Han Dynasty*, Vol. 22, "Li yue zhi" (Treatise on Rites and Music).

tuo geng:	the purple flesh from the hump of a camel, very delicious.[95]
sese:	woman's decoration, turquoise beads.
qin sheng:	to capture alive.
Tie ling:	The Iron Ridges of Fengtian, belonging to the *xian*.[96]
Hei he:	The Black River of the Eastern and of the Outer *sui*, both located southeast of the pasturelands.[97]
Gao liu:	A ruined city, now located west of Yanggao *xian*, Datong Prefecture.
she diao shou:	Xing Zigao said, "Hu Lüjin is a real vulture-shooter."[98]
Chile ge:	During the Northern Qi dynasty, Emperor Shenwu requested that Hu Lüjin sing the "Song of the Imperial Command."[99]
Tusu wine:	A kind of wine which helps keep the cold away.
Lilingtai:	Liling Terrace is located on Mount Yanran.[100]
huang yang:[101]	Animal, found beyond the Great Wall. No horns, aspect similar to river deer.
Jiaohe:	Name of an ancient city, Che Shi, in the Western Region.
jian lü:	*Jian*, lame. *Jian lü* means useless donkeys.
ruo li:	*Ruo* is the name of an herb, *Pollia japonica. Ruo li* is a rain hat made of this material.
"Liangyuan fu":	written by Xiangru.[102]

95. Purple camel hump is referred to in a poem by the celebrated Tang dynasty poet Du Fu, "Li ren xing," which has been translated as "The Ballad of Beautiful Women." See various editions of *Tang shi sanbaishou* (Three Hundred Tang Poems). *Geng* implies that it is stewed and not broiled.

96. The Fengtian in question was actually a *fu* or prefecture in Qing times; it corresponds to the present-day city of Shenyang.

97. The pasturelands in question were those established by the Qing, inside and outside the Great Wall, for raising horses. The *sui* were districts within a hundred leagues of the capital.

98. Xing Kang, *zi* Zigao, was a man of Northern Qi. For this anecdote, see the *Beishi* (History of the Northern Dynasties), Vol. 54.

99. Gao Huan (496–547) established the Eastern Wei dynasty; after his death he was canonized by his son, the first emperor of the Northern Qi dynasty, as Gaozu Shenwu Huangdi. For this incident, and the text of the song in question, see the *History of the Northern Dynasties*, Vol. 6.

100. Mount Yanran is the old name of a mountain now located in the People's Republic of Mongolia. Lilingtai is located in Zhenglanqi, Inner Mongolia.

101. Literally, "yellow sheep."

102. Sima Xiangru (179–117 B.C.), *zi* Changqing, was a poet of the Western Han dynasty. Toward the end of a very checkered career, during which he had briefly served Emperor Jing, and been given office by Emperor Wu, he addressed to the latter patron a remonstrance against the folly of wasting time in hunting, which may be alluded to here. He was not, however, the only writer who joined the gatherings in the garden of Prince Liang. Wu Weiye's essential point here appears to be that he will no longer be a member of court circles, joining such gatherings today. (This poem was written in 1657 as he was leaving the capital and making his way back to his home at Taicang.)

bi men: Yuan An of the Later Han dynasty was lying frozen on a snowy day behind closed doors.[103]

Preface to Collected Annotations on Sunzi, by Wei Yuan[104]

Huang Zhen: Native of Pucheng, Jian Prefecture, in the Song Dynasty (now Pucheng *xian*, Fuzhou Prefecture in Fujian), *zi* Boqi, was appointed commissioner of transportation for Guangdong.

Master Sun Wu thought that military force was the last resort, that it was not fitting to wage war for a long time and kill many people, and that awful military triumphs were shameful. "Was he only the father of military tactics and strategies? Wasn't he also a true gentleman [*junzi*] who has left us with some wise advice?"[105]

In the *Laozi* it is written: "In the world, there is nothing more submissive and weak than water. Yet for attacking that which is hard and strong nothing can surpass it."[106]

"To win one hundred victories in one hundred battles is not the acme of skill. To subdue the enemy without fighting is the acme of skill. . . . Therefore, the victories won by a master of war gain him neither reputation for wisdom nor merit for valor." From Sun Wu's "On Achieving Military Success."[107]

"Su Xun argued, If we judge a person's deeds by what he preaches, then Sun Wu cannot avoid responsibility for three errors: He let the army be exposed too long, thus giving the state of Yue the opportunity to invade; connived at [Zixu

103. Yuan An (d. 92), *zi* Shaogong. He held office as governor of several territories, and led the opposition against Dou Xian, the empress' brother, but his advice was rejected in favor of that of the eunuch Zheng Zhong. When he fell upon bad times, he lived alone in a room. In the incident referred to here, the magistrate of Luoyang passed his door after an accumulation of snow, and seeing no footprints, wondered whether he was dead. On entering, he found Yuan lying within, numb with cold.

104. Wei Yuan (1794–1856), *zi* Hanshi, *hao* Meishen. Although he served as magistrate, Wei Yuan owes his fame principally to his work as the effective compiler of the *Huangchao jingshi wenbian* (Collected Writings on Statecraft of the Reigning Dynasty), an important collection of documents on political and economic matters published in 1827. Much of the substance of Yuan's account of Sunzi is drawn from Wei Yuan's *Sunzi jizhu xu* (Preface to Collected Annotations on Sunzi), which can be found in the edition of his collected works known as the *Guwei tang ji*.

105. The central idea of this paragraph is drawn from Huang Zhen (1212–1280), *zi* Dongfa, *Huangshi richao* (Mr. Huang's Daily Jottings), Vol. 58, "Du Zhuzi" (Reading Notes on the Various Masters), and the final two sentences are quoted almost verbatim from this source. (The Huang Zhen in question is not the same as the one mentioned above.)

106. See chapter 78 of the *Daode jing* (The Way and Its Power), attributed to Laozi. Here we have used D.C. Lau's translation, Lao Tzu, *Tao te ching* (Harmondsworth: Penguin, 1963), p. 140.

107. These quotations are taken from Chapters 3 and 4 of the *Sunzi*, with slight verbal variations. See Samuel B. Griffith's version, Sun Tzu, *The Art of War* (Oxford: The Clarendon Press, 1963), pp. 77, 87. In noting the source of this passage, Mao has confused two characters pronounced *gong*, one meaning attack, the other success; in fact, Chapter 3 is entitled "Offensive Strategy."

and Bopi's] whipping [Emperor Ping's] grave, thus enraging the state of Chu; and broke relations with Qin to save Bao Xu. In discussing war, Wu [Qi] was inferior to Sun; but in practice, Sun was inferior to Wu. Even more, if we look back to the rest of his sayings, we must ask, were they wise?"[108]

"Wu was originally a marshland full of tattooed barbarians like big pigs."[109]

Sun Wu was only staying at Yue as a visitor. Since Yue could not follow all his advice, he declined their offer of a government position after he had won great victories for them.

"The hero who had learned to use the spear captured three hundred men-at-arms." This was the action of Ran Qiu. See the *Zuo zhuan*, the battle at Qing in the eleventh year of Duke Ai.[110]

The crossbow was developed from the bow, the bow was developed from the slingshot (catapult), and the slingshot was invented by a filial son. A slingshot was used to shoot someone, but had minimal effect, so it was improved into a bow. A bow could shoot farther, but because of the limitations of men's strength, the effect was still not great enough; therefore, it was further developed into a crossbow. A crossbow has a box containing a mechanism; when the mechanism is released, the arrow is shot out with great force, to a considerable distance. It was a good weapon of war during the middle ages. There are two legends about how the slingshot was devised in the olden days by a filial son. In ancient times, parents were not buried under the ground, and would be eaten by foxes. A filial son could not bear this, so he invented a slingshot to kill the foxes. This was one legend. When parents became old, the responsibility for taking care of them fell upon the son, so a filial son invented the slingshot to shoot birds to feed his parents. This was the other legend.[111]

To kill someone so that another may be born.

Injury begets grace, and grace begets injury. If we merely consider the origin of the mutual promotion and restraint of the five elements, in heaven and on earth there is no interaction without military force, there is no military force without the Way. and there is no Way without desire. "Absorb the weak, and

---

108. Su Xun (1009–1066), *zi* Mingyun, *hao* Laoquan, was the father of Su Shu and Su Zhe. He and his sons were fierce opponents of Wang Anshi and his reforms. This passage, which Mao has reproduced almost verbatim, is Wei Yuan's summary of Su's views, which can be found in his *Jiayouji*, Vol. 3, "Quanshu" (On Power), Part 2, "Sun Wu." The names given in brackets are mentioned in Su Xun's original text. The Wu who is said to be weaker in theory but better in practice than Sunzi (or Sun Wu) has a different character for his surname; to avoid confusion, we have therefore added his given name, Qi, in parentheses.

109. This sentence is a verbatim quotation from Wei Yuan; the following paragraph is a paraphrase.

110. The first sentence is quoted from Wei Yuan. The passage from the *Zuo zhuan*, XII, XI, to which Mao refers (Legge, Vol. V, pp. 824–25) says he captured 80, not 300. On Ran Qiu see note 36.

111. The first of these legends is to be found in the *Wu Yue chunqiu* (Spring and Autumn Annals of Wu and Yue), "Goujian yinmou waizhuan" (Unofficial History of the Strategems of [King] Gou Jian [of Yue]). The second has not been identified.

punish the wilfully blind; take their states from the disorderly, and deal summarily with those going to ruin."[112] Such is the Way of Heaven. If the world is without evil, then grace cannot be revealed. If there is no weakness, wilfull blindness, disorder and ruin, then is there any need for absorbing or taking states? Therefore we say injury begets grace. In history, the stronger nations have wiped out other countries. It is indeed injurious to destroy other countries, but as the stronger nations took over the weaker, colonized them, treated them as their own and brought prosperity to those people, as far as the people were concerned, it was grace. That is why we say injury begets grace.

Yiliao's pellets.[113] Yiliao, a brave soldier of Chu, good at shooting pellets.

Maiden of Yue's sword.[114] Fan Li told the King of Yue: There is a maiden in Yue who comes from the Southern Forests.

Book of Agriculture[115]

weng: pronounced like "old man," meaning to bank up.[116]

An old farmer said, after three seasons, the rice stalks will grow up to three sections high; after four seasons, the wheat stalks will grow up to four sections high. When planting, we have to wait for three seasons before the rice can be harvested, and four seasons before the wheat can be harvested, if we are to get a good crop.

ken gou chou gou (to dig and connect furrows): "chou" is pronounced the same as "worry," and means to bind or gather.[117]

lun: pronounced like "engulfed," third tone, meaning "ridge."

Early wheat has several advantages. It is best to dig and connect the furrows early. When it is done early, water is drained and the ridges will be dry. The harder you dig, the deeper the furrows will go. The deeper the furrows, the more fertile the soil. When the furrows are dug early, they will undergo the effects of the frost, and the earth will be looser; the roots of the wheat will go deeper, and this is even better than heaping fertilizer around them. The deeper the roots, the richer the plants, and the harvest will be at least double.

But if we can plant a hundred good trees in the cracks on the field and along the riverbanks, we will be able to earn more than a hundred gold pieces thirty years later.

---

112. The words in quotation marks are from the *Book of Historical Documents*, IV, II, IV (Legge, Vol. III, p. 181).

113. Xiong Yiliao is said in the *Zuo zhuan* to have been equal to 500 men, but there is no mention of pellets. See Legge, Vol. V, p. 847.

114. According to the *Wu Yue chunqiu*, "Goujian yinmou waizhuan," she could defeat any swordsman in the empire.

115. The reference is to the *Bu nong shu* (Supplementary Treatise on Agriculture) of Zhang Lixiang (1611–1674), *zi* Kaofu, *hao* Nianfa. Zhang, a supporter of Zhu Xi and critic of Wang Yangming, wrote his work as a supplement to a small monograph, entitled *Nong shu* (Treatise on Agriculture), by a writer of the clan name Shen. He himself frequently tilled the soil and planted mulberry trees.

116. Actually, this character should be pronounced *rong*, not like *weng*, meaning old man.

117. Pronunciation does not seem to be Yuan's strong point. The third character in the phrase he is commenting on should be read *jiu* rather than *chou*.

If you neglect farming, you will not know how difficult it is to sow and reap. If you stop raising silkworms and weaving, you will not know how our clothes are made. In "The Odes of Bin,"[118] on the origins of the rule of the ancient kings, the eight verses of "The Seventh Month" sing only of details regarding clothing and food. The seven sections in the *Mencius* regarding the essentials of kingly government also indicate that none are more important than agriculture, community living, trees, and livestock.[119]

The writings of the Confucian scholars are different from those of the men of letters. The former were translucent and pure, but the latter, unrestrained and argumentative.

The superior man seeks the truth, not food or drink. This is only relatively speaking, as compared with those who diligently seek after material gains. It does not mean that all literati care nothing for food and drink.

Our ambition is not merely to be clothed and fed. When we talk about establishing the will, however, if we speak of actions, even a kingly government takes as its ultimate goal to clothe and feed the people so that there is neither hunger nor cold. What is wrong with being concerned with clothing and food?

Chaff is alkaline and is best used as fertilizer. Put in the fields, chaff will loosen the earth and will not rot when soaked in earth for a long time.

There are merits in both Chinese and Western medicine. Chinese medicine stresses the vital energy of life and pulse; Western medicine stresses experiments. But the theory of vital energy and pulse is too subtle for the common people to understand, so it is dismissed as too abstract. When talking about experiments, we focus on substance but have departed from energy, so we tend to lose sight of the foundations. Thus, both are one-sided.

"Preface to Nishi Moroo's *Guide to Practical Studies*"[120]

Columbus: Spaniard. A famous contributor to knowledge.[121]

---

118. The reference is to the "Odes of Bin" in the *Book of Poetry*. The first ode, entitled "The Seventh Month," is devoted as Mao says largely to clothing and food. See Legge, Vol. IV, pp. 226–33. Bin was regarded as the ancestral home of the rulers of Zhou, and hence the domain of the ancient kings.

119. The reference appears to be to the various chapters throughout the *Mencius* dealing with this theme, such as III, I, III–IV, and VII, I, XIII–XXIII (Legge, Vol. II, pp. 239–56, 454–63).

120. This preface was by Wu Rulun (1840–1903), *zi* Zhifu, who had served under Zeng Guofan and Li Hongzhang. Under their influence, he became interested in Western civilization and studied the experience of Japan and Europe in modernization. To the end of his life, he was involved in bringing Japanese scholars to China to help establish modern schools. Wu's preface to Nishi's book, *Shixue zhizhen* (Tokyo: Huabei yishuju, 28th year of Guangxu [1902]), presented it as a compendium of knowledge about Japan and the West, and most of the foreigners mentioned below by Yuan appear there. Nishi Moroo, though Japanese, was a Sinophile who appears to have written the book in Chinese, and on the title page he used the pseudonym Jin Chengzi ("Child of the Golden City").

121. *Guangxue mingjia*. It is not clear whether Mao understood Yuan to be saying that

Newton: Englishman. Pioneer in pressure theory.

Franklin: American. Invented a powerful electric machine which could make steel needles magnetic, and also made kites to attract lightning.

Watt: Englishman. Invented steam engine, to which many of today's manufactures are indebted. Different from *Wa de*.[122]

Li Guinian: Musician of the Tianbao Period of the Tang Dynasty.

Fine writings have these features: Sentences are few but contents are rich. The words are few but the truths are many.

An American saying goes: "My country right or wrong."[123]

It is better to manage one's houses and clothes and shoes carefully, rather than spending money and losing the interest. Therefore, the principal is important. The Japanese value the principal so much that they hardly have any extra clothes in their closets, nor extra grain in their barns.

Hatred: There are two sides of hatred. It is all right to hate oneself, but not others.

"Preface to *Diary*"[124]

Zheng Qiao: *zi* Yuzhong, a native of Putian, Xinghuajun, under the Southern Song dynasty. He wrote two hundred volumes of a *General History*.[125]

Wang Yinglin: *zi* Bohou, native of Jianyuan Prefecture under the Southern Song dynasty. At nine, he mastered the Six Classics, and he was the most prolific writer of the Song dynasty.[126]

Columbus was a famous specialist in optics (*guangxue*), or whether he took the four words in the sense we have given them in the translation. That is, in any case, how Nishi Moroo presented Columbus (whom he also identified at the outset as an Italian, not a Spaniard); after recounting in outline the story of Columbus, Isabella, and the discovery of America, he concludes: "Hence, when we speak of civilization in the modern world, we cannot but begin by recognizing the great contribution of Columbus." See his *Guide to Practical Studies*, p. 12B.

122. It is not entirely clear to whom Mao is referring here. Transcriptions of Western names had not yet been standardized in 1913, and the editors of the *Wengao* provide no guidance. Watt, here written *Hua de*, is now commonly rendered *Wa te*, but the context makes the identification quite unambiguous in his case. The characters Mao uses for Watt are now employed for [Lester Frank] Ward (1841–1913), the American sociologist, and *Wa de* may stand for him.

123. This is undoubtedly paraphrased from the chapter on national opinion in Yan Fu's translation of Spencer's *Principles of Sociology*.

124. The reference is to Pan Lei's preface to his edition of the "Rizhilu" (Diary) of Gu Yanwu. Pan Lei (1646–1708), *zi* Cigeng, *hao* Jiatang, had been a student of Gu's. The next dozen paragraphs, through the one regarding Sima Lang, all come from this source. Gu Yanwu (1613–1682), *zi* Ningren, *hao* Tinglin, was perhaps the leading figure among the Ming loyalist scholars of the early Qing period. He blamed the decline of the previous dynasty on the influence of what he regarded as the impractical and unrealistic ideas of neo-Confucianism, and especially of Wang Yangming. Like Wang Chuanshan, he was to have a lasting influence on Mao. See below, Yuan's discussion of Gu Yanwu.

125. Zheng Qiao (1108–1166), *zi* Yuzhong, *hao* Jiaji, was a famous man of letters of the Song dynasty. His *Tong zhi* (General History) dealt, of course, only with China, and covered the period from the earliest legendary emperors down to the Tang.

126. Wang's dates are 1223–1296.

Wei Heshan: His given name was Liaoweng, and his *hao* was Heshan. He was a native of Pujian, Qiongzhou, in the Southern Song dynasty (today's Qiongzhou Prefecture of Fujian province). He was known as a child prodigy.[127]

Ma Duanlin: *zi* Guiyu, of the Yuan dynasty. Wrote *A General Study of Documents.*[128]

The drum and the satchels: A note regarding this topic in the *Book of Rites*: On the opening day of school, the drum is beaten to call everyone's attention, and then the students open their satchels and take out the classic works which they proceed to study.[129]

Tang Jingchuan: *ming* Shunzhi, a native of Wujin during the Jiajing period of the Ming dynasty. Wrote *Anecdotes of the Prominent Civil and Military Officials and Scholars*, in six volumes.[130]

Yang Yongxiu: *ming* Shen, of the Zhengde period of the Ming dynasty. A prolific writer.[131]

Wang Yanzhou: *ming* Shizhen, a native of Taicang, a *jinshi* of the Jiajing reign.[132]

Zheng Duanjian: *ming* Xiao, a man of Haiyan, and a *jinshi* of the second year of the Jiajing reign.[133]

[Tang] Jingchuan and [Zheng] Duanjian emphasized practical studies and that which can be found in reality. Yang and Wang were not their equals.[134]

The people during the Song and Yuan dynasties valued practical studies very much. Although a number of talents emerged during the Ming dynasty, their learning was not equal to that of former times.

"Mr. Gu Ningren[135] of Kunshan was born into an old and well-known family. When young, he was unusually gifted and devoted himself completely to the study of ancient texts; he could recite from memory most of the nine classics and

---

127. Wei Liaoweng (1178–1237), *zi* Huafu, *hao* Heshan. Yuan (or Mao) is in error about the location of his native place, which is in Sichuan, not in Fujian.

128. Ma's *Wenxian tongkao* (A General Study of Documents) was a huge encyclopedia.

129. See the *Book of Rites*, Chapter XVI, "Xue ji" (A Note on Schools). Couvreur translates the passage in question as follows: "Lorsque les élèves étaient entrés dans l'école, on battait le tambour; aussitôt chacun d'eux tirait de sa boîte ses livres et ses instruments, et se mettait au travail avec soumission." (Couvreur, *Mémoires sur les bienséances et les cérémonies*, Vol. II, part 1, p. 32.)

130. Tang Shunzhi (1507–1569), *zi* Yingde, *hao* Jingchuan.

131. Yang Shen (1488–1559), *zi* Yongxiu, *hao* Sheng'an, was indeed one of the most prolific scholars in Chinese history.

132. Wang Shizhen (1526–1590), *zi* Yuanmei, *hao* Fengzhou, another prolific and versatile writer. His works were published under the title of *Yanzhou shanren ji*; hence Yuan's reference to him here as Wang Yanzhou.

133. Zheng Xiao (1499–1566), *zi* Zhifu, *hao* Yanquan, was the first writer to attempt a comprehensive history of the Ming dynasty.

134. Here Mao has written the character *zhou* for *chuan* in the name of [Tang] Jingchuan, an obvious slip in Chinese which merely involves adding three dots.

135. On Gu Yanwu, see above, note 124.

the various histories. He was especially concerned about the events of his own time, and would copy the veritable records and memorials by hand. He also meticulously examined important matters of statecraft [*jingshi*]. During the last years of the Ming dynasty, he tried to establish himself, but in the end never received an appointment. Thus he remained poor until his old age. Nevertheless, his concern for his country and his people never diminished. As long as there were things concerning the people's livelihood and the people of the country, he would trace them back to the origins and discuss the causes. He had traveled through half of the empire. Wherever he went, he would make friends with sages, heroes, and elders, and study the mountains and rivers, as well as customs, people's sicknesses and sufferings, strengths and weaknesses. He knew all of these like his own hand."[136]

During the Wei dynasty, Sima Lang proposed to revive the "well-field" system, but this did not go into effect until after a change in dynasty. During the Yuan dynasty, Yu Ji proposed an irrigation plan for the east of the capital, but that plan did not go into effect until the next generation.[137]

Open fields: fields that have no trees planted in them. [Emperor] Xiaowen of the Northern Wei dynasty ordained that land be distributed evenly. Any male over fifteen years of age was allotted 40 *mu* of open land.[138]

During the Yuan and Ming dynasties, military offices were hereditary.

There is morality valid for a time, such as the master-slave relationship between prince and minister;[139] then there is morality valid for all time, such as benevolence, righteousness, the rites of proper conduct, wisdom, trust, providence, and the will of the people, etc.[140] When we talk about principles, we have to be up-to-date; when we study literature, we need to study the classics.

---

136. This passage is taken verbatim from Pan Lei's "Preface," as reproduced in the *Hanfenlou gujin wenchao* (Hanfenlou Collection of Ancient and Modern Literature), an anthology compiled by Wu Zengqi, Commercial Press edition, Vol. 17, p. 65B. There is only one divergence from the original: in Mao's notes, *guo ming* (the fate of the country) has been replaced by *guo min* (the people or the citizens of the country), as translated in the text. The rest is reproduced so accurately that Mao must have consulted it in the library, unless Yuan wrote the whole paragraph on the blackboard. Most of the substance of Pan's account is correct, though Gu's failure to hold a high appointment resulted not from his inability to obtain a post, but from his own refusal to serve under the alien Manchu dynasty, or to take the special honorary examination known as *boxue hongci*, to which he was invited in 1677.

137. For Sima Lang, *zi* Boda, see the history of Wei in the *Sanguo zhi* (History of the Three Kingdoms). Yu Ji (1273–1348), *zi* Bosheng.

138. Yuan Hongyan (d. 499) succeeded to the throne in 471 as sixth emperor of the Northern Wei dynasty. Apart from the land reform mentioned in Mao's notes, his rule was marked by an attempt to foster Chinese language, dress, and culture.

139. Such was the case under the Qing, between the emperor and Manchu officials.

140. The distinction between morality valid for a time *(yishi zhi zhengyi)* and morality for all time *(wanshi zhi tongyi)* appears to have been taken from Wang Fuzhi's *Du* Tongjian *lun* (On Reading the *Comprehensive Mirror of Good Government*), Vol. 14.

zou and *bao*: Memorials submitted to the throne by the higher-ranking officials were called "zou"; reports submitted to the higher-ranking officials by their subordinates were called "bao."

Though the systems have changed over time, the reasoning has not changed. For instance, the military, agricultural, financial, and tax systems have changed, but the justification for maintaining an army is to devise strategies, the purpose of agriculture is to enrich the people, and that of finances is to make the nation prosperous. Has the reasoning become any different?

Jingchuan[141] was talented both in literary and in military arts. He was good at archery and horseback riding.

A person is judged as to whether he has achieved any academic standing when he turns twenty-five.

The scholars of the Ming and Qing dynasties were useless because in their writings they only sought to follow the trend of the times.

The value of the books that have lasted for a long time lies in their practical nature. Those which are not useful but have nevertheless lasted for a long time are those that are superbly written. Han [Yu], Liu [Zongyuan], and Du [Fu]'s poetry are examples of this. The rest are as voluminous as the open seas, filling up heaven and earth.

A General Review of the Regulations and Institutions, *A General Study of Documents*, and *A General History*, called the "Three Generals,"[142] are required reading for scholars. These offer detailed study and evaluation of decrees and regulations, systems, rites, music, military affairs, agriculture, etc. They are very useful indeed.

When Chengzi read, he often stopped in the middle of his reading and tried to draw his own conclusions before he continued to read.[143]

During the Qian[long] and Jia[qing] periods, the scholars loved to research the texts to the extent that they would often tirelessly write tens of thousands of words for each word, each term, each piece of clothing, and each shoe.

Laozi was an idealist.

If a famous painter paints a cake, it may appeal to the eyes but is not edible. A certain Mr. Wang once painted a cake.

There are several categories of writing. The Confucian scholars of the Song dynasty were realistic. So were those in the Yuan dynasty. They truly had insights and developed them in theories.

The skills in writing also varied greatly.

---

141. Tang Shunzhi (see above, note 130).

142. The *Tong dian* (General Review of the Regulations and Institutions) is the work of Du Yu of the Tang dynasty. It is divided into eight sections, dealing with political economy, examinations, government offices, rites, military discipline, etc. The *Tong kao* (General Study of Documents), by Ma Duanlin, and the *Tong zhi* (General History), by Zheng Qiao, have already been mentioned above (notes 128 and 125, respectively).

143. Chengzi, or Master Cheng, is Cheng Yi. The passage in his works dealing with this point can be found in *Er Cheng ji* (Collected Writings of the Two Chengs) (Beijing: Zhonghua shuju, 1981), p. 258.

Zheng Yuzhong's *General History [of China]* is both factual and practical.[144]

General *(tong)*: substance and usage combined. Substance is material, the prerequisites; and usage, the actual practice, that comes thereafter.

December 13 Self-Cultivation

To be experienced and worldly wise is also a form of learning.[145]

It is a very difficult thing to know how to deal with people and things. This is something we need to study.

Changshi: the English term is comon [*sic*] sense.

One thing that is difficult for a man in establishing himself is to be meticulous. If a man does not overlook anything of which he is capable, and if he carries this through from small things to greater things, it will not be hard for him to be a sage. Otherwise, if one is not careful in small matters, one will fail in greater matters too. Mr. Tao Huan is a model for us of one who was successful by assiduous attention to small things.[146] Caesar is an example of how neglecting a small thing can lead to failure in greater things. Because Caesar did not take precautions the night before, he was assassinated in the legislature the next day. A certain army general who did not watch his step not only sacrificed himself and his whole army but also endangered his whole country. Shouldn't we take this to heart? To honor everything, to do small things faithfully, to give personal attention to everything, to separate words, to combine words, and to measure their significance are the basis of establishing oneself.

If you hesitate to make decisions, gradually you will fail. Therefore it is said, "Though he loved goodness, he did not act it out; though he hated evil, he did not do anything about it; that was the reason for Mr. Guo's ruin."[147]

Covet not gain, rise early, love to study, and be humble. These are good habits.

Good has to be accumulated. Therefore we say, a march of ten thousand *li* starts with a single step. A thousand *chi* of cloth is made up of single threads.[148]

---

144. The reference is, once again, to Zheng Qiao. (See above, note 125.)

145. This sentence appears to be inspired by the two mottoes cited at the beginning of Chapter 5 of the *Dream of the Red Chamber*: "True learning implies a clear insight into human activities. Genuine culture involves the skillful manipulation of human relationships." (Hawkes, *The Story of the Stone*, Vol. 1, p. 126.)

146. Tao Huan is the name under which Tao Kan (259–334), *zi* Shixing, was canonized after his death. A native of Jiangxi, Tao rose to high office from a background of poverty, becoming a highly successful governor and military commander. He declared, with reference to the saying attributed to the Shang dynasty emperor Yu the Great, according to whom one should be careful of every inch of time (on the sundial), that in modern times it was necessary for men to be careful even of tenths of an inch.

147. This quotation is drawn from the *Xin xu* (New Prefaces), Vol. 4, of Liu Xiang (80–9 B.C.), *zi* Zizheng, alternative *zi* Maojin.

148. A Chinese *li* or league is approximately one-third of a mile. A Chinese *chi* or foot is 13.1 English inches, or 0.33 meters.

Ten thousand *li*, short of one step, cannot be called such. A thousand *chi*, short of one thread, cannot be called such. Master Zhu's learning was accumulated from bits and pieces. If he did not store up the knowledge, he would not have been able to establish his position.[149]

If you keep at it, you will succeed. This is called perseverance. That means unremitting effort to the very end. That is also what is called "accumulation."

Just suppose that all in the past had died yesterday and all in the future were just born today.[150] This implies having no regrets, and moving forward.

Some philosophers say that the future is more important; others say that the present is more important. This is the big difference between Kidd[151] and Yang Zhu,[152] and the great distinction between the East and the West. But when we look at learning, we have to pay attention to the present. Why? Someone said, What is the point in regretting the past? What's the use worrying about tomorrow? If we want to grasp something real, we can do so only in the immediate present; if we have the present, we have a whole lifetime. How true are these words! If you study but do not stress the present, what is our life span? Even the sun and moon will grow old. Whose fault, then, is this? Hence the Great Yu's saying about cherishing time.[153]

Stressing the present has two important meanings. One is valuing oneself. (Seek within oneself.) (Do not depend on others.) The other is to understand the present age thoroughly. For instance, if we study history, we have to emphasize modern history, because it is closely related to us.[154]

If I survey physical space horizontally, there is not one thing in all the vast landscape I can rely upon except for myself (valuing oneself).

If I examine time vertically, from the most ancient times until today, there is nothing I can hold onto except for the immediate present. (To understand the present age thoroughly.)

---

149. The last two sentences appear to be borrowed from Zeng Guofan's *Za zhu* (Miscellaneous Works), "Biji" (Jottings), no. 27, "Keqin xiaowu" (Diligence in Small Things).

150. Mao has written at the head of this passage, "Zeng's words." See Zeng Guofan's letter of the 29th day of the second month of the sixth year of the Tongzhi Period (April 3, 1867) in his *Family Letters*.

151. Benjamin Kidd, English sociologist (1858–1915). Liang Qichao wrote an essay entitled: "Jinhualun gemingzhe Xiede zhi xueshuo" (The Theory of Kidd, a Revolutionary in the Discussion of Evolution).

152. Yang Zhu, a philosopher of the Warring States period, mentioned in the *Mencius* and the *Zhuangzi*, was reputed to be an absolute egoist who would not have parted with one hair of his body to save the whole world.

153. See above, note 146.

154. Yang Changji stated and elaborated the points made here regarding self-reliance and emphasizing the present in his article "Gao xuesheng" (An Exhortation to Students), published in 1919. See *Yang Changji wenji*, especially pp. 364–65.

Chinese Literary Works

"The Hall on Yunzhou Brook, with preface"[155]

yin:	pronounced like "sound," same as "dumb."
chan:	same as "land allocated to retainers." *Jiuchan* (nine "chan") is the same as *Jiuzhou* (the nine provinces).[156]

"You employ your resources wisely, and make good use of men."[157]

ping:	pronounced like "duckweed"; water chestnuts, whose roots float on the water.
gu:	pronunciation and meaning like *gu*, "wild rice."
wuwo yiyi:	The first *yi* is pronounced "yi," meaning to annoy. The whole expression means: "Do not weary of us."
ming te mou ze:	All belong to the locust family. *Ming* (snout moth's larvae) feed on the heart of the plants; *te* (a green worm), the leaves; *mou*, the roots; and *ze*, the stalks. Mou is also written in another form.[158]

"Cats Nurse Each Other"[159]

"The prince of Beiping. Refers to Ma Sui."[160]

"The government of the Xia honored loyalty; that of the Yin honored respect, and that of Zhou literary accomplishments."[161]

"Confucius, when writing the preface to the Book of the Emperors, mentioned

---

155. By Han Yu. See his *Collected Works*, Vol. 14, and also, for the significantly different version of this poem actually explained to Mao by Yuan, Gu Sili's edition of Han's poetry, *Changli xiansheng shi jizhu*, Vol. 11 (pp. 543–44 of the Taiwan reprint, Xuesheng shuju, [1967]). It is this text which is translated by Erwin von Zach, in his *Han Yus poetische Werke* (Cambridge: Harvard University Press, 1952), pp. 301–02. In the title, Mao has written a wrong character, pronounced "hun," instead of "yun." This hall was the residence of Han's friend Ma Cong, who had been appointed viceroy in the area in question, centered on Shandong. The following seven points also refer to this poem.

156. "The Nine Provinces" is another name for the core area of China. This comment relates to the first line of the poem, which von Zach translates "The Tang Dynasty has brought peace to the Nine Provinces." (Here and subsequently, we give the sense of his rendering in English, rather than reproducing the German text.)

157. This line, in praise of Ma Cong, occurs at the very end of the poem.

158. It is the alternate form of the character given here which is used in two lines from the *Book of Poetry* (II, VIII, 2; Legge, Vol. IV, p. 380): "We remove the insects that eat the heart and the leaf, and those that eat the roots and the joints." Han Yu uses this as a metaphor for harmful individuals and indicates that Ma Cong dealt with them as they deserved.

159. This is an essay by Han Yu; see his *Collected Works*, Vol. 14, pp. 3A–3B. (All page references are to the *Hanfenlou* edition published by the Commercial Press.)

160. From the notes to the title of this poem. Ma Sui (d. 769) was granted this rank by the Tang emperor for his services.

161. This and the following eight paragraphs are drawn from Han Yu's "Jinshi cewen shisanshou" (Thirteen Questions Set at the Examination for *jinshi*), in his *Collected Works*, Vol. 14, pp. 4A–8A. This sentence is quoted from question 2.

Qin and Lu, and the other nations' customs, but he singled out Song and Lu for praise."[162]

"Do those who value the Way not consider what is advantageous to others, as well as to themselves?"[163]

" . . . 'assembled all the princes together.' Gathering together [*jiuhe*] means the gathering of the armored chariots (three), and the war chariots drawn by four horses (six)."[164]

"The Qin adopted Lord Shang's laws; the people became prosperous, the country became strong, and the nobles did not dare to rebel. As a result, all the other seven rulers were subdued, and the whole country was unified under Qin. It was Lord Shang who made Qin the ruler of the whole empire."

"Those of later generations who proclaimed the Way were, however, ashamed to mention Guan and Shang.[165] Why? Wasn't it because they only sought after reputation and were not concerned with reality?"[166]

Confucius said, "From day to day you are saying, 'We are not known.' If some ruler were to know you, what would you like to do?"[167]

"If the dead could be resurrected, with which of them should I associate myself?"[168]

" 'They may speak when it does not come to them to speak.' This is also something the superior man would not do."[169]

These were all strong terms and great ideas, skillfully crafted like the classics. They showed that the high reputation of the Tang dynasty could be compared with that of the peak of the Han dynasty.[170]

This poem was written by Sima Qian, not [Sima] Xiangru.

---

162. The "Book of the Emperors" referred to is the *Book of Historical Documents*. This sentence is quoted from question 3 in the same text.

163. Quoted from question 5.

164. The five words at the beginning are quoted by Han Yu from the *Analects*, XIV, XVII, 2 (Legge, Vol. I, p. 282); the explanation which follows is from the notes to question 5, *Collected Works*, Vol. 14, p. 5B.

165. On Shang, or Lord Shang, see the note to Mao's essay of 1912 on his reforms. Guan is Guanzi or Guan Zhong (see note 62).

166. Both this and the preceding paragraph, which follow one another without a break in the original, are quoted word for word from the text of Han Yu's question 5.

167. From question 6 of the "Questions Set at the Examination for *Jinshi*," in Han Yu, *Collected Works*, Vol. 14, p. 5B. Han is quoting here from the *Analects*, XI, XXV, 3 (Legge, Vol. I, p. 247).

168. This quotation from the *Book of Rites*, I, II (part 2), III, 25 (Couvreur, *Mémoires sur les bienséances et les cérémonies*, Vol. I, p. 257) is part of the text of question 6, Han Yu, *Collected Works*, Vol. 14, p. 6A.

169. This is once again a word-for-word quotation from Han Yu's question 6 *(loc. cit.)* The first sentence is from the *Analects*, XVI, VI (Legge, Vol. I, p. 312).

170. From "Yuanhe shengde shi bingxu" ("The Sacred Virtue of the Yuanhe Emperor, with Preface"), in Han Yu, *Collected Works*, Vol. 1, pp. 7–11. See also von Zach, *Han Yus poetische Werke*, pp. 1–6.

"A man would not change his moral standards just because he lives in a different era."[171]

Though all the others sought after extravagance, Yangzi[172] took no pleasure in lust.

[Yang] Cheng loved to learn but was too poor to buy any books. So he asked to be hired as a scribe, and read the public books by stealth. After six years, there was nothing that he did not understand thoroughly.

If the people of Yue could see the rich and poor of Qin, they would suddenly forget about their joys and sorrows.[173]

"The skillful administration of a state is seen in rewarding without error and punishing without excess."[174]

"To toil diligently": *kuku* means to toil.[175]

"[The sage] hates to take his ease!"[176]

"Did this not offend against morals and waste words?"[177]

"Because Master Guo Wu loved to express himself provocatively and incite people, he was killed at Qi."

Duke Xiang said, "If you live in an immoral and chaotic society and yet love to express yourself provocatively and incite people, you have sown the seeds of grievances."[178]

---

171. This, and the following twelve paragraphs, down to the one beginning "The *Commentary* says . . . " are all derived, except where otherwise indicated, from the essay, "Zheng chen lun" (On the Disputatious Officials), in Han Yu, *Collected Works*, Vol. 14, pp. 8A–10B. (This sentence is quoted verbatim from p. 8B.) For further discussion of this text, under its alternative title of "On Imperial Censors," see below, the passage beginning with note 235.

172. Yang Cheng (736–805), *zi* Kangzong, a censor under the Tang dynasty noted for his rectitude. At an early age, he and his brother vowed never to marry; hence, no doubt, the ensuing comment by Han Yu. (Mao has used the wrong character for the surname Yang.)

173. The reference is to the Yue and Qin kingdoms of the fourth century B.C., before the Qin unification of the empire.

174. A quotation from the *Zuo zhuan*, IX, XXVI, 7 (Legge, Vol. V., p. 526).

175. These words occur in the context of a passage (Han Yu, *Collected Works*, Vol. 14, p. 9B) arguing that sages and worthies are concerned about the welfare of the realm, not about themselves, and is followed almost immediately by a reference to Yu, who passed his doorway without entering (see *Mencius*, III, I, IV, 7; Legge, Vol. II, p. 251).

176. This statement comes at the end of a passage declaring that sages are the eyes and ears of the people, who fear the Decree of Heaven, and mourn the poverty of the people. Hence their reluctance to be idle (Han Yu, *Collected Works*, Vol. 14, p. 10A).

177. In Han Yu's text, this sentence and the next follow one another without a break (*Collected Works*, Vol. 14, p. 10A). The antecedent of "this" is Master Guo's habit of forthright speech. Guo Wuzi is Guo Zuo, an official of the state of Qi during the Spring and Autumn Period. For the fact of his death, see the *Zuo zhuan*, VIII, XVIII, 3 (Legge, Vol. V, p. 408).

178. Duke Xiang is Duke Xiang of Dan. A note to Han Yu's text indicates that he addressed these words to Guo Wuzi by way of warning (Han Yu, *Collected Works*, Vol. 14, p. 10A).

"To have eyes that see Mount Tai, but not things which are near at hand — what shall we call this?"[179]

"The superior man remains in his own place, and thinks of his appointment; if he is not appointed, he thinks of cultivating his speech, in order to enhance his virtue."[180]

The *Commentary* says: "Only good men can accept radical proposals, and change according to what they hear."[181]

The time difference between the eastern and western extremities of our country is four hours and fifteen minutes. There is Kashgar in the west, and the Ussuri River in the east.

zhi: same as *zhi* (to roast). "Ten thousand oxen are cut up and roasted; ten thousand jars of wine are served."[182]

pa: pronounced [here] as *mai*. "They wrapped their heads in red kerchiefs."[183]

"A tempting bait will surely get fish hooked; a handsome reward will certainly attract a brave warrior."[184]

rangrang: in great numbers.

"Neck in a cangue and hands in chains."[185]

***Mencius* Classics**[186]

"Maledictions are uttered by one to another with eyes askance": *juan* means to look askance at somebody.[187]

---

179. A direct quotation from the notes to Han Yu's essay, *Collected Works,* Vol. 14, p. 10B.

180. Han Yu, *Collected Works*, Vol. 14, p. 10A.

181. The *Commentary* in question is the *Zuo zhuan*; this sentence is incorporated into Han Yu's essay on disputatious officials, *Collected Works*, Vol. 14, p. 10B. Mao has reproduced both this and the previous sentence verbatim.

182. This and the next four entries refer once again to Han Yu's poem "The Sacred Virtue of the Yuanhe Emperor." For the line quoted here see Han Yu, *Collected Works*, Vol. 1, p. 8A; von Zach, *Han Yus poetische Werke*, p. 2. The two characters pronounced *zhi* are the usual form with the fire radical underneath, and a variant, discussed in the notes to Han Yu, with the meat radical underneath.

183. The modern reading for this character, when it means a kerchief worn by men around the head as in ancient times, is *mo.*

184. This sentence, which is not from Han Yu, but from an ancient military writer, Master Yellow Stone, is quoted in the notes to Han Yu's poem (*Collected Works,* Vol. 1, p. 8B) to explain Han's statement that some people joined the rebel Liu Pi because they feared him, and others because they hoped for his bounty. See *Huang Shi Gong san lue* (Master Yellow Stone's Three Discourses on Strategy), Part 1. Mao (or Yuan) has modified only one character; the original has *si fu* (dead warrior) rather than *xiong fu* (brave warrior), but *si* should be understood here in any case as "willing to brave death."

185. This refers to Liu Pi after his defeat and capture.

186. The next five sentences come from the *Mencius*, I, II (Legge, Vol. II, pp. 150–79).

187. The reaction of the people, according to Mencius, when the ruler visits the countryside with too numerous a retinue. *Mencius* I, II, IV, 6; Legge, Vol. II, pp. 159–60.

"The rulers yield themselves to the current, or they urge their way against it; they are wild; they are utterly lost. . . . Descending along with the current, and forgetting to return, is what I call yielding to it. Pressing up against it, and forgetting to return, is what I call urging their way against it. Pursuing the chase without satiety is what I call being wild. Delighting in wine without satiety is what I call being lost."[188]

ke: means "possible," "can get by." "The rich may get through life well."[189]

zhao: When pronounced "zhao," means do not take what is not offered to you. Is pronounced "shao" in "zhi shao" and "jue shao" (ancient musical tunes). When pronounced "qiao," means loving to make extreme statements provoking people. That was how Master Guo Wu met his death at Qi.

si ji yong guang: To seek to gather the people in peace and to magnify one's country.[190]

Composition

"Preface to the *Humble Study Manuscripts*"[191]

Of all the classics and history and the hundred schools of thought, the natural and human sciences, regulations and institutions, anecdotes and legends, grasses and trees, insects and fishes, is there anything which is not material for writing? As for editing, adaptation, climaxes and anticlimaxes, opening and closing, and changes and intrigues, are there any of these which do not constitute techniques for writing?

The writings of the Ming period were deficient in techniques. The shortcoming of today's writers is lack of material.

Those who are critical of themselves are not self-satisfied. The more learned a person is, the more humble he becomes.

Therefore his diction was translucent and elegant, his writing skills and the content complemented each other. His craftsmanship was extraordinary and endlessly refined.

If only we can fully devote our energy to studies, and extend ourselves to the utmost possible limits, connect the natural and human sciences, gather together all the studies of the past and the present as our resources—as if we were taking

---

188. This is a direct quotation from the *Mencius* I, II, V, 6–7 (Legge, Vol. II, p. 160), with only one brief omission.

189. Mencius, I, II, V, 3 (Legge, Vol. II, p. 162), here quotes a line from the *Book of Poetry*.

190. Legge translates these four characters (Mencius I, II, V, 4), which are also quoted from the *Book of Poetry*, as: "That he might gather his people together, and glorify his state" (Legge, Vol. II, p. 163).

191. This preface, too, is by Pan Lei (see note 124). The "humble study" was, in fact, the very extensive library of the noted bibliophile and secretary in the Grand Secretariat Lin Ji (1660–1735), *zi* Jiren, *hao* Luyuan. The *Puxuezhai wengao* (Humble Study Manuscripts) was a collection of his prose works. The following six paragraphs refer to Pan's preface.

lumber from Denglin,[192] and quarrying stone from the Southern Mountain[193] to provide materials for the work of Chui[194] and Ban,[195] then we would be able to build ten thousand houses. If we could provide Yi Ya[196] with the rarest ingredients from the noblest places and gather the best foodstuffs from land and sea, then we would be able to have the most exquisite meal in the whole world.

I will not let myself be despised just so that I might barely survive.

Wei Bozi said, "A masterpiece's remarkableness lies in its commonness, its subtlety in its breadth. As for its ins and outs, and the relation between the whole and the parts, its splicing and transformations lie in its straightforwardness, its rich tastes lie in its blandness, and its glamour lies in its modesty."[197]

Wang Dunweng. *Ming* Wan, *zi* Tiaoren. A native of Wu. Became a *jinshi* during the year *yiwei* of the Shunzhi reign.[198]

"An inscription on the desk says 'Be neat, profound, generous, and even.' " Neat means to be simple and clean in heart; profound means to do things with sincerity and firmness; generous means to give when one has more than enough; and even means to be calm and at ease in deeds.[199]

Avoid writing awkwardly, or in too labored a style.

To pierce through a hair. During Wei's time there was a Korean guest who was adept at handling needles. He could pierce a hair right through the middle.

To shoot the fleas. *Liezi*. Fei Wei learned from Gan Ying how to shoot,

---

192. A forest described in the *Shan hai jing* (Classic of Mountains and Seas) by Guo Pu (276–324), *zi* Jingshun, a Daoist scholar. According to the account in this largely mythological work, Deng Forest sprang up magically from the staff of a spirit who had died of thirst. (See Vol. 7, on countries north of China.)

193. Old name of what is today called Zhongnanshan in Shaanxi Province. See the *Book of Poetry*, II, IV, VII, 1 (Legge, Vol. IV, p. 309): "Lofty is that southern hill, With its masses of rocks!"

194. A skilled artisan under the reign of the legendary emperor Yao.

195. Lu Ban, the name commonly used for Gongshu Zi, a famous artisan of the state of Lu during the Spring and Autumn period, long worshiped as the god of carpenters.

196. A famous cook, chief chef to the Duke of Qi, in the seventh century B.C. His personal name was Yi Wu; Ya was his *zi*.

197. Wei Bozi is Wei Jirui (1620–1677), *zi* Shanbo, *hao* Dongfang, alternative *hao* Bozi. For the passage referred to here, see his "Letter to the Duke of Zhou" in his collected works, *Wei Bozi wenji*, Vol. 2.

198. Wang Wan (1624–1691) was indeed a *jinshi* of the year indicated, which corresponds to 1655. The second character of his *zi* as noted by Mao is wrong; it should be Tiaowen. He also had various *hao*, including Yaofeng and Dun'an. The name by which Yuan calls him, Wang Dunweng (meaning "Old Man Dun"), derived from Dun'an, is that under which he published his collected works.

199. This reference is also to Wei Jirui; see his "Ming" (Inscriptions), in *Wei Bozi wenji* (Collected Writings of Wei Bozi), Vol. 10. Mao has, once again, made a minor error in transcribing this passage; in Wei's text, a "profound" person is *zhen* (upright or virtuous) rather than *zhen* (sincere).

and became more skillful than his master. Ji Changzhe, in turn, learned shooting from Fei Wei, and saw fleas as if they were as big as cartwheels. His arrows pierced their chests without cutting the [yak] hair on which they were hanging.[200]

sheng: pronounced "zong."[201] Eighty strands of cloth is a *zong*.

cong: pronounced "cong," meaning small tributaries flow into larger streams, and the waters are connected.

Dark wine and unseasoned thick meat soup.

bai bi: adorned, meaning adorned in white.

zang: the domain of the five elements. The heart corresponds to wood, the liver to fire, the spleen to earth, the lungs to metal, and the kidneys to water.[202]

The coming together of heavens and earth is called "tai."[203]

The heavenly lord is peaceful.[204] The heavenly lord is the heart.

jiju: centipede, feeds on snakes' eyes.[205]

dai: snake, the centipede eats its eyes.

The birds hated Xi Shi's charms: "Mao Qiang and Lady Li were beautiful in the eyes of men; but when the fish saw them they plunged deep, when birds saw them they flew high."[206]

yi: pronounced "yi," swallow.[207]

rou yuan: Of the family of monkeys. Good at climbing.

jue fu: macaque. *Jue* is also written as *jue*, meaning to capture. A macaque was said to have captured a woman to be his wife who gave birth to a son; hence the name.

guo ran: monkey. A good-natured animal.

---

200. This story is to be found in the *Liezi*, Chapter 5 ("The Questions of Tang"). For a translation, see Angus Graham (tr.), *The Book of Lieh-tzu* (London: John Murray, 1960), p. 112. The last sentence, describing the exploits of Ji Changzhe, is identical with that in the *Liezi* except that the original text refers to piercing the heart, not the chest, of the flea.

201. The character in question is normally pronounced "sheng"; its usual meanings are "to rise," or a unit of measure similar to a pint, but it may also have the sense given here.

202. This is not the usual order, or the usual correlation, which goes: heart = fire, lungs = metal, liver = wood, kidneys = water, and stomach = earth.

203. This quotation is from the *Book of Changes*, Chapter "Tai."

204. This passage comes originally from *Xunzi*, XI, 17, "Tianlun," which contains the sentence: "The heart dwells in the central void, and rules the five organs. Because of this, it is called the heavenly lord." According to the commentaries, Xunzi saw the five organs (ears, eyes, nose, mouth, and form) as capable of sensation, but not of communication with one another.

205. This is an allusion to the *Zhuangzi*, I, 2; the chapter title is "Qiwulun," which Graham translates as "The Sorting Which Evens Things Out." See Graham, *Chuang-tzu*, p. 58.

206. The passage in quotation marks is taken directly from the *Zhuangzi*, *loc. cit.* The introductory sentence is Yuan's; Xi Shi was a famous beauty of the fifth century B.C.

207. The fact that the character *yi* which appears here is a synonym for *yan* (swallow) is mentioned in the commentaries to the *Book of Poetry*, I, III, III (Legge, Vol. IV, pp. 42–43).

jiao rang: A plant whose leaves grow alternately.[208]

Wu Xun: *zi* Huaxi, a native of Tongcheng. Wrote "Huaxi's Leisure Talk."

The greatest virtue of Emperor Yao was his reverence; that of Emperor Shun, his filial piety.

Mr. Huntun. *Zhuangzi*, "Responding to the Emperors and Kings": The Emperor of the South was called Shu, and the Emperor of the North was Hu. The Emperor of the Center was called Huntun. Shu and Hu met in the land of Huntun, who treated them very generously. Shu and Hu were discussing how to repay Huntun's bounty. They said, "All men have seven holes through which they look, listen, eat, breathe; he alone doesn't have any. Why don't we try boring them?" Every day, they bored one hole, and on the seventh day Huntun died.[209]

Classics

gan ge qi yang: *qi* means axe; *yang*, battle-axe.[210]

can zei: He who outrages benevolence is called a robber [*zei*]; he who outrages righteousness is called a ruffian [*can*].[211]

yi. Twenty *liang*.[212]

"Mencius replied, 'If the people of Yan will be pleased with your taking possession of it, then do so. Among the ancients, there was one who acted on this principle, namely King Wu. If the people of Yan will not be pleased with your taking possession of it, then do not do so. Among the ancients there was one who acted on this principle, namely King Wen.

---

208. *Daphniphyllum macropodum*, a type of evergreen in which the old leaves commonly fall as the new ones begin to grow.

209. This is taken almost word for word, with a few minor changes, from the *Zhuangzi*, VII, "Ying diwang" (Responding to the Emperors and Kings). We have followed Graham's translation (*Chuang-tzu*, p. 98), except where it did not fit the text of Mao's notes. Graham translates the names of the first two emperors respectively as "Fast" and "Furious." Huntun, he notes, "is the primal blob which first divided into heaven and earth, and then differentiated as the myriad things."

210. This four-character line is from the *Book of Poetry*, III, II, VI, 1, quoted in the *Mencius*, I, II, V. Legge translates (Vol. II, p. 163): "With shields, and spears, and battle-axes, large and small." This and the following six paragraphs all relate to the same chapter of the *Mencius*.

211. This is drawn from one of the most celebrated defenses of regicide in the Chinese classics. The passage reads as follows: " 'May a minister then put his sovereign to death?' Mencius said, 'He who outrages . . . benevolence is called a robber; he who outrages righteousness is called a ruffian. The robber and ruffian we call a mere fellow. I have heard of the cutting off of the fellow [i.e., the notorious tyrant] Zhou, but I have not heard of . . . putting a sovereign to death' " (Legge, Vol. II, p. 167).

212. In ancient times, one *yi* was a piece of gold worth twenty (or according to some sources twenty-four) *liang* (taels, or Chinese ounces) of silver. This term appears in the *Mencius* I, II, X, 2.

" 'If you make the water more deep and the fire more fierce, they will in like manner make another revolution.' "[213]

"Master Zeng said, 'Beware, Beware. What proceeds from you, will return to you again.' "[214]

"A ruler does not injure his people with that wherewith he nurtures them. My children, why should you be troubled about having no prince?"[215]

The Philosophers

Though there is a difference between small and great, when everything occupies its place, then things will fulfill their nature, affairs will correspond to their potential, and each will play its proper role.[216]

Why do you put your heart in it?

Once the big bird takes off, it will not rest until it reaches the Heavenly Lake half a year later. As for the little bird, it will take it only half a day to dash to the elm and sandalwood. If you compare their capacities, there is a gap, but each acts according to its nature.

They say a *peng* does not know how far or how near the distance is. It only stops whenever it feels like it.[217]

"Is the azure of the sky its true color? Or is it that the distance into which we are looking is infinite? It [the *peng*] never stops flying higher until everything below looks the same as above."[218]

"If a mass of water is not bulky enough it lacks the strength to carry a big boat. When you upset a bowl of water over a dip in the floor, a seed will make a boat for it, but if you put the bowl there it jams, because your boat is too big for such shallow water."[219] When we read this saying, we sigh: How true this is! In history, there have been many who desired to be leading ministers. There have been some who succeeded with grace, sufficiency, skill, and ease, but there were more who stumbled with restlessness and imbalance, as if they could not set the big ships to sail. Wasn't it because they were lacking in resources? I think that

---

213. This is a direct quotation from the *Mencius*, I, II, X, 3–4 (Legge, Vol. II, pp. 169–70).

214. *Mencius* I, II, XII, 2 (Legge, Vol. II, p. 173).

215. *Mencius* I, II, XV, 1 (Legge, Vol. II, p. 176).

216. This, and the next five paragraphs, are all drawn from Chapter 1 of the *Zhuangzi*. This first sentence is a summary of the sense of the chapter as a whole, rather than a quotation.

217. This and the previous paragraph are based on the opening passage of Chapter 1 of the *Zhuangzi* (Graham, *Chuang-tzu*, pp. 43–44). The *peng* is a mythical bird, usually translated as roc.

218. This time, Mao noted down the precise textual quotation from the *Zhuangzi (loc. cit.)*.

219. This is, once again, an exact textual quotation from the same passage of the *Zhuangzi*.

Mr. Li of Hefei[220] was one of these. In the beginning, he was able to suppress the Taiping Revolutionary Army and the Nian Army. This was like a seed in a bowl of water. When he ascended to high places, ruled over the country, and got involved in diplomacy, he failed again and again. He was shamed to an extreme degree. Why? It was like setting a bowl in the water; the bowl gets stuck, because the water is too shallow and the ship is too big. Mencius said: "Flowing water is a thing which does not proceed till it has filled the hollows in its course. The student who has set his mind on the doctrines of the sage does not advance to them but by completing one lesson after another."[221] Shallow people should reflect on this.

Literary works

"The Sacred Virtue of the Yuanhe Emperor"[222]

gui: The ancient form of the character *gui* (jade tablet).[223]

pi: The parapet on top of the city wall. To throw the head over the wall.[224]

shaofu: According to the *Annals of the Tang Dynasty*, the *shao fu* was an officer in charge of costumes and ceremonial articles for the court officials. To serve as *shao fu.*[225]

pa: here pronounced *mai*. A cloth around the forehead, part of military dress. "They wrapped their heads in red kerchiefs."[226]

To go all the way to the source and to weed out the shallow lake overgrown with wild plants.

zhu: pronounced "zhu," commonly written [with the wood radical instead of the hand radical]. To support.[227]

leilei: pronounced "lei." *[Li]ji*: "linked together like pearls on a string."

---

220. Li Hongzhang (1823–1901), the celebrated statesman and diplomat.

221. This is a precise textual quotation from the *Mencius*, VII, I, XXIV, 3 (Legge, Vol. II, pp. 463–64).

222. Here Yuan returns to a poem by Han Yu he had already discussed earlier (see note 167). The next nine paragraphs all refer to this text.

223. The jade tablet or baton conferred upon feudal princes by the emperor, as a symbol of authority. Such tablets were given to officers and officials after the execution of Liu Pi, mentioned above (see notes 179 and 180).

224. The head in question was that of the leader of the rebels who had taken a city, after dissension broke out among them. See the Chinese text in Han Yu, *Collected Works*, Vol. 1, p. 7B, and von Zach, *Han Yus poetische Werke*, p. 2.

225. The context is that when Liu Pi (whose end is mentioned above) first sought to usurp the governorship of Sichuan the emperor, to avoid bloodshed, sent him, through the *shaofu*, a token of command (which he rejected with contempt). Han Yu, *Collected Works*, Vol. 1, p. 8A; von Zach, *Han Yus poetische Werke*, p. 2.

226. Yuan apparently forgot that he had already explained this line; see above, note 183.

227. The context makes plain why Han Yu used the variant of *zhu* which also has the meaning "to support" or "to prop up": "Next they executed [Liu Pi's] followers; they were so numerous that their bodies leaned against each other." (Han Yu, *Collected Works*, Vol. 1, p. 9B; von Zach, *Han Yus poetische Werke*, p. 3.

"Women crowded together."[228]

"[Everyone] feared the emperor's power, and was abashed before the emperor's virtue; they were all filled with respect and joy, cast away their weapons and shields, and privately gave themselves over to religious practices."[229]

ou: means friends.[230]

"A Proposal to Change Mourning Clothes"[231]

si: The mourning clothes to be worn for three months. The classics speak of changing the mourning *si*.[232]

mian: delayed. To change the three-months mourning clothes. The burial [of King Huan] was long delayed.[233]

This is the reason why a filial son expresses his feelings, and former Kings must [be dealt with] in good time.

To lay out a coffin in a memorial hall is called a funeral; to bury the body in the field is called interment.

If you stress mourning clothes, this is called dispensing with the indispensable, and stressing what shouldn't be stressed.

"I say, one cannot. When you compare deep sorrow and minute attention to observances, the latter is assuredly not as important as the former. Still, it is most admirable to conform with the rites. To be sure, compared to extravagance, thriftiness is better. And yet, it is most admirable to conform with the rites. This is what is meant by the saying that going too far is as bad as not going far enough."[234]

"On Imperial Censors"[235]

If aspirations cannot be put into practice, you had better not seek after them.

---

228. For the first quotation, from Chapter XVII, on music, of the *Book of Rites,* see Couvreur, *Mémoires sur les bienséances et les cérémonies*, Vol. II, p. 113. The second phrase, which Mao also quotes verbatim, is from Han Yu's poem (*Collected Works,* Vol. 1, p. 9A). The term *leilei* (linked together) appears in both passages.

229. This is a direct quotation; "everyone," Han Yu indicates in the previous sentence, means all between heaven and earth, including foreigners beyond China's borders. (*Collected Works,* Vol. 1, pp. 9B–10A; von Zach, *Han Yus poetische Werke*, p. 4.)

230. Actually, according to various passages in the classics, including one in the *Book of Poetry* pointed out by von Zach (*Han Yus poetische Werke,* p. 4), this character means "pair," originally two men pulling a plow together.

231. Essay by Han Yu; see his *Collected Works*, Vol. 14, pp. 10B–12A.

232. *Si* is also the kind of coarse cotton cloth from which such garments are made.

233. For this episode, see the *Zuo zhuan*, III, III, 3 (Legge, Vol. V, p. 75).

234. This whole passage is taken word-for-word from Han Yu (*Collected Works,* Vol. 14, p. 12A.) Quoting a sentence from the *Analects*: "In the ceremonies of mourning, it is better that there be deep sorrow than a minute attention to observances" (*Analects* III, IV, 3; Legge, Vol. I, p. 156), Han Yu asks the rhetorical question, "Can one then not also stress [mourning] clothes?" It is to this that he replies, "I say, one cannot."

235. As indicated above (note 168) this essay by Han Yu, called here "Jianchen lun" (On Imperial Censors) is also sometimes titled "Zhengchen lun" (On the Disputatious Officials). The next three lines refer to it.

"If Master Yang made such efforts [in spite of difficulties], this really passes our understanding."[236]

The master [Han Yu] tells us that Master Yang can be considered as a man who followed the Way. Though we cannot equal him, should we today not also regard him as a good man?

"Hence, to seek after fame but to hamper the whole world is not to respect the good."

"Inscriptions for Huang Zijiu's Painting"[237]

"There has never been one way in the world that was not true and did not have solid foundations, and yet worked."

"Alas, perhaps there may have been instances where one has learned and been familiar with the truth and put it into practice, but others could not copy him. But there have never been cases where you could gain the truth from looking at and imitating its semblance."

"On Xie An"[238]

"Those who succeeded to the empire in the old days had to get rid of the conventional ways and establish something new."

Moral capacity: "The superior men who ruled the world depended on imposing manners and moral capacity but not talents."

Talents: "But as far as talents are concerned, even though a prince does not rely heavily on them, they should not be ignored either."

"What do you think of our guest?" Meng replied, "He is hardworking and very imposing."[239]

"Emperor Yu of Xia was diligent and worked very hard. Emperor Wen used to eat his meals late and worked day and night. Today there are ramparts all around us, we should think of ways to help ourselves. Empty talk and verbiage are not appropriate today."

"The Qin dynasty used Shang Yang, but only lasted two generations. Did his

---

236. The "Master Yang" in question is Yang Cheng, mentioned in note 166. The whole of this essay is devoted to praising his courage in opposing wrongdoing by high officials, during his term as censor. This comment does not refer directly to the previous sentence.

237. By Hou Fangyu (see above, note 85). Huang Zijiu is Huang Gongwang (1269–1359), *zi* Zijiu, *hao* Dazhi, a noted painter of water during the Yuan dynasty. The previous sentence, as well as the following two paragraphs, are word-for-word quotations from this text. See Hou's collected works, published under the title *Zhuangmei tang wenji* (Collected Writings from Zhuangmei Hall), Vol. 7. The whole essay is about the *dao* or way of painting, referred to in the next sentence, and how the artist externalizes his observations of reality.

238. This is another essay by Hou Fangyu. (See his *Zhuangmei tang wenji,* Vol. 9.) Except where otherwise noted, the next thirteen paragraphs are verbatim quotations from it. Xie An (320–385), *zi* Anshi, was a high official of the Eastern Jin dynasty.

239. Meng is Wang Meng (309–347), *zi* Zhongzu. This exchange, quoted from the *Jin shu* (History of the Jin Dynasty), is supposed to have taken place when Wang's son asked him his impression of Xie An as a young man, when the latter paid his respects to Wang Meng.

honest advice bring disasters upon Qin?"[240]

"Was it something that could be predicted?"

"There have never been people who achieved great success without strength to carry the burden of the world, endurance to go through the sufferings of the world, and characters that could hold up a part of the world."

"[Xie An] has more than enough sincerity and loyalty, but not enough humility and experience."

"If a man does not seek after fame, but has acquired a lot of experience of the world, it is because of his upbringing."

"Those who are not tempted by fleeting fame have acquired discipline. Those who do not follow the current trends have gained self-control."

"Otherwise, how could he be profound, solid, and open-minded, make arduous efforts, and take the responsibility of the whole country upon his shoulders?"

"Dao had the insights of great achievers but did not have great talents. An had the capacity to do great things but did not have the skills to do so."[241]

[I], An, have heard that the princes are virtuous and are standing guard all around us, why do you, enlightened lord, need to deploy men behind the walls?[242]

Nothing was there before the chaos of the primeval era. That's why we say before chaos there was nothing. Hence, only after primitive chaos have there been things.

cai: Talent, used here in an economic sense. Talent can be acquired from learning. It can also be acquired from experience.

Xunyang: Used to belong to Anqing.

"A Proposal to Select Some Students through Examinations to Replace the Ceremonial Ministers"[243]

"They hold the bamboo fruit baskets for sacrifices and rush here and there to serve their superiors.

Jun, great.[244]

---

240. This and the previous paragraph represent an exchange, likewise recorded in the *History of the Jin Dynasty*, between Wang Xizhi (321–379), and Xie An; the first words are Wang's, the reply Xie's.

241. Dao is Wang Dao (276–339), long chief minister of the Eastern Jin dynasty. An is, of course, Xie An.

242. From the biography of Xie An in the *History of the Jin Dynasty*. The "enlightened lord" to whom he addressed these words was Xuan Wen (312–373), *zi* Yuanzi, who in 366 had deposed the emperor and set the latter's son on the throne as his puppet. According to the histories, Xie An thus frustrated Xuan's plot to murder him and others in order to strengthen his domination of the Jin court.

243. This is another essay by Han Yu (*Collected Works*, Vol. 14, pp. 12A–13A). The next eleven paragraphs relate to this text. As indicated by the use of quotation marks, the whole of what Mao copied down consists of sentences drawn from Han Yu's text, with only a very few minor verbal variations.

244. The explanation of the character *jun* is also taken from the notes to this text in Han Yu's works.

"This is indeed trivial.

"It is also clear that this cannot be changed.

"We cannot figure it out either.

"This may not be a proper method for choosing officials, but perhaps there are others that are even worse.

"There are no others.

"Isn't this near irreverence? There are also others that are even more improper. How can we state the truth?

"If there were any changes in the system or in the ordinances that were not very different from the old ones, then they were not worth trying.

"To act in accordance with[245] the ancient customs is not fit to serve as a model, and to examine the present is not profitable. To seek to find out reality by looking at the name is not proper. Therefore, [I] say, the proposal to remove the office of the ceremonial ministers and replace them with recommended students is not right."

leixi: vessel used in sacrifices.

zongyi: *Yi*, wine vessel. *Zongyi*, the wine vessel used in sacrificial ceremonies for the ancestors. It is the same as *leixi*.

Fu[246] "A 'Fu' on Two Birds"

"When the times are favorable, even a person of limited merit will prosper; when the times are not favorable, a person with much merit may not be able to do much."[247]

As the clear sky brightens the day, so does the magnificent scenery radiate over the whole country. Zuo Taichong.[248]

"People are gathering together, clamoring and sighing that they have grown old and their status has declined. But I am worried because the Way does not prevail in the world. I marvel that the divine Yao could take the empire with one brigade, and am concerned that his descendants cannot even unite the area north of the River with the empire." Li Ao.[249] "Alas, if the superior men of his time had been able to change their attitude of fretting about their old age and lowly status, and adopt [Li] Ao's attitude, how could the Tang dynasty ever have suffered from rebellions and destruction?"

---

245. Here Mao has substituted the character *wei* (to act, etc.) for the character *kao* (to examine) in the original.

246. A *fu* is a composition in rhymed metrical prose, interspersed with verse. For the first of the three *fu* by Han Yu discussed here, see his *Collected Works*, Vol. 1, pp. 1A–2B.

247. This is a word-for-word quotation from Han Yu, *Collected Works*, Vol. 1, p. 1B.

248. Zuo Si (c. 250–305), *zi* Taichong, was a well-known poet of the Jin dynasty.

249. Li Ao (772–841), *zi* Xizhi, was a Tang dynasty essayist. This whole long paragraph, before and after his name, is reproduced verbatim by Mao, with only one insignificant variation, from the notes to Han Yu, *Collected Works* Vol. 1, p. 2B. (In the notes to Han Yu, the attribution of these words to Li Ao precedes the passage quoted here.)

"Even so, you may argue that writings were often composed at the time when people were not yet in office. Once they became high officials and nobles and had successful careers, they wouldn't even have time to write unless they had the capacity and the bent to do so."[250]

"A 'Fu' on Renewal of One's Ambitions"[251]

"In the seventh month of the following year, he was too sick to carry the firewood on his shoulder. To carry firewood means to do menial work."[252]

Han and Peng's rebellions were considered as wild beasts rising to high positions. Zhang Huan's rising to power was considered as attaining high office through mastery of the classics. Don't you know that powerful people used their power to reach where they are? Liu Xiaobiao's *On Destiny*.[253]

If you understand the classics thoroughly, you can attain to high positions as easily as if you were merely bending to pick mustard from the ground. Xiahou Sheng to his disciples.[254]

"In the morning I hunt in a forest of books, and in the evening I fly around in the garden of the arts."[255]

"[Wang Mang] opened the imperial archives, and studied the innumerable books and writings to be found there; he was like a bird from afar, resting in the garden of literature or flying around in the theater of rites and music." *Ju qin mei xin*.[256]

---

250. This paragraph is reproduced without a single variant from the notes to Han Yu, *Collected Works*, Vol. 1, p. 2B, where it is identified as a criticism of Li Ao's view by Ouyang Xiu (1007–1072), *zi* Yongshu, *hao* Zuiweng, a noted writer and scholar-official.

251. This *fu* immediately follows the previous one in Han Yu's *Collected Works*, Vol. 1, pp. 2B–5A.

252. The first sentence is taken verbatim from Han Yu, *Collected Works*, Vol. 1, p. 2B; the following sentence of explanation is from the notes.

253. Liu Xiaobiao is Liu Jun (462–521), *zi* Xiaobiao, a scholar of the Southern Liao dynasty. According to his "Bian ming lun" (On Destiny), to be found in the *Wenxuan* (Anthology of Literature), Vol. 54, the rebel Peng is Peng Yue, and Han is Han Xin.

254. Xiahou Sheng, *zi* Changgong, was a scholar of the Western Han, and a founder of the "New Text" school. For his comments, quoted here, see the *History of the Han Dynasty*, Vol. 75.

255. This sentence is quoted word-for-word from Han Yu's poem (*Collected Works* Vol. 1, p. 4A).

256. This is a direct quotation from the *Ju qin mei xin* (The Excesses of the Qin and the Excellence of the New [Dynasty of Wang Mang]), by Yang Xiong (53 B.C.–A.D. 18), *zi* Ziyun, a Confucian scholar whose reputation was tarnished by the fact that he had accepted office under the usurper Wang Mang, and written essays such as this one in praise of Wang. This passage is included in the notes to Han Yu's poem (Han Yu, *Collected Works*, Vol. 1, p. 4A). Yang's original text appears in the *Anthology of Literature*, Vol. 48; for a translation, see Erwin von Zach, *Die chinesische Anthologie*, Vol. II (Cambridge, Mass.: Harvard University Press, 1958), pp. 898–905. (Our English version follows von Zach's reading.)

"Dance in the theatre of the arts. Relax in the garden of books." Ban Mengjian ("Games for the Guests").[257]

Those who compete for fame fight in the court; those who fight for profits fight in the marketplace. Today, the house of Zhou of Three Rivers is the court and the marketplace of the empire. *Records of the Historian*, biography of Zhang Yi.

You think you can move forward by holding back. But if you don't get closer, you will be farther and farther away.

Therefore, those who want to do as well as their ancestors but hesitate to move will never succeed. *Family Teachings*, chapter on the conduct of the scholar.[258]

To desire to do as well as their ancestors but hesitate to move. *History of the Former Han Dynasty*, biography of Liu Xiang.[259]

He detested the filth of greed and said, "I must work first before I can eat."

Even though there are disadvantages in being in a high position, there is the joy of fulfilling one's ambitions. Yi Yin's joy, nevertheless, came from farming. It could not be replaced by great wealth.

"A 'Fu' on Self-Exhortation"[260]

"In ancient times, Mr. Yan was noted for his self-effacing and liberal nature."

"Poor food and humble dwelling were enough for him to preserve health and enjoy life."[261]

"Our forefathers observed people on the basis of minor matters because people could be deceptive in bigger matters. A man can break a piece of jade that's worth a thousand pieces of gold, but can't help crying over a broken pot. A man can fight against a fierce tiger, but cannot help being alarmed at a scorpion. Don't you know that a single bamboo dish of rice and a single gourd dish of drink were big matters to a philosopher?" Su Zizhan[262]

"Guang says that Master Han wrote three letters to the prime ministers to beg for a position. In 'A Letter to Yu Xiangyang' he asked for wages to feed the

---

257. Ban Mengjian is Ban Gu (32–92), *zi* Mengjian, the celebrated author of the *Han shu* (History of the Han Dynasty). Mao once again quotes verbatim; the text can be found in the *Anthology of Literature*, Vol. 45, where it is entitled "Plays (or Games) in Response to Guests."

258. The family teachings in question are those of Confucius, *Kongzi jiayu*.

259. Ban Gu's *History of the Han Dynasty* is also known as the *History of the Former Han Dynasty*. Liu Xiang, who is referred to in note 147, was a descendant of Liu Bang, the founder of the Han dynasty, and held high office on various occasions.

260. Once again, by Han Yu. See his *Collected Works*, Vol. 1, pp. 5A–6A.

261. This and the previous sentence are quoted verbatim from Han Yu, *Collected Works*, Vol. 1, p. 5A. Mr. Yan is Yan Hui, Confucius' favorite disciple; for the reference in the *Analects* regarding his frugality, see above, note 91.

262. Su Zizhan is Su Shi (1036–1101), *zi* Zizhan, *hao* Dongpo. It is under the last of these names that he is best known as one of China's greatest poets. For the work alluded to here, see "Yan le ting shi bingxu (Poem on Yan's Joy Pavillion with Preface)," in *Su Shi shiji* (Poems of Su Shi), Vol. 15. This passage, which appears in the notes to Han Yu's text (*Collected Works*, Vol. 1, p. 5B), is reproduced here by Mao without a single variation.

animals and pay his servants. He also loved to please people, told them what his ambitions were, and accepted money from them. He was so worried about being poor. Didn't he know what Master Yan had done?" Sima Junshi[263]

"The comments of Mr. Sima and Mr. Su are right. Even so, Tuizhi, in his letter replying to Li Xizhi, said: 'Confucius praised Master Yan, saying that, with a single bamboo dish of rice and a single gourd dish of drink, while others could not have endured the distress, he did not allow his joy to be affected by it. Hui had the Sage as his model, and a ladleful of food and a gourd dish of drink to keep him alive. Wasn't it easy for him to be not sad but happy? Suppose there is a servant who has no one to serve as a model, does not even have a ladleful of rice or a gourd of drink, has no wages, and dies of hunger as a result. Isn't that difficult?' "[264]

"That prisoner of Chu is a superior man." A quotation from the *Spring and Autumn Annals*.[265]

---

263. Junshi is the *zi* of Sima Guang (1019–1086), *hao* Sushui, author of the great *Zizhi tongjian* (commonly translated as the *Comprehensive Mirror of Good Government*), a general history of China from the fifth century B.C. to the tenth century A.D. The passage cited here, from his "Yanle ting song (In Praise of Yan's Joy Pavillion)," is incorporated in the notes to Han Yu (*Collected Works*, Vol. 1, p. 5B), and has been reproduced by Mao word-for-word.

264. Tuizhi is Han Yu, and Li Xizhi is Li Ao. (For Han Yu's letter, see his *Collected Works*, Vol. 16.) Mr. Sima and Mr. Su are, respectively, Sima Guang and Su Dongpo. The whole of this passage from the notes, endorsing the criticism of Han Yu by these two writers, is reproduced verbatim by Mao.

265. See the *Zuo zhuan*, VIII, IX, 8 (Legge, Vol. V, p. 371).

1915

Letter to Wen Yongchang[1]

(February 24, 1915)

Mr. Yongchang:

Of the enclosed eleven books, the cloth case for *Shengshi weiyan*[2] is missing, and *Xinmin congbao*[3] has lost its front page. My sincerest apologies. I hope you will forgive me.

Respectfully,

Zedong

The eleventh day of the first lunar month

Also find enclosed two Chinese language textbooks, and one letter.

---

1. Wen Yongchang (1884–1961), *ming* Yinchang, was Mao's cousin.
2. *Shengshi weiyan* (Words of Warning to an Affluent Age), by the comprador Zheng Guanying, was one of the books Mao cited two decades later, in talking to Edgar Snow, as having greatly influenced his early thinking.
3. This fortnightly periodical, of which the title is variously translated as *Renovation of the People* and *New People's Miscellany*, was the organ of Liang Qichao, who soon acquired great ascendancy over Mao. (On Liang, see note 58 to Mao's "Classroom Notes" of 1913.)

Yang Changji's Record of a Conversation with Mao Zedong[1]

(April 5, 1915)

Student Mao Zedong said that he comes from a locality on the boundary between Xiangtan and Xiangxiang and that although these two places are divided only by a mountain, their dialects are distinctly different. His hometown is in the high mountains, where people live together by clans. Most of them are peasants and therefore can get rich easily. Once rich, they go to Xiangxiang to buy fields. Their customs are simple and pure, and very few indulge themselves in opium and gambling. His father, too, was previously a peasant, but has now become a trader. His younger brother is likewise a peasant. His mother's family is from Xiangxiang, and they are also peasants. And yet it is truly difficult to find someone so intelligent and handsome [as Mao]. Since many unusual talents have come from peasant families, I exhorted him, using the examples of Zeng Disheng and Liang Rengong. Student Mao had worked as a peasant for two years and had also been a soldier for half a year at the time when the Republic superseded the empire. He has truly had an interesting life history.

1. This is an extract from Yang Changji's "Journal."

In Memory of a Friend, Yi Yongxi[1]

(May 1915)

Repeatedly the barbarians have engaged in trickery,
From a thousand *li* they come again across Dragon Mountain;[2]
The scene of carnage, reeking of blood, awaits cleansing;
How can I alone save the world?

Why should we be concerned about life and death?
This century will see a war;
But you were a rare and precious flower beginning to bloom;
And your loss is particularly untimely.

1. Yi Yongxi, also known as Yi Changtao, was a student at First Normal School who had died of illness in March 1915. The school held a memorial meeting for him on May 23, 1915, and Mao contributed two of the 256 couplets contained in a pamphlet published on that occasion: this one, and that quoted in his letter of June 25, 1915, below.

2. There are many mountains in China called Longshan (Dragon Mountain), including one in Hunan, but Mao was probably thinking of that in Shandong, which would be crossed by Japanese or Russian invaders.

Letter to Xiangsheng[1]

(June 25, 1915)

Esteemed Xiangsheng:

I received your letter on the first of the month, and today is the twenty-fifth. I haven't answered until now because I had not decided on where I would be spending the summer vacation. A friend has invited me to Liuyang, but I do not want to go. Since I haven't any money to stay in the provincial capital, there is no alternative to going home for a spell. The school's examinations are over today; I have been very neglectful of my courses. In the past, I had some mistaken ideas, and I was confused regarding my studies. I was especially wearied by the burdensome details of science classes. Now I am learning from my teachers and friends, and moreover having grown up a bit myself, I have made some advances in my knowledge. I have come to the conclusion that the path to scholarship must first be extensive and later intensive, first Chinese and later Western, first general and later specialized. What is your opinion? What is past is past, and today I make a new start. Formerly, I favored an independent route, but now I know that approach to be wrong. I was especially contemptuous of the vanities of school grades and prizes, but now I know myself to have been in error. I once saw in the family letters of Zeng Wenzheng a passage which says, "When reading the Neo-Confucian works,[2] I also like to write essays; when writing essays, I must also attend to other duties. Thus, I have not accomplished anything to my satisfaction."[3] Are these words not equal in worth to gold and jade? If today I give up the sciences and don't strive for good grades, what else should I do? Perhaps others will say I have regressed, but I shall say I have progressed. When I read the study program you have arranged for yourself, and of the results achieved in your scholarship, I am amazed and ashamed. I don't know whether you have already fixed your plans both for school and for inde-

---

1. The editors of the *Wengao* have been unable to identify this individual. Xiangsheng could be a personal name, or it could be a pseudonym meaning "Hunanese student," "Hunanese scholar," or "born in Hunan."

2. *Xingli shu.*

3. From a letter by Zeng Guofan dated the fourteenth day of the twelfth month of the seventh year of the Xianfeng era (January 28, 1858), in Zeng Guofan, *Family Letters*. The passage in quotation marks is, for the most part, not a direct citation, but Mao's summary of Zeng's message. As indicated above (note 17 to the "Classroom Notes"), Mao had referred to this same letter in 1913.

pendent study. Judging from your wish to study English and mathematics, it appears that you are preparing to enter school. If you are considering independent study, let me suggest two men as examples. One is Kang Youwei.[4] Kang once said, "Before I was forty, I studied thoroughly Chinese works; after forty, I absorbed the essentials of Western knowledge." The other example is Liang Qichao.[5] Liang was assuredly a child prodigy. According to his own account, he too concentrated first on poetry and essays and only later applied himself to all the other subjects. Most likely, literature is the origin of all disciplines; I could not have been more mistaken when I previously said that poetry was without use. Do you have any ambitions in this regard? The difficulties which China faces in the future will be a hundred fold those of the past, and we will have no chance of saving her without extraordinary talents. Fortunately, you have not despaired. My classmate Mr. Chen[6] is a person of aspirations, a rarity among the others. In the midst of butchers, wine merchants, peddlers, and braggarts, there must be some extraordinary men. Pay attention to that! Except for the sages, men cannot be successful in isolation and, besides maintaining good relations with teachers, choosing one's friends is of primary importance, is it not? I have read your poetry: the tone is lofty and the meaning is profound, beyond my own capacities. Another classmate, Yi Changtao, has died of illness. He was an excellent calligrapher and a talented writer; we were very close. His death is truly to be lamented. I composed a poem for the school memorial service.[7] I beg you to correct it freely.

As time goes by, I am still absorbed in my thoughts of you,
I think of you, but you do not come;
As a friend of your youth desperately saddened,
I lament and sigh with boundless grief.
The Hengyang geese cry piercingly,
Spring silently returns to the shore of the Xiang River;
The things I see recall past joys,
And I pace back and forth at the bend of the southern wall.
At the bend of the wall the grass grows luxuriant,
And tears course down my two cheeks;
Splendid remains the lonely scene,

---

4. Kang Youwei (1858–1927), *zi* Guangxia, *hao* Changsu, alternative *hao* Gengsheng and Zuyi, a native of Guangdong, was the organizer and leader of the 1898 Reform movement. A *jinshi* of 1895, he had written on Confucius as a reformer and on the concept of *datong* or "Great Harmony." Mao had long been familiar with his ideas.

5. On Liang, see note 58 to Mao's "Classroom Notes" of 1913, and the many references to him in that text.

6. Chen Chang (1894–1930), *zi* Zhangfu, from Liuyang, Hunan, was to become a member of the New People's Study Society and of the Chinese Communist Party. He graduated from First Normal in 1915 and in 1917 began teaching at the attached primary school.

7. I.e., in addition to the previous text.

When the sun sets in the clouds west of Hengyang.
We were just planning to travel across the great expanse,
And never imagined we might be thus torn apart.
Our endless separation starts today,
And in the dead of night, I am startled by the crowing of the cock.
When I hear the cock's first crow,
It carries me across the eastern plateau;
I watch you gradually approach,
As we take each other's hands, the tears well up in our eyes.
Like a lame steed, I walk the mountain pass,
And a gust of wind blows up the spectral curtains;[8]
The feelings I hold in my breast are like fire,
Leaning against the rocks, I give vent to song.
The mountain ridge is green and luxuriant,
We pledged to try long swords;
The eastern sea holds island savages,
In the northern mountains hate-filled enemies abound.[9]
Together we denounced the licentious,
But how shall we purge the evils in ourselves?
When Ziqi died an early death,
[Bo] Ya stopped playing his lute.[10]
The halting of the lute causes extreme pain,
And this spring no red flowers will thrive;
There are a thousand days yet to come,
But with whom will I share this life?
I offer a cup of wine to the spirit,
And despondently watch the funeral streamers;
To what can I consign my desolation?
An eternal pool is left in nature.

These three books and the letter came from a certain Mr. Zheng today. I am also sending thirty sheets of oiled paper and three hundred cash. The amount is small and the road long: there is no need to return it. You might also read the lecture and the paper, "Baoming wan" (The Lifesaving Pill). If you gain any insights in your reading, I hope that you will write and tell me about them. I will send more later. Please accept my respectful wishes for your studies! I have also enclosed the volume *Mingchi pian* (Essays on the Sense of Shame). It was

8. Mao appears to evoke here the white cloth which traditionally surrounded a new grave.

9. The "island savages" referred to are the Japanese; the "hate-filled enemies" are the Japanese and Russians on China's northern frontier.

10. Bo Ya was a famous lute-player of the Spring and Autumn period. He formed a friendship with a woodcutter named Zhong Ziqi, who had such an understanding of music that he could visualize the scenery evoked by each piece. When Zhong died, Bo Ya broke his lute and never played again. The sense of these four lines appears to be that Mao valued the criticism of his essays by Yi Changtao as Bo Ya did Ziqi's appreciation of his playing.

compiled and published by our school and succeeds in conveying a general picture of the Sino-Japanese negotiations. From the last piece you will get an idea of the information within.

Zedong salutes you.

June 25

Postscript: Just in time, I have received a letter from the Advanced Normal School. Next semester they are going to establish departments of literature and history in order to remedy the shortcomings of recent years which have led to the loss of traditional teachings. Their system is largely like that of the academies,[11] emphasizing independent study rather than lectures. This should be an excellent place to study the classics. The school director, Mr. Wu, is the author of the lecture I have enclosed, and I have heard that the teachers are all quite distinguished in their fields. From the recruiting announcement, this school appears to be rather unusual. Your objectives and my own are similar; will you come and take the examination? I have enclosed the announcement. Please give it your close attention.

Once more, Zedong.

11. Presumably of the traditional-style academies, such as Yuelu Academy on the mountain of the same name, or Jiangnan (South of the River) Academy across the river. The second of these had been combined in 1903 with what ultimately became First Normal School. For more details on the Yuelu Academy see also the note to the text of September 1917.

Epigraphs to Mingchi pian *(Essays on the Sense of Shame)* [1]

(Summer 1915)

I

The seventh of May,
The Republic suffered extraordinary shame.
How to achieve revenge?
Through our students!

II

These words were written by Professor Shi Runshan of First Normal School. The professor's personal name is Guangquan, and he is a native of Baoqing. When the Sino-Japanese negotiations were concluded,[2] the entire school was enraged. This professor was especially anguished, so much so that he stopped sleeping and forgot to eat. Students and others raised a fund and printed this booklet. Professor Shi then wrote the preface, edited the text, and so on.

The piece entitled "Jiuguo chuyan" (A Modest Proposal on Saving the Nation) was also written by Professor Shi.

---

1. Regarding the book in question, see Mao's letter of June 25, 1915. The first of these two epigraphs was written on the outside cover of the volume; the second was written at the end of Shi Runshan's essay "Gan yan" (Emotional Words), which prefaced the collection. Mao also underscored various points throughout the book.

2. The reference is to Yuan Shikai's acceptance, on May 7, 1915, of Japan's "Twenty-one Demands."

Letter to a Friend[1]

(July 1915)

. . . regret it. In today's somber and repressive world, who can stop the coming of a violent flood if we do not persist in making a fuss?[2] A benevolent or superior man will do this to benefit his country and people, even at the sacrifice of his own life. Some might say this is merely perturbing the spirit and wasting time, and so it may appear. But this amounts to dismissing it as sophistry. Mencius was fond of disputing,[3] but he cannot be considered a sophist. Zigong's diplomacy preserved the Kingdom of Lu, created rebellion in the Kingdom of Qi, destroyed the Kingdom of Wu, strengthened the Kingdom of Jin, and made the Kingdom of Yue powerful,[4] and yet he cannot be considered a sophist. Who can say what is "perturbing the spirit"? Who can say what is "wasting time"? Moreover, I have often heard that making use of one's talents allows them to grow to

1. The beginning and end of this letter are missing, so the name of the recipient and the date of composition do not appear. Two references to "Zisheng" and other internal evidence make it, however, virtually certain that it was addressed to Xiao Zisheng. The editors of the *Wengao*, who also draw this conclusion, note that since Xiao graduated from the Normal School in June 1915, and this letter obviously precedes that of August 3, 1915, it can with some confidence be dated July 1915. Xiao Zisheng (1894–1976), also known as Xiao Xudong, was, with Cai Hesen, one of Mao's two closest friends during his student years in Changsha. Later their paths diverged, and they became bitter political enemies. This is reflected in Xiao's book about their youthful experiences: Siao-yu, *Mao Tse-tung and I Were Beggars* (Syracuse: Syracuse University Press, 1959). For details regarding his later role, see the note to Mao's letter of November 1920 to Xiao Zizhang.

2. The term *qiangguo* (to make a mighty clamor) is taken from chapter 33 of the *Zhuangzi* ("Tianxia"), where it is said of the philosophers Song Xing and Yin Wen that "even if the empire would not be converted, they were the sort that persists in making a fuss and will not give up" (Graham, *Chuang-tzu*, p. 278). Wieger renders the same words: "Éconduits, ils revenaient à la charge, et finissaient, à force d'importunités, par obtenir qu'on les écoutât" (*Les pères du système taoïste* [Paris: Cathasia, 1950], p. 503). Hence our translation of "fuss," which is close to Wieger's "importunités." More freely, Mao's point might be translated: ". . . if we do not persist in remonstrating (or stating our case)."

3. *Hao bian.* The allusion is to a passage in the *Mencius*, III, II, IX (Legge, Vol. II, pp. 278–79), which reads: " 'Master, the people beyond our school all speak of you as being fond of disputing. I venture to ask whether it be so.' Mencius replied, 'Indeed, I am not fond of disputing, but I am compelled to do it.' "

4. Zigong is the *zi* of Duanmu Ci (520 B.C. – ?), a man of Wei of the Spring and Autumn period and one of the four leading disciples of Confucius. The preceding part of this sentence is a direct textual quotation from the *Records of the Historian*, Vol. 67.

their full potential. The smith does not behave as if his arms are little, and they grow large and strong. The winnower does not behave as if his calves are spindly, and they grow stout. Su and Zhang[5] created great alliances, and their tongues were not therein exhausted. Li Zhu[6] excelled at using his eyesight, and his eyes did not therefore squint. There are many examples of talents which grew to their full potential through use, so one should not believe the argument about "perturbing the spirit." Of the little progress I have made in these last years, only the smaller part was achieved through books; the larger part of my gains were the result of questioning and seeking solutions to difficulties. Nothing would be worse for me than to give up discussion and debate and concentrate on books alone. Perhaps I may be just as muddleheaded now as I was in the past, but there is no way to know. And yet, I learn that [you], Zisheng, regret your words. Because you argued too much with people, when you parted you felt you had been much in the wrong, and this served as a warning to avoid such errors in the future,[7] and to be careful of your words. I say to Zisheng, if you had not first spoken out, how could you have known your mistakes? By knowing your mistakes, you have gained something; is this not a benefit from speaking out? If [you], Zisheng, have now sincerely learned from your errors in order to avoid them in future, they are no longer important. Therefore, one should not believe the argument about "wasting time" either. Thus, mutual questioning and interaction expand knowledge; making a fuss, if not avoided, can revive the nation; by rejecting such expressions as "perturbing the spirit" and "wasting time" we can improve the spirit and advance our studies. Is it not increasingly clear that discourse is invaluable! However, I do not insist on your consenting to my idea. I would rather entreat you, sir, to rectify my mistakes. I only present my trifling ideas for your consideration. The course of each man's life is different from another's, and only heroic individuals know that these diverging routes lead ultimately to the same place. I do not propose myself as a model for others so

5. Su Qin (? – 317 B.C.), a native of Luoyang, after being repulsed in an offer of his services to the Qin state, enjoyed a successful political career as the leading protagonist of the federation of six other states against Qin, though he ultimately perished by assassination. Zhang Yi (? – 310 B.C.), on the other hand, served the ruler of Qin, of which he became foreign minister. Mao's comment about his eloquence is inspired by a well-known anecdote according to which, after being wrongly beaten for an offense he had not committed, Zhang asked his wife on returning home, "Look and see if they have left me my tongue." When she replied that they had, he exclaimed, "If I still have my tongue, that is all I want."

6. Li Zhu, also known as Li Lou, flourished under the Yellow Emperor, said to have reigned 2698–2598 B.C.. It is reported that he could see the tip of an autumn spikelet at 100 paces.

7. Mao here uses an expression, *chengqian bihou,* which he was later to make famous during the Rectification Campaign of 1942–1943. In that context, it is commonly translated "learn from past mistakes to avoid future ones." (Speech of February 1, 1942, in *Selected Works of Mao Tse-tung,* Vol. III [Peking: Foreign Languages Press, 1965], p. 50.)

that they may take the same path as mine. Neither do I redirect my own path to conform to another's model. This is a universally true and fair statement. Throughout the ages, there have been struggles between different schools of thought. In the realm of government, superior men are distinguished from petty men, and the pure from the impure. In the realm of scholarship, the Han masters are differentiated from the Song masters, and Cheng and Zhu are differentiated from Lu and Wang.[8] Not to speak of government, scholarship has offered much room for criticism. Different people have different perspectives; masters and servants, they plant their banners, recruit friends and students, and rebuke one another unceasingly. Alas, for what reason? When I think of the greatness of Professor Yang, I feel that I will never be his equal. But you can be considered capable of following the master's teachings, and even further developing them. Your letter also mentioned that you had found great benefit and insight in my words. You believe my trifling ideas to be worthy of cooperative study for the promotion of knowledge. Your praise is too high for a person like me. Alas, what others can fully understand a person's affairs? Since ancient times, many have been contradictory in appearance and spirit, with mouths like Yao and Shun,[9] but hearts like Jie and Zhou.[10] Fan Ying[11] was famous . . .

8. The two main schools of thought in the late Qing, named after the periods when the thinkers they admired had lived, were the so-called Han school, which emphasized the investigation of facts, and the Song or neo-Confucian school, which stressed *li*, or principle. The individuals Mao goes on to mention represent the two main branches of the latter. The two Cheng brothers, Cheng Hao and Cheng Yi, have often been regarded as belonging, like Zhu Xi, to the current which regarded principle as the basis of the universe; Lu Jiuyuan of the Song, and Wang Yangming of the Ming, represented the view that principle was an emanation of *xin* or mind. All of these are mentioned in Mao's "Classroom Notes" of 1913, where further explanatory notes can be found.

9. Yao (d. 2258 B.C.) and his successor Shun (2317–2208 B.C.) are the two legendary sage emperors of early Chinese history. They are frequently referred to in the "Classroom Notes" and figure in the Confucian classics as models of virtue.

10. Jie Gui (d. 1763 B.C.), the last emperor of the Xia dynasty, and Zhou Xin (d. 1122 B.C.), the last emperor of the Yin dynasty, were notorious for their cruelty and extravagance. Both brought about the collapse of their respective dynasties by their misconduct, and their names are commonly used as symbols of everything evil.

11. A scholar of some renown at the time of the Eastern Han dynasty.

Letter to Xiao Zisheng

(August 3, 1915)

Esteemed Zisheng:

I don't know whether you have received the letter I sent you previously. The mail route is circuitous, and I expect it may not reach you easily. Today the sun is at its hottest; I feel too tired to study. There are no springs and hills in the city; the foul air and the noise are unbearable. The place I live may, however, be inferior to others. Recently, Mr. Fang Weixia[1] came to the provincial capital to declare that his *xian* had an opening for a higher primary school teacher of Chinese and would like to hire someone from the capital. He added that most teachers had just gone home for the summer vacation and good ones were hard to come by, so he had decided to take on whoever would come first. He raised this matter with me during his visit, and I immediately suggested your name, although I had not ascertained whether or not you would be available. My first consideration was that you were apparently interested in a teaching job in the capital, not elsewhere, so that you would be able to work for a famous school and cultivate some real talents. My second consideration was that to meet better teachers and friends is of great benefit to you both in teaching and learning. So, if the school in Pingjiang is out of the question, so be it. Time, however, brings changes, and perhaps you have changed your mind. Who knows? Therefore, I have decided to present the idea for your consideration, and let you decide for yourself. The position is head teacher of Chinese at the school in Pingjiang; the hours are fifteen per week; and the salary is 200 strings of cash each year, plus transportation expenses. According to Mr. Fang, there are many distinguished teachers among the staff. There is also a certain senior teacher who has been there over ten years and whose scholarship has a strong foundation. Therefore, if you are interested in further research in the field of Chinese studies, you will have a companion with whom to work. Please reply to me as soon as you receive this letter. School will be opening soon, and the principal is

1. Fang Weixia (1879–1934), a native of Pingjiang in Hunan, had studied in Japan and taught at First Normal School where he was also dean. He joined the Chinese Communist Party in 1926 and was killed in combat in 1934.

waiting. I had best not write any more. Please accept my best wishes for your studies and give my regards to my good elder brother Zizhang.[2]

Respectfully,

Your younger brother Zedong
August 3, 1915

---

2. Xiao Zizhang (1896–1983), also known as Xiao Zhifan and Xiao San, was born in Xiangxiang, Hunan. As the name Xiao San (Third Brother Xiao) suggests, he was a younger brother of Xiao Zisheng. He likewise graduated from Hunan First Normal School, and went on to teach at the attached primary school. In March 1917, he was a co-signatory with Mao of a letter to Miyazaki Tōten. For further particulars, see the note to Mao's letter of February 19, 1920.

Letter to Xiao Zisheng

(August 1915)

Esteemed Zisheng:

I received your letter on the seventh. After I read it, I jumped with excitement! Alas, except for Zisheng, who would be willing to speak to me of the Way? Except for you, who would be able to speak to me of the Way? After reading your precious statements, my heart feels lightened and refreshed. However, the knots which bind it are still thick, while the many heavy thoughts are deeply accumulated. They multiply and weigh down on me, and I am unable to free myself. Will you allow me to release them by talking to you? Today, I see that of all the myriad species, man is endowed with superior intelligence. The sounds we produce become speech. Having speech, we gather many others of our kind to form society. Speech is possible because of intelligence, and society is possible because of speech. Is speech not most valuable? Having recited the admonitions of Chengzi,[1] read the writings of Zeng Gong,[2] and tried to go back to the teachings of the Duke of Zhou and Confucius, I know that sayings such as "it is the mouth which gives rise to war"[3] and "be slow in speech and earnest in conduct"[4] have been recorded on bamboo tablets and disseminated for a thousand years. And now, when you implicitly call my attention to these principles which are in accordance with the teachings of the sages, do I dare not acclaim your wisdom? Bearing this in mind, I have thought things over. All the depths of wisdom found in heaven and on earth, and all the profundity of meaning accumulated throughout the ages, whether changeable and confusing, whether disorderly and obscure, are all without limit, whereas men's lives are limited. If one person who has obtained a pearl and another who owns half of a jade disk do not engage in mutual questioning and interaction, how can they broaden their knowl-

1. Cheng Yi.

2. Zeng Guofan.

3. A quotation from the *Book of Historical Documents*, II, II, II, 17 (Legge, Vol. III, p. 63). Book II is entitled "The Counsels of the Great Yu," and the words cited by Mao are not attributed either to the Duke of Zhou or to Confucius. Mao has left out two characters in the middle of the sentence; Legge's translation of the whole reads: "It is the mouth which sends forth what is good, and gives rise to war."

4. See the *Analects*, IV, XXIV (Legge, Vol. I, p. 172), where this quotation is attributed to Confucius: "The Master said, 'The superior man wishes to be slow in his speech and earnest in his conduct.' "

edge and achieve erudition? Perhaps this is what is known as inviting offense with speech. But even so, speech cannot be discarded simply because it can cause transgression, just as food cannot be discarded simply because it can cause one to choke. Furthermore, he who speaks does not necessarily transgress, and even if he does transgress, this is but a small matter to a wise man. Jesus was dismembered[5] for speaking out; Long and Bi were executed for speaking out.[6] From another perspective, one may also say that some people suffered bad ends not because they had transgressed through speech. Lu Yang and Yin Hao were famous among their peers, but as soon as they made a mistake in the eyes of the world, their standing was diminished immediately.[7] I am frightened morning and night and ashamed to face up to [the ideal of] the superior man [*junzi*]. Recently, I wrote a piece in my journal entitled "self-accusation." Read it and you will know the pain in my heart. The words are as follows:

> A guest said to me: "Do you know the bottle gourd? When the sun shines and the earth begins to warm, it sprouts and spreads. Intertwining with itself, it becomes a web of vines, each unable to extend itself on its own. If it is not interfered with by men, it will spread among the thorn bushes and reach out within the confines of the weeds. The seasons progress in good order, and it throws out a bud furtively, here and there. People will say, "This is only some type of weed," but when autumn descends and the leaves wither, a shepherd boy passes among the plants, cutting away the weeds and separating the shrubs. That substantial object, some as big as a crockery jar, is the vine's gourd. On the other hand, observe the peony which grows within the garden. Its green calyxes and vermillion blossoms lean this way and that, bursting with energy. Majestic and brilliant, the blossoms compete with one another in beauty and opulence. The unenlightened will say, "The fruit of this plant must be enormous." Who would think that when fall arrives and the cold weather returns, the flowers shrivel, and there is no fruit to harvest? Observing these two plants, which should we emulate?" I answered: "The peony flourishes first and later declines. The gourd declines first and later flourishes. The one has no end product and the other has. One should emulate the one with an end product, and is this not the gourd?" The guest said: "If that is your answer, I see that you have but one crude skill, and yet you make a treasured gift of it. You have not achieved any measure of virtue, and yet you wish to make a show for the crowds, gathering your kind around you and putting on airs by rolling up your sleeves and raising your eyebrows. You do not have the capacity for

5. No doubt this ancient Chinese punishment was the nearest equivalent to crucifixion Mao could think of.

6. Long is Guan Longxian; Bi is Bi Gan. Both of them were disemboweled for remonstrating with the tyrant Zhou Xiu for his excesses in the twelfth century B.C.

7. Duke Yang of Lu, a personage of the Warring States period, is mentioned in the *Huainan zi*, an eclectic work compiled at the court of Liu An (d. 122 B.C.), king of Huainan. It is related of him that he shook his spear at the declining sun and caused it to move back up in the sky in order to leave him more time for a difficult battle. Yin Hao (d. 356), a high military commander, was cashiered for incompetence.

> tranquility; you are fickle and excitable. Like a woman preening herself, you know no shame. Your outside looks strong, but your inside is truly empty. Your ambitions for fame and fortune are not suppressed, and your sensual desires grow daily. You enjoy all hearsay and rumor, perturbing the spirit and misusing time, and generally delight in yourself. You always emulate what the peony does, without hope for any end product, but deceive yourself by saying 'I emulate the gourd.' Is this not dishonesty?" Having no answer, I shrank back, sweating profusely, morose and frustrated.

Zhangfu[8] has gone home, and is expected to return in two weeks. It has been arranged that he should lecture at the affiliated primary school. I have already sent someone with a letter to take care of him. I enclosed your long letter and also a letter from Kunfu.[9] School vacation has been extended until the twenty-fifth. I am going home on the fifteenth to pay my respects to my parents and visit my brothers. You are right in declining the position at the Pingjiang school. I mentioned it only because I was uncertain whether everything had been settled with the Xiuye School.[10] I will stop here; for other news, see my letter to Zizhang. I respectfully submit this for your perusal.

Zedong salutes you.

---

8. Chen Zhangfu. See the note to Mao's letter of June 25, 1915.

9. Kunfu is Xiong Guangchu (1886–?), born in Xiangxiang, Hunan. He graduated from First Normal School in the summer of 1913, and went on to work as the school's librarian. In the summer of 1917 he successfully completed the Hunan Higher Teacher's College special training course on literature and history. He later joined the New People's Study Society, went to France on the work-study program, and died there.

10. The Xiuye xuexiao, literally the "Study School," had been established in Changsha in 1903 as a middle school, and expanded to include a primary school in 1904 and an accelerated teacher training department in 1906. According to Xiao himself, he had in fact been offered an appointment there two months before his graduation from First Normal, and taught there during the first semester of the 1915–1916 academic year. See Siao-yu, *Mao Tse-tung and I Were Beggars,* pp. 70, 182. Mao later taught history at Xiuye from April to December 1919.

Letter to Xiao Zisheng

(September 6, 1915)

Esteemed elder schoolmate[1] Zisheng:

I read in the *Doctrine of the Mean* about extensive study.[2] In his annotations to the *Great Learning*, Zhu Xi wrote[3] that, on the basis of first understanding their principles, all things found in heaven and on earth can be understood, even to the ultimate degree. Their outsides and insides, fine points and more general aspects, will all be arrived at; their entire substance and total functions will be illuminated. In the passage alluded to above, Confucius advocated "extensively studying all learning."[4] Mencius spoke of "learning extensively and discussing minutely what is learned."[5] I have taken this teaching as a matter of course and assumed it to be the path which all scholars must follow. Having heard that Mr. Li Shaoxi[6] was an enthusiastic scholar, I went to interview him. What he said seemed to be in agreement with these teachings, but his logic was more detailed. The practical method has also made his teaching more effective. I am extremely impressed with Mr. Li; in all my life, I have met only one person capable of expounding things in this way. You too are an enthusiastic scholar and a deep thinker. What I learned of his theories is still incomplete. Since I have been asked, I will recount it to you, but I will not be able to do justice to it. However, whenever I have some new understanding, I dare not fail to pass it along to you in order to repay your kind intentions and express my own sincerity. I asked Shaoxi how one gains knowledge. When the school is stagnant and corrupt, should one foresake it for deep mountains and serene springs, there to build a foundation by studying the writings of the ancients, and later, following in the footsteps of Mr. Kang and Liang Rengong, descend from the mountain and immerse oneself in the new learning? Shaoxi disapproved of this as reversing the

1. As noted above, Xiao Zisheng had already graduated in June 1915.

2. See the *Doctrine of the Mean*, XX, 19 (Legge, Vol. I, p. 413). The context is as follows: "He who attains to sincerity is he who chooses what is good, and firmly holds it fast. To this attainment there are requisite the extensive study of what is good, accurate inquiry about it, careful reflection on it, the clear discrimination of it, and the earnest practice of it."

3. The reference is to the paragraph in Zhu Xi's commentary dealing with the opening passage, especially the concept of "the investigation of things." See Legge, Vol. I, p. 358.

4. *Analects* XII, XV (Legge, Vol. I, p. 257).

5. See *Mencius*, IV, II, XV (Legge, Vol. II, p. 323).

6. On Li Jinxi, *zi* Shaoxi, see the note to Mao's letter to him dated November 9, 1915.

first and the last. In general, comprehensive study should be the foundation of specialization, and the new should be the foundation of the old. Politicians especially, and practical men, attach particular value to familiarity with and adaptability to all kinds of circumstances. Bismarck was richest in comprehensive knowledge. Today, even Yuan[7] also has much knowledge. If one fails in this, one will certainly be defeated. The example is Wang Anshi.[8] In order to carry out his own ideas, he found justification in antiquity. He annotated the *Rites of Zhou*, and wrote the *Zishuo*.[9] His writings could never match those of the Han and Tang dynasties. He deserves the title of a specialized scholar. He failed, however, because he was short of comprehensive knowledge and did not fully understand the real society around him, and consequently carried out inappropriate policies. Therefore, he made a turnabout and gave up his vain hopes, directing his energies to schools, with emphasis on comprehensive knowledge. This is the concrete aspect of his ideas. What about the abstract, and how should one set to work? To this, Shaoxi replied, "With the study of Chinese literature." First, it can endow one with the arts of clarity and conciseness and teach one to capture fully and convey common speech and events with just a few words. Second, the study of Chinese can enable one to understand the meaning and flavor of an essay, to judge the beauty, and to uncover the central ideas of each of the entire corpus of writings dating from ancient times to the present. The teachers and students of today fail to do this. "Expertise" is the so-called "comprehensive knowledge" of today; "strangeness" is the so-called "profundity" of today. Actually, so-called "expertise" is nothing but accumulation of the trivial and repetitious; accumulation of the trivial and repetitious cannot be considered "comprehensive knowledge." So-called "strangeness" is nothing but abstruseness and obscurity; abstruseness and obscurity cannot be considered "profundity." As for the steps to acquiring knowledge, there are those who are ignorant

7. The reference is to Yuan Shikai (1859–1916), *zi* Weiting, *hao* Rong'an, born in Xiangcheng, Henan Province. He occupied various high civil and military posts under the empire and became a favorite of the Empress Dowager in 1898 after betraying the reformers, who had sought his support. In the early years of the twentieth century, he built up the "New Army," which played an important role in the Revolution of 1911. Following Sun Yatsen's election as first president of the Provisional Government of the Republic, Yuan became involved in negotiations which led to his election, on February 14, 1912, as Sun's successor. In 1914, a new constitution was adopted which gave him dictatorial powers, but he soon began scheming to establish himself as emperor. These plans were frustrated by widespread public opposition and secret Japanese intervention, and he died of illness on June 6, 1916.

8. Wang Anshi (1021–1086), *zi* Jiepu, *hao* Banshan, a native of Jiangxi, was one of the most celebrated reformers in Chinese history. The changes which he introduced beginning in 1069, justified as Mao indicates by his interpretation of classical texts, were too bold for his contemporaries and were reversed before his death.

9. A work on Chinese characters, with particular attention to those formed by a combination of two or more others.

and inept even though they have read the entire corpus of writings dating from ancient times to the present. History is the observation of the evidence of the past and the application to the present of what is appropriate. Most crucial is the discovery of general principles and precedents. In order to grasp the outline and ascertain the details pertaining to the entire duration of a dynasty, there is no better way than to seek out its greatest and most powerful men. Great and powerful men are representatives of an era, and by assembling one by one every single piece of evidence relating to their lives, one will see that the whole era is but an accessory to these representative people. In Chinese history, one should concentrate on the descendants of the four tribes and build a foundation for the study of Asian history. In Western history, one ought to concentrate on the comparison of China with the West and choose from abroad what is useful at home. Geographical studies concern questions of space. History and all other subjects are each therein rooted. Maps are the most important tools of research, and filling them in by hand is the most efficient method of using them. Geographical studies encompass the greatest amount of comprehensive knowledge, and all newspapers and journals contribute to it. Newspapers and journals speak of education, and geographical studies include pieces on education; newspapers and journals speak of local customs, and geographical studies also include essays on local customs. Politics, military affairs, industry, transportation, religion, etc., all come within the scope of geographical studies. This is little understood by scholars today. They browse through newspapers and journals without comprehending their relevance. This is what is known as being unsystematic. Calisthenics, drawing, music, and handicrafts are types of skills and arts. The superior man can find in them the path to scholarship and self-cultivation. How is scholarship found in these activities? They require logic and order. If one does perform poorly, one will have no logic or order. Is there any greater path to scholarship than to expand the mind and improve the character through these activities? How is self-cultivation found in these activities? In the past, there have been men who practiced them, such as Tao Kan, Cromwell, and Washington. Tao Kan moved bricks as a form of manual labor;[10] Cromwell hunted in the mountains; and Washington chopped wood in his back garden. Men's spirits are limited, while those things which exhaust the spirit are limitless. One cannot rely on the limited to control the limitless. The sages knew this and renewed their spirits through these activities, thus making themselves inexhaustible. Furthermore, games, handicrafts, drawing, and music are forms of aesthetic education. Aesthetic education is the bridge between the present world and the essential world (see Mr. Cai's 1912 guidelines on the orientation of education),[11] and

10. On Tao Kan see note 146 to the "Classroom Notes." He used to carry a hundred large bricks out of his study every morning, and carry them back in the evening, to maintain his physical activity.

11. Cai Yuanpei had been in 1912 the first minister of education of the Nanjing

therefore, no subject can be done without in the schools. This is what Shaoxi had to say about his method of approach to various subjects and their utility. He further introduced me to the chapter entitled "On Perfecting Nature" in *An Introduction to Sociology*,[12] and I took this book and read it through. Afterward, I closed the book and exclaimed to myself, "Here lies the path to scholarship." For although this book is entitled *An Introduction to Sociology*, its scope is not limited to sociology; it can also be seen as an introduction to all scholarly disciplines. It indicates that the difficulties of scholarship are divided into three categories: those in the object, those in the subject, and those in the relation between subject and object. Those in the object are called "concealment of the object"; those in the subject are called "inhibition of feeling and knowledge"; and those in the relation between subject and object are called "academic distortion," "national bias," "customary prejudice," "political delusion," and "educational deficiency." In order to dispel these three difficulties, we must improve our nature. The nature is improved through learning, and learning is divided into three branches: the metaphysical, the relational, and the phenomenal. Logic and mathematics belong to the metaphysical; physics and chemistry belong to the relational; and natural history belongs to the phenomenal. Study these three fields, and the three difficulties will be dispelled. Only when the mind is refined and the intelligence is perfected can one speak of real scholarship. All this is linked together by psychology and physiology, which have great bearing on sociology. And what I am saying does not apply only to scholarship; virtue is also part of it. If a person does not suffer from concealment of object, or inhibition of feeling and knowledge, and if he furthermore displays no academic distortion, national bias, historical prejudice, political delusion, or educational deficiency, he is definitely a superior man [*junzi*]. What more is there to say? These days each time I speak to anyone about scholarship, I introduce him to this book, believing it to be most pertinent. If you have time, you should take a look at it. (Zhangfu has recently read this book too.) What I have laid out above may be divided into three parts: first, a discussion of the relation between specialization and comprehensive studies; then, an exposition of the methods of research applied to each subject; then, a recounting of what is to be prized about the book *An Introduction to Sociology*. However, something even more important than all of this is yet to be discussed, and that is Chinese studies. I speak of it last so as to command your greatest attention, and because of its great importance. Chinese studies are both broad and deeply significant. Altogether, the four categories of

---

provisional government. The guidelines referred to here were promulgated by him at that time under the title "Views regarding the orientation of education." Cai was also the translator of the book by Paulsen which Mao annotated in 1918. For a detailed note regarding him, see the text on the "Strengthen Learning Society" of July 21, 1919.

12. *Qunxue yiyan*, literally *An Introduction to Sociology*, was the title of Yan Fu's translation of Herbert Spencer's *Principles of Sociology*.

books[13] include the records of about five thousand years, and even if a person exhausts his life and intelligence, he can only understand a limited portion of them. Is this not amazing? There is the study of how to be a human being, the study of how to be a citizen, and the study of how to be an inhabitant of the world. The study of how to be a human being is the study of the relationships between father and son, husband and wife, elder and younger brothers, and the differences between cotton and silk, beans and rice.[14] The study of how to be a citizen is the study of the history, geography, political doctrine, and artistic climate of one's country. The study of how to be an inhabitant of the world is a matter of world view and of international relations. Certainly, the study of being a person or a citizen is easy, while the study of being a Chinese is difficult. There are five thousand years of history, the land extends over seven thousand *li*, political doctrine is extremely complex, and human feelings and customs are broad and convoluted. How can we approach all this? If we were Japan, with only three islands within our borders, or Germany, with a history of only half a century and land equivalent in size to our two provinces of Guangxi and Guangdong alone, how easy things would be! Yet how difficult it is to be a citizen of China! Therefore, general knowledge of Chinese studies is most crucial for our people. It has been said in the past that if one wants to know one of the classics, one must first know all of the classics. Today, if one wants to know Chinese studies, one must first possess general knowledge. Selecting books is of primary importance; they must include all manner of writings and encompass all manner of things. When the trunk shakes, the branches wave; when the general signals with his banner, the troops brandish their weapons. Mr. Zeng's *Zachao*[15] is such a book. In this book are selected the essential documents belonging to the four divisions, dating from the most ancient antiquity to the Qing dynasty. The method is as follows: For instance, "The Prince of Lü upon Punishments" comes from the *Book of Historical Documents*.[16] I have the *Book of Historical Documents* available while reading this piece, and by referring to details in related chapters from the *Book of Historical Documents*, I approach the entire work. It is the same in the case of other classics. The "Biography of Bo Yi" is from the *Records of the Historian*.[17] While reading this piece, I have the *Records of the*

13. Over the centuries, several different four-part classifications have been used in China, but Mao chooses here to follow that of Li Chong (fourth century A.D.), a scholar-official under the Jin dynasty. The four headings, enumerated below, were classics, histories, philosophical works, and literary collections.

14. These four commodities stand for the necessities of life, according to the biography of Cheng Yi in the *Song shi* (History of the Song Dynasty).

15. An abbreviated title for Zeng Guofan's *Jingshi baijia zachao* (Notes on the Various Schools of Classics and Histories).

16. See the *Book of Historical Documents*, V, XXVII (Legge, Vol. III, pp. 588–612).

17. The biography of Bo Yi (twelfth century B.C., son of the prince of the Guchu state) constitutes Vol. 61 of Sima Qian's *Records of the Historian*.

Historian at hand, and in referring to details in other chapters, I approach the entire work. It is the same with other historical writings. As for philosophical works, one starts with one philosopher and then goes on to other philosophers. As for the category of literary collections, one starts with one collection and then goes on to others. In this way, general knowledge of Chinese studies is ingrained in one's head. This is a broad summary. By following this method, one may well avoid the most threatening enemy of scholarship, narrowness. I have been reading Zeng Wenzheng on how to study books. He divided his studies into four fields. In studying ethics, he chose one or two primary books (the *Analects* and the *Jinsi lu*[18]), and supplemented them with others. In doing textual research, he did the same. In reading literature and economics, he did the same. This is similar to Mr. Li's approach, except that Li is concerned with only one branch, and this pertains to four. Li takes only one book as his primary source, while here the basic sources are not limited to only one book. Chinese studies involves both the philosophical and the literary heritage. Mr. Yao's *Classified Compilation*[19] places more emphasis on literature, while Zeng's writings can be valued for addressing both. His method may be called "deductive reasoning," which means to inspect one aspect in order to know the whole, to grasp one detail in order to understand the entirety. Or his method may be called "controlling the center," which means to hold on to the center and thus attain the totality, to apply to the inside and thus extend to the outside. This method may be applied to any other subject, not just this one. When I heard these theories I was truly startled! Think of all the old gentlemen of today, such as the provincial graduates, Hanlin scholars, and licentiates. One cannot say they are not proficient in their own fields of specialization. But as regards so-called general knowledge, seeking common principles and precedents, and linking the past with the present, how few are proficient! Spencer wrote that specialized study often leads to blindness to universal laws. How true! What I have said is rather tediously verbose and simple in meaning; it grasps what is crude and misses the subtleties. But having received your request, I dared not withhold it from you. I present this to you with the hope that you will correct my mistakes.

Zedong salutes you.
September 6

---

18. The *Jinsi lu* (Reflections on Things at Hand) is a compilation, by Zhu Xi and Lu Zuqian, of the writings of Zhou Dunyi, the Cheng brothers, and Zhang Zai.

19. The *Guwen ci leizuan* (Classified Compilation of Old-style Literature) is a work in seventy-five volumes by Yao Nai. For further details on Yao, see note 47 to the "Classroom Notes."

Letter to Xiao Zisheng

(September 27, 1915)

Esteemed Zisheng:

I have received your letter, and now I know how very busy you are with your teaching duties. The letter was written on the seventh, but the date was changed to the tenth. [I appreciate your thoughtfulness] very much. I sent my last letter on the ninth day of the month, and today is the nineteenth:[1] exactly ten days. Now I have also received another letter, and your kindness ought to be repaid. In expounding our ideas,[2] we should place primary importance on the cultivation of body and spirit, and on the acquisition of learning, and secondary importance on politics and current events. We should value substance over style, eschew embellishment, and keep only to the essential. In other words, every time we write a letter, it ought to convey some benefit; discourse should be laden with content. Otherwise, how are we different from the common masses? This day is like gold; how careful we should be of it! My self-discipline is very weak, and I look to the outer world to stimulate and encourage me. Therefore, I seek friends most enthusiastically. You, for example, are truly able to stimulate and encourage me. I have no merits other than my observance of the two sayings "share good with other people" and "emulate the good in others." Thus, when I have some gain, I would never dare keep it to myself; and if there is some goodness to be found in another, I will seek him out even if he is a thousand *li* away. It is my cherished hope and expectation that you will aspire in the future to the greatness of the men of antiquity. These days if one's friends are few, one's views cannot be broad, the learning of youth will achieve little success, and it will be hard to establish one's merit in middle age.[3] Therefore, I have circulated a personal notice, thus imitating the birds who call to seek friendly voices.[4] After several days, there are

1. According to the editors of the *Wengao*, the date of the nineteenth at the end of this letter means the nineteenth day of the eighth month of the lunar calendar, which corresponded in 1915 to September 27. On that basis, the letter of the ninth to which Mao refers here would have been written on September 17. No such letter appears to be extant.

2. The term Mao uses, *li yan*, means literally "to establish one's words"; this is the last of the three imperishable features of a man in the traditional view, the first two being, respectively, to establish one's virtue and to establish one's merit.

3. On *li gong* (establishing merit), see the previous note.

4. The notice in question was that about which Mao told Edgar Snow in 1936, signed with the pseudonmym Ershibahua sheng (Twenty-eight Stroke Student, twenty-eight

still very few responses. I have enclosed a copy, and if there are any worthy men[5] in your honorable school, please introduce them to me. For more, see my letter to Zanzhou.[6] With the chilly autumn weather, I have been suffering stomach trouble for a couple of days, but I am a little better now. Looking out for one's health is all important. One only knows the happiness of well-being when one is seriously ill.

Submitted by Dong
The nineteenth

---

being the number of strokes required to write the three characters of Mao's name). See below Mao's poem of 1918 addressed to one of the few who did reply. The reference to birds here is a paraphrase of two lines from the *Book of Poetry* II, I, V (Legge, Vol. IV, p. 253), which are translated by Legge as follows: " . . . ying goes its cry, seeking with its voice its companion." Interestingly, these two lines immediately follow the couplet about a bird issuing from a dark valley cited in Mao's letter of November 9, 1915, to Li Jinxi.

5. *Xianzhe*.

6. Chen Zanzhou (1892–1921), also called Shaoxiu, from Liuyang, Hunan, was a fellow student of Mao's at First Normal School. After graduation he became physical education teacher at the attached primary school. He was a founding member of the New People's Study Society and went to France in 1920 on the work-study program. He died of illness in Paris in 1921. Mao's letter to him is not available.

Letter to Li Jinxi[1]

(November 9, 1915)

Dear Elder Brother Shaoxi:

Month before last, Mr. Xiong[2] passed on to me a letter of yours, which is indeed instructive. Now, sir, I have something I wish to tell you. In these days, the voices of evil grow louder and louder, and justice is obstructed. In the face of such difficulties, and on the eve of the emergence of hidden dragons,[3] scholars, though ready for action, should not seek to advance hastily. Now, this business of yours, sir, is certainly a magnificent undertaking. While those on the other side, however, always use their craft to fool the people, is it right for you to submit your skills to help them? Their maneuvers for recruiting eminent personages are growing more clever every day. Is it possible that those whose ambition is to use the people of the whole country could be used by others? The Chiefs and Conquerors, as ministers of Shun, served virtue; Yang and Liu, as ministers of Mang, merely submitted to force.[4] If one is able to discriminate between Shun and Mang, one should be able to position oneself properly at present. That is self-explanatory. Beijing is like a crucible in which one cannot but be transformed. I am greatly frightened by what I have heard people say about it. The letter I received from you said you would soon return to teach; you added that Beijing stank with corruption and you could not bear it for long. But so far we have still not seen you return. I also heard that you were planning something and

---

1. Mao's former teacher Li Jinxi (1890–1978), *zi* Shaoxi, was born in Xiangtan, Hunan Province. He was a teacher at Hunan First Normal School and had left for Beijing in September 1915. Thereafter, he taught for a number of years at Beijing Normal University.

2. Xiong Guangchu. (See note to letter of August 1915 to Xiao Zisheng.)

3. This four-character phrase, *longqian bujian*, appears to be a conflation of several sentences in the opening passage of the *Book of Changes*. The paragraph in question, which is also quoted extensively in the *Zuo zhuan*, twenty-ninth year of Duke Zhao (par. 4, Legge, Vol. V, p. 731), after stating *qianlong buyong*, which Legge translates "The dragon lies hid in the water; it is not the time for active employment," goes on to discuss various circumstances in which the dragon is or is not seen *(jian)*.

4. The "Eight Chiefs" *(bayuan)* and "Eight Conquerors" *(bakai)* were the names commonly given to two related families, of eight brothers each, who served the legendary emperor Shun. Yang Xiong, mentioned above in the "Classroom Notes," and Liu Xin (? – A.D. 23) served Wang Mang, who usurped the throne in A.D. 8, and reigned until he was killed in A.D. 23.

would therefore be staying there for some time. My great puzzlement remains unresolved, and I feel I must speak out. I hope you will consider what I say and hurry back without lingering. At school, I have followed your counsels diligently without daring to violate them, but my nature is difficult to restrain. In the end I realized that this is no place to study: there is no freedom of will, the standards are too low, and the companions too evil. It is truly distressing to see my serviceable body and precious time dwindle away in pining and waiting. Master Zhu once said, "Those who do not know how to pilot a boat consider the stream too narrow."[5] Since I honestly cannot do what the ancients did, I ought to be held up to ridicule. But there is also the teaching of the "dark valley and lofty tree."[6] Schools like this are certainly the darkest of dark valleys. I must abandon it, make good plans, and establish far-reaching goals. I eagerly await your return so we can discuss this and make plans together. Throughout my life, I have never had good teachers or friends. Regrettably, I met you, elder brother, only late. How much I desire to seek your guidance every day! In the past two years, my desire to find friends has been most fervent. After I returned from the summer holidays, I posted a notice in several schools.[7] Five or six people responded. This is the only thing which makes my heart a little lighter these days. The year is drawing to a close, and the weather is getting colder. Take care of yourself, and watch out when traveling. I will stop here.

Your younger brother, Mao Zedong,
[styled] Runzhi, salutes you.

November 9, 1915

---

5. See Zhu Xi, *Zhuzi yulei*, Vol. 8.

6. Mao is alluding here to a couplet from the *Book of Poetry* II, I, V (Legge, Vol. IV, p. 253): "One [bird] issues from the dark valley, and removes to the lofty tree."

7. See the note to Mao's letter of September 27, 1915, to Xiao Zisheng.

Letter to Xiao Zisheng

(Winter 1915)

Dear elder schoolmate Zisheng:

Our meeting yesterday ended abruptly, and I was unable to discuss with you all I had wished. I would like to borrow *Saving the Nation Through Constitutional Monarchy*[1] to read. As you didn't have it there, please look for it at your leisure. The so-called five-part curriculum is actually light in terms of workload. Since I suggested to Mr. Chen that he use his spare time to study literature, I shall now talk about that. I am rather ashamed of myself to have spoken before acting. In the early morning, I study English; from eight in the morning to three in the afternoon, I attend class; from four in the afternoon until dinner, I study Chinese literature; from the time the lights are lit until they are extinguished, I do homework for all classes; and after the lights are extinguished, I exercise for one hour. These are the so-called five parts. Recently, our school has decided to print and distribute a collection of writings by Tang, Kang, and Liang.[2] The cover is to be inscribed with eleven characters reading "Painful Words on Current Affairs by the Three Scholars, Tang, Kang, and Liang." **We would be honored** if you would write them for us. The inscription must be **no longer than the length of the paper on which this letter is written, less one half inch.** The size and style of the handwriting we leave up to you. We need it in a hurry: may we have it tomorrow **morning**? I will stop here.

Your younger brother, Zedong
The twelfth

---

1. *Junxian jiuguo lun* (Saving the Nation Through Constitutional Monarchy) was a work by the conservative scholar Yang Du, which served to support Yuan Shikai's attempt at monarchical restoration.

2. Kang and Liang are Kang Youwei and Liang Qichao. (On Kang, see the notes to Mao's letter of June 25, 1915; on Liang, see note 58 to the "Classroom Notes.") Tang is Tang Hualong (1874–1918), a supporter of the revolution of 1911 who served as speaker of the National Assembly in 1913–1914 and 1916–1917. He and Liang Qichao were both members of the Jinbudang (Progressive Party), and in 1914–1916, he had worked together with Liang to oppose Yuan Shikai's attempt at monarchical restoration. Possibly that is why Mao groups them together here.

1916

Letter to Xiao Zisheng

(January 28, 1916)

Esteemed elder brother Zisheng:

These days I have been thinking of you quite a bit, and I want to move somewhere new. I am sure I will be happier. Ever since Mr. Xu left, I have not had the *Tiger Magazine* to read. I want especially to ask you, using your own name and at your convenience, to borrow issues 11 and 12 of this magazine from Mr. Xu.[1] I plan to pay my respects to you next Sunday afternoon. Please accept my best wishes for your studies. I will stop here. Your younger brother, Zedong, salutes you.

January 28

1. Mr. Xu's identity is unknown. *Jiayin zazhi*, called the *Tiger Magazine* because the name consists of the cyclical characters for 1914, a year of the tiger, when it was founded, had in fact ceased publication in October 1915 with issue no. 10. The two issues which Mao wanted had therefore never appeared. During its brief existence, the magazine had been in the vanguard of new intellectual trends in China. The editor was Zhang Shizhao (1881–1973), *zi* Xingyan, a Hunanese from Changsha. Zhang had edited the noted newspaper *Su bao*, and had been imprisoned on suspicion of complicity in an attempt to assassinate a Qing official in Shanghai. After his release, he went to Japan, and then to the University of Edinburgh, where he took a degree in law. Though he had participated in the anti-Qing movement before the 1911 Revolution, and he was an early advocate of a liberal constitutional government, he did not join Sun Yatsen's Tongmenghui. The *Tiger Magazine* was critical of Yuan Shikai's monarchical ambitions. In 1916, when the new president, Li Yuanhong, reconvened the National Assembly, Zhang went as one of the senators from Hunan who had been elected in 1913. In Beijing at this time he also served as professor of logic in the newly opened graduate school of Beijing University, when Chen Duxiu was dean of humanities.

Letter to Xiao Zisheng

(February 19, 1916)

Dear elder schoolmate Zisheng:

I received only yesterday the communication with which you favored me on the thirtieth of last month; I have respectfully taken cognizance of it and understand your whole meaning. I want very much to read issues 11 and 12 of the *Tiger Magazine* and would still like to ask you to borrow them for me from Mr. Xu when you have time. Will you be able to make a pleasure trip out of town on Sunday morning? In case you are able to borrow the magazines, please bring them along. If not, then I will have to borrow them from Mr. Yang.[1] If this Sunday's weather is fine, would you like to go with me? We have been separated only by a short distance, and only for a few days, yet it feels like a thousand miles and three years. Respectfully, I ask you to accept my best wishes for your studies. I will stop here.

Submitted by your younger brother,
Zedong.
February 19

1. Yang Changji was at this time living at Mount Yuelu just outside Changsha.

Letter to Xiao Zisheng

(February 29, 1916)

. . . above[1] are listed thirteen items in the category of "classics," sixteen in the category of "histories," twenty-two in the category of "philosophical works," and twenty-six in the category of "literary collections," making seventy-seven altogether. From today's point of view, these are all the Chinese books which one really ought to read. If one has ambitions in the way of scholarship, these certainly must be read, and none can be dispensed with. But it would take no less than ten years to read them through completely, and no less than two hundred gold bars to buy them. Yesterday, I received your notice that you want to give me some books; I dare not accept. For one thing, if you give them to me and I do not read them, or if I read them and do not gain anything from them, I would prove to be unworthy of your great kindness. For another thing, your wealth is less than copious and should not be squandered. Before, I suggested that you limit your gift to two or three strings of cash; thinking it over now, I ask you not to give me anything. It is just this kind of basic problem which must be researched. Therefore, I have written to inquire of you. I hope you will explain what is unclear, and correct what is wrong; I will then be most fortunate. I write to you, elder brother Sheng.

Your younger brother, Zedong,
bows to you yet again.
February 29, in the afternoon

1. The missing portion of this letter obviously included the list summarized here. The Chinese text begins with the character meaning "to the right," since it was written in traditional fashion from top to bottom and right to left.

Letter to Xiao Zisheng

(June 24, 1916)

To my dear kind elder brother Zisheng:

Since we said good-bye, the rains have been very heavy, and I have not been able to return home. Also, because robbery[1] continues and unrest is breaking out on all sides, I dare not risk traveling. These five or six days I have been reading newspapers and books, so you could say I have been well occupied. My mother, however, is ill at home, and she suffers thinking of me. How can a wandering son remain unmoved? And then, since school is closed for vacation and all of my classmates have gone home with one another, and since you have been fully occupied, I have no one with whom to talk. I rise early and retire late at night. My three meals come one after another. In normal times, I loathe the length of one day, but now each seems to pass in a twinkling of an eye. These bleak surroundings are depressing. In the vicinity are only soldiers, a rough crowd that comes from the mountain wilds. They talk like birds and look like animals. One cannot go near them, as you have already learned. What my eyes and mind encounter is mostly tragic. Suddenly, I hear the blowing of a trumpet, and then the clanking of army equipment, rousing martial sounds of fighting and battle. When I hear them in the deep of night, the tears begin to fall unawares. Even more hateful are the atrocious autumn rains. The ditches are filled and the gullies are overflowing, making it difficult to walk or travel. Otherwise, I would go to you and we could take hands and converse in person. If the rain stops tomorrow, I have decided to journey home. Regarding my earlier request that you write me, I hope you will not let me down. Also, please take care of your health. I have no way of revealing all that is in my heart.

Zedong bows to you yet again.
From First Normal School
The twenty-fourth

1. "Huanfu is not tranquil" — an allusion to a passage in the *Zuo zhuan*, twentieth year of Duke Zhao (Legge, Vol. V, p. 684): "The consequence [of the ruler's leniency] was that there were many robbers in the state of Zheng, who plundered people about the marsh of Huanfu."

Letter to Xiao Zisheng

(June 26, 1916)

For the perusal of my elder brother Sheng:

I reached the riverbank at nine o'clock this morning. I walked seventy *li* and stayed at Yintian Temple. As I was previously acquainted with the host, I feel quite comfortable here. Although my limbs really ache, my spirit is full of joy. I washed off the dust, shook out my clothes, and grasped a brush to write this letter. Thinking back to last night and this morning, the scenes, still vivid in my mind, evoke such feelings! I may decide to relate something of what I saw and heard on my journey. The Guangxi army is stationed outside of the city, where they swagger down the road, looking askance at those around them, gathering and gambling with other good-for-nothings in the big intersections. The patrolmen see them often, but dare not question them. This corroborates what we have heard at school. I am now convinced that gambling is rampant in Guangdong and Guangxi. In the region of Qilipu and Jiangche there are two divisions of the so-called National Protection Army.[1] One division, under Su Minghu, has approximately twelve hundred men. The other, under a certain Zhao, is about the same size. Having combined their forces, they are living in the hotels and eating without paying for it, and everyone complains. After questioning the men closely, I feel they are rather pitiful. They are hoping that they will get paid and discharged, but quite in vain. Their officers live in the hotels too; they put name cards on their doors saying "such-and-such official," but the placards they post verge on the incomprehensible. The scenery along the road is emerald wherever one looks. The water in the ponds runs clear, and the fields are luxuriant with sprouts. At dusk, when smoke hangs in the sky, the clear dew splashes down, and the warm air steams upward. The mountain mists unfold; the gorgeous clouds intermingle; and as far as one can see, everywhere it is like a painting. I am writing this tonight and will post it tomorrow. Two days on the road, and it should reach you around the twenty-ninth. I hope that it will bring a smile to cheer you and alleviate your cares a little.

Ze writes.[2]
The twenty-sixth.

1. The Huguo jun or National Protection Army was founded in Yunnan in late 1915 by Cai E as an instrument for struggle against Yuan Shikai's attempt at monarchical restoration. On Cai see note 5 to Mao's letter of July 25, 1916.

2. Literally, *Ze bai* — Ze who is without official rank, or by extension, "Humbly, Ze."

Letter to Xiao Zisheng

(July 18, 1916)

Esteemed elder brother Sheng:

I sent a letter from Xiangtan on the twelfth; I do not know if it has arrived or not? It has been seven days and I have had some new thoughts, so I respectfully recount them for you as previously agreed. Regarding the Hunan question, I still maintain that Military Governor Tang[1] should not have been sent away. Driving him out was an injustice, and the situation now is growing more and more chaotic. Why do I say it was an injustice? Tang was here for three years, and he ruled by the severe enforcement of strict laws. He swept away the oppressive and tyrannical atmosphere of earlier days, creating a tranquil and amicable environment. Order was restored, and the peaceful times of the past were practically regained. He controlled the army strictly, and with discipline. Even though Yuan[2] threatened him, he was able to plan expansion secretly and to attain independence. With just over fifteen thousand troops he was able to secure the provincial capital, defend Hubei, and look after the surrounding *xian*, but the officials in the towns around did not approve. If he was not extremely capable, could he have done all that? He appointed Zhang Shuxun[3] head of the police, and the city of Changsha became so honest that lost belongings were left on the street for their owners. Even chickens and dogs were unafraid. The city administration was the best among all the provinces! Anyone coming from Wuhan said that it could not compare to [the capital of] Hunan. When the armies of the north and south arose, Hunan became their battleground. Wave after wave hit the provincial capital, and in the period between spring and summer, the danger increased ten thousand fold. Yet he was able to maintain stability. When the

1. The previous governor, Tang Xiangming (1886–1975), *zi* Zhuxin, from Hubei Province, was a French-trained naval officer appointed by Yuan Shikai as successor to Tan Yankai on October 21, 1913. He was notorious for his harsh treatment of political opponents and pro-Guomindang elements, to such an extent that he was often called "Tang the Butcher." (Mao himself, who is relatively indulgent toward Tang here, applied this epithet to him in a letter of June 23, 1920.) Under pressure from his brother, Tang Hualong (see the note to Mao's letter of winter 1915 to Xiao Zisheng), Tang Xiangming declared Hunan independent on May 29, 1916, and fled the province on July 4, 1916.

2. Yuan Shikai.

3. Zhang Shuxun, *zi* Zhuqiao, a Hunanese, was head of the police in Hunan from October 1914 to July 1916. He later became head of the police in Hebei Province.

mine guards mobilized,[4] many of the students fled. He sent out a notice that they were not to miss classes, and when funds were required he issued them. Are these the accomplishments of a weak and cowardly person? He was especially painstaking in planning independence. He first raised the idea with Wang Yunting,[5] and had Wang declare independence. Afterward, he found a way to ward off the northern army while he brought back his own units. He contacted Guizhou and Guangxi, and they responded immediately. When Yuan unfortunately died early, the war was prolonged, and thus the contributions of Sichuan and Hunan in declaring independence were not less than those of Yunnan and Guizhou. Did they not have some districts that must be taken and cities which must be attacked, and are these two provinces not the key to the outcome of the struggle between north and south? Some partisans despise him for ingratiating himself with Yuan, but when did Tang really ingratiate himself with Yuan? Yuan had been suspicious of Tang for some time. First, he did not allow him to expand his army; then, he sent Cao Kun[6] to watch him; and then, he sent Shen Jinjian[7] to move in on his authority. The fact that he killed well over ten thousand people was the inescapable outcome of policy. Did he kill any more than Feng[8] in Jiangning? In the attack on Wujiang and the ransacking of Jiangyin, men were cut down like weeds. One can say that he manufactured public opinion, pandered to Yuan, and slandered good men. But did not this type of behavior also occur in Yunnan, Guizhou, and Guangxi? Those who plan far ahead will always have things for which to wait, and those whose accomplishments are great will always have things to endure. Without such behavior, the goal of national protection would be unattainable. Those who consider these things to be crimes do not comprehend the overall plan. (Under a strict interpretation of ethics, a different view should be taken of murder and slander.) When he fled, I

---

4. This refers to the attempted coup by the commander of the mine guards, Guo Renzhang, who led his guards into the city on May 14, 1916, with the aim of overthrowing Tang Xiangming and installing himself as governor. Tang's troops defeated the guards.

5. Wang Yunting, a Hunanese, was head of the Lingling garrison. Formerly a supporter of Yuan Shikai, in May 1916 he broke with the Beijing government and proclaimed the independence of surrounding *xian*.

6. Cao Kun (1862–1938), *zi* Zhongshan, was a native of Tianjin and a graduate of the Tianjin Military Academy. A longtime close associate of Yuan Shikai, he was sent to Hunan in 1913 as commander of the upper Yangzi military region. After Yuan Shikai's death, Cao moved his 3rd Division back to its permanent headquarters at Baoding. In September 1916, he became military governor of Zhili Province and was thereafter a leading figure in the Zhili clique, which stood in opposition to the Anhui clique of Duan Qirui.

7. Shen Jinjian, *zi* Shuzhan, from Zhejiang Province, was chief inspector general of Hunan from September 1915 to June 1916.

8. Feng Guozhang (1857–1919), *zi* Huafu, led his troops in attacking and occupying Nanjing in 1913. He was then appointed governor of Jiangsu Province by Yuan Shikai. Jiangning is the present-day city of Nanjing.

wrote that he was stupid. But it is precisely because he was stupid that one cannot say he is deceitful. Most of what was written in his Hankou cable was the truth: he did not fight, although he had over ten thousand troops, because he feared the destruction; he did not take the money that he could have, because he feared leaving disaster behind him. (When people in Hunan published a list of his crimes, they said he had embezzled several million, but I do not think this is likely.) Essentially, Tang can proclaim his innocence before the whole world, and before the people of Hunan. His departure from Hunan is a great misfortune for this province. Why do I say the situation is growing more and more chaotic? Tang called in the Guangxi army with good intentions, but the Guangxi army rebelled against him. This was not necessarily the idea of Lu Rongting. Chasing Tang to Xiangyin, seizing his provisions and weapons, adding them to all that was plundered from within the province, and carrying them home: this is what was called in the newspapers "the civilized army returning in triumph." At our school, even the grass was removed. There were some broken weapons belonging to the Xiang Army[9] in the junior school, with eight people guarding them. They took them all, and bound the eight men with the intention of executing them. Everyone felt that ridding themselves of the Guangxi army was like ridding themselves of tigers. Cheng Qian,[10] drunk with power, led his army to the capital with airs of extraordinary grandeur. He made enemies not only of Zeng Jiwu,[11] but also of Tao Zhongxun.[12] The likes of Tang Mang and Long Zhang[13] took advantage of the situation to rise up. They all wanted a taste of the governor's seat, and all had called up their own armies in order to expand their

9. Here the term refers not to Zeng Guofan's Xiang army, but to contemporary military forces from Hunan (particularly those loyal to Tan Yankai), as opposed to the various invading armies.

10. Cheng Qian (1882–1968), *zi* Songyun, from Liling, Hunan, was a graduate of the Japanese Officers' Academy, and an early member of the Tongmenghui. In 1916, having gone to Yunnan to join the anti-Yuan campaign, he was appointed Hunan pacification commissioner. On entering the province, he called himself, like many others at this time, commander of the National Protection Army for Hunan; though he finally arrived before Changsha in early July, his forces were defeated and he was obliged to retreat.

11. Zeng Jiwu (1873–1943), a Hunanese, was an early member of the Tongmenghui and a graduate of the Baoding and Japanese Officers' Academy. In June 1916, he became commander in chief of the first army of the Hunan National Protection Army. After the Hunanese forces had driven Tang Xiangming from Changsha, Zeng's army entered the city on July 5, 1916, and he served as acting governor of Hunan Province until Liu Renxi's appointment a fortnight later.

12. Tao Zhongxun commanded a unit of the northern armies which remained stationed just outside Changsha after Tang Xiangming's departure. His troops clashed with those of Cheng Qian, who had also approached the city, and defeated them.

13. Tang Mang (1887–1954) was a Hunanese graduate of the Japanese Officers' Academy. Long Zhang (1854–1918), *zi* Yanxian, a Hunanese, was a well-known merchant and cofounder of Mingde Middle School in Changsha in 1903. He was also active in the Society for China's Revival, and a member of the Tongmenghui. In July 1916 he

power. Cheng and Tao led their divisions to a place outside of the city and battled for two days and nights. If it had not been for Mr. Liu,[14] who went out to restore order, the situation would have been beyond saving. The Civil Affairs Agency and the Department of Civil Affairs were established simultaneously, and each issues its own orders and obeys its own orders. You have never heard of anything stranger. On July 7, rebel elements attacked the police station. The police scattered and fled, and their weapons were taken. In one single day, the success of ten years of diligent management was wiped out in violence, and after ten days of preparation since then, they are still unable to go back to their posts. Gamblers are emerging, and the atmosphere is white hot with debauchery. Both the merchant trade and police authority have been taken over by outsiders. The disorder is extreme. When Tang left, the gangsters tipped their hats and celebrated among themselves, resenting their previous oppression. They are everywhere, investigating and arresting people, and executing those they arrest. On the seventeenth was the memorial for Yang Deling,[15] and they caught six people and wanted to kill them as a sacrifice to his memory, but were stopped from doing so. Alas, it is like the Reign of Terror in France. In times like these, intellectuals must be cautious of how they situate themselves. I was in Xiangtan and too timid to venture to the capital, so I waited for the reports of friends before making the trip. I was truly frightened. There is talk from every sector of government officials robbed and *xian* magistrates defied. The magistrate of Ningxiang, Ding Xiangyi, is from Hubei and an appointee of Tang. Yi Kongshao had previously been appointed by the head bandit, Xie Wenlin. When Xie died, Yi was put in jail. Now Yi has secured the appointment of Long Zhang and incited other factions to send telegrams calling for the removal of Ding and for his own reinstatement. The governorship has already changed hands several times, and now there is talk of another replacement. When the province declared independence, Tang was accepted as governor. After chasing him out, Lu Rongting was welcomed. Before Lu got there, Zeng took his place. When Cheng Qian arrived, he had no choice but to step down. Then, when they were going to hold elections, Liuyang military officials, local legislators, provincial legislators, citizens' groups, and various local gentry and merchants, thousands in all, cabled in their

---

was elected head of the Hunan civil government by the Hunan United Association of All Circles, but never took up the post.

14. Mr. Liu, here referred to respectfully as Liu Gong, was Liu Renxi (1844–1919), *zi* Gensheng, from Liuyang, Hunan. He was a former Qing magistrate and a leading member of the Changsha gentry. In 1915 he was active in anti-Yuan activities, and later he joined in the movement to oust Zhang Jingyao. He was also involved in education, and had been principal of the First Central Circuit School, the predecessor of First Normal School. On July 6, 1916, he was elected provisional governor of Hunan by a "Joint Meeting of All Circles," and on July 19 this decision was endorsed by the Beijing government. He was eased out by Tan Yankai when the latter became governor in August 1916.

15. Yang Deling (1870–1913), *zi* Xingxun, a Hunanese, was head of the Department

candidacies and were all of a sudden suspicious of one another. When Chen Huan[16] arrived, tens of thousands of northern troops went to Yuezhou, where they convened another conference, and again called for Lu Rongting. For a long while, there were no problems, and then Huang Keqiang[17]was elected. How strange and crazy, the doings of Hunan! All things considered, the recent calamities in Hunan are worse than those of the 1911 Revolution. I thought you would like to hear these details since you are living in the countryside. The rights and wrongs of the situation are naturally being debated publicly, and although I am very tolerant in other matters, the Hunan situation angers and upsets me no end. I'm afraid I'll get myself in trouble. Don't let anyone else see this. It would be best if you burn it when you have finished reading it. I will write more later, and I am looking forward with great anticipation to your reply. Best wishes for a good summer. I will stop here.

Respectfully,

Your younger brother, Zedong
July 18

---

of Finance when Tan Yankai first became governer. He stood in opposition to Yuan Shikai's monarchical movement and was executed by the Hunan chief prosecutor in October 1913.

16. Chen Huan (1876–1939), *zi* Er'an, from Hubei Province, a Japanese-educated militarist, was a trusted subordinate of Yuan Shikai in the early days of the Republic. In 1915 he led the northern army into Sichuan Province, where he became military governor. In May 1916, in the context of the struggle against Yuan Shikai, he was forced to proclaim Sichuan's independence from the Beijing government, and was soon driven out of the province. In July 1916 he was appointed governor of Hunan by Yuan's successor, with Lu Rongting as his deputy, but was unable to establish himself in the face of Hunanese opposition. Duan Qirui (1865–1936), *zi* Zhiquan, one of Yuan Shikai's chief lieutenants, was premier for most of the time from April 1916 to October 1918, and subsequently provisional chief executive of the Beijing government from November 1924 to April 1926. A native of Hefei in Anhui Province, he was the head of the Anhui Clique during the struggles among rival factions of northern militarists.

17. On Huang Xing, here referred to by his *hao,* Keqiang, see the note to Mao's letter of March 1917 to Miyazaki Tōten. Huang, who died on October 31, 1916, was already too ill to accept the nomination by the "Joint Meeting of All Circles," which Mao calls an election, and recommended Tan Yankai instead. (On Tan Yankai, see the note to Mao's letter of July 25, 1916.) Tan assumed the functions of military and civil governor on August 20, 1916.

Letter to Xiao Zisheng

(July 25, 1916)

Esteemed elder brother Sheng:

I sent a letter on the twelfth from Xiangtan, and another on the eighteenth from school, both recounting current events in detail. I do not know if they have been lost or not? I keep expecting a reply, and it does not come. My anxiety is inexpressible. After the three great national problems of the Provisional Constitution, the National Assembly, and the cabinet were solved on the thirtieth of last month,[1] the southern provinces each successively rescinded independence. With the elimination of the Military Affairs Council, they have gradually moved toward unification. This was made possible by the deep understanding of the many heroes of the south, Duan's intervention at the center, and especially the influence of Mr. Li's[2] great sincerity. There are still those in each province who do not follow orders, for example, those who resist Shen Mingchang in Shanxi, those who resist Hu Ruilin in Fujian, those who attacked Long Jiguang in Guangdong,[3] the struggle between Chen and Zhou[4] in Sichuan, and those who drove out Tang Xiangming from Hunan. Except for the irrational events in Hunan, however, all these cases were connected with the monarchical system, or

1. When Yuan Shikai died in June 1916 and was succeeded by Li Yuanhong, the new president and Duan Qirui, who remained as premier, acted to restore the Provisional Constitution of 1912, summon the national assembly, and reestablish cabinet government.

2. Li Yuanhong (1864–1928), *zi* Songqing, *hao* Huangpi, from Hubei Province, had become head of the new revolutionary government in October 1911 much against his will. Elected vice president to Sun Yatsen, and then to Yuan Shikai in January–February 1912, he subsequently participated, reluctantly once again, in Yuan's attempt at restoration in 1915. On June 7, 1916, following Yuan's death, he became president in his own right.

3. Shen Mingchang, *zi* Miantu, from Zhejiang, was a former governor of Shanxi, and at this time was governor of Shandong Province. Hu Ruilin, *zi* Zihu, from Hubei, was governor of Fujian Province. Long Jiguang (1868–1925), *zi* Zicheng, from Yunnan, was a former Qing governor and Guangdong army commander. In 1913 Yuan Shikai appointed him governor of Guangdong. At about the time Mao wrote the present letter, Li Yuanhong removed Long from this post, because of widespread hostility from southern leaders, and transferred him to Hainan Island as commissioner of mining development.

4. Chen is Chen Huan, referred to in the previous text. Zhou is Zhou Jun, *zi* Jishan. Two days after Chen Huan proclaimed the independence of Sichuan on May 22, 1916, Yuan Shikai appointed Zhou Jun, the Chongqing garrison commander, to suppress Chen Huan. Zhou Jun led his army into Chengdu on June 25, and named himself governor of Sichuan.

were simply unavoidable, and can be forgiven. The central government must really be admired for appointing Ren Kecheng governor of Yunnan, Dai Kan governor of Guizhou, Luo Peijin governor of Guangxi, Cai E governor of Sichuan, and Lu Rongting governor of Guangdong.[5] The removal of Chen Huan, Zhou Jun, and Li Liejun,[6] and the appointment of Li as lieutenant general with second-degree honors can be considered good personnel management. I wrote in an earlier letter that the Hunanese had adopted a Monroe doctrine and elected Liu[7] in order to further their own private interests, and unfortunately I have been proven correct. Cai E has also already taken up his appointment. The only thing I did not foresee was that in Guangdong, Long and Li would both leave, creating a situation similar to that in Sichuan.

I was never in favor of the way the Hunan problem was handled. Although I have already given a fairly complete account of it in previous letters, I have more to tell here. Since the common gangsters drove out Tang for no good reason, the governorship has already changed hands twice, and Liu's acting position has been made permanent. One way or another, they should obey the central government and wait for further appointments. Now they are urging increased prominence for Huang Keqiang,[8] and seemingly adopting a system of the separation of powers. Thus, Long Zhang has been elected head of the civil government, but because he is under attack by public opinion, his appointment has hitherto remained pending, making him a laughingstock. Recently, the legislature has been coerced into electing him again and submitting his name to the central government for approval. Huang's name has been submitted for some time now, and Long's has been in for several days, but still the central government has given no

---

5. Ren Kecheng (1878–1945), *zi* Zhiqing, a native of Guizhou, an educationalist, was former counselor to the Yunnan governor. Dai Kan (1880–1917), had participated as a commander of the National Protection Army in the offensive against Yuan Shikai, leading his forces into Guizhou in March 1916. He was made governor of Guizhou by Li Yuanhong on July 6, 1916. Luo Peijin (1878–1922), from Yunnan, educated in Japan, was a Tongmenghui member who had participated in the 1911 revolution in Yunnan. Cai E (1882–1916), originally Genyuan, *zi* Songpo, was born in Shaoyang, Hunan Province. He was a graduate of the Hunan School of Current Affairs, studied in Japan, and on returning taught at the Guangxi and Yunnan military schools. At the time of the 1911 revolution, he became governor of Yunnan. In 1915 he was one of the leaders of opposition to Yuan Shikai's monarchical movement, and led the National Protection Army into Sichuan. He was appointed governor of Sichuan on July 6, 1916, but died shortly thereafter of illness.

6. Li Liejun (1882–1946), *zi* Xiehe, from Jiangxi, was a Tongmenghui member who had become governor of Jiangxi province in the aftermath of the revolution of 1911. He had fought against Yuan Shikai in 1913 and in 1915–1916, when he led the Second Army of the National Protection Army into Guangdong. His subsequent removal as commander of this force, which Mao regards here as correct, was brought about by Duan Qirui, whose warlord allies Li Liejun had defeated in Guangdong.

7. Liu Renxi.

8. Huang Xing.

order. I think it will be very difficult for them to accept. They cannot allow this trend toward nominating one's own superior officials to get off the ground. If natives of a given province serve as officials of that province, the damage will be very great. In Hunan especially, there are particular circumstances, and one does not have to look back any further than the 1911 Revolution for a good lesson. The causes for the calamities now before our eyes are again quite conspicuous and easy to see. An atmosphere of bias, framing, and interest-peddling has arisen. The Department of Civil Affairs produces one or several batches of *xian* magistrates each day, and even those who should be allowed to stay are replaced. The magistrate of Xiangtan, Zhang Qiju, was in office less than a month, and he earned praise for being a wise and capable man. Now he has been replaced. The customs agency has already had three replacements. The first obtained the position by using his connections; then, another used his connections to replace the first; now, the central government has appointed yet another. The mint has had four replacements, and the position is still unsettled; each of them lasted only a few days. Peng Zhengshu has been appointed headmaster of our school. The students are enraged and want to drive him out, but have not been able to do so. Liu and Wu are elderly men, and yet they, too, are behaving like this. It is all the fault of those gangsters. Liu wrote to Tan Zu'an[9] saying, "each day passes like a year," and that is the truth! I have selected only a couple of examples; the rest you can imagine. It is almost no better than the common saying: "Cracks your skull open!" In my previous letter I wrote that the gangsters were taking advantage of the situation to exact revenge. The most vicious of all are those in the so-called "Council for the United Relief of National Affairs." They arrest and execute people without distinguishing black from white. The arrogance of soldiers and politicians is out of control, and those tainted with the suspicion of monarchic leanings are simply thrown out. Shi Wenyao was actually executed by firing squad. I previously wrote a letter to Zhang saying that once the killing started, the revenge would never end. Calamities such as those that took place in France are to be feared the most. One would never have expected that we would now be playing out the same kind of tragedy. The independence of Hunan was only rescinded yesterday. This all seems quite strange.

I have said before that not every one of those who went along with the monarchic movement should be punished. Nevertheless, how can we do other-

9. Tan Yankai (1880–1930), *zi* Zu'an, *hao* Weisan, was born in Chaling, Hunan. A Hanlin scholar, he worked in the field of education in Changsha beginning in 1904. In 1909, he was elected president of the Hunan Provincial Assembly. His strong connections with the Hunan gentry enabled him to bring about the overthrow and execution of the young radicals who had taken power in Changsha following the outbreak of the 1911 revolution, and install himself as governor on October 31, 1911. He served as governor of Hunan from then until October 1913, when he was dismissed by Yuan Shikai; from August 1916 to August 1917; and from December 1917 to March 1918, although during this last period he never formally took up the post.

wise than deal with those whose crimes were greatest, and who were the originators of the disaster, so as to prevent future catastrophes, and uphold a sense of integrity, thus shaking the eyes and ears of the whole world and sweeping out the atmosphere of filth and corruption? For these reasons, when the order came down to punish the eight,[10] the people's hearts were greatly lightened. When I read about it in the newspapers, I was really startled. That these high officials, whose power was so fierce that their very touch burned people, should now face such an end! Thus history is a useless thing. After thousands of years of order and civilization, how could the lessons of past successes and failures, ups and downs, teach us so little that we did not know how to make wise decisions, how to situate ourselves, and how to behave? How can it be that the likes of Wang Mang, Cao Cao, Sima Yi,[11] Napoleon, and Metternich are not sufficient as examples from the past? If history were useful, we would not be where we are today. The stupidest of all was Yuan Shikai, but immediately after him come the eight. This punishment has not touched the military men like Duan Zhigui,[12] Ni Sichong,[13] Wu Bingxiang,[14] and others, none of whom were included among those proclaimed guilty, even though they are criticized by public opinion. And even among the eight, it is said that most have escaped.

These days there has been some astonishing news in the world I would like to tell you about. It is called the "Russo-Japanese Agreement." This agreement has already been concluded. In addition to both countries agreeing to respect each other's rights in Manchuria and Mongolia, Russia has given up its railroad line between Changchun and Bingjiang and navigation rights on the Sungari River, and Japan has agreed to assist Russia with weapons, ammunition, and other war materials. Until now, only a small part of this news has been published; the most important of it is being kept a secret. Our ambassador to Japan has sent back to Beijing an urgent telegram which was published in the *Dagongbao*. You should take a look at it. There is talk that the Okuma cabinet will be dissolved, but no matter who takes power, the policy toward China will not change. When you

---

10. On July 14, 1916, President Li Yuanhong ordered that the chief supporters of Yuan Shikai's attempt at restoration be punished, but this was never carried out. Chief among the eight was Yang Du, whose book *National Salvation Through Constitutional Monarchy* Mao wanted to borrow in the winter of 1915.

11. Sima Yi (178–251), *zi* Zhongda, was one of Cao Cao's generals. He commanded the army of the Wei dynasty under three successive emperors.

12. On Duan Zhigui, see the note to the text of July 14, 1919, "The Arrest and Rescue of Chen Duxiu."

13. Ni Sichong (1868–1924), *zi* Danchen, from Anhui Province, was a leader of the Beiyang warlord group and a close ally of Yuan Shikai. In 1913 he became governor of Anhui and in 1917 supported Duan Qirui's forceful unification of China, moving troops into Hunan. He was dismissed from office in 1920 after his power base, the Anfu clique, lost influence.

14. Wu Bingxiang, *zi* Jingtan, also from Anhui, was a former Beijing police chief and an enthusiastic supporter of Yuan Shikai's movement to restore the monarchy.

think of it, the Japanese are really our most formidable enemies! To think that our land, which stretches tens of thousands of *li* in all four directions, could submit to three islands, or that what is said to be four hundred million people could be enslaved by these thirty million. Manchuria and Mongolia are gone, and the north is in danger. The barbarians are riding into the central plains, not to mention that Shandong is already lost and that they have seized the Kaifeng-Jinan railroad, thereby entering Henan. Without a war, we will cease to exist within twenty years. But our countrymen still sleep on without noticing and pay little attention to the east. In my view, no more important task confronts our generation; if we wish to consolidate our own situation, in order to preserve our descendants, we must sharpen our resolve to resist Japan. The Japanese know all about our domestic circumstances, while many of us, ourselves, do not know; and their domestic situation is understood by very few of us. I hope that when you read books and newspapers you will pay attention to eastern affairs. I look forward to our encouraging one another in this. Do you agree?

It looks as if the West will not have a very terrible war. According to economists, from the perspective of the economy, the war cannot go on another year. At this point, Germany and Austria have yet to be defeated, the Dardanelles have yet to be broken through, and Serbia, Belgium, and Montenegro have already been lost. But ever since Romania joined in last winter, the prestige of the Allied Powers[15] has been bolstered. As for the Entente, they have repeatedly tried to persuade Portugal and Greece to mobilize, but until now, they have not done so.

The uprising in Mexico continues. The United States announced its intention to intercede militarily some time ago, but still has not gone through with it. In fact, there have been some incidents of Mexican rebels entering the southern part of the United States and recklessly murdering civilians. Wilson's term is already up, and they are in the midst of elections. The candidates are Wilson, Hughes, and Roosevelt. Wilson has been nominated and, in Chicago, Hughes was nominated too. Hughes is the chief justice of the Supreme Court and agrees with Wilson in favor of peace. The Americans fear that Roosevelt is too aggressive, and Roosevelt knows that he cannot win, and has therefore announced his withdrawal in favor of Hughes. I think that since the Americans are unwilling to enter the war in Europe, and public opinion on expanding military preparations is not yet mature, the policy will not change, even if Hughes defeats Wilson. Therefore, Wilson might as well continue in office for another term. As for Roosevelt's 1912 clash with Taft, and the subsequent splitting off of the Progressive Party from the Republican Party, this only allowed Wilson as a Democrat to reap the rewards of the struggle. I still remember the story about his going somewhere to make a speech and being stabbed by an enemy. Although his blood and guts were spilling out, he calmly finished his speech before attending to his wounds. I cannot help admiring his bravery and fortitude. I hear that he has

15. I.e., of the Triple Alliance of Germany, Austria, and Italy.

reached the fullness of his years, yet his courageous and dauntless spirit has not declined. I do not think they will use force at this time, and I do not think they will use force in Europe. Their time will come in ten years, and the place will be the Pacific. Rumors of war between Japan and the United States have been circulating for some time. In ten years, China will wage a war of revenge and they will respond to the righteousness of their comrades. We will attack on land, and they will attack on sea. When the three islands are subjugated, the two republics of East and West will draw close in friendship and cheerfully act as reciprocal economic and trade partners. This will be the great endeavor of a thousand years. What we give up now, we will no doubt see again at that time.

These days there are at least seven or eight newspapers in the Hunanese capital. The *Dagongbao* has a lot of spirit, but it is limited in space, and cannot carry very much news. The *Hunan gongbao*[16] is made up entirely of reprinted materials from other sources, but has a good deal of news. Recently, there have been several speeches by famous men in the coastal areas. For example, Sun Yatsen's[17] speech on local self-government is about ten thousand words long, and very informative. It was published in the *Hunan gongbao,* but did not appear in the *Dagongbao*. Moreover, it seems a shame that this paper never carries announcements of the visits of important personages, such as those found in the *Shibao.*[18] These last few days the original of the rough draft of the Temple of Heaven Constitution[19] has been published.

---

16. The *Hunan gongbao* was a daily paper started in Changsha in April 1912. Its first editor-in-chief was the Republic Party's Bei Yunzuo, though in 1913 it became an instrument of the Progressive Party. The paper later supported Yuan Shikai and Tang Xiangming, and ceased publication after Yuan's death in 1916.

17. Sun Wen (1866–1925), *hao* Yixian and Zhongshan, was born in Xianshan *xian*, Guangdong Province. We refer to him here, and throughout this volume, as Sun Yatsen (Yatsen being the Cantonese pronunciation of Yixian), the name by which he is commonly known throughout the English-speaking world. Mao first became aware of Sun's existence and activities at the time of the 1911 Revolution; he told Edgar Snow that he proceeded to write a "somewhat muddled" article advocating that Sun be made president of a new government, with Kang Youwei as premier (Snow, *Red Star over China*, p. 136). Although he did not actually organize the uprising of October 10, 1911, which led to the overthrow of the Qing dynasty, Sun is widely regarded as the father of the Chinese revolution. He was, for a brief period, the first president of the Chinese Republic in 1912, but was soon forced to resign in favor of Yuan Shikai. In April 1916 he had returned from exile in Japan to Shanghai, where he resumed his political activities. Mao is probably referring to Sun's speech of July 17, 1916, entitled "Zizhi zhidu wei jianshe zhi chushi" (A Self-Government System as the Foundation of [National] Reconstruction). See *Guofu quanji* (Complete Works of the Father of the Country) (Taibei: Jindai Zhongguo chubanshe, 1989), Vol. 3, pp. 164–69.

18. The *Shibao* was founded in Shanghai in 1904 by the reformer Di Baoxian with the support of Kang Youwei and Liang Qichao. It did not cease publication until 1939.

19. The draft Constitution of the Republic of China prepared in the fall of 1913 was known as the "Temple of Heaven Constitution" because the committee drafting it met in the Tiantan (Temple of Heaven) in Beijing. It provided for a cabinet-style government,

This is worth copying out. The minutes of the legislature are also worth your attention.

After writing this letter, I received word from you and Zhang,[20] and now I know that my last two letters have not arrived. The letter you sent to me at Yinshi has not been received either. I set out from home on the ninth, which was not long after you returned, so it is probably still in transit. At school, I feel that I am starting afresh with much enthusiasm, and I am studying from morning to night without rest. There are very few people here and the weather is fine. I only fear the beginning of the semester and the start of classes. Zhang is teaching at the same place, and it is going very well. I hope that you will provide me with advice in order to rectify my shortcomings. The soldiers have already pulled out, and therefore I am able to live here, as you already know. I have not expressed myself fully. I respectfully wish you well.

Your younger brother,

Zedong
July 25, under the lamplight

---

which would limit the powers of the president. Yuan Shikai, who intended on the contrary to expand his own powers, forced the abandonment of this draft early in 1914.

20. I.e., Xiao Zizhang, Zisheng's younger brother.

Letter to Li Jinxi

(December 9, 1916)

Esteemed Elder Brother Shaoxi:

I wrote you a letter last winter. Much that I said there was wrong; in your reply, you pointed out my mistakes, and I am indeed convinced by your views. Now I realize that what I said then was very inappropriate. Yuan[1] gathered eminent personages. For example, Wang, Liang, Zhang, Fan,[2] and others all fell for his tricks. This often makes me think about you, although you are not one of those who are called eminent persons today. Rank-and-file officials are, of course, different from those who take advantage of connections and power. What you do is no more than compile books, which suffices for a scholar's career.[3] Moreover, what difference does the fact that one is a rank-and-file official or not have on progress or regression? These are indeed very erroneous words I was saying. Your teaching runs thus: Scholarship should be a personal creation; one should not follow others. One's frame of mind should seek wholeness, and should not

---

1. Yuan Shikai. For a detailed note, see Mao's letter dated July 18, 1916.

2. Wang is Wang Kaiyun (1833–1916), *zi* Renqiu, a conservative scholar who was born like Mao in Xiangtan *xian*, Hunan Province. He participated in the suppression of the Taipings by Zeng Guofan's army and wrote a chronicle of that campaign. Later, he became a follower of Yuan Shikai. Liang is Liang Qichao, who long supported Yuan Shikai, though he had reservations about the attempt at restoration of the empire. (Regarding Liang, see note 58 to Mao's "Classroom Notes" of 1913.) Zhang is Zhang Binglin (1869–1936), *zi* Meishu, *hao* Taiyan, born in Zhejiang Province, an eminent scholar and historian. He was the prime mover in the introduction of the concept of nationalism *(minzuzhuyi)* into China at the turn of the century; his ideas on this theme were elaborated in the *Qiu shu* (Book of Raillery), first published in 1904, which attacked Manchu rule. Later he became a leading member of the Tongmenghui and editor of its journal *Min bao* in 1906–1908. After the 1911 Revolution he was adviser to the office of the president of the Nanjing Provisional Government and an early supporter of Yuan Shikai. In 1913 he was imprisoned after the assassination of Song Jiaoren. (Song, leader of the Guomindang in the parliament of 1913, in which it had won a clear majority, was shot by government agents on March 20, 1913, because of his opposition to Yuan Shikai and his policies.) Fan is Fan Zengxiang (1846–1931), *zi* Jiafu, *hao* Yunmen, a native of Hubei. Former governor of Jiangxi and Jiangsu provinces, Fan became a member of the Political Council *(canzhengyuan)* set up by Yuan Shikai.

3. In September 1915 Li Jinxi began working as head of the department of textbook compilers in the Beijing government department of education.

be one-sided. That has been talked about generally among scholars. You further advised me to write often, but without focusing on particular ideas. Actually, I had been preoccupied with a lot of things, but I was afraid they were not worth your attention, and I had best not write to you in order to save your pen, ink, and energy to reply. While reading newspapers this summer, I saw your article "On Substituting the Spoken Language for the Literary Language." I did not fully agree with you and made an attempt to put forward my views for discussion. But without any specialization in this subject, I was afraid that my superficial opinion, even though I assumed it to be correct, might be fallacious, and I therefore held back. Now what I want to present to you is as follows. In ancient times, there were three eternal virtues, namely wisdom, benevolence, and courage. Today's educationists hold that the three attributes, virtue, wisdom, and a strong body, are comparable to the former three virtues. Morality and wisdom do not reside outside of the body. Wisdom and benevolence are also attached to the body, but without courage, they become entirely useless. If we look at short-lived people since history began, they were short-lived not necessarily because they were fated to die early, but because of their bodily weakness. Master Yan died very young;[4] and Scholar Jia,[5] with the talents of a minister of state, died at the age of thirty-three. As for Wang Bo and Lu Zhaolin, one died young, and the other made an end to his life as an invalid.[6] All these people had profound morality and great wisdom. But once their bodies did not exist, their morality and wisdom evaporated. In one's life, the things one enjoys are those that materialize in one's lifetime. There is being outside of this world. Whether or not the soul remains immortal, although flesh and blood are dead, does not depend on the length of life, but on the amount of one's achievement, which is really immortal. However, if one's body is not perfect, one does not feel happy in one's mind; the primary substance has been injured. How could a cripple feel happy about the world? When one reads the collected works of Lu Shengzhi,[7] one feels how much pain he was suffering in his heart. In the past, in order to keep

---

4. Yan Hui, Confucius' favorite disciple. (See the repeated references to him in Mao's "Classroom Notes" of 1913.) He was physically weak, and died at the age of thirty-one.

5. The reference is to Jia Yi (200–168 B.C.), from Luoyang, who was made a doctor in the Imperial Academy at an early age, and was then appointed by Emperor Wen of the Han dynasty to the Privy Council. He was later demoted because of his reformist ideas and became tutor to the Prince of Liang. He died early because of his grief at the death of the latter.

6. Wang Bo (648–675), *zi* Zi'an, was an extraordinarily precocious scholar who began writing at the age of six. He incurred the emperor's displeasure with a satire on the Imperial princes and later drowned while on his way to visit his father, who had been banished because of the son's disgrace. Lu Zhaolin (c. 635–689), *zi* Shengzhi, *hao* You Youzi, was from the state of You. He suffered from rheumatism and committed suicide by drowning at an early age. Both of them were ranked among the "Four Heroes" of the Tang dynasty.

7. Lu Zhaolin, who, as already noted, suffered from rheumatism.

healthy, the Sage did not eat fish or flesh that was gone. The chapter "Xiang Dang"[8] describes this in great detail. Mencius said: "He who has the true idea of Heaven's decree will not stand beneath a precipitous cliff."[9] Some people may have a body which they can in no way make strong; others may have a body they could make strong, but take no care of it. The latter case is like eating spoiled meat or standing beneath the precipitous wall. What a great pity! Your morality and wisdom are perfect; only the health of your body is slightly deficient. I suggest that you exercise more often. Although I myself am not strong, I have gained much recently from physical exercise. I hear that even the weakest individuals may become very strong [through exercise]. The great athletes of the East and West like [Theodore] Roosevelt, Sonntag, and Kanō [Jigorō] have all developed mighty bodies out of frail ones. I have heard previously that body, soul, and spirit could not be perfected and integrated, and the work of organs, bones, muscles, and nerves could not be changed again after a certain time. Today I know that this is not so. Both mind and body may be perfected and integrated; organs and bones are subject to improvement at any time. This is my humble opinion; I know not whether it accords with yours. I'm not going to say more. I respectfully seek your instruction, and send you my best wishes.

Respectfully submitted by
Your younger brother, Zedong.

December 9

---

8. Of the *Analects*; see Book X, VII, 2 (Legge, Vol. I, p. 232).

9. *Mencius*, VII, I, II, 2 (Legge, Vol. II, p. 450; translation revised). (Mao has got the wording of this citation slightly wrong; the original refers to a wall rather than a cliff.)

1917

Letter to Miyazaki Tōten[1]

(March 1917)

Esteemed Mr. Hakurō Tōten:

We have long admired your lofty integrity, but fate has not granted us the privilege of a meeting. Even from afar, your reputation is a source of inspiration.

You, sir, supported Mr. Huang[2] in life with your spirit; in death, you mourn him with your tears. Now he is to be buried, and you return, across ten thousand leagues of billows, to stand at his grave and bid farewell to his coffin.[3] Your lofty friendship reaches as far as the sun and the moon; the sincerity of your mind moves demons and gods. This is something rarely heard of throughout the whole world and never before encountered either in the past or in the present. Zhifan[4] and Zedong are Hunanese students who have done some reading in the classics and have in substantial measure established their aspirations. Today we long for the opportunity to gaze upon your elegant countenance and to receive

---

1. Miyazaki Tōten (1870–1922), also known as Miyazaki Torazō, as well as by the name used in this letter, Hakurō Tōten, was a Japanese friend and supporter of the Chinese revolutionaries of the generation of Sun Yatsen and Huang Xing.

2. Huang Xing (1879–1916), *zi* Qingwu, *hao* Keqiang, originally named Zhen, was a Hunanese who had been, with Sun Yatsen, one of the two fathers of the Chinese Revolution of 1911. In 1903 he was one of the founders and president of the Society for China's Revival, and in 1905 in Japan he joined with Sun Yatsen in founding Sun's principal revolutionary organization, the Tongmenghui. He died from illness in Shanghai on October 31, 1916. Mao and Xiao here refer to him as "Huang gong"; the character *gong*, which also has the meaning of duke, is the most respectful of the various Chinese equivalents for "Mr." His funeral was to be held in Changsha on April 15, 1917.

3. Miyazaki had come to Changsha sometime before March 7, for on that date he sent a dispatch to a newspaper in Nagasaki giving his impressions of the city. For further details, see the translation of his son's article of 1967 on the subject, in M. Henri Day, *Máo Zédōng 1917–1927. Documents* (Stockholm: University of Stockholm, 1975), pp. 18–20 (Skriftserien för Orientaliska Studier no. 14). The precise date of Mao's letter is not known, but it was obviously written after Miyazaki's arrival.

4. Xiao Zhifan, the co-signatory of this letter, also known as Xiao Zizhang, was a friend and fellow student of Mao's. For further details, see the note to Mao's letter of August 3, 1915, to his elder brother, Xiao Zisheng, and (regarding later developments) the note to Mao's letter of February 19, 1920, to Tao Yi.

your magnificent teachings. If you, sir, actually grant our request for a meeting, we will count ourselves fortunate indeed.[5]

Respectfully submitted by Xiao Zhifan and
Mao Zedong, students at Hunan First
Provincial Normal School

5. Miyazaki Tōten did indeed visit the First Normal School, not only to meet with Mao and Xiao, but to give a talk there. See his son's account, already cited, Day, *Máo Zédōng*, p. 19.

A Study of Physical Education

(April 1, 1917)

Our nation is wanting in strength; the military spirit has not been encouraged. The physical condition of our people deteriorates daily. These are extremely disturbing phenomena. Those who promote [physical education] have not grasped the essence of the problem. Consequently their efforts, though prolonged, have proved ineffectual. If they refuse to change, the process of weakening will be aggravated. To attain our goals and exercise far-reaching influence is an external matter, an effect. The development of our bodily strength is an internal matter, a cause. If our bodies are not strong, we will tremble at the sight of [enemy] soldiers. How then can we attain our goals, or exercise far-reaching influence? Strength comes from drill, and drill depends on self-awareness. The [promoters of physical education] have not failed to develop many methods. The reason why they are ineffectual is that external forces are insufficient to move the heart. They do not understand the real meaning of physical education, its true value, its effects, or where one should start. In all of these respects, they are ignorant and lost in a thick fog. Naturally they are ineffectual. **If we want physical education to be effective, we must influence people's subjective attitudes and stimulate their awareness of physical education.**[1] If one has self-awareness, a program of physical education will follow without further discussion; similarly, we will attain our goals and exert far-reaching influence as a matter of course. I am deeply concerned about the importance of physical education, and I regret that those who promote it fail to achieve the results they should. I know there must be many comrades in our country who suffer from this as I do. I venture to offer my foolish opinions for debate. What I say here has not all been put into practice. Much of it consists of empty words and utopian ideas. I don't dare to deceive you. I'll humbly listen to whoever wishes to correct my errors, and bow to him a hundred times.

1. An explanation of physical education

Since mankind came into existence, there have been none, however limited their understanding, who did not know how to defend their lives. Thus it is that when hunger reached an extreme, they had to eat the ferns of the Western Mountains,[2]

---

1. This sentence, and all subsequent words and passages set in bold, were underscored by Mao in the original, using circles beside the characters.

2. The reference is to the brothers Bo Yi and Shu Qi, who, after the Zhou dynasty had overthrown the Shang, "disdained to eat the grain of Zhou" and stole away to the

and could not but gulp down the plums on the well.[3] They dwelt in trees and clothed themselves in skins. This was all a matter of instinct, and men did not know why they acted thus. It was spontaneous and unrefined. Then sages emerged, and there were the rites. Eating, drinking, rising, and retiring all were regulated. Thus "when the Master was unoccupied with business, his manner was easy, and he looked pleased."[4] "He did not eat rice which had been injured by heat or damp and turned sour, nor fish or flesh which was gone."[5] When he practiced archery in a vegetable garden in Juexiang, "spectators surrounded him like a wall."[6] There is no difference between the construction of a human body and that of the myriad animals. If animals cannot live as long as man, this results from the fact that they have no rules to govern their lives. Men, however, do have such rules, which become clearer with each passing age. Thus it is that physical education appears. Physical education is simply the way for preserving life. East and West differ in their understanding of it. Zhuangzi took the cook as his model.[7] Zhongni [Confucius] drew his examples from the archer and the charioteer.[8] Among the civilized nations of today, it is in Germany that [physical education] most flourishes. Fencing has spread to all corners of the country. Japan, for its part, has *bushidō*. Recently, basing themselves on what survives of the traditions of our country, they have developed *jujitsu* to an admirable degree. When we examine these examples, we see that they all begin with the study of physiology. They know in detail the structure of the body, the circulation of the blood, what parts of the body are most developed, and what parts are defective. Their program of physical education is based on these facts, and aims to reduce what is overdeveloped and strengthen that which is underdeveloped. Their conclusion is that **one must cause the human body to develop evenly**. Thus we see that physical education is the method employed by human beings to nourish their lives and cause their bodies to develop evenly, and that it possesses rules and an order of progression that can be discussed.

2. The place of physical education in our life

Physical education complements education in virtue and knowledge. Moreover, both virtue and knowledge reside in the body. Without the body there would be

---

Shouyang Mountain where they "plucked the ferns and ate them." (*Records of the Historian*, Vol. 61.)

3. See the *Mencius*, III, II, X, 1 (Legge, Vol. II, p. 284).
4. *Analects* VII, IV (Legge, Vol. I, p. 196).
5. *Analects* X, VIII, 2 (Legge, Vol. I, p. 232).
6. *Book of Rites*, Chapter XLIII, "Shi yi" (Significance of Ceremonies Relating to Archery), par. 7. See Couvreur, *Mémoires sur les bienséances et les cérémonies*, Vol. II, part 2, p. 674.
7. See the story of Cook Ding in the *Zhuangzi*, III b (Graham, *Chuang-tzu*, pp. 63–64).
8. *Analects* IX, II, 2 (Legge, Vol. I, p. 216).

neither virtue nor knowledge. Those who understand this are rare. People stress either knowledge or morality. Knowledge is certainly valuable, for it distinguishes man from animals. But wherein is knowledge contained? Morality, too, is valuable; it is the basis of the social order and of equality between ourselves and others. But where does virtue reside? **It is the body that contains knowledge and houses virtue.** It contains knowledge like a chariot and houses morality like a chamber. The body is the chariot that contains knowledge, the chamber that houses virtue. Children enter primary school when they reach the proper age. In primary school, particular attention should be paid to the development of the body; progress in knowledge and moral training are of secondary importance. Nourishment and care should be primary, teaching and discipline complementary. At present, most people do not know this, and the result is that children become ill, or even die young, because of studying. In middle and higher schools, stress should be placed equally on all three aspects of education. At present, most people overemphasize knowledge. During the years of middle school, the development of the body is not yet completed. Since today the factors favoring physical development are few, and those deterring it numerous, won't physical development tend to cease? In the educational system of our country, required courses are as thick as the hairs on a cow. Even an adult with a tough, strong body could not stand it, let alone those who have not reached adulthood, or those who are weak. Speculating on the intentions of the educators, one is led to wonder whether they did not design such an unwieldy curriculum in order to exhaust the students, to trample on their bodies and ruin their lives. If there is one who does not accept this, they punish him, and if someone has an above-average intelligence, they give him all sorts of supplementary readings. They fill his ears with sweet words and seduce him with generous rewards. Alas, is this not what is called "injuring a man's son?"[9] How stupid! The only calamity that can befall a man is not to have a body. What else is there to worry about? If one seeks to improve one's body, other things will follow automatically. For the improvement of the body, nothing is more effective than physical education. **Physical education really occupies the first place in our lives. When the body is strong, then one can advance speedily in knowledge and morality and reap far-reaching advantages.** It should be regarded as an important part of our study. Learning "has its roots and branches. Affairs have their end and their beginning. To know what is first and what is last will lead near to the way."[10] This is exactly what I have been trying to say.

3. Previous abuses of physical education and my method for remedying them

The three forms of education are equally important; students hitherto have paid much attention to moral and intellectual education but have neglected physical

9. The words quoted are from the *Analects*, XI, XXIV, 2 (Legge, Vol. I, p. 246).
10. *The Great Learning*, I, 3 (Legge, Vol. I, p. 357).

education. The unfortunate consequence has been that they bend their backs and bow their heads; they have "white and slender hands";[11] when they climb a hill they are short of breath, and when they walk in the water they get cramps in their feet. That is why Master Yan[12] had a short life and Jia Yi[13] died young. As for Wang Bo and Lu Zhaolin,[14] the one died young, and the other became a paralytic. All these were men of high attainments in morality and knowledge. But there comes a day when the body cannot be preserved, and then morality and wisdom are destroyed along with it. Only the men of the north are able "to lie under arms and meet death without regret."[15] In the regions of Yan and Zhao there were many heroes, and martyrs and warriors often came from Liangzhou. At the beginning of the Qing dynasty, Yan Xizhai and Li Gangzhu[16] practiced both the literary and military arts. Yan Xizhai traveled over a thousand *li* to the north of the Great Wall to learn the art of fencing. He contended with brave soldiers and won. Hence he said, "If one lacks either the literary or the military arts, is this the true way?" Gu Yanwu,[17] although he was from the south, liked to live in the north; he preferred riding on horseback to traveling in boats. All these men of old can serve as our teachers.

Since the introduction of [modern] schools, and the adaptation of the methods of various countries, customs have changed little by little. Nevertheless, those who are in charge of these schools belong to the category of those who are unwilling to give up the old habits. They are prisoners of the habits they have acquired, and are unable to change all at once. And if any of them devote a bit of attention [to this matter], **they do so only superficially; they do not go to the root of things, but attach importance only to petty details.** That is why, in my humble opinion, present-day physical education **is in general formal rather than substantial.** There is no lack of courses in gymnastics, or of teachers, but few are able to benefit from this. Not only is such physical education of no use, but it is even harmful. The teachers give orders, the students try to execute them, their bodies obey, but their hearts rebel. Their spirits suffer measureless misery,

---

11. An allusion to no. 10 of the *Gu shi shijiu shou* (Nineteen Old Poems), a famous collection of poems of the Han dynasty.

12. Yan Hui, Confucius' favorite disciple. (See the note to Mao's letter of December 9, 1916.)

13. On this Han dynasty philosopher and poet, see the note to Mao's letter of December 9, 1916, to Li Jinxi.

14. On these two Tang dynasty scholars, see the note to Mao's letter of December 9, 1916.

15. *The Doctrine of the Mean*, X, 4 (Legge, Vol. I, p. 390).

16. Yan Yuan (1635–1704), *zi* Yizhi, *hao* Xizhai, and his disciple Li Gong (1659–1733), *zi* Gangzhu, *hao* Shugu, were leading figures among the Ming loyalists of the early Qing period.

17. See above, note 126 to Mao's "Classroom Notes."

and when their spirits suffer, their bodies suffer too. As a result, when the gymnastics lessons are over, they are all exhausted and depressed. No attention is paid to the cleanliness of what they eat and drink, so inorganic matter and microbes get into their bodies, causing disease. In the classrooms the light is insufficient, thus causing serious harm to their eyesight. The tables and chairs are not of the right size, and their bodies are made to fit into this Procrustean bed.[18] Thus their bodies are harmed. There are innumerable such examples.

As far as we students are concerned, however, **the installation of a school and the instruction given by its teachers are only the external and objective aspect. We also have the internal, the subjective aspect.** When one's decision is made in his heart, then all parts of the body obey its orders. Fortune and misfortune are of our own seeking. "I wish to be virtuous, and lo! virtue is at hand."[19] How much more is this true of physical education! If we do not have the will to act, then even though the exterior and the objective are perfect, they still cannot benefit us. **Hence, when we speak of physical education, we should begin with individual initiative.**

4. The utility of physical education

Because man is an animal, movement is most important for him.[20] And because he is a rational animal, his movements must have a reason. But why is movement deserving of esteem? Why is rational movement deserving of esteem? To say that movement helps in earning a living is trivial. To say that movement protects the nation is lofty. Yet neither is the basic reason. The object of movement is simply to preserve our life and gladden our hearts. Zhu Xi stresses respect, and Lu Jiuyuan[21] stresses stillness. Stillness is still, and respect is not action; it is also merely still. Laozi said that immobility was the ultimate goal; Sakyamuni[22] sought quiet and methods of contemplation. The method of medita-

---

18. The corresponding Chinese metaphor, used here by Mao, is "cut the foot to fit the shoe."

19. *Analects,* VII, XXIX (Legge, Vol. I, p. 204).

20. "Animal" in Chinese is *dongwu,* literally "moving thing." Mao's statement is therefore rather like saying "An animal is naturally animated."

21. Lu Jiuyuan (1140–1192), *zi* Yujing, *hao* Xiangshan, was a successful official who entertained views which placed him in conflict with Zhu Xi, with whom he conducted a long and celebrated controversy. The essence of his views was that personal, subjective education, coupled with reflection, is the foundation of mental progress. The *jing* in his style Yujing is, obviously not by accident, the character which we have translated as "stillness" in Mao's discussion of his ideas. It is also part of the compound *jingzuo,* literally sitting in stillness or immobility, which signifies the "meditation" which Mao says characterizes the disciples of Zhu and Lu.

22. Mao here refers to the founder of Buddhism as "Mr. Shi," using only the first of the four characters (Shijiamouni) commonly employed to transcribe his name.

tion is esteemed by the disciples of Zhu and Lu. Recently there have been those who, following these masters, have spoken of methods of contemplation, boasted about the effectiveness of their methods, and expressed contempt for those who exercise, thereby ruining their own bodies. This is perhaps one way, but I would not venture to imitate it. In my humble opinion, **there is only movement in heaven and on earth.**

Movement as it applies to mankind, and when it is conducted according to rules, can be called physical education. As I have already stated, the efficacy of physical education consists in strengthening the muscles and bones. Formerly, I often heard it said that once the body and faculties of a man had been formed, nothing could be done to change them. By the age of twenty-five at most, a person was fully formed and could not change. Today, I know this is not so. A man's body changes every day. One never ceases to benefit from the renewal of what is old, and from the replacement of what is defective, in any part of the organism. If the eye cannot see clearly, it can be made clear; if the ear does not hear, it can be made to hear. Even people of sixty or seventy can benefit from improving their bodies. There is another aspect that should be mentioned. It is often said that he who is weak can scarcely become strong. Today I know that this, too, is false. Those who are born strong, if they misuse their strength, and do not resist all kinds of desires, can little by little ruin their bodies. Thus those who regard themselves as well endowed by nature, if they are satisfied with this and do not engage in training, may in the end change from strong to weak. As for the weak, if they consistently deplore the imperfection of their bodies, and are concerned about the brevity of their lives; if they cautiously and attentively exercise self-control, negatively by strictly restraining their appetites, and abstaining from harmful practices, and positively by diligently tempering themselves and remedying their incapacities, they can eventually become strong. Thus those who are born strong should not necessarily congratulate themselves, and those who are born weak should not necessarily despair. If I am born weak, perhaps it is because Heaven wants to encourage me to become strong. You never know. Eminent advocates of physical education in the East and the West, such as [Theodore] Roosevelt in America, Sonntag in Germany, and Kanō [Jigorō] in Japan, all began with very weak bodies, and succeeded in making themselves very strong. One often hears it said that the mind and the body cannot both be perfect at the same time, that those who use their minds are deficient in physical health and those with a robust body are generally deficient in mental capacities. This kind of talk is also absurd and applies only to those who are weak in will and feeble in action, which is generally not the case of the superior man. Confucius died at the age of seventy-two, and I have not heard that his body was not healthy. Sakyamuni traveled continually, preaching his doctrine, and he, too, died very old. Jesus had the misfortune to die unjustly. As for Mohammed, he subjugated the world holding the Koran in his left hand and a sword in his right. All these men were called sages in olden times and are among the greatest thinkers. Mr. Wu Zhiyong,[23] who is still alive today, is over seventy and says he might live to be a hundred. He is also a thinker. Wang Xiangqi[24] was over seventy when he died, but his health was extremely robust. How can those who preach the view mentioned above account for these cases? To sum up, regular physical education strengthens the muscles and bones; and when muscles and bones are strengthened, the whole constitution of the body can change. The weak can become strong, and body and mind can be perfect at the same time. All this is not a question of destiny,[25] but depends entirely on human effort.

Physical education not only strengthens the body but also enhances our knowledge. There is a saying: Civilize the mind and make savage the body.[26] This is an apt saying. In order to civilize the mind, one must first make savage the body. If the body is made savage, then the civilized mind will follow. **Knowledge consists in knowing the things in the world, and in discerning their laws. In this matter we must rely on our body, because direct observation depends on the ears and eyes, and reflection depends on the brain. The ears and eyes, as well as the brain, may be considered parts of the body. When the body is perfect, then knowledge is also perfect.** Hence one can say that knowledge is acquired indirectly through physical education. Physical strength is required to undertake the study of the numerous modern sciences, whether in school or through independent study. He who is equal to this is the man with a strong body; he who is not equal to it is the man with a weak body. The division between the strong and the weak determines the area of responsibilities each can assume.

Physical education not only enhances knowledge, it also harmonizes the sentiments. The power of the sentiments is extremely great. The ancients endeavored to discipline them with reason. Hence they asked, "Is the master [i.e., reason] always alert?" They also said: "One should discipline the heart with reason." But reason proceeds from the heart, and the heart resides in the body. We often observe that the weak are enslaved by their sentiments and are incapable of mastering them. Those whose senses are imperfect or whose limbs are defective

23. Wu Tingfang (1842–1922), *zi* Zhiyong, *hao* Wenjue, was a lawyer, journalist and diplomat. He had been foreign minister of the republican government in late 1911, and occupied the same post at the time Mao wrote this article. Shortly afterward, he was dismissed because he had supported President Li Yuanhong in removing the premier, Duan Qirui.

24. Wang Kaiyun. See the note to Mao's letter of December 9, 1916, to Li Jinxi.

25. Literally, *tianming* (the decree of Heaven).

26. This view may be compared with Chen Duxiu's advocacy, in an article published in issue no. 2 of *New Youth*, which Mao had certainly read, of the doctrine of the "savage" or "beastly" nature *(shouxing zhuyi)*, which he attributed to Fukuzawa Yukichi.

are often enslaved by excessive passion, and reason is incapable of saving them. Hence it may be called an invariable law that **when the body is perfect and healthy, the sentiments are also correct.** For example, when we encounter certain misfortunes, we experience disagreeable emotions, our hearts are agitated, and we find it difficult to control ourselves. But if we undertake vigorous exercise, we are able immediately to dissipate these former attitudes and to make our minds clear once more. Thus rapid results can be obtained.

Physical education not only harmonizes the emotions, it also strengthens the will. The great utility of physical education lies precisely in this. The principal aim of physical education is military heroism. Such objects of military heroism as courage, dauntlessness, audacity, and perseverance are all matters of will. Let me explain this with an example. To wash our feet in ice water makes us acquire courage and dauntlessness, as well as audacity.[27] In general, any form of exercise, if pursued continuously, will help to train us in perseverance. Long-distance running is particularly good training in perseverance. "My strength uprooted mountains, my energy dominated the world"[28] — this is courage. "If I don't behead the Loulan, I swear I will not return" — this is dauntlessness.[29] To replace the family with the nation — this is audacity. "[Yu] was eight years away from his home, and though he thrice passed the door of it, he did not enter"[30] — this is perseverance. All these can be accomplished merely on the basis of daily physical education. The will **is the antecedent of a man's career.**

Those whose bodies are small and frail are flippant in their behavior. Those whose skin is flabby are soft and dull in will. Thus does the body influence the mind. The purpose of physical education is to strengthen the muscles and the bones; as a result, knowledge is enhanced, the sentiments are harmonized, and the will is strengthened. The muscles and bones belong to our body; knowledge, sentiments, and will belong to our heart. When both the body and the heart are at ease, one may speak of perfect harmony. Hence, physical education is nothing else but the nourishing of our lives and the gladdening of our hearts.

5. The reasons for disliking exercise

Exercise is the most important part of physical education. Nowadays students generally dislike exercise. There are four reasons for this:

---

27. This practice had been recommended to Mao by Yang Changji.

28. From a poem attributed to Xiang Yu, the rival of Liu Bang, founder of the Han dynasty, in the *Records of the Historian.*

29. This statement is attributed to the famous commander Fu Jiezi, who served the Han emperor Zhao Di (86–73 B.C.). Fu volunteered for a mission to the king of the Loulan, in Central Asia, to punish him for killing some Chinese envoys, and returned with the king's head as proof he had accomplished his purpose.

30. *Mencius,* III, I, IV, 7 (Legge, Vol. 2, p. 251).

1) They do not have self-awareness. If a thing is to be put into practice, one must first take pleasure in it. One must understand in detail the whys and the wherefores. To know in detail the whys and the wherefores is self-awareness. People generally do not know the interrelation between exercise and themselves — or they may know it in general terms but not intimately. They do not develop their wisdom because their emotions are not involved. Thus the person who studies all kinds of sciences without ever being wearied is he who understands their relation to himself, knowing that if he does not study today, he will not be able to earn a living tomorrow. But as regards exercise, people do not have this awareness. The fault lies partly in their failure to think seriously about it, and partly in the inability of the teachers to enlighten them.

2) They cannot change their long-established habits. Our country has always stressed literary accomplishment. People blush to wear short clothes.[31] Hence there is the common saying, "A good man does not become a soldier." Even though they know why exercise should be carried out, and the effectiveness of exercise in strengthening a country, the force of the old ideas is still great. As regards the new conception of exercise, they half accept and half reject it. Thus there is nothing surprising in the fact that they do not like exercise.

3) Exercise has not been propagated forcefully. Here, too, there are two cases. On the one hand, those whom today we call educators are not well informed about physical education, do not know about it themselves, know about it only by hearsay, and engage in it only out of conformism. Thus those who speak of it are not sincere, and those who engage in it do not know the methods, and this deprives the students of the desire to study it. This is like a vagrant talking about independence, or a drunkard talking about sobriety; no one can take it seriously. On the other hand, teachers of exercise are often ill-educated, and vulgar in their mode of expression, so that the auditors close their ears. What they know is limited to this discipline alone, and even that they do not know very well. They see nothing every day but the mechanical movements of their students, and that is all. But **if there is only outward form, without the essential spirit which animates it, the thing in question cannot survive even a single day.** Thus it is today with exercise.

4) Students feel that exercise is shameful. According to my humble observation, this is really their major reason for disliking exercise. Flowing garments, a slow gait, a grave, calm gaze — these constitute a fine deportment, respected by society. Why should one suddenly extend an arm or expose a leg, stretch and bend down? Is this not strange? Hence there are those who know well that their

---

31. The dress of the swordsmen of King Wen of Zhao, according to the *Zhuangzi*, I, 4. For the whole of this picturesque episode, see Graham, *Chuang-tzu*, pp. 244–47.

bodies need exercise and, moreover, wish very much to engage in it, but they cannot. There are those who can exercise only with a group, not by themselves, and those who can exercise in privacy but not in public. In short, all this results from feelings of shame.

All four of these are reasons for disliking exercise. The first and the fourth are subjective, and changing them depends on ourselves; the second and third are objective, and changing them depends on others. "What the superior man seeks is in himself."[32] That which depends on others is of lesser importance.

6. The methods of exercise should be few

When I was myself distressed at the weakness of my body, and when I wanted to study the art of hygiene, I noted in looking at the writings of the ancients that already in former times it was much discussed. Modern schools have gymnasiums and books, but if hearts are not enlightened, and these facilities are treated negligently, it will be difficult to derive any benefit from them. For in such matters, the main thing is not words, but application. Zeng Wenzheng[33] practiced the method of washing his feet before going to bed and walking a thousand steps after meals, and derived great benefit from this. There was an eighty-year-old man who was still healthy. On being asked how he maintained his health, he replied, "I don't eat hearty meals, that's all." Nowadays the methods of exercise are very diverse, more than I can count. But although there may be several score or even several hundred, "A branch in the forest is sufficient for a nest, and a sip from the river fills the belly."[34] We have only this body and only these senses, bones, viscera, and veins. Even though there are several hundred methods of exercise, all of them **are aimed at stimulating the circulation of the blood.** If one method can accomplish this, the result of a hundred methods is the same as that of one. Therefore the other ninety-nine methods can be dispensed with. "Our eyes can see only one thing at a time; our ears can hear only one sound at a time."[35] To employ a hundred different methods to train the muscles and bones only disturbs them. One would like them to be effective, but one cannot see how they could be. Furthermore, the methods used for different purposes are not all identical to those which are appropriate simply to strengthen the body. A swinging bridge helps to train us for navigation, and a bamboo pole helps us to jump high. Walks and games are suited to primary school, while military training is

32. *Analects*, XV, XX (Legge, Vol. I, p. 300).

33. Yet again, Mao refers to Zeng Guofan by the honorific title bestowed on him posthumously, thus underscoring his respect for this great Hunanese predecessor.

34. This is a condensed paraphrase from the *Zhuangzi*, I, 4. The original reads: "The tit that nests in the deep forest wants no more than one branch, the mole that drinks in the Yellow River no more than a bellyful" (Graham, *Chuang-tzu*, p. 45).

35. *Xunzi*, Vol.1.

appropriate for middle school and above. These are methods useful in different ways. On the other hand, exercising the muscles and bones so as to promote the circulation of the blood serves to strengthen the body. It is appropriate to have different methods, useful for different purposes, but as far as strengthening one's body is concerned, it is best to have only a small number of methods. Students today have often not grasped this. In consequence, they suffer loss in two respects. On the one hand, those who like exercise consider that the best solution is to apply many methods, and all these methods are applied to a single body; the result is that they do not benefit at all. On the other hand, those who do not like exercise, when they see that the others know many techniques, while they know little, give up and do nothing. Those who do a lot do not necessarily benefit from this. If their activities are extensive but sterile, what value do they have? And those who do little do not necessarily derive no benefit. Even if they do no more than stretch out an arm and a leg, if they do this regularly, even that will be useful. When one has understood that, it can be said that one has begun to make progress in physical education.

7. The points to which we must pay attention when we exercise

We should have perseverance in all things. Exercise is no exception. Suppose there are two men who exercise. One practices and then stops, the other is unremitting in his practice. There will certainly be a difference in the results. First of all, perseverance in exercise gives rise to pleasure. In general, that which is at rest cannot set itself in motion; there must be something to move it. And this something can only be pleasure. All sciences must cause people to take pleasure in them in some respect, and this is even more true of exercise. When one is at rest, it is very agreeable, and it is most laborious to set oneself in motion. People always like to take their ease, and detest effort. If there is nothing pushing them forward, they cannot modify this fundamental tendency and change their natural penchant. Now, pleasure results from regular daily exercise. The best way is to exercise twice a day — on getting up and before going to bed — in the nude; the next best way is to wear light clothes. Too much clothing impedes movement. If one does this daily, the idea of exercise is continually present and never interrupted. Today's exercise is a continuation of yesterday's exercise, and thus leads to tomorrow's exercise. The individual exercise periods need not be long; thirty minutes is sufficient. In this way, a certain interest will naturally arise. **Second, perseverance in exercise can create pleasure. Exercise over a long time can produce great results and give rise to a feeling of personal worth. As a result, we will be able to study with joy, and every day will see some progress in our virtue. Our hearts are filled with boundless joy because we have persevered and obtained a result.** Pleasure and interest are distinct. Interest is the origin of exercise, and pleasure its consequence. Interest arises from the action, and pleasure from the result. The two are naturally different.

Perseverance without concentration of mind can hardly produce results. If we look at flowers from horseback, even though we may look daily, it is like not having seen them at all. The person whose mind is on a swan in the sky, although he is learning along with another, does not come up to him.[36] Hence one should concentrate all one's effort on exercise. During exercise, the mind should be on the exercise. Idle and confused thoughts should all be put aside. The mind should be concentrated on the problem of the circulation of the blood in the veins, on tensing and releasing the muscles, on the way the joints bend and straighten, on breathing in and out, and each exercise should be carried out rhythmically. The four actions of bending, stretching, advancing, and retreating should be carried out one after another. Zhu Xi explained that one must concentrate on one thing and ignore all the rest. He said that when you eat, you should think only of eating; when you get dressed, you should think only of getting dressed.[37] He who devotes himself with all his force to exercise is simply applying this principle.

The superior man's deportment is cultivated and agreeable, but one cannot say this about exercise. Exercise should be savage and rude. To charge on horseback, amidst the clash of arms, and to be ever victorious; to shake the mountains by one's cries, and the colors of the sky by one's roars of anger; to have the strength to uproot mountains like Xiang Yu and the audacity to pierce the mark like You Ji[38] — all this is savage and rude and has nothing to do with delicacy. In order to progress in exercise, one must be savage. If one is savage, one will have great vigor and strong muscles and bones. The method of exercise should be rude; then one can apply oneself seriously and it will be easy to exercise. These two things are especially important for beginners.

There are three things to which we must pay attention in exercise: (1) perseverance, (2) concentration of all our strength, and (3) that it be savage and rude. There are many other things that require attention. Here I have merely indicated the most important ones.

8. Discussion of the modest results I have achieved in the domain of exercise

I have already given a rough account of the various systems of exercise, but this has all been illumination from without, and not the fruit of my own thought. Adopting the strong points from each method of exercise, I have, however, put

---

36. This sentence evokes a paragraph in the *Mencius*, VI, I, IX, 3 (Legge, Vol. 2, p. 410) about two men learning chess, one of whom gives the subject his whole mind, while the other is thinking of shooting an approaching swan.

37. *Reflections on Things at Hand*, Vol. 4 (p. 86 of the Commercial Press edition).

38. Celebrated archer of the Spring and Autumn period.

together a system of my own, from which I have derived considerable benefit. The system as a whole is divided into six parts: the arm section, the leg section, the trunk section, the head section, the section for striking movements, and the section for harmonizing movements. Within these larger divisions, there are twenty-seven subdivisions,[39] making up the six divisions. Hence I have called it the six-section system of exercise. I have set it out in detail below; I will be grateful to all those men of virtue[40] among our contemporaries who may correct my mistakes.

a. Arm exercises. Squatting[41] position.

i. Make fists, alternately extend the arms to the front and retract them. Left and right, successively, three times. (Left and right, successively, means that when you exercise the left you rest the right, and when you exercise the right you rest the left, one after the other.)

ii. Make fists, bend the forearm, and then swing it to the rear in a semicircular movement. Left and right, successively, three times.

iii. Make fists, extend the arms forward and down, and then retract. Left and right together, three times. (Left and right together means that you exercise them at the same time, and not successively.)

iv. With the palms turned upward, make a movement as though grasping something toward the outside. Left and right successively, three times.

v. With the palms turned down, make a movement as though grasping something toward the outside. Left and right successively, three times.

vi. Extend the fingers, bend the elbow, and make a piercing movement forward. Left and right successively, three times.

b. Leg exercises. Squatting position.

i. Make fists, and let the left and right arms hang at the sides. Leaving one leg in its original position, extend the other out to the rear. Left and right successively, three times.

ii. Make fists and hold the arms straight out in front of you. Extend one leg to the side, and bend the other forward. The extended leg can be moved around, while you stand on the toes of the bent leg, with the heel touching the buttocks. Left and right successively, three times.

---

39. In fact, there are, as will be seen, thirty subdivisions.

40. *Junzi.*

41. Here, and in section b below, Mao uses the Chinese word *zuo*, which commonly means "sit." As pointed out by M. Henri Day, however, many of the exercises he describes simply could not be performed from a seated position. We have therefore followed Day (*Máo Zédōng,* pp. 30–31, and note 55, p. 38) in translating "squatting."

iii. Make fists, and let the left and right arms hang at the sides. Supporting yourself on one leg, lift the other. Left and right successively, three times.

iv. Make fists, and let the left and right arms hang at the sides. Supporting yourself on one leg, kick forward with the other. Left and right successively, three times.

v. Make fists, and let the left and right arms hang at the sides. Bend one leg forward, and extend the other to the rear. The bent leg remains in its original position, while the extended leg moves so that both are more or less in a straight line. Left and right successively, three times.

vi. Unclench the fists. Alternately raise the whole body to a standing position, and return to a squatting position. While squatting, the heels should more or less touch the buttocks. Three times.

c. Exercises for the trunk. Standing position.

i. Bend the body forward, and then backward. Three times. (In this and the following exercises, the fists should be clenched.)

ii. Raise one arm and let the other hang at the side. Tighten the chest muscles on the left and on the right. Once each on the left and on the right.

iii. Let one arm hang at the side, and the other extend down obliquely forward. Tighten the shoulder muscles on the left and on the right. Once each on the left and on the right.

iv. Place the feet in a "T" position. Swing the hands horizontally from side to side, twisting the waist and sides. Once each to the left and to the right.

d. Head exercises. Sitting position.

i. Bend the head forward, then back. Three times.

ii. Turn the head to the left and to the right. Three times.

iii. With the hands, massage the forehead, the cheeks, the nose, the lips, the throat, the ears, and the back of the neck.

iv. Free exercises. Keeping the head in more or less the same position, concentrate on moving the skin and the lower jaw. Five times.

e. Striking exercises. No fixed position. (Striking exercises consist in using the fists to hit the body all over. Thus the circulation of the blood is speeded up. The main object of this exercise is to strengthen the muscles and the flesh.)

i. Arm exercise. The right hand is used to strike the left arm, and the left hand the right arm.

a) Forearm. Hit the top, the bottom, the left side and the right side.
b) Upper arm. Hit the top, the bottom, the left side and the right side.

ii. The shoulders.

iii. The chest.

iv. The sides.

v. The back.

vi. The abdomen.

vii. The buttocks.

viii. The legs. Upper leg, lower leg.

f. Harmonizing movements. No fixed position.

i. Leaping. More than ten times.

ii. Deep breathing. Three times.

Foreword to Xiao Zisheng's[1] All in One *Self-Study Notes*

(Summer 1917)

You have entitled this book *All In One*, and have asked me to write the foreword. I think of the words of Zhuangzi: "My life flows between confines, but knowledge has no confines."[2] In today's world, learning is more and more highly developed, civilization is constantly progressing, and human affairs keep proliferating so that one can never study them exhaustively. But as civilization advances, our knowledge likewise increases, and there should consequently be some way to study it more systematically. Even though different people have taken upon themselves to study, some have results but others do not. It all depends on whether or not they properly accumulate what they study. Take, for example, a hundred-*zhang*-high platform.[3] When it is first built, it begins with a single stone; then there are two, three, four, and finally ten thousand stones. So it is with studies. Today we record one thing, tomorrow we comprehend another truth, and in time all this adds up to learning. Heights are built from low foundations, and greatness has humble beginnings. They all depend simply on men's quest for them. Once the basic knowledge is gleaned, there remain the differences of quality and scope of different works. As a platform is built with logs gathered from a thousand mountains, so is knowledge gathered together from many schools of thought. The more refined the knowledge we have extracted, the wider its usage; the deeper the roots of the tree, the better its fruit. This approach is definitely different from that which follows only one master and is self-complacent. Even if we have built a high platform or have gleaned a wide range of knowledge, however, we have not yet arrived, though we may think we have. A platform that is not securely built, or knowledge that is not carefully selected, is not very much different from having no platform or no knowledge at all. How do we achieve excellence in studies? It depends on the way we accumulate our learning. The way to accumulate it is to do it systematically. The defect of our country's ancient learning lay in its disorganized and unsystematic charac-

1. On Xiao Zisheng, see the notes to Mao's letters of July 1915 to a friend and of November 1920 to Xiao Zizhang.

2. See the *Zhuangzi*, Chapter 3, "On Nurturing Life," par. 1 (Graham, *Chuang-tzu*, p. 62).

3. The *zhang* is a measurement of length equal to 10 Chinese feet, or 3.3 meters.

ter. The only categories used were classics, history, philosophical works, and literary collections. Politics and religion were combined into one,[4] and no differentiations were made between the abstract and the empirical. This is why we have not made any progress, even in several milennia. As for Western studies, they are quite different. Each field of study is further divided into pure and applied, and also into explanatory and standard works. Each field is singled out from thousands of other fields of study. A field is further divided into branches, phylums, classes, genera, and species. The classifications are so clear that they sound like a waterfall dashing against the rocks beneath a cliff. Today, anyone who is resolved to pursue learning, and yet does not follow this principle, will not be able to attain excellence. Yet even striving for excellence is not enough. Breadth and excellence in learning cannot be achieved overnight; one must persevere. There is a saying, "Keep walking everyday, and do not be discouraged even if there are thousands or tens of thousands of *li* to go." Suppose you have already covered almost one thousand *li*; you are almost there, yet you turn back. Even if you have tried very hard, you have still not reached the goal. This is the difference between persevering and not persevering. I presume that you have completed this book with the intention of laying a foundation for further studies in the future and achieving excellence. It is clear that you will keep adding to it. Your book has incorporated all kinds of studies and will, without doubt, broaden the readers' minds. But it has collected both boulders and sand, big and small; although it is pleasing to the eye, it may not delight the heart. It would be good if these materials could be put in order, retaining the precious stones and discarding the dross. Moreover, you need to persevere and never give up halfway. If this could be done, I have no doubt that it would lay the foundation for a platform hundreds and hundreds of *zhang* high.

Your fellow student and younger brother,
Mao Zedong
Summer 1917

4. *Zhengjiao heyi,* the principle already alluded to in note 70 to the "Classroom Notes," which refers in particular to the fusion of political and religious (or spiritual-ethical) authority in the person of the emperor.

Letter to Li Jinxi

(August 23, 1917)

Esteemed Mr. Shaoxi:

After we met at the provincial capital,[1] I wanted to write you on several occasions, but never got around to it. There have been many different things on my mind lately. I do not have any close friends around, and there is no one to whom I can talk. Since I have known you, my respected friend, it has been like an infant finding a loving mother. Others confuse everything, tormenting my soul and depriving me of my ambition. There is nobody here with whom I can discuss scholarly issues, or talk about weighty affairs of state, the morality with which one may succeed, and the tactics of establishing oneself in this world. Alas, at an early age I was deprived of the opportunity to study, and now today I mourn the loss of my teacher. Who does not want to seek advancement? But when one's aspirations are continuously frustrated and when one gets lost in a maze of twists and turns, one's bitterness is too much to describe. For a very young man, all this represents a world of bitterness. I returned home this year during the summer vacation and stayed in the city for a few days; I toured Ningxiang, Anhua, Yiyang, and Hangjiang *xian*; this changed the atmosphere a bit and exercised my bones and muscles. I returned to the provincial capital on the sixteenth, and registered at school on the twentieth; school started on the twenty-second, and classes begin tomorrow. I seize a moment of leisure to write this letter in order to set forth the ideas in my mind; I venture to hope that in giving me your guidance, you will subject them to careful scrutiny.

Viewed from one standpoint, the divisions in today's world can be considered the natural outcome of change. From another standpoint, however, is it not that people lack the innate capacity and the methods by which to save the world from its distress, and that their attempts at partial cures through their own superficial understanding are inadequate — and yet they all claim that they have the means to cure all the world's ills! This is simply a lack of the clarity that comes from introspection, and of the knowledge that comes from observing the outside world. One should know one's own capacities. Those who, at best, are materials

1. Li Jinxi arrived in Changsha from Beijing on April 16, 1917, and met with Mao on April 23 to discuss scholarly matters. He left again for Beijing on May 15, 1917.

for making wine cups but who want to shoulder the responsibilities of the pillar have an empty mind but attempt to imitate the ambition of heroic rebels of old. They attempt to use clever tricks and sleight-of-hand as instruments to control an entire world. This is like the autumn pools of rain that have no source; it is like the rootless duckweed — how can they last long? Those that can be called men today are three in number: Yuan Shikai, Sun Yatsen, and Kang Youwei.[2] I won't discuss Sun and Yuan. Only Kang has something like ultimate principles, but looked at more closely, his ultimate principles cannot in the end serve as a guide to present reality. They are nothing but flashy words that sound brilliant, but lack the advantage of a single trunk to support branches and leaves. In my humble opinion, ultimate principles means simply the promotion of learning. Only learning is our foundation. People today have no learning, and therefore the foundation is not solid; it is in danger of frequent collapse. Of contemporary figures, I respect only Zeng Wenzheng.[3] Look at his handling of the campaign in which he disposed of Hong and Yang;[4] it was perfectly flawless. If anyone alive today were put in his position, could he do so well? The world is very large, social organization is extremely complex, and there are several thousand years of history. The wisdom of the people has been blocked, and it is very difficult to open it up again. Those who wish to move the world must move the world's hearts and minds, but instead of vainly attempting conspicuous acts, to move people's hearts one must have great ultimate principles. Today's reforms all begin with minor details such as the parliament, the constitution, the presidency, the cabinet, military affairs, business, and education — these are all side issues. Although details are indispensable, they are at most details, and ultimate principles are required. Without ultimate principles, such details are merely superfluous and of bad augury, so that you do not see the forest for the trees. Those who are fortunate get relatively close to the ultimate principles; those who are unfortunate travel in the opposite direction. Those who turn their backs on the ultimate principles and yet regard themselves as instruments of rule seldom avoid the fate of becoming laughingstocks of history who led a generation or a country to defeat. In their case, how can there be even the slightest modicum of wealth and

---

2. On Kang, see the note to Mao's letter of June 25, 1915; on Sun, see the text of July 25, 1916. In view of his long-standing admiration for both Kang and Sun, it is curious to see Mao lumping them together here with Yuan Shikai.

3. Zeng Guofan.

4. Hong Xiuquan (1814–1864), born in Guangdong Province, and Yang Xiuqing (1820–1856), born in Guangxi Province, were leaders of the Taiping Heavenly Kingdom. Zeng Guofan was appointed commissioner of local defense of Hunan and in that capacity built up a large and well-disciplined army commonly known as the Xiang jun (Xiang or Hunan Army) to fight the Taipings. In May 1854, this force turned back a Taiping invasion of Hunan. Yang rebelled against Hong in 1856 and was killed, but Zeng's campaign against the Taipings continued, culminating in 1864 with the capture of the Taiping capital, Nanjing.

power [*fuqiang*] or happiness to speak of? For the ultimate principles are the truths of the universe; the peoples who live in the world are each an integral part of the universe, so the universal truth resides in the heart of every man. It may be incomplete, but it always exists in at least some small measure. Today, if we appeal to the hearts of all under heaven on the basis of great ultimate principles, can any of them fail to be moved? And if all the hearts in the realm are moved, is there anything which cannot be achieved? And if the affairs of the realm can be dealt with, how, then, can the state fail to be rich, powerful, and happy? And yet today the realm is so divided. The reasons for this are first, as stated earlier, that people lack the clarity of introspection; and second, that people do not know what way should be employed to move the realm, in other words they lack the knowledge that comes from observing the outside world. Therefore, in my humble opinion, in today's world there should be broad-minded people who will begin with philosophy and ethics to reform philosophy, reform ethics, and change fundamentally the mentality of the whole country. This is like waving a huge flag to gather tens of thousands of men; this is like a flash of thunder and lightning that everyone hears in the dark; it is utterly irresistable.

In the past I was without knowledge; recently, I have gone through some books and newspapers, and made some comparisons of Chinese and world affairs. I feel that my countrymen have accumulated many undesirable customs, their mentality is too antiquated, and their morality is extremely bad. Inasmuch as thought rules the mind of man, and morality is the model for human behavior, if these two things are not pure, the entire world is corrupted. For the power of these two factors is all-pervasive. Thought and morality must be truthful and honest. The thought and morality of our country can be summed up as false rather than authentic, illusory rather than real. They have been in existence for five thousand years; their roots are deep and their leaves strong. They cannot be removed and purged without enormous force. According to Mr. Huaizhong,[5] a certain Japanese gentleman[6] says that Oriental thought entirely fails to correspond to the reality of life. This is well said. But in my opinion, Western thought is not necessarily all correct either; very many parts of it should be transformed at the same time as Oriental thought.

When we educate the young today, it is appropriate to cultivate their will. It is also said that when a certain individual has a will, foolish ideas cannot penetrate

---

5. Yang Changji.

6. The reference is manifestly to Fukuzawa Yukichi, about whose views Mao had heard from Yang Changji as early as the autumn of 1913. (See above his "Classroom Notes" of October–December 1913.) For Fukuzawa's own presentation of his ideas, see in particular *An Outline of a Theory of Civilization* (Tokyo: Sophia University, 1973), translated by David A. Dilworth and G. Cameron Hurst.

his mind. Will is the truth which we perceive in the universe. Accordingly, it may be called that which determines the tendency of our minds. What people today refer to as establishing the will, such as resolving to become a military commander or an educator, is the result of imitation, as when one sees and admires the enterprise of the previous generation, and the accomplishments of contemporaries, and then blindly follows this model as one's own will. Truly to establish one's will is not so simple. One must first study philosophy and ethics, from which one may gain truth, which in turn will become the standard for one's own words and actions, and one's goal for the future. Then one must choose an enterprise compatible with this goal and devote all one's efforts to pursuing it; only if one achieves this goal is it possible to speak of having a will. Only such a will is a true will, and not an impulse blindly followed. In fact, what is initially called will is simply an inclination to seek the good, or the true and the beautiful; this is nothing more than an impulse of passion, and not an authentic will. And yet, is such a will easy to establish? If, for a decade, one does not obtain the truth, then for a decade one will be without a will. An entire life without truth is an entire life without a will. That is why learning is as precious as youth itself. Today, what people study in the way of literature [*wen*] is simply the expression of opinions. Those who can distinguish between right and wrong and write copiously are regarded by today's world as possessing talent, and no one realizes how absurd this is. The opinions in question are their own subjective views, reflecting no concrete experience of today's universe. Since such people have not devoted the slightest effort to study, where does their truth come from? That is why a certain gentleman said that the challenge from yesterday's self to today's self has not yet been resolved. Nor can one know whether or not tomorrow's self will challenge today's self; that needs to be solved by further study, since I myself see the absurdity of my own previous subjective views. On the other hand, what I regard as mere talk, and others treat as the words of the sages, may have its absurdity revealed when it is applied in practice and thus no longer deceive the world. I also have a tendency of falling into such bad habits, which I ought to guard against in the future; I must devote all my efforts to exploring the great ultimate principles. The fruit of such exploration will be sufficient to explain everything. On the other hand, supporting details are like leaves and branches on which one should not waste time and energy. What do you think, sir?

The sages can master ultimate principles; the worthies[7] can master something of ultimate principles; fools can master nothing of ultimate principles. The sages

7. Mao evokes here the conventional Chinese hierarchy of "sage" *(shengren),* the truly exceptional individual such as Confucius who is intuitively wise, and "worthy" *(xianren),* a man of excellent virtue. Both of these, like the "superior man" or "Confucian gentleman" *(junzi)* referred to below, belong to an entirely different category from the "fool" *(yuren),* or the "petty man" *(xiaoren).*

have deep understanding of heaven and earth, and insight into the present, past, and future; they thoroughly understand the phenomena of the three realms. For example, Confucius said, "The affairs of a hundred ages can be known,"[8] and Mencius declared, "When a Sage shall again arise, he will not diverge from my words."[9] Confucius' and Mencius' answers to questions from their disciples were not difficult to understand. An ignorant person may be amazed and find them miraculous, not realizing that there is no clever artifice involved, but simply that they have grasped a great ultimate principle. By holding on to it, one can deal with all things, can master all situations, encompass all. How can this be a clever artifice? (Only theologians regard as gods ordinary individuals such as Christ, Mohammed, and Sakyamuni, and worship them as such.)

If we want everyone to act in accordance with his own true views, instead of blindly following other people's definitions of right and wrong, we must popularize philosophy. Today I see people being used by the strong; they may talk eloquently, but they have lost their subjective spirit; they confuse and manipulate things in the same way commercial goods and construction are handled. What a great pity! Everybody has philosophical views; naturally, when everyone's heart is at peace, conflicts are calmed, and truth prevails, the absurdities of the masses will die out of themselves.

Someone asked me why there were a lot of fools but very few wise men. As for the old and decadent, their intelligence has dimmed; they are incapable of accepting the truth even if you tell them; they are incapable of movement even if you urge them. This is only natural, and one must not be surprised. Among the young, however, there are many who pay no attention to reason, and merely want to act confusedly. This is like someone who goes to a philosophy class but dozes off and hears nothing. Life and death are momentous issues. They do not even seek to understand these questions, but instead concern themselves only with today's petty conflicts. They will not gain wisdom. I think most such individuals are pitiable. They do not care for reason; having been molded by thousands of years of an evil society, they are incapable of being their own masters. This is really pitiful. Several things are always fighting each other within their hearts: life and death is one of them; striving for personal gain is another; and praise and blame is yet another. There are several alternatives at the moment; are we going to be limited to these things? If we are, then we will be

8. A reference to the *Analects*, II, XXIII (Legge, Vol. I, p. 153). The passage reads: "Tsze-chang asked whether the affairs of ten ages after could be known. Confucius said, 'The Yin dynasty followed the regulations of the Hsia: wherein it took from or added to them may be known. The Chau dynasty has followed the regulations of the Yin: wherein it took from or added to them may be known. Some other may follow the Chau, but though it should be at the distance of a hundred ages, its affairs may be known.' "

9. *Mencius*, II, I, II, 17 (Legge, p. 192). Mao has modified this quotation slightly; the second clause of the original reads: "he will certainly follow my words."

pacing back and forth at a crossroads, without a real standard to be used as the criterion of judgment. This is akin to the weeds on the wall that lean both ways in the wind; it is by accident that they lean toward evil; it is also by chance that they lean toward the good. A loosely defined social sanction should praise and encourage the good, and punish and restrain the evil. All those placed under such a sanction will be more likely to be good than evil. Today, behavior such as observing chastity, rearing children, repairing bridges, and fixing roads, or even virtues like filial piety, loyalty to friends, love of one's neighbor, and generous charity are no more than blind acts. Although these deeds are laudable, in terms of the psychology of those enforcing the sanctions as well as those being sanctioned, they are rather aimless and are not based upon knowledge of the great ultimate principles of the universe. If we want to make these foolish people learn wisdom, this can only be done by popularizing philosophy.

When little people burden superior men, the gentlemen should be benevolent and seek to save these little people. Politics, law, religion, rites, systems, and all the superfluous agriculture, industry, and commerce that keep us constantly occupied day by day are not established for the superior man; rather, they are established for the little people. Superior men already possess lofty wisdom and morality; if there were only superior men in the world, then politics, law, rites, systems, as well as superfluous agriculture, industry, and commerce could all be abolished, and would be of no use. It is different when there are too many little people. This world's management follows the criterion of the majority, at the expense of the part made up of superior men; that is how little people burden superior men. But the little people are pitiable. If the superior men care only for themselves, they may leave the crowd and live like hermits. There were some who did so in ancient times, such as Chao and Xu.[10] If they have compassionate hearts, then they [recognize] the little people as fellow countrymen and a part of the same universe. If we go off by ourselves, they will sink lower and lower. It is better for us to lend a helping hand, so that their minds may be opened up and their virtue be increased, so that we may share the realm of the sages with them. By that time all under heaven will become sages. There will be no unenlightened. We may destroy all secular laws, breathe the air of harmony, and drink the waves of a crystal clear sea. Confucius entertained this idea, so he set up great peace as his goal, but did not do away with the two realms of chaos and tranquility.[11] The great

10. Chao Fu and Xu You were philosophers and hermits of ancient times who were said to have refused the throne when it was offered first to Chao, and then to Xu, by the legendary Emperor Yao.

11. Great peace *(taiping),* and the related term of great harmony *(datong)* are referred to frequently by Mao throughout this volume. The realms of chaos and of tranquility (or rising peace) are the first two of the three stages of history as laid down in the *Gongyang Commentary on the Spring and Autumn Annals*, which precede the final stage of great peace. Kang Youwei elaborated a variant of this idea in his *Zhongyong zhu* (Doctrine of the Mean Annotated), a work of 1901 which Mao may well have read.

harmony is our goal. Those who are virtuous, meritorious, and eloquent do their best to serve the world. We have compassion within our hearts, which makes us strive to save the little people.

There are many points about the school with which I am dissatisfied. I'll write again in the future to discuss this with you in detail. Now I am not too far from graduation. After graduation, I think it is better to continue to study than to teach or work. Of course, I have not yet established my will. I have not the slightest idea what to do about the universe, human life, the state, or education, so how could I go about teaching or working? Forcing myself to do so would be a pure waste of time. I find it all extremely confusing, and what has its source in confusion will certainly result in confusion. This worries me. I have long thought about setting up a private school, which would combine the strengths of classical education and modern schools. Provisionally, the course would be limited to three years, and the curriculum would aim at general familiarity with the essentials of Chinese studies. Afterwards the students would go abroad to study and learn the essentials of Western thought; then they would return to live in the private school, to deepen their preparation. Those who harbor such ideals would stay for four years. This should be put into practice a year from now, but the foundation has not yet been established. There are three worries. First, people. There must be teachers and friends in order not to feel lonely and isolated. Second, location. It must be convenient to reach, but not too noisy. Third, money. Those from poor families cannot afford to live there. Those who do not teach lose part of their income and increase their expenditures. Of the three worries, this is the most troublesome. However, if we want to imitate Master Yan's frugality[12] and Mr. Fan's [art of] cooking the rice he painted on paper, then we may just about be able to support this project. I wonder whether you, sir, would approve of this? As you are also preparing for the advancement of your own studies, I hope you will show me your plans, so that I may use them as a model. Your thoughts are profound and your writings far-reaching. Please express your thoughts at length; I shall never be wearied.

Respectfully submitted by your
fellow-villager
Zedong

12. Regarding the frugality of Confucius' favorite disciple, Yan Hui, see the *Analects*, IV, IX (Legge, Vol. I, p. 188), and Han Yu's commentary, note 255 to Mao's "Classroom Notes" of 1913.

Zhang Kundi's Record of Two Talks with Mao Zedong[1]

(September 1917)

I

Today is Sunday. I had an appointment with Cai Hesen,[2] Mao Runzhi, and Peng Zehou[3] to take a twelve-hour trip. After breakfast, Mr. Peng crossed the river to invite Mr. Cai to join us at Fishing Bay Marketplace. Mr. Mao and I arrived at the marketplace first. After a short while, Mr. Peng came alone, telling us that Mr. Cai could not make the trip because he was moving house today. The idea of taking this trip had originated with Mr. Cai; I agreed and discussed it with Peng and Mao. That all of us could not go together was truly unexpected. The three of us walked along the railway track. The weather was hot, but fortunately a strong wind relieved the heat somewhat. After walking more than ten *li*, we stopped for a break at a teahouse beside the railway, drinking the tea to quench our thirst and sitting for a moment before setting off again. After another ten *li* and more, we passed Datuopu. We walked six *li* more before we stopped at a restaurant for lunch. A big bowl of rice cost fifty copper cash, and a bowl of vegetables cost twenty cash. The three of us together ate five big bowls of rice and five bowls of pickled vegetables. We took a short rest after lunch and thought of having a swim in the big pond behind the restaurant. But since the water in the pond was shallow, only up to the hip, we went back to the restaurant to pick up our gear, and continued our trip. In less than three *li*, we found a boat dock, where the

---

1. This is an extract from Zhang Kundi's diary. Zhang Kundi (1894–1932), *hao* Zhipu, was born in Yiyang, Hunan Province. He was a student of Hunan First Normal School and a member of the New People's Study Society who went to France in 1919 on the work-study scheme. He was deported by the French government in the winter of 1921 for participating in communist activities, and joined the Chinese Communist Party in 1922. He was executed in 1932.

2. Cai Hesen (1895–1931), alternative name Cai Linbin, was born in Xiangxiang *xian*, Hunan. He was a classmate and close friend of Mao Zedong at First Normal School, and one of the principal organizers of the New People's Study Society. He went to France in 1919 on the work-study scheme, and joined the Chinese Communist Party after he was deported and sent back to China in October 1921. Thereafter he was a leading figure in the Party until his execution in 1931.

3. Peng Zehou has not been identified.

water was clear and deep. The three of us had a swim together, though I was hampered by the fact that I am not very good in the water. After that, we walked fourteen *li* and reached our destination as the sun was beginning to set in the west. Taking a rock-paved path on the back side of the mountain, we climbed the mountain, the clear waters of the Xiang River just below, and the beautiful peaks of the mountain called Zhaoshan rising above. On the mountain, there is a temple, called "Zhaoshan Temple," in which there are three or four monks. We told them that as it was very late we would like to spend the night in the temple. At first, the monks would not accede to our request, so we thought of sleeping outside in the woods. Later, the monks allowed us to spend the night in the temple, and the idea of sleeping outside was abandoned. After supper, the three of us went down the front of the mountain and took a swim in the Xiang River. Following our swim, we sat on the beach and talked. A cool breeze dispelled the heat, and the rippling waves of the river accompanied our talk like music coming from an unknown source. After quite a long time, we returned to the temple by the same path, talking as we climbed, oblivious to the precipitousness of the slope. The monks were waiting for us at the front gate of the temple. Under the bright starlight, the trees were a deep green and seemed full of vitality. Soon, we went into the temple and followed the monks to a guestroom. They pointed to a huge bed to sleep on and lent us one small cotton quilt. Outside our room, there was a small pavilion, to which we went to enjoy the cool air. With a south wind blowing sporadically, the three of us sat there for a long time, talking and laughing and thoroughly enjoying ourselves. We talked for a long time, benefiting a lot from each other's company. Mr. Mao said, "The Westerners have a highly advanced material civilization, but as it is limited to clothing, food, and housing, it provides only for the development of fleshly desires. If human life is just having enough of these three things, clothes, food, and housing, then human life has no value." "We must figure out the easiest way," he continued, "to solve the economic problem. Only then can we realize our ideal of cosmopolitanism." Mr. Mao also declared, "If man's mental and physical powers are concentrated together on one task, no task will be difficult to accomplish." I agreed completely with what he said. Besides, I have long believed in the theory of the power of the human mind. Thus I mentioned Tan Sitong's book *Renxue*,[4] in

---

4. Tan Sitong (1865–1898), *zi* Fusheng, *hao* Zhuangfei, Hunanese philosopher and reformist, was perhaps the most radical of the three leading figures of the Reform Movement of 1898. In 1894 he founded a society for the promotion of western learning, and in 1897 he edited Hunan's first newspaper, the *Xiangxue xinbao* (Hunanese Study), which was published every ten days. Following the collapse of the reforms, he did not flee the country like Kang and Liang, and was executed by the Qing authorities. *Renxue* (The Study of Benevolence), written during the last two years of his life, was the most sweeping and systematic of his attacks on traditional Confucian attitudes and customs. In it, he called for "complete Westernization." Mao Zedong admired Tan's courage in dying for his ideals, and was significantly influenced by his thought.

which he says that the mental abilities can be trained and tempered. My friend Dingcheng[5] also agreed. Moved by the clear night, Mr. Peng told us about his long-cherished desire to be a monk and also said that, some years later, he would invite all of us to come to study on some famous mountain. Mr. Mao and I also have such a desire, but Mao's desire is much stronger than mine. I, too, was moved at that time, and the lines came to me:

> Wind blowing in the trees, music of the heavens,
> Desires and rewards cannot be perceived, and shed their forms.

But I did not reveal them to my friends. It was deep night before we slept.

Written on the seventeenth
(September 16)

II

Yesterday afternoon, I went swimming with Mr. Mao Runzhi. After swimming, we went to Mr. Cai Hesen's place at Mount Lu. As it was near dusk, we stayed for the night. We had a rather long talk in the night. Mr. Mao Runzhi said, "At present, the Chinese people are indolent and indulge in false mutual admiration. They are slavish in character and narrow-minded. How can our people produce great revolutionaries in the domains of philosophy and ethics, like Tolstoy in Russia, who will cleanse our people of the old ideas, and explore the new thought?" I thought that what he said was very true. The Chinese people are gloomy, stubborn, and unaware of their own backwardness. They have become accustomed to acting like the master at home, but slavishly outside. Where shall we find men like Russia's Tolstoy, who will break through the net of appearances and develop their ideal world? Men who, in their personal lives and in their writings, have sought after truth and abided in the truth, not caring what others might say. Tan Sitong in the past, and Chen Duxiu today, are such people; their spirit and courage are great, and truly, today's common scholar cannot compare with them. Mr. Mao proposed, too, that all the anthologies of prose and poetry published since the Tang and Song dynasties be burned in the same fire. He also advocated a family revolution and a revolution of teachers and students. Revolution does not mean using troops and arms, but replacing the old with the new.

Today, we got up very early. Mr. Cai, Mr. Mao, and I climbed Mount Yuelu by the slope beside Cai's house. We followed the ridge until we reached the

5. Zou Yiding (1894–1919), *zi* Dingcheng, was born in Xiangyin, Hunan. A graduate of First Normal School, he was a member of the New People's Study Society. He was soon recruited to teach Chinese at the evening school organized by Mao. (See below, the *Evening School Journal*, Vol. I, November 1917, in which his name appears.)

academy,[6] and then came back down the mountain. A cold, strong mountain wind came up, and the air was clean and crisp. Bathed by the air and the wind, our minds were lucid, and the worries of the ordinary world seemed far away. It was eleven o'clock in the evening when we got back.

On returning from Mount Lu, I wrote a letter to my family. I took the letter to Jin city and asked Mr. Hu[7] to take it back with him.

(September 23)

6. The reference is to the Yuelu Academy, one of the most famous academies of the Song dynasty, founded in 976.

7. This individual has not been identified.

Chinese Language Teaching Plan (Second-Year Chinese Language Class) [1]

(September 1917)

Text: Volume Four, Lesson Ten, "Clothing" (review).

Review:

1. Reading: individually, by rows, and all together.

2. Grammar: (The original text: As material for making clothes, silk may be used, or cotton cloth. Silk is very expensive, and moreover cannot be washed frequently. Hence, for making everyday clothes, it is better to use cotton cloth.)

> 1) Dividing into sentences: the first three phrases, which point out that there are two kinds of material for clothes, namely, silk and cotton cloth, form the first sentence; the two middle phrases, which simply state the defects of silk, that it is expensive and cannot be washed frequently, and lead to what comes after, form the second sentence; the last two phrases, which draw out the conclusion of the whole passage that it is better to use cotton cloth for making clothes, form the third sentence, ending the whole text.[2]
>
> 2) Change the order: As material for making clothes, cotton cloth may be used, or silk. Silk cannot be washed frequently, and furthermore it is expensive. (balance omitted)

---

1. This is the teaching plan that Mao Zedong wrote during his practice teaching in the primary school attached to Hunan First Provincial Normal School. There is no indication on the original manuscript as to when it was written. Mao's classmate Li Duanlun made the following note about this practice teaching on September 22, 1917: "Mr. Mao's attitude, teaching method, and language are all excellent. The only pity is that he does not yet have an appropriate position." This teaching plan must have been prepared shortly before that date.

2. The sentence structure of the translation, and the division into phrases and clauses, can obviously not follow exactly that in the Chinese, but we have tried to adopt the same pattern as much as possible, so that Mao's points can be understood. Similarly, in points 2 (2) and 2 (3), and 3 (1) and 3 (2), we have made the English wording identical with that in the translation of the "original text" whenever the Chinese was the same.

3) Add and subtract words and phrases: The material for making clothes may be either silk or cotton cloth. Silk is very expensive, and furthermore, it is difficult to wash it frequently. So for everyday clothes, it is better to use cotton cloth.

3. Selected examples:

1) For the talented pupils: As material for making umbrellas, cotton cloth may be used, or paper. Cotton cloth is very expensive, and moreover is not good against wind and rain. Hence, for making umbrellas for everyday use, it is better to use paper.

2) For the less able pupils: The material for building the fence around the well may be wood, or rock.

4. Supplementary information not covered in the text for the use of the teacher:

1) Advocate the virtue of frugality (use cotton cloth instead of silk).

2) Encourage the use of products made within the country (Chinese cotton cloth).

3) Add a discussion of cloth made from animal hair (sheep's wool, ox hair, pig hair).

5. The addition and subtraction of numbers:

1) Eight feet of white cloth and nine feet of blue cloth make how many feet of cloth in all?

2) Nine square ink sticks and seven round ink sticks make how many ink sticks in all?

3) Of sixteen sheets of paper, seven have been used up. How many sheets are left?

4) Of eighteen pupils, nine (words missing). How many pupils are left?

5) A trip is fifteen *li* long, and seven *li* (words missing). How many *li* are left?

Public Announcement Inviting Students to the Workers' Evening School[1]

(October 30, 1917)

Gather round, all of you, and listen to me say a few words in the spoken language:

What is the greatest source of inconvenience from which you all suffer? Do you all know what it is? As the popular saying goes, you can't write what is said, you can't read what is written, and you can't do figures. All of you are men, and yet from this perspective, aren't you just like sticks or stones? So all of you demand a bit of knowledge; you want to be able to write a few characters, recognize a few characters, and do a bit of arithmetic. Only thus can you rid yourselves of this inconvenience. Though this is the case, all you workers must toil, and you are also without anyone to teach you. How, then, can you obtain this really hard to get thing? Now there is an excellent way to do it, for we of First Normal have set up an evening school. We had a great many students during the first half of the year. Probably some of you have come to those classes. This evening school is set up especially for you workers. There are two hours of classes every evening, from Monday to Friday. We teach writing letters and adding up accounts — things which all you gentlemen have need of all the time. We provide the instruction completely free of charge. Attending classes at night will also not interfere in the least with your work. If there are any of you who want to study, hurry along to the Normal School in the course of the next week to sign up at the registry. Think about it, all of you. Why are we doing this?

---

1. This announcement was issued by the Students' Society (Xueyouhui) of First Normal School. Originally called the Skills Society (Jinenghui), when it was set up in 1913 by the principal of the Normal School, this society had changed its name in 1915 and at the same time defined its aims as: "to perfect morality, to study education, to advance knowledge, to prepare for an occupation, to temper the body, and to unite sentiments." Mao had played a leading role in it from November 1915, but in October 1917 the organization of the society was changed so that fourth- and fifth-year students, instead of teachers, took up positions as heads of the various departments. Mao became concurrently general affairs officer and head of the department of educational research, and in this capacity he drafted the text below. For further information about the Students' Society, see the following text, dated November 1917, that dated May 29, 1918, and Li Jui [Li Rui], *The Early Revolutionary Activities of Comrade Mao Tse-tung*, (White Plains, N.Y.: M.E. Sharpe, 1977) pp. 51–65; hereafter Li Jui, *Early Mao*.

It is for no other reason than that, thinking of what you workers suffer, we want all of you to be able to write and do arithmetic. Why don't all of you gentlemen come quickly to register and attend our courses? There are those who say the times are not propitious and fear they might be violating martial law. In this respect, we can serve as your guarantors. Each person, as soon as he begins attending school, will be issued an auditor's card; if you are stopped and questioned by the military or the police, you can say that you are a student of First Normal evening school, and there will be no problem. Should, however, any difficulty arise, we will serve as your guarantors, so you can set your minds at rest on this point. Hurry along to register, and don't put it off any longer.

Evening School Journal,[1] *Volume One*

(November 1917)

It has been half a year since the first term of our school's evening course started. The teaching staff are faculty members both of the Normal School and of the higher primary school attached to it. But Mr. Zhou Weihang[2] is actually in charge. The students are divided into two classes, A and B. Each class meets two evenings a week. At the beginning, it was very lively, with an enrollment of sixty to seventy persons. After a while, however, the number gradually declined. There are three probable reasons for this. First, the students have rough jobs in different places, and few have the persistence and patience to give up their evenings. Second, because laborers do not have steady employment, and most of the students are those who have come to the province from various places looking for a job, when they leave their jobs and go elsewhere, they quit the evening school. Third, the teaching staff are the faculty members from the two parts of our school who have a heavy schedule during the daytime, and may be exhausted in the evening, or sometimes miss classes when there is a storm, and unavoidably lose some credit with the students. This situation is discussed in the report made by Mr. Zhou, which may be used as a reference for further study. There are three courses: general knowledge, arithmetic, and Chinese. Teaching materials for all three courses take the form of lectures, which are mimeographed on loose pages lesson by lesson, because there are new students joining the old students all the time. During the re-election of the students' society this term, several plans were worked out. One of them is the plan for the evening school. At the beginning of the founding resolution, we expressed the belief that education should be the ultimate goal for the Normal School. Under the circumstances currently prevailing in our country, the core of our society is truly the great majority of the people who do not have a chance to go to school. This presents a powerful obstacle to the implementation of government policies, to organizing for self-rule, to the reform of customs, and to universal education. At this moment, therefore, schools and education are extremely critical for creating a new generation of citizenry, and obtaining talented people capable of promoting development. In order to fulfill this goal, however, the obstacles have to be removed. That is one

1. The *Yexue rizhi* (Evening School Journal) is distinct from the *Xueyouhui jishilu* (Records of the Students' Society) from which the text dated May 29, 1918, is drawn.

2. Zhou Weihang, also known as Zhou Zhenkun, from Ningxiang, Hunan, was teaching at this time at First Normal School, where he had formerly been a student.

of the reasons why we set up the evening school. The Europeans and the Americans claim that they have universal education, but they still have evening schools, open-air schools, half-day schools, and school camps. Besides, they have nurseries, special schools for the deaf and blind, for the handicapped, and for mental patients. Even for those who are ineducable, they will not give up, but try to find some line that they are able to learn. Plants and trees, birds and animals all nurture and care for their own kind. Must not human beings do the same? Little men [*xiaoren*] were not originally inferior. They are not evil by nature. Some of them are out of school simply because there is some lack in their natural endowments, or they come from less fortunate circumstances. It is precisely for such people as these that the humane person should show sympathy, rather than shift the responsibility to them. This is another reason why we set up the evening school. Furthermore, we are studying education, and those of us who are in our third and fourth years have already finished the study of theory and started our practice teaching. So establishing this evening school as a place where we can do our practice teaching is like an industrial school setting up a workshop, a commercial school setting up a store, or an agricultural school setting up a farm. This is yet another reason why we set up the evening school. An even greater incentive lies in the extreme decadence of the schools at the present time, and the fact that school and society constitute two poles, two things separated by a huge gulf. Upon entering a school, the students look down on society as if they had climbed into the heavens. Society, too, looks on the schools as something sacred and untouchable. This mutual alienation and suspicion causes three evils. One is that the students cannot find jobs in society. When the students approach society, society keeps them at a distance; when the students become intimate with society, society rejects them. They can never communicate or cooperate with each other. Another evil is that society does not send its children to school. One reason for this is that the schools are not good, but the most important reason is that society does not know very much about the schools. Since the people in the schools and the people in society have in the past never communicated or exchanged views with each other, how would society know about it even if there were a good school? The third evil is that this situation has led to incidents, such as the burning of schools and the blocking of funds. If these three evils can be removed, and the misunderstandings resolved, so that society and the schools can join together, people in society will look on the students as their eyes and ears and will rely on their guidance to reap the benefits of prosperity and development. The students will look on the people in society as their hands and feet, whose help will make it possible for them to accomplish their goals. Finally, all the people in society will have graduated from school. One part of schooling will be the small school one attends for a while, and the whole of society will be the big school that one attends forever.[3]

3. The opposition between "little school" *(xiao xuexiao)* and "big school" *(da xuexiao)*

This is the very achievement we expect will result from hundreds of years of reform and progress, and that is another reason why we set up the evening school. When this proposal was made, we consulted the faculty and staff of the school, not one of whom failed to support it. Last term, the management of the evening school was therefore turned over to the students' society, because if the two schools[4] were placed on the same footing, it was feared there would be difficulties with the students and with the expenses. Consequently, one of them was placed under the sole management of the students' society, which has continued to be involved in its organization.

November 5

So far, the number of people who have registered for the evening school has reached 102. First, we put out two advertisements. The first time, in addition to posting it in the streets, we asked the police to distribute copies and had the students of Guomin School[5] take copies home and urge people to register, but there was no response for a long time. The second time, apart from printing leaflets, we wrote some big posters and put them up in conspicuous places, again without result. The total number of the people who registered, including those who registered after our first advertisement, was only nine. One reason is that society did not know anything about the school, and in spite of the advertisements, people remained skeptical. The second reason is that just putting up posters does not get the attention of the people. They paid no attention to them, just as we pay no attention to the notices posted by the government. We asked the police to distribute the advertisement for us, but there is some doubt as to whether they actually did it or not. Even if they did, since people tend to see the police as severe government officials, whom they have always feared, how could they have confidence? The third reason is that the advertisement was not distributed widely, so the people did not get a copy to read with their own eyes. Starting from October 3,[6] we rewrote the advertisement in the vernacular and distributed it ourselves. While distributing the copies to the people, we also explained the advertisement to them. They liked it very much, asking us questions one after another and shouting, "We're going to take evening classes!" From the area of Tongyuanju on both sides of the railway tracks to Hongen

---

evokes the Chinese terms for primary school and university, but it is plain that Mao is mainly concerned with the idea of life in society as a "great school," which he sought to apply half a century later, during the "Great Proletarian Cultural Revolution."

4. I.e., the Normal School itself and the workers' evening school.

5. As indicated below, Guomin School was the higher primary school attached to First Normal School. Mao himself was to become principal of this school in 1920.

6. According to *History of the Hunan First Provincial Normal School,* published in September 1918, this should read 30 instead of 3 (*Wengao,* note 3, p. 108). This fits with the ensuing text, which says that in three days a large number of students were recruited.

Temple, from Dachun Bridge on the left to Shetan Ridge and Swan Pond on the right, six hundred copies were distributed and posted in the streets with dense coverage. That is how, in less than three days, the number of applicants reached this figure.

In the evening, more than ten people, including faculty members of Guomin Higher Primary School and some of the third- and fourth-year students, gathered for a meeting to discuss how to proceed.

November 6

A notice was posted to inform the students: To all who have registered, the quota has been filled, so you must come to school. The first class will meet in Guomin School, attached to the Normal School, at seven o'clock in the evening, on the twenty-fifth day of the ninth lunar month. Please bring your own brush, ink-stick, and ink-slab. It is important that everyone be present.

November 7

A meeting was held this evening to discuss how to proceed. Another twenty or more students registered.

November 8

Twelve teachers held a conference this evening to discuss school affairs.

At the meetings on successive days, a great many matters were discussed and resolved. The main points are as follows:

1. Each class will meet for two hours three evenings a week, six hours in all. There will be three courses: Chinese, arithmetic, and general knowledge. There will be three hours for Chinese, an hour and a half for arithmetic, and an hour and a half for general knowledge. Every evening, the course in general knowledge will be taught for thirty minutes, following the Chinese and arithmetic classes. The time schedule is shown below:

Day[7]	Monday	Tuesday	Wednesday	Thursday	Friday	Saturday
Class	Class A	Class B	Class A	Class B	Class A	Class B
Time						
One and a half hours	Chinese	Chinese	Arithmetic	Arithmetic	Chinese	Chinese
	Chinese	Chinese	Arithmetic	Arithmetic	Chinese	Chinese
Half an hour	Geography (General knowledge)	Geography (General knowledge)	History (General knowledge)	History (General knowledge)	Science (General knowledge)	Science (General knowledge)

7. The days of the week are here indicated by the characters in common use in Japan, meaning (in order): moon, fire, water, wood, metal, and earth. This may reflect the influence of the several teachers who had studied in Japan.

2. For the Chinese and arithmetic courses, teaching materials will be compiled by selecting excerpts from the textbooks used in lower and higher primary schools and from miscellaneous word books and dictionaries.

3. The division into subjects of the classes in general knowledge and the schedule for them (lasting nine months in all, from the first day of the tenth month this year to the thirtieth day of the sixth month next year according to the lunar calendar) are as follows:

First three months

History
Geography
Science

Middle three months

Moral cultivation[8]
Hygiene
Industry and commerce

Last three months

Politics and law
Economics
Education

4. In each class, there are two teachers for Chinese, one for arithmetic, and three for general knowledge.

5. Each of the general knowledge teachers will be responsible for one branch of study, with specified times allotted to the individual topics. The history class, for instance, will be taught in the first three months; during the twelve sessions planned, it would be possible to cover something like twelve events.

6. The general knowledge class is meant to expand the students' general knowledge and nurture their minds. In history, for instance, the teaching should focus on the great events in every age and the most important incidents in recent years, in order to nurture an historical perspective and a patriotic spirit. (In the past, we used to learn about a number of fragments of events from legends and plays, but there was no systematic perspective or patriotic spirit.)

7. General knowledge will emphasize content. It is better to cover less material, one page each time. All illustrations and charts must be printed.

---

8. The *xiushen* which Mao had studied with Yang Changji in 1913.

8. General knowledge will emphasize spirit, as distinct from Chinese and arithmetic, which are like skills. Thus it will be the evening's entertainment, half an hour each time, to be taught in the form of lectures.

9. Since there is much to be taught in all these subjects of general knowledge, and the time is limited, it is imperative to select those things that are important and closely relevant to the students of the evening school.

10. The subjects to be taught in the Chinese class include character recognition, writing characters (paper will be handed out), writing short essays, notes, letters, etc.

11. The arithmetic class will concentrate at first on teaching the students how to use the abacus; later, there will be a bit of work on how to do written sums.

12. The teaching will mostly use a spoon-feeding style, but sometimes an effort will be made to stimulate the students' intelligence.

13. Teaching materials will be discussed and prepared by the two instructors teaching a given course.

14. The format of teaching materials shall always be left up to the teachers to decide.

15. The original manuscript or source of all teaching material must be preserved.

16. The instructors are responsible for the printing and preservation of the teaching materials. They should consult with those who are doing the copying and printing whenever necessary.

17. Those who take the reference books are responsible for their safekeeping.

November 9

Today, the evening school started classes. Yesterday afternoon, six hundred notices were printed and posted everywhere. The faculty and staff of the evening school were completely organized. The following is a list of their names:[9]

Teachers

Class A, Chinese	Zou Yiding[10]	Monday
	Ye Zhaozhen	Friday
Class B, Chinese	Peng Zongliang	Tuesday
	Tang Fuyan	Saturday
Class A, Arithmetic	Luo Zonghan	
Class B, Arithmetic	Fang Wei	
Class A, History	Mao Zedong	

9. All twenty-eight of the people listed below were at the time students at Hunan First Normal School.

10. See the note to Zhang Kundi's "Record of Two Talks" of September 1917.

Class B, History	Shan Chuanshi
Class A, Geography	Xiao Xuexiang
Class B, Geography	Liu Daikun
Class A, Science	Zhang Chao[11]
Class B, Science	Zhou Mingdi[12]

Administration

Monday	Zhang Kundi,[13] Deng Xianyou
Tuesday	Zhou Shizhao, Zeng Yilu[14]
Wednesday	Li Duanlun, Xiao Zhenyuan
Thursday	Sun Mohan, He Ti
Friday	Liu Zhan, Guo Yiqin
Saturday	Li Shengxie, Huang Qiansheng
Copying	Tian Siqing, Yang Shaobing
Printing	Zeng Zhengbang, Liao Heng

The program for the opening session was as follows:

1. The faculty and staff of the evening school gathered together at the Guomin School after supper.
2. Registration.
3. The students were tested in order to divide them into two classes, Class A and Class B, on the basis of the following criteria:

    a) Write down five street names.
    b) Write their home address and occupation.
    c) Write their own name.

4. The faculty and staff made speeches.
5. Admission cards and regulations were distributed.
6. Dismissal.

At the same time, administrative assignments were made as follows:

---

11. Zhang Chao (1892–), also known as Quanshan and Jisan, was a native of Xiangxiang, Hunan. After graduation from First Normal School he taught at the attached primary school, and continued to work in the educational field. Deceased.

12. Zhou Mingdi (1895–), also known as Xiaosan and Xiaoyan, from Xiangtan, Hunan, went to Japan in 1918 after graduating from First Normal School and enrolled at Tokyo Teachers' College.

13. For information on Zhang, see the note to his "Record of Two Talks with Mao Zedong" of September 1917.

14. Zeng Yilu (1896–), also known as Xinghuang and Zhaizhong, was a native of Wugang, Hunan. After graduating from First Normal School, he joined the New People's Study Society and went to France on the work-study program in the fall of 1919.

Registration	Zhang Chao, Li Duanlun
Testing	Zou Yiding, Ye Zhaozhen, Peng Zongliang, Tang Fuyan
Class assignments	Mao Zedong, Shan Chuanshi
Filling out admission cards	Tian Shiqing, Yang Shaobing

At 6:30, it was almost dark. The faculty and staff of the evening school arrived at Guomin School one after the other; the students started to come in; when all were assembled, the test was carried out. The items for the test were written on the blackboard. Each student was provided with a piece of paper. Some of the students wrote down everything that was required clearly and correctly; some wrote down two or three street names, and their name and address; some were not even able to write their names correctly. When the test was over, several people went around to inspect and collect the tests and lead the students into the auditorium, where they sat down. It was all finished in about one hour. All the test sheets were graded A or B, and the students were divided into the two classes, forty-four people in Class A and forty-one in Class B. Every test sheet was marked Class A or Class B. After that, all the students lined up and bowed three times to the national flag and the portrait of Confucius; the faculty, staff, and students bowed to each other once. Mr. Fang Weixia, chief dean of the Normal School and acting head of the students' society, delivered some words of guidance, mainly encouraging the students to study hard by citing Zhu Maichen[15] and Li Mi[16] as examples. Then Mr. Zhou Weihang, the director of the evening school, also made a speech, explaining everything about the school. The two of them introduced the faculty and staff of the evening school, praising them for their ability to write, to calculate, to get things done, for their commitment to teaching, and so on. The students assigned to Class A were called by name to pick up their admission cards and then stood in a line on the left, across the front. The students of Class B were then called up by name to pick up their admission cards and stand in a line on the right. The assignment to classes having been completed, the course instruction manuals were distributed to the students. Mao Zedong explained the items in the course instruction manuals one by one. At the end, the whole assembly was dismissed and went out. On this occasion, the

15. Zhu Maichen (? – 115 B.C.), *zi* Wengzi, was originally a poor woodcutter who read books whenever he could take a break from his work. By diligent study, he became governor of Guiji in Zhejiang Province, and ultimately minister of state.

16. Li Mi (582–618), *zi* Xuansui and Fazhu, was originally from Liaodong. Though he inherited the title of Duke of Pushan from his father, his family was too poor to send him to school, and he earned his living by herding cattle for other people. Every day he would hang books on the horns of the cattle and read while riding on their backs. After participating in several rebellions, he submitted in 618 to the founder of the Tang dynasty and was ennobled as duke. Unsatisfied with his lot, he again raised the standard of revolt and was slain.

registration went better than anyone had expected, being very lively, yet very orderly. Of the students this time, three-tenths were thirteen- or fourteen-year-old youngsters. Some of them had gone to lower primary school for a year or two. So many of these children who are not in school would remain illiterate forever if this evening school did not exist to rescue them. Countless middle-aged people who had missed the chance to finish school have also been asking permission to register since the day before yesterday, the deadline set for registration. Because they are prevented from doing so by the limit on the number of available slots, they are like infants, crying to be fed.

The course instruction manual is reproduced below:

Our school has begun this evening, and class assignments have been made. Now you are students of this evening school. In two days, next Monday (that is, on the eighth day of the ninth month, according to the lunar calendar), you must attend classes. Here are explanations regarding various matters:

1. The evening school is divided into two classes, A and B.

Class A will meet on Mondays, Wednesdays, and Fridays (i.e., on the twenty-eighth and thirtieth days of the ninth month, and the second day of the tenth month, according to the lunar calendar; the ensuing days can be calculated similarly).

Class B will meet on Tuesdays, Thursdays, and Saturdays (i.e., on the twenty-ninth of the ninth month and the first and third of the tenth month, according to the lunar calendar, and so on).

2. Classes will meet for two hours every evening, from seven to nine o'clock.
3. There are three courses, including Chinese, arithmetic, and general knowledge.
4. The teaching materials and exercise books will be provided by the school.
5. You must bring your own brush and ink-stick to class.
6. Whenever coming to class, students may dress to suit their convenience. There is no need to dress up.
7. Every student will be issued a card for admission to classes.
8. The school has already sent a letter to the police, requesting protection. You do not have to be afraid when you come to class or go home.

November 10

Twelve reference books were purchased. Here is the list:

The Five-Character Epigrams, Young Student's Treasury, Children's Letter Writing, A Guide to Arithmetic, Chinese-Western Everyday Words, Easy Words, Elementary Words, A Comprehensive Dictionary, A Dictionary of Four-Character Phrases, A Dictionary of Six-Character Phrases, Shortcuts You Should Know.

In addition, the following reference books were obtained from the school library the day before yesterday:

Textbook and Teaching Method for Chinese in Lower and Higher Primary School, sixty copies.

Textbook and Teaching Method for Arithmetic in Higher Primary School, thirteen copies.

Textbook and Teaching Method for History in Higher Primary School.

Textbook and Teaching Method for Geography in Higher Primary School.

Textbook and Teaching Method for Science in Higher Primary School.

After the roll call, the twelve members of the administrative staff held a meeting in the office of the students' society and made decisions on the following matters:

1. Four lamps will be placed in the classroom, one at the front door and one at each of the three side doors.

2. The evening school will hire one janitor, who will be in charge of supplying tea, and oil for the lamps, and doing other things. Guomin School will designate another janitor to be on call when necessary.

3. The faculty and the administrative staff will go to the evening classes together, so that the students will not be kept waiting long.

4. The administration will adopt a strict attitude, so as to strengthen the students' trust.

5. The teaching material will be distributed by the administration, which will also prepare a student roll book to record attendance.

6. Students will be told to shake out their rain gear, place it under their desks, and look after it themselves.

7. The students will use the restrooms in the street when the weather is good.

8. It is the responsibility of the administration to keep an eye on the clock and ring the bell.

9. When the work is over every evening, administrative staff should brief those on duty the following day and turn the attendance book over to them.

November 11

Yesterday, the notice was posted: Students who have not yet registered will be allowed to take a make-up test this evening. Assignments to Class A and Class B, as determined the night before last, were also listed.

At seven o'clock this evening, the make-up test was conducted. Forty-four people who had registered the night before last did not show up. Ten [new] people came tonight.

November 12

Class A attended courses. [Blank] were present; [blank] were absent.[17] Zou Yiding, the Chinese teacher, came and taught lesson one, "Savings." At the end, he taught four extra sentences to the students. First he carefully explained the difficult characters and their meanings; then he read them aloud and had the

17. These two figures are missing from the original document.

students read after him. After this, he gave each student two sheets of exercise paper, one with a grid of square boxes. When one hour and thirty minutes had passed, the bell rang for a ten-minute break. Xiao Xuexiang came to conduct the general knowledge of geography class. He talked about the main features of the five continents and distributed a map outline to each student. Because there was so much to cover, the class ran over for about half an hour. Zhang Kundi and Deng Xianyou were the administrative staff on duty.

The roll call was taken after the break was over (the roll call was taken at this time because the students straggled in one after the other at the beginning of the class).

At the beginning and end of the class, students were asked to stand up and bow to the teacher. Brief instructions were given beforehand.

At the beginning of their classes, Zou and Xiao were introduced to the students (by Mao Zedong).

When the class was over, Mao Zedong told everybody: You must not make a lot of noise. You should attend every class. Whoever skips class three times will be dismissed, and the slot will be given to someone else. You may use the outside restrooms. When it rains, you should put your rain gear under your chairs and look after it yourselves. Today, some people did not bring their own brushes and ink-sticks. Be sure to bring them next time. You may take the exercise paper with you and finish it at home, but bring it here next time because it will be graded A or B.

The class lasted more than two hours. The students listened very attentively.

There were four kerosene lamps in the classroom, but two of them were not bright. The lamps were in the four corners of the room, so it was rather dark in the middle of the room. Another lamp should be added.

Several of our classmates came to observe.

The students drank tea during the break.

During the geography class, the students were told to correct wrong characters in their text first. The teacher drew a map on the blackboard and showed the students a globe.

The teaching materials had not been punctuated in advance. The students added the punctuation in class (as dictated by the teacher).

The teaching materials for the geography class were not good. The characters were too small, and not clear.

November 13

The B class met. Forty people were present. Peng Zongliang conducted the Chinese class, while Liu Daikun conducted the general knowledge of geography class. In the Chinese class, lesson one was "Cheng Palace," along with some proverbs. The geography lesson was the same as for the A class. Zhou Shizhao and Zeng Yilu were the administrative staff on duty.

A special martial law was imposed in the provincial capital. Sentry guards were deployed all the way to Shetan Ridge. The students were told to come to class earlier than usual. At the same time, the school sent a written request to the provincial government asking for protection and notified the students [of the B class] about the various regulations, as in the case of the A class.

As the educational level of the students in the B class is rather low, most of them do not read much Chinese.

Some students of the A class were shouting along the railway tracks after they left school last night. The police had something to say about this, so we made a point of warning the students of the B class about it.

November 14

The A class met. Luo Zonghan conducted the arithmetic class, explaining different ways of calculating, the basic idea of addition, and the Arabic numerals. Mao Zedong conducted the class in general historical knowledge and talked about the major events of the different dynasties and the achievements of remote antiquity. Four students had not brought their own abacuses, so we borrowed some temporarily from the primary school. The class was dismissed half an hour early, because of the martial law. Li Duanlun and Xiao Zhenyuan were the administrative staff on duty.

After three days of experimenting, it seems that the Chinese class is too much and too difficult. The fact that there is too much can be remedied by reducing the quantity of material taught; the fact that it is too difficult can be remedied by using the common language[18] instead (intermediate between spoken and classical Chinese). The load for the general knowledge classes is also too much (meaning the written material). Fewer written materials should be used, and in the commentary on them, the vernacular should be employed to explain things in a few simple sentences. Don't give the teaching materials to the students at the beginning, just use your own heads to lecture. Toward the end of the class, it will be sufficient to read the commentary through once cursorily. This method was used for a change in today's history class, and the atmosphere seemed to be much more alive.

Today's arithmetic class, however, seemed to be too simple. When the students were asked how many of them knew division, no fewer than nineteen raised their hands. Thus, the degree of difficulty should be gradually increased.

Tonight, everyone was provided with a piece of exercise paper for arithmetic.

Principles should be explained in depth, while the language and characters used should be simple (the view of Mr. Zhou, the director).

---

18. *Tongsuyu.*

On the Occasion of a Memorial Meeting for Students of Hunan First Normal School Who Died of Illness[1]

(1917)

Wherefore did seven of our fellow students die?
Merely for lack of a ten-minute exercise break!

1. During the course of this one year (1917), seven students at Hunan First Normal School died of various illnesses. This aroused the indignation of certain students and teachers against the school authorities who, they felt, callously ignored the students' need for physical exercise to the extent of denying them even a ten-minute exercise break between classes.

Mourning Couplet for a Student

(1917)

Rather than drift through an ignoble existence, a life of no account,
Struggle to the death, a death more than worth mourning.

In Praise of Swimming[1]

(ca. 1917)

Surely if I lived two hundred years,
I'd thrash a wake of three thousand miles.[2]

1. This couplet is all that Mao himself could remember in later years of a longer poem on the same theme. See Mao's note to his poem "Changsha" of autumn 1925. These "author's notes" *(zuozhe zizhu)* are to be found in all recent Chinese editions, including *Mao Zedong shici duilian jizhu* (Annotated Edition of Mao Zedong's Poems and Couplets) (Changsha: Hunan wenyi chubanshe, 1991) (hereafter *Poems and Couplets*), which, as indicated in the "Note on Sources and Conventions" (above, p. xliv), we have taken as our basic text for Mao's poetical writings. (We also follow that source in dating this couplet.) Mao's notes are not commonly reproduced in English versions of his poems, but all of them relating to poems written before October 1949 will be included in our edition. "Changsha," and the note containing this couplet, will appear in Volume II.

2. A reference to the first chapter of the *Zhuangzi*, which Mao had studied in 1913 (see note 217 to the "Classroom Notes" and the accompanying text). The relevant sentence reads: "When the P'eng travels to the South Ocean, the wake it thrashes on the water is three thousand miles long" (Graham, *Chuang-tzu*, p. 43). As Graham puts it, the pieces in this section are "on the theme of soaring above the restricted viewpoint of the worldly."

In Answer to Mr. Xia Mo'an[1]

(1917)

Birds chirp and chirp on the poplar's green branches—
  Is spring coming or is spring going?
Frogs croak and croak in the green grassy pond—
  Is this public or is this private?[2]

1. Xia Mo'an was from Anhua county, Hunan, where he was head of the Education Commission. In the autumn of 1917, while on a study tour investigating conditions in the countryside there, Mao and Xiao Zisheng went to call on him. Xia was reluctant to receive them at first, but changed his attitude after observing the sincerity and unusual manner of the visitors. This couplet is the result of Xia's challenging Mao to "answer" or "match" the first line of his own composition.

2. Here Mao is throwing a barb at his host for his conceited attitude by referring to a story about Emperor Hui of the Jin, a figure known for his ignorance and stupidity. Strolling through the gardens on the outskirts of Luoyang shortly after the beginning of the summer rains, the Emperor heard frogs croaking. He asked his attendants: "Is this call in an official capacity or a private capacity?"

1918

Advertisement Regarding Evening School Enrollment[1]

(March 2, 1918)

—Students enrolled last year may register in the reception room of the normal school.

—Any new students wishing to attend the evening school, regardless of their age or how many characters they know, may register in the reception room of the normal school and write down their name, address, occupation, age, and other personal information.

—Classes begin on the fifth day of the second month according to the lunar calendar. When you come for registration, bring your own brush and ink-stick. Classes will take place in Guomin School, which is next to the Normal School.

—Classes will last two hours every evening, from 7:00 to 9:00;

—Classes will run six evenings a week this year, every night with no breaks;

—No tuition will be charged, and the teaching materials will be provided;

—Every evening in the evening school, people are welcome to listen in whenever there are empty seats.

---

1. The entry for March 8 in *The Journal of the Evening School Run by the Students' Society of the First Hunan Provincial Normal School*, Volume I, published in 1918, from which this text has been taken, also contains the following explanation: "The advertisement was first written by Mr. Mao Zedong on March 2, but it was recorded in the journal later."

Seeing Off Tate Uichirō[1] *on His Journey to the East*

(An old-style poem with seven characters to the line)

(1918)

The clouds have parted, and Mount Heng once again stands revealed;
  the sky is no longer overcast.[2]
The mantis and the phoenix[3] have appeared in the spring trees.

Lofty young talents such as Qu and Jia[4]
Were drawn together here by the majestic and spectacular scenery.

---

1. Tate Uichirō (meaning something like "he who ranges over the universe") was the Japanese-style name taken by Luo Zhanglong (1896–), born Luo Aojie, *zi* Zhongyan, *hao* Wenxian. A native of Liuyang, Hunan, and a graduate of the Changjun Middle School, Luo was one of the founders of the New People's Study Society. In May 1915, he had gone to First Middle School in Changsha to visit a friend, and had seen there the letter which Mao had written, using the pseudonmym "Twenty-eight stroke student," expressing his desire to meet congenial spirits. (On this episode, see the note to Mao's letter of September 27, 1915, to Xiao Zisheng.) On returning to his own school, Luo immediately wrote a reply, signing it Tate Uichirō. In the spring of 1918, in accordance with a decision of the New People's Study Society, Luo was preparing to go to Japan. The Society gave a farewell dinner party in his honor in the outskirts of Changsha, and on that occasion Mao Zedong wrote this poem for Luo, addressing him by his Japanese-style name, and signing it with his own pseudonym, "Twenty-eight stroke student." On May 7, 1918, the anniversary of the Twenty-one Demands, the Japanese authorities beat up patriotic Chinese students in Tokyo. When he arrived in Shanghai, Luo joined the widespread protest movement against this action, and then, abandoning his plan to visit Japan, went to Beijing instead, where he studied the humanities in the Beijing University Literature Department. He joined the Chinese Communist Party in 1921.

2. Mount Heng is one of the five sacred mountains of China, located to the southwest of Changsha. There is also an allusion here to a poem about clearing skies written by the Tang poet Han Yu while climbing Mount Heng.

3. These are the names of two similarly shaped small peaks located near Changsha.

4. Qu Yuan (c. 340–278 B.C.), original name Qu Ping, *zi* Yuan, was a native of the state of Chu. After enjoying high office, he was dismissed as a result of the intrigues of rivals. He thereupon expressed his feelings in the famous lament *Li sao*. As already

Your leaving inspires me to lift up my voice in song,
Henceforth the *kunpeng*[5] will hit the waves and start its journey.

The waters of Lake Dongting and the Xiang River have risen to meet
the skies,
And the great warship[6] will dash straight eastward.

For no reason I have scattered sorrow enough to fill the sky.
Fortunately it is driven ten thousand *li* away by the east wind.

What is worthy to occupy the thoughts of a true man?
He should regard the whole universe as a grain of rice.[7]

Though the seas flow turbulently, why be concerned?
Neither should one attend to the diverse and confusing affairs of human life.

But if you are mindful of your own body and spirit,
The sun and moon in your heart will shine ever brighter.

It has been five hundred years since men of talent arose,[8]
Apart from you, those in the public eye today are of no account.[9]

---

indicated, Mao had copied this poem in 1913 into the book in which he wrote his "Classroom Notes," and Qu Yuan remained one of the poets he most frequently read and cited to the end of his life. Regarding Jia Yi (200–168 B.C.), see the note to Mao's letter of December 9, 1916, to Li Jinxi.

5. This is yet another reference to the opening passage of the *Zhuangzi*. The bird called *peng* is presented there as a metamorphosis of a giant fish called the *kun*. Here Mao uses the composite name *kunpeng*, which evokes both the creature's forms. The image of the *peng* or roc striking the waves with its wings is a metaphor for a mighty will.

6. *Mengchong*, the term used by Mao, is an ancient name for a warship. Here, it refers to the steamer which will take Luo Zhanglong to Japan. The *Wengao*, and some other editions, have *chongmeng*; *Poems and Couplets* regards this as simply a typographical error.

7. This line is a conflation of two sentences from chapter 17 of the *Zhuangzi* which read as follows: "If you measure the Four Seas against heaven and earth, are they not like an anthill on the wide moors? If you measure the Middle Land against the Four Seas, is it not like a rice grain in a vast granary?" (Graham, *Chuang-tzu*, p. 145.) The Chinese term for universe, *yuzhou*, includes the character *yu* (read *u* in Japanese) which Luo Zhanglong had used in his Japanese name, and Mao probably also intended an allusion to this here.

8. An allusion to *Mencius*, II, II, XIV, 3 (Legge, Vol. II, p. 232); the relevant sentence reads: "It is a rule that a true royal sovereign should arise in the course of five hundred years, and that during that time there should be men illustrious in their generation."

9. Mao has taken the expression *lulu*, which we have rendered as "of no account," from the biography of Lord Pingyuan in the *Records of the Historian*. Yang Hsien-yi and Gladys Yang translate the relevant sentence: "You yes-men [*gong lulu*] can only reap what others have sown" (*Records of the Historian*, p. 131).

Many are the friends gathered in front of the Pinglang Palace,[10]
Narrow is the belt of water that separates Chongming Island from
the Tsushima Strait.[11]

Waiting for your letters to come from the Eastern Sea flashing like a sword,
I will turn back from the shore, while you go on.[12]

---

10. The place where the farewell dinner was held, which was also the pier for the river boats.

11. Chongming Island, located at the mouth of the Yangtze River, and Japan's Tsushima Strait are separated only by a narrow strip of water. According to the account in the *Nanshi: Chen Houzhu ji* (History of the South: Chronicles of the Later Ruler of Chen), Emperor Wen of Sui said that Sui and Chen were separated only by "a strip of water as narrow as a belt," thus comparing the Yangtze to a belt.

12. The last line draws on a passage in Chapter 20 of the *Zhuangzi*, in which a Daoist philosopher named Yiliao is advising the Marquis of Lu as to how he can escape from the cares that burden him. Mao's wording comes from the italicized sentences, but we give the whole of the relevant paragraph (Graham, *Chuang-tzu*, p. 173), in order to provide the context:

> Reduce your expenditures, lessen your desires, and even unprovided you will have enough. May my lord ford the river and drift out over the ocean, gaze into the distance beyond sight of shores, go farther and farther in ignorance where there is an end. *Those who come to see you off will all turn back from the shore. You will be far indeed from here.*

Students' Society Records *for May 10*[1]

(May 29, 1918)

On May 10, Mao Zedong and other staff members turned all the funds, equipment, books, and account records of our society over to the safekeeping of the two auditors, Mr. Yu Heng and Mr. Pi Wenguang.[2] Thus, one year's business of the society ended on this day, and the work of the former director was completed. First, this term began with a staff members' meeting on February 19 that continued carrying on the business of the society. The overall plan was: (1) that every department should carry on as in the past; (2) that a deputy director should be elected for the evening school, so the evening school can be run like a school; (3) that a sports meet and exhibition of achievements be prepared; (4) that grades be published in the school bulletin (the magazine has ceased to appear for lack of funds); (5) that more books be obtained for the library of the society; and (6) that the statutes of the association be revised. Less than a month after activities began, under the influence of the war, the retreat of the southern army to defend Hengyang and Yongxing, and the northern army's arrival and stationing of troops at our school, the students scattered.[3] The one hundred or so students who remained could not continue their studies, so just like everything else at the

---

1. The *Records of the Students' Society of First Provincial Normal School* was the object of a resolution adopted after Mao had become general affairs officer in October 1917. Its purpose was "to record current affairs, for the sake of future reference." Issue no. 2 of the *Records*, the only one which has been preserved, was written in turns by the staff members of the evening school. Originally, this text was a speech delivered by Mao Zedong at the handing-over meeting of the society on May 10. It was written into the *Records* on May 29. This issue of the *Records* also contains information about other activities carried out by Mao Zedong when he was in charge of the students' society, but since these records were written by other people, they are not included in the *Wengao*.

2. Yu Heng, *hao* Shaoqin, was from Pingjiang, Hunan Province; Pi Wenguang, *hao* Liukun, was from Yuanjiang, Hunan Province. Both of them were students of First Normal School and worked as auditors in the students' society.

3. The reference is to the war waged in Hunan in the spring of 1918 between the southern "Law-Protecting Army" and the northern warlords. The southern army was defeated, and on March 31, the northern warlords headed by Zhang Jingyao entered Changsha. Zhang's younger brother, Zhang Jingtang, quartered his troops in First Normal School. For a detailed note on Zhang Jingyao and his brothers, see the text dated January 18, 1920.

school, the business of the society came to a halt. At present, all classes under grade three will be released for a vacation because the school is unable to continue providing meals. As the students of grade four are about to graduate and leave the school, it is urgent that we find a way to let them finish as soon as possible. To this end, we are calling all staff members who are still at the school to meet with the head of the society. In addition to a formal resolution to turn the business of the society over to Mr. Yu, Mr. Pi, and the head of the society, they should discuss various issues raised by Mao Zedong and others.

The first issue is to increase the funds of the society. Nothing can be done without money. The funds of the society come mainly from three sources: first, the funds left over from the previous term; second, donations from ordinary members (schoolmates); third, contributions from sponsoring members (the faculty and staff). Of the three, the first is not very considerable, and then it is necessary to turn it over to a successor. Unless there is a special reason, this money should not be spent. The second source is the money collected, based on the statutes of the society, from the annual membership fee of twenty cents per person. Last year, the annual membership fee was decreased to 200[4] per person. The total amount collected was less than 100 strings. Paper silver currency converts to silver dollars at 30 percent of face value, while paper copper currency is worth 40 percent of its face value. The third source can generate a little more money. If each individual gives 2 *yuan*, and there are sixty contributors, the total amount could reach 120 *yuan*. But these are voluntary contributions in paper currency, so it is not possible to predict how much money will actually be collected. This year, because of the impact of the current situation, we have collected a total of only 2 *yuan*. Looking at the matter in the light of these facts, how can our society, lacking a **regular, and fairly reliable income base**,[5] carry out all of its activities, and make successful progress in reform? This year, for instance, because these funds are insufficient, we have to be frugal in everything, and some things, for which costs cannot be cut, will have to be abandoned when there is too little money. This year, we had two plans, to publish a magazine and to purchase more books for the library, but even though both of these were truly most advantageous things, they could not be done for lack of funds. Similarly, the evening school, which helps poor people who do not have a chance to go to school, and which in fact is an extremely important public service, can scarcely be run well, even if the spirit is there, because it has not really been able to establish its own independent funding, and must look to the Normal School for small donations just to survive. In addition, there is another matter, namely, the plan for an **independent office** of our society, to maintain links with schoolmates who have already graduated from our school, in order to promote the study and development of education throughout the province. This certainly

4. This must refer to copper cash, as is confirmed by the reference to 100 strings.

5. Emphasis in original.

cannot be undertaken without a large sum of money. In my view, therefore, the original rule in our statutes of **20 cents** per person for the annual membership fee should be restored, and the initiation fee of 50 cents should be doubled to **one *yuan*** in silver dollars. It should be paid along with the identity card fee by everyone on entering the school, making a total of 2 *yuan*. With one *yuan* as the initiation fee and one *yuan* as the annual subscription, a person who stays in the school for five years will receive so many benefits from the society that it is really not excessive to ask everybody to assume this obligation on entering the school. Thus, if we have two classes every year, of 60 people each, that will make 120 people, from whom we will be able to collect 240 *yuan*, moreover in cash. By thus increasing the fund for annual expenses as much as possible, we shall have more than enough. Then the money left over from the previous term, and the money donated by the sponsoring members, can be used to set up an independent society office. Thus all aspects of this matter will be adequately dealt with, the task of management will certainly not be excessive, and our successors will have the good fortune to take over and complete the work.

The next issue is to set up a communications department.[6] As specified in our statutes, the organization of our society is composed of two parts: those who are still in the school, and those who have already graduated. Thus, to maintain links with people both inside and outside the school, to encourage the exchange of ideas between new and old students, and to plan ways for combining theory and experience is of great significance. The actual situation in our society at this moment, nevertheless, is that not one of the existing fifteen departments can be expected to establish liaison with the graduates. Even the department of educational research is not really able to carry out this task. It is evident, therefore, that we have one-sidedly put the emphasis on the students who are in school, while neglecting the graduates, and the latter, though they have a deep love for their alma mater, have no way to express it. In schools in different countries, East and West, there are very strong feelings between teachers and students, and among the students themselves. They are anxious to keep in touch with each other, and opportunities for liaison are numerous. Thus, it is common for the graduates of a school to support and promote its expansion, and for schoolmates, even though living in different places, to maintain their ties, encouraging and learning from each other. For example, Yale University of the United States, which has a branch school in our province, is a case in point.[7] But for schools in our country,

6. As will be seen from Mao's discussion of the tasks of this department, it was in effect to be an office of alumni affairs. We have nevertheless preferred to translate the Chinese title more literally.

7. The branch of Yale referred to here comprises Yale University in Changsha (sometimes known as "Yale in China") and the Hunan-Yale Medical School. Both of these institutions were established jointly by the Yale Overseas Missionary Society (later known as the Yale Society), which had been organized by a group of graduates from Yale University in America, and the Hunanese gentry.

the situation is just the opposite. The students have a mechanical relationship with each other while they are in school, but once they graduate, their relationships are over, and there is no contact, no unity, and no desire whatsoever to work together out of love for their alma mater. What a pity! As a normal school, our need to maintain liaison is more urgent than in the case of other schools. In education, it is important to compare and observe what others are doing, to exchange information, and to discuss methods. Since our school is located in the provincial capital, it is the pivot of popular education for the whole province. If we make contacts effectively, and do our research properly, it will not be hard to give education a bright new outlook throughout the province. Recently, some schools, such as First United Middle School, have established alumni associations, surveyed their graduates, and displayed the results with illustrations and tables that immediately elicit memories of their old school days and inspire them to develop further. Some time ago I went to the Changjun Alumni Association, where I met the secretary, Mr. Li, and asked him about how they do this. Since my return, I have been thinking about using their method and setting up a communications department. I planned to present this idea to the administration and to my fellow schoolmates but procrastinated and never did it. Today, as we are about to leave our positions, we only hope that all of you who will take over after us will do your best to accomplish this. The broad outlines of how to go about it are sketched out below:

<u>The specific rules of a Communications Department</u>

Article One — This department is established for the specific purpose of maintaining liaison with graduates, in order to plan for educational reform and universal education.

Article Two — There shall be one director of this department, to be chosen from among the graduates who are living in the vicinity of the provincial capital. There shall also be a number of staff members, selected from among the graduates, one graduate from each class, as well as two current students in the school.

Article Three — The activities of this department shall be as follows:

1. To make preparations for an office for the society;
2. To conduct a survey of the past and present circumstances of graduates;
3. To make arrangements for graduates visiting our province;
4. To prepare and distribute reports.

Article Four — Every graduate is expected to assume the obligation of writing at least one letter a year to the society, providing us with information about himself and his places of residence, past and present, to facilitate the publication of the report. Personal information should include the following items:

1. Name;
2. Other names used;
3. Age;
4. Native place;
5. Residence;
6. Mailing address;
7. Past circumstances;
8. Present circumstances.

Article Five — The report shall include tables based on the individual reports submitted by the graduates, along with information about the recent operations and activities of the society. The report will be published and sent to the graduates.

Article Six — In accordance with the statutes, each graduate shall pay annually a membership fee of 20 cents in cash. He shall also make a donation of one percent of his income, which can be handed over directly or through another person, or be sent in the form of a postal money order.

Article Seven — These rules shall remain in effect indefinitely, but may be revised at any time.

Mao Zedong
May 29, 1918

Letter to Luo Xuezan[1]

(August 11, 1918)

To Senior Classmate Rongxi for his inspection:

I have received a letter from Mr. Cai[2] and learned that you have already sent me a reply. I can raise the 200 *yuan* for travel to Beijing and France, but the 100 *yuan* for travel to Baoding[3] I cannot raise. This is one problem. When my talented brother Cai gets to Beijing, I will discuss with him raising or borrowing the money, or if at any time I am able to get it, I will let you know. The diploma must be mailed to me immediately; if it is sent double-registered at the post office, it can't get lost. I have another point to discuss with you. You specialize in the techniques of industrial production; this seems not suitable to your talent. Your strength is in education. I, your younger brother, have discussed this with Mr. Cai and others many times; he has many friends, but few of them are engaged in primary education. Our future is rather empty, and we have no definite plans. Recently, Mr. Zhou Shizhao[4] was hired as the dean of remedial education; I deeply approve of this and feel relieved. I heard something about your assuming a teaching position at the Huang Family School;[5] I wonder whether that has become a fact. Of course, going to Baoding is one thing to do, but it is not as beneficial as engaging in education. First, education is inherently superior. Second, it facilitates the study of related subjects such as the humanities. Third, to educate the young is to build up the future support of the association. For all these reasons, it needs to be thought over. Between going to a place

1. Luo Xuezan (1893–1930), also known as Luo Rongxi, was born in Xiangtan, Hunan Province. He was one of Mao's classmates at Hunan First Normal School and later studied at Self-Study University. An early member of the New People's Study Society, in 1919 he went to France on the work-study program, but was expelled by the French government in November 1921. He joined the Chinese Communist Party on his return to China and was involved in the Hunan workers' movement. He was killed by the Guomindang in Hangzhou. (This letter was actually a postcard.)

2. Cai Hesen, Mao's intimate friend from the Normal School in Changsha. (See the note to Zhang Kundi's "Record of Two Talks with Mao Zedong" of September 1917.) At this time he was in Beijing making arrangements for the work-study in France program.

3. At this time preparatory classes for students planning to go to France on the work-study scheme were being held at the Yude Middle School in Baoding, Hebei Province.

4. See the note to Mao's letter of March 14, 1920, to Zhou Shizhao.

5. I.e., the Xiangtan Huang Family School.

afar and a new place, one ought not to decide in haste ([going to] Southeast Asia also means education, or to wait a while for the message from Southeast Asia is also another way). There are many things I will discuss with you in the future. This is only one of them; I omit the rest.

Your Younger Brother,

Zedong

Letter to Seventh and Eighth Maternal Uncles

(August 1918)[1]

To the Honored Seventh and Eighth Uncles:[2]

It has been several days since I said good-bye to you at your house and arrived in the provincial capital. I have decided to go to Beijing by boat, along with twelve or thirteen other people, on the seventh day of the month.[3] Sightseeing is the only aim of our trip, nothing else. I am deeply grateful that my mother has lived in your house for a long time, and has been well taken care of during her illness. There are not many good doctors in the countryside, and I am afraid that my mother's long illness may be difficult to cure; consequently, I had decided earlier to bring her to the provincial capital. Today, I got a special prescription from someone, which I think may be effective if administered properly. If she still does not recover, I plan to ask Runlian[4] to bring my mother to the provincial capital after the autumn harvest. I hope that you two uncles will help make this possible.

Your nephew respectfully salutes you.

---

1. This letter is undated. In the light of Mao's statement that he had decided to go to Beijing by boat, it must have been written during the first half of August 1918, before he went to Beijing for the purpose of organizing the young people from Hunan to join the work-study program in France. (See also note 3 below.)

2. The seventh uncle (on the mother's side) is Wen Zhengxing (1853–1920), *zi* Bosheng, *hao* Yuduan. The eighth uncle (also on the mother's side) is Wen Zhengying (1859–1929), *hao* Yuqin. Both of them were farmers in Tangjiatuo Township, Xiangxiang *xian*, Hunan.

3. In August 1918, Luo Xuezan wrote a letter to his grandfather, saying: "Your grandson bid farewell to you on the sixth day of the seventh month . . . , and arrived in Changsha early in the morning of the seventh day. I stayed in Changsha for a day and joined Mao Zedong and twenty other people. On the morning of the ninth day, we left by boat" for Beijing. The date on which Mao Zedong and others actually went to Beijing can therefore be taken as the ninth day of the seventh month of the lunar calendar, or August 15.

4. Runlian is the *zi* of Mao's brother Mao Zemin (1896–1943), also called Yonglian.

Marginal Notes to: Friedrich Paulsen, A System of Ethics

(1917–1918)

Introduction

1. The concept of ethics.

2. The place of ethics is among the sciences. There are two kinds of science: one mainly theoretical, the second mainly practical. The former is called the study of science, the latter is called the art of science; the former belongs just to knowledge, while the latter shows that man also uses his ability to manipulate things and make them suitable to the purposes of human life.

This says that ethics belongs to the arts.

Seen in this way, ethics without doubt belongs to the arts. Since ethics shows what human life should be, so that it will be suitable to the purposes of human life, ethics stands at the head of the arts, and broadly speaking, may indeed embrace all the arts. Why is this so? All those things that are called arts are used by man to achieve the perfection of his life. From commerce and industry to education and government, this is true for all of them. Hence, we can make the statement that all things called arts come within the jurisdiction of ethics, and are part of ethics.

This speaks of the relationship between the arts and learning.

All the arts are based on learning, since they apply theory to the solution of practical issues. And ethics is based on anthropology and psychology. The purpose of ethics is to determine our knowledge of human nature and the laws of human life, and to use it to explain in what way the life and actions of mankind as a whole and as individuals may contribute to or impede the development of human nature. This relationship will become clear by comparing it with other arts. . . . Based on a knowledge of the human body, the art of medicine is used to improve human bodily life, to make the body healthy. Based on a knowledge of human nature in general, especially its spiritual and social sides, ethics is used to improve and perfect all aspects of human life. We might therefore call ethics the art of universal hygiene, in which not only medicine, but all the other arts such as education and politics may be seen as parts of ethics, or as its auxiliary arts. The founder of the study of ethics, Aristotle also held this view.

This says that the arts are not a new science.

This is the difference between the arts and learning, but the arts are not an independent new science. Why is this? Science studies the nature of things, but the modifications of things made by man should not be regarded as part of their nature. Scientific writings may also add remarks about the corresponding applied arts. For example, a work on physics, after discussing the theory of steam, may add a comment on the applications of steam. It is quite natural to treat technologies as corollaries to theories.

This says that all learning comes from practical problems; thus it all comes under ethics.

If the essence [*benti*] of human beings were strictly theoretical, it would be sufficient to study theory alone. But such is not the case. What we call our essence is the practical side. Practical problems always occur before, and are more important than, theoretical problems. What we call the sciences come later, in the attempt to explain the practical problems. . . . Thus, the origin and end of all philosophy is to be sought in ethics. (pp. 1–3;Thilly 1–3)

This talks about our two kinds of knowledge.

deduction induction

4. The method of ethics. Our knowledge may be divided into two kinds: one is that obtained from experience, and the other that obtained from intuition.[4] Mathematics is the prototype of intuitive knowledge. It first sets up units from which, by deduction, it then logically proves various general rules[5] and, in accordance with the principles of thought, demonstrates their necessary causal relations. Empirical knowledge[6] is the opposite, as in the case of physics or chemistry which must first observe the general constitution of things, and seek the rules of their natural interrelationships, before attempting to reduce them to universal formulas, or causal laws. The proof of these formulas lies not in their logical connection with presupposed definitions, but in demonstrating that they agree with observed causalities.

This states that the study of ethics comes from experience.

I am convinced that the methodology of ethics is different from that of mathematics, and resembles rather that of physics and chemistry. The physicist or chemist does not deduce definitions from concepts, but rather demonstrates from actual experience the relations that exist among facts. . . . (p. 4; Thilly 6)

This explains the theory of intuitionism.[1]

The view of intuitionism is that ethics does not deal with empirical knowledge, but that it sets up moral propositions that are neither capable nor in need of empirical proof. Ethical imperatives come from the human conscience [*liangxin*], which is *a priori* in nature, an innate faculty that judges and legislates. And it asserts that it is a fact that all persons have a concept of right and wrong without any experience. What is advantageous and what is disadvantageous is known through experience, but what is good and what is bad is fully known before experience. It is for this reason that neither man's real actions nor his concepts of the various causal effects of his actions can in any way affect his intuitive knowledge.

Mencius' "Righteousness is internal," and Wang Yangming's "Mind is principle" both appear to be [forms of] intuitionism.[2]

Not necessarily.

The statement of intuitionism, that mankind did not await the coming of moral philosophy to distinguish between good and bad, is indeed true. What we call morality existed before there was moral philosophy, and if there had not first been what we call morality, there definitely could be no moral philosophy. Moral philosophy can only be established as a reflection on an already existing positive morality that governs our lives and wills. We do have an inner mind [*xin*] that indeed seems to give commands about what things we ought to do and what things we ought not do, which is called the conscience [*liangxin*]. . . . (p. 5; Thilly 7)

This asserts that morality came before moral philosophy. Thus, moral philosophy comes from experience, as expanded upon below.

Good and bad are born from advantage and disadvantage; advantage and disadvantage are born of joy and suffering; joy and suffering are born of life and death; life and death are born of formation and disintegration; formation and disinte-

gration; formation and disintegration are born of attraction and repulsion; attraction and repulsion are born of small and great; small and great are born of being and non-being; being and non-being are born of mind and principle.[3]

Both these passages assert that morality arose before moral philosophy.

Human beings did not await the discovery of moral philosophy before distinguishing between good and bad, just as they did not await the discovery of the art of hygiene before being able to take care of the body. Before the art of medicine existed, hungry men ate, those who were cold sought to clothe themselves, all of their own accord. If the question were asked, Why is it that eating cures hunger? or Why is it that clothing keeps out the cold? it would be like asking school children, Why is stealing wrong? They would think, Why bother asking further about something that is self-evident to everyone? Taking things that people had never thought worth inquiring about, as problems for investigation, is the work of science. . . .

The origins of science.

The same is true for moral philosophy, that before moral philosophy was invented, there already existed an unexamined, naturalistic morality that was publically accepted. Social life, like the human body, was also guided by a moral instinct that did not depend on science. It was from this moral instinct bringing together all kinds of life that society was formed. And the moral laws existed in our consciousness as unquestionable commands, no different from the laws of hygiene. For example, do not kill, do not steal, do not lie, all come simply from the conscience, and require no further justification but nat-

The formation of society comes from the moral instincts.

Here and elsewhere I do not think it is the conscience, but rather the human desire to preserve one's life that comes from the concept of advantage and disadvantage.

rally must be obeyed, no differently from the cases of eating when hungry or putting on clothing when cold. (p. 6; Thilly 9)

This refers to the basic function of moral philosophy.

Is it true, then, that what we call moral philosophy can do nothing but collect the various positive and negative commands given by the conscience, and that it cannot be called a science? I say: No, No, Not so. All natural morality frequently simplifies its truths and puts them into proverbs. As in the case of, the best staff is credibility. The saying that the best staff is credibility is not an imperative, but it indeed contains a truth. An analysis of it would show that it means, you should keep your word. You know that a walking staff will support you, and do you not know that credibility will support you even better? This illustrates a truth. The basic function of moral philosophy is to expand upon the truths contained within this kind of natural morality to determine the strengths and weakness of various kinds of actions. (p. 7; Thilly 9)

. . . Moral philosophy is based upon natural morality, which it then elaborates upon and develops, and shows that a particular action is permissible or impermissible, and determines the boundaries within which it may be applied, like demonstrating that lying is wrong but then pointing out that there are times when one must lie. Furthermore, when things get very complicated, natural morality inevitably leaves too many roads open, from among which only a very experienced person can choose the right one. In laying down the general rules of

The above says that the methodology of ethics is experiential, not intuitive.

experience, moral philosophy too must leave particular decisions to someone familiar with the situation, but in comparison with natural philosophy, it makes the choices clearer.

What follows raises other issues.

The rules of experience are the function of the doctrine of virtues and the doctrine of duties. All propositions in the doctrine of virtues and the doctrine of duties are teleological and causal: in order to reach such and such a goal, such and such a behavior is necessary. But what really is the relationship between this goal and my knowledge? From what source does ethics derive knowledge of the perfect life? And how does it prove that its rules for attaining the highest good are correct?

These two passages say that purpose is unrelated to knowledge and is related only to feeling and will.

For such problems as these the case is inevitably somewhat different. Determining the character of the highest good is not a function of my intellect, but is actually a function of my will. I have an ideal of the perfect life, which appears before my eyes and which, without any thinking or deliberation, I believe to be my highest goal. Such ideals as these, although they appear within the realm of consciousness, they are definitely not intellectually arrived at, but in reality are a reflection of my inner essence [*benti*]. At this point, there are people whose ideas are very different from mine, whose errors I would like to correct, but neither the rules of logic nor empirical experience are sufficient to move them. I might try to move their feelings by revealing my highest ideal, and perhaps they will be won over. At this point, the value of the ideals they hold is not determined by their intellect but entirely by the force of their wills. The intellect determines truth and falsehood, but cannot distinguish good from bad.

Is the source of morality the reason, or is it the feelings? This has been discussed by ethics since ancient times. But actually both are involved. The determination of what constitutes the perfect life comes entirely from the unquestioned feelings. Although various kinds of arguments might be raised, it is not these that arouse the feeling of respect for an ideal, just as the power of argument will not change a bitter taste into a sweet taste. Habit can change somewhat my taste in food, and the same is true of the taste of morality, but this can occur only by changing the internal content of the person who is doing the tasting. But once the ideal of the highest good is established, the intellect easily determines whether any action will help realize the greatest good or obstruct it.

This says that the ideal of the highest good is fixed in all people because human beings share common impulses.

Scientific laws cannot be used to prove an ideal of the highest good.

What makes an ideal of the highest good most universal, most correct, is not something that can be proven by scientific law. The only thing that can prove it is those tendencies that are common to the human will. Human capabilities and his laws of living are common to all, so there is always a certain degree of common agreement, just as other animals to a certain degree have similar desires. But the study of such impulses belongs to natural history. It is the task of natural history to discover the common ways in which all human beings realize their ideals of the highest good. If the moralist were to engage in this task then he would not be any different from the biologist, in that his task would be not to prescribe the impulses of mankind but merely to discover them. If we could discover the common impulses of human beings, and then found an occasional few persons whose impulses varied greatly from the common ones, they would have to be regarded as abnormal. . . . (pp. 7-9; Thilly 9-12)

This speaks of the broad and narrow definitions of natural law.

5. Comparison between moral laws and natural laws. When I look at the various phenomena of the natural world and see that they change according to fixed laws, and then express these in terms of a general formula, this is a natural law. Natural law has two meanings, one broad, one narrow. Used in the narrow sense, a certain cause must have a certain effect, with no individual variation. . . . In the wider sense, although its formulas adequately embrace all things, this does not guarantee that there will not be a few variants. . . . (p. 10; Thilly 13)

This says that morality is also a natural law in the broader sense.

Seen from this perspective, the moral laws may also be called natural laws. The laws of ethics are mainly involved with the circumstances of human life, and express the different kinds of human actions and the effects these actions usually have. For example, lying destroys trust, and when trust is broken social relations are damaged, much like the disorder that alcohol induces in the nervous system. Or, the fact that habitual idleness impairs the reason and weakens the will, which is a biological law that applies to psychology. Thus, we say that moral laws are natural laws in the broad sense. Some question this by saying that moral laws explain what ought to be, and not what is, as do natural laws. But, as in the case of the law, "Thou shalt not lie," although there may indeed be a few exceptions, it is indeed universally valid. Or, there are some who believe that moral laws are closely related to legal statutes, and unlike natural laws. Indeed, moral laws are related to legal statutes, and furthermore, proper and true legal statutes are perhaps simply a section of the moral law, but this does not stop them from being related to natural law. And the fact that legal statutes also express what ought to be, does not prevent them from having a few exceptions. . . . (pp. 10-11; Thilly 13–14)

I suspect that the words "what ought to be" should read "what is."

This says that moral laws, like natural laws, describe what is.

This is also true of moral laws, that they describe not only what ought to be, but what is. . . . Moral law is based on laws of causality, just as in medicine and jurisprudence. If the connections between cause and effect, between the actions and life of the individual and society did not conform to natural law, there would be no moral law. Consequently, moral law is not invented by man himself, nor is it arbitrarily defined by divine command or by the conscience, but is indeed one of the inherent qualities of human life that conforms to natural law, and that is simply manifested as moral law. . . . (pp. 11-12; Thilly 15–16)

This states that grammar also describes what is.

The category of moral law may be understood by comparison with grammar. Grammar is popularly thought to describe what ought to be. But when we study the history of language, we discover that what we call grammar was not created to prescribe a way to speak but is specifically a description of the rules inherent in language. . . . Thus the grammarian seeks to describe a real language and obtain its general rules, and when he has to select from among various different forms, he must take common usage as the standard, and he may adopt the forms that appear in the works of famous writers that are followed by many people. At which point, this form becomes the standard, and grammar becomes finally a normative science. When we correct ı speech or article, we judge it against standard grammar. Here there is a very important connection, which is the purpose that makes this form necessary. The purpose of language is to communicate with others, and ungrammatical language, being incomprehensible, would be misunderstood and rejected.

Morals are not prescriptive; they are descriptive.

The same is true of moral philosophy. The average person believes that the task of moral philosophy is to prescribe to us the rules of living, but the evidence of anthropology and history reveals that the job of moral philosophy is not primarily to prescribe to us how we should act or how we should make judgments, but is actually simply to describe the most general forms of real life. . . . (pp. 12–13; Thilly 17)

The highest good can only be explained formally.

6. The concept of perfection. Above, we said that the goal of ethics is the highest good, and that the highest good is the perfect life. What is the perfect life? The perfect life means developing all the human bodily and mental powers without exception to their highest, with no apologies for

doing so. What the real content of this is, will be discussed later, but here I shall talk first of its formal connections. . . . Here I should like to show that it is impossible to give anything but a formal explanation of the highest good. . . . (pp. 13–14; Thilly 17-18)

There is no one perfect life, so ethics can only describe it formally and cannot set up a concrete model.

It is impossible for there to be one and the same perfect life for everyone. If there were a nation of people in which everyone had the same perfect life, it would be a bore. What kind of a nation would it be in which all individuals had the same inner nature, the same life, and were distinguished only by their numbers. Thus, what is called the perfect human life is made up of the many different perfect lives of many different individuals, which are not identical with each other. Thus, if we wanted to describe the concrete perfect life, we would have to include all the many different forms of it conceptualized by mankind. We would have to include all the different ways of living of each individual, clan, and nation. This would be the function of a philosophy of history that had a creative goal. It would be extremely difficult for us just to list the life of people in the historical past, the life of all the nations of people in order to construct a concept of humanity, much less to construct the new forms of history and humanity in the future. (p. 14; Thilly 18)

Develop individuality.

Perfect dissimilarity is perfect similarity; perfect non-unity is perfect unity.

General rules (the necessary conditions of the perfect life).

It would be impossible for aesthetics to attempt to list all the ideas of beauty of all the paintings, sculptures, poems, and musical compositions that exist, and of what should appear in the future. The creation of beauty is the business of the genius. Aesthetics takes what past genius has created and studies it, with the task of describing generally the necessary conditions of art. At this point, although ethics cannot suggest artistic phenomena for the future, it can help the artist know these necessary conditions and avoid mistakes. Ethics is the same. Although it cannot describe the content of the perfect life of the future, but rather sets out the general rules that describe the necessary conditions of the perfect life, so that we individuals in our particular lives may observe these conditions and not violate them.

In the broad sense, there is no universal human morality.

The view of Kant.

This was also the view of our early Confucians.

7. The universal types of ethics. There is no so-called universal morality for all humanity. What each nationality regards as the universal model comes from its own particular morality. For example, it is an undoubted fact that the Englishman and the African each has his own ways and virtues, and that since the circumstances of their lives are different they subsequently have different moralities. The question can also be asked whether their differences ought to be, or just are. Wise men in the past, such as Kant, have all thought that the essential meaning of morality lies within human rational nature, and that it must have one universal, unvarying reality. If morality can vary from place to place, then would there not be different moralities for men and for women, for artists and for merchants, according to their sex or occupations? I would reply that this is indeed so, but that different moralities for different people does not necessarily rule out an ideal of the perfect life. Since the circumstances of human life are different for each person, his rules of life must naturally also be different. . . . (p. 15; Thilly 19)

In the narrow sense, there is a universal human morality. But when it is put to direct use it must be flexible.

Although this is true in the broad sense, in the narrow sense it is possible to speak of a universal morality. Since the fundamental nature and laws of life are the same for all humanity, the guidelines for maintaining a healthy life are the same. Thus dietetics may prescribe universal rules, such as types and quantities of drink and food, certain amounts of activity and rest, that we should all observe. Likewise with morality, as in carefully considering and taking precautions, or as in educating the young, or as in resolving differences between husband and wife, or as in the prohibition against harming your own kind, all of which are universal rules, but which if abused may be very harmful. The fact that murder and adultery, robbery and cheating are bad, and that being upright and kind and truthful are good, also imply this. When these universal rules and their formulation as cautionary prescriptions are applied directly to actual affairs, they must be used flexibly, taking into consideration the differing qualities of the people involved and the differences in the everyday circumstances. . . . (p. 16; Thilly 20–21)

Morality differs with the times, but it none the less remains morality.

This is not at all difficult to explain, and is in fact explained below.

Looked at in this way, morality inevitably changes with the changing times, and although the reasons for this may not be well understood, the fact that it occurs is indisputable, even though the wisest philosophers seem to have found it difficult to explain why it is that morals inevitably change with the times, and that even though morals do change, morals still continue to exist. The average person tends to feel that if what those in the past did is incompatible with today's morality then it must be rejected as wrong. When we read the history of the Middle Ages, and see that Christians hated those of other beliefs and often arrested and tortured heretics and witches, and even killed and burned them, we strongly condemn them. Such brutality was truly barbarous. But the use of barbarous punishments in a barbarous age was not impermissible. And perhaps it was inevitable that such means were employed in the process of advancing from barbarism toward civilization. If the brutal punishments of the past had not existed, perhaps the cities of the Middle Ages would not have been able to move toward the complex social life of today. . . . (p. 17; Thilly 21–22)

Morality is different in different societies, and with different persons.

We shall even further say that even the individual societies and individual persons within one nation may have their own particular moral codes. Different dispositions and conditions of life require different bodily diets, and also different spiritual morals to sustain them. It is often the case that what is beneficial and necessary for one may be unsuitable and injurious to another. This is also true when making real judgments. The same action may be permissible for this person but not for another. It would be impossible to have all individuals act the same. . . . When we see that the conduct of all persons is largely similar, we are looking only at the outside. When we seek to probe their inner feelings, we find that each one is unique. The inner feelings are man's essense, and it is his unique individuality that makes him complete and real, and it should not be

Few understand this principle.

An important point.

regarded as a defect. Only where the basic ethical meaning has disappeared, where it approaches the domain of law, does conduct become totally the same.

This asserts that individuals need moral teachers to admonish them, but that moral teachers must respect the uniqueness of each individual.

Every moral teacher emphasizes the universal nature within the special nature of the indivdual. Individuality comes from the human being's natural constitution and temperament, but the general rules do not take into account the temperament. If human beings all took just their own particular dispositions into account when dealing with the external world, if on the grounds of their own special natures and positions in society, they each demanded a special moral code, it is very easy to see that, from the point of view of the judgments of others and of a conscience based upon a higher moral code, there would be frequent conflicts of all kinds. This being true, Kant's rigorism is fully adequate to curbing his excesses. In the view of Kant, the will, which is the ruler of the senses, is subservient to universal laws, and this is indeed the origin of the individual's realization of the highest moral code. This realization of the highest moral code is, in the words of the Christian Bible, not the destruction of the law but its fulfillment. But the moral code does not tell man how to fulfill it, as the above shows. The moral code simply points to the universal laws. Following these laws and adapting them to particular events is the task of the conscience and the knowledge of the individual. But the individual is not without need of guidance, so he needs a moral instructor, just as he needs a doctor to advise him on his medical health. . . . (pp. 17-18; Thilly 22–24)

This is why one should not rashly comment on others.

The view of Kant.

Educators.

This discusses the limits on the application of moral philosophy.

However, looking at the matter more carefully, the rules of moral philosophy are not valid for all. What we have called the universal human morality is a rational entity which, although everyone can conceive of it, in the last analysis, has never been realized. The feelings and thought of the moral philosopher cannot reach beyond the nation and era which define them. There are two reasons for this. The first is that since his childhood it is the ideals of his nation that have gradually molded his own ideals, and second, his ideas of good and bad are inevitably conditioned by his times. This went unnoticed by the rationalists of the eighteenth century, who thus committed this error, including Kant. As the age of history, the nineteenth century is no longer able to believe in a universal human morality. It is for this reason that the sphere to which a moral philosophy is applicable is limited to the civilization of this philosophy, and cannot transcend it, no matter whether its moralists are aware of this boundary or not. The task of the moral philosopher is limited to pointing out to his compatriots within his own culture the most suitable mode of life that will give them a healthy, peaceful, and happy existence.

The goal of ethics lies in practice, not in study.

8. Why ethics is a practical science. It is asked, Can ethics be called a practical science, not only in that it deals with the methods of practice, but also in greatly influencing the practical world? Yes. And this was the original meaning of ethics. As Aristotle said, The goal of ethics is practice, not

study.[7] Schopenhauer, in his work *The Foundation of Morals,* takes issue with this view. All philosophy, he says, is theoretical; upon mature reflection, it ought finally to abandon the old demand that it become practical, guide action, and transform character.[8] Morality is not constructed of concepts, nor judged by the reason. Morality cannot be taught, just as genius cannot be taught. Thus, moral philosophy cannot make one a virtuous or gentle person or a saint, just as aesthetics cannot make one a great poet or sculptor or painter or musician.

This is what is meant by empty words are useless.

Knowledge assists the will.

But ethics definitely cannot be so fainthearted. The most important task of ethics is to offer man knowledge about action, that is, about what modes of action necessarily have what kinds of relations with the external world and events, and what their effects are upon the conditions of life of the individual and of society. All human knowledge is basically useful to action; why should ethics alone be different. . . . If human beings understand that the vices of indolence, hatred, indiscretion, envy, and falsehood are obstacles to life and that the virtues of prudence, politeness, modesty, uprightness, and amiability promote the development of life, how can this not but influence the will? The will cannot of course be totally determined by knowledge. Natural capacities, education, and examples, and the admiration and contempt of the external world, all play their part. Thus, knowledge assists the will, but cannot oppose it.

Ethics shows the goals of human life, and contributes to conduct.

Ethics contributes to conduct by causing us to have a real feeling for the goals of human life, rather than just giving them lip-service. It would be futile for a physician to advise a man who does not care about his health and bodily welfare. Similarly, it would be useless for the moral philosopher to advise someone on the importance of ethics who did not understand "the pleasure of righteousness." But if one day such a person is enlightened, and shown what the goal of human life is, how do we know that he will not be converted and turn away from evil to follow the good? . . . (pp. 19–21; Thilly 24-27)

The importance of moral philosophy in an enlightened [*kaifang*] age.

The skeptic might again say that, moral philosophy not only is not beneficial to conduct, it is on the contrary dangerous. Why? Human beings are moral because they have faith in and obey the forces of conscience and custom. Any attempt to probe into its origins, and its meaning and value will kill that faith. I would reply: This too is not so. All such questions are not the product of philosophy, but rather it is indeed these questions that gave birth to philosophy. Although human beings may want to avoid probing, this is impossible. Whenever something happens or there is a decision the right and wrong of which must be determined, it is necessary to probe its principles. Moral philosophy simply follows this tendency to inquire and clarifies the principles involved. Furthermore, the clarification of such principles is an especially urgent task today. The contemporary social mind has an increasing tendency to seek what is new, to reject the old accepted *a priori* truths. There are many evidences of this tendency, such as the statements of Nietzsche, the view of the age of youth that everything should be transformed, of socialism that would change the old customs of state and society. These are but the most obvious examples. The contemporary age, whether in thought, in morality, or in life styles, is rejecting all things old and seeking the new. As for the authority of religion and its ancient proverbs, everyone regards them as worthless. Having been so excessively repressed, in reaction they rebel and become skeptics, and their subjective ideas are breaking down the walls and escaping in all directions, in reaction to the old unthinking learning and the religions of unquestioning faith. These are the characteristics of the Enlightenment. The Enlightenment of the past still exists, is reappearing again today. At first taking hold of the young people, today it is spreading among the common people. Those who have been oppressed by the thought and prescriptions on living of the past, regard this as the blind leading the blind, and inevitably want to do their own thinking and open up another world. Such is the right of freedom. Free thought, free living, is the first right of human life, and the first duty. The most precious quality of the realm of the spirit is none other than independence, independence of the spirit lies in the freedom to think, not in relying on ready-made beliefs. The problem of ethics is to help those who have fallen into skepticism to discover the true purpose and task of life and to give it a foundation in free investigation. (pp. 21–22; Thilly 28–29)

All our nation's two thousand years of scholarship may be said to be unthinking learning.

This is the situation in our nation today.

FUNDAMENTAL CONCEPTS

Metaphysical and psychological introduction

This regards feelings as part of the will.

7. Psychic life has two phases, will and knowledge. The will is expressed as impulses[9] and feelings. Knowledge manifests itself in sensation, perception, and thinking.

. . .

All persons have the goal of self-preservation.

10. The development of the will has three stages: (1) unconscious impulses, (2) the desires of the senses, and (3) the rational will. And the goal at which it aims, throughout all three stages, is the preservation and promotion of the individual and the race.

The origin of pleasure and displeasure.

11. The original form of the will is unconscious impulse. In consciousness, the unconscious impulses appear as conscious impulses. If our life activities satisfy our impulses, a feeling of pleasure accompanies them. If these activities are obstructed or go against our impulses, it is accompanied by a feeling of displeasure. (p. 24; Thilly 220)

. . .

On the distinction between good and evil.

Chapter I: Good and Bad. Teleological and Formalistic Conceptions

What is the criterion for distinguishing between good and bad—one view is that it is only the motive, the other says that it includes the result.

1. The distinction between conceptions of good and bad. Where does ethical thought come from? It springs from two questions. The first is, what is the ultimate ground of moral value distinctions? The second is, What is the ultimate end of human life? These two questions have often guided thinking people to the path of ethics. The former question springs from the function of moral judgment, while the lat-

ter has its origin in volition and action. (p. 26; Thilly 222)

The world view of these two philosophers.

. . . What we call ethics originated in the Platonic and Aristotelian theory of the universe, which has often been thought of and called teleological because it is associated with purpose. In the view of these two philosophers, all existence, all human beings in the universe, have their own tasks. This is a fundamental insight of their ethics. And all the various problems of ethics address the elucidation of these tasks, and of the forms and functions of life that arise from them. (pp. 27–28; Thilly 223–24)

Purpose.
Method.

The sense of this section has already been outlined in the previous section.

2. The meaning and power of the teleological view. Popular opinion inclines more to the formalistic view: Acts are not morally good or bad acccording to their results; they are good or bad in themselves. Differences in moral value depend upon intent, not the effects. Even if the compassion of the good Samaritan in the Gospel had not saved the man who fell among thieves, but on the contrary had caused his death, this would not diminish the moral worth of the act. Or again, if a slanderous remark on the contrary reveals the virtues of the person slandered and destroys the credibility of the slanderer, even though the result might be very good, this does not alter the fact that slander is evil.

This section repeats the objections

We would answer: This is indeed true, but this is not an objection against the teleological way of examining things. The teleological determination of whether a particular act is good or bad does not rest on its actual

to this view.

result, but upon the fact that acts of that type tend to produce certain results. It lies in the very nature of slander that it may have the effect of hurting another person's credibility and good name. Where the effect is the opposite, as in the example raised above, this occurred for a particular reason, such as the conscience and caution of the listener and his experience and understanding of the world, and certainly not because of anything inherent in the nature of slander. In Aristotle's terms, this slanderous remark was an accidental cause of the good effect, not its true cause. Thus morality has to do not with actual effects, but with the effects that may be expected to come from the very nature of the act. (pp. 28–29; Thilly 224–225)

The writer emphasizes objective, material judgments.

3. Subjective, formal judgments, and objective material judgments. A further objection to my view might be: The facts are not like this. Moral judgments are concerned with intention, not with acts. If the motivation for an act is good, we know that it was done with good intentions. If the intent springs from a consciousness of duty, we need not inquire into its content or effects. This is what Kant meant when he said that there is no good other than what is a universally good intention. (p. 30; Thilly 226–27)

This section develops these two statements.

Finally, the subjective, formal judgment itself is reduced to the teleological view. To act from conscientiousness or respect for duty is called good. This is upheld by the subjective formal view. But why is conscientiousness good? Some might say that this is an absurd question, but I do not think so. The an-

The above section says that objective material judgments have a teleological foundation, and this section says that subjective formal judgments also must be reduced to the

teleological view.

swer to this question is that conscientious acts are objectively good. Why? Conscientious intentions, in determining our acts, have the effect of promoting the welfare of ourselves and our surroundings. Although inclinations are inevitably diverse, conscience is the same for all the individuals of a people, and therefore actions that are determined by the conscience have the quality of universality. Furthermore, the content of my conscience comes from the positive morality of the people to whom I belong, which is inculcated by education, example, and public opinion. But the general moral code simply contains the moral laws of a people or of an entire civilized society. The investigations of anthropology conclude that everything which is called morality is a moral instinct of social relations that impels one to act so as to preserve individual and social life. For this reason, the conscience simply determines the principles of action that promote my own most vital interests and the vital interests of the society to which I belong. I shall discuss this in detail in chapter five. (p. 35; Thilly 232–33)

This section says that only at the most appropriate times do the ends justify the means.

4. The relationship between ends and means. Before further discussing the content of the highest good, I shall first raise and respond to a few objections to my view.

The objection is made, Is not the general teleological principle the same as the saying of the Jesuits (a medieval Catholic sect that flourished in Spain, the strengh of whose disciples made the conquests of such places as the Philippines possible, whose teachings and actions have been rejected, and today no longer exist) that the ends justify the means. If the value of conduct depends upon its effects, does not the value of all kinds of particular acts depend upon their effects? I would reply that there are two interpretations of the Jesuit morality of what is called the ends justifying the means. One is that if the end is good then no matter what means are used to achieve it, these means must be good. Consequently, any improper illegal action could be regarded as good.

. . .

. . . A contradiction in the meaning of the terms. The words murder and falsehood signify not merely an objective fact, intentional killing or intentional deception, but they likewise imply condemnation. The judgment "Murder is wrong" is an analytical judgment. This judgment can also be used in instances in which homicide is not considered legally or morally wrong. In order to make a pure judgment the implication of condemnation must be eliminated from the term, and judgment must be pronounced solely on the objective fact of intentional homicide. Then it becomes clear that some cases may be considered good. . . . (pp. 36–38; Thilly 233–36)

This is a particular proposition and does not mean that all homicide is wrong.

6. A brief discussion of egoism. Looked at from one aspect of moral philosophy, we can supplement the above. To the question: What is the ultimate objective of the will? the answer is simply, The welfare of the individual and of other human beings.

There is also an opposing view which says that it is the nature of the will to regard the welfare of the individual as its end, not universal welfare. This view states that everyone strives for what is agreeable or useful to oneself, regardless of whether it furthers or detracts from the welfare of others. This view, formulated as a theory, is known as egoism; it is also called individualistic utilitarianism. In the early period of modern philosophy, Hobbs [*sic*] was a representative of this view. He stated that the real will of every animal takes self-preservation as its end, and that this is a natural law. Therefore, whatever really benefits oneself is good, and whatever benefits others is indirectly good if it also serves to preserve oneself indirectly.

Hobbes' theory.

I really feel that this explanation is incomplete. Since human beings have an ego, for which the self is the center of all things and all thought, self-interest is primary for all persons. That this serves the interests of others is due to the fact that those others who belong to the same category as the self share related interests. Thus we may say that the self cannot but benefit others. The starting point of altruism is the self, and altruism is related to the self. It is impossible to say that any mind is purely altruistic without any idea of self-interest. Nothing in the world takes the other as its starting point, and the self does not seek to benefit anything in the world that is totally unrelated to the self. Otherwise, such concepts as "individual personality", "self-discipline", and "free-

I do not believe that we can maintain this theory without flying in the face of the facts. The egoistic impulses of the mind [*xin*] have as their goal self preservation, and are inherent in all human life. All human beings without exception tend to stress self-interest over the interests of others. But is there any human being who is only aware of what is beneficial or detrimental to himself, and is unaware of what is beneficial or detrimental to others? All human beings are as concerned about the welfare of kin and friends as about their own. And our feeling of concern for the welfare of society too is clearly obvious, as in the case of our extreme disgust and anger at someone who betrays his country for personal gain, which shows that this action is absolutely intolerable to our consciences. Thus we may say:

dom" would be absurd. These concepts are indeed a noble egoism, an egoism of the spirit. If I open my eyes wide and say that mankind is the greater self, and say that all living things are the greater self, and then say that the universe is the greater self, does this negate self-interest? Why should self-interest be unworthy?

The human will seeks the welfare of the individual and of others as its goal, and although the relationship between how much something benefits oneself and how much it benefits others may be highly complex and variable, there is nothing in which the two are not interrelated. Thus those we call unselfish[33] tend to stress altruism, while the so-called egoist simply leans toward emphasizing self-interest. (p. 44; Thilly 244–45)

[Next to the words in the text, "the welfare of the individual and of others as its goal" is the comment:] Ultimately the individual comes first.

. . .

In our consciousness, individual stimuli and social stimuli, egoistic feelings and altruistic feelings, are usually both present, mixed together. Human beings cannot live apart or in isolation from others; they can exist only as members of a whole society. This is a biological fact. Objective biological factors manifest themselves in the subjective psychological realm, in the constitution of the will and the feelings. The impulse of self-preservation in all animals coexists with the impulse to preserve the species. (p. 45; Thilly 245)

This is indeed so, but we cannot say that they are equal, but rather that one comes before the other. For animals the impulse for self-preservation comes first, and the impulse to preserve the species comes second. When young, animals cannot be said to have an impulse to preserve the species. Alas! At this point I have a very strong feeling that there are many who use the excuse of altruism to seek their own egoistic gain. Truth

is good; falsehood is bad. To act in self-interest may be small-minded, but is at least true. To pretend to be benefiting others when really acting in self-interest is a great falsehood. To extend self-interest to the greater self of benefiting all mankind, to the greater self of benefiting all living things, and to the greater self of benefiting the universe, this is to go from a small truth to a great truth. The progress of human wisdom can achieve this. When self and other are equal, their order is not clear and it is easy to pretend to be acting for others when actually acting in self-interest, in which case it is impossible to achieve the highest self-interest. I think that the theories of our Confucian scholars are based on egoism, as in the saying, "The way of heaven and earth has its origin in the relation of man and wife,"[10] and can be seen in, "He who first cultivates himself may afterward bring peace to the world,"[11] and "He is first affectionate to his parents, and then benevolent to the people and kind to creatures."[12]

The theory of universal love[13] is not altruism, for universal love includes the self, is to extend the love of self to loving all men.

By basing the theory on self, it has a starting point, a criterion. If self and other are treated as having equal weight, there is no starting point, and the criterion is lost.

As animals evolved into *homo sapiens*, the impulse to preserve the species became stronger. All human beings regard themselves as being

This kind of statement fully proves the validity of egoism.

Quite true, quite true!

Except for those who are sick and crazy, there definitely are no such persons.

Love of wife and parents is inescapable. Lions and tigers seem to have this; can human beings not have it?

members of the entire society. Every human being thinks of himself as belonging to a clan or society or nationality, and consequently human beings always take the goals of their society as their own personal goals. It is indeed clear that the interests of the individual are mutually interwoven with the interests of society, so that it is impossible to draw a line demarcating the two. For this reason, it may be said that the goal of my will is the common shared welfare of the individual and of society, or we may say that the welfare of society includes the welfare of the individual. It is true that there are persons in this world who are totally devoid of feelings for the interests of others, who are oblivious to the interests of their neighbors, who even take pleasure in the suffering of others. But this does not threaten this view, any more than the existence of idiots in this world threatens the common principle that mankind possesses reason and speech. The person who lacks sympathetic feelings for others is ethically an abnormal person, just as the idiot is abnormal. Physicians and anthropologists would simply call them abnormal people.

After the concept of welfare has been more clearly defined, I shall come back to the antithesis between egoism and altruism. Here I should simply like to state that in my view the antithesis between these two is not as important as contemporary moral philosophers make it. Schopenhauer and his followers regard this as the foundation of moral philosophy. In their view, the natural man is simply and solely egoistic, and therefore without moral worth. To have moral worth, the motivation for an act must be the interests of others. But since such motivation necessarily cannot exist in the natural constitution of mankind, morality is supernatural. I do not think that this is true. Is the world in which we live really so degenerate? What we call compassion does indeed exist within the natural order. Only pessimists like Schopenhauer believe that compassion is supernatural. Schopenhauer once said that, "The natural man would, if forced to choose between his own destruction and that of the world, annihilate the whole universe merely for the sake of preserving himself." If forced to make such a choice under the threat of imminent danger, perhaps there are some who would do this. But if the world were annihilated, how could I alone exist? The unbearable senselessness would make him regret the error of his choice and force him to seek an immediate end to his life. At this point, even the egoist would also realize that living in isolation from others is unbearable. The desires of human beings to be admired or feared or envied all depend on other people. Not only do we depend on others, it is also clear that there is no human being who can totally ignore the interests of others and deny human nature. (pp. 45–46; Thilly 246)

This is treating others as I would want to be treated.

To live in isolation divorced from others is indeed unbearable. Thus society is created by individuals, not individuals by society.

This is what is meant by mutual assistance, and the basis of mutual assistance is fulfillment of the individual.

This is what is meant by sympathy, and sympathy arises from the self.

I too disagree with Schopenhauer. There are two points here. The first point is that natural man is only egoistic, and that since the existence of the individual is incompatible with the universe, he must

preserve himself. I say this is not true. Self-interests are indeed primary for human beings, but it does not stop here. It is also of our nature to extend this to helping others. This is one and the same human nature, so working for the interests of others is in my own self-interest. Self-interest is primarily benefiting one's own spirit, and the flesh is of no value in benefiting the spirit. Benefiting the spirit means benefiting the feelings and will. For example, since I cannot forget the feeling I have toward the one I love, my will desires to save her and I will do everything possible to save her, to the point that if the situation is desperate I would rather die myself than let her die. Only thus can my feelings be satisfied, and my will be fulfilled. In all times, there are filial sons, faithful widows, loyal ministers, and devoted friends, those who die for love, for their country, for the world, for their ideals—all to benefit their own spirits. I do not agree with the first point, that moral values apply only to those acts that are motivated by altruism. Morality does not necessarily depend on others. What depends on others is objective moral law; what is independent of others is subjective moral law. My desire to fulfill my nature and perfect my mind is the most precious of the moral laws. There are assuredly human beings and objects in the world, but they all exist because of the self, and the image I have of them disappears when I close my eyes; thus the objective moral law is also the subjective moral law. If I were the only person

in the world, I could not fail to fulfill my nature and complete my mind, simply because it would be no loss to others. I would still have to fulfill and complete them. Such things are done not for others, but for ourselves.

The welfare of the individual and the welfare of society are closely interwoven, in the narrow sense with family and friends, and in the larger sense with community and country. If others do not fare well, then the individual too cannot fare well. This is recognized by the great majority of the people. This is true not just for objective events, it is true also for the feelings. Such purely egoistical people may exist in theory, but they do not exist in reality. Thus the egoist school of ethics manufactures them in order to justify their false theory.

In a certain sense, egoistic feelings are humanly inevitable. Even the most unselfish person desires the welfare of others because he knows that it will also benefit himself. Alleviating the woe of others and bringing others happiness also brings one pride and satisfaction. If this were not true, if he were indifferent to the pain and pleasure of others, they could not become an object of his willing. My will can only be moved by my feelings; I cannot have and feel the feelings of others. Thus, the ego remains the center of things. This, however, is not the ordinary meaning of the word egoism, which is that one is not saddened by the misfortunes of others, nor pleased by their good fortunes. The abstract moral philosophers, who believe that conflict with one's natural will is a characteristic of fulfilling one's duty, and that it is an

This, the narrowest form of egoism, does not exist in this world.

article of moral value that the self must have no sense of pleasure, will be troubled by the fact that giving happiness to others invariably gives oneself a feeling of pleasure. In order to maintain their false theories, they disregard the evidence of the facts.

Is this indeed the philosophy of Schopenhauer? The theories concocted by the abstract moral philosophers do not agree with reality. Why is conflict with the natural will a necessary characteristic of the fulfilment of duty? To take conflict as a characteristic is to take falseness as a characteristic. Is there really any morality that believes that it is an article of moral value that the self must have no sense of pleasure? When one already has a sense of pleasure, why get rid of it? This is an extreme kind of altruism. The abstract moral philosophers who are troubled by this, like Schopenhauer when he says that only an altruistic act has moral value, do not understand true egoism.

Let me add another statement. It has been said that utilitarian moral philosophy cannot explain self sacrifice, that the Roman legend of Regulus necessarily contradicts utilitarianism.

However, if we do not regard pure egoism as central to the theory of utilitarianism, there is no contradiction. Having been captured by the Carthaginians, upon the conclusion of a cease-fire between the two states, Regulus returned to Rome where he argued against the peace agreement so that the Romans disavowed the agreement and declared war, whereupon he had to return to Carthage to meet his death. This act may be as easily explained by teleological moral philosophy as by the formalistic theory of ethics. Regulus' martyrdom had indeed a high and lofty purpose, that of being willing to sacrifice himself for the good of his state as an example for

In the past, teleology was called utilitarianism, to emphasize the result of actions.

This was the inherent result of this kind of act.

If you want to achieve a certain result, you must engage in an action

that implies that result. Thus sacrificing oneself for a good cause is also respected by teleological ethics.

citizens of his own state, and he also wanted to show the enemy the high and lofty character of the Roman people. I doubt that the idea of just rigidly abiding by an agreement could have prompted so lofty an act.

This statement is very well put.

Besides, every real sacrifice also implies preserving the ego, that is, it is a means of preserving that person's concept of his ego. The reason that Regulus' goal was not life, was simply because his goal was his spiritual life, rather than his material life. His service to his state, whether in peace or in war, required total dedication to his efforts, even unto death. Thus he felt that anything short of bringing honor to the Roman people, of glorifying their name, would have been not fulfilling his duty. And this is why for the Roman nation his name has remained immortal over the years.

This statement shows that Paulsen, too, takes individualism as his foundation. This is an individualism of the spirit, and may be called spiritual individualism. There is no higher value than that of the individual. All values depend on the individual. If there were no individuals (particulars) there would be no universe. Thus, it can be said that the value of the individual is greater than that of the universe. Thus there is no greater crime than to suppress the individual or to violate particularity. Therefore our country's three bonds[14] must go, and the churches, the capitalists, monarchy, and the state constitute the four evil demons of the world. Some say that the individual's dependence on the group for his existence is as important as the fact that the group exists because of the individual, that they are mutually dependent on each other, and that neither should be over-emphasized. This is not true. It is a fact that there are individuals before there is a group, and that the individual cannot exist alone apart from the group, but the group in itself has no meaning, it only has meaning as a collectivity of individuals. The individual may rebel against the group, but

there is no such thing as the group rebelling against the individual, since this would make the group meaningless. Furthermore, a group is an individual, a greater individual. The human body is constructed of the aggregation of a number of individual parts, and society is constructed of the aggregation of a number of individual persons, and the nation is constructed of the aggregation of a number of societies. Separated they are many, together they form a single whole. Thus the individual, society, and the state are individuals. The universe is also an individual. Thus, it is also possible to say that there are no groups in the world, only individuals.

7. Conclusion. The conduct of any person is morally good if, in the objective realm, it is able to increase the happiness of the self and others, and is directed toward perfecting life and if, subjectively, it is in conscious fulfillment of his duty. Otherwise it is bad. If just the objective quality is absent it is bad, but if it also lacks the subjective quality, then it is evil.

These words contain the true features of Paulsen's thought.

Thus, we call a person good or bad depending upon whether or not there was an objective quality, and virtues and vices are also explained in terms of the different kinds of good and bad. Corresponding to the many different problems of life there are forces of the will that are equally complex. The complexity of the virtues and vices is similar.

This passage again raises my doubts.

Only when both the objective and subjective are satisfied is someone called good.

The concept of good, therefore, presupposes a point of relation, or

This term "point of relation" is most important.

point of reference; it means good for something. It is commonly said that something is good when it is proper for the use to which it is put, and that a person is good when he is able to fulfill his function. For example, a good businessman, a good official, a good father, a good friend, etc., means that that person is able to fulfill the function of businessman, official, father, or friend. The same is true in ethics. Good means that a certain action is proper. A good person is thus one who can fulfill his human function. These all refer to their particular points of reference. It is for this reason that something is regarded as good, when it is good not just for some particular thing but for the perfect life of society as a whole. Every particular action, every particular virtue, every particular person, is a reference point of goodness. The good person is the person who combines all these points of reference, takes them as his function or duty and is able to fulfill this function.

It is not that any particular thing in itself contains a transcendent good, rather it is called good simply because of its relationship to life.

At this point, I also have a sense that people casually say that a particular thing is good or not good depending on the way in which it is related to human life, and that this does not refer to any intrinsic reality in the thing itself. Thus, people say that a particular event or thing or action, that may not be bad in itself, is bad because it hurts life. How unjust!

Each individual.

But we must add that, in the moral world, each human being is one entity within the whole moral world, and thus each is part of the highest good. If we address those ends that are not relative to something else, then one's own ends are also part of the highest good.

Every virtue.

The same is true of the virtues. All the virtues are aspects of the good person, and thus, referring to those ends that are not relative to something else, they are not just external functions, they are also themselves a part of the perfect life and also a kind of end in themselves. Therefore, moral actions are not just external means, they may also be said to be realizations of this end. As in a work of art or poetry, everything is both a means and an end. The same is true of the moral world. Thus nothing can be said to be exclusively an external function. Thus, from the perspective of the final end, a work of art, a poem, and morality are all part of the whole, and the value of each part is derived from their relationship with the whole. Just as when reading a poem we realize that a particular stanza is indispensible to the whole piece. So too, are virtue and duty indispensible to the perfect life of the individual and of society.

Ends.

This is excellent. It may be called one of the great discoveries of ethics.

This section has the defect of praising blind morality. What people today call good deeds, such as building bridges and repairing roads, is just blind morality. A moral action depends on feeling and will, which must precede the moral action about which there must be a conscious decision followed by this action that is done voluntarily. Blind morality has no value at all.

The discovery of the preceding section, that the spirit includes both means and ends, could bring about a change in the meaning of humanity's view of life. How? In the past, everyone thought that ultimate ends have not much value before something occurs. Consequently, everything that takes place before the objective is attained is utterly meaningless, and the road traveled is seen as worthless. Now we know that both the ends

However, we need not be conscious of this relation of ends for our actions to have moral value. As in the case of the good old mother mentioned above, who despised theft simply because it violates the Christian eighth commandmant [the Chinese has "seventh commandment"], not because it is her ideal, yet whose actions are moral. It is only the philosopher who comprehends the importance of the property system among the laws of human life, and abides by it. But what makes him abide by it is not his knowledge, but rather his instincts. But the moral value of his action is not thereby diminished. (pp. 44–50; Thilly 246–50)

and the means are ever enjoyable. Since every day of life is valuable, people will not fear death. Living another hundred years is fine, and dying today is fine.

The above talks of the morality of the person of great wisdom, even though the average person, who for the most part just does things by instinct, is also able to lead a full life. This instinct is the experience of our ancestors passed down from generation to generation, which in the beginning was self-conscious, but which over time has become social habit that, in the brain of the individual, has become a kind of unthinking and automatic reflex that is called instinct.

On what the ends are.

Chapter II: The Highest Good. Hedonistic and Energistic Conceptions

1. For utilitarianism, pleasure is not the purpose of action. . . . There is a school of thought that is more influential than our view, which says that the highest good does not consist in the objective content of life, but in the feeling of pleasure which life produces, that the feeling of pleasure in itself has value, and that everything else has value only as it produces pleasure. This view we commonly call hedonism, and the theory opposed to it is energism. (p. 50; Thilly 251–52)

Here the schools of thought are described very clearly.

The antagonism between these two schools is of long standing; it runs throughout all of Greek philosophy. The former are the Cyrenaics and the Epicureans; the latter are the followers of Plato and Aristotle, and include the

Stoics. This antithesis appears in the modern world, with on the one side the empirical psychologists, and on the other the seventeenth- and eighteenth-century rationalists, and the German philosophers following Kant. According to the former, the subjective feeling of pleasure, regardless of how it is produced, is the highest good. According to the latter, the highest good lies in the objective condition of the individual and of society, regardless of whether it yields pleasure or not, though they do believe that actually it will bring a subjective sense of satisfaction.

This statement is very true. Whether or not something has value is man-made, while whether it is true or false is natural. Thus the scholar should seek the truth in the natural properties of something, and then ask whether or not it has value.

If we wish to understand hedonism better, we must ask whether the hedonistic view is true or false, not whether or not it has value. Scholars have long attempted to prove that hedonism is false by saying that it is worthless. A maxim of the Stoics that rejects both hedonism and atheism in the same breath is not a legitimate argument. Theories are worthless only if they are false. Any attempt to prove that something is false by saying that it is worthless is nonsense. The proponents of hedonism have never been lacking in fine upstanding persons. Epicurus lived a pure and blameless life. Bentham and Mill throughout their entire lives worked hard to realize their practical observations.

What proof is there that pleasure is the highest good? As I see it, only by showing that human nature actually values pleasure. The proponents of this view are ethicists, whose function is not to be lawgivers, but strictly to explain the natural world. It would be absurd to say that human nature seeks pleasure, but does not regard it as the highest good, and then to add that it ought to regard pleasure as the highest good. The arguments of all hedonists are generally of this sort. They all say that all human beings, all living things seek pleasure, that to seek pleasure and avoid pain is mankind's greatest desire, and that all other things are simply the means by which human beings seek pleasure and avoid pain. (pp. 51–52; Thilly 252–53)

Hedonists believe that everything is a means to seek pleasure and avoid pain.

. . . Did Goethe (great German poet who believed in Mill's theory, and said that whenever a person does something, he inevitably measures it by the criterion of what gives the greatest sense of pleasure), in his poetry, in his amours and travels, and in his studies of natural science and history, think that they were all means to the attainment of the greatest sense of pleasure? It is clear that this is absurd. There were in Goethe's constitution impulses and powers that demanded development and exercise. These impulses and powers are like those contained within the sprouts of young plants. When these are developed and fulfilled, a feeling of pleasure naturally ensues, but this sense of pleasure is certainly not a pre-existing idea that is the end of which all other things are but the means. These impulses, and the desire to carry them out, precede the appearance of the idea of pleasure, and the idea of pleasure cannot come before, or be independent of, the impulse that gives a sense of pleasure. Only the indolent idlers of the world first experience a desire for pleasure and then seek a means to procure pleasure. Healthy persons do not act in this way.

This section directly attacks the fallacies in the hedonist view.

This is similar to the story of Taigong going fishing in the River Wei.

. . . There was an Englishman who was seated on the bank of a lake, fishing. A German approached him and informed him that there were no fish in the lake, and asked, "Why are you fishing?" The Englishman calmly replied that he was fishing not for fish, but for pleasure. This Englishman had clearly transcended the common conceptual association in which the pleasurable end is attained only by the means of fishing for fish. Do other people have this feeling of seeking the pleasure and the fish? I think that upon hearing the words of this Englishman, all persons would laugh, which proves quite adequately that they have a different view. As I see it, the will and desires never take pleasure as their end, but rather the end is in an event, such as an activity or change of one's condition. Thus, although the idea of a thing may indeed precede the desire, the idea of pleasure is not in the consciousness, and does not appear as a desire prior to the idea of the thing. (pp. 52–54; Thilly 254–55)

This says that the concept of a thing comes first, and that the desire for it occurs afterward.

An idea is a concept.[15]

Consequently, hedonism must modify somewhat its claim and say that pleasure is not the conscious goal, but is the actual goal or end. Although the actual goal does not appear in the consciousness, it is still the underlying goal or cause, like a mechanical weight that though unseen by the observer is really what makes a machine move. Although such things as food, riches, and honor appear in the consciousness as ends, they are but pretexts to mislead the intellect, while the true end of the will is really pleasure. A lover goes out on business and quite

Objective facts are but pretexts to mislead the intellect. This is a very strange theory.

This is not a common event.

unconsciously passes by the home of his love, much to his surprise, whereupon he realizes that his reason for going out on business was a means, a deception by which his impulses anticipated the objections of his reason. Is it true that pleasure is the mistress of the will, and that the will then uses other pretexts to delude the reason?

Opponents of my view, wishing to prove that this theory is not false, must say that whatever we do realizes not the pretended goal but rather the goal of the hidden desire, as in the case of the lover whose pretext was going out on other business, but who unconsciously was seeking his love. Can this be proven in fact? Hardly. The human will always attains its ostensible goal, and seldom what it fundamentally desires. The miser may accumulate great wealth, but the happiness he had expected escapes him. The ambitious person may gain fame and honor, but his suffering from his worry about losing it, is probably greater than his concern about getting it. Sexual desire leads to the propagation of the species, but once satisfied, the happiness ends and feelings of sadness abound. This is not made very clear in their exposition.

Certainly not.

People cannot attain their fundamental desires, and it may be said that people cannot attain their fundamental ideals. People can only achieve those things that take the place of attaining ideals, and once achieved, the ideal is again one level higher. Thus ideals can never be attained; only things can be achieved.

. . .

. . . Several thousand years ago, Aristotle had already explained the relationship between pleasure and the will. He said: Pleasure is not an end, but a manifestation [in the consciousness].[34] When the will is carried out, and it is accompanied by the appropriate manifestation, this is pleasure. Thus pleasure

Knowledge or knowing.

The term "a sign" is really like making a report to the will that the goal has already been attained.

is simply a sign that the will has achieved its objective. Pleasure is that by which we recognize that the will has been satisfied. But hedonism regards this recognition as good, as if to say, value does not lie in things, but in being of value, that satisfaction is not in the activity but in being satisfactory. Is this not tautologous?

The statement of negative hedonism that what drives human beings to action comes entirely from dissatisfaction would also seem to be founded in part.

Hedonism also appears in a negative form which says that what drives living things to proper action is not our idea of pleasure, but our feeling of pain, or the sense of dissatisfaction. Thus, the end that motivates us to action is getting rid of pain.

But this form of the theory likewise suggests that hedonism does not explain the facts. We know that the discomfort of pain may be a spur to action, as when ill we seek a doctor, or as when one who is idle seeks diversion or work. But is this the motivation for all activity? If we say that it is always discomfort that impels human beings to action, did Goethe write his poetry or did Dürer[35] paint just out of unhappiness? Is it pain that impels a child to play? I don't think so. The impulses of the will have nothing to do with pain; it is when the impulses are not satisfied that pain ensues. Human activities arising from the impulses always occur before the onset of pain. The farmer does not wait until he is hungry before he plants the fields. He sees the sun rise and breathes the clear morning air, and without thinking about it picks up his hoe and goes out into the field. What does this have to do with pain? When obstacles come between the impulses and their fulfillment, this may give rise to a feeling of

The motivation for such things is indeed not pain.

This has two interpretations: one says that it is determined by unfavorable conditions, and the other says that it is determined by favorable conditions.

Pain arises when the impulses are not satisfied. To say that impulses arise from pain is to turn cause and effect upside down.

pain. Otherwise, how is it painful? The impulse to fulfill one's hopes can only fill one with pleasure.

This paragraph is the conclusion of this section.

Thus, I do not believe that feelings, be they pleasure or pain, are the cause of action. For action in the basic sense, impulse and the will are primary, and feelings are secondary. The feeling of pleasure is a phenomenon that occurs when the will achieves its goal, and pain is the phenomenon that occurs when the will is unable to achieve its objective. This is what biology teaches, as I shall show presently. (pp. 54–57; Thilly 255–58)

2. On the function of pain as a goal of human impulses.

This is the reason for our love of change, our sense of curiosity. Human beings cannot be without change for long.

. . . If all the causes of pain, all danger, all resistance, all failures, were to be avoided, then struggle, competition, the feeling of adventure, the longing for battle, the joy of victory and the loathing of defeat would all be eliminated. This is a natural principle. But we would then inevitably be terribly bored by satisfaction without obstacles, by success without resistance, as we are with a game that we always win. If a chess player knows that he will win every game, he takes no pleasure in the match. If the hunter knew that every shot would hit its mark, he would take no pleasure in the hunt. What makes the chess game or the hunt fun is the fact that the outcome cannot be anticipated, that victory or defeat, winning or losing, cannot be predicted, otherwise they would be of no interest. Human life, too, is like this. . . . (p. 58; Thilly 260)

3. Using the laws of biology to confirm the hedonistic view. . . .

This is true.

. . . Biology says that pleasure attracts us, just as pain serves as a warning. Pain shows us what lessens life, while pleasure shows us what furthers life. The one warns us to flee, while the other guides us forward. The two may be said to be the primitive forms of the knowledge of good and bad.

The will or impulses contain no elements of feeling or of intellect.

The will or impulses contain no elements of feeling or of intellect. The newly hatched chick instinctively picks up kernels of grain not because it is hungry or likes to eat. Its actions, just like the falling of a stone, or the formation of a crystal, or the growth of a plant, are determined by natural forces. The same is true of the sexual impulse. In lower forms of animals, there is no prior sense of pain or pleasure. The evolution of life is accompanied by the development of the feelings. From the higher stages of animal life to human beings, everything has its own special feeling. These feelings give rise to the phenomena of pain and pleasure, according to whether its life functions are obstructed or furthered. . . .

This is a summary; each point is discussed separately below.

With the gradual evolution of the life of the spirit, from the feelings intellect is born. The function of intellect is to manage the activities of the feelings and to perfect them, to cause the will to know the difference between what is beautiful and what is ugly and make it possible to choose between them. . . .

Biology also suggests this.

It is for this reason that biologists do not regard pleasure to be the ultimate end of human life, but regard it to be the complement of pain, both of which function as guides to the will. The will, under the guidance of the sense of pleasure, exercises a function

The sense of pleasure is an indicator of the gradual attainment of the

highest good, and the hedonists take the indicator to be the ultimate end.

that moves life forward. Thus, the sense of pleasure is an indicator, a sign, of the gradual attainment of the highest good, and the hedonists take the indicators to be the ultimate end. If it is then asked, What is the function of pain? it is as the complement. Pleasure and pain are inseparably related. Since pain is very clearly a guide to avoiding harm, is not pleasure a guide to moving forward?

For those who maintain the hedonist position, pleasure never ceases.

Furthermore, there is also one kind of fact that, from the biological perspective, definitely cannot be explained in terms of hedonism, which is that once our impulses are satisfied, the pleasure ceases. To continue eating after one is already full is painful, not pleasurable. Only something that stimulates the palate can diminish this pain. The desire of male and female is the same. Whenever the organs of reproduction are used as instruments of pleasure, disturbances and disease ensue, and those who are not enlightened will clearly lose their function, and their lives as well. (pp. 62–64; Thilly 264–68)

5. A positive definition of the highest good. Now that we have rejected the hedonistic theory, let us give a positive definition of the highest good. It is my view that our human end, expressed in the most general form, is to let our human life functions operate within the laws of our natural constitution. Every animal desires to live as is suited to its natural endowments, to let its impulses, which manifest its nature, define its activity. The same is true of human beings. Human beings desire to use fully their mental powers, to live an historical life according to their

These are all what is called the objective content of life.

This section is very well done.

original nature. It is for this reason that we desire to play, to study, to work, to acquire wealth, to possess and to enjoy, to form and to create, and also to love and to admire, to obey and to rule, to fight and to win, to make poetry and to dream, to think and to investigate. And he desires to pursue all these things in their natural order of development. All human beings desire the experience of human relations. Thus brothers desire to be brothers and friends desire to be friends and companions desire to be companions and citizens desire to be citizens, and even enemies desire to be enemies. To wife and children, he desires to be a good husband and kind father. He desires all these experiences to maintain the content of his life, and then he desires to rear and educate sons and daughters to continue after him. If his experiences have indeed been exemplary, so as to prove that he was indeed an upright and true human being, he has then achieved the goal of human life and can die without remorse. However, what the content of his life is, is obtained from the history of the life of the people. Thus, we may also say that the human will is his personal form of expressing, and of maintaining and developing, the life of his people. (pp. 65–66; Thilly 270–71)

. . . Human beings are different from other animals in that from the animal impulse of self-preservation has grown a conceptual self-preservation impulse. For all subhuman animals the will that determines their actions is an unconscious impulse, but human beings can be conscious of it. We must think about how to express and carry out our aims in life which then become the forms of our life content that then make up the ideals that appear in our minds.

Liang Rengong's[16] article on the concept of the future and the belief in the present [*xianzai zhuyi*] contains this idea.

It is then the realization of these ideals that forms the basis of our attempt to perfect our constitution, and the development of our life activities and the definition of its value. Mankind indeed has a great many such ideals. The Greeks and the Romans, the Spartans and the Athenians, each had different ideals. There is a different ideal for men and women, for soldiers and scholars, for peasants and fishermen.

Their simplicity.
Their origins.

But they all come from one fundamental type, just as the features of human beings are very diverse, but if we look at them in the context of anatomical-physiological types they are all the same.

I would say that the human race has only a spiritual life, and not a bodily life. It is clear that though the spirit has changed frequently, the body has remained unchanged for thousands of years.

I would say that there are also differing degrees of depth in the ideals themselves.

As the spirit develops, the ideals become diverse.

With the gradual development of the life of the spirit, ideals become more diverse, and with the diversity of ideals, their realization becomes increasingly individualized. The direct perception of ideals as displayed in the consciousness is seen in varying degrees of clarity with each person, and the ability to resist corrupting influences and to pursue one's ideals also varies from individual to individual. However, all human beings have ideals, and furthermore everyone uses his ideals as the basis of perfecting his basic constitution and developing his life activities. It is indeed a fact that this is true for every human being.

It is concepts that create civilization. Indeed, indeed.

. . . As nations evolved, they were then able to form ideals from their past history. But in actuality, the historical life of world civilization is governed by concepts. Types of behavior for perfecting the basic human qualities

New ideals.
Life ideals.

and developing life appear that can overcome the old views and give rise to new ideas, that are ultimately realized in human activity. Consider the fifteenth-century movement inspired by the doctrine of universal brotherhood.[36] Did it not arise from the contemporary ideal of life? Did not the Reformation come from a newly constructed ideal of life of the believers in Christianity? . . . Such facts, arising from the great enterprise of real history, which have inspired the will of individuals and forced their acceptance, have all been due to the power of new ideals of the human race.

Historical life must be interpreted in this way for it to approach the truth or have value.

Thus, it is plain to see that the goal of realizing our ideals is not just a concept of assorted obsessions. When a people has an ideal of freedom or power or glory, and engages in realizing it, this certainly is not just an arbitrary wish for pleasure or happiness. Even when the ideal is realized, there is yet always a sense of satisfaction, but no one cares whether or not this is the greatest pleasure of the entire human race. A nation does not reckon the cost of its ideal. It strives for freedom, or power, or glory, without calculating how much happiness is gained or lost. In striving to realize its ideal, a nation will push straight forward, offering up the interests and lives of its individuals in sacrifice, and the individual willingly sacrifices his interests and life, without regrets. Even though they may dread the sacrifice as individuals, as members of the nation they inevitably are willing to accept their own death. The historical judgment, like the historical will, accepts this as its standard. A nation does not

See the introduction.

judge its own past by the standard of pleasure, but rather it determines the value of its historical persons and events according to the concept of its current basic character. Thus our judgment of Frederick the Great and his wars is not based on a computation of the pleasures and pains which they caused, but upon the honor and dignity they achieved, upon whether or not the nation advanced closer to its objective goals. The scientific historian does the same. He indeed knows that there is absolutely no hope of applying the standard of pleasure. Only philosophers hold on to this hope. But, so far as I know, not one of them has ever achieved this hope.

Thirteen philosophers, nine groups.

6. The historical arguments. The view here advanced of the ultimate end of the human will and the ultimate standard of the behavior value is not new. The Greek moral philosophers formulated it long ago, and additionally, all moral philosophies, with the exception of hedonism, accept this view. In the words of Plato and Aristotle: The highest good is natural character and life and action in harmony with the concept. The happiness of the human race consists in upholding and practicing all the human virtues. The Stoics taught the same, that living in accord with nature consisted of regarding all real things as the end of the will; thus, our ultimate end is to live in accord with reason. To live in accord with reason is the way that we find tranquility . . . (pp. 66–69; Thilly 271–73)

Natural.

7. The positive meaning of the highest good, in detail. Someone might query: But has this not commit-

ted the fallacy of circular argument? Did you not say earlier that the value of virtue lay in the fact that it aided in the development of life? And now you say, being virtuous, which is simply a kind of means, is also an end?

Behavior that is good and kind.

All positive virtues are both means and ends.

As I have already said, my reply is that this is true. The various parts of all organic entities are means, and at the same time they are also ends. As parts of the whole, they are like the bodily organs, all of which exist to support physical life, and at the same time are parts of the body. The body cannot exist independent of the organs of which it is composed. It is the whole of these organs that form the body. Thus, the activities of these organs are in themselves means that maintain life, and at the same time they take these activities as their life. . . . The moral life of the spirit in itself is an organism whose every power and every function are both means and ends. Thus each part has its own inherent highest value, but if its relationship to the whole is severed it becomes meaningless. . . . Negative virtues, such as not stealing or not committing adultery, have value only as means to such goods as truth, property, and marriage; they have no value in and of themselves. Such positive virtues as respecting truth, preserving justice, and upholding family relations are means of perfecting life, and at the same time are part of the content of life. The exercise of all such virtues as the search for knowledge, the acquisition of property, and maintaining the social order in family life and raising children are means to life and at the same time are important ele-

Negative virtues are indirectly related to the perfection of life.

Negative virtues are not "good" in and of themselves.

ments of life. (pp. 71–72; Thilly 275–76)

I would further say that although all virtues and motives are both means and ends, their value as means have differences of degree. The relationships of the different parts of a living thing to the whole differ in importance. The various scenes of a play vary in the respect to which they express the central theme of the play as a whole. Similarly, some functions of moral life are more central to life's ultimate end than others. Some are secondary means, while others are means that are closely tied to the ultimate ends. . . . (p. 72; Thilly 277)

Similarly, some persons are honored more than others according to their different degrees of wisdom or stupidity.

A similar conclusion discovered by evolutionists and historians is that later forms of life are superior to earlier forms of life. The life activities of the lowest forms of animal life are simply to get food and avoid harm. As they gradually evolved, the reproductive organs gave birth to love for one's own species. As the senses of the sensory organs developed into a higher capacity for knowing, this laid the basis for social and intellectual life. With the highest development of human social and intellectual life, based on our ability to remember the past, this development could be known directly, which is part of the content of the history of evolution, or what is called the history of man. One important part of the historical life of the human race is the expanding and deepening of our knowledge of reality, and another is the more comprehensive, more integrated growth of social relations, both of which are derived from the development of reason and social virtues. The

This section gives a clear and thorough account of evolution.

rational knowledge of things guides the will in the attainment of its goals. It is only when the social virtues serve family, state, and society, that the human essence as historical reality can be perfected.

It is for this reason that that human life which is able to develop these higher powers and subordinate the lower powers to them is higher in human character. Otherwise, that life in which the vegetative and animal functions and the sensory impulses and blind passions are dominant is a lower form of life. The perfect human life is one in which our spiritual abilities are developed to their highest, in which thought and imagination and action are developed to the highest degree. Seen from the perspective of human history, the social virtues are indeed an important part of life, for it is they that make possible a peaceful environment for human life and its mutual support. Thus, the common saying that truth and goodness are the two sides of the perfect life. However, the reader should not for this reason think that my view is the same as that of idealism, for I certainly do not denigrate the sensory side of man (i.e., the animal functions). The childhood pleasures of perception and play are also part of life. And eating and drinking and happiness have their place in the perfect life, as long as they do not become the whole of life.

This says that the sensory side cannot be denigrated. This differs from the view of the Song Neo-Confucians.

From this, we may further discuss the life of the individual in terms of its two sides of ends and means. The perfect life is the ultimate end of life. But as a part of the state or of civilized society, the individual is but a means.

Thus ends and means have no fixed position. Ends are everywhere, and means are everywhere.

Plato said that the state is a human being on a larger scale. Thus, the functions of the state are similar to the functions of the individual. The relationship between the community and the individual is much like the relationship between ends and means, except that as means the individual is part of the ends, since the whole is formed of the totality of the individual parts. Thus, we obtain a new standard for defining human character: The more a person fulfills his duty to his people, the more he contributes to the spiritual and historical life of his people, to their scholarship or ethics or art, the greater will be his historical value. Moral worth in the narrower sense does not depend on this, but upon fulfilling his duty to his state. The reader, however, should not think that this is idealism. (pp. 73–74; Thilly 278–79)

Benevolence [*ren*].

It is when we progress from the state to yet a higher stage, and become members of the world, that we reach what is called the human way [*rendao*]. The human way, the concept of benevolence expressed concretely, is the ultimate goal of the results of our search for the highest good within the realm of experience. The perfect human way, or, in Christian phraseology, the kingdom of God on earth, is the highest good, the final end of human beings. And because of this, the morals of nations are related to it as a means. But though they are its means, we must understand that they are also parts of the end. The character of each nationality takes this end as its highest criterion for judging the degree to which its concept of humaneness has developed. Although no nation or

However, does perfecting the human way also include the way of all things? If not, how do we explain that killing things is inhumane [*buren*]?

stage of development is totally devoid of value, the quality of the character of a people nevertheless inevitably differs according as the development of its political, spiritual, moral, aesthetic, and religious life approaches the concept of humanity.

We still do not know what humanity's ultimate purpose really is.

We cannot express concretely the concept of humaneness, but can only outline its general concept in human spiritual, historical life. All anthropological and historical studies furnish us with materials, but we cannot construct the idea. . . . Although we can see and compare fragments of the divine ideal in human history, these assorted fragments and their varying functions cannot provide us with an understanding of the organization of the whole. We can never have a concept of the organization of the whole. . . . (pp. 75–76; Thilly 280–81)

To explain it.

But the human life is but one part of the life of all real things. We can only have a formal concept of the totality of the life of all real things. We cannot perceive it directly, and can only describe it by analogies, thus it is called the inconceivable. It is called God. . . . (p. 76; Thilly 282)

Chapter III: Pessimism

This passage proves that mankind values surprise. Surprise is what the life of mankind is all about.

1. The theory of pessimism. . . .

2. The realm of sense perception proves the view of pessimism. . . . All those who have strong desires receive only a small amount of pleasure when their desires are realized. It is only those who quietly wait who experience the purest, the fullest pleasure when they receive what they did not expect. We see this in children. It is always

clear that those with the strongest desires are the least satisfied. (p. 81; Thilly 292)

Not so. Mature people too sometimes want to be children again. In their maturity, people undergo all kinds of changes, and since the period of childhood does not have these changes, adults look back on their childhood with longing.

. . . Elderly people often have the wish to be young again. Mature people never want to be young again, and the young do not have the desire to be children again, unlike the elderly. Is it not because having enjoyed a period of rest they have already nourished the courage to go out into the world again. (p. 84; Thilly 297)

Indeed, indeed. People really do take developing courage as their final objective.

3. The argument for pessimism in the moral domain. . . . Just as wild beasts must be kept behind iron cages, human beings must use the iron bars of fear to make cages of criminal laws to prevent them from acting aggressively against each other. Whenever they can escape the restraints of the criminal law, they will immediately attack each other. Even what they call virtue, if exposed to the light, is similar in nature. They are sociable from vanity. They are sympathetic from self-love. They value their reputations out of fear. They remain peaceful out of cowardice. They are benevolent out of superstition. Among them there are a few whose malice preponderates over their ignorance, and since those who have stronger wills invariably are more intelligent, the laws do not restrain them, so they burst from the cage like wild animals and pounce on others stopping at nothing. The many are like sheep, cowardly and stubborn and narrow; the few like wolves and foxes, ferocious and deceitful. Only those with wisdom and virtue stand outside these two categories. Nature hardly ever creates two or three geniuses in one cen-

Such things really do happen. In 1918, when the troops were routed in Changsha, this phenomenon did occur.[17]

tury. The same is true for saints. (p. 85; Thilly 298)

. . . The habit of sham and deception is strong today, but was there ever an age that was free of this habit? And was there ever an age in which those who saw behind the scenes did not have plans to reform it? It is doubtful, however, whether any age can dispel our illusions. Today, condemning mankind and exposing the evil side of mankind is a popular theme in the literary world. Showing the falsehood and coarseness of mankind is the task of poetry. Is this a sign that people's minds are turning toward the truth? I'm afraid that I am not convinced of it. Besides the craving for truth, there is another impulse in us that takes pleasure in the dark side of life, that feeds upon gossip and scandal. I doubt that this new school of art, which calls itself the realistic school is either healthy or worth welcoming. Falsehood is indeed false, and we should not close our eyes to reality. . . . (p. 91; Thilly 304)

Paulsen is a supporter of idealism.

. . . It is indeed a fact that even if people could dispel their sense of fear of each other, there are some who would not take pleasure in helping others, but that there are also those who would delight in helping others without being asked. Likewise, if you do not expect gratitude, when someone who has sincerely received your assistance shows his thanks in his countenance you will have a feeling of joy. . . . (p. 92; Thilly 306)

Mutual distrust and deception.

We furthermore often feel that it is quieting and consoling to form a universal conclusion about the baseness of life and mankind. For example, when a man has been deceived by his wife, he often declares that women are good for nothing. When a writer is ignored by the public he often says that ordinary people can't tell the difference between black and white. Another example is the fact that if, upon meeting someone who has been disappointed, we tell him that what he has suffered is an exception, his suffering is increased, while if we say that such a fate is common to all, his pain is mitigated. . . . (p.93; Thilly 307–8)

A penetrating insight into human nature.

4. The argument for pessimism in the historical-philosophical domain. . . . The poet Hesiod once described the ages of the world as beginning with the golden age and ending with the iron age, and bemoans the fact that he was unfortunately born into the iron age. Such a conception may be explained physiologically. The temperament of old age is always optimistic about the past, and unable to keep in touch with the present. Because he is powerless to do things in the present, and finds the cause of this not in himself but in the times, he often longs for the glowing age of his youth. The elderly are the bearers of history from whom the young receive knowledge of the past. They are the light of history. The tendency of youth in particular to admire, and the tendency to glorify one's own forbears, is also relevant. And the fact that the institutions of moral instruction tend to make use of history serves the same function. All those who for their own particular reasons are dissatisfied with the present love to humiliate it by praising the past. (p. 95; Thilly 309)

Such notions of praising the past and denying the present are held not just in our nation but in the West as well.

To sum up: As civilization advances, both the varieties and the degree of suffering increase. The same is true of pleasure. Thus the historical optimists say that the advance of history brings an increase in happiness, while the pessimists say that it brings an increase in suffering. I regard both positions as incapable of proof. Although both may refine their arguments, in reality neither can be proved. Only one conclusion seems certain to me, that the so-called advance of civilization brings with it greater sensibility, and also an increasing intensity of both suffering and pleasure. . . . (p. 99; Thilly 313–14)

A compromise position.

5. Morality and historical pessimism. . . . It is only particular personalities that can clearly distinguish between good and evil. On the one hand, we have reverent love, self-sacrificing loyalty, and passionate devotion to the truth and to justice; on the other, terrible depravity, even though, when the two are compared, there is more good than evil, and the abnormality of evil is in obvious contrast to the good as undoubtedly has always been the case. . . . (p. 102; Thilly 317)

More good than evil.

Chapter IV: Bad and Evil

1. Physical flaws. I distinguish between two kinds of human flaws: physical flaws and moral flaws. Physical flaws also come in two varieties: external flaws deriving from the world of nature, and internal flaws due to our bodily or spiritual weaknesses.

. . . All events in the world and civilization begin in obstacles and struggle. If the fields automatically grew

Where the river emerges from the Tong Pass, because Mount Hua is an obstacle to it, the force of the rushing water is much greater. When the wind blows back through the Three Gorges, because it is blocked by Mount Wu, the angry howling of the wind increases in intensity.

rice or the vegetable garden grew vegetables by itself, there would be no agricultural or horticultural arts. If the climate were always suitable to the body there would be no buildings. If all implements and articles were provided naturally by heaven and earth there would be no handicrafts. If this were true this would be no different from what the alchemists call paradise. This world that we live in is different from paradise precisely because of the obstacles and all the activities relating to these obstacles. Thus our present constitutions are more suited to living in this real world than to living in paradise. As for extraordinary obstacles, their effect on human beings is no different from that of ordinary obstacles. Floods teach us the art of building dikes. Fires are the germ of the evolution of building. Although we cannot tell a particular individual that a particular calamity from which he has suffered losses is good for him, it is possible to turn bad fortune into good. As he looks back on what happened in the past he may see that what was clearly an unfortunate occurrence might even have been a blessing. An evil that has been overcome by one's own efforts, and with help from others, is no longer an evil but has been transformed into a blessing which, recalled later, gives immeasurable pleasure. Is there anyone who has not experienced this?

From this we understand that it is the same with the effects of the flaws that are inherent to ourselves, what we have called physical and spiritual weaknesses. If there were people who were physically able to conquer the external world, who had the strength and endurance to resist harmful influences, and if there were people whose intellect surpassed others in understanding so that they never made an error, the result would be the same as living in the paradise mentioned above. The increase of power would have the same effect as the decrease of obstacles, to the point that would be the same as being in paradise. The value of the rice comes from the effort put into tilling it. If it could be harvested with no labor, it would have no value. The same is true of the human capacities. Our bodily organs are suited to life in this world, and thus our various kinds of life activities are responses to our will and feelings. Those living in a different world would have organs and functions different from those of mankind. But our functions are appropriate to our tasks. Moreover, the fact that our physical functions have illnesses, blindness, and handicaps that are greater than our nature and our powers yields an effect similar to that of accidental external evils. . . . Although we cannot say that all illnesses are useful to us, if we can make use of our inherent flaws, it is not impossible to turn weakness into strength, as we have already seen. Looked at in this way, evils are not only real, but necessary.

This is not true. As mankind's powers increase, external obstacles also increase. Great power faces great obstacles, and great obstacles face great powers, as inevitably as ordinary people face ordinary obstacles. For example, a great new continent to the West confronted Columbus, Yu[18] was faced with the great flood, and a host of European nations rose up to surround Paris and defeat Napoleon.

"The light dove dividing the air in her flight and feeling its resistance might perhaps imagine that she could suceed much better in a vacuum." Thus Kant chides men, showing that the activity of our understanding must come from the facts of experience. Similarly, human intent [*yisi*] must

A very true principle, very well expressed.

have obstacles to oppose it. Without resistance there is no motive force, without resistance there is no happiness. Pure happiness, like pure truth, exists only for God. For human beings, real happiness requires obstacles and loss, just as the knowledge of truth requires ignorance and misunderstanding.

2. Moral flaws. Physical flaws are unavoidable in life, but what about moral flaws, what we call evil?

The fleshly desires concern the individual, and selfishness concerns social relations; fleshly desire is related to personal virtue, and selfishness is related to public virtue.

I believe that evils, too, are inevitable ingredients of mankind's historical life. Why do I say this? There are two basic forms of evil: the desires of the flesh, and selfishness. The desires of the flesh, or sensuality, are sensory impulses that the powers of reason and morality cannot control, exposing their weakness, such as dissipation, indolence, frivolousness, and cowardice, and all kinds of intemperance. Selfishness, hurting others to benefit oneself, is the source of such evils as greed, injustice, and malice. If all sensual desires and selfishness were eliminated, since the world would contain no evil, it would also contain no good. The virtues of prudence, patience, and fortitude necessarily exist only in opposition to their corresponding fleshly evils. If human beings had no fear of suffering, there would be no fortitude, and without the stimulus of pleasure, there would be no moderation. Thus if there were no potential of evil, there could be no virtue. Perhaps good without evil is what is meant by divine virtue? But it is inconceivable to us human beings. The human social virtues presuppose the natural selfishness of the senses as their opposing counterparts. Without selfishness there could be no

Personal virtues.

Only afterward is it clear that the qualities of the sagely person, who "is born with the knowledge [of those duties]," "without an effort, hits what is right, apprehends without the exercise of thought, and naturally and easily embodies the right way"[19] are not believable.

Public virtues.

The sagely person is formed in the resistance to great evils.

virtues of justice and benevolence. All the virtues contain an ingredient of self-control.

The above talks of the types of evil, and this talks of actual evils.

Not only is this true, the actual evils outside us are also indispensable to the formation of virtue. Virtue grows strong in the battle against actual evils. Injustice arouses in the spectator or victim an increasing idea of the right. Falsehood and deceit reveal the value of truth and honesty. Cruelty and malice are the foil for kindness and broadmindedness. (pp. 105–8; Thilly 323–26)

All things in the world are realized from their differences and comparisons. The Buddhists say that we should extinguish differentiation. I wonder how they would deal with the problem of moral good and evil?

But if this were true the inequality, the lack of freedom, and the great wars that have existed in the world from time immemorial could never be ended, so how could the world be one of pure equality, freedom, and universal love? If it were, it would simply be a paradise. But is not the theory that is touted as the Great Harmony[20] a false ideal?

Thus if we eliminate all evil from history, we at the same time eliminate all the traces of the struggle of good against bad, and all of humanity's greatest phenomena of moral heroism are also lost.

Since today we do not live in the age of Great Harmony we wish for the Great Harmony, just as those who suffer strife wish for peace. But a long period of peace, pure peace without any disorder of any kind, would be unbearable to human life, and it would be inevitable that the peace would give birth to waves. Could human life stand the Great Harmony? I am sure that once we entered a reign of Great Harmony

But not this alone; the content of historical life is also lost. The forms of historical life are nothing other than the forces of the struggle between good and evil that develop with the times. If states had no schemes for aggression there would be no military preparations. If no one acted improperly there would be no need for laws. Military forces and laws are the means by which the state fights against foreign and domestic disorder. If all

waves of competition and friction would inevitably break forth that would disrupt the reign of Great Harmony. It is for this reason that the conception of a society in which the sage is exterminated and the wise discarded, and the people of one state grow old and die without having had any dealings with those of another, put forward by Laozi and Zhuangzi,[21] remains but an ideal society and nothing more. The realm of Tao Yuanming's peach-blossom spring[22] is also simply an ideal realm. This also shows that human ideals are seldom realistic, that they are mostly false. This is the reason for the natural alternation between order and disorder, and the cycle of peace and war. Since the earliest of times, when a period of order is followed by a period of chaos, human beings always hate the chaos and hope for order, not realizing that chaos too is part of the process of historical life, that it too has value in real life. When we read history, we always praise the era of the Warring States, the time of the rivalry between Liu [Bang] and Xiang [Yu], the time of the struggle between Han Wudi and the Xiongnu, the era of the struggles among the Three Kingdoms. It is the times when things are constantly changing, and numerous men of talent are emerging, that people like to read about. When they come to periods of peace, they are bored and put the book aside. It is not that we like chaos, but simply that the reign of peace cannot last long, is unendurable to human beings, and that human nature is delighted by sudden change.

disorder, both domestic and foreign, were eliminated, and all observed the way of justice, peace, kindness and tolerance, then war and diplomacy, courts and police, and all the aggressive features of government would disappear, and the perfect state would also vanish. Religion, too, is nothing but a form of the struggle between good and evil. If there were no evil acts, human beings would all be gods, and religion too would vanish. (pp. 109–10; Thilly 327)

I once dreamed of everyone being equal in wisdom, and of the whole human race being made up of sages, so that all laws and rules could be discarded, but now I realize that such a realm cannot exist.[23]

Something that is evil is so because it is inferior to something that is good. It is not evil by nature. Because it is inferior to the good, it cannot be equal in value to the good. But it cannot be said to be without value. At a particular time we may feel that it is totally without value, and not only that it has no value, but that it is very harmful. This refers just to that particular time, and in relationship to something else. This does not mean that by nature it is valueless in itself.

Evil is inevitable, but is evil normal? Does it have equal value to good? I think it is not. Evil has no value or right to exist in itself. It exists only for the sake of good, as a means to the realization of good. Good is to bad as light is to darkness. If the painter does not paint the shadows he cannot show the light, but his intention is to paint the light, not the shadows, just as in the old saying, the clouds take their light from the moon. The same is true of the poet, who cannot portray the grand, the beautiful, or the good without describing also the vulgar and ugly. But though his intention is to portray what is beautiful and good, he can only do so by setting them off against the vulgar and ugly. Both in life and in history, it is only the good that exists, while evil is subservient to it and functions as a stimulus, an obstacle to it. Thus evil is negative and has no value in itself. It is realized only as the opposite of good. This inherent quality of contradiction is without constructive power. As Kant said, evil cannot escape its own contradictory and self-destructive nature. Thus there is no positive antimorality.

That there is no principle of antimorality, or unvirtuousness, is like the case of falsehood. All truth forms a unified system, but there is no system of falsehood or error. As Epictetus (Epictetus, of the Stoic school, was

Because of such phenomena, my friend Zou Panqing[24] has a pessimistic view (referring to such things as those mentioned in these three sentences).

There is indeed a question here: Of what use to us is this historical reputation, and what is wrong with an evil person gaining a bad reputation?

I do not think a theory should be based on this. We should emphasize only whether or not the reality at the time was good or evil. If the actual activity is good then it is good, if evil then it is evil. We should not think about being good in order to leave behind a good historical reputation or about evil leaving behind a bad reputation historically. When we judge history and say that someone was good or that someone was bad, we are referring to the good or bad actions of that person. There is no goodness or evil apart from real actions. Thus it is stupid to think of leaving behind a reputation for all time, and it is also stupid to envy the reputation that others may leave behind them.

born in the year 60 A.D. and died in 120) said, there is no mark for the misses. In the present, a good person may be vilified and a bad person may be honored, but history is just. Even when the lives of humane and upright people are full of suffering and they are rejected everywhere, their virtue still stands, immortal and untarnished. The evil persons of their age, though they may attain the highest position and honors, will be unknown after they die. This is the admonition of history. Consider the case of Jesus, whose truth was bright and clear. The record of history moves our highest thoughts, and makes strong our will, though indeed no one has ever suffered as cruelly as he.

When Pilate sat in judgment on Jesus and said, Do you not see that I have the power to condemn you or to set you free? how great Pilate seemed to himself. At the time, he saw before him only a madman who was called king of the Jews, whose life or death would hardly affect the Roman Empire. But as we look back on it today, not only are the roles changed, Pilate who would otherwise have been consigned to oblivion long ago, along with all the other petty functionaries, is known to the world centuries later, just because of the story of this madman who was nailed to the cross. The tragic death of Jesus cannot be told without mentioning the name of Pilate, and so the foul stench of Pilate must accompany the sweet fragrance of Jesus for a thousand generations. His name will be known for generations, not for his honor or glory, but to let later people know that a judge and procurator of that time was not capable of passing the final judgment. (pp. 109–11; Thilly 326–31)

Augustine, using the words of Aristotle, once criticized the Persian religion, the Manichaeans, saying, "Evil has no real essence, but the loss or the absence of the good has received the name of evil." Spinoza and Leibnitz also believe that only in God is there perfection and reality. The difference between good and evil lies solely in the fact that our ways of looking at things are incomplete. In the unity of all things, God, everything is necessary and perfect. We cannot get away from ourselves to observe things, but we understand that our conception of things is in images that are not their essence. Also, we understand that evil does not have the same kind of value as good, and that it does not possess any real power in relation to good. Thus, it is clear that even though both evil and good appear in the world, we cannot conclude that the world is worthless.

I agree very much with this statement.

What we call evil is only the image, not the essence.

3. My view is not quietistic. Some may think that my view is quietistic because I say that evil is by nature unavoidable, but this is not true. My view does not say that because evil is unavoidable we should just sit down and accept it, but rather that since evil is unavoidable we have the responsibility to attack and suppress it whenever and wherever it occurs. The existence of evil in the world presents us with the goal of attacking and suppressing it. It would be a great mistake to say that because evil is inevitable we should accept or tolerate it. Disease that fails

Here too, my view is different. If disease inspires the medical arts and teaches a sense of patience and benevolence, if suffering is able to move the heart and instill patience, if falsehood is conquered by truth, if evil thoughts submit to one's conscience, is this not precisely because they are evil? Do not people everywhere say "we can't . . ." and "don't . . ." about other evils besides these? When evil does occur, do not "we still cannot . . . " or "still are not . . ." mean the same as "we can't . . ." or "don't . . ."? Those things about which we say "we still cannot . . ." or "still are not . . .", are similar in nature to those about which we say "it's already possible . . ." or "already happened . . ."; they are all bad. The reason we cannot do without evil is that it is capable of assisting our resistance and struggle, and thus every kind of evil is always under attack and being suppressed; it is not just that it is inevitable. (A close reading of this passage shows that the words are not clear, and this may not be what Paulsen meant.)

to arouse the medical arts or to teach a sense of patience and benevolence, poverty that is accepted without moving the heart, falsehood that is not conquered by the truth, and evil thoughts that do not submit to one's conscience, these are real evils. We must exert every effort to attack and suppress them. How could we just sit down and be indifferent to them? (pp. 111–12; Thilly 332)

Some might question this saying, since evil is inevitable in this world, then there is no way to eliminate evil as long as the world exists. Even though we work hard to attack and suppress it, it is but wasted effort. . . .

My answer is: Our impulse to combat evil does not come from the conception of satisfaction after the battle, but from being oppressed by this evil. It is clearly understood that satisfying one need, or removing one obstacle, will inevitably be followed by yet another new need, another new obstacle.

Do not worry about the harvest, just about the planting.

We want to do away with evil because it is enemy to the fulfillment of life. Thus we eliminate evil in the process of fulfilling life, not just to eliminate evil. In wishing to live a full life, how am I to know whether the evils are many or few, or whether I shall totally eliminate them or not.

Is this the inner peace of he who has the strongest, greatest powers?

But this does not diminish the strength to press forward. No matter what the circumstances, there is one inevitable result, which is the reality that right will conquer wrong, that good will conquer evil. Our most important task is not to bring perfect happiness to the human race, but to live our own lives properly. This purpose can be achieved under all conditions, in all times. Goethe says, he who is capable does what is right, without worrying about the results. Indeed! Those who are silently passive and simply accept being oppressed by evil, will not only be unable to overcome it, they will submit to it without courage and without spirit, which is the source of decline and weakness. But those who constantly strengthen themselves, not only feel that they can rely on their abilities, they often feel that evil is giving way before them. The satisfaction they get from this is not diminished by the fact that another evil will follow closely upon the defeat of the first evil. Future evils concern future human beings, and I should not attempt to anticipate them. My task is to eliminate present evils. (pp. 112–13; Thilly 333–34)

The good persons of whom poets write are those who die content, without bitterness for their opponents, even though they have suffered cruel wrongs. Such are Cordelia and Desdemona. Thus in the end they are able to overcome evil with good, and evil has no power to destroy their inner peace. It was a means of testing and perfecting their character. Sooner or later, evil does not wait to be destroyed, but destroys itself. (p. 113;

Thilly 334)

4. On life and death. Some people regard death as a great evil. Neither the individual, nor the nation, nor all humanity can avoid death.

But this is a false view. Death should not be viewed simply as an external necessity, but as an inner teleological necessity. Goethe says that death is the plan of nature that provides for the diversity of life. The plan that gives nature historical life is indeed not good for those who are dying, but without the change of generations there would be no history. The content of an unhistorical life, of the human race without death, is inconceivable to us. Moreover, if there were no death, I fear there would also be no life as we know it. If there were no family relationships, I fear there would likewise be none of the deep moral feelings, such as the love of parents for their children or the love of children for their parents. Thus, it is clear that if we wish to have human historical life we cannot hate death. Furthermore, human life is not infinite in its nature. Its powers and contents are limited. Biology and psychology tell us that every action tends to be cyclical. Thus there are fixed forms of thought and action, for which there are also corresponding principles. Cyclical actions invariably lead to contraction or involution, and finally torpor. The will and understanding are in ever-changing motion, which over time leads to a loss of the ability to respond flexibly to change. As people get older, even though they continue to come into contact with external things, they are no longer capable of receiving the new

Only the rocks in the ground do not die, but what human being would wish to live the life of a rock?

Cyclical

Contraction

influences, nor can they make use of them, and they gradually, imperceptibly, become strangers to the world. The decline and death of human beings is not due to an invasion of some external force but rather is inherent to our very essence. From the perspective of the living, as part of the completion of life, death is not to be despised. From the perspective of the dying person, the same is true. Thus both the living and the dying regard death as a natural law. How can it be evil? What the dying person wished to be, he has already experienced, and what he has lived for has already appeared in the world. His descendants, his nation, the truth, the good, and the beauty that he has lived for continue on after his death, so what regrets are there? (pp. 114–15; Thilly 335–36)

To accept it and die, what is there to regret?

Human beings are part of nature, are supported by the laws of nature. That the living must die is the law of all natural things, that what comes into being must perish. All natural laws have the quality of necessity. We human beings also have the necessary, inevitable desire to achieve. What more can we desire than to fulfill that which is fundamental and essential, and discard that which is inessential. Furthermore, our death is not death, but simply a dissolution [*jiesan*]. All natural things are not destroyed; neither are we human beings destroyed. Not only is death not death, life too is not life, but simply a uniting. Since a human being is formed of the uniting of spirit and matter, what is there to dread when the decline of old age leads to their dispersal? Moreover, dispersal is not a single dispersal that is never united again. This dispersal is followed by that uniting. If the world contained only dispersal without reuniting, how could we then see every day with our own eyes phenomena that represent unitings (I do not mean reincarnation)? The universe does not contain

only the world of human life. There are many other kinds of worlds in addition to that of human life. When we have already had all kinds of experience in this world of human life, we should leave this world to experience other kinds of worlds. If human life knew no dying, and if we were to live forever on this venerable world, we cannot imagine what the content of such an ahistorical life without the changing of the generations might be like, but even if we could imagine it, what point would there be in forever experiencing one kind of life? Would we then think that dying was painful? Certainly not. Never having experienced death, what makes us think it is painful? Furthermore, pursuing it logically, it would seem that the event of death is not necessarily painful. Life and death are two great worlds, and the passage between these two worlds, from life to death, is naturally very gradual, and the distance is by nature barely perceptible. Elderly people peacefully come to the end of their years and enter a natural state, an event that is necessary and proper. Where is the pain and suffering? I would guess that people fear death so much not because it is painful, but because it is such a great change. From the realm of life it is an enormous change for human beings suddenly to enter the realm of death. But if we could have some idea of what it would be like after the change, then it would not arouse so much fear. But we today still cannot know at all what happens after death. Where is the vast universe

heading? This truly is enough to evoke a sense of sadness and pain in life. However, I do not see it this way. Human beings are born with a sense of curiosity. How can it be different in this case? Are we not delighted with all kinds of rare things that we seldom encounter? Death too is a rare thing that I have never experienced in my entire life. Why should it alone not delight me? Whether it is painful or not, and even if it is, this pain will indeed be a wonderland. Even though the future is dark and unknowable, is not this dark and unknown world also a wonderland? Some may fear the great change, but I think it is profoundly valuable. When can such a marvelous great change be found in the world of human life? Will it not be truly valuable to encounter in death what cannot be encountered in the world of human life? When a storm rolls over the ocean, with waves criss-crossing in all directions, those aboard ship are drawn to marvel at its magnificence. Why should the great waves of life and death alone not evoke a sense of their magnificence!

In reference to a life fulfilled.

Here, I would explain it using natural phenomena, by the natural law of the rise and demise of things. Everything in the natural world comes into existence not without cause, and goes out of existence not without cause. Human beings are born not without cause, and die not without cause. Since there is a cause of death, one's death is explained by its cause. The purpose or reason why

But the above cannot explain the case of an early death in the prime of life, before one's tasks have been completed, or perhaps in early age when one's life has barely begun. And even the wise and great cannot help being confused by the fact that in an epidemic, the young and old, the wise and stupid may be brought to their deaths one after the other. It is indeed not easy to find theoretical evidence for the purpose of such particular cases.

one's life was not fulfilled is also the cause. Since this cause is the reason that a life was not fulfilled, what is there to regret?

At such times, we can only have a feeling of the frailty of man's powers and the inscrutability of the ways of heaven and be even more in awe of God's meaning. For those who have died prematurely, the grief of the living is double what it would be ordinarily. The Greeks often felt that the early demise of a young man or woman was not necessarily a misfortune, as the words of Solon indicate. Moreover, the fact that death comes not just to old people alone, but may strike those who are young and strong, enjoying life, and full of potential, may be looked at in another way. The purpose of such cases in the common order of life may also, to a certain extent at least, be proved logically. As the Greek wise man, Bias of Priene, said, You should live every day to the fullest, so that if you die in the morning you will have no regrets, and the same if you live to one hundred. This explains it somewhat. We cannot know whether our lives will be long or short. If we die young, to have no regrets, and if we live long, not to lose courage, this is our proper task. To not worry about whether one's life will be long or short, but to be prepared for it, then one may die without regrets. (This is precisely what Confucius meant when he said, "If a man in the morning hear the right way, he may die in the evening without regret.")[37]

When a person dies leaving behind achievements that will benefit later generations, we may say that his life continues on in his descendants and nation. But what if nations in time perish and what if the world in time perishes? Does this not then destroy the very foundation of all human life values? We cannot escape the fact that the cyclical stages of the life of a nation are the same as those of the individual, that the only difference is one of scale. This is not easy to explain. History proves that all nations inevitably go through the stage of old age and decline, of withering and contraction. As the fixed habits of thought and action, the historical stock of ideas, of structure and authority, increase with time, tradition acts as an obstacle to the forces of renewal, and the past oppresses the present, opposing the powers of the new age, gradually grinding them down, until this historical organism inevitably collapses. At this time, do the individuals have the ability to give life to the basic elements of the old civilization and create a new historical reality? The same is true for the entire human race. Although history cannot prove it, it can be deduced that humanity too will come to an end. Physics shows that the stars and the solar system all go through stages of birth and growth, of decline and death. They come into being by separation from other stellar systems, after which they develop and mature, and after an immeasurable life, grow old and decline, wither and contract. And the same is true for the earth and for humanity.

This is precisely the position of the Republic of China.

My interpretation here would be the same as above. The idea of the life and death of the individual is based on the indestructibility of spirit and the indestructibility of matter (spirit and matter are not two absolutely separate things; actually, there is only one thing, in which both exist). All phenomena in the world are simply a state of constant change for which there is no birth and death, no formation and demise. Life and death are both change. Since there is no birth and destruction, but only change, and change is inevitable and necessary, the formation of this necessarily means the destruction of that, and the destruction of that necessarily means the formation of this. Formation is not birth and demise is not destruction. The birth of this is necessarily the death of that, and the death of that is necessarily the birth of this, so birth is not birth and death is not destruction. The demise of a state is a change in its manifestation. Its land is not destroyed, nor are its people. Changes in a state are the germ of its renewal that is necessary for the

evolution of society. Today's German Reich is the same as the former German states.[25] The land is the same, and so are the people. I used to worry that our China would be destroyed, but now I know that this is not so. Through the establishment of a new political system, and a change in the national character, and a reforming of society, the German states became the German Reich. There is no need to worry. The only question is how the changes should be carried out. I believe that there must be a complete transformation, like matter that takes form after destruction, or like the infant born out of its mother's womb. The state is like this, and so are nationalities, and so too humanity. In every century, various nationalities have launched various kinds of great revolutions, periodically cleansing the old and infusing it with the new, all of which are great changes involving life and death, formation and demise. The demise of the universe is similar. The destruction of the universe is not an ultimate destruction. It is certain that its demise here will necessarily be a formation there. I very much look forward to its destruction, because from the demise of the old universe will come a new universe, and will it not be better than the old universe!

If the destruction of humanity is similarly inevitable, then is not human life also worthless? I do not think so. The flower blooms for just a few days, the dance performance lasts just a couple of hours, but they have value. Anything that is finite cannot exist forever. This is also true for the life of an individual, of a nation, and of the human race. Their essence is finite, so how could their development be infinite. Everything finite is perishable; only the infinite reality is forever and unperishable. But the fact that humanity must inevitably perish does not mean that all its values perish with it. Otherwise, why has humanity labored, and suffered and battled? . . . Death is simply the cessation of the continuation of life, and cannot influence past life. If the past life is worthless, and the present alone is real, is it only myself and my life, as they exist in my present consciousness, that alone have the quality of reality? But the present is just a single point with no breadth. My life is formed of a process that includes the past and the present. It cannot be formed of just that single point that is the present. If this means that my past life is regarded as being unreal, then is not what we call all of life devoid of the quality of reality? (pp. 115–17; Thilly 336–39)

Although it is not forever, yet it is forever. This finite reality can never be destroyed.

The past and future of time are arbitrary divisions that human beings make in the present, but in reality time is one indivisible span. And thus our life within the single span of time is all real. How can it be said that past life is not real?

In the realm of ethics, I advocate two principles. The first is individualism. Every act in life is for the purpose of fulfilling the individual, and all morality serves to fulfill the individual. Expressing sympathy for others, and seeking the happiness of others, are not for others, but for oneself. My heart contains this love of others, so I need to fulfill it, for if it cannot be fulfilled then there is something lacking in my life, I have not achieved my ultimate end. This is how both Sakyamuni and Mo Di[26]

achieved their ultimate ends. The second is realism. In terms of time, we see only past and future; we do not even see that there is a present. Realization does not refer to this; it refers rather to the spiritual and physical experiences that I bring together in the course of my life in the universe, and which I must make every effort to actualize. For example, a particular action is an objective proper real thing, which I should pursue with all my energies, and a particular idea is a subjective proper real thing, which I should apply my energies to realizing. I am responsible only for my own subjective and objective reality; I am not responsible for whatever is not my subjective and objective reality. The past that I have not known, and the future that I do not know, are irrelevant to my individual present reality. Nor do I believe the saying that historical human beings are responsible for continuing the past and leading the way to the future. I develop only my own self, so that internally my thoughts and externally my actions achieve their ultimate ends. After I die, I place myself in history where later people may see that I had indeed fulfilled myself. Because I have thus perfected myself, later generations may speak well of me, but I derive no pleasure from this, because it belongs to the future and not to my present reality. The same is true of things that happened before in history. I take from history whatever may be used as resources in the fulfillment of my life. Nor do I believe that I have a responsibility to

reproduce. If I myself desire to reproduce, this becomes one fragment of my entire life. To whom am I responsible for carrying out my own desires? Only what is in accord with these two ideas can be called true freedom, can be called true self-perfection. Paulsen says that though human beings die they leave behind achievements that benefit later generations, that one lives on within the sons and grandsons of one's people, and that this may be called immortality. This may only be a description of the objective aspect of reality, but it certainly cannot exist in the subjectivity of the person concerned. We do not strive for achievements for the sake of leaving a legacy to future generations. The capacity to benefit future generations is contained within the inherent nature of these achievements themselves. Likewise, the fact that I am not destroyed is simply because my body inherently contains these properties that are not destroyed. Paulsen also has these two ideas, but he just does not state them very clearly.

Chapter V: Duty and Conscience

1. The Origin of the Feeling of Duty. . . .

How does the willing being come to have a feeling that something ought to be done? Where does the conflict between the feeling of duty and natural inclination really come from? Is it that something supernatural enters into the system of the willing being? Religion says that conscience is the voice of God.

I.e., the conscience [*liangxin*].

I.e., sense of duty.

A kind of realm.

Although this is a good idea, it has no value as an explanation. Ethics cannot use God as a reason any more than physics can. The foundation of both natural law and moral law are indeed in the supernatural world.[38] But we want to explain it in terms of the facts of experience, and thus must not base it upon the transcendent world, but must seek it within the realm of the world of experience, and furthermore, I believe we can find it within the world of experience.

I.e., fundamental essence [*benti*].

See below.

Darwin said this in the fourth chapter of his *Descent of Man*, where he proved that the development of the feelings of animals is similar to that of human beings. He says that a female dog lying down with her puppies sees her master going out to hunt and wants to go with him, but out of love for her young does not go with him. When she sees her master return, with her tail between her legs, she seems to beg his pardon, as if she is very ashamed of not being faithful to her master. Domestic animals have two kinds of impulses: (1) those that are natural, and (2) those that come from training or habit, and they often vacillate between the two impulses. Darwin believes that this is the sense of duty in its primitive form, in which a resolution that is based on a learned habit comes into conflict with a natural impulse. At this point, there is a kind of inner feeling that compels one to ignore the natural impulse and follow the resolution that is based on learning or habit, which is the primitive sense of duty. Although we can also oppose the resolution that is based on learning or habit, nevertheless, if we do just blithely follow the

A conclusion.

An example.

The sense of duty.

Natural impulse.

The manifestation of conscience.

Inborn nature.
Secondary nature.

The sense of duty acts as judge or arbiter between the two sides A and B.

A noun.

This is like speaking of constantly striving to improve oneself.

I suspect that natural instincts are not necessarily false, and that the sense of duty is not necessarily true. The sense of duty, which derives from training or habit, is *a posteriori*, is acquired or artificial. Natural instincts come from Nature, and are inborn or *a priori*, not acquired or man-made. Whatever derives from Nature is a real thing that actually exists in the natural world. That which is artificial or man-made is obtained from experience, is created from conceptual thinking, in order to adapt to one's surroundings and better one's life and development. Such things do not necessarily exist in the world of Nature. If such things do not exist in the world of Nature, they simply are not real. But why say that, though the instincts are natural, they cannot better my life development, and that it is the sense of duty, though not natural, that can actually contribute to bettering the development of my life? I think that this view would cause us to adapt poorly to our surroundings, and not to develop our lives well. Even though the instincts are natural, it is not necessarily true that they cannot contribute to the development of life. Whatever is natural

natural impulses, this arouses a sense of uneasiness or shame, which is the most basic form of the troubled conscience. A troubled conscience may also be said to come from social or artificial instincts that are always at work, and which therefore oppose and suppress the very strong natural impulses of the moment. In human beings these kinds of feelings are especially strongly developed. Human beings remember the past longer and more accurately than other animals, and so the opposition of their wills to the natural impulses of the moment are powerfully determined by education and habit. (pp. 118–21; Thilly 340–42)

is both true and real. Can something that is both true and real fail to contribute to improving my life? Besides, my life and development ultimately depend on just such things. The desire to eat contributes to my life, sexual desire is good for my development, and both of these come from natural instincts. Since the will is based on instincts, how can the conscience, which is part of the will, be an exception? Since the conscience too originates from the instincts, it should in principle be consistent with the instincts. The inconsistencies that we sometimes encounter come from our knowledge and experience. Living in this world of continuous change and diversity is indeed not easy. Under the demands of a particular time and place, when we seem really to rely on our instincts, it is inevitable that we get ourselves into situations that threaten our lives and their development. Progressively subjected to the constraints of training and habit, the conscience, although it is also based on the instincts, may also, in special conditions, get into situations that conflict with instinct. This may be because we do not understand the laws governing the events we are experiencing, or it may be that there is no fundamental conflict with our instincts and simply that we cannot yet see how this may also contribute to our life and development. In short, the two are originally one entity, and our many different activities both create and in turn are driven by many different instincts. The conscience recognizes all of

them. The conscience certainly always sees our appetite for food and for sex for what they are. It is only at a particular time and place that the conscience will suggest restraining the impulses, as when the desire for food or sex becomes excessive. And then the conscience acts only to restrain or moderate the excess, certainly not to oppose or deny these desires. It is this restraint that perfects the job of the instincts. Thus, the instincts and the conscience are consistent as a matter of course, in harmony, rather than in conflict. *A posteriori* training and habits that are rigid and excessive will lead to incidents that deny nature and instinct, and will cause the conscience, which derives from the same source as instinct, which is likewise true and natural and real, to become warped and unnatural and false. This is the tragedy of excessive rigidity.

A situation in which the conscience commands the will to do something.

It is explained below how duty has a special authority.

The objection is raised: This cannot explain the special authoritative character of the human sense of duty. The authority that compels us to do what one ought to do does not derive from the life of the natural instincts, and the reactions of the conscience come from a different source than the feelings aroused by the natural instincts. Thus how can the authority that duty exercises over one's own will come from the system of natural instincts? (p. 120; Thilly 342)

Various other customs are, I suspect, also based on the instincts [*benneng*]. The long-standing prohibitions against such things as murder and robbery belong to this category. Such customs as these, I suspect, also derive from the animal herd instinct. The relation of authority and obedience, which is the basis of the state, is also present, in germ, in the animal herd. From this perspective, it is clear that duty does not arise from the inner will of the individual but is really formed by an external absolute authority. . . . (p. 121; Thilly 345)

I have doubts about this passage.

2. The relation between duty and inclination. We here return to the earlier problem, to discuss the relationship between the good that is in harmony with duty, and the good as that which agrees with inclination and contributes to human welfare and happiness.

My above argument is in complete accord with this idea.

From our discussion above, we may conclude that the conceptions of habits and customs act as the mediators between good as duty and good as inclinations. Those human habits and customs which come from our animal instincts are modes of behavior that promote various life activities and bring them into harmony with our ends. The force of habit and custom acts to benefit the preservation of society and the normal development of the individual. And duty is not seen as requiring human behavior that is contrary to habits and customs. . . . (p. 122; Thilly 346)

. . . All consciousness of one's duty regarding property involves rules that limit it, such as: Thou shalt not steal, cheat, be greedy, or stingy. Our consciousness of our duty concerning speaking is the same, as in: Thou shalt not be garrulous or rash, and thou shalt not lie. From this perspective, duty is the limitation of the impulses. Duty presupposes the impulses, and without the impulses there would be no duty.

This agrees with what I have said above.

The origin of duty is essentially negative, as in the prescription, Thou shalt not do something or other. So it is only when the impulses go too far that human beings are conscious of the duty to limit them. The positive formula does not state that, You should do such and such, but rather that, I want to do such and such. It is only when the natural impulses are in some way deficient that duty changes from, I want to do such and such, to You should do such and such. (pp. 124–25; Thilly 348–49)

. . . When we look at a people as a whole, the matter becomes perfectly clear. The natural inclinations of a people as a whole are always consistent with duty, and the common will of a people represents the moral law. The moral laws are not imposed from without, but represent the will of the people themselves. It is only for the individual that there may occasionally be a conflict between his inclinations and duty, as when he should do something but does not want to do so, or when he wants to do something that he should not do. It is at this point that he often feels that the moral law is imposed from the outside and that it limits his will. But if we look at the will in general, we will always find that the individual usually agrees with the commands of the moral law, and also that the individual will not hesitate to act or speak or have thoughts opposing any violation of the moral law by others. (p. 125; Thilly 349)

This is why the theory exists that society is more important than the individual.

3. Critique of the Kantian view. According to the Kantian view, the foundation of morality lies in the con-

flict between inclination and the feeling of duty. He thinks that in order for human actions to have moral value, they must spring from the feeling of duty, in a situation in which those actions are not motivated by inclination, or when they are contrary to inclination. To act benevolently out of natural inclination cannot be called moral. . . . Kant says that an action is moral when the person involved receives no feeling of pleasure from it, when he has no thought for the fact that it provides others with relief from suffering or danger, but acts simply because he considers it his duty to help others.

Self versus self.

The same is true of preserving one's own life or augmenting one's own happiness. To act according to inclination cannot be considered moral. The act of an unfortunate person who has fallen into great misfortune and who would rather die than live, who yet out of a sense of duty preserves his life, is indeed truly moral.

I would say that this kind of sense of duty can only be sought in the world of the unconscious, or in the world of the dead.

Thus in Kant's opinion, a human act has value only when the will contains a conflict of the inclinations or impulses, but one acts purely from a feeling of duty. But a humanity that is good solely for the sake of duty would be dry and insipid, like so many wooden manikins.

Quite so!

The unreasonableness of this position goes without saying. But there is also something that can be taken from this view. Although conflict between duty and inclination is not the general rule, and although the control of the feelings by duty is not necessarily an absolute law of moral value, nevertheless, moral character is only expressed when there is a conflict between duty and inclination. We cannot say of the rich man

Such cases do exist, but they have only a secondary relationship to morality.

who picks up ten dollars from the street and returns it to its owner that he is an upright person, because a mere ten dollars would in no way affect the rich man's finances. But if a poor man picked up ten dollars, and though it would be very useful to him, he nevertheless out of a sense of duty returns it, we would think him an upright, or perhaps good, person. Thus, when there is no conflict between the inclinations and duty, there is no opportunity for a person's actions to be determined by his will and sense of duty, so we have no way to evaluate this person's character. It is only when there is a conflict between duty and inclinations that we can judge whether a person's character is moral or not. (pp. 125–26; Thilly 350–51)

I still have doubts about this passage.

Actually, there need not be a conflict, as even when inclination and duty are basically one entity, there are still distinctions of gradation, degree, time, and place. These distinctions are sufficient to evaluate a person's character.

Kant over-emphasized the consciousness of duty, and Fichte was even worse. Our actions are not all due to a consciousness of duty, and even where this is true, it cannot be considered a fault. It is neither possible nor necessary that all natural impulses should be controlled by motives of a will determined solely by moral law. Moral philosophers have always considered that perfection could be attained only when all actions of the will were determined by the idea of duty. Spinoza's sage is governed wholly by the dictates of reason, and his impulses have no effect whatsoever on his behavior, and the wise man of Bentham or Mill differs little from him. They

The view of our Song Neo-Confucians was the same as Kant's.

Because these have all insisted on separating and setting natural will and the sense of duty in opposition to each other, they have failed to recognize that they are one, that the differences are only ones of degree, and of time and place.

are both modeled on the Stoic and Epicurean sage. In reality, reason, or the idea of duty, is not necessarily this important. Reason, or the idea of duty, regulates the impulses, but it cannot replace them. The impulses are the hanging weights of the clockwork of life. Reason definitely cannot replace them. Why? Reason has no motive force of its own.

This is the idea that regulates me.

Excellent point!

. . . So, too, the most perfect morality is to live naturally by realizing one's instincts, rather than by being concerned with ethics. Both aesthetics and ethics possess no creative power. It is their job to guard against going beyond the bounds of beauty and morality. Thus they are restrictive, not creative. The realization of beauty and of morality does not wait upon the rules of aesthetics or of ethics entering into the consciousness, or upon their becoming the central focus of attention. Moreover, when the rules of aesthetics or of ethics enter the consciousness, or become the focus of attention, they invariably become obstacles to the realization of one's art or morality. It is well known that when writing, getting mired down in the rules of writing leads to uncertainty and confusion. The best way to answer a question in orthography is to take up your pen and write it properly. The best way to answer a moral question is by performing the act rather than reflecting upon it.

I strongly support this view.

Beauty existed long before there was a field of aesthetics, and every human being had virtue and attained his ultimate end long before there was a study of ethics. All the many writings merely outline actual situations and describe their natural principles. All books of all kinds merely describe; they do not act or do. It is of the basic nature of our minds that they operate within a limited realm and cannot create anything at all! If the universe had always existed in this same state, it would not have had the capacity to create. If spirit is not destroyed and matter is not destroyed, spirit cannot be born and matter cannot be created, and if there is no destruction how can there be any birth? There can only be change. Our minds are limited to concepts, and concepts are limited to phenomena, and phenomena are limited to reality. Our minds contain only changes; how can they create anything whatsoever?

An unbiased mind will say that the moral value of human beings certainly does not depend on thinking a lot about duty or on a consciousness of the motivation for one's actions. One whose actions are forced is totally different from someone whose actions are natural. I have no way of knowing whether the descriptions of Kant given by his biographers are really true or not, or whether Kant the person really took duty as the motivation for his actions. In any case, I must confess that these descriptions have never pleased me. Although the sense of duty may serve to prevent evil, the truly great person is certainly never one who acts from a sense of duty, but rather is one who is primarily molded by the vitality of the impulses of his feelings. (pp. 128–29; Thilly 355)

The truly great person develops the original nature with which Nature endowed him, and expands upon the best, the greatest of the capacities of his original nature. This is what makes him great. Everything that comes from outside his original nature, such as restraints and restrictions, is cast aside by the great motive power that is contained within his original nature. It is this motive power that is the strongest and truest reality, that is the spring that fulfills his character, what this work calls natural impulses or inclinations. He then judges whether or not it is right and proper to exercise this motive power. If it is right and proper he upholds it; if not, he reforms or changes it so that it is made right and proper. This comes solely from his own judgment, not in obedience to an external moral law, or to what is called here a sense of duty. The great actions of the hero are his own, are the expression of his motive power, lofty and cleansing, relying on no precedent. His force is like that of a powerful wind arising from a deep gorge, like the irresist-

ible sexual desire for one's lover, a force that will not stop, that cannot be stopped. All obstacles dissolve before him. I have observed from ancient times the fierce power of courageous generals on the battle line facing undaunted ten thousand enemies. It is said that one man who scorns death will prevail over one hundred men. This is because he fears nothing, because his motive force presses forward in a straight line. Because he cannot be stopped or eliminated, he is the strongest, the most powerful. This is true also of the spirit of the great man and of the spirit of the sage. For Paulsen, the great man is not one who acts according to a sense of duty that would temper and constrain the vitality of the impulses of his feelings. How true, how true! (Note: I see this as quite similar to the view that Mencius puts forward in the two chapters "Haoran zhi qi" and "Da Zhangfu."[27])

4. On the errors of the a-prioristic-intuitionalistic moral philosophy. . . .

I think that in reality, anyone can immediately recognize the truth of the moral laws without having sought their purpose or understanding. In content, they are no more than the positive and negative expressions of customs and habits, and these customs and habits exist in the consciousness of every member of the entire society. A person knows of customs and habits through the many particular judgments by which others and he himself approve or disapprove of different kinds of actions. The fact that whenever a particular event is encountered it is immediately judged with certainty is something that comes with practice. The same is true of human knowledge of the general forms of morality, which are impressed on us from childhood up. Schopenhauer says, not without reason, that truths that we do not remember having learned are erroneously regarded as innate. Moreover, all words that refer to actions contain within their meaning moral judgments of right and wrong, such as the fact that the terms falsehood and greed imply disapproval, while fairness and frugality imply approval. . . . (pp. 129; Thilly 355–56)

That such terms in their origins do indeed agree with objective facts is due to the fact that they are derived from all kinds of experience. As far as the individual is concerned, since they have been practiced since childhood, they seem to be *a priori* truths. Historically speaking, however, they are derived purely from experience, and are not intuitively known *a priori* truths.

. . . There is unquestionably an objective ground for the existence and validity of the moral laws, which appear in the consciousness of the individual in the form of what we call inconceivable[39] commands and prohibitions; they are the condition of the welfare of the individual and of society. The task of moral philosophy is to validate their foundations, just as the task of legal philosophy is to validate the foundations of the content and form of laws. . . . (p. 130; Thilly 356–57)

Only to validate.

This refers to the ultimate great purpose of humanity.

I believe that it is indeed difficult to know what will bring true and durable advantage, but to say that human beings know easily the imperatives of duty is not in accord with the facts. There are some activities about which everyone knows what their duty is, but this is not true for all actions. For any-

Knowledge of it comes from experience.

thing that is somewhat complex it is never easy to know where one's duty lies. . . . (p. 130; Thilly 357)

Suppose that a politician disagrees with one of the positions of the party to which he belongs, and his party drafts a platform that expresses the great achievements of the party, and requires him to sign it. If he goes along and signs it, he is cheating himself; if he refuses to sign it, he will lose his political influence, and this will be a great obstacle to his future. Kant's categorical imperative cannot help him decide how to deal with this problem. In my view, he should first ask himself, How important is this issue? If it is not of great importance, it is not impermissible for him to give in and go along with the party's position; otherwise, he cannot do it. If the issue is of great importance, then rather than give in to the party's position, it would be better to leave the party and issue a statement of his own views.

Even though his words may not be believed and his actions may not be effective, he simply does what is right.

The objection may be raised that, if morality is uncertain, all kinds of doubts will appear to which there can be no resolution. I would reply that, it is not we human beings that make them uncertain; they are uncertain in and of themselves, and will always remain so. Morality is not a simple mechanical function that is based on some innate power, called practical reason or the conscience, that can be appealed to in an instant. Nor can every particular case be subsumed under a general rule. (pp. 132–33; Thilly 359–60)

True statement.

The central axis of Kant's entire philosophy is the absolute universal and necessary quality of the moral

Respect for particularity, a good proposal by Paulsen.

laws. Their absolute and logical quality is perfectly consistent with their legal and moral quality. For teleological ethics, on the other hand, the moral laws are derived from empirical rules, in the same way that hygiene is based on the laws of physiology. Thus, there are always exceptions to the moral laws just as there are to empirical laws. There is indeed a common rule for the way in which any particular action works to promote or injure life. But since human affairs are extremely complex, it is unavoidable that at times, the same action may have the opposite effect. Thus, a formal breach of the moral law may not necessarily be immoral, and indeed may be the only way to be truly moral. We often see that this is true in actual practice and in actual judgments. And that intuitionist ethics cannot explain this is a further proof of the inadequacy of its views. (pp. 133–34; Thilly 361)

Let us take an example. The first duty of a soldier is obedience, absolute obedience in his work. That the soldier takes obedience as his duty is essential to the existence of the modern state. Because this duty is so important, even a slight deviation from it incurs severe punishment. However, there are times when the breach of this duty brings neither remorse nor reproach. In the convention of Tauroggen, General York (on December 30, 1812, the Prussian General York signed a treaty of neutrality with the Russian General Diebitsch at the Russian Palace of Tauroggen which soon forced Napoleon I to retreat from Russia), based on his own observations and understanding of the political situation, publicly disobeyed the king's order, violating his duty to observe military obedience, by signing a peace treaty with the enemy. Was this action still in accord with duty, and was it permissible morally? According to the Kantian formula, certainly not. It is bad for the country for a general knowingly to act contrary to his king's order. Moreover, if pursued to its limit, at another time it might become impossible to use the universal formula to keep the Prussian soldiers under control.

Only after much hesitant deliberation did the general decide to take this action. What made the general hesitate was his thought, "To disobey my orders and ignore my duty to obey, is a gross abuse, and might destroy my country." But then he decided to do it, saying, "If I do not act contrary to the orders of my king, my country will be quickly destroyed." In the end, the general's action was accepted by popular opinion. After having wanted to rebuke him, the Prussian king also admitted that he was right. And today, there is no historian who does not think that this action benefited Prussia.

The same was true of the dissolution of Parliament by Cromwell.

And even though this action was most disadvantageous for the French, French historians do not question it. Thus, the example of an official being immoral and violating the state's commands in pursuing his own policy in order to save the state in an emergency has been publicly accepted. All similar situations cannot be dealt with by

This is necessarily true in the case of a revolution.

using the universal principle. If the universal principle were to be upheld no matter what, then a soldier would have to obey no matter what the outcome might be. He absolutely could not violate his duty to obey and pursue an independent policy. However, when the situation is an emergency that involves the life and death of the state, and the state cannot be saved except by disobeying the chain of command, then one has no choice but to break the universal rule. The highest among all the laws, what is called the law of the universal welfare, is a condition that even the wise sage cannot violate, and if a soldier mistakenly violates this condition, then it is proper for the government to punish him with death.

The moral laws are also subject to this condition, and so there will always be exceptions. The moral laws are made for man, not man for the moral laws. The jurists have an old maxim, *Fiat justitia, pereat mundus.*[40] The Kantian moral philosophers have also said, *Fiat lex, pereat vita.* This means that the laws are more important than any particular purpose. But the law really exists for the sake of the people, to preserve them, not to destroy them. The same is true of the relation between the moral laws and human life. They exist to preserve life, not to destroy it. Thus if following the moral law should result in destroying life, then the form must give way to the content, the means to the end. (pp. 134–35; Thilly 362–63)

Only when it is just [*yi*].

5. Conscience [*liangxin*]. We stated above that conscience comes from a consciousness of social custom, that it is the existence of social custom within the consciousness of the individual. The so-called authority of the conscience exists within the entire human race to restrain the will of those

who would oppose the moral laws, and thus is the guarantor of the moral laws. It exists within human beings first as the authority of parents and teachers who impress the various objective virtues of the social customs upon the child. And then, as the authority of society, which is wider in scope, it expresses its judgment of individual behavior in terms of praise and blame. And further, it becomes the authority of the judiciary. . . . The content of conscience differs with each nation of people. Each nation of people has its own different characteristics and its different conditions of life, from which are formed its different social customs. Although the content of the conscience may be different, its form is always the same: the consciousness of a higher will that works internally within the individual to restrain the will from immoral intentions. This higher will is always regarded as emanating from a superhuman divine power.

This refers to the origins of the conscience and the origins of the authority of the conscience.

Those who say that conscience comes from a divine voice, not only think that the historical and psychological explanation is incomplete, they further think that it is dangerous, and say that it robs conscience of its sanctity and destroys its efficacy. Those who explain the conscience in historical and psychological terms also frequently accept this conclusion. P. Rée (whose work *Origin of Conscience* was published in 1885), who studied the origins of the conscience and wrote about the results of historical and psychological studies, says that, when the commands of the conscience lose their sanctity, all those who know that the conscience is man-made will violate

The reason for the theory that conscience originates in a divine voice.

its commands and act shamelessly.

However, I do not agree. Responsibility to obey the commands of the conscience cannot be erased just because of the logical conclusions of anthropological theory or because of its psychological definition. I indeed believe the logical conclusion which says that the conscience is an expression of a people's accumulated experience, and that virtue maintains human life, while a lack of virtue destroys it, and that the true nature of the conscience is not thereby diminished. Thus we would argue that the inherited wisdom of the people is strong proof that the natural order of morality comes from an objective self-examination, so how can this interpretation destroy the true nature of the moral order? As for psychology, whatever its view of social customs is, it too will not be opposed to them. The effect on the spirit of what is inherited or learned will not cease just because we suddenly discover that it is false or irrational. There are some scientists who are not free of superstitious habits, and there are some people who do not believe in ghosts yet have hidden fears much like those of ordinary people. In any case, we are dealing here not with the false or meaningless elements of concepts and feelings, but with really important elements. All human beings know that if everyone were without morals and conscience, and all behavior were determined by calculation and apprehension, a nation could not exist for a single day. Even the great philosophers have never been guided by moral philosophy in their everyday lives, but by impulses and feelings,

Paulsen's argument here is indeed quite true, but it is false to say that knowledge has no influence whatsoever on the mind, for knowledge definitely has a great influence on the human mind. The human mind is moved half by feeling impulses and the conscience, and half by newly obtained knowledge. The progress of the human race, its revolutions, its spirit of reform, depend entirely on being guided in its actions by new knowledge.

Beliefs must be preceded by knowledge which is known and then believed. Although there are superstitious people, this is a pejorative term we have applied to them, and they do not consider themselves superstitious. Rather they say that they already have a very intimate knowledge of something and therefore firmly believe it. We, on the other hand, point to their attitude of firm belief and call it superstitious. Knowledge comes before belief, and a particular kind of knowledge becomes the foundation for a particular kind of belief, which is then expressed in a particular kind of action. Knowledge, belief, and action are the three stages of our spiritual activity. All knowledge that leads to

belief, when it becomes known, the mind regards as true, and it is this condition of thinking that something is true that constitutes belief. When through moral philosophy we come to know the content of the conscience, this gives us even greater courage to follow the dictates of the conscience. Otherwise, knowledge without belief invariably leads to contradictions that necessarily create vacillation and indecision. Looked at in this way, the view that clarifying something logically and psychologically necessarily destroys the true nature of the moral process is wrong. And Paulsen's view that even those who understand logic and psychology do not rely on them in their actions, but rather rely on their original impulses, their feelings, and conscience, is also not the best of theories.

morality and conscience, by feelings of love for the good and hatred for evil. Chemistry has made great advances, but the human organs of smell and taste have not become superfluous because of this. In our daily meals we still distinguish between sweet and bitter, fragrant and foul smelling through the functions of our organs of taste and smell. Moreover, they are more discriminating than a chemical test can ever be. In preparing food human beings all rely on traditional knowledge passed down over hundreds of years, rather than just on chemistry. The task of chemistry is to explain, not to discover. It may, of course, be used as a compass to revise our eating habits, but anyone who discarded his ordinary appetite and inherited knowledge, and tried to eat solely by the principles of chemistry, would be a fool. Would it be any different if someone attempted to do away with the forces of conscience and social custom and tried to live solely by moral philosophy? (135–38; Thilly 363–65)

Very true, very true!

The phenomenon is the noumenon,[28] and the noumenon is the phenomenon. The sum total of all the infinite number of phenomena are the one great reality [*da benti*], which is divided into the infinite number of phenomena. The human race is directly related to reality, and is a part of it. Human consciousness and the consciousness of reality are interconnected. Reality is also called "the divine."[29]

Some might object that this is all very well, but what if the inconceivable sanction disappears? I would reply that that will not happen. In my opinion, there will never be a day when human beings will cease to believe that the feeling of morality and holiness derives from the divine. If these feelings were not deeply and permanently rooted in the nature of the universe, how could they appear from nowhere in the human consciousness? Is the human race really an anomaly in the universe, having only a superficial accidental relationship to it, and lacking any relation to the divine essence? . . .

The objection might also be raised that, if the origin of conscience is as empiricism says, then humanity is ultimately likely to think that anything that is not illegal is all right. When someone who originally thought that the moral laws came from the command of God, now doubts the existence of God, or perhaps even believes that God does not exist, would it not be natural for him to despise and reject these so-called commands? I would reply, yes, this indeed would be natural, but it certainly would not be true. If, as the empiricists suggest, the moral laws are not just an accidental arbitrary system, but have their foundation in the very nature of the universe, in the very nature of humanity itself, then what we call conscience is the reflection within the individual human consciousness of the natural correspondence of the moral life with the objective world. Its great value for preserving life cannot be destroyed by examining its origins. For example, the ancients thought that human language was a divine gift, and today, even though we know that this theory is groundless, this in no way diminishes the value of language. (pp. 138–39; Thilly 366–67)

Some say that we must believe that the moral law comes from the command of God, for only then can it be carried out and not be despised. This is a slavish mentality. Why should you obey God rather than obey yourself? You are God. Is there any God other than yourself?[30] Our study of the origin of the conscience shows that this problem also comes from ourselves, so we should obey that which comes from ourselves. All the myriad things that exist in space and time should obey what comes from themselves, for there is nothing that is greater in value. Throughout our entire lives, all of our activities obey the ego. The activities of each and every thing in the universe all submit to the ego of that particular thing. In the past, I emphasized altruism, believing that there was only the universe, without self. Today I realize that this is not so, that the self implies the universe. Without the self, there would be no universe. The universe is formed of the collectivity of all selves, and each self exists for itself. Without the self, there would be no selves! It is for this reason that within the universe, only the self can be honored, only the self can be feared, only the self can be obeyed. There is nothing other than the self to honor, except as designated by the self; there is nothing other than the self to fear, except as designated by the self; there is nothing other than the self to obey, except as designated by the self.

This statement is very true. All things human are natural.

. . . Thus the starting point of the evolutionists' study of history is the belief that all things human develop strictly according to natural forces. A man like Voltaire swept away superstition, but at the same time, because a basic premise of his philosophy was the rejection of the conscience as blind and worthless, his theory failed, just as did that of the theologians. The evolutionists firmly believe that a universally existing organ must have an *a priori* basis, and that it must perform a function related to the preservation of life. Thus it is the business of science to explain the significance of these functions for the development of human life. (p. 139; Thilly 367)

6. The differentiation of conscience.

. . .

This section on the differentiation of the human spirit is excellent.

With the increasing development of the human spirit and historical life, this ideal becomes increasingly specific and individual. All historical development is a function of differentiation. It is the assumption of scholars that as the various different races and nations of mankind became differentiated from primitive man, their different social customs came to express their mental individuality. And as evolution advanced still further, the basic national mentalities became further differentiated as individual mentalities. In a less civilized nationality, the people are basically the same, and all individuals have the same concepts, thoughts, judgments, habits, and behavior, the same mental life. As they evolve further, the content of life becomes increasingly richer and more complex. As the differences among individuals become greater, individuals look at things differently, and they become dissatisfied with the common view of life presented by their national religion and myths, which is the beginning of philosophy. All philosophies originate in the conflict between the beliefs of individuals and the common beliefs of their nationality. And as the judgments of the individuals become less tied to social custom, the individual becomes increasingly particularized, and life activities or livelihoods become particularized. The sphere of freedom of life-activity expands, and the area of life that is controlled contracts. The relationship of the life of the individual with the lives of others becomes one in which the particular character or personality of the individual is not lost, as in the case of parents and children or husband and wife, so that it becomes increasingly difficult to apply the old formulas or laws, and particular rules are developed. (pp. 140–41; Thilly 369–70)

. . . The religious morals of Jesus were much higher than the religious morals of the nation at that time. His concept of God was much higher than the concept of God of the people of his time. He thought that what his people called righteousness was despicable and lamentable and unsatisfactory. Thus he and his disciples placed themselves outside the laws of their people, violated the Sabbath, broke the eating restrictions, and replaced them with the new commandment to love one another. The conservatives were greatly frightened, and to preserve their old laws did battle with Jesus and killed him. But although Jesus suffered greatly and gave his body in sacrifice, his way [*dao*] ultimately triumphed and his believers founded the

This truly brings out very well the mentality of all those great men of the past and present who sacrifice themselves for benevolence.

theory of the heavenly mandate of the new kingdom of love. This then became the prototype for later generations, for those who thirsted for the truth and righteousness of the kingdom of God, for those who feel that there is not enough of divine love and freedom in their lives, for those who are tortured and burned for ardently expressing themselves and yet do not repent. (p. 142; Thilly 370–71)

Every great genius can become either a tyrant or a wise sage. Goethe's Faust portrays the spiritual transformation from extreme evil to extreme good. In the first part, Faust is described as a person who despises his people for believing in their customs, and who abandons himself to his desires. . . . The second part describes the transformation of this thoroughly evil person into one who knows self-control and respect for what is right, although he is never able fully to realize this concept. The Faust of part one could have been saved only by striving for some high end, by great suffering and great battle, not by becoming in his later years just a great hydraulics engineer. That so great a genius as Goethe left it at this was a consequence of the fact that in his own life Goethe had never experienced great suffering or great struggle, and thus he dared not write about something that was so far from his own subjective realm.

Quite true, quite true.

Although the two types of great evil and great good appear similar outwardly in their disregard for the social customs, they are very different inwardly in their relationships to social customs and the people. What makes a tyrant a tyrant is that he despises social custom and vio-

Yuan Shikai.

lates it in order to pursue his own desires; he seeks only pleasure and power. . . . (p. 143; Thilly 372–73)

This section is not very good.

8. The sphere of the meaning of duty. There are one or two questions concerning the concept of duty. What do we mean by meritorious duty? Can human beings do more than duty? What actions does duty allow? Are there actions that duty neither enjoins nor prohibits, that can be said to be neither good nor bad? All such questions deal little with reality and mostly with semantics. They can be explained clearly by defining the terms more carefully.

I, however, think that we have a duty only to ourselves, and have no duty toward others. We have the duty to do whatever we have thought about, that is, we have the duty to do whatever we know. This duty arises naturally within my spirit, such as repaying debts, keeping promises, not stealing, not being false, and although they are things that involve other people, it is also my wish that they be done. The meaning of duty to oneself means no more than just developing fully one's own physical and spiritual powers. Helping those in need, perfecting those things that are humanly beautiful, treading fearlessly in the face of danger and sacrificing oneself to save others, are no more than duty, since I desire to do them, and only then will my mind be at rest. If I see someone in danger and do not try to rescue him, even if not doing so would not be considered wrong, will I really think in my own

The concept of duty, in its narrowest sense, means considering what is in the interest of others, and determining that something should or should not be done, such as paying your debts, keeping your contracts, not stealing, and not cheating. As for rescuing someone who is in danger, or doing someone a favor, these are above and beyond duty, for they are purely voluntary, and unlike the former which are obligations. In this sense of the term, there can be no duties toward the self. . . . (p. 146; Thilly 377)

mind that not helping him is right? The fact that I think it is not right is what makes it my duty to try to rescue him. We rescue those who are in danger to set our minds at rest, and to develop fully the capacities of our spirits.

If doing something is considered meritorious, then it should be considered a duty. How can failing to do it not be a breach of the principle of duty? If we think wise or great people do it, then we should think that ordinary people do it. To call someone a wise or great person is to say that his or her spiritual and physical capabilities have been developed to the fullest. Everyone should seek to develop his or her spiritual and physical abilities to the fullest. To say that only the wise or great people would risk their lives to rescue someone and that common people do not need to do so, is to imply that the wise and great people develop their mental and physical abilities to the fullest, but that the common person need not do so. How can this statement be regarded as compatible with ethics?

Duty in a wider sense means all life and actions that are in accordance with social custom and the laws of morality. If someone should ask me what road to take, and I refuse to tell him, this would be a violation of duty. The concept of duty contains the commandment to love your fellow man. But to risk your own life to rescue someone is beyond the call of duty; to do so is to perform a meritorious act, but to not do so is not a breach of one's duty. These are the actions of the wise or great man. In this wider sense, I have a duty to myself to develop my own capacities. It is a violation of duty to ruin one's body out of negligence, or to damage one's mental capacities by idleness or dissipation. But in the responsibility to carry out this duty there is a degree beyond which is meritorious conduct. At this point we can define the concept of actions that duty allows. Although there is work that must be done, and we have the ability to do it, duty does not prohibit us from taking a break temporarily. And although there are other things we should use our money for, duty does not prohibit us from spending some money on recreation. As long as we seek to stay within the boundaries of moral behavior, duty tolerates minor differences.

In the widest sense of the term, there is no distinction between what is allowable and what is meritorious. Christianity admonishes its disciples:

"Be ye therefore perfect even as your Father which is in heaven is perfect." No imperative can go further than this. Thus, there can be no merit before God. Whoever has kept the commandments, can only say, I have done my duty. But human beings can never be totally pure and without blemish, so even the saint will also say, I am an unworthy servant. (pp. 146–47; Thilly 378)

What here is called duty is really the laws. Laws are made only to forbid people to do evil, and not to encourage people to be good. How can this be the most important of the ethical duties? Duty is directed toward oneself. Duty to oneself cannot be a matter of degree. Our duty should be to put the highest good into practice, that is, to develop our mental and physical capacities to their highest, and to experience life to the fullest. If I have a job to do and the ability to do that job fully, my sense of duty forbids me to slack off or fail to do it. Duty does forbid us to spend our money on frivolous pleasures when there are other things we should buy. Why? To be slack in doing our jobs or to be without the things we should have bought would create a lack, a defect, in the full life. Duty means more than just not doing something or other; it also means that there are some things that ought to be done. Duty is not just negative; it also has a positive meaning.

Chapter VI: Egoism and Altruism

1. There is no absolute conflict between egoism and altruism. . . .

. . . In fact, all our actions arise from and are determined by our own

But of these two, it is egoism that pursues life, and altruism is simply one of the methods it employs to attain one's life objectives. It goes without saying that there is absolutely no basis for pure altruism. Pure egoism is also merely a theory that definitely cannot be realized in this world of multiple individual entities and diverse activities. Although it cannot be realized, although it is not a factual reality, it does still have meaning. The basic meaning of human life still lies in fulfilling the individual. In order to achieve this objective, what methods should we choose? Should we choose the method of pure egoism? In the beginning, a people, and the individual person when first born, do indeed select this method, but after a while run into a great many obstacles, so they discard this pure egoism and choose instead the method of combining egoism and altruism, and thus all people pursue life. It is for this reason that we sometimes use altruistic methods to attain our own egoistic objectives.

The members of a nation or people do in reality join together and

will and feelings; they are never first determined by the will and feelings of others. However, this statement is not sufficient to reconcile the difference between egoistic and altruistic feelings, because if this statement were true, then the egoistic will would still unavoidably contain differences between the directly egoistic and indirectly egoistic impulses, and the latter would correspond to the altruistic impulses of the will. And then we would have to say that without the altruistic impulses of the will, human life would be just as impossible as it would be without the egoistic impulses of the will. For the individual and for society as a whole, both together are necessary to make life possible. Pure altruism and pure egoism are both erroneous as moral principles, and both are based on a false anthropology. They both presuppose the old rationalistic individualism that treats each individual human being as an absolutely independent being, that has only accidental relations with others. And the relationships between one person and another are either egoistic or altruistic. Those who claim they are altruistic say that altruistic behavior is moral and that other actions are either indifferent or bad. The defenders of egoism counter by saying that the whole of a person's relations with others consists simply in the pursuit of one's own interests, and nothing else. Both theories are based on one concept that appears at the beginning of Jeremy Bentham's *Principles of Morals and Legislation*, where he says, "A community is a fictitious body, composed of individual persons who are considered as consti-

live together. But I do not agree with the idea that the life of the individual derives from the life of the nation in the same way that the four limbs derive from the body. The life of a nation, including its politics and language, all began well after the human race had evolved and did not exist in the beginning. Furthermore, these later activities were created by individuals joining together, for the benefit of the individual. The individual came before the nation; the individual did not come from the nation. The life of a nation is the total life of its individuals, is formed of the combined lives of individuals. The life of the individual does not derive from the life of the nation. Once a nation or society is organized and comes into being, the individual cannot help but live within it. If we look just at the situation as it exists today, the inevitable effect is that the nation is great and the individual is small, that the nation is important and the individual is unimportant. A closer look would show that this is not really so. Paulsen's view reflects the fact that he lived in Germany, which is highly nationalistic.

tuting, as it were, its members." This conception has been abandoned in Germany since the end of the eighteenth century. In fact, a people is not a fictitious body, and the individual is not a fictitious member. A people is a real unified being and its relationship to the individual is like that of the body to its limbs. The limbs are brought into being by the body; they have life because the body has life. The individual is produced by the people, and has life and movement because the people has life. The individual acts as a member of the people, he speaks its language, he upholds the philosophy of his people, and his feelings and hopes are the feelings and hopes of the people. And the existence of the people results from the propagation and education of the individual. These are the relations between the individual and society in the objective realm. And in the individual's subjective realm, of the will and feelings, there is no distinction between the self and others. We all experience this personally. Only the moral philosophers deny it. All the inconsistencies between pure altruism and pure egoism are no more than their erroneous opinions that turn their backs on the facts. In reality, no one ever acts purely out of either altruism or egoism. And the motives and the effects of our actions always vacillate between altruism and egoism until the boundaries between them gradually disappear. (pp. 147, 150–51; Thilly 379, 381–83)

2. A summary of the effects of actions.

. . .

So we may assert that human qualities and actions that are of benefit to the health of the individual also benefit the progress of society, and that what is an obstacle to the health of the individual is also harmful to society, or as Spinoza put it, we should take what is of benefit to ourselves and apply it to the benefit of others. But the converse is also true, that virtues that benefit society also necessarily promote the welfare of those who exemplify them, and that those who turn their backs on these virtues also hurt themselves. (pp. 151–52; Thilly 383–84)

There is truth in this.

. . . Dishonestly acquired property loses its true commercial quality, so a life of cheating is always very precarious. The fruits of honest endeavors increase one's well-being, but this is not true if acquired by theft. If the argument were made that this is not true, then even if something has been stolen only once and it has been preserved and not wasted, why is it that everyone still looks upon it as dishonest property? What is true and false, praised and blamed, by the society as a whole always has an effect on the conduct of the individual. One may be lucky for a while, but sooner or later his day of judgment will come. Secret actions have never, in the past or in the present, resulted in happiness. Everyone knows that it is his duty to be considerate, fair, and kind toward others, and that this is the way to achieve happiness for oneself. If a person is able to extend his own feelings to others, and bring peace and prosperity to his kind and to his friends, then their peace and prosperity will inevitably reflect back on himself. And conduct that is haughty, deceitful, and malicious, that

The reason why stealing is not permitted concerns primarily human character, and secondarily happiness. Being a dark malevolent act, a despicable method, stealing quickly destroys a person's self-respect.

brings suffering to others, will also bring suffering to oneself. Looked at in this way, duties toward others and duties toward oneself are certainly not mutually exclusive. The individual's welfare is inter-connected with the welfare of his family, society, and nation. Whoever is able to fulfill his own duty to self, thereby increases the welfare of society, and by fulfilling his duty to society he increases his own welfare. (p. 153; Thilly 385–86)

3. Summary of the motives of conduct.

. . . Human inclinations, whether they come from his nature or from life, have many diverse causes. And the situation at the moment also contains direct and indirect demands, in the form of entreaties and admonitions, praise and blame, that are especially complex. When the peasant plows and harvests the fields, working all year long without resting, is he motivated by egoistic or by altruistic motives? This is an absurd question. If we were to ask the peasant himself, Do you work so hard in the fields for yourself, or for others? he would be puzzled by the question, or else he would reply, If I don't the fields will go to ruin. And if we were to ask, But why not let the fields go to ruin? he would reply, For a peasant, that would be disgraceful. He would give the same answer if we asked why he keeps his family and home in order. And if the same moralist were to investigate further, he would find that this peasant was working hard in the fields to benefit his village, that he was rearing his sons for his country, and that he was doing these things because he really wanted to. His motivation for increasing his income ultimately cannot

Reality itself does not make distinctions; the distinctions are only conceptual, in order to facilitate language and memory. Ethical qualities such as public and personal, great and small, or good and bad, are distinguished according to their usefulness to a person. This is true not just in ethics. All distinctions in the universe are simply those different aspects of it that appear to us when we observe and react to it. In its basic nature it is simply one single form. This is true of such things as the *yin* and the *yang*, of top and bottom, big and small, high and low, this and that, others and self, good and evil, positive and negative, clean and dirty, beautiful and ugly, bright and dark, and victory and defeat. Our various forms of human mental activity are composed of these distinctions and comparisons, and without these distinctions and comparisons historical life would not be possible. Evolution is the succession of differentiation. Only after there are distinctions can there be language and thought, without distinctions they would not be possible—

Not all the distinctions we human beings make about matters of fact are correct, and even more of the conceptual distinctions we make are incorrect. The reason for this is that we leap to conclusions based solely on superficial judgments of the usefulness of something, as in the case of public versus private virtue. We all know of such errors—

be that he says that so much of his work is for himself and so much is for others. All of his actions are both for himself and for others. They are determined by the total weight of his conscious and unconscious purposes taken together. Any listing of his actions that distinguishes so much for himself, so much for his family, and so much for society is like trying to calculate pleasure; they are just the conceptual distinctions made by moralists who mistakenly believe that they are real distinctions. (pp. 153–54; Thilly 386–87)

Distinctions arise from the drawing of boundary lines. Since human beings live within boundaries, their thoughts are limited, their abilities are limited, and their activities are limited. They divide up in many and various ways that part of the objective world that lies within the reach of their mental capacities and activities. This is how the world of distinctions is formed.

This section is argued very lucidly. The only goal of human beings is to realize the self. Self-realization means to develop fully both our physical and spiritual capabilities to the highest. Action is the means by which this goal is achieved. Action relies on the various organizations of the nation and society, the joining together of human beings. But to say that one writes for others is really very superficial. Our various kinds of activities, such as writing, use this as a means of displaying our own abilities. When engaged in writing, the writer is oblivious to both the past and the future, concentrating so intently on the writing that he is unaware of anything or anyone else except himself and his writing. This is the way it must be if the writing is to be true and honest, and not false and superficial. Other activities are the same. The same is true of a craftsman, even if he is working to make a living. Once he starts working, he must have no thought that this is being done for someone else. Zhuangzi says: "A hunchback was catching cicadas, . . .'I know only the cicada's wings.' "[31] Everything in

And what is it like for the scholar, the artist, or the statesman? When a scholar reaches his seventieth birthday, or on some other occasion, someone praising him will inevitably say that this person exerted his efforts for the happiness of the nation and humanity. And perhaps that person says this himself, as when Christian Wolff says in his preface to one of his works, I love humanity, and all my works have been written for others. Not that I question Wolff's word, but I wonder if when he started to write, he first raised the question of human happiness and then made a plan as to how he could benefit the human race, and if he picked up his pen to write only after discovering his so-called rational thoughts? This is doubtful. I imagine that Wolff must have first run into a problem that he wanted to clarify, and then, having a bright idea, he felt like expressing it in writing. At this point, was he not sometimes pleased with the thought of publishing his lucid thesis in a learned journal so that the readers could appreciate it, and he could strike back at the attacks of his opponents? And sometimes he probably thought that by striving to explore the truth and

the world that is accomplished and has value is done in this way (by being oblivious to the distinction between the self and others, by concentrating solely on the true nature of real things). This is why things in the world fail and are worthless. This is the difference between true and false, and the difference between excellent and inferior.

writing these several books he was making a contribution to human knowledge and increasing its value. The worth of these books is not diminished by the fact that they were written in response to these various hopes. Works that are written solely for altruistic purposes are inevitably far inferior to those written by a writer who seeks fame. Schopenhauer did not worry about the weal or woe of others. He wrote simply to reveal the great secret he had glimpsed and to make it known to the world, with no goal of benefiting others. His writings, like the verse of the poet or the canvas of the artist, simply express the marvels of his spiritual world. If there were only the self and no others in the world, there would be no writing at all. Without an audience, the lecturer would not open his mouth. If there were no readers of poetry, then the poet would not pick up a pen. But once the process starts, the writer does not need to imagine that this is being done for others alone. Goethe once said to Eckermann, I never thought that it was the responsibility of a writer to pay any attention to what will please others, or how I can benefit others. I simply always endeavored to enrich my personality, and to say only what I had found to be good and true. (pp. 154–55; Thilly 387–88)

I have questions about this. I suspect that negative suicide is also a form of self-preservation. He who cannot solve the problems confronting him, or is ashamed of sins he has committed in the past, may conclude that death is preferable to life, and thus he ends his life. This judgment that he would rather be dead than

. . . Those who sacrifice their lives also do so for self-preservation, to preserve their conceptual, intellectual selves. They have no regrets in sacrificing their lives because they wish to preserve the self that is greater than life, higher than life. Negative suicide has nothing to do with self-preservation, and cannot be called self-sacrifice. All

alive is egoistical. Even if we think that a difficult problem might be solved with some effort, that a shameful sin could be erased with effort, that self-preservation is still possible, he does not see it this way. This being the case, it is not impermissible for him to act according to his view of the situation. As for suicide committed for a cause, its value as self-preservation is self-evident.

The statement that the difference between the superior man and the petty man lies in what they consider happiness to be, and that human character is higher or lower accordingly, is quite true. The superior man and the petty man are one in their desire to manifest their egos; it is just that their understanding and experience may be higher or lower. Where there are higher or lower levels of understanding and experience, the methods employed differ similarly as a result. Our judgments of human character consequently also distinguish between higher and lower. Someone who does not really know himself may think that he is among the highest in character, and only when a great person comes forth does his own low character become evident. He who betrays his friends and country does not think that this is a sin. The fact that it is a sin becomes evident when we compare it with someone who does not betray friends and country. Therefore we say that there is no evil in the world, just lesser goodness, and that there are no evil persons in the world, just people of lesser goodness.

self-sacrifice contains an element of egoism. Unselfish martyrdom is a contradiction in terms. Self-sacrifice always seeks self-preservation. The reason that someone willingly gives up property or life is that he has something greater than these to preserve. The little man, on the contrary, will sell out his friends, or his good name, or his country, for material profit, not because he hates his friends or his reputation or his country, but just because he lusts after material things. Thus, the difference between the great man and the little man lies in what they regard happiness to be, and human character varies accordingly. Thus you can know the innermost disposition of a person by examining the value of what he thinks happiness is. (p. 156; Thilly 388–89)

The comparison with physics is very good.

Physicists claim that there is no isolated point in the universe, that every bit of matter in the physical universe has a reciprocal influence on all other matter. The same is true in the moral world as well. The actions of each individual necessarily have an influence on the entire moral world, and all phenomena of the moral world necessarily affect the conduct of the individual. . . . All phenomena are interrelated. No one can be totally indifferent to the actions of others. Upon hearing of someone else's actions, he makes a judgment that it is good or bad. And the result of all judgments is public opinion, which acts to further or retard all actions. Thus everyone feels that the conduct of other people concerns himself directly, and thus promotes or opposes it.

Judgment plays a really powerful role.

A question.

Is the difference between egoism and altruism therefore meaningless? Are there no differences between motive and result that can be called egoistic or altruistic?

I do not agree. This is not what I mean to say. There are always those cases in which there is a conflict, or apparent conflict, between my interests and the interests of others. At such times, one either acts in one's own interest at the expense of others, or sacrifices one's own interests to those of others, and there is no doubt that this is very much related to moral values. However, conflict between one's own interests and the interests of others, conflict between egoistic and altruistic motives, is not the rule but the exception. As a rule, egoistic and altruistic motives are consistent with each other. The way of life is not as intensely antagonistic as most moralists claim, with no peace at all. Although no one can escape the competitive struggle, most human beings do not depend on intense competitive struggle in order to be able to live. It is the experience of those who live in healthy families and an orderly society and that have regular occupations, that they generally follow a path that is of benefit both to the self and to others, and that they are seldom forced into a situation in which they cannot benefit others except by making some self-sacrifice.

The path that benefits both oneself and others is mutual aid.

4. Moral judgments. . . . Any altruistic act of self-sacrifice that results in benefiting others must be called good, righteous. However, what about an act that gives others a little pleasure and ignores my own important interests? Should I sacrifice my property, my health, and my life for the sake of the whims of a sick person or to lessen his illness a little? Is that my duty, or if not my duty, yet a fully moral act? Or should I sacrifice the interests of my own family to fulfill the wishes of others? The unprejudiced answer must be, no. My family and kin are closer to me than others, and to sacrifice the welfare of family and kin for the sake of others is not only not my duty, it would violate it. Thus, it is not necessarily good just to sacrifice one's own wishes and interests. In order to be good such an act must promote the important interests of others. Sacrificing one's life to save the lives of others, or for the public interest of one's nation, these are great and good acts. Not to

This is in agreement with our Confucian theory of ethics.

It also agrees with Mozi's universal love, because the mutual aid of Mozi's universal love does not ignore my own important interests for the minor interests of others, but is altruistic self-sacrifice that results in benefiting others.

be able to control one's desires even when it endangers the well-being of others, this is evil. (pp. 156–58; Thilly 389–92)

This is the Confucian righteousness [*yi*].

. . . The first of my duties are those imposed on me by my calling and position, and next come those that involve my special relations with others, and then those that arise from my occasional relations with others. If the interests of the latter are seen as more important than those of the former two, I would have to make a special effort to distance myself from the core of my ego. In the real world we easily make decisions on such matters. The relation of human beings to others is like that of concentric circles in which the centripetal force of the circles depends on their distance from myself at the center and determines the rate of their motivating force. . . . (p. 159; Thilly 393)

Mutual aid.

Sociableness is a factor in self-preservation, quite true.

5. The effect of the theory of evolution on ethics and on altruism and egoism. . . . The reason that the human race is superior to other animals, and that poisonous snakes and wild beasts cannot threaten it, is entirely due to the collective social capacities to provide mutual support, including such capacities as language, intelligence, and the discovery of tools. There is no power stronger than that of joining together to achieve a common purpose. Hence, sociableness is a self-preserving factor, which is exhibited in many different qualities, such as trust, friendship, and the sacrifice of personal interests for the common good. And the deepest foundation for these various qualities

is in following the social love of companions, from which comes the ability to implement social morality, rather than being eliminated by nature, and also to attain a superior position in the competition to exist among the various nationalities. . . . (p. 160–61; Thilly 394–95)

True.

. . . If human beings did not have feelings of mutual love, but were driven solely by egoistic feelings, there would still be order and common tasks. For example, there is much more mutual suspicion and envy in today's commercial and industrial society than there was among the agricultural peasants of the past. In German agriculture of the past, there was no such thing as competition or cheating between landlords and tenants, no threats of public disturbances or disorder. There was very rarely contact between one household and another. As systems of cooperation become increasingly complex the points of collision multiply. In all societies today where are there the most collisions? Among officials and teachers and clergymen, or among peasants and soldiers? Everyone is able to answer this question. The reason for this is that the society of commerce and industry is not nearly as simple as that of the peasants. On the one hand there is an increase in friendship and trust, but on the other hand there is also an increase in feelings of jealousy and envy.

This is really true.

Spencer appeals to the development of family relations as proof of his view. I believe that family relations have also developed in two directions.

This is the reason for discord.

In the world today, there are families that are in greater discord than the ancients could ever have imagined. This is quite natural, for with the appearance of increasing individuality, the mutual feelings of love and hatred also become increasingly intense. Wild animals live together in the hills and forests in far greater harmony than do human beings. (p. 163; Thilly 397–98)

This is quite true.

. . . If the world of the future attains perfect happiness and morality, this would in no way diminish the happiness and morality of past humanity. The kind of life they lived was suitable to their kind, and moreover was an inevitable stage in the evolution of the human race. And their condition does not lose its value, just as the age of youth, of taking pleasure in playing, does not lose its value. . . . (p. 164; Thilly 398–99)

This chapter is extremely well done.

Chapter VII: Virtue and Happiness

. . . .

There is a similar saying in our country: "On the good-doer He sends down all blessings, and on the evil-doer He sends down all miseries." [32]

1. The effect of virtue on happiness. The first truth that all peoples rely upon as the basis of examining all things in the moral world is that goodness brings happiness and evil brings misfortune. This conviction that is the conclusion of all forms of life experience has been expressed in proverbs. In the first chapter of his *Ethics of the Greeks*, L. Schmidt[41] includes an exhaustive collection of Greek proverbs and passages on this idea. Moreover, his introduction states that the Greek people were firmly convinced that the fate of the human race was perfectly just and correct, that good is rewarded

and evil is punished. (Pp. 164–65; Thilly 401)

. . . The basic nature of all things contains a force that connects virtue and happiness. But the conception of happiness tends to be focused within the internal nature of things, and thus the so-called direct effect of virtuous conduct is not necessarily an external happiness, but an internal happiness, or what is called internal peace. The humane and great person does not necessarily attain external happiness, though his virtuous conduct is certainly affected by external happiness. And even if he can never attain external happiness, he is sure to find internal happiness within his own heart. This truth is also in accord with the general position of modern ethics. (p. 166; Thilly 401)

The unity of happiness and virtue.

Between optimism and pessimism, is the pessimist correct and the optimist wrong? I do not think so.

All the pessimistic views of individuals and of nations may be reconciled within optimism. We cannot of course say that good people will never have misfortunes, just as he who is careful with his hygiene may even so fall ill, while those who are lax and dissolute may remain healthy. The great man may fail while the little man may succeed. The loyal and upright minister may incur the hatred of his prince, while the flatterer may be given high position. Such things are unavoidable in the human world. However, the fact that such things are always closely noted and regarded as injust demonstrates that they are not the general rule but the exception. When frivolousness or recklessness

Indeed, indeed.

lead to ruin, everyone says: Of course! But when someone who has been just and righteous meets with misfortune and even death, all persons will sigh: How inscrutable the ways of heaven! When the good person succeeds and the bad person fails, everyone thinks it quite normal. When some illegitimate action leads occasionally to amassing a fortune, people talk about it forever, precisely because it is not normal. (p. 167; Thilly 402–3)

Like the government of Yuan Shikai.

Whenever, wherever there is a society in which vice is upheld, those who are upright and virtuous will not be respected or loved, but will be treated with contempt and persecution. But those who follow vice will unavoidably be in conflict with each other, and will be judged before the court of the entire society, with the result that they shall crumble and fall. (p. 168; Thilly 404)

Excellent.

. . . He who acts virtuously takes only virtue as his goal, and if external happiness eludes him, and his senses suffer hardship, nevertheless his virtuous conduct brings him spiritual happiness. Spinoza said that the reward of virtue is not happiness, but virtue. This is true. (p. 171; Thilly 406)

2. The effect of happiness on character.

. . . Happiness and success often and easily make people self-satisfied and can lead to arrogance. The prosperous person is prone to criticizing others, and often lacks self-knowledge, so that he boasts of his own achievements and looks upon the failure of others as being due to their own lack of ability. Thus he belittles the efforts of others, has no compassion for their difficulties, and becomes insolent so that he is hated by both the gods and men. All those who become arrogant in victory are contemptuous of their neighboring states, abuse the weak, and insult the vanquished. Their own sense of careless security will one day be their downfall. (p. 171; Thilly 407–8)

As in the case of Germany.

What is true of individuals is also true of collective bodies, of nations, societies, and parties. Their common prosperity is an omen of ruin. They will then lose their capacity for self-criticism and self-control, they will end up by being overrun by the enemy they so despised. The world has always detested nothing more than those who are self-satisfied and arrogantly extravagant.

This proves that prosperity is the agent of ruin. On the other hand, we can learn from misfortune, be it failure or adversity, the results of which strengthen and purify. Misfortune can teach and temper us in the strength to stand up under pressure, the patience to be flexible. It also nurtures strength of will, the ability to be patient, and the virtue of modesty. Prosperity feeds the divisive qualities of human beings, while misfortune makes human beings draw upon the qualities of friendliness, patience, and justice that bring them together. When a storm suddenly drenches travelers with rain on a summer day, those who have mutually despised each other crowd together under the same roof, talking and laughing without rancor. When a city or nation meets with misfortune, those

Cause the blind to see and the deaf to hear, as it is said.

who ordinarily hated and despised each other all work together to help each other. These are all evidence for this view. The highest morality cannot be matured without great pain and suffering. (p. 172; Thilly 410)

In the past I was in this situation.

There are people who are dissatisfied with the present world and have visions of another world of perfect pleasure. There is no basis for their imaginings, but even if there were such another universe and they could go live there, I fear that when they recalled this old world they had despised, they would regard it as the better of the two. There are indeed those who hate their own country and move to live abroad. But before long they begin to think of home, and want to maintain a close relation with their homeland throughout their entire lives. The same is true of those who say they hate the world. If they could leave the earth to live among the stars, they would soon long for earth and regret the errors of their view. (pp. 174–75; Thilly 413)

This chapter talks of philosophical problems; fairly good.

Chapter VIII: The Relation of Morality to Religion

1. The historical relationship between morality and religion and its effects. . . . (p. 175)

Even before its full flowering, religion was a force that restrained naked violence and protected the young and weak.

. . . The gods are the enemy of insolence, and so become the protectors of morality. All those who are weak, without rights, strangers in another land, and helpless are protected by the gods. Those who persecute strangers, the old, or young, will be punished by the gods. This is its greatest significance.

This section discusses the evolution of the relationship between morality and religion; fairly good.

An exploration of the relation between religion and morality brings us even closer to this. All religions instruct us to have faith in a transcendent reality. All religions presuppose a feeling of dissatisfaction with the empirical world of experience. Fetichism and shamanism also assume a transcendent power or a reality that natural forces cannot reach, that can only be reached with magic. As human life develops, the will is gradually spiritualized. In the very beginnings of human civilization, the objectives of the will were solely concerned with the animal needs. With the advance of civilization, these objectives turned toward the beautiful and good life, or what is called the ideal human way of life. With the change in the direction of the human will, the form of the transcendent world that man imagined also changed, beginning with polytheism. Polytheism moved away from the vague indefinite magic of fetichism, and toward realization of the personal, historical. The gods of polytheism represent the human ideals of the beautiful and good life objectified. The Greek world of the gods was an objective representation of the national ideals of the human world. Thus each of the various gods takes the form of some aspect of the Greek ideal of human life. And this transcendent world could not but have an influence on the empirical world. These various gods were always mindful of human life, guiding, protecting, admonishing, leading human beings toward perfection. The magic character, though, had not been totally eliminated; prayers for the health, prosperity, success, and victory of their people were predominant. But the intellectual leaders gradually did away with magic and led the common people to regard the gods as a representation of the perfect human life, that is not necessarily to be expected, and treated reverence and admiration alone as the function of religion. Monotheism, the highest development of religion, contains even more elements of the ideal. Christianity does away with magic entirely. Jesus and his disciples seek only that the will of God be realized. Christian prayer presupposes that whatever comes from God's will is good. And ultimately, he who is sincerely submissive to God's will believes that it is holy, just, and kind. When I realize my will as an objectification of the will of God, as His revelation, this is truly the purest, most profound goal of mankind.

I would therefore conclude that the religion of any people is the reflection of its will in a transcendent world that expresses its deepest yearnings. . . .

Thus, it is clear that in the relationship of morality and religion, the two come from a single source, the fervent desire of the will to attain perfection. What in morality is just a demand, in religion becomes a reality. Perfection is described by morality in abstract terms, but in religion it is a concrete intuition. . . . (pp. 176–78; Thilly 418–19)

Form without content.

2. On their necessary internal relationship. . . .

There are two views of the world that are diametrically opposed to each other. The one regards it as most important that good exists in the world,

These are two of the great currents of philosophy.

that reality is itself good and that it exists for the good. Taking Plato's conception of the world as based on the idea[42] of the good, we may call this view the idealist world view. The reason human beings believe in God is because good is the foundation or goal of the world, or as Fichte put it, that morality is the ultimate basis of the world order. Thus the idealist world view is also called the theistic world view. Diametrically opposed to this view is the materialist world view. The materialist view says that the principles of reality are absolutely indifferent to distinctions of value; the whole of reality, which is composed of atoms moving in conformity with laws, has nothing to do with good and evil, and simply that all things are produced in the course of time. Living things are formed entirely from the accidental conjunction of atoms, and the feelings of pain and pleasure that living things have are no more than variations in the movements of atoms. What we call pleasure and pain, good and bad, are no more than this. All atoms combine accidentally and disperse accidentally, so all objects must die, and species must also perish. This is also true of the conditions of the formation of living things. Thus what we call pleasure and pain, good and bad, will also perish, leaving only the unfeeling atoms and the natural laws.

We must choose between these two opposing world views. And the choice cannot but be related to one's inclinations and conduct. A person whose life contains ideals must be inclined to the idealist view of the world, while the person whose life is purely materialist must be inclined toward the materialist world view. This is quite natural, for it is the inclinations that come first, and then one's world view. Thus, it is life that determines faith, not faith that determines life. As Fichte said, the philosophy a person chooses depends on what kind of a person one is. Truly. If a person just follows his unconscious impulses and momentary desires, how can he have a higher conception of the world? A person judges the worth of the world according to the worth of human life, and his evaluation of the worth of human life depends on his own experiences of life. If his own life merely follows unconscious impulses and momentary desires, then he will view the world as no more than the conjunction and dispersal of atoms. Likewise, if he has great ideals with lasting purposes. As for life itself, he knows first his own life, then the life of humanity, and then he knows how noble, how great, the world is. Such a person, then, will know the meaning of historical life, and that the whole of reality moves forward in the same direction as his own inclinations. And in this way, the value of his own life is influenced by the value of the entire world. (p. 182; Thilly 423–24)

Words are the sounds of the heart, and the sounds of the heart are the expression of the inherent capacity of the basic nature of the heart.

Thus life influences faith, and faith in turn affects life. If a person believes in the power of good, believes in God, this gives him courage and arouses hope. I dare say that no one in this world has ever accomplished anything of greatness without this kind of faith. All religions are founded on faith. Their teachers and disciples have conquered the world by faith. The fact

We can do without religion, but not without faith.

that, in the past, as in the present, the faithful have devoted their whole lives to their ideals, have resisted adversity, have overcome danger, and even willingly given their lives, is indeed due to the faith that good will be victorious over evil. . . . (p.183; Thilly 424–25)

3. The relationship between religion and science.

. . .

The feeling of awe.

This feeling of awe is the source of religion. Awe contains two meanings, humility and trust. Humility is thinking of the infinity of the universe and seeing oneself as no more than a ephemeral mayfly. Trust is the feeling not only of the great power of the universe, but that it really has the great capacity of giving birth and nourishment. This is the beginning of religious feelings. . . . (pp. 188–89; Thilly 431–32)

Resides in occupational differences.

4. The reason for not believing. It may be said that there are also upright and great human beings who do not believe in religion, and who advocate not believing in religion. Why is this? I would reply that there are indeed such persons, and the reason for it is that the capacity of religion is not equally present in all persons. Where the intellect and will are excessively developed, they may inhibit the higher, freer feelings. There was a great mathematician who, after listening to the reading of a poem, was unmoved, and asked, But what does it prove? Because his daily occupation had to do with proofs, and did not involve being interested in anything else, over time he seemed to have forgotten that anything existed outside of mathematics.

Darwin once related that his ability to be moved by poetry had disappeared over the years. This is likely to be true of anyone who devotes his entire life totally to the pursuit of science. And there are some who are so engrossed in practical problems that they regard anything that is not relevant to them as dull and boring. Such persons may be great and good human beings, but they are not normally developed. A most important aspect of their inner lives has not been able to develop fully, that part which is most beautiful, noble, and free. This is especially true of many people today. The strong point of the present, the division of occupations and specialization, and the use of mechanistic principles to prove the conditions of life, have contributed to this one-sided development. Many scholars praise the uniqueness of the modern age. The ancient Greek philosophers, the scholars of the middle ages, and the thinkers of both the seventeenth and eighteenth centuries had a much broader view of the world than today's scholars. The development of anyone who is addicted to one thing or one occupation will inevitably be one-sided. This indeed is not as good as in ancient times, when life on the one hand was simple, yet varied, when human beings had more diverse contacts with things, and for this reason had active imaginations and rich feelings, and they developed equally. Modern specialization is most prone to killing off religious feelings, and especially the scientific specializations. Salamanders living in the stalactitic caves of Carniola have lost their sense of sight and even have no eyes. This is

Paulsen emphasizes inner cultivation to correct the defects of materialist civilization.

Not bad.

a rule of biology, that organs that are not used will disappear. . . . (pp. 190–91; Thilly 433–34)

5. The relationship between belief in the immortality of the soul and morality.

. . . Faith in the immortality of the soul is very relevant to life as a whole, but not to moral philosophy. Whether or not there is life after death in no way changes the principles of ethics. The moral laws are the natural laws of historical life, of human beings living in this age, on this earth. Even if this present life is simply preparation for a life after death, we must still do so by following the moral laws. And should there be only this life, and no life after death, the moral laws should still be obeyed. Obeying the moral laws for the sake of this life brings its own reward that does not depend upon what happens after death. (p. 191; Thilly 439–40)

Quite true.

What is time? An inherent form of reality? If so, then to be in time would be a condition of being real. We might further say that something has to be in the present in order to fulfill the condition of being real. Why? What is not in the present must be either past or future, and the past is no longer, while the future is not yet. Thus, it must belong to the present. However, if we pursue this further, there is no so-called present, because this momentary instant that we call the present is already past. Thus, present is a point that does not occupy space. Being in the present cannot be a condition of reality. If reality is not to dissolve it must be real both in the past and in the future. Thus, being in time is not a con-

The question of life and death is a question of time.

I think that the question of life and death is a question of time, and that the question of formation and dissolution [*cheng-hui*] is a question of space. For the world, there is formation and dissolution, not life and death; there is only space, not time. By extension, we may infer an entirely different sort of world. I can imagine space without time, and feel that I am placed in an infinite, unbounded, broad, and expansive great place that has no present, no past, and no future. In this context, it is possible to maintain the view that both body and spirit are immortal. Is this not an entirely different world?

dition of reality. As Kant said, Time is not a form of reality, but a form of our sense-perception. Our consciousness is bound to this form of intuition which then appears as the experience of time. Its essense or noumenon continues forever, quite untouched by our thoughts of death or destruction. Life is definitely not destroyed by death. Since this life is a part of eternal reality, it is neither destroyed nor changed. How can this be affected by Karl Moor's statement that one bullet makes the wise and foolish, the courageous and the cowardly, the noble and the villain, entirely equal. Although death may sever the connection of this life with the future, the content of life can be neither changed nor destroyed, since it is of the nature of reality that it can be neither changed nor destroyed. (pp. 192–93; Thilly 440–41)

I would say that the discovery of the concept of time comes from a kind of physical mechanical change that exists in the objective world. The earth revolves around the sun and creates day and night. If there were only daylight or only long night, there would be no concept of time, and this proves that there is no such thing as time. The revolution of the earth around the sun is merely motion in space.

Some might say that if reality is completely without consciousness, I too would be without it. And furthermore, if I have no consciousness, then others also lack it, in which case, what connection do I have with reality?

I would say: I am reality, so reality is myself. I have consciousness, thus reality has consciousness. I have life, so reality has life.

I would disagree. Can the questioner prove that reality does not have consciousness? Otherwise, how does he know that reality cannot have absolute consciousness as its inherent essence? Can the commonly recognized view of the great philosophers of the past and present be mistaken? The divine consciousness is different from the temporal consciousness of earthly human beings, which is the reason that human beings cannot conceive, imagine, or describe it. But dare we say that there is nothing outside of what we can conceive, imagine, or describe?

It cannot be proven.

We dare not say it.

Temporal consciousness must be based in real consciousness before its origin and existence can be explained.

And who would dare to claim that this earthly temporal consciousness is not part of an eternal consciousness, or that all that exists in time cannot exist forever? And if this were to be denied, how would the questioner explain the origin and the existence of temporal consciousness? (pp. 193–94; Thilly 442)

The same is true of the faith of Christianity when expressed in philosophical terms. The eternal life of Christianity is not a sensory temporal life; it transcends the senses and time. It does not consist of clothing and food, but of a solemn blessing. With the end of this earthly life, the essence does not revert to a state of change. The temporal life cannot but undergo changes, so after death there can be no temporal life. The faith of Christianity is not just an abstract and negative function that just expresses the fact that the eternal life transcends the senses and time. It also presents an idea of the life that transcends the senses and time, and imagines it using the forms of sensory temporal life. Its kingdom of heaven has streets lined with gold, with gates of pearls, and angels clad in white robes, God the Father, and God the Son. And the hell it speaks of is composed of things that are repulsive and horrible to human beings. These are mental images, but not just mental images. It is a peculiar quality of faith that it steps outside the sensory world, yet cannot help but hold on to it. What faith throws away with the right hand it snatches up with the left hand. All religious faith vacillates between the sensory and super-sensory, alternating between imagination and thought. What it calls God, on the one hand transcends the temporal senses, is infinite and unchangeable, while on the other hand it is finite, changing, thinking, feeling, and willing, and so is described as being moved to joy and sadness. Polytheism attributes to the gods human sensory qualities, and gives them freedom. This gives them that aesthetic perfection that we so admire in the Greek gods. The spread of Christianity, from the beginning, had a special relationship with the inner sensory world, at a time when thought and imagination had long been divorced from each other. . . . (pp. 194–95; Thilly 444)

I say: the concept is reality, the finite is the infinite, the temporal senses are the super-temporal senses, imagination is thought, form is substance, I am the universe, life is death and death is life, the present is the past and the future, the past and the future are the present, small is big, the *yang* is the *yin,* up is down, dirty is clean, male is female, and thick is thin. In essence, the many are one, and change is permanence.

I am the most exalted person, and also the most unworthy person.

Chapter IX: The Freedom of the Will

1. The history of the question of free will. . . .

Since ancient times, the metaphysical freedom of the will has been the most difficult and greatest problem for philosophy, but I do not regard it as such. . . .

I agree with this view.

Greek philosophy did not address this as a distinct problem, but only touched on it occasionally. The Greek philosophers for the most part clearly believed that human beings are part of the natural universe, and thus that they are subject to the universal rules that govern the natural world. (p. 197; Thilly 454)

2. The question of using the facts to evaluate the freedom of the will.

. . . Human beings are born of their parents, just as are other animals. In body and spirit, they resemble their parents. And their temperament, their desires, their feelings, and their intellect are all inherited from their parents. At the same time, they are imbued with the physical and spiritual habits of the nation to which they belong; these are not determined by themselves. And their sex, as male or female, for whatever unknown reason, is not chosen by the individual, so it is clear that human beings cannot escape the jurisdiction of natural law. (p. 200; Thilly 457)

That human beings are subject to natural law is compatible with my view.

. . . Society constantly uses words and deeds to show us the difference between what is right and what is wrong, what is proper and improper, what is attractive and repulsive, and always commands or requests that we perform certain specified tasks. Is there anyone who does not receive instructions from his times? The builder does not build as he chooses, but as the age chooses, as in the fourteenth century in the Gothic style; in the sixteenth century in the Renaissance style; in the eighteenth century in the scientific style.[43] The same is true for the scholar who does not choose his own scientific questions, but has them chosen for him by his age. . . . (p. 201; Thilly 458)

In short, each and every structure of the self depends entirely on external materials, and we can in no way escape this world outside the self.

. . . The difference between an organic and inorganic structure is that the former is determined by external mechanical effects, while the structure of the latter comes from the force of internal causes.[44] For example, a sculpture can be fashioned with a chisel, but though mechanical effects can destroy an organism, they cannot create one. Thus the human race is created not by external mechanical effects but by internal effects. This is what our consciousness tells us. This is not to say that all particular processes arise without cause. Nor does it mean that the various momentary experiences of life are unrelated to the past. Nor does it mean that the inner principles, what is called the ego, are all uncaused. Nor does it mean that the ego enters this world as an independent entity. The human body is formed of matter, and becomes an organism only after it is matured. Although during the early stages of its development, it is greatly affected by material influences, as it evolves to a higher degree it is gradually able to resist material forces, and through the will, it becomes capable of changing its close ties to the external world, and indirectly its own form. Is what our will tells us in conflict with the above view? (pp. 202–3; Thilly 459–60)

I still suspect that human beings are powerless from beginning to end. Even after the development of the human spirit, are we not still defined by the natural world?

After writing the above, I got another idea, as follows: Although we are defined by Nature, we are also part of Nature. Thus Nature has the power to define us, and we have the power to define Nature. Although our power is very small, it cannot be said to have no effect. Nature without us would be incomplete. Our relationship to Nature is like that of the individual to his people. The individual is influenced by the people in many kinds of ways, but he is also a part of the people. A people without its individuals loses its power. From this derives the significance of both our responsibility and our freedom. All our various kinds of knowledge and social relations are molded by the external influence of parents, friends, etc. Indeed, but since it is essential that we ourselves have this basic nature [*benxing*] that can be molded in order for this to happen, what is there for completely external

shaping to rely on? This basic nature that is capable of being molded, I call our potential nature, and it is to this nature that I have responsibility.

4. The definition of human freedom.

The definition.

. . . The conceptual ability that determines all particular acts is what we call the free will. Thus we say that a person's acts are free when they are determined by purposes and ideals, by duty and conscience, not by the stimuli and desires of the moment.

This is free will explained through evolution.

The animal part of man is the track of natural experience. That part which is in Nature is still moved by external stimuli. With the evolution of the human race, it became possible partially to escape from the forces of Nature, to stand above it, and thus to determine and use it, rather than being determined by Nature. This is what is called personality. And it is this that makes it possible for human beings to become masters of all their own actions, and with this comes responsibility for one's actions.

Secondary nature.

At this point, it becomes quite clear that it is in this sense that we recognize that freedom of the will is not an original endowment of human nature but is acquired through training. . . . Human beings develop this ability in differing degrees. Those who are wholly controlled by the animal impulses and cannot attain mastery over them are vulgar barbaric people. Those in whom such impulses are wholly absent are dry and insipid people. Neither of these is normal. Thus, humanity stands between the animal and the rational. (pp. 209–10; Thilly 467–69)

Humanity is both animal and human.

This being the case, can human beings determine themselves by their wills? To this question, it is possible to say both yes and no. Yes, for every human being has the capacity of educating and aiding himself, and thus one's own life, both external and internal, through the function of consciousness, is formed by the ideals one embraces, and the natural impulses can always be suppressed or controlled. He cannot do this just by purely wishing or resolving it, but must examine himself and practice it constantly over time for it to become possible, just as in athletic training. . . . Demosthenes, the famous Greek orator, is said to have originally had a bad speech defect, but having resolved to become a public speaker, he worked at it arduously and with determination and finally achieved his purpose, becoming world famous. This is the only way for us to train our inner natures. He who has a quick temper, if he recognizes that it is wrong and wishes to control it, cannot accomplish this overnight, but must take appropriate measures to guard against and get rid of it gradually. By avoiding the occasions that arouse anger he may over time get rid of his quick temper, which is the principle that human organs decay with lack of use. Or if when such occasions cannot be avoided, he always reminds himself of many examples of the injurious effects of blind rage, and of the virtue of controlling oneself, and repeats them over and over to himself so that he cannot forget them, then a quick temper may also be gradually overcome. Looked at in this way, there is no doubt that human beings are capable of changing their basic natures by using their wills. . . . (p. 210; Thilly 469–70)

The method of self-denial and self-cultivation.

This is the origin of the theory of the omnipotence of education.

The power of the will.
The power of the mind.

Notes

1. Here Thilly has "rationalism."

2. For Mencius' view that not only benevolence, but righteousness, are "not infused into us from without," put forward in a discussion with the philosopher Gaozi, see the *Mencius,* VI, I, IV–VIII, especially VI, 7 (Legge, Vol. II, pp. 394–95, 397–409). On Wang Shouren, commonly referred to as Wang Yangming, see note 16 to Mao's "Classroom Notes" of 1913 and note 8 to Mao's "Letter to a Friend" of summer 1915.

3. *Xin li.*

4. Thilly's English text (p. 6) has "empirical and rational."

5. See Thilly, p. 6: ". . . mathematics . . . deduces propositions from definitions and axioms, and demonstrates them logically . . . "

6. Here Cai Yuanpei uses the standard Chinese term for empirical, which more literally means "experiential."

7. *Jiangqiu,* literally attempt to understand; here the Thilly translation has "theorize."

8. Here, exceptionally, we have reinstated the preceding two sentences, beginning "Schopenhauer," which are omitted from the extracts given in the *Wengao,* because otherwise the impression is created that the conclusion of this paragraph represents the ideas of Aristotle.

9. *Chongdong* is used here where Thilly has "strivings"; throughout the work, Cai Yuanpei employs it variously for "impulses," "instincts," or even "inclinations."

10. See *The Doctrine of the Mean,* XIII, 4 (Legge, Vol. I, p. 393). Mao has recast the citation and presented it in such a way as to stress the central importance of family relationships like that between husband and wife. The point of the original text is rather that, as Legge translates, "The way of heaven and earth may be found, in its simple elements, in the intercourse of *common* men and women." Cf. also Couvreur's Latin version, which says the way "habet initium in vulgaribus viris et mulieribus." (S. Couvreur, "L'invariable milieu," in *Les quatre livres* [Paris: Cathasia], p. 35.)

11. A reference to the *Great Learning,* 4–5 (Legge, Vol. I, pp. 357–59). This passage, one of the most famous in the entire Confucian canon, reads as follows: "The ancients who wished to illustrate illustrious virtue throughout the kingdom, first ordered well their own States. Wishing to order well their States, they first regulated their families. Wishing to regulate their families, they first cultivated their persons. Wishing to cultivate their persons, they first rectified their hearts. Wishing to rectify their hearts, they first sought to be sincere in their thoughts. Wishing to be sincere in their thoughts, they first extended to the utmost their knowledge. Such extension of knowledge lay in the investigation of things. Things being investigated, knowledge became complete. Their knowledge being complete, their thoughts were sincere. Their thoughts being sincere, their hearts were then rectified. Their hearts being rectified, their persons were cultivated. Their persons being cultivated, their families were regulated. Their families being regulated, their States were rightly governed. Their States being rightly governed, the whole kingdom was made tranquil and happy." The cultivation of the self, or person *(xiushen)* alluded to here is the same concept on which Yang Changji had lectured to Mao in 1913.

12. The reference is to the *Mencius,* VII, I, XLV (Legge, Vol. II, p. 476). Mao's paraphrase is reasonably close to the meaning of the original.

13. *Jian'ai,* the doctrine of Mozi (468–376 B.C.).

14. The relations between prince and minister, father and son, and husband and wife, which constituted the core of Confucian morality.

15. Here, and in Cai Yuanpei's text, on which Mao is commenting, the Chinese used for "idea" in Thilly's English version is *xiexiang,* which has a literal meaning closer to "image." The same two characters in Japanese, read *shashō,* stand quite definitely for image, as in "imagists."

16. Liang Qichao.

17. For an account by Mao and others of the depradations inflicted by warlord soldiers at this time, see the "Appeal to the Central Government in Beijing by Hunanese Citizens in All Walks of Life Accusing Zhang Jingyao of Ten Major Crimes," dated January 19, 1920.

18. The legendary emperor.

19. From the *Doctrine of the Mean*, XX, 9 and 18 (Legge, Vol. I, pp. 407, 413).

20. The chief promoter of the idea of Great Harmony *(datong)* at the time was Kang Youwei. Mao had earlier expressed admiration for Kang, but see his two brief, barbed articles of July 14, 1919.

21. In fact, the language and ideas here are taken from Laozi. The passages evoked are to be found in Chapters 19 and 80. The first of these begins: "Exterminate the sage, discard the wise, and the people will benefit a hundredfold." The relevant portion of the second reads: "Though adjoining states are within sight of one another, and the sound of dogs barking and cocks crowing in one state can be heard in another, yet the people of one state will grow old and die without having had any dealings with those of another." (D.C. Lau, *Tao te ching*, pp. 75 and 142.)

22. Tao Qian (365–427), original name Yuanming, *zi* Yuanliang, *hao* Wuliu Xiansheng, an outstanding poet, described an ideal kingdom, reached through a peach-blossom spring. The metaphor has long since passed into the common language in China to designate a utopia.

23. For a statement to this effect, see Mao's letter of August 23, 1917, to Li Jinxi, above, p. 135.

24. Zou Panqing refers to Zou Yunzhen (1894–1985), *zi* Panqing, alternative *ming* Bangeng, a Hunanese who graduated from First Normal School in the eighth class. He became a member of the New People's Study Society.

25. Mao here uses the Chinese transcriptions *Deyizhi*, meaning "deutsch" or "Deutschland," and *Ri'erman*, or German, to designate these two entities, but the distinction he wants to make is clearly that between the situation before and after Bismarck's unification.

26. Mozi.

27. See the *Mencius*, II, I, II, 11: "I venture to ask wherein you, Master, surpass [Gao]." Mencius told him, "I understand words. I am skillful in nourishing my vast, flowing passion-nature *[haoran zhi qi]*" (Legge, Vol. II, p. 189). Also III, II, II, 3: "To dwell in the wide house of the world, to stand in the correct seat of the world, and to walk in the great path of the world; when he obtains his desire for office, to practise his principles for the good of the people; and when that desire is disappointed, to practise them alone; to be above the power of riches and honours to make dissipated, of poverty and mean conditions to make swerve from principle, and of power and force to make bend—these characteristics constitute the great man *[da zhangfu]*" (Legge, Vol. II, p. 265).

28. The Chinese is *benti*, meaning noumenon, *Ding-an-sich*, or ultimate reality. (*Bentilun* is the term for ontology.)

29. *Benti huo mingzhi yue shen*.

30. Mao's handwritten text actually has "Is there any God other than God?" As the Chinese editors point out, the second "God" must represent a lapse on his part, and should read "self."

31. The reference is to a story in Chapter 19 of the *Zhuangzi*. Confucius encountered a hunchback catching cicadas on a sticky rod with the greatest of ease. Asked about his Way, the hunchback replied: ". . . out of all the vastness of heaven and earth, the multitude of the myriad things, it is only of the wings of a cicada that I am aware. I don't

let my gaze wander or waver, I would not take all the myriad things in exchange for the wings of a cicada. How could I help but succeed?" (Angus Graham, *Chuang Tzu,* p. 138.)

32. From the *Book of Historical Documents,* IV, iv; Legge, Vol. III, p. 198.

33. *Boaijia,* literally "persons [animated by] universal love."

34. This reference to an accompanying manifestation *in the consciousness,* which appears both in Thilly, p. 257, and in the German original, p. 258, has disappeared in Cai Yuanpei's text.

35. The footnote to this name in the Beijing edition of Mao's notes wrongly identifies the painter in question as James Turner, instead of Albrecht Dürer.

36. The old Chinese concept of *boai* ("universal love," "love without distinction") serves more than one purpose in Cai Yuanpei's translation. Earlier in this text, he used it as an equivalent for Paulsen's word "unselfishness" (see note 33). Here he has employed the same term to render Paulsen's "Humanist movement," which becomes *boaizhuyi yundong*. We, in turn, have freely translated this back into English as "movement inspired by the doctrine of universal brotherhood."

37. This is Cai Yuanpei's note; the quotation is from the Confucian *Analects,* IV, VIII (Legge, Vol. I, p. 168).

38. Compare with Thilly (341) "Both the natural law and the moral law may point to something beyond them, to something transcendent."

39. Cai Yuanpei introduces the term *buke siyi,* rendered here as "inconceivable," where Paulsen, in the original and in Thilly's English translation (as well as in Kanie Yoshimaru's Japanese version), speaks merely of commands and prohibitions which appear to the individual as "absolute." More precisely, *buke siyi,* originally a Buddhist concept, refers to that which cannot be grasped by thought or expressed in words, and thus hardly seems in harmony with Paulsen's view that the "categorical imperatives" of moral philosophy are grounded in objective reality.

40. The maxim appears in Latin both in the German and in the English editions of Paulsen; the sense of Cai Yuanpei's Chinese exactly corresponds to it. The same applies to the ensuing quotation from the Kantian school.

41. The reference is to L. Schmidt, *Die Ethik der alten Griechen,* 2 vols., 1882.

42. The Chinese is *guannian,* "concept" or "idea." Thilly has "idea"; the sentence referring to Plato does not even appear in the German edition.

43. Here Cai Yuanpei has *kexue shi,* "scientific style," for what in both the German and the English editions is "Rococo." The reasons for this rather inappropriate emendation are obscure.

44. Cai Yuanpei's version here inverts the meaning of Paulsen's text. The relevant sentence in Thilly's translation (p. 459) reads: "The organic differs from the inorganic in that the former is not determined by external, mechanical effects, but by the action of an inner principle." The sense of the Japanese translation, and of the German original, is the same. Since the Chinese sentence also contradicts the thrust of the ensuing paragraph, Cai's formulation must result from an accidental confusion of "former" and "latter."

1919

Letter to Seventh and Eighth Maternal Uncles and Aunts

(April 28, 1919)[1]

Respectfully submitted for the perusal of Seventh and Eighth Uncles and Aunts:[2]

One year has quickly elapsed since your nephew bade farewell to you last summer. Since then, I have written you a letter to express my regards. I am sure that your days have been full of happiness and good fortune. Thinking of your many blessings gives me joy and comfort. My mother lived with you for a long time, and you looked after her well. I am most grateful. Now her illness has reached a turning point; her throat has largely recovered, but the treatment of her gastric ulcer has not produced any effect. As she has long been suffering from this disease, it will certainly take some time before we see any results. I had a position in Beijing as a staff member of Beijing University[3] when I heard that my mother's illness had become serious, and had to rush back home to look after her. I set out on March 12, by the Western calendar, and arrived in Shanghai on the fourteenth. I was detained there on business for twenty days, and arrived in the province from Shanghai only on April 6. I have been waiting on my mother, giving her draughts, and have not left her side. I hope this will allay your worries. I send you my respectful good wishes. Please give my regards to my cousins and their wives.

Please give my regards to Fourth, Fifth, and Tenth uncles,[4] for I shall not write to them separately.

Your nephew,
Mao Zedong

1. This letter carries no indication of the year in which it was written, but the references to the passage of one year since Mao parted from his uncles and aunts, and the information about his return to Changsha from Beijing, make plain that it should be dated 1919.

2. The uncles are those to whom Mao's letter of August 1918 was addressed. The seventh and eighth aunts were both *née* Zhao; they were peasant women from what is now the Shaoshan district of Xiangtan in Hunan.

3. Mao had been working as a library assistant since his arrival in Beijing the previous autumn.

4. Mao's fourth uncle was Wen Zhengru (1844–1919), *hao* Yushan. His fifth uncle was Wen Zhengmei (1847–1922), *hao* Yuli. His tenth uncle was Wen Zhenghua (1864–1930), *hao* Yusen. They were all peasants.

Manifesto on the Founding of the Xiang River Review

(July 14, 1919)

Since the great call for "world revolution," the movement for the "liberation of mankind" has pressed forward fiercely, and today we must change our old attitudes toward issues that in the past we did not question, toward methods we would not use, and toward so many words we have been afraid to utter. Question the unquestionable. Dare to do the unthinkable. Do not shrink from saying the unutterable. No force can stop a tide such as this; no one can fail to be subjugated by it.

What is the greatest problem in the world? The greatest problem is that of getting food to eat. What is the greatest force? The greatest force is that of the union of the popular masses. What should we not fear? We should not fear heaven. We should not fear ghosts. We should not fear the dead. We should not fear the bureaucrats. We should not fear the warlords. We should not fear the capitalists.

Since the Renaissance, thought has been liberated, and the question "How should mankind live?" has become a great issue. From the examination of this issue some have concluded that "man should live like that" or "man should not live like this." Some scholars have suggested, and a majority of the popular masses have agreed with, reforms in many domains, which have been implemented or are about to be implemented.

In the area of religion, the Reformation resulted in freedom of religious belief. In literature, the literature of the aristocracy, classical literature, dead literature, has given way to a literature of the common people, contemporary literature, a literature imbued with vitality. In the political arena, autocracy has been replaced by representative government, and a restricted suffrage has been replaced by universal suffrage. In the realm of society, the dark society of the dictatorship of a minority class has been transformed into an enlightened society in which all the people can freely develop. In education, we now believe in education for the common people, and in economics, we now believe in equality in the fruits of labor. In the area of thought, we have moved forward to pragmatism, and internationally, there is now a League of Nations.

In a word, these various reforms represent simply "emancipation from oppression." The basic ideology of these various forms of resistance to oppression is that of "democracy." (Compare the different renderings for democracy [in Chinese], *pingmin zhuyi* [the rule of the common people],[1] *minben zhuyi* [the people as the basis], *minzhu zhuyi* [people's rule — the usual term today], *shumin zhuyi* [the rule of the common people]). Religious oppression, literary oppression, political oppression, social oppression, educational oppression, economic oppression, intellectual oppression, and international oppression no longer have the slightest place in this world. All must be overthrown under the great cry of democracy.

There are two views about how they will be overthrown, one extreme, one moderate. We must make a choice between the two. (1) We accept the fact that the oppressors are people, are human beings like ourselves, and that the abuse of oppressive power is an unconscious error or misfortune on their parts, an infection or hereditary disease passed on to them from the old society and old thought. (2) We use oppression to overthrow oppression, with the result that we still have oppression. This would be not only self-contradictory, but also totally ineffectual, as witness the European war between the [Triple] Alliance and the [Triple] Entente,[2] and China's war between the North and the South.[3]

Thus it is our position that as regards scholarship, we must uphold thorough study. Unfettered by any of the old views or superstitions, we must seek the truth. In dealing with people, we advocate uniting the popular masses, and toward the oppressors, we believe in continuing the "sincere admonishment movement." We put into practice the "cry of revolution" — the cry for bread, the cry for freedom, the cry for equality — the "bloodless revolution." Thus we will not provoke widespread chaos, nor pursue that ineffectual "revolution of bombs," or "revolution of blood."

The international oppressor staring us in the face is Japan. The effective way of dealing directly and indirectly with the Japanese oppressors is through such movements as boycotting classes, merchants' strikes, workers' strikes, and boycotting Japanese products.

---

1. This was the term which had been used by Mao's mentor, Li Dazhao, as the title for a long article on the subject in 1918. Li Dazhao (1889–1927), *zi* Shouchang, a native of Hebei, studied political economy at Waseda University in Tokyo from 1913 to 1916, and during this period contributed to Zhang Shizhao's *Tiger Magazine.* In 1918, he accepted an appointment as head of the Beijing University library, and in this capacity he provided employment for Mao as a library assistant during Mao's first visit to Beijing in the winter of 1918–1919. Li had become a member of the editorial board of *New Youth* in 1916, and in this periodical he published, in 1918, an article entitled "The Victory of Bolshevism." Thereafter, he evolved rapidly toward a Marxist position, and was, with Chen Duxiu, one of the two principal founding fathers of the Chinese Communist Party. His intellectual and personal influence on Mao remained strong.

2. Mao uses here the terms "Alliance" and "Entente" which were current at the time, respectively, for the Triple Alliance of Germany, Austria-Hungary, and Italy, and the Triple Entente of France, England, and Russia. Since it is now common to refer to the "Allies" (including the United States) and the "Central Powers," we have sometimes translated in subsequent texts "Allies" where Mao has "Entente" *(Xiehe).*

3. See the note to the text dated May 29, 1918.

As for the Xiang River, it is but one river in the eastern part of the Eastern Hemisphere of the planet earth. Its waters run clear; its course is long. The popular masses living on and near the river are simple untutored folk who understand little of the affairs of the world. They do not have a highly organized society. The population is scattered, each person making his own living, knowing only of what immediately relates to himself and his life, in a very short span of time. Most have never even dreamed of life in a community, or of long-range perspectives. Their politics does not include negotiation and full resolution of disputes. They only understand private quarrels. Swept up in the great currents of the outside world, they have also established some education, but it has had little effect on them. Generally speaking, bureaucratic-style educators, rigid and dry, turn schools into prison cells and treat students like inmates. Their industry is underdeveloped. There are some among them who have useful talents, who in various countries and places have mastered learning and the arts. But they are given no scope to use these tools and are easily restrained within a kind of Lake Dongting.[4] They are also extremely parochial and live by the idea of Hunan rice for the Hunanese, so that education and industry are unable to take in many people from outside. Their brains are weak and rotten, and none of them would even suggest that there might be a need for reform or change. Young people among them truly in search of knowledge are numerous and able, but no one uses effective methods to instruct them in new knowledge and new skills. Ai! Xiang River, Xiang River! Your very existence on this earth has truly been in vain.

The time has come! The great world tides are rolling in even more insistently! The floodgates to Lake Dongting are moving, and have indeed opened! The vast and furious tide of the new thought is already rushing, surging along both banks of the Xiang River! Those who ride with the current will live; those who go against it will die. How shall we greet it? How will we propagate it? How will we study it? How will we carry it out? This is the most urgent, most pressing problem for all of us Hunanese, and hence the most urgent, most pressing task of our *Xiang River Review*.

---

4. Lake Dongting, the largest lake in Hunan, can also be taken, like the Xiang River, as a symbol for the province.

The Waves of Strikes in Various Countries

(July 14, 1919)

Just when the political magnates and financial tycoons of France, Britain, and the United States were having a great time concentrating all their efforts on the Paris Peace Conference, attempting to oppress defeated Germany and Austria with harsh measures, a wave of strikes broke out suddenly in their own countries. Strikes are actually a common occurrence in those countries. It is true that governments and financial tycoons dare not take the laborers too lightly. Whenever the laborers unite and go on strike, raising issues such as low pay, overly long work hours, inadequate housing, unemployment, and various other grievances, they can't avoid giving them some small benefits. It is just like when a child is hungry and cries so hard that the adult can't help but give him a piece of bread with a smile. But at most this is only trying to put out a burning cartload of faggots with a cup of water; how is it going to help? So the mainstream faction[1] all laugh at the workers of Britain and France as simpleminded. It is impossible to get chewed-up meat from a tiger's mouth.

[As regards] the present wave of strikes in various countries, immediately after the end of the World War (last December), a big strike involving various transportation agencies and the fuel, mining, and shipbuilding industries took place already in England and Scotland. For that reason, the strike this time around does not involve England[2] proper. The strike in France was quite serious in the beginning, but ended with small gains and did not have very good results. Some members of the mainstream faction argued that they should have seized this opportunity to start a political movement in Paris, but that did not become a reality. A portion of the telegraph and telephone employees in the United States had a strike, with the intention of supporting the majority of the Congress in opposition to joining the League of Nations. It certainly was different in purpose

1. For the translation of *guangyi pai* as "mainstream faction," in the sense of "genuine socialists," see the note to the next text, "The Arrest and Rescue of Chen Duxiu," relating to the assassination of Rosa Luxemburg. Here and elsewhere, Mao advances the view that though England and France had won military victory, Germany and her Eastern neighbors were politically more advanced because of the oppression visited on them by their adversaries.

2. The Chinese here is *Yinglun*, not the transcription commonly used *(Ying'gelan)*, but as we have noted already such things were not yet standardized in 1919. There can be no doubt from the context that Mao is referring to England, as distinguished from Scotland, rather than to Great Britain in general.

from the strikes that took place in Britain and France. The strike in Italy was a movement started by its Socialist Party out of protest against the things done by the government. Since the great defeat of Germany's minority Socialist Party last winter, the widespread strikes also have not had any good results. Since the reign of the majority Socialist Party, it has been as silent as a cicada in cold weather, and dares not speak up. This time, signing the peace treaty could trigger strikes. But Scheidemann's cabinet fell, and the succeeding Bauer cabinet plays no different tune from the former one. They are firmly in control of military forces that, though not strong enough to defend against foreign invasion, are more than sufficient to suppress domestic rebellion. Who dares to touch them? The mainstream faction's radical political strategies certainly have no chance of being put into practice for the time being. It is no wonder that their strikes did not materialize. Hungary has not been greatly affected by the strikes. The cause of the strikes was entirely lack of food. Below I will describe separately the strike situation in each country since January of this year.

France

Since the wave of strikes broke out on June 3, it has spread very fast. In Paris alone, 200,000 men and women workers walked off their jobs. There were different demands from different walks of life, but they were unanimous in advocating the eight-hour day. On the fourth it spread even more widely. It was estimated that 500,000 workers were on strike. On the fifth, the laundry workers went on strike. Later, the number of workers on strike increased. The subway, trolley, and street car employees decided to continue the strike. The subway workers demanded that their minimum monthly salary be set at 450 FF (at a rate of 1 FF = 0.4 *yuan*, this is equivalent to 180 *yuan* a month), that they be entitled to an old-age pension at fifty, and that after fifteen years of service they should also be entitled to a certain pension. On the seventh, the tide of the Paris strike turned. The workers and employers of the metal and machinery industries agreed on several points. On the eleventh, the metal workers and subway employees went back to work. The authorities took some necessary measures to deal with the railroad strike. It looked as though all the coal miners might go on strike. On the twelfth, **the Chamber of Deputies passed a bill providing that the miners should work only an eight-hour day**,[3] but the Miners' Union was still not satisfied and decided that the whole membership would go on strike, starting from the sixteenth. So did the Sailors' Federation. The General Confederation of Labor claimed that the cost of living was extraordinarily high [Note by the author: Recently someone who has just returned from Paris gave an example to

3. This and the subsequent passage in bold, like the names of the countries discussed, were underscored by Mao in the *Xiang River Review*, using dots alongside the relevant characters.

show how expensive things were there: an old toothbrush cost 2 FF and a pair of leather shoes, 60 FF.], and that at all the African ports, there were thousands of tons of wheat piled up rotting. The goods and merchandise were piled up at various ports like mountains, but neither the ships nor the trains were willing to transport them. Shouldn't we quickly stop the waste, trickery, and monopoly of such a government? On the fourteenth, the wave of strikes gradually subsided. **The radical faction had a plan to seize the opportunity to start a movement to overthrow Clemenceau's authoritarian regime**, but this was rejected by the Railway Workers' Union. Nevertheless, since the miners were dissatisfied with the explanation of the government about the law regarding the eight-hour day, they decided to go on strike on the sixteenth. It was feared that the workers of the railroads, the mines, and the Transportation Federation would also strike in sympathy. Old man Clemenceau panicked, got the representatives of the transportation companies and the transportation workers together for negotiations and pleaded with them to show some patriotic fervor during the national crisis. The workers ate up this crude flattery and decided to behave conscientiously, and go back to work.

Britain

May 30 London wire: A strike on the third by the police of the entire nation has been brewing. The government has promised to increase their wages and add some benefits, but it will not recognize the Police Federation nor rehire the dismissed police. There are also waves of strikes in the British colonies of Australia, Canada, and Suez. On June 4, the workers of the Vickers armaments factory in Canada went on strike, demanding a forty-hour work week. On June 5, the Suez Canal workers went on strike, and the situation was rather atrocious. On June 9, the navigators of Australia walked out on their work with a fierce momentum threatening to paralyze all industries. On the 1[X],[4] the wave of strikes was still serious, and as a result more and more workers of other industries are going idle every day.

America

On June 7, the Chicago telegraph operators scheduled a strike for eleven o'clock. There were about 60,000 of them in all, 25,000 of whom belonged to the Telegraph Operators' Union. The president of this union, Mr. Cunningham,

4. In the Chinese texts from which our translations have been made (both the *Wengao* and the *Mao Zedong ji*), characters in the original sources which the editors could not read are represented by lightly outlined squares. This symbol fits neatly into a line of Chinese characters, but would not have been appropriate here. We have therefore adopted the combination [X] instead. In this instance, 1[X] stands for a two-character number beginning with 1, i.e., a number between 11 and 19.

drew up strategies for a nationwide strike. On the same day, the telephone operators of the entire nation were ordered out on strike starting from the sixteenth, to show sympathy for the telegraph operators. On the eighth, the secretary of the Telegraph Operators' Union proclaimed to all telegraph employees that everyone should go on strike, including the telegraph receptionists. The aim was to stop the telegrams sent by President Wilson back and forth to Paris, in order to make him pay attention to the fact that the people of the country did not approve of the proposals he had made at the Peace Conference. On the twelfth, all the telegraph companies announced that the telegraph operators' strike had failed.

Italy

On June 13, in La Spezia, Italy, riots erupted and shops were smashed because of high prices for food. On the fourteenth, the workers in Genoa demonstrated, and several hundred were arrested. The banks and shops were closed, and trolleys stopped operating. Most of the workers in Turin stopped work on this day, in memory of [Rosa] Luxemburg, the leader of the German Spartacists. The workers in Milan went on strike in protest against the actions of the authorities of Genoa and La Spezia.

Germany

On June 13, the Greater Berlin Citizens' Congress held a secret meeting and resolved to go on strike. People in all professions and among the military agreed to support the plans to stop all kinds of industrial work. Some expected that this would trigger a civil war, and that middle-class society would seize power.

Hungary

On May 31, riots caused by hungry workers broke out in the capital of Hungary. The Army of the Red Flag, under orders from the Communist government, entered all the factories and suppressed the riots. There was hardly any food in the Hungarian capital.

The Arrest and Rescue of Chen Duxiu[1]

(July 14, 1919)

The former dean of humanities of Beijing University, Chen Duxiu, was arrested at the Beijing New World Market on June 11.[2] According to the police report, the reason for his arrest by secret agents was that on this evening leaflets containing a manifesto of the townspeople were being distributed at the New World. Only after inquiry at the police station was it discovered that the person arrested was Mr. Chen. The text of the so-called manifesto of the Beijing townspeople, as disseminated by Chinese and American news agencies, reads as follows:

> 1. Abrogate all of the Sino-Japanese secret treaties negotiated during the period of the European war.
>
> 2. Dismiss from office Xu Shuzheng, Cao Rulin, Zhang Zongxiang, Lu Zongyu, Duan Zhigui, and Wang Huaiqing,[3] and have them expelled from Beijing.

---

1. Chen Duxiu (1879–1942), originally Chen Qiansheng, *zi* Zhongfu, *hao* Shi'an, pseud. Zhongzi, was born in Huaining, Anhui Province. Chen was educated in the Chinese classics but sought a modern education, which he received at the Qiushi Academy in Hangzhou before studying in Japan. Returning to China in 1903, he established the revolutionary newspaper *National Daily News* in Shanghai as a forum for discussion of new ideas. (The paper was closed within a few months.) Chen began his academic career as dean of studies at Anhui Higher Normal School in 1910, at the same time developing his contacts with the publishing world. In 1914 he became junior editor of *Jiayin zazhi* (the Tiger Magazine). (For details, see the note to Mao's letter of January 28, 1916.) He was best known as founder and editor of *Qingnian*, later *Xin qingnian* (New Youth), the most influential organ of the literary and cultural movement leading up to May Fourth. In 1917 he accepted Cai Yuanpei's invitation to serve as dean of humanities at Beijing University, but was forced to resign in March 1919 under pressure from leading conservative intellectuals, backed by the warlords. In 1920 Chen moved to Shanghai, where he continued to publish *New Youth*, and in August organized the Socialist Youth League. He coordinated the organization of Communist study groups throughout China. In July 1921, although Chen was not able to be present at the First National Congress of the Chinese Communist Party, he was elected secretary of the Party's Central Bureau, a position he took up in August 1921.

2. Chen was arrested at 2 P.M. on June 11 at the Xin Shijie (New World) Market situated at Qianmen in Beijing. He was released from prison on September 3, after being imprisoned for eighty-three days.

3. Xu Shuzheng (1880–1925), *zi* Youzheng, was born in Jiangsu Province. Xu was a chief military adviser to Duan Qirui's Beiyang army in its early days. In September 1918 he was appointed codirector of the War Bureau and commander in chief of the Northwest Frontier Defense Army, and in November 1919 he forced the Mongol princes and

3. Abolish the General Office of the Infantry and the Headquarters of the Garrison Command.

4. A Beijing Security Force should be organized by the merchants.

5. Press for a peace agreement between north and south.

6. The people have an absolute right to freedom of speech, publication, and assembly.

The above six articles are the people's minimum demands of the government, and it is hoped that these objectives will be achieved by peaceful means. If the government does not accede to the will of the people, the people of the city of Beijing will have no choice but to take direct action to achieve fundamental reform.

The above text is the leaflet containing the manifesto of the townspeople of

---

ministers to sign a petition for the abolition of Mongolia's autonomy. This action played a key role in turning the Mongols against China.

Cao Rulin (1877–1966), *zi* Runtian, born in Shanghai, was one of the principal targets of the May Fourth demonstrations. He studied law in Japan, returning to lecture at Beijing University in 1905. In 1911 he became a personal adviser to Yuan Shikai on foreign, particularly Japanese and Mongolian, affairs. Yuan and Cao were responsible for the Chinese side of the negotiations with Japan over the Twenty-one Demands of 1915, and for this Cao later came under fierce attack. In 1918, as minister of communications and acting minister of finance, he was also largely responsible for negotiating the series of loans from Japan known as the Nishihara loans which were to finance Duan Qirui's army, and his plans to unify China militarily. In return, China made valuable land, mining, and communications concessions to Japan. It was not until the 1919 Paris Peace Conference that the full extent of China's concessions, especially regarding the Shandong peninsula, to Japan became known. His home, where Cao, Zhang Zongxiang, and Lu Zongyu were meeting, was stormed by student protesters on May 4. Cao escaped without injury, but continued agitation led to his being dismissed from office on June 10, 1919. Zhang Zongxiang (1879–1962), *zi* Zhonghe, was born in Zhejiang Province. Zhang studied law at Imperial Tokyo University with Cao Rulin, returning to hold various government posts. In 1916, when the Nishihara loans negotiations began, Zhang, as Chinese ambassador to Japan and an old friend of Cao, handled the affair at the Japanese end. He was hurt by students on May 4 as they stormed Zhang's house, and was relieved as ambassador on June 10, 1919. Lu Zongyu (1876–1941), *zi* Runsheng, was born in Zhejiang Province. An old friend of Cao Rulin, Lu preceeded Zhang as ambassador to Japan in 1913. He ratified the Twenty-one Demands in Japan in May 1915 and played a prominent role in the Japanese loans negotiations. In 1919 he was head of the Beijing government Financial Office, until his dismissal in June 1919. Duan Zhigui (1868–1925), *zi* Xiangyan, was born in Anhui Province. A trusted lieutenant of Yuan Shikai, military commander of the Northeast and civil governor of Fengtian, he later became a close associate of Duan Qirui. During the May Fourth period he was commander-in-chief of the Armed Forces for the Protection of the Capital, and enforced a policy of mass arrests. Wang Huaiqing (1886–), *zi* Maoxuan, born in Zhili, studied at the Tianjin Military Academy and became renowned for military achievements as a Beiyang Army commander under Yuan Shikai. On May 21, 1919, Wang was appointed acting police inspector general, and on July 31 his post was made official. The police inspector general petitioned to by the Beijing students would have been Wang Huaiqing.

Beijing. We have seen it and find nothing all that extraordinary in it. The arrest of Mr. Chen by the government has been reported in all the papers, and he has been seriously mistreated. The entire Beijing student body has presented a public petition to the police station requesting his release, the text of which reads as follows:

> To the Police Inspector General: Most respectfully, we have recently heard of the arrest by military police of the former dean of humanities of Beijing University, Chen Duxiu, on serious false charges. Students and others find this impermissible and raise the following two major points. (1) Mr. Chen is highly respected in academic circles, and his words and ideas are known and well regarded both at home and abroad. Should he be falsely accused of any crime, it is feared that this would incite yet another nationwide student uprising. Coming just at the height of the present student movement, this is hardly a measure designed to calm things down. (2) Mr. Chen is despised by most of those of the old school for promoting the new literature and modern thought. We truly fear that his arrest at this time will make people at home and abroad suspect that the military police authorities have intentionally manufactured this ruse as one step in stamping out modern thought. At present, a variety of problems have already made the situation very complex. Why make the situation even more divisive by creating yet another issue? For these two reasons the students and others petition your honorable office for the early release of Chen Duxiu.

The Beijing students have also sent the following telegram to the newspapers, schools, and others in Shanghai:

> Mr. Chen Duxiu has been the most effective advocate of modern thought and is indeed highly respected in the academic world. He has today been arrested, and his home has also been searched. This has caused widespread anxiety. In addition to attempting to find a way to rescue him, it is hoped that all citizens will take notice.

The Shanghai Industrial Association has also sent a telegram requesting Chen Duxiu's release. It reads in part, "Venting your anger over the Beijing student movement on one man, Mr. Chen, is the germ from which great chaos will begin." The government is not yet so befuddled as to be completely out of touch with the general situation outside and may be expected to release him soon. Even if it is absolutely bent on setting up a prison for words, I'm afraid that the government will not have the stomach to wage a life-and-death struggle against the tide of the new thought movement, which is sweeping the whole world. Zhang Xingyan[4] has been an old friend of Mr. Chen for many years. When Chen was appointed dean of humanities at the university, Zhang was director of the

---

4. On the early career of Zhang Shizhao (1881–1973), *zi* Xingyan, see the note to Mao's letter of January 28, 1916, to Xiao Zisheng. During the years immediately preced-

university library and professor of logic in the graduate school. When Mr. Chen was arrested, Zhang sent a long telegram to Wang Kemin[5] in Beijing, asking him to deliver it to the police station and seek Chen's release. The sense of it was:

> . . . Mr. Chen has always devoted himself to teaching, and throughout his life has stayed clear of the stench of political cliques. On this occasion, even if he used some inappropriate language, why should he be thrown into prison like a common criminal, and deprived of his normal contacts? Moreover, just as the student movement was about to die down, how could you suddenly exercise literary censorship, and incite the masses to renewed anger? This is hardly something that wise men would do.

Mr. Zhang has also sent a letter to Acting Premier Gong Xinzhan,[6] in which he puts it even more urgently:

> To the honorable Mr. Xianzhou. Though it has been many years since I received your valued instruction, it lives in my memory. In all sincerity, I have heard that the former dean of humanities of Beijing University, Mr. Chen Duxiu, has been arrested on suspicion of being involved with distributing a leaflet, and that he still has not been released. From so far away I do not yet know just what the details of the case really are. I do recall though that Mr. Chen always devoted himself exclusively to teaching. Even though the new thought movement he promotes and his writings and theories may not be

---

ing the May Fourth movement, he served as professor of logic in the newly opened graduate school of Beijing University, and thus worked closely together with Chen Duxiu to promote the movement for academic reform. Although he was, as Mao states in this article, a good friend of Chen's, and also of Li Dazhao's, he was not in the mainstream of the May Fourth movement in one important sense: he considered that the beauty of the Chinese language was to be found in the classical style, and therefore did not support the use of *baihua*. With the dissolution of the assembly by Duan Qirui, Zhang moved to Guangdong and was chosen to represent the southern military government at the north-south peace talks in Shanghai in February 1919. In 1922 he became minister of education in the Duan Qirui government, and was severely criticized for this by the radical intellectuals.

5. Wang Kemin (1873–1945), *zi* Shulu, was born in Hangzhou. Wang held various financial positions under the Republican government, including minister of finance in the administration of Wang Shizhen from December 1917 to the resignation of the cabinet in March 1918. His next official assignment was as a Beijing government representative to the north–south peace negotiations on February 20, 1919. He probably renewed contact with Zhang Shizhao there.

6. On June 13, 1919, Qian Nengxun, who was appointed acting premier on Duan Qirui's resignation October 10, 1918, resigned. The then finance minister, Gong Xinzhan, succeeded him as acting premier. Gong Xinzhan (1871–), *zi* Xianzhou, was a member of Duan Qirui's Anfu clique, and a former diplomat. He remained in the position for only three months. He was, like Chen, a native of Anhui—hence Zhang's reference below to the consideration which rulers should have for their fellow countrymen.

without their excesses, they really involve only the field of literary usage, and certainly are not tainted with the stench of politics. This is clearly verifiable. These are troubled times in our country, and now that the student movement has just died down, how could you follow the old tactics of criticizing behind people's backs and vilifying those you are supervising, thereby further inciting the people's emotions? Wise men would assuredly never do this. History shows that when those who wield political power make life difficult for men of letters over literary trivia and institute literary prisons, if they are fortunate enough to win out they will not have to resort to military force. If they fail, popular morale crumbles and the network of authority collapses, and even a worthy person cannot remedy the situation. A look at the past and present, in China and abroad, shows that literary censorship is most likely to be established just at that point when a state is in the last stages of decline and exhaustion. The end of the Ming dynasty is just such a chilling example. Today rumor and slander abound, and good people are menaced by fear. That there are such cases of educated people being charged with crimes is truly an ill omen for the state and the basis for great chaos throughout the realm. You must nip these errors in the bud, and dare to confront all aspects of the present situation. Mr. Chen is, moreover, heroic in bearing and extremely cultivated, and has mastered both Chinese and Western cultures. [His native] Anhui Province links north and south, and constantly produces men of talent and military prowess, but one of such scholarly attainment is rare indeed. That the holder of power should regard with equanimity all worthy men from his native place I trust you will agree. Whether throughout the country, or near at hand in a single province, to cultivate one man of talent is by no means easy. Could you then bear to have him suddenly destroyed? I have specially written this letter and had it delivered to request that the police release Mr. Chen quickly. Mr. Chen and I are childhood friends, and fellow students at the university. I am thoroughly familiar with his character and conduct. I would willingly vouch for his innocence, and testify on his behalf. . . .

Most respectfully,

Zhang Shizhao
June 22

We regard Mr. Chen as a bright star in the world of thought. When Mr. Chen speaks, anyone with a reasonably clear mind assents to the opinions he expresses. China today can be said to be in an extremely dangerous situation. The danger does not result from military weakness or inadequate finances, nor is it the danger of being split up into many small fragments by domestic chaos. The real danger lies in the total emptiness and rottenness of the mental universe of the entire Chinese people. Of China's 400 million people, about 390 million are superstitious. They superstitiously believe in spirits and ghosts, in fortune-telling, in fate, in despotism. There is absolutely no recognition of the individual, of the self, of truth. This is because scientific thought has not developed. In name,

China is a republic, but in reality it is an autocracy that is getting worse and worse as one régime replaces another. This results from the fact that the masses of the people haven't the faintest glimmer of democracy in their mentality, and have no idea what democracy actually is. Mr. Chen has always stood for these two things. He once said that our only crimes against society have been for the sake of "science" and "democracy." For these two things, Mr. Chen has offended society, and society has repaid him with arrest and imprisonment. This can truly be considered a case of the punishment not fitting the crime! Thought knows no boundaries. Last December, the head of the mainstream faction[7] of the German Socialist Party, Rosa Luxemburg, was killed by the [Social]-Democratic Party government.[8] In the middle of last month, people from the Turin area of Italy, the enemy of Germany, held a large demonstration in her memory. There was a similar demonstration in Zurich, Switzerland, as a memorial to her. If it was like this in countries hostile to Germany, it must be all the more so in countries not hostile to Germany. If it is like this in other countries, how much more so in her own country? The arrest of Mr. Chen will certainly not diminish him in the slightest. On the contrary, this has created a great memorial for the new thought movement, causing it to spread its splendor even farther. The government definitely will not dare to execute Mr. Chen. And even if they should, his death would in no way diminish the strength and greatness of his spirit. Mr. Chen has himself said, out of the laboratory and into prison, out of prison into the laboratory. He has also said, death is something I do not fear. Now Mr. Chen can put his words to the test. I wish Mr. Chen a long, long life! May Mr. Chen's eminent and lofty spirit live on for ten thousand years!

---

7. Literally, "in the broad sense" *(guangyi)*. Mao appears to be using the term to mean "mainstream," in the sense of all those committed to "real" or "full-blooded" socialism, and we have so translated it here, and in the text dated July 21, 1919, on the signing of the Versailles Treaty, where it occurs frequently. Rosa Luxemburg's organization called itself the Spartacus Union, and then, shortly before her death, became the German Communist Party, but Mao manifestly regards it as a component of the "real" socialists.

8. In fact, Rosa Luxemburg was assassinated by right-wing officers on January 15, 1919, while under arrest by the Socialist government following the failure of an insurrection.

The Threat of Force

(July 14, 1919)

At the beginning of last month, when the price of Japanese rice was very high, one picul cost over 40 *yuan.* The Japanese authorities were at a loss. The newspapers confirmed that the food crisis was already very serious. Poor Japan! Your guts will be wracked with hunger, but you still flaunt your might before your benefactors. Since when will the threat of force get you more in charity?

Study the Extremist Party

(July 14, 1919)

The Russian extremist[1] party has been the principal architect behind the Afghan invasion of India, so the extremist party has reached South Asia. It is said that the extremists were also involved at the height of the "Cry for Revolution" in Korea, so they have already reached East Asia. That's how fearsome the extremist party is! Each of us should examine very carefully what kind of thing this extremist party really is. We cannot just close our eyes and spout empty pronouncements such as: "It's the same as wild beasts during a flood," or "Put them down," or "Reject them." In the twinkling of an eye, the extremist party, to everyone's amazement, has spread throughout the country, to the point that there is no place to hide from them.

1. "Extremist" *(guoji)* was the term commonly applied at this time, both in China and in Europe, to the Bolsheviks. (In France, the newspapers spoke of *"les Maximalistes."*) The idea behind this terminology was, of course, that they were so extreme as to be beyond the pale of civilization or of political debate.

The Blockade

(July 14, 1919)

Last month the high-level economic conference in Paris passed a resolution to institute a blockade against Hungary, saying the blockade will last until the Hungarian government[1] announces that it is willing to accept the will of the people. This should be examined at two levels. First, the Allied countries are mistaken in thinking that the goals of the Hungarian government are not in accord with the wishes of the Hungarian people. The goals of the Hungarian government are indeed not in accord with the wishes of Hungary's bourgeois and aristocratic[2] minority, but they are assuredly not in conflict with the wishes of the vast majority of the proletariat and common people, because it is they who organized the government of Hungary in the first place. Second, a blockade would be a real boon to the propagation of extremism. I fear that the Allies will also fall into this whirlpool. Consequently, implementing a blockade would really be "a matchless achievement."

---

1. The reference is, of course, to the Communist government led by Bela Kun, which held power from March to August 1919.

2. Mao uses here the term *shenshi*, which strictly speaking refers to the specifically Chinese social stratum of landlords linked to officialdom sometimes translated as "gentry," but he clearly has in mind the Hungarian landowning aristocracy.

Proof of the Equality and Justice of the Allies

(July 14, 1919)

The German reply to the Peace Conference demands that after the German army is reduced in size, the Allied countries must also make similar reductions. Who dares to say that this is wrong? The Allied countries talk a lot about equality and justice. We shall see what the Allies do subsequently about their military forces. That will be the proof.

Afghanistan Picks Up the Sword

(July 14, 1919)

When a tiny Afghanistan goes to war against a mammoth England, monarch of the seas, there must somewhere be an important reason for this. But the teletypes from the British side are not reliable. Turkey is about to be cut up and devoured by some ferocious beasts. India, risking its own life to help Britain, has earned itself a clown wearing a flaming red turban as representative to the Peace Conference.[1] The demands of the Indian people have not been granted. They want to suppress the political movement of the Indian people with military might. Afghanistan is a Moslem country. When the fox dies the hare grieves,[2] so how could she fail to pick up the sword?

1. Mao is referring to the Indian representative included in the British Dominions party, the Major-General His Highness Maharaja Sir Ganga Singh Bahadur, Maharaja of Bikaner. He was one of the great princes of India, famous for his Camel Corps.

2. A Chinese saying evoking fellow feeling between different creatures.

The Rhine Republic Is a Grotesque Country

(July 14, 1919)

If the Allies want to turn the Rhine valley into their own Great Wall against the enemy, they must first tear it away from Germany and turn it into a separate country. It is said that a provisional government has already been set up in Wiesbaden with a Dr. Dorten as president. How happy this Dr. Dorten must be! The Jin set up Liu Xiang,[1] and the Khitan set up Shi Jingtang.[2] China has also had a number of such states.

---

1. Liu Xiang (1073–1146) was an official of the Northern Song dynasty who went over to the Jin invaders and was set up by them as a puppet emperor.

2. Shi Jingtang (892–942), a general of Turkic descent, and son-in-law to Emperor Ming of the Later Tang dynasty, bribed the Khitan to help him to the throne, and in 936 proclaimed himself first emperor of the Later Jin dynasty. He, like Liu Xiang, enjoyed no real power and was said to have died of frustration at his own subordinate position.

So Much for National Self-Determination!

(July 14, 1919)

Poland and Czechoslovakia, in reestablishing their national existence, have presided over the death of Germany. The Allies did their utmost to help them in this, in the name of "national self-determination." The Arabs benefit from the splitting up of Turkey, and therefore were allowed to become semi-independent. The desire of the Jews to restore their nation in Palestine will not succeed because it is of no great concern to the Allied powers. The Siberian government[1] has acquired merit by attacking the extremist party and as a result has now been recognized *de jure*. Wishing to gain a foothold in Siberia, Japan has to make a show of its goodwill, so it was the first to propose recognition. Korea bewails the loss of its independence; so many of its people have died, and so much of its land has been devastated, but it was simply ignored by the Peace Conference. So much for national self-determination! I think it is really shameless!

1. The reference is to the so-called Far Eastern Republic, which existed at this time as a buffer state between Soviet Russia and China, with the tacit agreement of Lenin as well as of the Allies.

Poor Wilson

(July 14, 1919)

Wilson in Paris was like an ant on a hot skillet. He didn't know what to do. He was surrounded by thieves like Clemenceau, Lloyd George, Makino, and Orlando. He heard nothing except accounts of receiving certain amounts of territory and of reparations worth so much in gold. He did nothing except to attend various kinds of meetings where he could not speak his mind. One day a Reuter's telegram read, "President Wilson has finally agreed with Clemenceau's view that Germany not be admitted to the League of Nations." When I saw the words "finally agreed," I felt sorry for him for a long time. Poor Wilson!

Savage Bomb Attacks

(July 14, 1919)

Everyone has heard that in the very civilized, very wealthy United States of America "savage bomb attacks" occurred in eight cities simultaneously. Anarchist parties have spread very widely. In the vicinity of the bomb explosions there have been anonymous posters saying that the "class war" has already begun, and will not cease until international labor has won complete victory. The bombs were often hidden in the home of an official, on the roof of which was found a human head. How horribly frightening! I worry about how the little sons and daughters of those officials can sleep at night. Some congressmen, who get a lot of votes because they have a lot of money, and get elected because they have a lot of votes, are still sitting there roundly condemning the instigators of violence and passing bills inflicting stiff punishment. I formally announce to all of you gentlemen that your "day of judgment" is at hand! If you want to save your lives, and want something to eat and something to wear, you had better wash your brains very thoroughly, take off your top hats and put away your tails, join together with the common people of your countries, work with them in the factories, and go to the countryside and till the soil with them.

The Despotism of Industry Is Unacceptable

(July 14, 1919)

The head of the American Labor Party,[1] Gompers, said in a speech, "The Labor Party is determined that in the enterprise of reconstruction it will have the right to speak out. The despotism of industry is unacceptable." The United States is the first nation of the globe to be an industrial despotism, and it is from this that the evil system of the trusts has arisen. For the pleasure of a few, ten million must weep. The more industry develops, the greater will be the number of those who must weep. What means will Gompers employ to make this "unacceptable"? We do not know yet. But it is a good thing that there is someone to take the lead in calling it "unacceptable." From the mouth of one man saying "unacceptable" it will spread to ten million all saying "unacceptable." "Unacceptable" will spread and rise from a low murmur to a loud and a very loud and finally to a wild cry of "Unacceptable!" Only then will the day of mankind's true liberation dawn.

1. Samuel Gompers was, of course, the president of the American Federation of Labor, not of a party. Perhaps Mao's sources did not make this clear, or perhaps he did not at this time regard the difference as very important.

The Cession of Territory and Reparations Are Mutually Incompatible

(July 14, 1919)

Germany has replied to the Allies that if it loses Silesia and the coal mines of the Saar, it will be unable to pay the reparations. I suspect that when they heard this the Allies were extremely vexed. Why? Territory can be ceded, reparations can also be obtained, above all with regard for both sides. But Germany says the two are inversely proportional. How could the Allies not be vexed? Nevertheless, I venture to urge their excellencies, the high officials of the Allies, to consider where on earth there is anything so excellent as being acceptable to both sides?

A Bloodletting for the Socialist Party

(July 14, 1919)

Austria's chief delegate, Dr. Renner, has replied to the Peace Conference, "Austria today is in the process of consuming its capital, which is already greatly diminished as compared with the past. If there is further devastation, it will set the stage for a bloodletting for the Socialist Party." Stupid Dr. Renner! Don't you realize that the Allies' true objective for the last year has been precisely to cause a bloodletting for the Socialist Party?

Bernstein

(July 14, 1919)

The German Dr. Bernstein[1] has said in a speech, "The conditions of the peace agreement are the result of a barbaric war, for which it is most fit that Germany assume responsibility. Article 19 of the peace treaty is necessary."[2] To be sure, we oppose the oppressive treaty imposed by the Allies, but these words of the doctor regarding a barbaric war are refreshing to hear.

---

1. For details on Eduard Bernstein, see the note to Mao's article of July 21, 1919, "For the Germans, the Painful Signing of the Treaty."

2. The Covenant of the League of Nations was incorporated into the treaty, of which it constitutes the first twenty-six articles. Article 19 reads as follows: "The Assembly may from time to time advise the reconsideration by Members of the League of treaties which have become inapplicable and the consideration of international conditions whose continuance might endanger the peace of the world." By invoking it, Bernstein suggests that, while Germany must accept responsibility for her past acts, she may, and no doubt should, be treated differently in future.

There Are No Temples to Illustrious Virtue Abroad

(July 14, 1919)

When they were about to tear down the Temple to Illustrious Virtue (Mingluntang)[1] to make way for a new road in Guangzhou, Kang Youwei[2] got very agitated. He sent a telegram to Cen and Wu[3] accusing them of "insulting the Sage and destroying morality," something "unheard of in all my travels abroad." Kang Youwei's words are quite true. In what other country in the world would you find a Confucius, much less a Temple to Illustrious Virtue?

---

1. Mingluntang was the name of the main audience hall of Confucian temples in imperial China.

2. Kang, the initiator of reform in China, had always been opposed to revolution and had no sympathy with the "new thought" of the May Fourth era.

3. Cen is Cen Chunxuan (1861–1933), original name Chunxi, *zi* Yunjie. At this time he was chairman of the directorate of the military government in Guangzhou, a post to which he had succeeded Sun Yatsen in May 1918. (For more details see the text of April 27, 1920.) Wu is Wu Tingfang (1842–1922), *zi* Wenjue, *hao* Zhiyong. He had also been one of the seven directors of the southern opposition government, as well as its foreign minister, but he left Guangzhou for Shanghai in March 1919 and did not return until October 1920, together with Sun Yatsen.

What Is Fitting in a Republic?

(July 14, 1919)

Mr. Kang also says, "It is not fitting in a republic that things be forcibly destroyed." How strange! Does he really mean to say that it is only "fitting in a republic" to retain such things as "the prince guides the ministers" or "let the prince be prince and let the ministers be ministers"?

Probably Not a Human Being

(July 14, 1919)

At the new National Assembly, Deng Rong[1] said, "It's not necessary to appoint a special official to honor Confucius. We can save on expenses." Zhang Yuanqi[2] said, "In the Department of Internal Affairs, the prayers to Confucius are carried out by a clerk in the tearoom. Neither the head of the Department nor his first assistant pay any attention to it. It is necessary to appoint a special official." Most likely the tearoom clerk of the Department of Internal Affairs is not a human being. If he were a human being, how could he be incapable even of offering up the prayers to Confucius? I think that old man Confucius' bureaucratic airs must be somewhat attenuated after all these years.

1. Deng Rong, *zi* Shouxia, a native of Sichuan Province, was a graduate of Meiji University in Tokyo. At this time he was a lawyer, a member of the National Assembly, and an active participant in government and political affairs.

2. Zhang Yuanqi (1858–1922), *zi* Zhenwu, was a former governor of his native Fujian Province. At this time he was deputy director of the Department of Internal Affairs.

From the Kunlun Mountains to Europe

(July 14, 1919)

Zhang Yuanqi also said, "What is all this talk about seeking the new learning and going along with the new current? I think we should honor Confucius and go against the current." Not bad, not bad at all! If Mr. Zhang really is that strong, then the Yangzi River could be made to flow back in the opposite direction from the Kunlun Mountains, and we could get to Europe by just taking a boat over the Kunlun range.

A Good Scheme

(July 14, 1919)

A student at a certain school said to me, the administrators and teachers at our school are afraid that we students might learn about new doctrines that they have not yet learned about themselves, so they closed the library. Any magazines, newspapers, or books from outside that were even a tiny bit new we were not allowed to see. When I heard this I nodded my head and sighed in admiration. A very clever scheme! But is it just one particular school? All of the schools in Hunan province would appear to have joined together in this.

The Instant Transformation

(July 14, 1919)

There are some bureaucratic-style educators who, caught up in the tide of world events, will have their rice bowls broken if they do not take defensive measures. Such people undergo an instant transformation in which they just quietly put away their decadent bureaucratic airs of the day before. Some of them make the change in all sincerity, and this is very admirable. Others, whose transformations are phoney, easily give themselves away. As for this type of people, I blush for them, and I fear for them.

We Are Starving

(July 14, 1919)

We young people locked up behind the great gates of Lake Dongting are truly starving! Our stomachs are assuredly hungry, but our brains are hungrier still! The cooks preparing our meals have far too few resources! The situation is hopeless! Our only recourse is to rise up and take matters into our own hands! This is the pitiful voice of us who are starving! Make no mistake about it!

Do You Mean to Say That Walking Is Only for Men?

(July 14, 1919)

The administration of one women's school hides the students away as if they were land deeds, afraid that if let out they would come in contact with something evil. Such evil magazines as *New Youth*, in particular, they are not even allowed to glance at. During the latest earth-shaking student movement, women students from Beijing demonstrated at the Xinhuamen,[1] and the girls from the School for Poor Children were willing to go to jail as surrogates for the male students. The students from this girls' school were tightly locked up and not allowed to take a single step outside, as if walking were only for males.

1. After President Xu Shichang issued mandates on June 1, 1919, praising those responsible for the 1918 Japanese Nishihara loans (see the notes to Mao's article of July 14, 1919, "The Arrest and Rescue of Chen Duxiu"), denouncing the anti-Japanese activities of the students, and imposing martial law, thousands of students took to the streets in protest and were subsequently arrested. The prisons in Beijing were soon overcrowded, and the Law School and the School of Science building at Beijing University were turned into temporary student shelters. On June 4, female students joined in the protests for the first time as a unified group. On June 5, over one thousand from fifteen girls' schools assembled to march to the president's palace to protest against the ill-treatment of students and the use of school buildings as prisons. They requested the release of the male students being held prisoner and demanded freedom of speech.

Ha! Ha!

(July 14, 1919)

When the question of Qingdao[1] arose, Hunan students were greatly aroused, and new plays and speeches were all the rage for a time. One friend told me that there was an old gentleman who got really angry about his son being made up for a play. He went to the school and burst out at the teacher, "Why is it that I should have to suffer such a fate? That the son I have raised should do something so low!" When I heard this I couldn't help laughing. Ha! Ha!

1. I.e., the controversy over the German concessions in Shandong, handed over to Japan at the Paris Peace Conference, which had provoked the May Fourth demonstrations.

The Women's Revolutionary Army

(July 14, 1919)

If a woman's head and a man's head are actually the same, and there is no real difference between a woman's waist and a man's, why must women have their hair piled up in those ostentatious and awkward buns? Why must they wear those messy skirts clinched tightly at the waist? I think women are regarded as criminals to start with, and tall buns and long skirts are the instruments of torture applied to them by men. There is also their facial makeup, which is the brand of a criminal; the jewelry on their hands, which constitutes shackles; and their pierced ears and bound feet, which represent corporal punishment. Schools and families are their prisons. They dare not voice their pain, nor step out from behind closed doors. If we ask, how can they escape this suffering, my answer is, only by raising a women's revolutionary army.

Notice from the Xiang River Review

(July 14, 1919)

1) This newspaper takes as its main purpose the propagation of the newest currents of thought. In addition to each weekly issue, if there are important articles we will publish a supplement. All articles will be in the colloquial language [*guoyu*]. We welcome contributions in harmony with our paper's purpose. For the time being, there will be no material reward for articles; we can only express our gratitude in spirit and will also send you the paper.

2) If there are those who are willing to help in distributing the paper, we will regard them as benefactors. Those who distribute many copies will receive a discount. As soon as we receive your letters, we will send the necessary number of copies.

3) The newsprint for this paper is supplied by the Hankou Paper Factory.

What Kind of Talk Is This?

(July 14, 1919)

Zhang Jian[1] says: "A government can be likened to a father and elder brother, and students to sons and younger brothers. If the country is fortunate, father and elder brother take the lead in educating, sons and younger brothers strictly adhere to their guidance, and the nation will prosper. If, unfortunately, father and elder brother act inappropriately, and sons and younger brothers are to remedy the situation, they must adopt the attitude as in the 'Minor Odes' of harboring resentment but not giving vent to their anger. In this way the nation will be at peace. If this is not done, there is great danger."[2] Think about it, dear reader—what kind of talk is this?

The Japanese Lieutenant General Horiuchi has stated: "At this time it is imperative that we adopt decisive measures and demand that China's government punish all those perpetrators of violent acts. We must also teach them to stand in awe of Japanese authority. We should dispatch troops to Beijing and Tianjin, send a fleet to the Yangzi, and absolutely prevent the occurrence of any anti-Japanese rebellion." Think about it, dear reader—what kind of talk is this?

Zhang Zuolin says: "Now that the peace conference has begun, the President must, from above, promote a benevolent attitude of sincere compassion. Once the people of the whole nation understand clearly how to hold fast to loyal devotion and show sincere feelings, they will offer support and praise from

---

1. Zhang Jian (1853–1926), *zi* Jizhi, *hao* Se'an, Seweng, a native of Nantong in Jiangsu Province, was one of China's early modernizers and reformers. After obtaining the *jinshi* degree in 1894, he turned his back on an official career to establish a cotton mill in Nantong. Zhang served briefly in 1912 as minister of industries in Sun Yatsen's provisional government, and later for two years (October 1913 to December 1915) as Yuan Shikai's minister of agriculture and commerce. He became best known, however, as an educator, conservationist, and public benefactor. He founded several schools (including China's first normal school) in his native district of Nantong, where he also undertook numerous charitable works. During the last decade of his life, he consciously sought to make Nantong a model for all of China.

2. The view criticized here had been put forward by Zhang Jian following the May 4th demonstrations, in an open letter entitled "Jinggao quanguo xuesheng" (Warning to the Students of the Whole Country). See *Zhang Jizi jiaoyu lu* [Writings of Zhang Jian on Education], Vol. IV, pp. 16B–18B.) The words following the allusion to the "Minor Odes" (Part II of the *Book of Poetry*) are not quoted from that work, but reflect Zhang Jian's reading of it.

below. Clouds come with the dragon, wind with the tiger, a rare opportunity is at hand. . . . " What an amazingly slavish tone of voice. Think about it, dear reader—what kind of talk is this?

Wang Zhanyuan says: "Hubei is Wang Zhanyuan's Hubei." Think about it, dear reader—what kind of talk is this?

For the Germans, the Painful Signing of the Treaty

(July 21, 1919)

Before the treaty was signed: Rantzau[1] and the other representatives of the defeated but not broken Germany arrived in Paris at the beginning of May. The solemn ceremony of the treaty exchange took place at the Palace of Versailles on May 7. The German representatives maintained a very dignified demeanor. Clemenceau stood up to announce the opening of the session. The chief German delegate, Rantzau, seated, then read the following statement:

> The German army has been broken and the extent of Germany's defeat is clear to us. But Germany is not solely responsible for this European war; all Europe shares the guilt. For the last fifty years, the imperialism of all the nations of Europe has truly poisoned the international situation. Germany's crimes in the war cannot be denied. In the course of war, the conscience of the people is clouded by passion, and crimes are committed. But after November 11 of last year, no German was fighting, while the Allied powers looked on with cold deliberation as many died from the effects of the blockade. The Fourteen Points of President Wilson were accepted by the entire world, and the Allied nations announced that the peace treaty would be based on these principles. Now Germany cannot be left completely without the means to avoid starvation. The League of Nations should be open to all nations. Germany cannot be left outside. Germany is willing to study the peace treaty in a spirit of good intentions.[2]

Paul Dutasta, general secretary of the peace conference, picked up the treaty, a large volume bound in a grayish yellow cloth, and handed it to Rantzau. Rantzau then returned to his residence and ate dinner in silence. After dinner, he immediately had people begin translating the treaty. The translation was completed at three o'clock in the morning and sent to Rantzau's sleeping quarters. It was daylight by the time he finished reading it. He had several copies made which were sent by courier to Berlin. On the eighth, the German cabinet met in a

---

1. Ulrich Karl Christian, Count von Brockdorff-Rantzau (1869–1928), foreign minister and head of the German delegation.

2. This is a greatly condensed paraphrase of some points in the original. For the full text of Rantzau's speech, see Graf Brockdorff-Rantzau, *Dokumente und Gedanken um Versailles* (Berlin: Verlag für Kulturpolitik, 1925), pp. 70–73.

long session. Chancellor Philipp Scheidemann,[3] in a speech before the committee studying the peace treaty, said:

> The peace treaty is simply a sentence of death for Germany. The government must adopt a politically very calm attitude in discussing this detestable, mad document. . . .

He then telegraphed the terms of the treaty to each of the [German] state governments and asked them to express their views. Because of the profound sense of suffering, a special proclamation was announced stopping all public entertainments for one week. The opera and theater were permitted to perform only tragedies of extreme suffering similiar to that of this day. The stock exchange, also in reaction to this painful shock, was closed for three days. News that the treaty was going to be signed angered people from all walks of life. Everyone talked about the possible implications of refusing to sign the treaty. No one believed that Germany could accept these conditions. All the Berlin newspapers attacked the treaty. One said, "The actual treaty far exceeds our most pessimistic expectations. If this vicious benighted document cannot be revised, the only word of reply must be 'rejected.' " Another paper said, "If we sign this treaty, it will be submission to naked coercion. In our hearts we should firmly reject it." Only the organ of the Independent Socialist Party advocated signing the treaty, saying, "From experience, we know that refusing to sign will only increase our problems later."

Most worth noting at this time is the attitude of the German political parties.[4] The government faction of the Majority Socialist Party did not advocate signing. The same was true of the People's Party and the Centrist Party. The only exception was the Independent Socialist Party. On the twelfth, the Independent Socialist Party passed a resolution advocating accepting the treaty and stated, "The return to belligerent behavior on the part of the present German government would strengthen the suspicion and fear that other peoples feel toward Germany. Germany has no choice but to bow to the coerced signing. The German-Russian treaty and the German-Rumanian

---

3. Philipp Scheidemann, Social Democratic Party, chancellor of the first cabinet of the German Republic formed February 13, 1919, following the election of Ebert as president on February 11.

4. The composition of the National Assembly elected on January 19, 1919, was as follows:

Social Democratic Party 163
Catholic Centrist 90
Democratic 75
Five other parties 93
(including 22 Independent Socialists; the Spartacists boycotted the elections)

Total 421

treaty[5] will soon be defunct. And there is nothing to stop the developing revolution from canceling the Versailles Treaty." If we look at it from Germany's point of view, if she doesn't want to abide by the treaty, she must follow in the footsteps of Russia and Hungary and carry out a great social revolution. This is precisely what the Allies fear the most. The fact that Russia and Hungary did not send representatives or make peace proposals is an obvious and courageous defiance of the Allies. The Allies still don't know what to do about it. If the social revolution of the mainstream faction[6] of the German Socialist Party had succeeded last winter, Germany would have been allied with Russia in the east and with Austria in the south and would have had even closer ties to Hungary and Czechoslovakia, and the news of their ideology of world revolution might have aroused a response in the long pent up socialist parties of England, France, and the United States. Could the Allied governments have swallowed that? The Independent Socialist Party and the mainstream Socialist Party were originally one party that split into two. It is not strange that they should talk like this. This talk about using the development of the revolution to abrogate the peace treaty should not be taken lightly.

On the same day that the German National Assembly was discussing the articles of the treaty, Scheidemann spoke out:

> This is a day of life or death for the German people! We must unite! To keep our nation alive—that and nothing else—is our duty. Germany has no plan to pursue any nationalistic dreams. Nor is it a question of prestige or of a thirst for power. Today everyone feels a throttling hand at his throat! The dignity of humanity is placed in your hands. Preserve it.

The fourteenth: Rantzau sent a note to Clemenceau, the content of which was essentially as follows:

> The items in the peace treaty regarding territory would strip from Germany extremely important productive lands. The grain and potato supply would be cut by 21 percent, coal by one-third, iron by three-fourths, and zinc by three-fifths. The loss of her colonies and commercial shipping would paralyze the German economy. If we now cannot get sufficient raw materials, the situation will deteriorate to the extreme limit. At the same time imports of foodstuffs would have to be greatly reduced. If the many millions who rely on transportation and commerce for their livelihoods cannot be given jobs and food by the German government, they will be forced to seek their livelihoods in other countries. But most of the major countries prohibit German immigration. Thus,

---

5. I.e., the Treaty of Brest-Litovsk signed on March 3, 1918, between the German Empire and Soviet Russia, and the German-Rumanian treaty signed in Bucharest on May 7, 1918.

6. See above, the note to the text of July 14, 1919, "The Arrest and Rescue of Chen Duxiu."

> signing the peace treaty would be tantamount to a sentence of death for many millions of the German people. . . .

In addition to this note, Rantzau sent two other notes to Clemenceau. The first said in essence that, "The occupation of German territory by the Allies violates the principles announced by President Wilson." The second note, expressing opposition to the reparations payments, said, "Germany is willing to pay reparations, but not because it admits responsibility for the war." We see that Germany's opposition stressed (1) that it was not solely responsible for the war and, (2) that it did not want to part with territory that produced raw materials. Although it did also object to other items, they were not the most important ones.

The thirteenth: In the evening, there was a great demonstration in Berlin. At the demonstration, the Majority Socialist Party mounted the stage and declared, "The peace treaty is more venomous, more despicable even than that forced on Carthage by Rome." The masses paraded through the streets, stopping finally in front of the Hotel Adlon, where the members of the Allied delegation were staying. Someone spoke to the crowd, saying that their forces were very powerful and that anyone wanting to attack the hotel would be stopped by the police. They then went to the general offices of the cabinet, where Scheidemann appeared at the windows and spoke to them. Another large group of people went at dusk to sing songs in front of the Hotel Adlon. They shouted, "Overthrow the ruthless peace settlement, down with Clemenceau, down with the English thief." The crowd went again to Scheidemann's place and asked him to speak to them. When Scheidemann brought up the Fourteen Points of President Wilson, the crowd shouted, "Down with Wilson." On that day the Independent Socialist Party held fourteen meetings in Berlin and the countryside.

The nineteenth: One of the Berlin papers carried the speech of the leader of the Socialist Party, Dr. Bernstein,[7] in which he said: "The extraordinarily burdensome conditions of the peace treaty are not purely the product of anger and revenge. We have been treated in this way because German policy was not trusted by others. All the destruction is Germany's fault. The fulfillment of all these demands is but repayment for what Germany has stolen from others. I entirely disagree with the impassioned words of most speakers. I tell them that never again must we have the arrogant bluster of August 4, 1914!" This was like a glass of cold water on the impassioned voice of German opposition.

The twentieth: Rantzau sent a letter to the peace commission requesting a revision of the deadline for examining and discussing the peace treaty.

The twenty-second: Clemenceau's reply granted permission to extend the deadline until May 29.

---

7. Eduard Bernstein, long a leading "revisionist" of Marxism in the German Social-Democratic Party, worked with moderates among the Independent Socialists in an attempt to approve signing the treaty.

The twenty-third: In the evening, the German plenipotentiary left for Spa to meet and make all final decisions with several cabinet members from Berlin.

The twenty-fourth: Scheidemann[8] and Mathias Erzberger went by car from Berlin to Spa. Rantzau and sixteen members of the delegation also arrived, and they met in an extraordinarily long session chaired by Scheidemann that passed the German counterproposals. At the end of this session, the government members of the delegation returned to Berlin, and Rantzau returned to Versailles.

May 27: The German reply was presented to the peace conference. The essentials of the first part of the reply were:

1. Germany agreed to reduce its military forces to 100,000 men.
2. Agreed to turn over the large military naval ships, but retain mercantile shipping vessels.
3. Opposed the decision concerning the eastern territories, and requested that the people of East Prussia set up a popular assembly or congress.
4. Recognized Danzig as a free port.
5. Requested that Allied troops be withdrawn four months after the signing of the treaty.
6. Requested membership in the League of Nations.
7. Strongly desired to be given the right to administer her colonies.
8. The total sum of reparations must not exceed 100 billion marks.
9. Refused extradition of the Kaiser and other personages.
10. Germany must have the right to engage again in overseas commerce.

The second part of the German counterproposals may be summarized as follows:

1. In the transition period, it would be necessary to maintain a large army to preserve civil order.
2. The German people should be allowed to convene a national assembly to discuss the question of territorial cession. And Austrians should be allowed convenient entrance to Germany.
3. Rejected the cession of Upper Silesia.
4. Did not recognize that Russia had any right to claim reparations.
5. Germany had no duty to make reparations to Italy, Montenegro, Rumania, or Poland.

---

8. Different characters are used here to transcribe Scheidemann, a not uncommon anomaly at the time.

After long discussions, the representatives of the four Allied powers drafted a reply to the above German counterproposals that rejected the German peace proposals item by item. The entire document is very long. Throughout it makes the impossible claim that Germany bears sole responsibility for the war. Germany must use every effort to repair all losses, must turn over its military leaders and all those who committed acts of violence during the war period to be punished according to the law. For a number of years Germany must be subject to special restrictions. The fundamental position held by the Allied powers in constructing the treaty cannot be changed in any way. Concessions may be possible only in regard to concrete German suggestions, etc., etc.

After May 29: In response to repeated requests of the German representatives for further extensions of the deadline for signing the treaty, it was finally agreed that the date would be put off until June 28. The entire first half of June was taken up by repeated replies and counter-replies.

When the German delegation returned to Germany from the French capital on June 18, it unanimously advised the German cabinet that it should refuse to sign the treaty. The German cabinet then made preparations to convene the National Assembly at Weimar to decide on this momentous problem. By this time, the Allies had already made military preparations, and the moment Germany should express opposition to signing the treaty, their troops would march in. Germany was already in a position in which it had no choice but to sign.

June 22: The Allies gave their "final reply" to Germany[9] and on this day communicated to the German representatives that Germany must accept the treaty within five days. The "final reply" made the following concessions:

1. A plebiscite would be held in Upper Silesia.

2. The western boundary of Prussia would be redrawn.

3. The German army could be temporarily increased to 200,000 men.

4. The German army must promise to produce within one month the list of persons accused of breaking the law in wartime.

4. [*sic*] Minor revisions regarding questions of finances.

5. Germany could be admitted to membership in the League of Nations on condition it fulfilled its duties.

Knowing that there was no further possibility of redeeming the peace treaty, the Scheidemann cabinet decided to resign.

The twenty-second: A new German cabinet was formed, with [Gustav Adolf] Bauer as chancellor, [Hermann] Müller as minister of foreign affairs, [Mathias] Erzberger as minister of finance, [Eduard] David as minister of the interior,

9. In fact, what was called a "final reply" was handed over on June 16, but some further concessions were made in an Allied note of June 22. The deadline for German acceptance was June 23.

[Gustav] Noske as minister of defense, [Johannes] Bell as minister for the colonies, Giesberts as minister for post and telegraph, Senschnan as minister of labor, Schlicke as minister of public works, Wissell as minister of public welfare, Meyer as minister of the treasury, and Schmidt as minister for food supplies. Bauer and most of his cabinet belonged to the Majority Socialist Party and had been members of the previous cabinet. Now, in this very tense international atmosphere, they had to come forth and face the difficult task of signing the peace treaty. When the new cabinet was formed, it was already clear that it was prepared to sign the treaty. When Scheidemann resigned, those of his cabinet who had been representatives in the peace negotiations of course also resigned. Thus the German peace negotiating delegation changed personnel. The new delegation was composed of the new cabinet's foreign minister, Müller, the minister of post and telegraph, Giesberts, etc.

At this time, the National Assembly was still in session at Weimar. Mr. Bauer appeared before the National Assembly and delivered a very agonized speech. He spoke in extreme terms about the anguish of forming the new government, and besought the National Assembly to come to a decision; otherwise warfare would break out all over again. Bauer said, "For the last time in free Germany, I stand up to oppose this brutal and destructive treaty! I stand up against this travesty of the right of self-determination! Against this scheme to enslave the German people! Against this new device to subvert world peace!" Amidst cries of "yea" and "nay," the motion to sign the treaty was passed.

After the motion to sign the treaty was passed, on the twenty-third, Bauer again appeared before the National Assembly to explain that it was necessary to sign the treaty unconditionally. In his speech he said, "That nation which is defeated in war will be humiliated by the world! In signing the treaty we gain a reprieve for a while. In the end, he who does damage to my honor will get his just deserts!" At this point the parties of the right raised objections. A vote was taken. The result confirmed permission to sign the treaty. The president of the Assembly, Fehrenbach, rose and declared briefly, "We entrust our fatherland to the mercies of the Lord!" He continued, "The leaders of all parties have been in touch with military circles. The entire nation hopes that the example of the sacrifice of the army and navy at Scapa Flow will help labor to rebuild the fatherland!" Germany's decision to sign the peace treaty, an event so closely tied to the peace and stability of the entire world, was finally taken to the accompaniment of this extremely painful speech. For the German people, there is no memorable occasion since the beginning of history that surpasses this day!

The National Assembly having passed the bill to sign the treaty, the new German delegation went to Paris and delivered the "Note of Approval to Sign the Treaty" to the peace conference. In its essentials, the note read:

> The government of the Republic of Germany recognizes that the Allied states are determined to use military force to coerce Germany into accepting the

> conditions of the peace treaty. Although these conditions have no great significance, their real intent is to deprive the German people of their honor. While submitting to superior military force, the German government does not withdraw its reservations regarding the unprecedented violation of justice of the conditions of the peace treaty! We hereby declare acceptance of the conditions imposed by the Allied states.

The joy of other countries at the proclamation of the above note was of course indescribable. Then on the twenty-eighth, the very last day of the extended deadline, the greatest ceremony in history was held in the Palace of Versailles for the signing of the peace treaty.

The ceremony for the signing of the peace treaty: At 3:05 P.M. on June 28, 1919, the conference opened in the Versailles Palace. In the Hall of Mirrors, a high dais had been set up, an imposing and solemn setting. The heads of the Allied plenipotentiary delegations assembled first. Next came the German plenipotentiaries, who included only the minister of foreign affairs, Müller, and the minister of transport, Bell.[10] The others refused to attend. As president of the peace conference, Clemenceau first delivered a brief address. "The governments of the Allies and states participating in the war have come to an agreement on the conditions of peace. Now the signatures will be given, expressing mutual faith solemnly to abide by the understanding." He then continued, "I invited the representatives of the German Republic to sign first." Suddenly there was a loud shout from the seats of the German delegation, "Deutschland! Deutschland!" At this Clemenceau changed the appellation to "Deutschland." The German representatives then rose and put their signatures to the treaty. Bell signed first. The time was 3:12 in the afternoon. In the gardens, the fountains sent up four jets, to the thunderous sound of the canons. By the time the German delegates had returned to their seats, everyone in the place was smiling. The United States signed next, and then Britain, followed by France, Italy, and Japan, with the Republic of Czechoslovakia signing last. At 3:35 the signing was completed, and Clemenceau announced the close of the meeting.

After the signing: When the news was announced that the German National Assembly had approved the signing of the peace treaty, patriotic demonstrations and marches took place throughout Germany. Groups of the common people sang war songs and the national anthem and shouted out their respect and praise for the elderly war veterans. The newspapers expressed extreme anger about the question of bringing the Kaiser to trial. One paper made a plea to the army officers of 1914, saying that if the Kaiser was put on trial that they should be willing to be put on trial by the Allies also. It even suggested the formation of an organization that might go to Holland and protect the Kaiser. Strikes broke out in

10. Johannes Bell of the Centrist Party was concurrently minister of colonies and minister of transport in the Bauer cabinet. The Ministry of Colonies was abolished on November 7, 1919.

many places one after the other. When on the twenty-eighth the news of the signing of the peace treaty reached Berlin, one Berlin newspaper printed an article that read, "The German people must eventually take revenge for the humiliation of 1919." The government suppressed circulation of this paper. On the twenty-ninth the newspapers all had a "black rule" to express their bitter grief. All the papers ran extremely pessimistic editorials. The railroad and trolley workers in Berlin and other places went out on strike. Transportation ground to a complete halt within the city of Berlin. There were riots in Hamburg and other places. Strikes spread throughout the entire nation.

Editorial Comment: In this account, I have described only the German side of the treaty signing. And in describing the German side of the treaty signing, I have focused solely on the pain and suffering inflicted on the spirit of the German people. Why? Aside from setting up the League of Nations, the entire peace treaty was written to deal with Germany. Germany is made up of the Germanic peoples, who have long been celebrated in history for possessing the characteristic of towering strength. When one dynasty is on the brink of collapse, a new sharp sword appears, which the peoples of the whole world can scarcely resist. We do not see the bellicose spirit of of Germany as having been unleashed solely by one man, the Kaiser. The Kaiser is the crystallization of the German people. Because there is a German people, there is a Kaiser. The German people have in recent years been molded by the philosophical ideas of "striving upward," of "action," of Nietzsche, Fichte, Goethe, and Paulsen. The call to arise when opportunity strikes has been loud and clear. Even today, they still do not admit defeat. "No war guilt." Of all the peoples of the world, the spirit of the German people is richest in "greatness." A spirit of "greatness" alone can overcome all difficulties, can seek to realize, bring to fruition this "greatness." Even while detesting the Kaiser's bellicose spirit and indiscriminate use of force, we can also shed tears of warm sympathy, moved by his spirit of "greatness." The German people have been defeated, and that is over. They have accepted even these humiliating painful conditions. With this first turnaround, they have already changed from an imperial monarchy into a republic. In the second turnaround, perhaps they will not even want to be a republic.[11] I would venture to make a rough judgment on this. We can see that England and France to the west are their enemies, can we not? If England and France are Germany's enemies, are not Russia, Austria, Hungary, Czechoslovakia, and Poland to the east and south its friends? Where else would they turn if not to countries such as Russia, Austria, Hungary, and Czechoslovakia? If they are to become associated with

11. *Minguo,* literally "people's country" or "citizens' country," the term commonly used at the time for Western-style republics, and which had been used since 1912 in *Zhonghua minguo*, the Republic of China. Mao goes on to contrast this type of "republic" with that of Soviet Russia, which he calls (as in the title of the regime he himself was to set up in 1949) *gongheguo.*

Russia, Austria, Hungary, and Czechoslovakia, they must change into a system that is compatible with that of Russia, Austria, Hungary, and Czechoslovakia. That the social revolutions in Russia and Hungary have been successful goes without saying. The same trend also exists in Hungary[12] and Czechoslovakia. The other day, the teletype said that Czechoslovakia had already become a republic [*minguo*] of the workers and soldiers. The fierce uprising of the Spartacus Union[13] of the mainstream faction of the German [Socialists] last winter came very close to succeeding. With the establishment of the Ebert government, the Majority Socialist Party holds power and depends on just a few soldiers, a few guns, to keep the mainstream socialists under control. When the peace treaty is concluded, the soldiers will want to demobilize, and their guns will be handed over. Then what can the government depend on? If German industry and commerce want to recover from the crushing blow they have suffered, they will have to rely entirely on the toilers who provide their labor power. From this point on, a major task of the government will be to kowtow a great deal to the laborers. And the weapon of the mainstream faction is precisely these laborers. Thus, examined from the perspective of trends in foreign relations, I suggest that Germany must ally herself with Russia, Austria, Hungary, and Czechoslovakia and become a communist republic [*gongheguo*]. Similar conclusions may also be drawn if we think in terms of the trends in internal politics as well.

Before 1919, Germany was the most powerful nation in the world. After 1919, the greatest powers in the world will be France, England, and the United States. Germany's power was political and international. The result of this great war has been the use of the political and international power of the Allies to defeat the political and international power of Germany. After 1919, the power of France, England, and the United States will be social and economic power. If there is war after 1919 it will be class war. The result of class war will be the victory of the ideology of the states of eastern Europe, the victory of the socialists. We must not underestimate the Germans of the future. We should not overestimate the strutting and prancing men of the present peace conference. Their days of famine will come soon! Their day of headaches will arrive!

Thus, don't even count on this peace treaty "lasting five years." If we truly extrapolate from the examples of the "German-Russian Treaty" and the "German-Rumanian Treaty," I'm afraid it is only a question of time. Ignorant old man Clemenceau, clutching this grayish-yellow thick volume under his arm, thinks that the signatures on it make it as stable and solid as the Alps. How pitiful!

---

12. The editors of the *Wengao* suggest that the character for Hungary is a misprint for that representing Austria.

13. The Spartakusbund of Rosa Luxemburg and Karl Liebknecht had become, in January 1919, the German Communist Party.

Joy and Suffering

(July 21, 1919)

When Clemenceau received the telephone call in his office telling him of Germany's acceptance of the peace treaty, he was beside himself with joy. He stood up and shook hands with the cabinet members and other officials in his office and said, "Messieurs! I have been waiting for this moment for forty-nine years!" What joyous words. The greatest joy, however, also contains within it a certain amount of suffering. In 1871, how elated Wilhelm I and Bismarck were when they occupied the seat of power in Versailles and accepted the French document of submission. The result, however, was to bring about this war. Even though the delight of Wilhelm I and Bismarck was unmatched, a certain amount of suffering was inherent in it. From 1800 to 1815, Napoleon trampled over the German people, divided their country, occupied their lands, and disbanded their armies. The King of Prussia submitted, and proclaimed himself a vassal. How elated Napoleon was! The result was the war of 1871. Even though the delight of Napoleon was unmatched, it contained within it a certain amount of suffering. From 1789 to 1790, the mighty armies of the Holy Alliance, Germany and Austria, inspired by deep hatred for democracy and freedom in France, invaded French territory several times and surrounded Paris. The result was the rise of Napoleon, who in turn invaded Germany, much to the distress of the German people. When we look at history in the light of cause and effect, joy and suffering are often closely interrelated, inseparable. When the joy of one side reaches an extreme, the suffering of the other side will inevitably also reach an extreme. When we look at the contents of this peace treaty, is it any different from the way that Napoleon treated Germany? Is there any difference as regards the dismemberment of Germany, or German lands being occupied, or the German army being disbanded? Clemenceau's great joy is the Germans' great sorrow. I guarantee that in ten or twenty years, you Frenchmen will yet again have a splitting headache. Mark my words.

Karl and Puyi

(July 21, 1919)

A newspaper reporter, seeking an interview with Karl, the former emperor of Austria, now in exile in Switzerland, was met by his chamberlain, who stated, "The emperor did not retire of his own accord and thus hopes for the restoration of the monarchy. His seclusion, and lack of involvement in politics, are only temporary." No one who has once been emperor does not want to be emperor again. No one who has once been an official does not want to be an official again. This is simply a long-established psychological bent. Westerners like to be thorough in doing things. Historically, many kings have been put to death. The execution of Charles I by the English in 1648, of Louis XVI by the French in 1793, and of Nicolas II by the Russians in 1918 all took place because it was felt that this was the only way to stamp out the roots of trouble. Napoleon was imprisoned on St. Helena, and today, Wilhelm II, in being submitted like a latter-day Napoleon to the judgment of the Allies, can on the whole be regarded as having been let off very lightly. Both Karl in exile in Switzerland and Puyi in seclusion in Beijing[1] will sooner or later make trouble if the people do not take the necessary precautions.

---

1. Puyi was the personal name of the former Xuantong Emperor, who had abdicated in February 1912 and was then still living in the imperial palace in Beijing. In 1924, he was forced by Feng Yuxiang to vacate these premises, and sought refuge in the Japanese concession in Tianjin. He did indeed "make trouble" when he became head of the Japanese puppet government of Manchukuo in 1932, and was proclaimed emperor in 1934.

The Founding and Progress of the "Strengthen Learning Society"

(July 21, 1919)

The Hunan Intellectual World Before the Strengthen Learning Society

For the last twenty years, the intellectual world of Hunan has been extremely dull and dreary. Twenty years ago, Tan Sitong[1] and others founded the Southern Study Society[2] in Hunan, gathered together such well-known people as Liang Qichao[3] and Mai Menghua[4] in the Changsha School of Current Affairs[5] and published the *Xiangbao*[6] and the *Shiwubao*.[7] At the time, these were highly important, successful, and well-known groups. They were formed in response to the anger and humiliation imposed at the time on the ancient Chinese empire by the repeated attacks of the foreign powers. They realized that the Great Wall and the broad oceans were no longer proof against the iron horses and fearless

---

1. See the note to Zhang Kundi's record of two talks with Mao Zedong, September 1917.

2. The Southern Study Society was formally founded in Changsha in February 1898 by Tan Sitong and Tang Caichang. The Society aimed to promote new learning and discussed the issue of a new government for Hunan until it was banned after the failure of the 1898 Reform movement.

3. On Liang Qichao, see the note to Mao's letter of June 25, 1915.

4. Mai Menghua (1875–1915), *zi* Rubo, *hao* Jiameng, was a native of Guangdong and a student of Kang Youwei at his school there. He supported the 1898 Reform movement and devoted himself to the propagation of new ideas. He worked closely with Liang Qichao as editor of various publications.

5. The Changsha School of Current Affairs was founded by Jiang Dejun and Xiong Xiling in October 1897 in Changsha. Xiong Xiling was president, Liang Qichao was head of the Chinese department, and Li Weige was head of the Western-language section. Classes were held on economics, Western politics and government, and natural science, and the school aimed to spread ideas of constitutional reform and modernization. It was closed in November 1898.

6. The reformist paper *Xiangbao* (Hunan Daily) was Hunan's earliest daily paper, established in March 1898 by Tan Sitong, Tang Caichang, and others. It was forced to cease publication on October 15, 1898, having published 177 issues.

7. The *Shiwubao* (known in English as "The Chinese Progress") was established on August 8, 1896, in Shanghai to promote political reform. It aimed to publish every ten days, and Liang Qichao was the editor-in-chief. It closed in November 1898, following the repression of the reforms.

warships of other peoples, and that the old ways of China were really somewhat inadequate. The call for reforms and self-strengthening at that time became a great chorus that spread throughout China. This was a moment of great and pivotal change for China. And the accompanying changes in Hunan were likewise pivotal.

Ideas changed. What were the ideas at that time? What was the central point of the world of thought at that time? To these questions, one must first reply as follows:

1) The ideas of that era were of attaining greatness. Such slogans as "seek Western learning," or "examine with an open mind," were merely ways of getting "respect through learning." Everyone thought that the new foreign ways could be mastered in ten to twenty years, and with this new learning the self-strengthening of China would be possible. Once the goal of self-strengthening was achieved, China would be able to wage a last desperate battle[8] against the foreign devils, or at least fend them off. This was just like a little child who has been bullied by the child next door, and in the night secretly takes out his stick with the idea of running out the next morning to teach the other a lesson. "Western studies" and "new ways" were simply equivalent to the little child's stick.

2) The thought of that era was empty and vacuous, as we can see by just a glance at the publications of the time that promoted the reforms. They uniformly appealed to the emotions with "disaster and grief." In content they were totally hollow, having very little that even touched on real life or society. At the time, there was an atmosphere of "founding schools," of "establishing self-rule," of "calling conferences," most of which was, in the last analysis, much ado about nothing. When all this commotion reached gale force, it was not easy for anyone in the intellectual world actually to examine the facts and the truth.

3) The philosophy of the time followed the pattern of "Chinese studies as the foundation, Western studies for practical use."[9] "China is a nation famous for its culture. The traditional Chinese ethical system is number one in the world. The West only has powerful scientific armaments. We only need to learn about these." Anyone whose ideas deviated even a little from this would be regarded as a "European fanatic," someone to be spit upon and reviled his entire life.

---

8. This is an allusion to the *Zuo zhuan*, Year II of Duke Cheng (Legge, Vol. V, pp. 341 and 346). The leaders of a neighboring state, invaded by Qin, are there quoted as saying, "If you will not grant [our plea for peace], then we will collect the fragments of our forces, and ask for another battle before the walls of our capital." The final four characters of this sentence, cited here by Mao, have come to mean a desperate last stand.

9. *Zhongxue wei ti, xixue wei yong*—the formula identified with Zhang Zhidong (1837–1909), governor-general of Hunan and Hubei from 1889. Zhang was in favor of industrial development and economic modernization, but broke with the reformers in 1898 because he regarded them as too radical. Both this slogan, and Zhang's contribution to China's industrialization, were points to which Mao repeatedly referred until the end of his life.

4) The philosophy of the time was centered on Confucius. Politically, those times saw the movement to expel the Manchus and the movement for representative politics. In the scholarly realm, there were the movements to abolish the imperial examination system, to found schools, and to make use of science. But no one dared say anything at all negative about old man Confucius. The popular formulation was "new studies and old morality." "Old morality" was another way of saying "the morality of Confucius."

This situation prevailed throughout China, and Hunan was part of this situation. Thus, although thought did change, the change was not thoroughgoing. The most we can say is that the changes were rather general, blind, and transitional. From 1898 to the present, the intellectual world of Hunan has been totally under the control of these vague, blind, and transitional changes.

Hunan has been talking about seeking the new learning for more than twenty years and still does not have a really new intellectual atmosphere. In Hunan twenty years ago the intellectual climate was that of the old studies, and its two branches, Song studies and Han studies. Twenty years later, that climate has still not totally dissipated. Although academies have given way to schools and the students have been drawn away by the sciences, they are still submerged at the bottom of society. An examination of the reasons why the new studies have not taken hold would show that this results entirely from the fact that the new studies have never had a well-established central core of thought. Such an intellectual core has not been established for the following reasons: (1) There is no study group or association that is devoted purely to the new studies. (2) There are no colleges or universities of the new studies. (3) Very few students study abroad. There are also those who do not continue in the pursuit of their specialties because of the problem of making a living, or because the pursuit of vain glory takes precedence over the path of studying something that is useless. Those who went to study in Japan have been drawn into politics by Huang Xing.[10] (4) Political turmoil and the lack of peaceful days in which to study. This is the reason it has not been possible for those involved in the new studies in Hunan to establish a central core of thought, that is to say, a distinctive study climate. Ever since 1911, most of those filling the ranks of education have been philistines whose views and opinions are based on a little bit of knowledge half digested, creating an environment of ignorance and vacuity. As for a central core of thought or a new climate of study, it is pointless even to talk about it.

In the past few years, the situation in China has been changing. Cai Yuanpei,[11] Jiang Kanghu,[12] Wu Jingheng,[13] Liu Shifu,[14] and Chen Duxiu were

---

10. See the note to Mao's letter of March 1917 to Miyazaki Tōten.

11. Cai Yuanpei (1868–1940), *zi* Heliao, *hao* Jiemin, a native of Zhejiang, was a scholar of the Hanlin Academy, and also studied in Germany from 1908 to 1911. An eminent educationalist, he became the first minister for education of the Nanjing provisional government. In 1916 he was appointed chancellor of Beijing University, to which

the first to call for reforms [*gexin*]. Not just partial or piecemeal reform. Everything must be changed, from thought and literature to politics, religion, and art. Even such questions as whether or not to retain the nation, or the family, or marriage, whether property should be private or public, are all issues that are open to examination. And even more important are the great European war and the Russian Revolution it sparked, the waves of which are moving from West to East. Scholars of Beijing National University were the first to welcome it, and young people from schools throughout China have responded to it, and its roaring tidal wave has reached Hunan, prompting the founding of the Strengthen Learning Society.

The Founding of the Strengthen Learning Society

On June [1]5, the chairman of the provincial education association, Chen Runlin,[15] invited faculty from various provincial and city schools to gather together to found the Strengthen Learning Society. Among these were Xu Teli,[16]

---

he brought Chen Duxiu as dean of humanities. Under his leadership, Beijing University emerged as a center of intellectual freedom and a key influence in the new culture movement. He was one of the instigators of the work-study in France program in which many Hunan students participated around 1920.

12. Jiang Kanghu (1883–1954), original name Shaoquan, was born in Jiangxi Province. He was strongly influenced by socialist and anarchist ideas while a student in Japan and founded the Chinese Socialist Party in Shanghai in 1911.

13. Wu Zhihui (1866–1953), *zi* Jingheng, was born in Jiangsu Province. In 1902 he joined the Shanghai Patriotic Study Society and worked at the *Su bao*. He joined the Tongmenghui in France in 1905 and in 1907 organized the anarchist *Xinshiji* (New Century) magazine. He later worked for the Guomindang government.

14. Liu Shifu (1884–1915), also known as Liu Sifu, was a prominent radical of the early Republican period. A disciple of Kropotkin, who dedicated his life to the propagation of the anarchist cause, he was one of the founders of the Conscience Society (Xin She) in 1912, and of the Anarchist-Communist Comrade Society in the same year. He advocated abolition of family and class divisions, and the creation of equal education.

15. Chen Runlin (1879–1946), *zi* Suhuang, *hao* Liyuan, also known as Chen Sufang, was a well-known Hunanese educationalist who had studied in Japan. He participated in the 1911 revolution and later became active in Hunan affairs. In 1918 he became head of the provincial Council on Education, and he was president of the Chuyi School from 1919. As well as being active in the organization of the Strengthen Learning Society, he was involved in the movement to expel Zhang Jingyao and in the Cultural Book Society. (On Governor Zhang Jingyao, see the note to the text of December 24, 1919.)

16. Xu Teli (1877–1968), original name Maoxun, also known as Lihua, was born in Changsha. Xu was one of Mao's teachers at First Normal School, where he taught ethics and education from 1913 to 1918; in 1918 he was principal of First Women's Normal School in Changsha. Before the 1911 revolution, he and other teachers at Zhounan Girls' School established an elementary adult education school in Changsha. He was one of the oldest of those who went to France on the work-study program in 1919. He joined the Chinese Communist Party in 1927.

Zhu Jianfan,[17] Tang Song,[18] Cai Xiang,[19] Zhong Guotao,[20] Yang Shuda,[21] Li Yunhang, Xiang Shaoxuan,[22] Peng Guojun,[23] Fang Kegang, Ouyang Ze,[24] He Binglin, Li Jingqiao, and Zhao Yi. The meeting was held at the Chuyi School. The purport of Chen Runlin's presentation on organizing the study society, as reported in a newspaper, is recorded below:

> When we were last in Beijing, we had an unexpected feeling of great optimism. Just four years previously, the only goal of students at Beijing University was to become an official. This was not true only in the universities. Outside the universities, it was the same everywhere. On our last trip to the capital, what we observed was quite different. The tide of thought among university students had undergone a great change, and they were all thinking about the purpose of human life. This thought tide was already manifested in a number of magazines and periodicals. Because of this, students of many schools in the capital had already changed their old views all of a sudden, and the present great movement to save the nation had emerged. The reason for this is that since Mr. Cai Yuanpei became chancellor of the university the infusion of philosophical thought and the concept of a philosophy of life has brought about a complete change in the old thought. Some mistakenly think that the student movement to save the nation has been manipulated by the politicians and do not realize that it really came from the students themselves, and from the clash between the old and new ideas. Following the change in the political structure of the Russian government, socialism has gradually been transported into East Asia. Although there are many different factions, the flow of this tide cannot be stopped. For example, the Japanese government, which previously dealt out the death sentence to those who supported a socialist

---

17. Zhu Jianfan (1883–1932) was a Hunanese educated in Japan. In 1916, he became principal of Zhounan Girls' School in Changsha. He was very active in the movement of 1919–1920 to oust Zhang Jingyao. In 1922 he became a member of the Hunan Provincial Assembly established by Zhao Hengti.

18. Tang Song (1887–), *zi* Shoujun, a native of Changsha, studied at the Tokyo Commercial School and then in America, returning to China in 1915. He was editor-in-chief of the Shanghai Commercial Press and one-time head of Changsha Commercial Vocational School. At this time he was working in Shanghai for the Hunan branch of the Sino–French Educational Association.

19. Cai Xiang was president of Jiazhong Technical School at this time.

20. Zhong Guotao (1889–1961), also known as Chusheng, a native of Hunan, graduated from Nanjing Higher Normal School. He was an early member of the New People's Study Society. In 1920 he was teaching at the Zhounan Girls' School; he went on to work at the primary school attached to Hunan First Normal School.

21. See the note to the text of January 19, 1920.

22. Xiang Shaoxuan (1884–1946), *zi* Fu'an, was a Hunanese who worked at Mingde Middle School in Shanghai after returning from study in England.

23. Peng Guojun, a returned student from Japan, established Changjun Middle School in Changsha. In 1918 he became principal of the school, after serving on the Hunan Provincial Assembly. He was a strong advocate of the new thought movement, and in 1919 his Changjun school was the first to adopt *baihua* (the vernacular) in all its classes.

24. For details on Ouyang Ze, see Mao's letter to him dated November 25, 1920.

party, can no longer do so, and today finally allows activities by members of the socialist party. Another example is that of Dr. Yoshino,[25] who advocates tempering extremism with national socialism and going along with world trends and accepting changes in the Japanese polity that would make it an English-style pseudo-monarchy. This demonstrates just how great is the force of the rapid change in world thought tides. The new thought tide in our country is also very well developed, and cannot be held back much longer. We Chinese must study it in a timely fashion, and guide it along the proper path. The colleagues who have organized the study society will adopt sound and correct theories with which to make a thorough investigation of it. . . .

It is said that at the meeting held on this day, Mr. Zhu Jianfan gave a talk "proposing that everyone put aside his prejudices and submit to truth in the study of the worldwide new thought," and Mr. Xiang Shaoxuan made a speech "advocating the adoption of national socialism." These were indeed unprecedented new ideas in the Hunan intellectual world. Below are the society bylaws issued at this meeting:

1. Comrades have come together in this society, in view of the influx of the new world thought tide, to study it together, and to select those ideas which will be propagated as our platform.

2. This society will be called the Strengthen Learning Society.

3. The society will be temporarily located at the Chuyi Elementary School at Chuyingyuan, Changsha.

4. Those wishing to join the society must truly intend to engage in scholarly study and will be admitted for membership in this society through the introduction of one of its members.

5. On methods for introducing the new thought tide:

1) The society will collect all the newest books and magazines and make them available to members to read. The personal books and periodicals of members must be loaned to members of the society to read. The society particularly welcomes contributions.

2) There will be a periodic examination and reporting of correspondence with comrades both at home and abroad.

3) Well-known people will be invited to speak.

6. On methods of research:

1) The areas of study will primarily be problems in philosophy, education, psychology, ethics, literature, aesthetics, sociology, political studies, economics, for the study of which members will divide into individual groups.

2) Important questions will be studied by the whole membership together.

---

25. Yoshino Sazō (1877–1933) was a Japanese politician, doctor of law, and a professor in the law department of Tokyo Imperial University.

3) Members of the society wishing to study foreign languages will be taught by the society's members.

7. On methods of dissemination:
1) Lectures. Both scheduled and unscheduled. The regularly scheduled lectures will be given once a week, between eight and ten o'clock on Sunday morning. Members will take turns being responsible for them. The speaker and the topic will be decided the previous Sunday. The speaker should prepare a manuscript of his talk to be given to the society for publication. Unscheduled lectures on important topics to be given by either members or well-known persons. Times and places to be announced.

2) Publications.

8. The society will have one treasurer and one librarian. The responsibility for other tasks of the society will be shared by the members. Each meeting will be temporarily chaired by one of the members.

9. Members of the society should abide by the following regulations:

1) Be prompt.

2) Have the true spirit of research.

3) Help each other in learning.

4) Freedom of scholarly discussion.

5) Avoid formal, empty politeness. Stress frankness and honesty.

10. Membership dues will be at least 2 *yuan* yearly. Special contributions to help with expenses will be very welcome.

11. When important matters of this society come up and need to be discussed, the entire membership should be notified following the scheduled talks and a consensus arrived at.

Of the society's bylaws, numbers 5, 6, 7, and 9 are extremely important. Under number 9, having the true spirit of research is a very good idea, in order to break through preconceived and self-satisfied opinions. We wish that after a spirit of "research," they had added a "critical" spirit. The development of contemporary scholarship is, for the most part, the result of the learning of single individuals. Most important is the "I," or "individuality," which is precisely the opposite of the Chinese habit of not commenting on someone unless he is dead, and of not citing the viewpoints of contemporaries. Our own individual thoughts should be at the center of our actions, like the sun spreading its light through the heavens, like a beacon at sea shining far into the night. Do not worry about whether it is really right or wrong (by what is today regarded as right), or whether it agrees or not with someone else's view. We should only worry about whether or not it accords with the truth. What the old gentlemen dislike most is arrogance. Are they not aware that, both in the past and in the present, all truly correct principles, all really great enterprises, have been discovered or created by arrogant individuals who were labeled as such by others? Living in this complex society, this ever changing world, if we lack a critical spirit we will easily become the slaves of others. One gentleman has said that most Chinese are slaves. That's not a bad way of putting it. The item under number 9 on freedom of scholarly discussion is very much in accord with the principle of freedom of thought and freedom of speech. This is mankind's most precious treasure, the source of utmost satisfaction. Scholarly research most abhors a deductive, arbitrary attitude. Chinese cliches like "respect your teacher and you will be honoring the Way," "the Master says," "Confucian orthodoxy," "such-and-such a sect" are all diseases arising from an "arbitrary attitude." They are the repressive despotisms of the intellectual world, and we must smash them with all our might. For example, we oppose Confucius for many other reasons as well, but for just this one reason alone, for his hegemony over China that has denied freedom to our intellectual world, that has kept us the slave of idols for two thousand years, we must oppose him.

The Progress of the Strengthen Learning Society

According to the bylaws of the Strengthen Learning Society, the business of the society is primarily the study and dissemination of the latest in scholarship, with an emphasis at present on study. It is said that people have already been sent to Beijing, Shanghai, and other places, to select and buy books, newspapers, and magazines. In the provincial capital they have started a class in English so that the members of the society can learn English in preparation for studying Western learning directly. Members forty and fifty years of age enjoy studying it. They have also started a lecture group in which the members take turns presenting their views and exchanging information and knowledge. Those gentlemen who had a thoroughly bureaucratic demeanor have suddenly become humble in their respect for and openness to studying, although some of the others are still not totally satisfied because they feel that the attitude of these gentlemen is still 50 to 60 percent bureaucratic, as their talks still tend to adopt the style of orders and admonitions. There are those who say that they are camouflaging themselves, like green bugs on green leaves. But I don't think it is necessary to reproach them in this way for not being perfect. For something like this to take place in such an effeminate and lethargic place as Hunan is quite enough to draw people out of their confinement and cheer them up. We should applaud and welcome the light of dawn in the East, the sound of footsteps in the empty valley. We hope that this will be the prelude to the "reform of Hunan." Looking at the topics of four of their talks, "The Mistaken Chinese View of Life and Death," "How to Act as Becomes a Man," "Education and the Vernacular Language," "Adopting John Dewey's Philosophy of Education," they are all very much to the point. If they could change their present practice and open their lectures to the public so that everyone could come and listen, then there is no telling how fast [these ideas] would spread, and how great the benefits might be.

Explanations by the Xiang River Review

(July 21, 1919)

I

This paper is concerned purely with academic theories and with social criticism. We do not meddle at all in practical politics.

II

The inaugural issue of this paper was printed in two thousand copies, which have now all been sold. At present, we are printing another two thousand, but because the press is very busy, it will require several days before they can be produced. We beg the indulgence of our readers.

The Great Union of the Popular Masses

Part I

(July 21, 1919)

The decadence of the state, the sufferings of humanity, and the darkness of society have all reached an extreme. Where is the method of improvement and reform? Education, industrialization, strenuous efforts, rapid progress, destruction, and construction are, to be sure, all right, but there is a basic method for carrying out all these undertakings, which is that of the great union of the popular masses.

If we look at the course of history as a whole, we find that all the movements which have occurred throughout history, of whatever type they may be, have all without exception resulted from the union of a certain number of people. A greater movement requires a greater union, and the greatest movement requires the greatest union. All such unions are more likely to appear in a time of reform and resistance. In all hitherto existing cases of reform and resistance in religion, science, politics, and society, the partisans on both sides necessarily had their great unions. Victory and defeat are decided by the solidity or fragility of the unions on each side, and by whether the ideologies which serve as their foundation are new or old, true or ill-founded. Both sides, however, are alike in that they must employ the technique of union.

Among the various unions that have existed since antiquity, those of the oppressors, the aristocrats, and the capitalists have been most numerous. For example, the various "alliances" and "ententes" in foreign relations are unions of the world's great powers. The so-called "Beiyang Faction" and "Southwestern Faction" in our country, and the Satsuma and Chōshū clans in Japan,[1] are unions of oppressors within a country. The political parties and legislative assemblies in various countries are unions of aristocrats and capitalists. (The upper house or senate is naturally a lair where aristocrats gather; similarly, the lower house, because of the property qualifications for the vote, is largely occupied by capitalists.) As for the so-called trusts (railroad trust, oil trust) and companies (Nippon

1. Satsuma and Chōshū were clans in late Tokugawa Japan which seceded from the central government and set up their own feudal domains, giving them the power to carry out comprehensive reforms independent of the central authorities. Their actions spearheaded a political development which led to national rejuvenation. In 1897, Liang Qichao proposed that Hunan should follow this example and declare independence from the Beijing government as the only way for China to prevent national subjugation by foreign powers.

Yusen Kaisha, the Manchurian Railway Company), they are purely capitalist unions. In recent times, the union of the oppressors, the aristocrats, and the capitalists has reached an extreme, and in consequence the decadence of the state, the sufferings of humanity, and the darkness of society have also reached an extreme. It is then that reform and resistance arise; it is then that the great union of the popular masses is called into being.

After the victory of "political reform" had been obtained in France by the opposition of the great union of the popular masses to the great union of the adherents of the monarchy, many countries followed the French example and undertook all sorts of "political reforms." After the victory of "social reform" had been obtained last year in Russia,[2] by the opposition of the great union of the popular masses to the great union of the aristocracy and the great union of the capitalists, many countries — Hungary, Austria, Czechoslovakia, Germany — likewise followed the Russian example and undertook all sorts of social reforms. Although this victory is not yet complete, it may certainly become so, and it is also conceivable that it will spread throughout the whole world.

Why is the great union of the popular masses so terribly effective? Because the popular masses in any country are necessarily more numerous than the aristocracy, the capitalists, and the other oppressors in a single country. Since the aristocrats, capitalists, and other oppressors are few in number, they rely, in order to maintain their own special interests and to exploit the collective assets of the majority of ordinary people, first on knowledge, second on money, and third on military force. Education in the past was the privilege of the aristocrats and capitalists; the ordinary people had absolutely no opportunity to get any. Since they were the only ones who had knowledge, there arose the classes of the wise and of the ignorant. Money is the intermediary in life. Originally, everyone could get it, but those aristocrats and capitalists with their knowledge thought up various methods for something called "the concentration of capital," and as a result the money gradually flowed into the hands of the landlords and the factory bosses. They took all the land, machines, and houses for themselves, baptizing them "real property." They also took the money, which they called movable property, and stored it up in their treasure-houses (the banks). Thus the millions of ordinary people who worked for them had, in contrast, nothing but a meager salary of a franc or a penny. Since those who worked had no money, the classes of the rich and the poor emerged. Having knowledge and money, the aristocrats and the capitalists set up military camps to train soldiers, and factories to make guns. Making use of the signboard of "foreign outrages," they recruit dozens of divisions and hundreds of companies. They have even gone so far as to invent a method for levying more troops known as "conscription." This means that strong vigorous sons become soldiers, and when a problem arises, they take their ma-

2. This error in dating on Mao's part undoubtedly resulted from the fact that it was only in 1918 that Li Dazhao first published his article "The Victory of Bolshevism."

chine guns and go attack their feeble old fathers. For example, if we look at what happened last year, when the defeated southern army was retreating from southern Hunan, did they not kill a great many of their own fathers? When the aristocrats and capitalists employ such admirable schemes, the common people are even more afraid to raise their voices. Thus the classes of the strong and the weak emerge.

Now, it happens that these very three methods of theirs gradually cause the common people to learn a good deal in their turn. The common people, too, read a bit of these textbooks which they have made their "secret pillow books," and gradually acquire knowledge. As for the land and factories which are the source of their wealth, the common people have long been entombed in them, and look with envy on the comfort of the capitalists, wanting to have a finger in the pie themselves. Even the soldiers in the military camps are, after all, their sons, brothers, or husbands. Should the soldiers turn their machine guns against them, they will let out a big shout, and at this their bullets will immediately turn to mud. Spontaneously they will join hands and turn the other way instead, becoming together valiant fighters resisting the aristocrats and the capitalists. We have, in fact, seen Russia's hundred thousand brave warriors suddenly exchange the imperial standard for the red flag, and from this we may know that there is deep truth in what I say.

Thus the common people have seen through the three methods of the aristocrats and the capitalists, and they have also perceived that in order to apply these methods, the aristocrats and capitalists employ the technique of union. The common people are also conscious of the fact that the number on the other side is so small, and the number on our side is so big. Thus we must unite on a very large scale. As to the actions which should be undertaken once we have united, there is one extremely violent party, which uses the method "Do unto others as they do unto you"[3] to struggle desperately to the end with the aristocrats and capitalists. The leader of this party is a man named Marx who was born in Germany. There is another party more moderate than that of Marx. It does not expect rapid results, but begins by understanding the common people. Men should all have a morality of mutual aid, and work voluntarily. As for the aristocrats and capitalists, it suffices that they repent and turn toward the good, and that they be able to work and to help people rather than harming them; it is not necessary to kill them. The ideas of this party are broader and more far-reaching. They want to unite the whole globe into a single country, unite the human race in a single family, and attain together in peace, happiness, and friendship — not friendship as understood by the Japanese — an age of prosperity. The leader of this party is a man named Kropotkin, who was born in Russia.

We must know that the affairs of this world are, in themselves, very easy to deal with. If there are cases when they are not easy to deal with, this is because of the difficulties caused by the force of history — habit. If we can only give a

3. Literally, "deal with that person according to his own principles" — from Zhu Xi's commentary to Chapter 13 of the *Doctrine of the Mean.*

shout together, we will shatter this force of history. Let us forge an even greater union, coming together as we have never thought possible, and then we will draw up our ranks and give a great shout at the opposing side. We already have experience: the bullets of Lu Rongting[4] will never overcome traitors like Cao Rulin.[5] As soon as we arise and let out a shout, the traitors will get up and tremble and flee for their lives. We must know that our brothers of other lands have often employed this method to secure their interests. We must arise and imitate them; we must carry out our great union!

Part II: Taking Small Unions as the Foundation
(July 28, 1919)

In the previous issue of this paper, I have already concluded my discussion of the possibility and the necessity of the "great union of the popular masses." In the present issue, I shall consider what method we should employ for carrying out this great union. The method is that of "small democratic unions."

If we truly want to achieve a great union, in order to resist the powerful people confronting us who harm their fellow men, and in order to pursue our own interests, we must necessarily have all sorts of small unions to serve as its foundation. The human race has an innate talent for uniting together, that is to say, a talent for constituting groups, a talent for organizing societies. "Groups" and "societies" are precisely the "unions" I am talking about. There are big groups and small groups, big societies and small societies, big unions and small unions — they are merely different names for the same thing. So if we want to establish groups, societies, unions, it is because we are desirous of securing our common interests. Because our circumstances and professions are different, there are also some differences, large or small, in the sphere of our common interests. Because there are differences, large or small, in our common interests, the method (union) for securing our common interests also displays certain differences, large or small.

Gentlemen! We are peasants, and so we want to establish a union with others who cultivate the land as we do, in order to promote the various interests of us tillers of the soil. It is only we ourselves who can pursue the interests of us tillers of the soil; others who do not cultivate the soil have interests different from ours and will certainly not help us to seek our interests. Gentlemen who cultivate the

4. See note to text of April 27, 1920.

5. For details regarding Cao Rulin, see the note to the text of July 14, 1919, "The Arrest and Rescue of Chen Duxiu." Cao is called a "traitor" here because of his policy of concessions to Japan. Mao's statement that he will be overcome not by bullets, but by the action of the "great union," is based, of course, on the fact that the May Fourth student demonstrations actually did bring about Cao's overthrow.

land! How do the landlords treat us? Are the rents and taxes heavy or light? Are our houses satisfactory or not? Are our bellies full or not? Is there enough land? Are there not some in the village who have no land to cultivate? We must constantly seek solutions to all these problems. We must establish a union with others like ourselves, to seek clear and effective solutions.

Gentlemen! We are workers. We wish to form a union with others who work like ourselves, in order to promote the various interests of us workers. We cannot fail to seek a solution to such problems concerning us workers as the level of our wages, the length of the working day, the equal or unequal sharing of bonuses, or the progress of recreation facilities. We cannot but establish a union with those like ourselves to seek clear and effective solutions to each of these problems.

Gentlemen! We are students. Our lives are extremely bitter; the professors who teach us treat us like criminals, humiliate us like slaves, lock us up like prisoners. The windows in our classrooms are so tiny that the light does not reach the blackboard, so that we become "nearsighted." The desks are extremely ill-adapted, and if we sit in them for very long we get "curvature of the spine." The professors are interested only in making us read a lot of books, and we do read a great many of them, but we don't understand any of it, we merely exercise our memories to no good purpose. Our eyes are blurred, our brains are confused, our blood supply is insufficient, our faces are ashen and we become "anaemic." We become "feebleminded." Why are we so lethargic, so lacking in vivacity, so withered? Oh! It is all because the professors force us to refrain from moving or speaking out. And so we become "petrified unto death." And yet this bodily suffering is only secondary, gentlemen! Look at our laboratories! How cramped they are! How lacking in equipment! Only a few worn out instruments, so that we cannot conduct experiments. Our teachers of Chinese are such obstinate pedants. They are constantly mouthing expressions such as "We read in the *Book of Odes*" [*Shi yun*], or "The Master says" [*zi yue*], but when you come right down to it, the fact is that they don't understand a word. They are not aware that this is already the twentieth century, and they still compel us to observe the "old rites" and to follow the "old regulations." They forcibly impregnate our minds with a lot of stinking corpse-like dead writings full of classical allusions. Our reading room is empty. Our recreation room is filthy. The country is about to perish, and yet they still stick up proclamations forbidding us to love our country. Just see, for example, what great favor they have shown to the present movement of national salvation! Alas! Who is it that has frustrated us and made us unhappy in both body and mind? If we do not unite in order to attend to our own "self-instruction," then what are we waiting for? We are already sunk in an ocean of suffering, and we demand that attention be given to the means for saving ourselves. The "self-instruction" invented by Rousseau is most appropriate for this purpose. We will unite with as many comrades as possible and study by ourselves. As for those professors who bite people, we must not rely on them. If an event occurs such as the present trampling on our rights by the oppressors of Japan and of our own country, then we will marshal our forces and direct at them a great and powerful shout.

Gentlemen! We are women. We are sunk even more deeply in an ocean of suffering! We are also human beings, so why won't they let us take part in politics? We are also human beings, so why won't they let us participate in social intercourse? We are gathered together in our various separate dens, and we are not even allowed to go outside the front gate. The shameless men, the villainous men, make us into their playthings, and force us to prostitute ourselves to them indefinitely. The devils, who destroy the freedom to love! The devils, who destroy the sacredness of love! They keep us surrounded all day long, but so-called "chastity" is confined to us women! The "temples to virtuous women" are scattered all over the place, but where are the "pagodas to chaste men"? Among us there are some who are gathered together in schools for women, but those who teach us there are also a bunch of shameless and villainous men. All day long they talk about something called being "a worthy mother and a good wife." What is this but teaching us to prostitute ourselves indefinitely to the same man? They are afraid that we will not allow ourselves to be fettered, so they intensify their indoctrination. O bitterness! Bitterness! Spirit of freedom! Where are you? Come quickly and save us! Today we are awakened! We want to establish a union of us women! We want to sweep away all those devils who rape us and destroy the liberty of our minds and of our bodies!

Gentlemen! We are primary school teachers. All day long we teach; we are terribly busy! All day long we eat chalk dust, and yet we have no place to relax. In a big city like this, there are several hundred, if not several thousand, primary school teachers, and yet there is no place of recreation specifically set aside for our use. If we are to teach, we must constantly increase our knowledge, and yet there is no study organization set up for our use. There are so many periods when we must go to teach precisely as the bell rings, we have absolutely no time left over, no energy left over, to study and acquire knowledge — our spirits are simply not up to it! Thus we turn into phonographs, doing nothing all day long but putting on a performance of the lectures correctly transmitted which the teachers of former days taught to us. Our bellies are hungry. Our monthly salaries are 8 or 10 *yuan*, and even on this there are deductions. Moreover, there are some of these gentlemen among the principals who imitate the method of "reducing the soldiers' pay" and take the money provided by the government to line their own pockets. Because we have no money, we find ourselves moreover in the position of widowers with wives. We and our beloved wives live in solitude, separated by several tens or hundreds of *li*, gazing toward one another. According to educational theory, teaching students in a primary school is the task of a lifetime; they can hardly expect us in addition to spend all our lives as widowers and widows, can they? According to educational theory, the teachers' families should live at the school if they are to serve as a model for the students, but today this is not possible. Because we have no money, we can't buy books either, nor can we travel and observe the world. There is no use saying any more. Primary school teachers are in all respects slaves, and that's all there is to it! If we want to cease to be slaves, there is no way save to unite with others like ourselves and to realize a primary school teachers' union.

Gentlemen! We are policemen. We also wish to unite with others like ourselves in order to realize a union which will benefit our bodies and our minds. The Japanese say that those whose lives are hardest are beggars, primary school teachers, and policemen. We are also inclined to feel somewhat the same.

Gentlemen! We are rickshaw boys. All day we pull our rickshaws until the sweat pours down like rain! The rent which goes to the owners of the rickshaws is so much! The fares we get are so small! How can we make a living? Is there not some way for us to form a union too?

The foregoing are the lamentations of the peasants, workers, students, women, primary-school teachers, rickshaw boys, and others of all sorts. They are unable to bear such hardship, and so they want to set up all sorts of small unions adapted to their interests.

Hitherto I have been talking about various small unions, such as the union of the workers. This is still a very broad and general term. If one goes into greater detail, such organizations as the following correspond to the lowest level of small unions:

Union of railway workers
Union of mine workers
Union of telegraph employees
Union of telephone employees
Union of shipbuilding workers, union of merchant sailors
Union of metal workers
Union of textile workers
Union of tram workers
Union of rickshaw boys
Union of construction workers . . .

The workers in various Western countries all have small associations of the workers in each trade and industry. Everywhere there are to be found such organizations as the association of transport workers, the association of tram workers, etc. From many small unions one advances to form a great union, and from the many great unions, one advances to form the greatest union. It is thus that what are called "federations" or "alliances" come into being one after another. Because common interests are limited to a small part of the people, it is small unions that are set up. The interests of many small unions have points in common, so it is possible to set up big unions. For example, the pursuit of learning is the particular concern of us students, so we set up our unions for the pursuit of learning. Such things, on the other hand, as the pursuit of liberation and freedom are the concern of everyone, whoever he may be, and therefore people of every kind must be brought together to form a great union.

Thus, the great union must begin with small unions. We must arise and follow the example of our brothers in other lands. We must promote many, many small unions of our own.

Part III: The Present Status of China's "Great Union of the Popular Masses"

(August 4, 1919)

In the previous two issues of this paper, I have already discussed (1) the possibility and necessity of the great union of the popular masses, and (2) the fact that the great union of the popular masses must begin by taking small unions as its foundation. In continuing today my discussion of the great union of the popular masses of our country, I shall consider such questions as: Do we, in the last analysis, have the requisite consciousness? Do we have the requisite motive force? Do we have the requisite capacity? Can we succeed?

1. In the final analysis, do we have the requisite consciousness regarding the "great union of the popular masses" in our country? The 1911 revolution had the appearance of a union of the popular masses, but in reality it was not so. The 1911 revolution was the work of Chinese students abroad, who initially showed the way, of the Gelaohui, which responded with enthusiasm to their call, and of a few soldiers of the New Army and of the provincial forces who fought with their swords and crossbows. It had no connection whatsoever with the great majority of us popular masses. Although we approved of their principles, we nevertheless did not act. Nor did they need us to act. And yet we have acquired a certain level of consciousness. We know that even sage emperors (such as Wen and Wu) can be overthrown. Moreover, democracy, the great rebel [*dani budao*] can be established. If we have something we want to say or do, we can say or do it at any time. Following the 1911 revolution, we overthrew another emperor, the Hongxian Emperor,[6] in 1916. Although this was still the work of a minority, once again we became conscious of the fact that the Hongxian Emperor, with all his awesome majesty, could nevertheless in fact be overthrown. And when we come down to the last few years, with the wars between the South and the North, and the World War, things have changed even more. As a result of the wars between the North and the South, it has been demonstrated even more irrefutably how the bureaucrats, military men, and politicians harm, poison, and mutilate us. As a result of the World War and the bitterness of their lives, the popular masses in various countries have suddenly undertaken all sorts of action. In Russia, they have overthrown the aristocrats and driven out the rich, and the toilers and peasants have jointly set up a Soviet government. The army of the red flag surges

6. Yuan Shikai.

forward in the East and in the West, sweeping away numerous enemies. The countries of the Entente have been transformed as a result, and the whole world has been shaken. Hungary has risen up, and a new toilers' and peasants' government has also appeared in Budapest. The Germans, Austrians, and Czechs have done the same, exerting their utmost strength in the battle with the enemy party within each country. The raging torrent advances in the West, and then turns eastward. After many great strikes in England, France, Italy, and America, several great revolutions have also taken place in India and Korea. New forces have arisen, and within the area enclosed by the Great Wall and the China Sea, the May Fourth movement has broken out. Its banner has advanced southward, across the Yellow River to the Yangzi. From Guangzhou to Hankou, many real-life dramas are enacted; from Lake Dongting to the Min River, the tide rises ever higher. Heaven and earth are aroused by it, the wicked are put to flight by it! Ha! We know it! We are awakened! The world is ours, the state is ours, society is ours. If we do not speak, who will speak? If we do not act, who will act? We must act energetically to carry out the great union of the popular masses, which will not brook a moment's delay!

2. Is there already the requisite motive force for the great union of the popular masses of our country? To this question I answer directly, "Yes." If you gentlemen do not believe it, listen to what I have to say.

If we wish to go back to the source of the union of the popular masses of our country, we must look to the establishment of the provincial assemblies at the end of the Qing dynasty, and to the organization of the Revolutionary Party — the Tongmenghui. The provincial assemblies having been established, the assemblies of the various provinces allied themselves to petition for the early opening of a parliament. The Revolutionary Party having been established, it called on all those within and without the country to raise troops to fight the Manchus. The 1911 revolution was a drama entitled "Swallowing the Yellow Dragon" played in concert by the Revolutionary Party and the provincial assemblies. Afterward, the Revolutionary Party turned into the Nationalist Party [Guomindang], and the provincial assemblies turned into the Progressive Party [Jinbudang]; such was the origin of political parties among our Chinese people. From this time forward, the Republic was established, the central government convoked a parliament, and the various provinces also called together provincial assemblies. At this time, each province also set up three other bodies: a provincial education association, a provincial chamber of commerce, and a provincial agricultural association. (There are a number of provinces that have a provincial industrial association; in several of them, it is combined with the agricultural association, as in Hunan.) At the same time, each *xian* also set up a *xian* education association, a *xian* chamber of commerce, and a *xian* agricultural association. (There are a few *xian* that don't have them.) This constitutes a very firm and powerful kind of union. In addition, bodies of various kinds have been set up according to the circumstances and position of each category of people, such as:

Associations of alumni of various schools

Associations of fellow villagers traveling outside their native places [*Tongxianghui*]

General associations and branch associations of Chinese students abroad

The General Association of Shanghai Newspapers

The World Association of Chinese Students

The associations of students [returned] from Europe and America in Beijing and Shanghai

The Sino-French Educational Association in Beijing.

The various study societies such as the Self-Strengthening Society [Qiangxuehui], the Christian Literature Society [Guangxuehui], the Southern Study Society [Nanxuehui], the Aspiration Society [Shangzhixuehui], the Chinese Professional and Educational Society, the Chinese Scientific Society, the General Association of Asian Culture. . . .

The various professional associations (of the various branches and professions of industry and commerce), such as the Banking Association, the Rice Dealers' Association. . . .

The study societies in various schools, such as the Society for the Study of Painting and the Society for the Study of Philosophy at Beijing University —there are dozens of them. . . .

The various clubs. . . .

All these are products of the recent flowering [*kaifang*] of political and intellectual activity, which were not allowed to exist and could not have existed in the era of autocracy. The examples listed above are all very simple, more or less like the "small unions" referred to in the previous issue of this paper. It is only recently, because of political disorder and foreign oppression and the resulting rise in consciousness, that there has been a motive for establishing great unions. Such organizations as the following all belong to this category:

National Federation of Educational Associations

National Federation of Chambers of Commerce

The Guangzhou union of seventy-two guilds [*hang*], the Shanghai union of fifty-three public bodies

Union of Commercial, Educational, and Industrial Journals

National Union of Journalists

National Association for Promoting Peace [Hepingjichenghui]

National Union for Peace [Hepinglianhehui]

Sino-French Association in Beijing

Citizens' Association for Foreign Affairs

The Hunan Reconstruction [*shanhou*] Association (in Shanghai)

The Shandong Association (in Shanghai)

United students' associations in Beijing, Shanghai, and various other places

The Union of All Circles, the National Union of Students. . . .

All such associations, societies, clubs, general associations, unions must inevitably include a considerable number of gentry [*shenshi*] and "politicians" who do not belong to the popular masses (such organizations as the parliament, the provincial assemblies, the provincial educational associations, the provincial agricultural associations, the National Association for Promoting Peace, the National Union for Peace, etc., are entirely associations of gentry or of politicians), but the associations of the various professions and industries, and the various study and research societies, are purely groupings of common people or of scholars. As for the recently created United Students' Association, Union of All Circles, etc., they are even more purely great unions of the popular masses, who have risen up to resist the oppressors within and without the country, and in my opinion, the motive force for the great union of the popular masses of China is to be found precisely here.

3. Do we really have the capacity to carry out the "great union of the popular masses" in our country? Can we really succeed in this? When we come to talk about capacity, then some doubts may well be expressed. Hitherto the people of our country have known only individually run enterprises, with the unworthy aim of maximizing individual gain. Those engaged in business did not know how to set up a company; those engaged in labor did not know how to set up a Labor Party; those engaged in studies knew only the old method of working alone in one's closet, and not joint research. Organized undertakings on a large scale were something of which the people of our country were quite simply incapable. As for how badly our political affairs were managed, that goes without saying. If there was a degree of success in the postal service and the salt monopoly, it was thanks to the foreigners. The prohibition of oceangoing trade has been lifted for such a long time, and still we have not even one little boat going to Europe. Even the few lone countrywide undertakings such as the "China Merchants' Steamship Company" and the "Hanyeping Mines" show capital losses every year, and when the losses are too great they call on investment from abroad. On all those railroads managed by foreigners, the standard of cleanliness, equipment, and service is bound to be a bit better. As soon as a railroad comes under the control of the Ministry of Transport, it goes to pot [*zaogao*]. Among those who ride on the Beijing-Hankou, Tianjin-Pukou, and Wuchang-Changsha railroads, there is none who does not snort with contempt and gnash his teeth. Moreover, such things as schools are not well run, self-government is not well implemented, and even a single family or the life of an individual is not well ordered. It is all very much the same, monotonously uniform. Is it not all too easy, then, to talk about the great union of the popular masses? Is it so easy to stand up and resist the deeply entrenched and well-established oppressors? Although things are like this, we are not at all fundamentally incapable. There is a reason for our lack of capacity, namely, "We have had no practice."

In reality, for thousands of years the Chinese people of several hundred millions all led a life of slaves. Only one person, the "emperor," was not a slave (or rather one could say that even he was a slave of "Heaven"). When the emperor was in control of everything, we were not allowed to exercise our capacities. Whether in politics, study, society, or any other domain, we were not allowed to have either thought, organization, or practice.

Today things are different, and in every domain we demand liberation. Ideological liberation, political liberation, economic liberation, liberation [in the relations between] men and women, educational liberation are all going to burst from the deep inferno where they have been confined and demand to look at the blue sky. Our Chinese people possesses great inherent capacities! The more profound the oppression, the more powerful its reaction, and since this has been accumulating for a long time, it will surely burst forth quickly. I venture to make a singular assertion: one day, the reform of the Chinese people will be more profound than that of any other people, and the society of the Chinese people will be more radiant than that of any other people. The great union of the Chinese people will be achieved earlier than that of any other place or people. Gentlemen! Gentlemen! We must all exert ourselves! We must all advance with the utmost strength! Our golden age, our age of glory and splendor, lies before us!

France Fears Germany as If It Were a Tiger

(July 28, 1919)

France fears Germany as if it were a tiger or a wolf. Even after Germany has suffered such a great defeat, France is still terribly afraid of her. They have taken the coal mines of the Saar. They have detached the left bank of the Rhine from Germany and made it into an independent country.[1] They have destroyed the fortifications on Heligoland. They have helped Poland to become independent in order to restrict Germany in the east. They have helped Czechoslovakia to become independent in order to prevent Germany from moving south. The desire of the German and Austrian peoples to join together as Germany has been obstructed on every hand, heedless of the fact that the ideal of national self-determination was thus sabotaged. Germany's colonial territories, together with her land, sea, and air forces, have been pared away on all sides. She has had to turn over much of her commercial shipping to prevent her from recovering her foreign trade. But even this is not all. France also wants guarantees from England and the United States. The other day the teletype noted that Wilson had agreed that before leaving France he would sign a treaty guaranteeing that if France is attacked in the future, the United States will come to her aid. In the name of England, Lloyd George has also signed an identical treaty. The significance of this is profoundly disturbing! Unless France has some great weakness that cannot be disclosed to others, why should she have such fear? The French are a very proud and heroic people. Why are they begging for protection like women and children? I think this phenomenon bodes no good for France!

---

1. See above, the article dated July 14, 1919, "The Rhine Republic is a Grotesque Country."

Contents of the Treaty

(July 28, 1919)

General Smuts[1] said: "I have signed the Peace Treaty, not because I consider it a satisfactory document, but because it is imperatively necessary to close the war." He also said, "The promise of a new life, the victory of the great human ideals, . . . the fulfilment of [the peoples'] aspirations toward a new international order, are not written in this Treaty. . . . A new spirit of generosity and humanity, born in the hearts of the peoples . . . can alone . . . be the solvent for the problems which statesmen have found too hard at the Conference." He further stated: "I deeply regret that in the treaty the abolition of militarism is limited to the enemy."[2] Smuts is a British military man, one of the signers of the treaty, and these, his comments delivered after signing the treaty, give us an idea of the contents of the treaty.

---

1. General Jan Christiaan Smuts, Minister of Defense of the Union of South Africa, represented that country in the delegation acting for the British Crown.

2. The previous passages in quotation marks have been reproduced from the English text of Smuts' statement of June 29, 1919 (H.W.V. Temperley, *A History of the Peace Conference of Paris*, Volume III [London: Henry Frowde and Hodder and Stoughton, 1920], pp. 74–76), to which Mao's Chinese translation almost exactly corresponds. The immediately preceding sentence has been left as Mao recast it; the original reads: " . . . the abolition of militarism — in this Treaty, unfortunately, confined to the enemy — may soon come as a blessing and relief to the Allied peoples as well."

The Secret Treaty Between Japan and Germany

(July 28, 1919)

A Reuters teletype from Paris states, "Recently there have once again been rumors abroad of a secret treaty between Japan and Germany." What kind of a thing is a secret treaty? What presumptuous persons are thinking of making an appearance on the international scene tomorrow? Above all, what is the secret treaty between Japan and Germany? The secret treaty between Japan and Russia was publicized by the Lenin government and not only failed to be concluded, but caused a great loss of face. The secret treaty between Japan, England, and France did go through, and is a threat to our Shandong Province. The year before last there were several rumors of some kind of secret treaty between Japan and Germany. It was said that in 1917 Germany gave Japan permission to occupy the Dutch colonies at will, including Java and Sumatra, but the British government heard about it, and informed Holland, so the plot was stopped. We must realize that Japan and Germany are a couple of dogs, male and female, that have tried to mate on a number of occasions, and that although they haven't made it up to now, their lusting after each other will never go away. If the militarist adventurers of the authoritarian Japanese government are not exterminated, if the German Ebert government is not overthrown by revolution, and if this lustful stud and lascivious bitch are still not separated, the danger will be truly great.

Politicians

(July 28, 1919)

Smuts says that it is only the new truths of the people that "can be the solvent for the problems which statesmen have found too hard at the peace conference." How is it that the truths of the people and the opinions of the politicians[1] are so different? Why does it seem so hard for the politicians, but not for the people? Is there another level of explanation somewhere in all this? I have always been suspicious of so-called "politicians," afraid that this was not a good kind of thing to be. Today, I've truly been given proof of it. After the signing of the peace treaty in Paris, Lloyd George returned to England, where he delivered the following speech: "The many successes of this England of ours show what can be achieved by a great people united and inspired by a common purpose. Let us rejoice over the victory, but let us rejoice as men who are not under the delusion that all our troubles are over, but rather like men who feel that the first and the worst of our troubles are past, and that the spirit, courage, and resolution which enabled us to overcome these will also enable us cheerfully to face what is to come. Let us not waste our strength prematurely in fighting each other."[2] Such is the great talent of a politician. Such is the great magic of a politician. Don't waste our strength fighting each other means, in fact, that you the people should not trouble the government with your boring problems concerning the suffering of your daily lives or the true wishes of the citizens. These are all little problems not worth worrying about. In the future, following the natural development of things, we will still have to go to war with other countries. Patriotism, inspiration, uniting, foreign affairs, these are what is most important of all. I hereby formally announce to politicians such as Lloyd George that we reject all your big speeches as nothing but "lies" and "nonsense." We have already awakened. We are not as we used to be. You can just pack up and go now, and don't ever come back again.

---

1. The term used by Mao, *zhengzhijia*, can mean either "statesmen" or "politicians." In the previous sentence, we have rendered it as "statesmen," because that was Smuts' own word, but hereafter it is translated as "politicians," since Mao manifestly has in mind that concept, with all its negative connotations.

2. As in the text entitled "Contents of the Treaty," we give the original English of Lloyd George's speech of July 3, 1919 (Temperley, *Peace Conference*, Vol. III, p. 97), rather than a literal translation of Mao's Chinese, since the sense is virtually identical.

Those Who Don't Believe in Science Will Die

(July 28, 1919)

Two weeks ago, several people were killed by lightning during a big thunderstorm in Changsha. Several people were also struck by lightning inside a house under an old tree on Mount Yuelu. In the city, where the streets and ditches are filled with garbage and the electrical potential is especially high, tall towers with lightning rods should be erected in many places. Old trees have a high electrical potential, so houses should not be built beneath them. This is scientific common knowledge that everyone should know. But among the Changsha police, and among the more than 300,000 inhabitants of Changsha, not one has the time to take notice of it. There are even some who say that "the heavens punish with five hundred bolts of lightning." People have died but the cause of their death is still unknown. How pitiful!

Dead Rats

(July 28, 1919)

Rats are one cause of epidemics. Everywhere in the city of Changsha, you can see dead rats. They stare at the police with wide open eyes, and yet the police stand right next to these dead rats. Just a few years ago, Changsha was not like this. Gentlemen of the police! We ask you please to pay just a little bit of attention to this!

Petition of the Hunan Students' Association to the Governor of Hunan

(July 30, 1919)

The purpose of this petition is to plead for the punishment of local scoundrels and for the rehabilitation of the newspaper office.[1] Since the recent Qingdao incident, students all over China and various public organizations have made their voices heard, even at the risk of the greatest sacrifice, to awaken their compatriots for a common effort to rescue the country from perishing. We students of Hunan are unanimous in our actions. Inspired by sincere patriotism, we have explained and propagated our goal of saving the motherland. After several months, we were beginning to see results. We were ready to step up our efforts and were hoping for a speedy reconciliation of the North and the South so that we could unite against the foreigners. Who could have foreseen that the remnants of the imperial system, and the old partisans of the Anfu clique, thinking only of their personal interest, would not scruple to lobby in such deceptive language as to hoodwink Your Honor. Illegal elections that were canceled in departments at all levels are resurrected, like dead ashes rekindled into a fire. There are even cases where the results of the primary elections were reinstated. Our Association holds that since the peace conference is still adjourned, since Hunan Province is still divided, and since the continuance or dismissal of the old or the new parliaments[2] is yet to be decided by resolutions, long and difficult negotiations are likely to delay the peace conference. Just at this precarious moment, there suddenly popped up this illegal election, which is not only an obstacle to the peace conference, but also an impediment to your abundant virtue. We, the students, have long been worried about the Honorable Governor. We were just going to air our opinions frankly to you, Chen Ming[X], and others, when local thugs Gu Tianbao, Huang Zhong, Li Fanxi, and others called a fraudulent Citizens' Assembly at the fake "Council on Education" set up on the basis of forged "public opinion." Our Association knew very well that this was a vital issue, since one can never tell what kind of plans such murderous thugs may

1. The newspaper in question was the *Dagongbao*. See below.

2. I.e., of the "old" parliament originally elected in 1913, which had been dissolved after Yuan Shikai expelled the Guomindang, but whose members still claimed at this time to represent the only legitimate legislative authority in China, and of the "new" parliament, elected in 1918 in two stages, amidst gross corruption, under the domination of the Anfu clique.

have in mind. Consequently, we sent our representatives to attend the assembly. The meeting place was heavily guarded by policemen and army people. Gu and Huang were the first to take the platform. They attacked the people of Hunan viciously for opposing their illegal election. On behalf of all the students, the chairman of our Association, Peng Huang,[3] and representative Qiu Weiqin expressed the genuine opinion of the people. They were immediately arrested by soldiers, acting on the orders of people like Gu and Huang, who threatened to shoot them on the spot. They would have been martyred if it had not been for the intercession of Regimental Commander Zhang, who was there to safeguard the assembly. We at the Student Association are extremely grateful to Your Honor for your absolute approval of, and manifold support for, this action of the students. Although they claimed to be leaders, local thugs like Gu Tianbao, Huang Zhong, and Li Fanxi are actually slighting the people of Hunan, hoodwinking Your Honor, and insulting the students. This is why we at the Association have made a brief statement of the facts. We humbly plead that Your Honor punish the local thugs severely in order to warn anyone who might be tempted to follow their example. Also, there are some people in our Association who do not quite understand Your Honor's intentions. The *Dagongbao*[4] is the organ which expresses the true opinions of the people of Hunan, and it has long been praised by readers both inside and outside the province. We did not in the least expect that the paper would be banned, and its editor arrested, just because it published a manifesto by various organizations and associations expressing their opposition to the illegal election, and that this situation would last for several days. We students thought that this could not have been Your Honor's intention, and that the matter would be resolved in no time at all. Hence, for some time we did not submit any petition to express our opinions. In any case, not only did various organizations compose the manifesto, but the people of Hunan opposed the illegal election with one voice. We sincerely hope that Your Honor, for the sake of both interest and profit, will reach a correct decision. In that case, the people of Hunan will forever remember your virtuous action. Otherwise, in a republic that has the right of free speech, when a well-known newspaper is banned, ill-informed outsiders may proclaim that this government is abolishing the right to free speech. We should guard against evil tongues more than a flooding river, and we cannot stop the pot from boiling by merely scooping up the water and pouring it back. Your Honor is enlightened and farsighted, and it is impossible

3. Peng Huang (1896–1921), *zi* Yinbo, was a native of Xiangxiang *xian*, Hunan Province. He was a close friend of Mao from an early date, and a student leader in Hunan during the time of the May Fourth movement. For details on his various activities, see the text of February 19, 1920.

4. The *Dagongbao* (commonly translated, like the newspaper of the same name in Tianjin, *L'Impartial*) was the most prestigious and influential paper in Changsha. Mao published many articles in it himself during this period; see, in particular, later in this volume, his numerous pieces on the suicide of Miss Zhao.

that you do not agree with us on this. It was fortunate for us that Your Honor listened to public sentiments and postponed the election. The editor of *Dagong*bao has, however, still not been released, thus obliging the paper to cease publication for many days. The masses are terrified and do not know what to do. Therefore our Association has prepared this petition beseeching Your Honor to yield magnanimously to public sentiment, free the editor, and rehabilitate the newspaper. We have known for a long time that Your Honor hates evil as if it were an enemy and spontaneously follows the good. Perfect sincerity prompts us to petition for the rehabilitation of the newspaper and the punishment of the local hooligans. It is our fervent hope that Your Honor will look into the matter and grant us a speedy answer. Respectfully we present this letter to Your Honor, governor and commander in chief of Hunan.

An Overall Account of the Hunan United Students' Association

(August 4, 1919)

It is necessary to keep a record of the history of our Association. But because of the limitations and lack of knowledge of the author of these notes, there are probably things that are not exactly right or things that are incomplete in this article. I hope those of you who are familiar with the history will supply me with more materials, and also make suggestions and criticisms about what is recorded here. The Association would be very grateful for this. (Author's note.)

Student Circles in Hunan Before the Founding of the Association[1]

The very first school in Hunan, called the School of Current Affairs, was founded in the spring of 1898.[2] Though short-lived, it nevertheless trained some courageous and active youth. During Tang Caichang's battle for Hankou,[3] several students from that school were martyred. The school at that time advocated revolutionary ideals. Students all studied thoroughly what is called statecraft.[4] The topics they often argued about and discussed comprised such things as how corrupt the affairs of state had become, how to overthrow the Manchu government, how to deploy military forces, and how to build up the country. Later, the

1. This, and all subsequent words or sentences set in bold, are underscored with dots beside the characters in the Chinese text.

2. This important institution was in fact founded in the autumn of 1897 with the support of the reformist governor of Hunan, Chen Baozhen. See the note to the text of July 21, 1919, on the Strengthen Learning Society. A clear and well-documented account of the events discussed by Mao in the present document can be found in Joseph Esherick, *Reform and Revolution in China. The 1911 Revolution in Hunan and Hubei* (Berkeley: University of California Press, 1976), especially Chapter 2 (pp. 34–65).

3. An uprising at Hankou in August 1900 led by Tang Caichang (1867–1900), *zi* Pucheng, a young Hunanese scholar trained in Western learning who had been one of the founders of the School of Current Affairs, the Southern Study Society, and the daily *Xiangbao*. Tang's attempt was supported by Kang Youwei, but ended in failure and the execution of over a hundred reformers.

4. The school of thought evoked by the term *jingshi* (statecraft), which dated from the seventeenth century, had reemerged in the early nineteenth century. Of Confucian inspiration, it emphasized practical application and this-worldly activism in the light of current reality.

Mingde School[5] was founded. Its goals were similar to those of the School of Current Affairs. The Mingde students, in the last years of the Guangxu era, were highly esteemed by all the other students in the provincial capital. Most of the students at that time were characterized by their willingness to get involved, and the fact that they did not fear death. Outwardly, their behavior was marked by rebellion against the official bureaucracy, and by refusal to submit to oppression. When Chen Baozhen was governor of Hunan,[6] he took upon himself the task of developing Hunan, and he was in reality the first to promote the establishment of the School of Current Affairs and other schools. When the reform movement broke out in 1898, Chen Baozhen left, Tan Sitong died,[7] Liang Qichao fled, Xiong Xiling[8] was stripped of his membership of the Hanlin Academy, and a great pile of Sage Kang [Youwei]'s writings was burned in the schoolyard outside of the Small Wu Gate. Thus the School of Current Affairs collapsed.

Though the School of Current Affairs was gone, Mingde was just then rising. At this time, several official schools, such as Qiuzhong ["Seeking Loyalty"] Middle School, Youji ["Superior"] Normal School, and the Higher Academy had been founded. There were even more private schools, such as Zhounan, Chuyi, and all the *xian* schools in Changsha.[9] It goes without saying that **official schools** were heavily bureaucratic. There were the "superintendents" and "supervisors," who wore red-topped peacock-feathered caps, horsehoof-patterned patched gowns and inch-high-heeled official boots. Every first and fifteenth of a month, they would lead the students (in long gowns with mandarin jackets) in the ritual of the kowtow,[10] first before [a tablet reading] "Long live the Emperor, may he reign forever," and then to [one dedicated to] "the Greatest Sage and Teacher, Confucius." A big board was usually hung in the central hall of the school, on

5. The Mingde ("Illustrious Virtue") Middle School, which was founded in 1903 by a group which included Tan Yankai, had a reputation for radicalism. Huang Xing taught there briefly, but was obliged to resign when it was discovered that he was reprinting the writings of Chen Tianhua, whose death is discussed by Mao below.

6. Chen Baozhen (1831–1900), *zi* Youming, a reformist from Jiangxi Province, was governor of Hunan from 1895 to 1898.

7. Tan was executed on September 28, 1898, in the aftermath of the reforms.

8. Xiong Xiling (1870–1937), *zi* Binsan, from Fenghuang, Hunan, was a *jinshi* and a bachelor of the Hanlin Academy. He was head of the School of Current Affairs in 1897, organized the Southern Study Society, and ran the *Xiangbao* for a time. He returned to his native province during the 1898 reform movement to work with such leaders as Tan Sitong to promote reform in the educational field. In the aftermath he fell into disgrace for a time, but later became minister of finance. He was appointed premier of Yuan Shikai's first cabinet in 1913, but abandoned that post in 1914, having compromised himself by countersigning Yuan's order expelling members of the Guomindang from parliament.

9. This apparently refers to schools for natives of the various *xian*.

10. Literally, "three bowings and nine knockings of the head on the ground," as in prostrating oneself before the emperor.

which the "Sacred Edicts" were inscribed: "First of all, value loyalty; second, value honesty; third, respect Confucius. . . ." They were all in dazzling gold and green, fantastically beautiful! Every day, the students had to wear long gowns at mealtimes. If you happened to visit them in the hottest days of June at their mealtime, it was also quite a sight! When the time came for graduation, the "heralds" would ask the "student affairs officer" or the "gatekeeper" to do them a favor and let them copy a large number of graduates' names and addresses, and would rush to make many "notices of the herald," on which they wrote things like: "Congratulations to young master so-and-so from such-and-such a family who has risen high by obtaining a superior first place in the examination given by the imperial commissioner, the army envoy, the first deputy court censor, so-and-so from the Hunan government, along with so-and-so from Hunan official such-and-such school." Full of zeal, the herald would run to the countryside and, doing obeisance, hang a notice high up in the central rooms of a graduate's house. The whole family of the graduate, beaming with delight, would come out to look at those golden characters on red background with white edges and decorative patterns. What a joy! After receiving the good news, the graduate would hop on the sedan chair (if the family did not have one, a new one would be made immediately) in red-topped cap and horsehoof patterned gown (most of the time they are newly made) and go around "paying respects" to relatives and old family friends. On the back of the sedan chair, there would hang a lantern with "Secretary of the Imperial Patent Office"[11] inscribed on it. Having received the respects of the graduate, the relatives and old family friends, "feeling greatly honored," would go to the graduate's home to congratulate the family. By then, on the top of the portal of the graduate's house would be hung a small horizontal board with *"juren"*[12] or *"bagong"*[13] inscribed on it. With golden lettering on red, this board looked even more beautiful! After a feast of celebration, each went on his way home. This is called "offering wine," or "giving a banquet," or "beating the autumn wind."[14]

Aside from the bureaucratic teachers and staff, if we still want to seek for **vigor, courage, and vitality** amidst such rampant corruption in student circles, we need only look for two things that were often secretly hidden in many students' messy piles of books on their desks or in their drawers. One was the *Xinmin congshu* [Collected Writings for the New People], written by Liang Qichao and others; the other was the *Minbao* [People's Newspaper] of Wang

---

11. *Zhongshu ke zhongshu.* This was the appointment granted, after a further test, to those who had passed the second-level imperial examinations for the degree of *juren*, with second-class rating.

12. A successful candidate at the second or provincial level.

13. Provincial government nominee from among the unsuccessful candidates for *juren*, sent to the national capital to be considered for an appointment.

14. To be given free material help or money by others.

Jingwei,[15] Song Jiaoren,[16] et al. These two were forbidden publications but somehow got spread around fast from Japan to Hunan. At the same time, dauntless and invincible, Huang Xing and Yu Zhimo[17] still remained in Changsha engaging in all kinds of underground activities. This continued until the events of 1904, when the Ping[xiang] and Li[ling] uprisings failed, Ma Fuyi was executed outside of Liuyang Gate, and Huang Xing escaped in a small sedan chair out of Small West Gate, disguised as a foreigner.[18] But Hunanese morale had been strengthened by ever-growing persecution. At this point, Yu Zhimo was the sole leader of the Hunanese students. Thus began **the following earthshaking incident which is worth recording.**

Chen Tianhua[19] and Yao Hongye[20] were students from Xinhua and Yiyang

---

15. Wang Jingwei (1883–1944), *zi* Lixin, *ming* Tiaoming, was a native of Guangdong. He graduated from the Tokyo Law College in 1906 and became an active member of the Tongmenghui while in Japan. Returning to China, he became a close collaborator of Sun Yatsen and editor of the *Minbao*. He also made himself notorious by an abortive attempt to blow up the prince regent in 1910. He was a leading figure in Guomindang politics in the 1920s, when he took up a position on the left of the party. He ended his life as premier of the Japanese puppet government in Nanjing.

16. Song Jiaoren (1882–1913), *zi* Dunchu, *hao* Yufu, a native of Hunan, was one of the organizers of the Society for China's Revival (Huaxinghui) in 1904. He joined the Tongmenghui in 1905 and was in charge of general affairs for the *Minbao*. In 1912, he was instrumental in organizing the Guomindang and was the chief architect of its victory in the elections of 1913. Indeed, his very success led Yuan Shikai to have him assassinated, as indicated in the note to Mao's letter of December 9, 1916.

17. Yu Zhimo (1867–1907), *zi* Qiting, was a native of Xiangxiang *xian* in Hunan. After studying textile manufacturing in Japan, he returned to Hunan in 1902 and began a dual career in business and education. This dual orientation is symbolized by the fact that he soon became both chairman of the Hunan Council on Education and head of the Changsha Chamber of Commerce. He was also active in the Tongmenghui. He was arrested on August 10, 1906, charged with inciting demonstrations over the deaths of Chen and Yao (described below) and other antigovernment activities. He was executed in January 1907.

18. Mao here telescopes events which took place between 1904 (Huang Xing's escape) and 1906 (the Ping-Li uprisings). On Ma Fuyi, see the note to the text of September 6–7, 1920.

19. Chen Tianhua (1875–1905), *zi* Xingtai, *hao* Sihuang, a Hunanese from Xinhua *xian*, was an important radical student leader in the early twentieth century. His two pamphlets *Meng huitou* (Wake up!) and *Jingshi zhong* (Alarm to Arouse the Age), published c. 1904, were among the most influential publications of the time. He was a student in Tokyo at the time of the Chinese students' strike of 1905, provoked by the promulgation of drastic new regulations by the Japanese authorities in November 1905 for controlling Chinese student activity. Outraged by the reference of a Japanese newspaper on December 7, 1905, to the "self-indulgent and mean self-will that seems peculiar to Chinese nationals," Chen committed suicide by drowning himself in Ōmori Bay, after writing an inflammatory testament which incited two thousand of his fellow Chinese students to leave Japan for home.

20. Yao Hongye (1887–1906), *zi* Jiansheng and Jingsheng, was from Yiyang, Hunan Province. In 1904, after graduating from the Changsha Mingde Middle School, he went to study in Japan, where in the summer of 1905 he joined in the protests over the

respectively. Both had studied in Japan. On their journey home, they committed suicide by throwing themselves into the sea, furious at the desperate situation of the motherland.[21] When this news reached the students of Hunan, and when their bodies had been shipped back along the Xiang River, the students demanded of the government that they be buried on Mount Yuelu. The apathetic and heartless Hunanese governor, Yu Liansan,[22] and the education commissioner turned a deaf ear to the plea, hoping to shed more blood of the revolutionary party and the students, thus gaining promotion for themselves. The students, sensing that they were getting nowhere, decided to "take things into their own hands." On the first day of the fourth month in the thirty-second year of the Guangxu era,[23] all students in Changsha, from primary schools to colleges, were mobilized. They crossed the river from two points, Juzhang Ferry and Small West Gate. With bright banners and spotlessly white clothes reflecting the blazing-red sunshine, they loudly sang songs of mourning in a line stretching over more than ten *li*. The military and police forces stood along the roads watching, but dared not say anything. Thus on this occasion they successfully buried Chen and Yao after all, while the government took it very hard, but dared not blame anyone. The morale of Hunan at this time, as if in a frenzy, had reached its peak. But after some time, the government, having harbored resentment for a long time, found an excuse to kill Yu Zhimo! Later, they also dug up Chen's and Yao's bodies!

After the "righteous burial of Chen and Yao," the next event that is worth recording about Hunanese student circles was the **Students' Sports Meet of all schools in the provincial capital** in the fifth month of the second year of the Xuantong era.[24]

We are used to students' sports meets, so what is worthy of note about this?

Guangdong-Hankou railway agreement. He returned to China at the end of 1905 in protest at the new restrictions on Chinese students mentioned in the note on Chen Tianhua. Settling in Shanghai, he became disillusioned with talk of constitutionalism and angered at the scarcity of student scholarships and the resistance to his plans for public schooling in that city, where there were a large number of students returned from Japan. He saw no hope for China under the dominance of Japan, and on May 6, 1906 (the thirteenth day of the fourth month by the lunar calendar), he drowned himself in the Huangpu in Shanghai.

21. As will be seen from the preceding notes, Chen and Yao committed suicide for similar reasons, but not in the same place or at the same time. Their coffins were, however, returned to Hunan together. The events described by Mao below took place on May 23, 1906.

22. Yu Liansan, a native of Zhejiang Province, succeeded Chen Baozhen as governor of Hunan in October 1898. During his rule, the consitutional reform and modernization initiatives of Chen Baozhen were stopped, and any anti-Qing uprisings were brutally suppressed. He had, however, been replaced in February 1902, and the governor of Hunan in 1906, when the events described here took place, was Pang Hongshu. Mao's reference to him in this context must be simply a lapse.

23. As noted above, this event took place on May 23, 1906, which corresponded to the first day of the fourth *intercalary* month, inserted that year after the normal fourth month.

24. 1910.

This particular sports meet, which took place in the second year of the Xuantong era, was quite different. It was imbued with the significance of a "demonstration," and had a "revolutionary" character. The government bureaucracy had great fear of it; the education commissioner, a certain Wu, was particularly terrified. The promoters succeeded in mobilizing the students by exhorting them in every way, arguing that our nation was in peril, and foreign insults were getting worse. The site of the Sports Meet was the large open space outside of Small West Gate in Changsha where the New Army used to drill. All the students, neatly lined-up, performed all kinds of sports, taking advantage of the cool morning breeze in the beautiful early dawn. Most memorable of all was their solemn and stirring singing of the sports song, reaching up to the clouds. I have forgotten who wrote the song, but for ten years now, my fellow Hunanese students have remembered it very well. I am going to write the words down below:

How great is Hunan, with Mount Yue rising to the heavens
and Lake Dongting carrying your imagination far away.
The angelicas of the Yuan River and the orchids of the Li
River spread their fragrance far and wide.
Strong and brave are we, innumerable are our talents, our
fame tempered in a hundred battles.
The brave Xiang Army pacified the empire;[25] we of this
generation are also heroes.
Harken to the military songs, impassioned and stirring,
our banners all unfurled.
A forest of guns and a rain of bullets, like bloody campaigns
on a battlefield.
The militaristic spirit has given a new aspect to the civilization
of the sons of Hunan.

The so-called "militaristic spirit" was the guiding theme of education at that time. It was also the goal of the students themselves in pursuing their studies. This spirit was aimed, on the one hand, at the foreign powers, and on the other, at overthrowing the Manchu Qing dynasty. In fact, as soon as Wuhan put forward the cry of revolution, Hunan was the first to respond to it. In the south, there was support from the overseas Chinese; to the north, the reaction extended as far as Beijing. Within four months, support came from seventeen provinces, the autocrat was overthrown, and the Republic was founded. The contribution of education, and of the efforts on the part of the students, must be considered as an important factor.

25. I.e., the Hunanese Army under the overall command of Zeng Guofan put down the Taipings.

At this point, I would like to recount the activity of the Hunan student movement between the fifth month and the end of the eighth month of the third year of the Xuantong era,[26] prior to the Revolution, which consisted in the **Movement of Resistance against the Nationalization of the Railroads.**

On the nineteenth day of the third month[27] of the third year of the Xuantong era, Huang Xing led the uprising in Guangzhou which rocked the whole nation. When the news reached Hunan, many students with revolutionary ideals were eager to follow suit. The muddleheaded Qing Court, ignoring the trends of the time, adopted Sheng Xuanhuai's[28] plan to nationalize all the important railroads (author's note: The railroads should be nationalized, but the Qing court's timing was bad in this case), including the Sichuan, Guangzhou, and Hankou railroads. Sichuan was the first to defy this, and the situation became acute. Then Hunan followed suit. The students in particular were indignant. They advocated going on strike[29] and held meetings and made speeches everywhere. The incompetent and ignorant Hunan governor, Yang Wending,[30] immediately stepped in. Since it was forbidden to meet openly, students met secretly. Since it was forbidden to meet in the city, they met on Mount Yuelu. I was a minor figure among these many people then. Every day we made speeches behind the closed gates. Many fellow students fervently advocated revolution. I still remember how one student, while making a speech, ripped off his long gown[31] and said, "Let's hurry to get some military training, and be ready to fight." One night, many of us were awakened by loud shouting to learn that some of the student representatives of our school and of some neighboring schools had been captured by the military

26. 1911.

27. This is an obvious misprint for the twenty-ninth day of the third month of the lunar calendar, which corresponds to April 27, 1911, in the Western calendar. These events, which Sun Yatsen called the "tenth uprising" of the revolutionaries prior to October 1911, have, however, often been referred to as the "March 29 Revolution." See Hsueh Chun-tu, *Huang Hsing and the Chinese Revolution* (Stanford: Stanford University Press, 1961), pp. 78–93. The seventy-two rebels (out of a "Dare-to-Die Corps" of eight hundred) who perished on this occasion have been commemorated ever since as martyrs to the revolutionary cause.

28. Sheng Xuanhuai (1844–1916) was the earliest major promoter of merchant enterprises supervised and supported by the officials of the imperial bureaucracy. His companies included the Hanyeping Mines in Hunan and the Shanghai Cotton Cloth Mill. (See Albert Feuerwerker, *China's Early Industrialization. Sheng Hsuan-huai 1844–1916 and Mandarin Enterprise* [Cambridge, Mass.: Harvard University Press, 1958].)

29. I.e., boycotting classes *(bake)*, the type of student strike which was to be so important during the May Fourth movement and after.

30. Yang Wending, *zi* Puyang, from Yunnan Province, was governor of Hunan from April 1910 to July 1911.

31. This gesture should no doubt be read in the light of Mao's remark, in his "Study of Physical Education" of April 1917, that conventional literati in their long gowns scorned to wear the "short clothes" adapted to combat.

police during a secret meeting. Many said that probably they would be shot. Our principal stuck out his tongue nervously and said repeatedly, "This is extraordinary!"[32] He immediately invited the other principals to ask the government to let the students out on bail. Finally at dawn, the student leaders were bailed out, and we went back to sleep happily. This time the disturbance was really great. Not until the nineteenth day of the eighth month[33] did Hubei get independence, and Hunan echoed this on the first day of the ninth month.[34] Let me leave the backdrop aside and return to our theme — it was then that in Hunan we discovered the student army.

Now I want to go ahead and record the facts regarding the Hunan student army. (To be continued.)[35]

---

32. *Liaobude*. On the many possible meanings of this Chinese expression, see the note to "The Founding of the Cultural Book Society," July 31, 1920.

33. October 10, 1911, the date of the Wuhan uprising, which marked the beginning of the revolution.

34. October 22, 1911, the date on which the New Army entered Changsha and overthrew the old order. Hunan was thus, as Mao states above, the first province to respond to Hubei's initiative.

35. The second part of this article presumably appeared in issue no. 5 of the *Xiang River Review*, which was confiscated by Zhang Jingyao and of which no copies are known to be extant. Thereafter, the newspaper was, as already indicated, closed down.

Statutes of the Problem Study Society

(September 1, 1919)

Announcement by Deng Kang:[1]

My friend Mr. Mao Zedong has sent from Changsha the Statutes of the Problem Study Society, amounting to over ten pages. Friends in Beijing have looked at them, and all say they are very good, and should be studied. Everyone has asked me for a copy, and I now have only one left. Since quite a few people still want copies, I have had them printed in the daily paper of our school,[2] in reply to the request of all those who are concerned with finding answers to the problems that concern us in this present age.

Article I All things and all principles, whether essential or nonessential to contemporary human life, that have not yet been solved yet influence the progress of contemporary human life, are problems. Together we today found this society, emphasizing that the solution to such problems as these starts first with study, and name it the Problem Study Society.

Article II The various problems listed below, and other problems that are deemed worthy of study to be continually added, are problems to be studied by this society.

1. Educational Problems
(1) The problem of universal education (of compulsory education). (2) Middle school education problems. (3) Specialized education problems. (4) Higher education problems. (5) The problem of educating people about society. (6) The problem of compiling textbooks in

1. Deng Kang (1894–1933), a Hunanese, later took the name Deng Zhongxia. Deng was, in 1919, a student at Beijing University. While at the university he was active in various societies, including the Beijing University Mass Education Lecture Corps and the Society for the Study of Socialism. He and Mao maintained regular contact during this period. He was later an important labor organizer and the author of a history of the union movement in China which remained the standard work for several decades. Though the paragraph which follows is not by Mao Zedong, it accompanied the first publication of this document and is therefore included here.

2. I.e., the *Beijing daxue rikan* (Beijing University Daily).

the national language. (7) The problem of teaching the Chinese language in middle school. (8) The problem of nonpunishment. (9) The problem of abolishing examinations. (10) The problem of improving teaching methods at all levels. (11) The problem of the knowledge, health, and salaries of elementary school teachers. (12) The problem of building public athletic stadia. (13) The problem of building places of public amusement. (14) The problem of building public libraries. (15) The problem of revising the educational system. (16) The problem of sending large numbers of students to study abroad. (17) The problem of how to implement [John] Dewey's educational doctrine.

2. Women's Problems

   (1) The problem of women participating in politics. (2) The problem of education for women. (3) The problem of women and a career. (4) The problem of women and social intercourse. (5) The problem of chastity. (6) The problem of the freedom to love and the sacredness of love. (7) The problem of coeducation. (8) The problem of female makeup and adornment. (9) The problem of education and the family. (10) The problem of mothers-in-law and daughters-in-law living together. (11) The problem of abolishing prostitution. (12) The problem of abolishing concubines. (13) The problem of abolishing footbinding. (14) The problem of establishing public nurseries. (15) The problem of establishing public kindergartens. (16) The problem of the way children born out of wedlock are treated. (17) The problem of birth control.

3. The Problem of the National Language

   (The problem of the colloquial language [*baihua*])

4. The Problem of Confucius

5. The Problem of Combining Eastern and Western Civilizations

6. The Problem of Reforming the Marriage System, and Whether or Not the Marriage System Should Be Abolished

7. The Problem of Reforming the Clan System, and Whether or Not the Clan System Should Be Abolished

8. The Problem of Reforming the State System, and Whether or Not the State System Should Be Abolished

9. The Problem of Reforming Religion, and Whether or Not Religion Should Be Abolished

10. The Labor Problem

    (1) The problem of working hours. (2) The problem of educating workers. (3) The problem of housing and entertainment for workers.

(4) The problem of dealing with unemployment. (5) The problem of the value of labor. (6) The problem of child labor. (7) The problem of equal value for the work of men and women. (8) The problem of labor organization. (9) The problem of an international alliance of labor. (10) The problem of the political participation of workers and peasants. (11) The problem of forced labor. (12) The problem of the equal distribution of the surplus. (13) The problem of public ownership of the organs of production. (14) The problem of worker retirement annuities. (15) The problem of inherited property reverting to the public domain. (to be continued)

11. The Problem of the Self-Determination of Nations
12. The Problem of Economic Freedom
13. The Problem of Freedom of the Seas
14. The Problem of Limiting Military Armaments
15. The Problem of the League of Nations
16. The Problem of Free Emigration
17. The Problem of Racial Equality
18. The Problem of Whether or Not Socialism Can Be Implemented
19. The Problem of How to Advance the Union of the Popular Masses
20. The Problem of How to Universalize the Work-Study Philosophy
21. The Problem of Russia
22. The Problem of Germany
23. The Problem of Austria and Hungary
24. The Problem of Indian Self-Rule
25. The Problem of the Independence of Ireland
26. The Problem of the Partition of Turkey
27. The Problem of the Egyptian Riots
28. The Problem of How to Deal with the German Emperor
29. The Problem of Reconstruction in Belgium
30. The Problem of Reconstruction in Eastern France
31. The Problem of Dealing with the German Colonies
32. The Problem of Public Ownership of Harbors

33. The Problem of Air Flight Across the Atlantic Ocean
34. The Problem of Air Flight Across the Pacific Ocean
35. The Problem of Air Flight Over the Tianshan[3]
36. The Problem of Drilling Traffic Tunnels Under the Bering Sea, the English Channel, and the Straits of Gibraltar
37. The Problem of Siberia
38. The Problem of Philippine Independence
39. The Problem of Food Supplies in Japan
40. The Japan Problem
41. The Korea Problem
42. The Shandong Problem
43. The Hunan Problem
44. The Problem of Abolishing Governors-General
45. The Problem of Demobilizing the Troops
46. The Problem of a National Defense Force
47. The Problem of the New and Old Parliaments
48. The Problem of Unifying the Railroads
    (The problem of dissolving the spheres of foreign influence)
49. The Manchurian Problem
50. The Mongolian Problem
51. The Tibetan Problem
52. The Problem of Returning the Boxer Indemnities
53. The Problem of the Chinese Laborers[4]
    (1) The problem of educating the Chinese laborers. (2) The problem of the savings of the Chinese laborers. (3) Resettlement of the Chinese laborers after they return home.
54. The Problem of Local Self-Government
55. The Problem of the Central versus Local Governments and the Centralization versus Decentralization of Power

---

3. The mountain range running between Xinjiang and Central Asia.

4. I.e., of the coolies sent to dig trenches for the Entente during the First World War.

56. The Problem of a Bicameral versus Unicameral System

57. The Problem of General Elections

58. The Problem of Limitations on the Power of the President

59. The Problem of Examinations for Civil and Legal Officials

60. The Problem of Eliminating Bribery

61. The Problem of a Cabinet with Collective Responsibility

62. Industrial Problems
(1) The problem of reforming sericulture. (2) The problem of reforming tea production. (3) The problem of reforming cotton planting. (4) The problem of afforestation. (5) The problem of opening mines. (6) The problem of setting up more silk and cloth factories. (7) The problem of foreign trade. (8) The problem of establishing national factories.

63. Transportation Problems
(1) The problem of reforming the railroads. (2) The problem of getting large foreign loans to expand the railroad tracks and equipment. (3) The problem of setting up radio stations. (4) The problem of adding to electric power lines over land and over water. (5) The problem of increasing merchant shipping. (6) The problem of building commercial ports and highways. (7) The problem of building automobile roads in the countryside.

64. Problems of Public Finance
(1) The problem of paying foreign debts. (2) The problem of getting more foreign loans. (3) The problem of repaying and raising more domestic loans. (4) The problems of reducing interest and increasing taxes. (5) The problem of overhauling the salt administration. (6) The problem of drawing a line between the financial powers of the capital and those of the provinces. (7) The problem of overhauling the tax system. (8) The problem of land surveying. (9) The problem of unifying and collecting the land tax.

65. Economic Problems
(1) The problem of the basic unit of the currency. (2) The problem of establishing a central bank. (3) The problem of recalling paper currency. (4) The problem of establishing people's banks.[5] (5) The prob-

5. Here, and in item 5 which follows immediately, the term translated "people's" is *guomin*, literally "citizens' " or "national," but Mao appears to be contrasting the "people's" banks with the central bank referred to earlier.

lem of people's savings.

66. The Problem of an Independent Judiciary
67. The Problem of Abolishing Extraterritoriality
68. The Problem of Establishing Public Town Parks
69. The Problem of Model Villages
70. The Problem of Self-Rule in the Southwest
71. The Problem of Whether or Not to Implement a Federal System

Article III The study of problems should be solidly founded on academic principles. Before studying the various problems, we should therefore study various "isms."[6] The isms listed below are those we should pay special attention to studying.

1) Philosophical theories.
2) Ethical theories.
3) Educational theories.
4) Religious theories.
5) Literary theories.
6) Aesthetic theories.
7) Political theories.
8) Economic theories.
9) Legal theories.
10) Scientific laws.

Article IV Any problem may be suggested for study, whether large or small, so

6. This is clearly a reference to the famous controversy about "problems" *(wenti)* and "isms" *(zhuyi)*, launched by Hu Shi's article "More Study of Problems, Less Talk about Isms," published on July 20, 1919. Hu Shi (1891–1962), *zi* Shizhi, was a native of Anhui. After undergraduate studies at Cornell, he was influenced by the thought of John Dewey, under whom he took his Ph.D. at Columbia in 1917. While still a student in New York, he wrote an article in *New Youth* advocating the use of the spoken language, and following his return to China in July 1917 he played a leading role in the intellectual controversies of the May Fourth period. In 1919–1921, he served as Dewey's intepreter during his lecture tour to China. Understandably, divergences opened up between him and the more radical members of the *New Youth* editorial board, such as Li Dazhao and Chen Duxiu, who had comitted themselves to Marxism. In the controversy evoked here, Hu's view was that the most important task of Chinese intellectuals was to study concrete problems; Li Dazhao and other future Communists argued that without theory or ideology, it was impossible to understand problems. The term "ism" *(zhuyi)* recurs in subheadings 1 through 9 below, but because this reads oddly with some of the adjectives, we have preferred to translate it as "theories." As will be obvious from the name of this society, and the whole thrust of the statutes, Mao was much influenced by Hu Shi at this time, but clearly he had some sympathy with Li Dazhao's view as well.

long as it is relatively broadly general in nature, such as the problem of Japan.

Article V In studying problems, those that require on-the-spot investigation should be investigated on the spot, and those that do not require on-the-spot investigation, or for which on-the-spot investigation is presently impossible, may be studied from books, magazines, and newspapers, as for example the problem of Confucius and that of the three underwater traffic tunnels.

Article VI The emphasis will be on the study of problems related to contemporary human life, but we shall also take note of those for which projections about the future can be made. Problems of the past that have no relevance to the present or future will not be examined.

Article VII The methods of problem study take three forms.

1) Study by a single individual.
2) Study groups of two or more persons.
3) Study by correspondence among two or more persons in different locations.

Article VIII The Problem Study Society will be limited to the "theoretical solution of problems." "Solving problems in practice" will take place outside the Problem Study Society.

Article IX Anyone interested in studying one or more of the above-mentioned problems, and who wishes to be involved in the Problem Study Society, will be considered a member of the Problem Study Society.

Article X The relation of the Society to its members and the relations among members of the Society will be limited to just "problem study." Any other kind of relationship will be outside the Problem Study Society.

Article XI The Problem Study Society will have two secretaries, who will administer the Society's business.

Article XII The Problem Study Society was founded on September 1 of the eighth year of the Republic of China, 1919 by the Western calendar. The Regulations of the Problem Study Society were adopted and announced on this day.

Letter to Li Jinxi[1]

(September 5, 1919)

Mr. Shaoxi,

Your instructions have been respectfully received. Your encouragement is greatly appreciated. The *Xiang River Review* was banned and stopped publication after issue no. 5. Issue no. 5 has already been mailed to you, and I assume you have received it by now.[2] Meanwhile, *Xin Hunan* (New Hunan), from issue no. 7 onwards, will be edited by your younger brother.[3] Right now it is being reorganized, and in half a month or so the issue will be published, at which time I will submit a copy to you for your suggestions. Issue no. 6 of *Minduo* (The People's Tocsin)[4] contains your brilliant article, "Research on National Language Studies."[5] I have read it, and benefited in no small measure. Together with the "Brief Survey of Trends in Russian Literary Thought" published in the same issue, it may be considered among the few important articles of the last several

---

1. Mao's former teacher at First Normal School in Changsha, who later moved to Beijing and became prominent in the language reform movement at Beijing University. See the note to Mao's letter to him dated November 9, 1915.

2. Issue no. 5 was, of course, confiscated, so neither Li nor anyone else ever received it.

3. *Xin Hunan* was the organ of the schools commonly known as "Yale in China," located in Hunan. (For details regarding the links of these institutions to Yale, see the note to the extract from *Students' Society Records* dated May 29, 1918.) On Mao's editorship of it, see Li Jui, *Early Mao*, p. 118. The full text of Mao's editorial in no. 7 (one of the four he edited before this periodical, too, was shut down by Zhang Jingyao) appears on p. 418 of this volume. By "your younger brother," Mao means, of course, "my humble self."

4. *Minduo* was founded in 1916 in Tokyo by the China Academic Research Society (Zhonghua xueshu yanjiuhui), an organization of Chinese students studying in Japan. In principle a quarterly, it appeared in fact approximately twice a year. In May 1918, beginning with the fifth issue, it was moved to Shanghai. No. 6, to which Mao refers here, appeared in 1919. In addition to Li Jinxi and Yang Changji, it numbered among its contributors many celebrated scholars, including Zhang Binglin, Cai Yuanpei, Liang Shuming, Li Dazhao, and Gu Jiegang.

5. "National language" (*guoyu*) means in the first instance the language of Beijing (often called "mandarin"), as opposed to regional dialects. Here, and elsewhere in this volume, however, it refers to the colloquial language, *baihua*, as a vehicle of expression, as opposed to the literary language (*wenyan*). Li Jinxi's article corresponded to the text of a speech he had given in October 1918 and January 1919 at Wuhan and Taiyuan National Language Institutes. It was later published by Commercial Press.

years. The problem of the national language is one that I, too, would rather like to study. As a student of education myself, I would say that nothing can be done unless textbooks are compiled in the national language. The difficult thing about studying it, though, is collecting materials. If you, sir, should happen to encounter any materials on the "national language," please be so kind as to send me a few. There seem to be good hopes of putting together a group of students from Hunan to study in France. Sending students to study in France would bring new life to education in Hunan, and you have long been interested in this matter. By the way, I have already received a good number of issues of *Pingmin*.[6]

Submitted by Zedong
September 5, 1919, from the Study School[7]

---

6. The reference is to the *Pingmin zhoukan* (Common People's Weekly), founded July 1919 and published by the Beijing Institute of French Language and Literature. The aim of the publication was "to be the companion of the common people, and the advocate of the new culture movement."

7. Regarding the Study School (Xiuye xuexiao) in general, see the relevant note to Mao's letter of August 1915, to Xiao Zisheng. Mao Zedong himself taught history in its elementary school section from April to December 1919.

Expressing Sympathy for the Students of the Normal School[1]

(September 21, 1919)

Students of the normal school, because they love to study, and also sympathize with the more than one hundred primary school students, assuming that they share their love of knowledge, oppose the disbanding of the primary school attached to the normal school.[2] (For details see yesterday's issue of our paper.) Just look at their words: "The innocent young children are very attached to the school. They gathered in front of the school gate, weeping. They wanted to go in, but the gate was closed tight. The staff and officials tried to disperse them, but to no avail. When their former teachers met them in the street, the pupils came to clasp their hands, and said: 'Teacher, what about teaching me?' " No one who ever saw or heard about it could keep back his tears. Educators of our Hunan Province have some brains and should show some sympathy for the students.

1. The school in question is Hunan First Provincial Normal School, from which Mao had graduated the previous year.

2. Mao himself became principal of this primary school in the summer of 1920. In autumn 1919 the primary school was forced to close because of classroom and financial difficulties. In response, the Students' Society of First Normal School wrote a long petition to Governor Zhang Jingyao calling for government support for the primary school. It was published in the *Dagongbao* on September 20, 1919, and the next day Mao wrote this article.

It Was He

(September 26, 1919)

The rickshaw boy had been pulling his carriage all day long, pulling until he was dizzy, running around aimlessly, oblivious of what was going on. Suddenly, some heavy blows landed on his back. "Ai-yo," he cried out, "this is terrible!"[1] Tears ran down his cheeks. At first, he was ready to take up the quarrel, but after one glance, he saw that it was he![2] Then he dared not utter a word, but fled as fast as he could, pulling his rickshaw.

1. *Liaobude.*

2. Presumably, the mysterious aggressor was a policeman, rickshaw owner, or other person having authority over the hero, whom he could not venture to resist.

Revised Manifesto for Xin Hunan *on the Occasion of the Publication of Issue No. 7*[1]

(September 1919)

Beginning with issue no. 7, the guiding principles of this periodical will be:

1) to criticize society,
2) to reform thought,
3) to introduce [the new] learning, and
4) to discuss problems.

From issue no. 7, those associated with this periodical will bend all their efforts to act in accordance with these principles. Naturally we will not be concerned with "success or failure, or whether things go smoothly or not." Still less will we pay attention to any power (authority)[2] whatsoever. For our credo is: "Anything may be sacrificed save principle, which can absolutely not be sacrificed."

---

1. As indicated in his letter of September 5, 1919, to Li Jinxi, Mao assumed the editorship of this weekly with issue no. 7. Like the *Xiang River Review*, it was soon closed down by Zhang Jingyao.

2. The Chinese expression *shili*, which means power, force, or influence, is followed by the English word "authority" in the original text.

Mao Zedong's Funeral Oration in Honor of His Mother

(October 8, 1919)

Alas, mother died suddenly at fifty-three.[1] She had given birth to seven children, of whom only three survived. They are Dong, Min, and Tan.[2] The others, two daughters and two sons, all died. Worn down by the many hardships she had suffered in raising us, her sons, mother became ill. The heartrending details of her sufferings are too numerous for me to write down here. Later I will recount them little by little.

Now I will only mention two salient points—her abundant virtues and her hatred of injustice. The noblest aspect of mother's character was her impartial love that extended to all, far or near, related or unrelated. Her motherly kindness moved a great many people. Wherever her love reached, it was genuine. She never lied or cheated. She was always neat and meticulous. Everything she took care of would be put in order. She was clear in thinking, adept in analyzing matters. Nothing was neglected, and nothing was misplaced. She was well known among her relatives and neighbors for her cleanliness. Both her outward appearance and her inner being were spotless. The five constant virtues, all alike remarkable, were her salient points. They fitted her personality, which was like that of a noble. Her hatred for lack of rectitude resided in the last of the three bonds.[3]

She left the world without fulfilling her wishes and completing what she wanted to do. This was her greatest mental anguish. O Heaven! O men! Now mother is lying in a corner of the earth. Her next regret was that her children

---

1. In the original Chinese, this whole text, apart from the "mourning couplets" at the end, consists of four-character lines of blank verse. It would be difficult to produce an English translation in this form which did not sound like doggerel, so we have preferred to render the funeral oration in prose.

2. I.e., [Mao Ze]dong, the second brother, [Mao Ze]min, and the youngest surviving brother, [Mao Ze]tan.

3. The third and last of the "three bonds" *(san gang)* or ethical relations was that between husband and wife. (The first two referred to the relation between sovereign and minister, and between father and son.) Mao's relationship with his father was notoriously stormy, and he often took his mother's side in their quarrels. Among the many sources on this, see in particular Mao's own account, as told to Edgar Snow and published in *Red Star over China.*

were just growing up, still like unripe fruit or the new crop only in the blade. During her illness, she used to hold our hands, heartbroken. She kept calling on us to do good, and to be kind to all the close relatives and dear ones in the family. Whether out of simple benevolence, or because they were weary and sick, both young and old, related or unrelated, deserved their reward. In sum, the radiance of her abundant virtues was so sincere that its effect will last forever. As for her unaccomplished wishes, we pledge to fulfill them. As I think of them now, my heart is set and determined. How deep was mother's kindness in raising us! It was like the sunshine in spring and the morning clouds. When can I ever return her love? Alas, mother! You have not died after all! Although the body is gone, your spirit lasts forever. As long as I live, I will return your love; as long as I live, I want to accompany you. I have many words to say, yet time is too short! I have simply mentioned the main points briefly.

At this time of our family mourning, may I empty this glass of wine! I will tell you many things as the days wear on.

May I now present the offerings!

Mourning Couplets

(1)

In her last illness mother called out the names of her sons.
How boundless was her love!
I suffer endless remorse at a thousand expressions of gratitude unuttered.
Late in life, she again sought comfort in Buddha,[4]
Yet she could not remain in this world after all!
I weep, but where can I find mother's face?

(2)

Only the glow of her spirit lingers with us now on the southern shore in the spring breeze,
Many tears I shed at Shaoshan in the autumn rain!

4. Mao's mother had always been a fervent Buddhist. This line must mean, not that she had returned to her faith after turning away from it, but simply that like many people she had sought particular consolation in religion at the end of her life.

Commentary on the Suicide of Miss Zhao[1]

(November 16, 1919)

When something happens in society, we should not underrate its importance. The background of any event contains the multiple causes of its occurence. For example, the event of a "person's death" can be explained in two ways. One is biological and physical, as in the case of "passing away in ripe old age." The other goes against biological and physical factors, as in the case of "premature death" or "unnatural death." The death of Miss Zhao by suicide belongs to the latter category of "unnatural death."

A person's suicide is determined entirely by circumstances. Was it Miss Zhao's original intent to seek death? No, it was to seek life. If, in the end, Miss Zhao chose death, it was because circumstances drove her to this. The circumstances in which Miss Zhao found herself included: (1) Chinese society, (2) the family living in the Zhao residence on Nanyang Street in Changsha, (3) the Wu family of the Orange Garden in Changsha, the family of the husband she did not want. These three factors constituted three iron nets, which we can imagine as a kind of triangular construction. Within these triangular iron nets, however much Miss Zhao sought life, there was no way for her to go on living. The opposite of life is death, and so Miss Zhao was obliged to die.

If one of these three factors had not been an iron net, or if one of the iron nets had opened, Miss Zhao would certainly not have died. (1) If Miss Zhao's parents had not used excessive compulsion, but had acceded to her own free will, she would certainly not have died. (2) If, while exercising compulsion, Miss Zhao's parents had allowed her to put her point of view to her fiancé's family, and to explain the reasons for her refusal, and if in the end her fiancé's family had accepted her point of view, and respected her individual freedom, Miss Zhao would certainly not have died. (3) If, even though neither her own parents nor

1. On November 14, 1919, Miss Zhao Wuzhen (1896–1919), a native of Changsha, had committed suicide in protest against a marriage arranged by her parents. She was to have been the second wife of Wu Fenglin, the son of a wealthy antique dealer, but though the first wife was dead, she rejected this status. She also objected to the fact that Wu was old and ugly. When her parents refused to change the wedding arrangements, she therefore slit her throat with a razor in the bridal sedan chair. These events were reported in the press on November 15, and inspired intense discussion for the next fortnight. Mao was moved to write no less than ten articles on this topic, and there were many other contributions to the debate, some of which are mentioned below by Mao.

her husband's family could accept her free will, there had been in society a powerful segment of public opinion to back her, and if there had been an entirely new world to which she could flee, in which her act of flight would be considered honorable and not dishonorable, Miss Zhao again would certainly not have died. If Miss Zhao is dead today, it is because she was solidly enclosed by the three iron nets (society, her own family, her fiancé's family); she sought life in vain, and finally was led to seek death.

Last year in Tokyo, Japan, there was the case of the double suicide of the wife of a count and a chauffeur who had fallen in love. The *Tōkyō Shimbun* published a special issue, following which a number of writers and scholars discussed the incident for several months straight. Yesterday's incident was very important. The background to this incident is the rottenness of the marriage system, and the darkness of the social system, in which there can be no independent ideas or views, and no freedom of choice in love. As we discuss different kinds of theories, we should discuss them in the light of real, living events. Yesterday, Mr. Tianlai[2] and Mr. Jiangong[3] have already provided a short introduction. In continuing this discussion and presenting some of my own views, I have done so with the express hope that others will earnestly discuss the case of this young woman, a martyr to freedom and to love, from many different perspectives, and will cry "Injustice!" on her behalf. (See yesterday's issue of this paper for details.)

---

2. Mr. Tianlai's article entitled "The Pernicious Influence of the Old Marriage System" was published in the *Dagongbao* on November 15, 1919. His identity is unknown.

3. Mr. Jiangong is Long Yi (1888–1951), *hao* Shouyi, commonly known by his pen-name Long Jiangong. A native of Xiangtan, Hunan Province, he was at this time one of the three chief editors *(zhubi)* of the *Dagongbao*, then Changsha's most influential newspaper. In addition to the piece alluded to here by Mao, entitled "A Victim of the Reform of the Marriage System," Long wrote two other articles concerning this incident in the paper. He was very active in the Hunan self-government movement and was one of the members of the preparatory committee for self-government in October 1920, along with Mao and Peng Huang.

The Question of Miss Zhao's Personality

(November 18, 1919)

The day before yesterday, I wrote a commentary in which I said that the cause of Miss Zhao's death was entirely determined by her circumstances, that is, by the society in which she lived and by the two families, those of her own parents and of her fiancé. Consequently, I would like to say a few words about the personality of Miss Zhao.

Someone asked me whether Miss Zhao had a personality or not. I said that I had two replies, one, that Miss Zhao did not have a personality of her own, the other, that she did have a personality.

What did I mean by saying that Miss Zhao did not have a personality? If Miss Zhao had had a personality, she would not have died. Why not? Having a personality requires respect from those one deals with. Its prerequisite is freedom of the will. Was Miss Zhao's will free? No, it was not free. Why wasn't it free? Because Miss Zhao had parents. In the West, the free will of children is not affected by the parents. In the Western family organization, father and mother recognize the free will of their sons and daughters. Not so in China. The commands of the parent and the will of the child are not at all on an equal footing. The parents of Miss Zhao very clearly forced her to love someone she did not want to love. No freedom of will was recognized at all. If you do not want to love me, but I force my love on you, that is a form of rape. This is called "direct rape." Their daughter did not want to love that person, but they forced their daughter to love that person. This, too, is a kind of rape, which is called "indirect rape." Chinese parents all indirectly rape their sons and daughters. This is the conclusion which inevitably arises under the Chinese family system of "parental authority," and the marriage system in which there is the "policy of parental arrangement." For Miss Zhao to have had a personality of her own she would have had to have a free will. For her to have a free will, her parents would have had to respect her and accede to her wishes. If Miss Zhao's parents had respected her, had acceded to her wishes, would she have been put into that cage-like bridal sedan chair in which she finally committed suicide? But it is now a fact that this happened. Thus, my first reply is that Miss Zhao did not have a personality of her own.

Why do I also say that she did have a personality? This is with reference to Miss Zhao herself. Although Miss Zhao lived for twenty-one years (she was twenty-one *sui*) in a family that did not allow her to have a personality, and for twenty-one years her father and mother kept her from having a personality, in that last brief moment of her twenty-one years, her personality suddenly came forth. Alas, alas, death is preferable to the absence of freedom. The snow-white knife was stained with fresh red blood. The dirt road of Orange Garden Street, splashed with blood, was transformed into a solemn highway to heaven. And with this, Miss Zhao's personality also gushed forth suddenly, shining bright and luminous. Consequently, my second reply is that Miss Zhao did indeed have a personality of her own.

Thus, my conscience forces me to utter the following two sentences:

1) All parents who are like the parents of Miss Zhao should be put in prison.
2) May the cry of all humanity fill the heavens, "Long live Miss Zhao!"

The Marriage Question—An Admonition to Young Men and Women

(November 19, 1919)

Three days ago, the Casual Comments section of this paper carried a piece by Mr. Jiangong, "Those Sacrificed to Reform of the Marriage System."[1] Referring to the suicide of Miss Zhao, he addressed a warning to parents. It read as follows:

> . . . not all Chinese are deaf and blind. Anyone with even a little tiny bit of conscience should be thoroughly awakened, and refrain from interfering in the marriages of his sons and daughters. This young woman did not die for nothing. . . . We must not fail her, we must not allow the sacrifice of her life to have been in vain.

The words of Mr. Jiangong say half of what must be said, but he left out the other half. Let me add the following:

> Dear young men and women throughout China. None of you are deaf and blind. Having seen such a tragedy of "blood splattering the city of Changsha," you must be stirred to the depths of your souls, and become thoroughly awakened. See to it that you arrange your own marriages yourselves. The policy of letting parents arrange everything should absolutely be repudiated. Love is sacred, and absolutely cannot be arranged by others, cannot be forced, cannot be bought. We must not fail her, we must not allow the sacrifice of her life to have been in vain.

Readers, what are your views?

---

1. Long's piece, which had already been mentioned by Mao in his article of November 16, appeared on November 15. This article must therefore have been written on November 18, though it was not published until the following day.

The Question of Reforming the Marriage System

(November 19, 1919)

Yesterday, my piece on Mr. Jiangong's "Those Sacrificed to Reform of the Marriage System," and his words on which I was elaborating, offered an appropriate proposal for young men and women.[1] Today I would like to say that since we have already mentioned "reform of the marriage system" we should proceed to discuss "How to reform the marriage system." I really hope that all of you young men and women will come up with solutions to this question. This newspaper would of course greatly welcome your essays on such solutions.

1. As already noted, the article which Mao says he wrote "yesterday," i.e. on November 18, appeared on November 19, in the same issue of the *Dagongbao* as this one.

"*The Evils of Society*" *and Miss Zhao*

(November 21, 1919)

My friend Mr. Yinbo,[1] in his editorial comments published the day before yesterday in this paper, criticized my article, "Commentary on the Suicide of Miss Zhao," saying that I had placed all the blame on circumstances, letting Miss Zhao off scot-free, and that this was not right. He wrote, "The action of Miss Zhao was a weak and negative action. Such actions must never never be advocated." I am basically in total agreement with this positive critique, forcefully put forward by Mr. Yinbo. On the question of the suicide of Miss Zhao, I had originally intended to criticize her on several different small points. Among the several small points that I was considering, one was precisely "against suicide." Mr. Yinbo's view and my view are really identical.

In the end, however, I cannot let "society" off. No matter how weak you might say Miss Zhao's act of committing suicide was, you cannot say she "died without cause." And the "cause" of her death, to one degree or another, indisputably did come from outside of herself, from society. Since society contains "causes" that could bring about Miss Zhao's death, this society is an extremely dangerous thing. It was able to cause the death of Miss Zhao; it could also cause the death of Miss Qian, Miss Sun, or Miss Li. It can make "women" die; it can also make "men" die. There are still so many of us who today have not yet died. We must be on our guard against this dangerous thing that could find the occasion to inflict a fatal blow on us at any moment. We must protest loudly, warn and awaken those fellow human beings who are not yet dead, and cry out: "Society is evil!"

I said that there were three factors that drove Miss Zhao to her death. One was her parents' family, one was her fiancé's family, and one was society. Ultimately, both her parents' family and her fiancé's family are part of society. Her parents' family and her fiancé's family are each one component of society. We must understand that the parents' family and the fiancé's family are guilty of a crime, but the source of their crime lies in society. It is true that the two families could themselves have perpetrated this crime, but a great part of their culpability was transmitted to them by society. Moreover, if society were good, even if the families had wanted to perpetrate this crime, they would not have had the opportunity to do so. For example, if the Zhao family had heard that Madame Wu, the

1. Peng Huang.

prospective mother-in-law, was bad, the go-between, Fourth Madame She, would have insisted that it was not true. If this had taken place in Western society, there would have been no system of go-betweens to force them together, and no lies to trick them. Or again, if this had been in Western society, and Miss Zhao's father had slapped her in the face when she refused to get into the sedan chair, she could have taken him to court and sued him, or she would have resisted in some way to protect herself. Or yet again, when Miss Zhao wanted the Wu family to change the date, the wife of the eldest brother of the Wu family had the right simply to "refuse adamantly," and the other side was forced to accept this "refusal," and go ahead with the marriage. All these are dirty tricks peculiar to the evil society of China.

Mr. Yinbo wonders why Miss Zhao didn't just run away, and he says that it would have been possible for her actually to do this. I say, true enough, but first let me raise a few questions, after which I shall present my view.

1) Within the city of Changsha there are more than forty peddlers of foreign goods. Within a 30-*li* radius of Shaoshan Village where I live there are seven or eight peddlers of mixed foreign and domestic goods.[2] Why is this?

2) Why is it that all the toilets in the city of Changsha are for men only, and none for women?

3) Why is it you never see women entering a barber shop?

4) Why is it single women are never seen staying at hotels?

5) Why is it you never see women going into teahouses to drink tea?

6) Why is it that the customers hastening in and talking business in such silk shops as the Taihefeng or in stores selling foreign merchandise such as Yutaihua are never women, always men?

7) Why is it that of all the carters in the city not one is a woman, they are all men?

8) Why is it that at First Normal School outside South Gate there are no women students? And why are there no male students at Old Rice Field First Normal?

Anyone who knows the answers to these questions will understand why it was that Miss Zhao could not run away. The answers to these questions are not

2. The peddlers to whom Mao alludes were those who brought cotton cloth, particularly that used for women's undergarments and for children's clothes, to people's homes. The point of this reference is that, unlike the men referred to under item 6 below, who hung about silk shops, women were sequestered in their houses and could only wait for the peddlers to come to them.

difficult. There is only one general answer, that "men and women are extremely segregated," that women are not allowed a place in society. In this society, in which "men and women are extremely segregated" and women are not allowed a place, even supposing Miss Zhao had wanted to run away, where would she have run to?

To those who say that there are examples in this world of those who have run away, I again reply, yes there are. Once more, I will give you an example. "In our village of Shaoshan, there is a young woman of eighteen named Mao who is both intelligent and good looking. She was married to a man named Zhong who was both extremely stupid and extremely ugly. This young woman was extremely unwilling. Finally she threw off her husband and had an affair with the son of a neighbor named Li. In August of this year she ran away from her home to exercise the freedom to love."

> You certainly must think that this was very good. But . . .
>
> "In less than two days, she was surrounded by some other people who notified her family. Her family then sent someone to catch her."
>
> Just being caught wouldn't have been so bad.
>
> "She was dragged home, where she was beaten very severely and locked in an inner room, where as before she was left with her stupid husband to fulfill that 'most proper' marital relationship."
>
> This still wasn't much.
>
> "Zhang San says, 'She deserved to be beaten. She ran away. She's shameless.' "
>
> "Zhang Si[3] agrees. 'If you don't beat her now, when will you! If a family produces a girl like this, it's really a miserable disgrace to their whole clan.' "

This Miss Mao should be seen as putting into practice a positive view of things. Not afraid of danger or stopped by difficulties, she did everything possible to struggle against the evil demon. But what was the result? As far as I can see she got only three things: she got "caught," she got "beaten," and she got "cursed."

If we look at it in this perspective, how could Miss Zhao have done anything else but commit suicide? Alas for Miss Zhao! Alas for the evils of society!

After I had finished writing the draft of this article, I saw the critique of Mr.

---

3. Zhang San and Zhang Si (literally "Third Brother" and "Fourth Brother" Zhang) are names like John Doe or Bill Smith commonly used in Chinese to represent typical individuals.

Rulin.[4] He also emphasizes the aspect of society, on which our views agree. But from the standpoint of Miss Zhao, as to whether or not there were other means by which she could have fulfilled her free will, and what the relative value of the different means might be, I will discuss that next time. Any further details on what Miss Zhao's personal name was, or what school she graduated from, or whether she had bound or natural feet, would be most welcome.

---

4. Mr. Rulin is believed to be Xiao Rulin (1890–1926), a native of Hunan Province. After the 1911 revolution he became editor-in-chief of the Changsha *Junguomin ribao* (National Military Daily), and was deputy chief of the office of Governor Tan Yankai in 1917. The *Dagongbao* published his article entitled "My Views on the Suicide of Miss Zhao" on November 19, 1919.

Concerning the Incident of Miss Zhao's Suicide

(November 21, 1919)

In recent days there have been many commentaries on the incident of Miss Zhao's suicide, and I too have written a few comments on it that have been published in this city's *Dagongbao.* This is a public event that concerns all mankind, and leaving aside those who advocate extreme individualism and living alone, everyone should pay attention to it and study it. But Chinese women should devote particular attention and study to it. Because for several thousand years perverse customs based on the [Confucian] rites have prevailed in China, women have had no status in any area of life. From politics, law, and education, to business, social relations, entertainment, and personal status, women have always been treated very differently from men, and relegated to the dark corners of society. Not only are they denied happiness, they are also subjected to many kinds of inhumane mistreatment. That this incident of a woman being driven to suicide should occur at a time like this, when the truth is very clear and there are loud calls for the liberation of women, shows just how profound are the evils of our nation's society. Today we need not express more pity for the deceased, but rather we should look for a method that will thoroughly correct this problem so that from now on such a tragedy as this will never happen again. But before we look for a method, we must first search for the controlling root causes of this domination.

Let us consider why it is that women have been bullied by men and have not been able to emancipate themselves [*fanshen*][1] for thousands of years. Regarding this point, we must examine the question of what, in the last analysis, are the defects of women? Looked at superficially, women have a lower level of knowledge than men, and are weaker willed than men. Women have deep emotional feelings, and when the emotions well up, one's conscious awareness recedes. In this respect, they are psychologically not the equals of men. Also, women are physically somewhat weaker, and to this must be added the suffering and painful difficulty of walking with bound feet. These are the physiological defects of women. Actually, none of these are inherent defects. Generally speaking, the

1. This is the term used after 1946 to characterize the transformation of the lives of the peasants as a result of land reform, which William Hinton took as the title of his book on the subject.

psychological processes of women are not much different from those of men. This has already been proven by the fact that the effects of education in all countries show no differences based on gender. The last two items of physical weakness are the result of custom. The binding of women's feet was not practiced in antiquity and cannot be regarded as a basic biological defect. The search for any inherent biological deficiency in women finally comes down solely to the question of childbearing.

The relationship between men and women should, according to the contemporary view, center on "love," and apart from love, must not be governed by "economics." Thus the contemporary position is, "Each is economically independent, sharing the fruits of love." Before modern times, this was not the case. No one knew of the principle "Love is sacred." In the relationship between men and women, love was considered to be only secondary, while the core relationship remained economic, and was thus controlled by capitalism. In antiquity, eating was a simple affair. People picked fruit and caught wild animals and fish, and were easily satisfied. Men and women were equals, and economically women asked nothing of men and men asked nothing of women. Men and women sought of each other only "love." Thus woman sometimes, on the contrary, used her physiological strengths (physiologists say that in sexual physiology women are stronger than men) to control men. Later, as population increased, and food supplies became inadequate, the competition for survival made it necessary to emphasize work, and with this arrived the terrible age in which women became subjugated to men.

In doing physical labor, women are not inherently inferior to men, but because women cannot work during the period of childbearing, men took advantage of this weakness, exploited this single flaw, made "submission" the condition of exchange and used "food" to shut them up. This then is the general cause that has kept women subjugated and unable to emancipate themselves. On the one hand, what member of the human race was not born of woman? Childbearing by women is an indispensible element in the survival of humanity. That men should have forgotten this supreme act of benevolence, and on the contrary should have wantonly and unscrupulously oppressed them, merely for the sake of petty economic relationships, is truly a case of returning evil for good. On the other hand, childbearing is an extremely painful event. "The pangs of childbirth" is a term that frightens every woman who hears it. Despite the medical discoveries that have changed the "difficulty of childbirth" into the "ease of childbirth," we should show great reverence and compassion. How can we instead take advantage of trivial economic benefits to press the other down?

Having presented the "reasons" above, we can now turn to the "methods." The methods by which women can become free and independent and never again be oppressed by men may in general be listed as follows:

1) A woman must never marry before she is physically mature.

2) Before marriage, at the bare minimum, a woman must be adequately prepared in knowledge and skills to live her own life.

3) A woman must prepare herself for living expenses after childbirth.

The above three items are the basic prerequisites for a woman's own personal independence. In addition, there is a further condition of "public child support," to which society should pay close attention. If women themselves are able to fulfill the above three conditions, and if society, for its part, provides for the public rearing of children, then marital relationships centered on love can be established. This will depend on the efforts of all of us young men and women!

Against Suicide

(November 23, 1919)

I have placed the blame for Miss Zhao's suicide on the circumstances that forced her to this. I have said nothing so far about "suicide" itself. On the question of suicide, scholars of ethics, ancient and modern, Eastern and Western, have presented who knows how many arguments. Whether extolling or condemning suicide, their point of departure has always been their philosophies of life, how they viewed human life. My attitude toward suicide is to reject it, on several levels.

1) Ethics is the science of defining the objectives of human life and the methods for attaining the objectives of human life. Aside from a small number of pessimistic moral philosphers, the majority hold that the goal of man is "life." Some may define that as meaning "for the public good, freely develop the individual," and others may define it as meaning "the life and development of the individual and all mankind." But Paulsen says it is "developing all the human bodily and mental powers without exception to their highest, with no apologies for doing so."[1] I feel that Paulsen's words, as a concrete expression of the objective of human life, are most apt. But this objective is definitely not attainable through suicide. Not only is suicide not a means for "developing to their highest the powers of the human body and spirit, with no apologies for doing so," it is ultimately the opposite of "developing to their highest the powers of the human body and spirit, with no apologies for doing so." This principle is very easy to understand.

2) As to what is going through the mind of the person who commits suicide, we cannot really judge, since we have not had the experience of committing suicide. Living persons generally reject the concept of "death" and welcome the concept of "life." The vast majority of human beings welcome the concept of "life" and reject the concept of "death." Thus we have to say that those few who welcome "death" and reject "life" are exceptions to the rule. These exceptions

1. For this precise statement in Paulsen's *System of Ethics*, see our translation of Mao's marginal annotations to the book, pp. 185–86. Mao himself said something very similar in his marginal notes to another passage: "Self-realization means to develop fully both our physical and spiritual capabilities to the highest" (our translation, p. 285.) It is most likely that Mao consulted his annotated copy of Paulsen in writing this article, for his notes included an extensive commentary on the meaning of suicide (our translation, pp. 286–87) which is not without relation to his argument here.

may be seen as persons having a kind of mental abnormality.

3) Physiologically, a person's body is composed of cells, and the life of the person as a whole is the composite of the lives of the individual cells. The natural condition of cellular life is to continue living until a certain age, at which time one dies of old age. Suicide is a revolt against this natural physiological condition. This natural physiological condition falls under the control of a kind of abnormal mentality, and is thereby terminated. We may say that this is a kind of physiological irregularity.

4) In the world of living things, very few of them commit suicide. Although there are tales about so-called loyal dogs or animals who have been faithful unto death, these are not common occurrences. Ordinarily animals delight in life, are adapted to their environments, and strive in every way to seek life.

To summarize the above, suicide has no place in ethics, in psychology, in physiology, or in biology. Thus the criminal law of many nations includes prohibitions against suicide. Social custom, too, celebrates life and grieves at death, and both of these attitudes are rooted in the "principle of seeking life."

Today we are concerned with why there are, after all, suicides in human society, and why they are not altogether rare, and also with the question of why we invariably express a feeling of respect for heroic suicides, and sometimes even suggest that it was "a good suicide." What is the reason for this?

My response to these two points is:

1) Before the idea of committing suicide develops, a person does not want to commit suicide, but rather wants to seek life. Moreover, his hope for life is unusually strong. Such an unusually strong hope as this can only be fulfilled under conditions which are at least adequate. If one's environment or poor treatment causes one's hopes to be repeatedly frustrated and turn into disappointment and loss of hope, then one will invariably seek death. Thus a criminal cannot be told that he has been given a death sentence very many days before the sentence is actually executed. Therefore, we know that the motivation for a person's suicide is absolutely not to seek death. Not only is it not to seek death, but it is actually an urgent striving toward life. The reason why there are suicides in human society is that society has robbed that person completely of his "hope" and has left him "in utter despair." When society robs someone completely of his hope, leaving him in despair, then that person will surely commit suicide. Such was the case of Miss Zhao. If society robs a group or clan of people completely of hope, and leaves them in utter despair, then this group or clan will inevitably commit suicide, as in the case of the 500 Tianheng martyrs who all committed suicide at the same time,[2] or of Hong and Yang's army of

2. Tianheng (?–202 B.C.) was a nobleman of the state of Qi and a supporter of the king of Qi during the war between Chu and Han. When Liu Bang became king, Tianheng was unwilling to act as his subject, so committed suicide. Five hundred of his followers, on hearing of this incident, also took their own lives.

100,000 who set fire to themselves,[3] or the beginning of the Dutch war with a certain other state when they declared that if pressed too hard they would breach the sea dikes and drown themselves. If society in a certain place leaves more people in despair, then there will be more suicides in that society. If society in a certain place leaves fewer people in despair, then there will be fewer suicides in that society.

2) We respect the heroic suicide for the following two reasons. First, because that person dares to do what others dare not do, we recognize that his spirit surpasses our own, and thus a feeling of respect arises unwittingly within us. Second, because of his spirit of rebellion against oppression, we recognize that although his body is dead, his aspirations live on (they do not actually continue to exist, but his suicide makes us feel as if they do), and the powers oppressing him are thus foiled. We derive a feeling of happiness and comfort from this, which turns into respect for the person who has committed suicide. Consequently, we respect only heroic suicides, which represent the triumph of righteousness over treachery.

At this point, I would like to explain the topic under discussion, "against suicide."

First, as has been proved in many ways, our goal is the search for life, so we ought not turn around and seek death. Therefore I am "against suicide."

Second, the condition of suicide is that society robs a person of hope. In such circumstances, we ought to advocate struggle against society, to take back the hope that has been lost. To die in struggle is to "be killed," it is not "suicide." So I am "against suicide."

Third, we do not feel respect for "suicide" as such, so if we respect a heroic suicide, it is because he has "performed a difficult action," and "resisted oppression." If it were not for these two aspects, suicide would be easy. Furthermore, if there were no oppression in this world, there would be no need to resist it; in that case, even though suicides might take place, how could they inspire a feeling of respect? Since we have no feeling of respect for "suicide" as such, we ought to oppose this thing called "suicide." Regarding the first point, respect for a "difficult action," we should look elsewhere for it, rather than in the callous act of suicide. As for the second point, "resistance to oppression," we should seek it in struggle. Thus I am "against suicide."

3. The "army of Hong and Yang" refers to the forces of the Taipings. In July 1864 the capital of the Taiping Heavenly Kingdom was taken by Zeng Guofan's forces, after the campaign for which Mao earlier expressed such admiration. On the day the city fell, the Xiang Army ravaged the city, looting shops and killing many people. On seeing this, officers of the Taiping army gathered up all remaining valuables and set fire to the lot, including themselves. As indicated in the note to Mao's letter of August 23, 1917, Yang Xiuqing had, in fact, died in 1856, though the supreme leader Hong Xiuquan was still alive.

Finally, let me return to Miss Zhao. It is already clear that suicide in general is not proper. Miss Zhao committed suicide and therefore is among those who did something improper. As I see it, there were four ways in which Miss Zhao herself might have dealt with her situation:

1. By living her life in terms of her own personality.
2. By being killed in struggle.
3. By suicide.
4. By submission.

She was not willing to bend in submission. To live life in terms of her own personality, she would first have had to create a new society for herself. Miss Zhao had neither the strength nor the preparation to accomplish this. Had she fled somewhere else, she would have been shamed and forced into submission. This is why Miss Zhao preferred not to flee. The fulfillment of the personality by suicide is not a natural turn of events psychologically, physiologically, ethically, or biologically and was not her original intention. It is better to be killed in struggle than to die by suicide. The goal of struggle lies not in "wanting someone to kill me," but rather in "making it possible to live life in terms of one's own personality." In the end this was impossible, and despite all her efforts, a final heart-rending struggle led to her destruction like a shattered piece of jade.[4] This was a real-life act of true courage and a tragedy most capable of imprinting itself on people's minds. Thus I say that in order to preserve her personality, fulfill her free will, and conform to the natural laws of human life, Miss Zhao had four options which can be ranked as follows in terms of their value:

First, to live life in terms of her own personality.
Second, to be killed in the course of struggle.
Third, to commit suicide.
Fourth, to bend in submission.

There is no place in the personality or free will for submission. There is no place among the natural laws of human life for suicide. As for being killed in the course of struggle, although there is no place for the result among the natural laws of human life, there is a place for the motivation that leads to it. In the case of living one's life in terms of one's own personality, both motivation and result are good. Unfortunately, this is inconceivable in the case of contemporary Chinese society and Miss Zhao. So in the end Miss Zhao dealt with her situation by killing herself. Therefore, my conclusion concerning Miss Zhao is:

4. *Yu sui*. This is an allusion to the proverb: "*Ning wei yu sui, bu wei wa quan*" (It is better to be a shattered vessel of jade than an unbroken piece of pottery) — in other words, better a glorious death than a life of dishonor.

> "Her suicide had only 'relative' value in terms of 'preserving the personality.' "

The above article, drafted in haste, presents my own personal views. The reader is invited to judge whether, in the last analysis, I am right or wrong. I do find it difficult to express agreement with the view of Mr. Xinman,[5] who sees suicide as "a most happy and joyous event." In case of glaring errors, corrections would be extremely welcome.

5. Mr. Xinman's identity is unknown. He was one of three authors whose articles were published in the *Dagongbao* under the heading "Public Opinion on the Suicide of Miss Zhao" on November 20, 1919. In his piece, he praised Miss Zhao for being a resolute person who refused to bow to circumstances, and criticized the "erroneous arguments" of Mao and others, who failed to grasp that her suicide (not suicide in general) was a "joyous event."

The Question of Love—Young People and Old People

Smash the Policy of Parental Arrangement

(November 25, 1919)

I often feel that in matters of all kinds, old people generally take a position of opposition to young people. From such things in daily life as eating and dressing, to feelings about society and the nation, and attitudes toward mankind in the world at large, they are always drearily, rigidly, and coweringly passive. Their views are always ingratiatingly humble. Their position is always negative. I think that if young and old are none the less able to live together, it is mostly because of a relationship of mutual benefit. The old rely on the young to provide their food and clothing, while the young rely on the elderly to provide experience and wisdom. Although you may feel that this is an "extreme" way of putting it, this very peculiar phenomenon does exist in China, thanks to an evil system and evil customs. It is a fact that there are fundamental differences between the life of the old and that of the young. This proposition has physiological and psychological foundations. The reason why human life is different for the old and for the young lies in the differences between the physiology and psychology of the old and of the young. Generally speaking, human life is the satisfaction of physiological and psychological desires. Desires differ according to differences in sex, differences in age, differences in occupation, and differences in beliefs. The difference in desires resulting from age differences is, however, the most pronounced. This has already been proven by both Eastern and Western scholars.

We have many different kinds of desires, such as the desire to eat, the desire for sex, the desire to play, the desire for fame, and the desire for power and influence (also called the desire to dominate), and so on. Of these, the desires for food and sex are fundamental, the former to maintain the "present" and the latter to open up the "future." Of these two desires, there is no absolute difference in the desire for food according to age. Sexual desire does, however, differ with age.

The expression of sexual desire, generally speaking, is love. Young people see the question of love as being very important, while old men don't think it's worth worrying about. The relationship between husband and wife was originally meant to be totally centered around love, with everything else being subordinate. Only in China is this question put to one side. When I was young, I saw many people getting married. I asked them what they were up to. They all replied that a person takes a wife to have someone to make tea, cook, raise pigs, chase away the dogs, spin, and weave. At this I asked, wouldn't it be a lot easier just to hire a servant? It wasn't until later that I heard that people got married to "carry on the family line." This left me still perplexed. And right down to today, when you look at what society says about marriage, you still can't find even a hint of anything about love. Society does not regard love as being important, and thus, except for the slave's work of making tea, cooking, and so on, marriage is nothing but that base life of fleshly desire. (What we call sexual desire, or love, involves not only the satisfaction of the physiological urge of fleshly desire, but the satisfaction of a higher order of desires — spiritual desires and desires for social intercourse.) The slave's work of making tea and cooking is a result of capitalism. Old people pay no attention to love, only to "eating." Thus when their sons want to take a wife, they say they are taking a daughter-in-law. Their goal in getting a daughter-in-law is to have the daughter-in-law do the slave's work for them. A passage in the *Book of Rites* says, "Even if a son is very pleased with his wife, if his parents are not, he repudiates her. A son should not be pleased with his wife."[1] This is firm proof of the fact that the question of love between the son and the daughter-in-law is to be put to one side, and that a wife is only for doing the slavework. When a woman is given in marriage, her parents don't say that they have chosen a husband for their daughter, but rather that they have selected a happy son-in-law. A "happy son-in-law" means only that this will make the parents happy. It doesn't matter whether their daughter will be happy or not. And even all the dowry payments are just so that they themselves can eat well. In short, capitalism and love are in conflict with one another. Old men are in conflict with love. Thus there is a tight bond between old men and capitalism, and the only good friends of love are young people. Wouldn't you say that old men and young people are in conflict with each other?

Observing that the Zhao family forced their daughter to commit suicide, Mr. Pingzi[2] strongly opposes parents' controlling the marriage of their children, but

---

1. Mao has truncated and slightly altered the sense of this quotation, though it supports his argument. It appears in the chapter "Nei ze" of the *Book of Rites*, paragraph 12. Couvreur, who renumbers this section as paragraph 16 of Chapter X (*Mémoires sur les bienséances et les cérémonies,* Vol. I, p. 634), translates the relevant lines as follows: "Lors même qu'un fils est très satisfait de sa femme, si ses parents ne le sont pas, il la répudie. Lorsqu'un fils n'est pas satisfait de sa femme, si ses parents lui disent, 'Elle nous sert vraiment bien,' il continue à remplir envers elle ses devoirs d'époux jusqu'à la fin de la vie, sans se relâcher."

2. Mr. Pingzi is Zhang Pingzi (1885–1972), *zi* Qihan, like Mao a native of Xiangtan *xian*, Hunan. A member of the Tongmenghui, he became in 1919 one of the chief editors of the Hunan *Dagongbao*. His own article entitled "I Do Not Approve of Parents Controlling Marriage" appeared in the November 22, 1919, issue.

he does not bring out the real reasons for this position. The arguments of others like Messrs. Yunyuan, Weiwen, and Buping[3] mostly vacillate back and forth on the issue of parents interfering with the marriages of their children, and do not take a firm stand against such encroachment. (Mr. Buping's suggestion that parents act as participants with a strong say in the matter goes even farther.) I have adduced physiological and psychological evidence to prove that parents absolutely cannot interfere in the marriages of their sons and daughters. On their side, sons and daughters should absolutely refuse parental interference in their own marriages. This must be done, for only then can capitalist marriage be abolished; only then can marriage based on love be established, so that loving and happy couples may truly appear.

---

3. The identities of Yunyuan, Weiwen, and Buping are unknown. On November 20, 1919, the *Dagongbao* carried an article by Weiwen, "The Problem of the Reform of the Marriage System," as well as a brief note by Buping under the heading "Public Opinion on the Suicide of Miss Zhao." An article signed Yunyuan, "My Views on Reform of the Marriage System," was published the following day.

Smash the Matchmaker System

(November 27, 1919)

Speaking of this thing called a "matchmaker," this is another cheap trick of Chinese society. Chinese society contains a great many cheap tricks. Things like those literary essays, imperial examinations, local bandits, and bureaucrats are all nothing but a bunch of tricks and games. The same is true of things like exorcizing devils, sacrifices to appease the gods, dragon lanterns, lion dances, and even doctors treating patients, teachers teaching classes, and men and women getting married. A society like that of China should really be called a society of cheap tricks. This trick called marriage is connected with the problem of men and women, and also gives birth to a bunch of smaller games, such as "crawling in the dust," "robbing the sister-in-law," "raising the hero," "fighting the wind," "wearing a green bandana," "making the genie jump," and so on. But as regards marriage, standing above all these little tricks, so that it may in all conscience be called the "ultimate cheap trick," is that three-headed six-armed ubiquitous demon, the "matchmaker."

The Chinese matchmaker has the following strange features:

the basic philosophy is "successfully dragging them together";
each marriage is at least 80 percent lies;
the "gods" and the "eight characters"[1] are their protecting talismans.

In China, it is always said that the major power over marriage is in the hands of the parents. In actuality, although the parents are nominally the ones in control, they do not really make the decision. It is in fact the matchmaker who has decision-making power. In China anyone is qualified to be a matchmaker. Moreover, matchmaking is recognized as a kind of duty. As soon as someone has a son who needs a wife or a daughter who needs a husband, everybody and anybody around them, no matter who, is eligible to step in and join the search. For this kind of matchmaker the first thing is to have the basic philosophy of "successfully dragging them together." Going around selling both parties on the idea that she genuinely wants the marriage to be a "success," the matchmaker always says forcefully, you two families must make up your own minds. In fact,

1. I.e., the characters representing the year, month, day, and hour of the birth of the prospective bride and groom, which must stand in the proper relationship in order to create a favorable horoscope.

however, after all her badgering, even parents with iron ears have long since become limp rags. I have seen a lot of matchmakers, 80 or 90 percent of whom have been successful. The matchmaker thinks that if she can't get the couple together it is her own fault. In the event that they do come together, and the two parties go from "unmarried" to "married," she will have a meritorious deed to her credit. At the bottom of such a philosophy of dragging people together, one thing is indispensable: "telling lies." Since the two families of the man and woman are not close to one another, there are many things that they do not know about each other, and the girl is locked away in the inner chambers, making it even more difficult to find out about her. So the matchmaker rambles on, making up all kinds of stories, so that on hearing them, both sets of parents will be happy. A marriage contract is written up on a sheet of paper, and thus the affair is concluded. As a result, it is frequently the case that after the marriage, the two turn out to be completely incompatible. This case of Fourth Madame She bringing together Miss Zhao and Fifth Son Wu is a perfect example of such lying. Some even go so far as to substitute another bridegroom, or switch the bride. This constitutes "a match between unmatchables," and not just "a few little lies." Totally incompatible marriages in which the matchmaker has simply "dragged" the couple together and then lets out a futile fart to the heavens (country people call a lie a "futile fart")[2] practically fill Chinese society. And why is it that one never hears of the man or the woman picking a quarrel with the matchmaker, or that of all the lawsuits in the courts, one rarely hears of one against the "old man of the moon"?[3] On the contrary, such people get off scot-free, with money in their pockets from the fee for their services. Why is this? Thanks to the blessings of the "gods" and the "eight characters," the responsibility is placed on the supernatural. Quite apart from the fact that the parents as usual do not blame the matchmaker, even the son and daughter can do no more than bemoan their sins in a previous life. The wrong has already been cast in bronze, and all they can do is to make the best of a bad job. This is one of the main causes preventing suitable marriages. I have already discussed this at length in yesterday's paper.

Since matchmakers are as bad as all this, when in the future we think about marriage reform, it is imperative that we immediately do away with the matchmaker system. Vocabulary such as "matchmaker" and "the old man of the moon" must be expunged from dictionaries of the Chinese language. With the establishment of a new marriage system, provided only that the man and the woman both

---

2. *Baipi*. This term is obviously related to another popular Chinese idiom, the use of *fang pi* ("to let a fart") to mean "to talk nonsense." (For Mao's use of this expression, see his "Hunan Peasant Report" of 1927.)

3. Mao writes simply *yuelao*, "the old man in the moon," who was supposed to unite by an invisible thread the fortunes of those about to be married. The term is also used, however, for the matchmakers who claimed to be able to detect these links by casting horoscopes, etc., and should be so understood here, and in its subsequent appearances in this and the next text.

know in their hearts that they have a deep and mutual affection for each other they should be fully able to mate freely. If and when they want to make this clearly known to their relatives and friends, the best thing is to place a public announcement in the newspapers, declaring that the two of us want to become man and wife, and that the wedding date is set for such-and-such a month on such-and-such a day, and that's that. Otherwise, it should also be sufficient just to register at a public office, or in the countryside to report to the local authorities. This thing called the matchmaker should be hurled beyond the highest heavens and forever forgotten. If the atmosphere in the countryside is not yet receptive, so that it is difficult for the time being to abolish the system completely, the couple should at least meet face-to-face to prevent the matchmaker from lying. And if the marriage does not work out, an inquiry can be requested in which the matchmaker cannot escape responsibility. An examination of the origins of the matchmaker system would show that it came about because the line separating men and women is drawn too deeply. Therefore, if we want to abolish the matchmaker system we must first thoroughly crack open the great prohibition against men and women meeting. In the past few days Messrs. Xincheng,[4] Yuying,[5] Borong, and Xitang[6] have already discussed this in detail, so I need not go over it again here.

---

4. Xincheng is Shu Xincheng (1893–1960), a Hunanese who was editor of *Hunan Jiaoyu* (Hunan Education), a monthly critical of the existing education system founded on November 1, 1919, and suppressed after its fifth issue in March 1920. At this time he was teaching at Changsha Fuxiang Girl's School. The article to which Mao refers had appeared on November 23, 1919, in the *Dagongbao*.

5. Yuying is Long Bojian (1879–1983), a Hunanese who had been editor-in-chief of the weekly *Xin Hunan* (New Hunan). His article entitled "A Question" was published in the *Dagongbao* on November 22, 1919.

6. Borong is Li Borong (1893–1972), and Xitang is Li Youlong (1881–1953), *zi* Xiaoshen, *hao* Xitang. Their articles on the incident were published in the *Dagongbao* on November 22 and November 24 respectively.

The Problem of Superstition in Marriage

(November 28, 1919)

In studying the reasons why it is still possible to maintain the old marriage system, I frequently think that it is because of one enormous superstition.

Why do I say this? At the center of marriage is love. The power of the human need for love is greater than that of any other need. Nothing except some special force can stop it. Since love is an extremely important human need and is extremely powerful, everyone should be able to find what he's looking for, and after marriage, the relationship between husband and wife should be full of love. Why is it that, carrying a lantern as big as a house and searching the far corners of all of Chinese society, we find not even the faintest shadow of love? The two phoney billboards of "the parental command" and "the matchmaker's word" are easily capable of completely blocking even such a great power as this. Why?

Some reply that it is "because of China's religion of the rites."[1] But how many of our 400 million people really understand what the so-called "religion of the rites" is? It goes without saying that all of China's 200 million women are totally illiterate. All of China's peasants and all of China's workers and merchants can recognize only a few big characters. If we eliminate all of these, those who really understand the religion of the rites are only a small portion of those self-styled scholarly gentlemen dressed in long dark robes. Apart from the "scholarly gentlemen," for the vast majority of uneducated women, peasants, workers, and merchants, what controls their spiritual world, and enables the two phoney billboards of "the parental command" and "the matchmaker's word" to block this surging tide of the need for love, is none other, I believe, than "superstition."

The greatest superstition is the theory that "marriages are determined by destiny." Of an infant who has just dropped out of its mother's belly, it is said that its marriage is already predestined. When the child gets a little older and develops its own need to be married, it dares not propose a partner itself, but leaves it up to the parents and a matchmaker to make arrangements. The child believes that making his own choice and leaving it up to the parental and matchmaker intermediaries amounts to the same thing, since it is already predestined and everything will be fine no matter what. The wedding is held, and the husband and wife are united. Except for those who have yielded to the irresistible

1. *Li jiao,* i.e., Confucianism.

natural force of love, people either throw out everything and start a big ruckus, turning the bedroom into a battleground of deadly mutual hostility, or find themselves another world outside the home, among the mulberry fields on the banks of the Pu River, where they carry on their secret amours.[2] Apart from these, those numerous husbands and wives who are called good couples with harmonious families have the words "marriage is predestined" writ large in their brains. Thus they frequently commit to memory such maxims as, "Each generation cultivates sharing the pillow as those who cross over in the same boat have cultivated it for a hundred generations," "The old man in the moon knots the threads," "A match made in heaven." Such marriages that obey the theory of destiny probably account for 80 percent of Chinese society. For these 80 percent of Chinese couples the flavor of love is an obscure mystery. You might say their marriage is good, but then again, they are often known to sigh and moan. But if you say it's no good, they are, after all, a couple who live together in the same room, eat and sleep together, give birth to children and raise them as if their marriages really had been "made in heaven." Following their periodic quarrels and fights, when they have calmed down a bit, they recall that "each generation cultivates sharing the pillow" and that "matches are made in heaven," at which point they return to their original state, and go on eating and sleeping as before. It is because of this theory of predestination that the matchmaker is able to avoid responsibility. Any Chinese, even the blind and deaf, is qualified to be a matchmaker. Marital predestination is implanted in everyone's mind, and when there is a wedding in some family, everyone always goes along with it, whether or not the match is appropriate. You think that if you don't go along with it, you're certain to be condemned by the gods. You hear the saying everywhere "go along with marriage, don't work against it." Anyone who "investigates the prospective spouse" by inquiring from the neighbors will never hear anything bad from them. Once the bride enters the bridegroom's house, it is considered "determined by the trigrams *qian* and *kun*,"[3] and "celebrated with bell and drum."[4] After that, no

---

2. In ancient times, the mulberries on the banks of the Pu River in the state of Wei were known as a favorite haunt of men and women engaged in clandestine meetings. The "Treatise on Music" of the *Book of Rites* declares: "Dans le pays des mûriers, sur le bord de la Pou, les airs étaient ceux d'un État qui tombe en ruine." (Couvreur, *Mémoires sur les bienséances et les cérémonies*, II, XVII, I, p. 49.) The "Treatise on Geography" of the *History of the Han Dynasty* indicates, in its coverage of the state of Wei, that the mulberries on the banks of the Wu were a place where men and women gathered for debauchery. (Perhaps, for the ancient Chinese, the ruin of the state and the violation of family relationships were much the same thing.) Thus the four characters used here by Mao, *sangjian Pushang*, had long been a synonym for secret amours.

3. The four-character expression translated "determined by the trigrams *qian* and *kun*" is from the chapter "Xi ci" of the *Book of Changes*, which is devoted to prognostications. *Qian* stands for heaven, or the male principle *yang*; *kun* stands for the earth, or the female principle *yin*.

4. The four-character expression translated here as "celebrated with bell and drum" is

one would dare back out, no matter how bad it is. All they can do is remember that "marriage is determined by destiny." It is this theory of predestination that gives rise to such extremely irrational practices as "marriages decided in the womb"[5] and "choosing a partner in infancy." Everyone thinks, however, that it's all a matter of "perfect destiny." No one has even considered that it might be a big mistake. If you ask someone for a reason, the reply will be that "marriage is determined by destiny." Oh, how powerful you are, "marital destiny."

The theory that "marriage is determined by fate" is an overarching superstition, to which many other small superstitions are appended:

> 1) "Matching the Eight Characters."[6] When arranging for the marriages of their sons and daughters, it is not that Chinese parents are utterly unselective. On the contrary, they waste a lot of effort worrying about the selection of a mate for their sons and daughters. Their criteria for selecting, however, are not looks or disposition or health or learning or age, but rather only whether or not the eight characters match. So the first step in arranging a marriage is "matching the eight characters." There are two ways of matching the eight characters. One is to ask a fortune-teller to match them, the other is to ask a "Buddha" to match them. As long as the eight characters can be matched, even a demon can be dragged into becoming a husband or wife. In society there are many cases of a young girl being mated with an elderly husband, or of a young man taking an elderly woman to wife. In our village there is a joke, "Eighty-year-old Grandpa produced a baby, and the hundred thousand families of Changsha laughed themselves to death," which refers to the story of an eighteen-year-old girl, married to an eighty-year-old man, having a baby. In addition, there are frequent instances of an ugly husband matched up with a beautiful wife, or a beautiful wife matched up with an ugly husband, with the consolation that "happiness and wealth come to the ugly." None of the other factors, such as disposition or learning, are regarded as significant criteria.
>
> 2) "Registering the Dates." After the eight characters are matched, the second step in the marriage procedure is "Registering the Dates," in which the eight characters of both the man and the woman are written down in the Book of Dates in the presence of "the illustrious spirits." Incense is burned and prayers

---

from the first ode in the *Book of Poetry* (I, I, 3; Legge, Vol. IV, p. 4), in praise of the bride of King Wen. Legge renders this and the preceding line of the poem as follows:

> The modest, retiring, virtuous young lady—
> With bells and drums let us show our delight in her.

5. *Zhi fu wei hun*. For an anecdote illustrating the origins of this practice, see the biography of Wang Yuxing in the *Wei shu* (History of the Wei Dynasty).

6. See the note to the previous text.

are invoked that the couple may "live together to a ripe old age." From this stage forward, the marriage is considered an ironclad case. Registering the Dates originally meant sealing the contract, but in the Book of Dates itself nothing is said about contracts. The only thing that is written down is eight big characters indicating the year, month, day, and hour. All the many really essential conditions of marriage count for nothing. How can this be considered anything but superstition?

3) "Selecting an Auspicious Day." After registering the dates, and the exchange of presents, it is necessary to select a lucky day. It must be a day of no "evil spirits" or "taboos." The almanac is commonly consulted for "suitable" and "impropitious" days. Next, a fortune-teller is asked to calculate the position of the stars. Then the Buddha's permission is asked. It was at this point that Miss Zhao begged her parents to change the wedding date, to which her mother replied, "The auspicious day has already been determined and is virtually impossible to change." Had they agreed to change the date, and waited for her elder brother to return home, it might not have been necessary to bury her on this "most auspicious day."

4) "Sending the Sedan Chair." This is even stupider. There is some tale to the effect that when King Zhou of the Shang dynasty was receiving his concubine, Daji, a fox-spirit changed places with her during the journey. Ever since, whenever a bride is on the way to her groom's house, it is feared that she might become a second Daji. First, therefore, a heavy closed sedan chair must be used; second, its door must be locked tightly; and third, the "god of good luck" is entreated to offer proper protection. Some say that if on this occasion Miss Zhao had been in a light open sedan chair, not tightly locked and sealed, so that she could have been seen from outside, she might not have committed suicide.

5) "Greeting the God of Good Luck." Seated in the dark inside a sealed sedan chair, a bride is already very depressed, but when she arrives at the bridegroom's house and the sedan chair is set down, she must also calmly greet the "god of good luck," requesting him to "ward off unlucky influences." On this occasion, when Miss Zhao arrived at the Wu family home, she was already about to expire, but the Wu family was just getting ready to greet the "god of good luck," in order to "ward off unlucky influences."

6) "Worshiping Heaven and Earth."[7] Worshiping heaven and earth means

7. *Baitang* (literally "worshiping the [ancestral] hall,") designates the ceremony in which the new husband and wife first worshiped heaven and earth together, and then presented their respects to the groom's parents.

being presented to the ancestors. It is said that when a new bride is added to a household it is necessary to ask the ancestors to protect and assist in "giving birth to many heirs," so that "abundant descendants may glorify the ancestors." In the West, they do not report to their ancestors, but they do thank some God, and say that the love of the bride and groom is a gift from God, and their marriage relationship has been put together by God.

These superstitions are really just so many cheap tricks of marriage, and have no other purpose than to be the rope that tightly binds a man and woman together. Between the matchmaking and the exchange of gifts, the bride and groom are so tightly bound by the bonds of superstition that they can't even breathe, and afterwards, they become a stable, proper, and very harmonious good couple. Miss Zhao's marriage had, of course, gone through all the "big ceremonies" except that of "worshiping heaven and earth."[8] Her choice of death was certainly closely related to these superstitions. As we put forward our call for the reform of the marriage system, it is first of all these superstitions about marriage that must be demolished, above all the belief that "marriages are decided by destiny." Once this belief has been demolished, the pretext behind which the arrangement of marriages by parents hides itself will disappear, and "incompatibility of husband and wife" will immediately start appearing in society. As soon as incompatibility between husbands and wives manifests itself, the army of the family revolution will arise in countless numbers, and the great tide of the freedom of marriage and the freedom to love will sweep over China. Riding the crest of this tide, new husband and wife relationships will be formed wholly on the basis of a philosophy of love.[9] At this point, I could not help associating this with a subject that everyone is talking about, "universal education."

---

8. There is an apparent contradiction between Mao's observation here and the statement, not only in all the other sources on the suicide of Miss Zhao, but in Mao's own article of November 18, to the effect that the victim cut her throat in the sedan chair while being carried to her future husband's house, so that Orange Garden Street was "splashed with blood." The explanation apparently lies in the account published in the *Dagongbao* on November 16, 1919, according to which Miss Zhao was still bleeding and did not appear to be dead when the chair was opened in front of the Wu family home, and medical attention was sought. In a macabre twist to the tale, she was taken first to the Red Cross infirmary, and then (because they had no woman doctor to treat her) to the Hunan-Yale Medical College outside the north gate, where it was too late to save her. This version is compatible with Mao's statement, in paragraph (5) above, that when she arrived at the Wu family home, she was already "about to expire." Assuming it is accurate, Miss Zhao did indeed live to complete all but the last of the marriage ceremonies.

9. Literally, "love-ism" *(lian'aizhuyi)*.

The Work of the Students

(December 1, 1919)

For several years now I have been dreaming about life in a new society, but I did not know how to go about it. In the spring of 1918, I had intended to invite some friends to found a work-study society of comrades on Mount Yuelu opposite the provincial capital, and to spend half the time tilling the land, and half the time studying. Since most of them could not stay in Hunan longer, and I was also going to visit Beijing, this plan was not carried out. Such a thought came to me once again this spring when I returned to Hunan. I have a proposal to build a new village at Mount Yuelu. The first step will be to start a school, which will apply an educational doctrine based on the principles of social thought. The fundamental ideal of this new village is to fuse together new families, new schools, and other new social forms. I have drafted a proposal concerning the methods for running this school. Now I am going to reproduce the chapter on "The Work of the Students" from the proposal and ask the comrades to comment on it. I think we can take the building of a new village at Mount Yuelu as a problem for consideration. If any comrades have detailed plans, or any practical ideas for resolving this problem, I will sincerely welcome their suggestions.

(I) Teaching time at the school should be reduced as much as possible, so that students may do independent research and work. The daily schedule should be divided into six parts. The time allocations are as follows:

sleep	2 parts
relaxation	1 part
study	2 parts
work	1 part

The two parts devoted to study consist of one part of self-study and one part of lectures. In terms of hours, the distribution is as follows:

sleep	8 hours
relaxation	4 hours
self-study	4 hours
lectures	4 hours
work	4 hours

The four hours of work is one of the essential requirements for putting this work-study concept[1] into practice.

(II) Work will be purely agricultural in nature. For example:

(A) Gardening
  (1) Flowers and trees
  (2) Vegetables
(B) Farming
  (1) Cotton
  (2) Rice and other crops
(C) Forestry
(D) Animal husbandry
(E) Mulberry-tree planting
(F) Poultry and fishery

(III) The work must be productive and practical. The handicraft courses offered nowadays in the schools aim at training students to be agile with their hands and eyes, training them to think precisely, and stimulating their concern with order and their appreciation of beauty. These are the merits of the handicraft courses, but most of them are unproductive — the things made (e.g., of paper, clay, plaster, and the other materials) can only be played with but cannot be used. They are also irrelevant to real life situations. The things students learn in school and the reality of society are inconsistent. As a result, the students are not familiar with the inner workings of society, and society also loathes the students.

At present in our country, there is yet another bad practice, which is that once the students have graduated, the great majority prefer to live in the cities rather than in the rural areas. They are not used to village life and therefore do not like it. (There are other reasons why they do not enjoy rural living, but I won't discuss them now.) This is linked to the establishment of local autonomy. If most of the students are scattered among the villages, either as initiators, or as interpreters and executors of ideas, they will constitute the nucleus of local autonomy, and it will be carried out. If there are no students in the villages, local autonomy will lack a nucleus and there may be trouble in carrying it out properly. [The fact that students do not like living in the villages] also has implications for politics. Today's politics is representative politics, based on elections. Neither of the two elections held since the founding of the Republic has truly represented the will of the people. As for the local preliminary elections, only the bad gentry, the bullies, and the military cast their votes, while most of the villagers did not even understand what the elections were all about, so there was no popular will worth speaking of. The reason lies in the lack of

1. *Gongduzhuyi,* literally "work-studyism."

participation by people with an elementary grasp of politics. If there were students to offer guidance and supervision, the incidence of giving up the right to vote in this way could gradually be reduced.

In order to do away with the defects mentioned above (activity which is unproductive and unrelated to real life, preference for cities, and dislike of rural areas), what is needed, first of all, is economic work directly linked to production, so that the energy exerted, no matter how much or how little, no matter how great or how small, will bear visible fruit. Second, the product of this work must satisfy a general need of present-day society. Third, this work must be performed in the villages; such work must be agricultural in nature.

The first aspect mentioned above leads to direct production; the second links the work to practical living; and the third fosters a taste for village life.

(IV) Apart from what has been mentioned above, there is one more important point, which I shall now discuss. It is well known to all who advocate world reform and progress that all this starts from popularizing[2] education and equipping people with knowledge. In order to popularize education, one needs first to establish schools. This is indeed true, but establishing schools is only one aspect of conducting education. The educational process as a whole is not confined to the schools. At one end, there is the family, and at the other, there is society. If the members of a student's family are illiterate (and as a result the organization and habits of the family are poor), the knowledge he acquires in school will be incompatible with that of his family. This can only lead to one of two consequences: (1) He will be absorbed by the family and molded to be a hypocrite who is a filial son and obedient grandson and, at the same time, a strange mixture of the new and the old value systems. (2) He will break off entirely from his family. That is why we have heard so much about "family revolutions" and "father and son conflicts" recently. It is the same with society. On leaving school, the student enters society. If the members of society are ignorant (and as a result the organization and habits of the society are poor), there will be conflict between society and what the student learns in school. This also leads to one of two consequences: either fusion or rupture. All the weaklings and sly crooks of the past are the products of the former. All the hermits of the past are the results of the latter. (Most hermits withdraw from society because their ideals are incompatible with those of society.) Therefore, if we only talk about the reform of education in the schools, but not about reform of the family and of society at the same time, that is like picking up something from the middle but leaving the upper and lower ends untouched. You gain one but lose two.

---

2. "Popularization" is the term commonly used for the Chinese expression *puji* in Mao's *Selected Works* and elsewhere, and we have so rendered it here. Actually, the literal sense of *puji* is "universalization," and popularization should therefore be understood as making learning (or literature) widely available, rather than as "vulgarization."

Is it going to get us anywhere if, given the present situation, we aim at reforming families and society by the power of the schools, if those who run the schools try at the same time to be the reformers of the family and the society? I can tell you right now that it is impossible. Because, given the present situation, the relationships among the family, the school, and society are not organic but inorganic; they are not relationships of the spirit, but purely formal ties. Although formally they are completely united, on the spiritual level there are often clashes. The aim of today's schools is to raise "persons of independent and sound character." But the aim of the family as regards its children is "to raise persons able to provide for the family." (For example, the father and older brother merely expect the son or younger brother to make money to provide for them, but never ask where the money comes from.) Similarly, society's aim for the individual is not that society should be a place where the individual can develop, but that the individual is a thing to be sacrificed for society. (For instance, the factories enslave the laborers, and most lower-ranking staff of organizations of all kinds lead miserable rather than happy lives.) Isn't this clear proof of spiritual conflict? Given present ways, and no change in present customs, families, schools, and society will grow farther and farther apart. Where, then, is the hope of reform?

Now let us explain what we mean. Those of us who truly want to help families and society to progress cannot merely talk about "reforming what is old," but must resolve to "create the new" and then to improve upon it. For what is called reforming the family or reforming society is nothing but reforming "life," but the old family life and the old life of society cannot in the end be reformed. Old forms of life were suited only to the former era. The times have already changed, so we need a new and different life, adapted to these new times. Have there ever been instances since ancient times of old things truly reformed? Yes, but they have all involved the creation of something new. We have known for some time that old plays[3] cannot be reformed to produce new ones, but we do not seem to know that the various kinds of old life can none of them be reformed to produce new life. On the basis of the evidence presented here about the facts of the family and society, we all know that it is impossible to discuss with present-day patriarchs the personal independence of their offspring, or to seek for the workers an equitable distribution of the fruits of their labor from the current factory owners. Therefore, the toilers will not be able to win a completely equitable distribution of the product of their labor until the social system is reformed, and sons will not be able to attain full personal autonomy until the family system is reformed. The main feature of a social system is its economic system. The main feature of a family system is the marriage system.

3. The Chinese is *ju*, which can refer to any theatrical form; presumably he means that, for example, Beijing opera *(Jingju)* cannot easily be transformed into Western-style spoken drama *(huaju)*.

How can a systemic transformation on such a grand scale be achieved by partial measures such as "reforming the old"?

To create new schools and to practise new education must be closely connected with creating new families and a new society. The main theme of the new education is to create a new life. The "productive work," "practical work," and "village work" referred to in the previous section are salient features of the new life.

Each and every student in the new schools will be a member of the new family he creates. As the number of students in the new schools gradually increases, the number of new families created will also gradually increase.

Several new families joining together can create a new society. There are so many kinds of new societies that I cannot name them all. To mention some notable examples, there are: public childcare centers, public nursing homes, public schools, public libraries, public banks, public farms, public factories, public consumers' associations, public theatres, public hospitals, public parks, museums, and autonomous associations.

The combination of such new schools and new societies will give rise to a "new village." I consider the area around Mount Yuelu to be the most suitable location near Changsha for establishing such a new village.

France is the exemplar of a political revolution, and Russia is the exemplar of a social revolution. They are the so-called "model countries." Berlin is famous for the cleanliness of its streets, and Paris for being a magnificent commercial city. They are the so-called "model cities." Our own Nantong *xian* is much admired for its autonomous education, and can be called a "model locality."[4] The reason lies in its outstanding results in training excellent students, which have attracted everyone's attention. In order truly to transform morality, a certain force needs to be cultivated, a force that should be tightly controlled, with no room for laxity. It needs a clear-cut stand and yet needs to be pragmatic in implementation. If today we scarcely venture to talk of a "model country," "model city," or "model locality," but rather of a "model village," it is because modest plans are easier to implement.

In order to spread their socialism, many Russian youth have gone to the villages to live among the peasants. Among Japanese youth, there has recently flourished a so-called "New Village Movement." The United States of America and one of its colonies, the Philippines, also have popular "work-study programs." Our students studying abroad have also followed suit: They have formed the "Work-Study Club" in America,[5] and the "Work-Study Association" in

---

4. The reformer Zhang Jian was engaged at this time in an effort to turn his native *xian* of Nantong in Jiangsu Province, where in 1902 he had established China's first normal school, into a national model. For more details, see the note to the text "What Kind of Talk is This?" of July 14, 1919.

5. The Work-Study Club was organized by Chinese students studying in America. It

France.[6] Therefore, if we are truly sincere about creating a new life, we should not be afraid that we will not have supporters.

(V) The various gardening and husbandry programs given in section II have all followed conventional farming practices, and are not a new way of life. But if we carry them out with a new spirit, then it will be a new way of life. In the old days, scholars never participated in gardening. Now, if we study and work simultaneously, regarding work as sacred, then this is a new way of life. Most of the class of intellectuals known as scholar-officials[7] pursue their careers in business and official circles and do not breathe the fresh air of the villages, or enjoy the beautiful scenery. If we breathe this fresh air and enjoy this beautiful scenery, it will be a new way of life.

There are two kinds of gardening: (1) To plant flowers and trees, i.e., flower gardens. (2) To plant vegetables, i.e., vegetable gardens. Combined, they are equivalent to what are now called school gardens. If further expanded, they will be botanical gardens. Cotton and rice will be the major crops in farming, and barley, wheat, sorghum, and corn can also be planted between times. If some rough work is too hard for the students, hired hands should be employed to assist them.

Forests should be planted in the hills. The trees a student plants on one occasion will remain even after he leaves the school, thus increasing his remembrance of and love for his alma mater.

Cattle, sheep, and pigs can all be raised within the available limits.

To raise silkworms, one needs to plant mulberry trees. When mulberry trees are grown, their leaves can be fed to the silkworms. This work can be done by both male and female students.

Raising poultry and fish is also a line of production, one that students will enjoy doing.

(VI) Not every individual is required to do every type of work. There should be a division of labor. Each person may do only one kind of work, or several kinds.

---

was formed in 1914 and was initially called the Diligent Study Society (Qinxuehui); its name was changed to the Work-Study Club in 1916. It advocated the idea of part-work part-study as a way of helping students lessen expenses, and thereby facilitating studying abroad.

6. This organization, called Qingong jianxue hui (literally, Diligent Work and Thrifty Study Association), was organized in France in 1915 by Cai Yuanpei, Wu Yuzhang, Li Shizeng, and others, with the aim of "promoting knowledge among the toilers," including the coolies who had been brought to France during the First World War to dig trenches, etc. The Association called on Chinese students to come to France on the work-study program, and in March 1916 the Sino-French Educational Association was set up, with Cai Yuanpei as president, to administer the program.

7. *Shidafu,* a term which may refer either to high officials or to literati both in and out of bureaucratic office. Obviously Mao is using it in the latter sense, since some of the people he refers to are in business rather than in government service.

The students will regard the school as their family, and the crops, gardens, and forests as their private possessions. All of the students' private possessions and private belongings can be pulled together to form a common body. This body can be called the "Work-Study Comrades' Society." This society should have production, consumption, and savings departments. After the students have left school, they are not allowed to withdraw the savings they put in the Society within a certain period of time. After that time, they may withdraw a part of it and leave a part there. This is a way to have the students maintain a lasting relationship with the school.

(VII) As was said in section III, the handicraft courses offered in schools nowadays are unproductive, and the energy exerted wasted. It is indeed "uneconomical energy." Besides the handicraft courses, it is the same with gymnastics. Most gymnastics belongs to a second category of "uneconomical energy." Now that we have various kinds of work, we may do away with these two courses. The same benefits gained through these two courses will be obtained in the process of doing various kinds of work.

(The end.)

Zhang Jingyao's Smuggling of Opium Seeds Uncovered

(People's News Agency dispatch,[1] December 24, 1919)

Information from the People's News Agency. An express letter from Hankou dated the twenty-fourth reads as follows: This afternoon students went to the Zhanyutao train station in Wuchang, where fifty bags (big gunny sacks) of opium poppy seeds have been detained. The seeds, which Hunan Military Governor Zhang Jingyao[2] had shipped from Fengtian,[3] arrived yesterday evening (the twenty-third) and were to be shipped to Hunan on the Changsha–Wuchang railroad line, but they were detained at the station for lack of a permit. This morning (the twenty-fourth), Mr. You Yong,[4] a Fujian student, learning of the incident at the station, ran to spread the news to the higher normal school. The Wuhan Student Association has already put forward its demands to the Opium-Prohibition Office of the provincial assembly and has decided to distribute leaflets tomorrow to inform the people of the three cities.[5] It is said that the Hunanese residing in Hubei will also meet and discuss how to deal with the situation. Another communication reports: a large quantity of poppy seeds has

1. The *Pingmin tongxinshe* or People's News Agency was organized by Mao, Zhang Boling, and others as the news agency of the Hunan Petition Delegation in Beijing calling for the ousting of Zhang Jingyao. Every day, it despatched news on the movement to oust Zhang Jingyao to papers in Beijing, and also in Tianjin, Shanghai, and Wuhan, as well as to Hunan.

2. Zhang Jingyao (1881–1933), *zi* Xunchen, from Anhui Province, graduated from the Baoding Military Academy and rose quickly in rank thanks to the patronage of Duan Qirui. In 1917 he was sent to Hunan during the north–south hostilities, where he contributed little to the success of the northern armies. Despite this, when Duan Qirui once again became premier in March 1918, he proceeded to appoint Zhang Jingyao, a trusted member of the Anfu clique, governor of Hunan. Zhang's brutal nature and artibrary rule provoked the intense hatred of the Hunanese. The defeat of the Anfu clique by the Zhili clique in the continuing struggles among the warlords undermined Zhang's position, and he was obliged to flee the province at the end of June 1920.

3. Old name for Liaoning Province, or its capital, Shenyang, formerly Mukden.

4. For more details on Mr. You Yong and this incident, see the text of January 4, 1920.

5. I.e., the three cities making up the conurbation known as Wuhan: Wuchang, Hankou, and Hanyang.

recently been discovered and seized at the Wuhan railway station. When the news reached here, seven people, Yi Lirong, Li Weixiang, Zhang Maoxun, Chen Haiting, Yuan Dawei, Liu Shengdong, and Yang Bojuan, were delegated to go to the Zhanyutao station where they examined 50 big sacks, weighing over 200 *jin* each and totaling over 10,000 *jin*, all contained in gunny sacks. The students took a handful of seeds out of the sacks and shot a few photos for evidence. According to Zhao Fenglou, a police guard at the station, the seeds arrived more than ten days ago and were to be sent to Hunan and turned over to Military Governor Zhang. Since there was no permit accompanying them, the matter was reported to Military Governor Wang,[6] and the seeds were detained. Governor Wang has already cabled the central government asking for instructions on what to do with them. Whether they will be shipped or burned, concludes Zhao, depends entirely on the governor's orders. There is, however, as yet no news as to whether or not Governor Wang has actually cabled the central government. Some people say that another 25 sacks (about 5,000 *jin*) of the seeds sent from Fengtian by the Beijing–Wuhan line have reached their destination. The entire military escort (all Governor Zhang's men) has fled. Governor Zhang is reported to be exerting his influence on the Ministry of War for a permit to be issued to Wuhan so the seeds may be shipped to Hunan. The Wuhan Student Association has adopted a resolution, which will be sent to the central government in the form of an open telegram, and submitted to the governor as well. The Association of Hunan Students Residing in Hubei has also made preparations for issuing a telegraphic statement, and has made contact with the General Association of Fellow Hunan Provincials, suggesting at the same time that this can all be carried out today or tomorrow. The telegram of the Wuhan Student Association reads as follows: To all provincial assemblies, all provincial education societies, all provincial chambers of commerce, all newspaper offices, the General Student Association, all provincial student associations: Hunan Governor Zhang Jingyao, acting in collaboration with Zhang Zongchang, commander of the Sixth Mixed Brigade stationed in Hunan, has detached troops to escort with a permit a shipment of opium poppy seeds into Hunan to force the people to grow them in vast areas. The crime of bringing calamity to the nation and the people must not go unpunished. He has already brought in many shipments without being discovered. Yesterday, he brought yet another 50 sacks from the north to the Zhanyutao station in Wuchang, on the Wuhan–Changsha line, and brazenly demanded railway cars for their transport. Such flagrant actions as these truly display a total disregard for law and order. Fortunately, our association was informed by an attendant at the station, whereupon we promptly requested the station to detain the shipment. Apart from a special telegram we have sent to the president in

6. Wang Zhanyuan (1861–1934), *zi* Zichun, was born in Shandong Province. A former Beiyang Army leader and supporter of Yuan Shikai, he was at this time military governor of Hubei. In 1920, he became concurrently high commissioner of Hunan and Hubei.

Beijing asking him to send someone to investigate and deal with the matter, we are circulating this telegram to the people of the whole nation. Let us rally together and rise up against an affair in which there is already material evidence amounting to an ironclad case. We hope that our fellow countrymen will take immediate action.

Respectfully,
the Wuhan Student Association

Petition Opposing Zhang Jingyao's Secret Agreement to Sell the Mines

(December 27, 1919)

Petition submitted to the Presidential Office, the Cabinet, and the three Ministries of Foreign Affairs, Finance, and Agriculture and Commerce. We request that severe punishment be meted out to the officials who have signed a secret agreement to sell the mines, as a warning to corrupt officials and to protect the mining industry of Hunan. Most respectfully submitted.

We venture to inform you that Zhang Rongmei, director of the Hunan Mining Bureau, is a man of base character and greedy disposition. Taking advantage of his personal ties with the military governor of Hunan, Zhang Jingyao, he came to Hunan and was made the chief of the Administrative Department, an office for which he was not qualified, where he gained a bad reputation for helping the wicked and taking bribes. Then, coveting the huge profits of the Hunan mines, he schemed with ulterior motives to worm his way into the post of director of the Mining Bureau. In Governor Zhang's earlier secret talks with Grant,[1] an English businessman, about buying the province's mining rights, he in fact acted as the chief plotter, hoping to receive big bribes. Fortunately, the affair was discovered by the Ministry of Agriculture and Commerce and was opposed by all the people of Hunan, and the deal was terminated. Unbelievably, Zhang Rongmei did not give up his ambitions and continued to contrive all kinds of new schemes. He colluded secretly with Weigeke,[2] a German mining engineer of the Bureau at Shuikoushan, who introduced him to the American businessman Meyer Blukin,[3] and others, in order that they might use the name of a joint-capital venture in the

---

1. Archibald Morsley George Grant, a mining engineer, had concluded a draft agreement with Zhang Jingyao which would have given him a concession to develop all the mines in Hunan, except those already in operation, for a period of fifty years, for a sum of 30 million *yuan*. The terms of the agreement were extraordinarily generous, even to the point of exempting Grant from the effects of any mining laws which might in future be adopted by the government in Beijing. Public opposition prevented the deal from going ahead. For the text, see *The Far Eastern Review*, December 1919, pp. 781–82.

2. The transcription is "Wei-jia-ke"; Weigeke appears the most likely German name.

3. "Mai-yi-er Bu-liu-jin" was a trader with the American Pacific Enterprise Co. in Shanghai at this time. In December 1919 he signed a joint venture agreement concerning the Shuikoushan Zinc Smeltery with Zhang Rongmei. No English-language source has been found, and "Meyer Blukin (or Bljukhin?)" is merely a guess.

management of the Hunan Zinc Smeltery[4] as collateral for a loan. It is reported that, according to the loan contract, the Hunan government's stock shares are the lead ore, valued at U.S.$800,000, while the investment of the American businessmen is to be U.S.$1,400,000. Zhang Rongmei and the American businessmen secretly signed the draft agreement in Beijing at 1 P.M. on December twelfth of this year. The term is five years, at the end of which it may be extended for another ten years; during this term, the lead ore of Hunan Province is all to be sold to the Smeltery at U.S.$10 per ton. On the day of the signing of the draft agreement, U.S.$60,000 were paid in. It has been agreed that on the conclusion of the formal agreement, another U.S.$140,000 will be handed over. A limit of three weeks from the signing of the draft agreement is set for the formal agreement to be approved and sealed, after which time the contractual agreement will be null and void. It is known that the lead mine at Shuikoushan is the sole source of revenue for Hunan, and the zinc smeltery the sole lifeline of the province's mining industry. If it should ever fall into foreign hands, not only would the people of Hunan lose forever their last hope for relief, but the province would also lose forever the resources for regulating its finances. Zhang Rongmei has taken leave of his senses and, in pursuit of wealth to line his own pocket, he has rashly and with no qualms given away the important rights and interests of Hunan Province. This is an act of robbery and theft, a crime that can by no means go unpunished. The mining regulations stipulate that in all joint-capital mining ventures between Chinese and foreigners, both parties must remain equal in terms of capital, so as to protect the nation's sovereign rights. Under this contract the American businessmen would have an excess investment of U.S.$600,000, thus clearly violating the mining regulations by giving up sovereignty to the foreigners. That is the first reason why the Hunan people can never accept the contract. Shuikoushan in Hunan is one of the mines under provincial administration. This contract gives the Smeltery a purchasing monopoly and a pre-fixed price on the lead ore, so that the price is tied down by the contract, even if the market price of lead rises considerably in future. Thus the disaster of the contract made with the Japanese at Hanyeping will be repeated at Shuikoushan. Apart from the inevitable losses, the Smeltery's purchasing monopoly will in actuality turn Shuikoushan into an appendage of the Smeltery. Thus, in addition to the loss of the rights to the Smeltery, the mining rights are also forfeited. The consequences are too ghastly to contemplate. That is the second reason why the Hunan people can never accept it. Furthermore, seeing that the U.S.$200,000 that the American businessmen will have paid to the Hunan government on concluding the contract is clearly a loan against the joint-capital Smeltery, but the money is to be used for something other than the Smeltery, why is it that the Americans are so willing to render this service? What will Governor Zhang do with this money? No inquiry is needed to understand the

4. I.e., the Shuikoushan Zinc Smeltery.

inside story behind this murky deal. The insatiable greed of one or two corrupt officials is being satisfied by sacrificing the rights to the biggest mine in the province, before the people of Hunan are told anything about it. That is the third reason that the Hunan people can never accept it. All in all, this agreement concluded by Zhang Rongmei is a joint-capital mining enterprise in name, but in reality it is a sellout of the mining rights. Governor Zhang's two-year tyrannical rule over Hunan has been marked by vicious exploitation of every possible kind. Zhang Rongmei plays the jackal to his evil superior and is so intent on profit-making that he gives not the least consideration to the public welfare or to the miseries of the people. Who could trust a person capable of such deceit? The millions of Hunan people who have suffered hardship and misery throughout their entire lives see that unlike other short-term embezzlements this contract will have endless consequences, affecting not just themselves but their sons and grandsons as well, not just a few individuals but the whole population. The masses are angry and indignant, and would rather die than accept it. Three weeks will pass in a twinkling. It is still possible now to annul the contract without endangering our foreign relations. We beseech Your Excellency (and distinguished premier and ministers) to condescend to take up the matter personally. Please cable Governor Zhang before the contract is sealed, instructing him to annul the draft agreement immediately, return the money, and withdraw from the arrangement. Ask the governor also to dismiss Zhang Rongmei from office, and to punish him as a warning to corrupt officials, and to protect the mining administration. We urgently await your instructions. Submitted to the president[5] (and to the Cabinet, Ministry of Foreign Affairs, Ministry of Finance, and Ministry of Agriculture and Commerce), with greatest respect.[6]

Hunan citizens residing in Beijing:
Mao Zedong, Zhang Boling, Wu Qilin,
Chen Shaoxiu, Wang Yunjun, Zhao Xianpu,
Liu Tianhui, Huang Dugu, Bin Zuoshi,
Zuo Du

---

5. The president of the Beijing Government at this time was Xu Shichang (1855–1939), *zi* Bowu, *hao* Juren, an ex-Qing bureaucrat who was elected president by the Anfu parliament on September 4, 1918. He was forced to resign after the Zhili-Fengtian War of 1922 when Li Yuanhong resumed the presidency.

6. For background information regarding the Shuikoushan lead and zinc mines, and more generally on the economic and political foundations of Zhang Jingyao's rule, see Angus McDonald, *The Urban Origins of Rural Revolution* (Berkeley: University of California Press, 1978), especially pp. 34–35 and 188–89.

Public Indignation of the Hunan People at Zhang Jingyao's Smuggling of Opium Seeds

(December 31, 1919)[1]

The case was recounted in our earlier report that Zhang Jingyao, the military governor of Hunan, in collusion with Zhang Zongchang,[2] had illegally shipped from Fengtian a large quantity of poppy seeds, which were discovered and detained at the Zhanyutao station near Wuchang. It is known that the Hunanese residing in Beijing are enraged by this matter, and the Association of Hunan Students Residing in Beijing[3] has already dispatched three telegrams, one to Wang Zhanyuan, one to the inspector of the Jianghan Tax Office, and one to the Hunan Anti-Opium Society.[4] The Hunan petition delegates who went to Beijing have also sent three telegrams: (1) To Hubei Military Governor Wang: Hunan Governor Zhang Jingyao's smuggling of opium seeds, fortunately, has been uncovered. You are earnestly requested to pursue this rigorously and not to allow him to get away with it. Otherwise, if evildoing is indulged and the law subverted, Your Excellency cannot but be held responsible. Respectfully, the Hunan Petition Delegation. (2) To the Wuhan Student Association, care of Mr. Yi Lirong,[5] Mingde University, Dazhi Gate, Hankou: Fortunately, you gentlemen have discovered the poppy seeds shipped secretly by Zhang Jingyao. Please guard them with your lives and do not let him get away with this. As your fellow Hunanese, we pledge to back you up. Respectfully, the Hunan Petition Delegation. (3) To the Changsha Anti-Opium Society: There are forty-five sacks of

1. In the *Mao Zedong ji*, this document is dated January 6, 1920, the day it was published in the *Shenbao* (Shanghai Daily News). According to the *Wengao*, the correct date of composition is as shown here, and the dispatch was distributed on January 2, 1920.

2. Zhang Zongchang (1881–1932), *zi* Xiaokun, from Shandong Province, was at this time a commander in the Beiyang Army. He and members of his forces escorted Zhang Jingyao's opium shipments from Fengtian to Wuchang.

3. This was an association in support of ousting Zhang Jingyao formed in November 1919 by Hunan students resident in Beijing.

4. This Society was formed on November 18, 1919, in Changsha by the Hunan Christian Association (Hunan jidujiao gegonghui) and aimed to "assist the government in the prohibition of opium."

5. At this time Yi Lirong was living in Hankou at Mingde University and was working as liaison officer in Hubei for the Hunan Petition Delegation. For more details on Yi Lirong, see the note to Mao's response to a letter from him dated November 1920.

opium seeds at the Zhanyutao station in Wuchang, which were about to be shipped into Hunan but have been detained. Please send an investigation team to Hubei to examine them and administer justice. Respectfully, the Hunan Petition Delegation. Mr. Yi, representative from Hankou, arrived in Beijing on the thirtieth and immediately reported this to the International Anti-Opium Society.[6] On the thirty-first, he went to call on Premier Jin,[7] and was received by his secretary, Wang.[8] He related the story of the discovery of the poppy seeds, and asked if the government had received the telegrams from Governor Wang and from the Wuhan Student Association. Secretary Wang replied: The telegrams may possibly have arrived, but I have not yet seen them. I would be glad to let the premier know the purpose of your visit. Because the premier is very busy at the turn of the year, he is unable to receive you in person. In the meantime, representatives of the students residing in Beijing, Yi Xiangyang, Li Shi, and Miss Yang Rongzhen, also came to see Mr. Jin. In addition, Hunan citizens residing in Beijing Peng Huang and Zhang Boling also went to the Cabinet on the same matter. In short, Hunanese residing in Beijing are greatly concerned at this incident.

There follows a copy of the statement submitted by the Hunanese residing in Beijing:

We sincerely request that the military governor, who is violating the prohibition and is smuggling opium, be removed from office and punished, so that the nation's laws may be observed fully and the lives of the people may be saved. Ever since his arrival in Hunan, Hunan Governor Zhang Jingyao has ignored the will of the people, and his evil actions of all kinds are too numerous to relate. The one that will have the most pernicious effects is opium. From the day of his arrival in Hunan, the ban on opium has been widely ignored. The number of opium-smokers, among both the gentry and the common people, has increased greatly. No one knows what quantity of opium and poppy seeds has been shipped into Hunan from other parts of the country. Governor Zhang has encouraged the people to grow opium. He summoned the *xian* military commanders, distributed the seeds to them, and ordered that they be planted. In the single *xian* of Changsha, as many as 40,000 packets of seeds were handed out. The people of Hunan have been puzzled as to the means by which such large quantities of seeds have been smuggled in under so strict a ban on opium, but had long sought in vain to obtain evidence of this traffic. On December 24, a large amount of poppy seeds was discovered at the Zhanyutao station in Wuchang. There were 45 gunny sacks weighing about 200 *jin* each. The sacks were marked: Dis-

---

6. This organization was formed in Shanghai on January 17, 1919.

7. Jin Yunpeng (1876–1951), *zi* Yiqing, from Shandong Province, graduate of the Beiyang Military College, former Beiyang Army commander and governor of Shandong, was at this time premier of the Beijing Government.

8. I.e., Wang Lei.

patched from Fengtian to the general command headquarters of the Second Route Army of Hunan for inspection and receipt. The station attendant You Yong[9] reported this information. He wrote an emotional letter of accusation; the Wuhan Student Association and Hunan students residing in Hubei took photographs and kept some of the seeds as evidence, and also informed the Cabinet and notified the whole nation of the case. For many days in succession, the Beijing and Wuhan newspapers have given it full coverage. This is a case of openly defying the national prohibition and flying in the face of world condemnation, smuggling the poisonous stuff and bringing disaster to the whole of Hunan. Having learned of this, the Hunan people are filled with rage. In a matter that affects international relations as well as a major national prohibition, we respectfully urge the Cabinet to petition the president without delay to announce publicly that Hunan Governor Zhang Jingyao is to be dismissed from office and handed over to the courts to be punished according to law, so that the nation's laws are fully observed and the people of Hunan may be saved. We urgently await your instructions. Respectfully submitted to the premier.

Lou Shaokai, Peng Huang, Xiao Ba,
Mao Zedong, Chen Shaoxiu

Hunan citizens residing in Beijing:

Ouyang Jiaoru, Luo Zonghan, Xiong Guangchu, Wu Junchen, Chen Wen'ne, Zhang Boling, Wang Renda,[10] Peng Xianze, Liu Mingyan[11]

December 31, 1919

(People's News Agency dispatch no. 10, January 2, 1920)

---

9. On You Yong, see the note to the text dated January 4, 1920.

10. Wang Renda, a Hunanese, was one of the youths who went to France on the work-study program. He joined the Socialist Youth Corps in 1922, and the Chinese Communist Party in 1924.

11. Liu Mingyan (1899–1977), also known as Wangcheng or Ruoyun, a Hunanese, was a classmate of Mao at First Normal School and an early member of the New People's Study Society. In 1920 he went to France on the work-study program. He was one of the organizers of the Socialist Youth Corps in France (with Zhou Enlai, Wang Ruofei, and others).

Zhang Jingyao Smuggles Opium Seeds (continued)

(People's News Agency dispatch, January 4, 1920)

A report from the People's News Agency states: Our previous dispatch has already reported that Zhang Jingyao was discovered smuggling a large quantity of opium poppy seeds at the Zhanyutao railroad station in Wuchang. Since their discovery, these seeds are said to have attracted widespread attention among all circles of people in Wuhan and among the Hunanese residing in Beijing. The following is a more detailed report. Opium poppy seeds had already been shipped to Hunan on the Beijing-Wuhan line more than once before, but had never been discovered. Zhang Jingyao, in forcing the planting of the poppy seedlings, had called together [X] head [X] of the *xian* [X] and ordered as many as 40,000 packets [of seeds] to be planted in the single *xian* of Changsha. The people of Hunan have been puzzled as to the means by which such large quantities of seeds have been smuggled in, but had long sought in vain to obtain any evidence of this traffic. The present large quantity of poppy seeds shipped from Fengtian, originally 70 or more sacks in all, arrived in Hubei before December 20. People at the station have asserted that 25 sacks were sent on prior to December 24. On the twenty-fourth, the rest were discovered by the railway attendant Mr. You Yong at the Zhanyutao station, when they were transferred from the Beijing-Wuhan line to the Wuhan-Changsha line. (Yesterday's dispatch mistook You for a student.[1] Mr. You, whose *hao* is Runtao, is from Minhou, Fujian Province.) There were 45 gunny sacks weighing over 200 *jin* each. Marked on the bags were the words, "For the attention of the general command headquarters of the Second Route Army." The commander of the Second Route Army is Zhang Zongchang. But the men who were escorting the seeds said before the discovery: "These items are being sent to Changsha to be turned over to Governor Zhang." As soon as the discovery was made, the escort immediately fled and disappeared. Most likely, when these items sent from Fengtian reached Hunan, they were to be received by Zhang Zongchang and then turned over to Zhang Jingyao.

On the twenty-sixth, leaflets were printed by representatives of the Wuhan

---

1. The reference is to the text dated December 24, 1919, which was published in the *Shenbao* on January 3, 1920, and refers to You as a student from Fujian. He was in fact, as stated below, a graduate of the Railway Management School of the Ministry of Communications.

Student Association. One of the leaflets was signed at the bottom: With tears of blood, respectfully reported, You Yong, graduate of the Railway Management School of the Communications Ministry. The full text reads:

"On the twenty-third of this month, the subordinates of Zhang Zongchang, the commander of the Sixth Mixed Brigade stationed in Hunan Province, escorting forty-five sacks of opium poppy seeds, arrived at the Zhanyutao station and asked the Hunan–Hubei Railroad Bureau for cars in preparation for sending them to Hunan. It is a story modeled on Chen Shufan's[2] example. Zhang Jingyao grows poppy extensively throughout Hunan in order to make a huge profit; in order to provide for his army for five years, he is sowing the seeds of an evil fruit that will hurt China for tens of thousands of years, bringing calamity to the country and misery to its people, a crime that must not escape punishment. If the seeds are not burned today, the whole country will suffer disaster when the poppy flowers next year. Having notified the Wuhan Student Association, together with the students, I am watching over the seeds, and at the same time I have sent a cable requesting the government to remove Governor Zhang of Hunan from office and punish Zhang Zongchang. Alas! The military have brought disaster upon the nation for far too long. And Chen Shufan and Zhang Jingyao are especially vicious. However, to the urgent petition of the people the government has paid no heed, but rather glosses over their crimes. This evidence today is irrefutable proof of their crime. At the risk of death, I have tried to entreat the government. Elders, brothers and sisters, of the whole country, rise up together against it. With tears of blood, respectfully reported, You Yong, graduate of the Railway Management School of the Communications Ministry."

As soon as the Wuhan students heard this news, a large group of them went right away to the station to investigate. When the Hunan students residing in Hubei learned of this shipping of poppy seeds, they redoubled their efforts. On the morning of the twenty-fourth, Yi Lirong, a student of Mingde University in Hankou, Luo Jian, a student of the Higher Normal School, and some others went to the station and removed a small quantity of the opium seeds. In addition, they sent a photographer to the station that afternoon to take pictures of the poisonous stuff. At first, the stationmaster forbade them to do this, and they only got permission after considerable [X] effort. No sooner had they taken the photos than soldiers suddenly arrived, snatched away the film, and sought to apprehend Yi Lirong. Fortunately, a station attendant who had heard of the plan a bit earlier opened a back door, through which Mr. Yi escaped in disguise. When the incident became known, the Hunan students residing in Hubei were extremely indignant. They promptly sent a petition to Wang Zhanyuan, the military governor of Hubei, reading:

2. Chen Shufan, *zi* Bosheng, was military governor of his native province, Shaanxi, from 1915 to 1921. As governor he kept most of the revenue from the heavy opium tax he imposed in the province, thus amassing a large personal fortune.

We respectfully request that the opium poppy seeds be confiscated and burned at once. While seeing a friend off to Hunan at the Zhanyutao railroad station at 4 P.M. on the twenty-fifth of this month, [X] happened to notice in the railway warehouse a pile of forty-five gunny sacks marked for shipment to Hunan. Upon closer inspection, he discovered they all contained opium poppy seeds, whereupon he took some as a sample to present to you for [X]. We understand that, since the ban on opium in our country, the government has vigorously pursued the state policy of proper punishment for smugglers. If such a large quantity of poppy seeds as has been uncovered in the railway warehouse is allowed to be shipped to Hunan and sown among the people, not only will the success the state has achieved in banning opium be ruined overnight, but also 30 million people in Hunan will be destroyed by the opium poison. Furthermore, there is the treaty signed with the British banning opium. If shipments are allowed to pass freely, it will seriously harm the nation and give other people a real excuse. Therefore we request that you send someone to investigate, and that the opium seeds be confiscated and burned, so as to avert future disaster. We would be most grateful if Your Excellency would do as we implore, look into the matter thoroughly, find out by whom the seeds are being smuggled, and expose the arch criminal [X] according to the laws of China. This petition is submitted to Military Governor Wang by the Hunan students residing in Hubei.

The telegram sent to the government reads: To the president and the Ministry of Internal Affairs in Beijing: We students have inspected forty-five sacks of poppy seeds found at the Zhanyutao station for transhipment to Hunan. [XX] Hubei, [X] be confiscated and burned. Respectfully, the Hunan students residing in Hubei.

The Hunan students residing in Hubei, fully conscious of the seriousness of the case, selected Mr. Yi Lirong on the twenty-ninth as their representative to go to Beijing to petition [X] the government, [X] the law. Please allow us to report at a later time on his actions in Beijing and on the indignation of the Hunan people residing in Beijing.

Letter to Yi Lirong

(January 13, 1920)

Elder Brother Runsheng:

I received your letter two days ago, and sent you a reply yesterday. I expect it has reached you. I hear Mr. Zhang Shen'an[1] of Changsha is coming to Beijing. When he passes through Wuhan, please hand him a letter from me. There is little to do in Beijing. It is better that Zhang not come to Beijing, but go straight to Shanghai. Please give him this message.

Your younger brother
Zedong

1. Zhang Xiaomin, *zi* Shen'an, was editor-in-chief of the Changsha *Minzhi ribao* (People's Rule Daily). He later settled in America.

Expel Zhang Jingyao: Express Communiqué

(January 18, 1920)[1]

To: Mr. Xiong Binsan, Mr. Fan Jingsheng, Mr. Guo Tongbo, and Mr. Liu Aitang in Tianjin; Mr. Zhang Qiutong, Mr. Peng Yunyi,[2] and Mr. Xu Fosu[3] in Shanghai; Mr. Tan Zu'an in Chenzhou; the Hunan Reconstruction Association of Shanghai;[4] the Hunan Fund-Raising Society of Beijing;[5] the associations of Hunan students residing in Beijing, Shanghai, Nanjing, Hubei, Tianjin, and Guangdong; to the Union of All Circles, to all societies of fellow provincials, and to all fellow Hunanese in all parts of China, for their perusal.

Alas, our Hunan, ravaged by repeated wars for many years, presents a scene of utter devastation. Since coming to Hunan last year, Zhang Jingyao has unleashed his troops of hungry wolves, raping, burning, looting, and killing, and has given free rein to his government, a fierce tiger that pillages, plunders, cheats, and exacts taxes. Public lands, reclaimed paddies,[6] mines, and textile

---

1. This date has been adopted instead of that given in the *Mao Zedong ji* (December 18, 1919), because, as indicated in the *Wengao* (note 1, p. 657), many of the organizations referred to had not yet been founded in December 1919. The *Mao Zedong ji. Bujuan* in fact prints it twice, once (Vol. 1, pp. 173–74) under December 18, 1919, and once (Vol. 9, pp. 89–90) under May 24, 1920, which is the date it was reprinted in the Shanghai *Minguo ribao* (Republican Daily).

2. Peng Yunyi (1878–1943), *zi* Jingren, Hunanese educator, subsequently became minister of education in the Beijing government.

3. Xu Fosu (1879–1943), *zi* Yunkui, from Changsha, Hunan, studied in Japan. He was an early associate of Liang Qichao, and an ardent advocate of constitutional government. While a political councilor in the government of Yuan Shikai, he was instrumental in the overthrow of Yuan's monarchical movement. In September 1918 Xu was elected president of the New Parliament, and at this time was a member of the northern delegation to the North–South Peace Conference. He retained ties with Hunan and in 1920 was one of those who drafted the new Hunan provincial constitution which was adopted by the Provisional Assembly. Subsequently, he devoted his energies to the promotion of a federal system throughout the different provinces.

4. The Hunan Reconstruction Association (Hunan shanhouhui) of Shanghai was an anti-Zhang organization set up by upper-class Hunanese in December 1918. It called for the removal of Zhang Jingyao as a precondition for solving the problems of Hunan. It published the book *A Brief Account of Calamity in Hunan.*

5. This Society was organized to raise funds for Hunan, and at this time its director was Xiong Xiling.

6. *Hutian,* literally "lake paddies," are low-lying rice paddies reclaimed from lakes, and surrounded by dikes.

mills have been sold off, exhausting all the public property. Taxes have been raised on rice, salt, paper, and land, wringing the people dry. By now, the rich have become poor and the poor are dying, their stories of misery and destitution so bitter that one cannot bear listening to them. The thieving Zhang brothers[7] have each amassed tens of millions, yet far from being satiated, they are now planning to seize for their private purses the only thing remaining, the public rice and salt fund. Last year, thief Zhang instigated Li Mingjiu, a Hunan ruffian, and others to cable Beijing to inquire about the fund, and in Changsha he set up a Rice and Salt Public Stock Inspection Office. It is reported that he recently bribed Guo Renzhang[8] and others, in the name of the Association for Assisting Hunanese Travelers in Beijing,[9] to inquire of Mr. Xiong Binsan concerning this fund. There was no reason for this provocative action. Their intention, as can be inferred, is none other than the seizure of all Hunan public property, devouring the Hunan people in order to satisfy their avaricious greed. How can our Hunan, which has suffered such terrible blows, and those who have survived this misery be revived without this substantial amount of money? The public rice and salt fund represents savings we 30 million people have put aside by enduring hunger and living on simple food. It was not easy to come by, and will be very useful in many ways. Were the money to be gobbled up, it would be very difficult to get it back. The thieving Zhangs have long been ruthlessly and cruelly hurting us Hunanese. What is hard to understand is why some people, who eat the same food grown from the same land with us, would be so degenerate, would destroy the land of our parents, and serve as lackeys to our hated foe. That a human being can fall so low! The citizens will never accept this vicious conduct of Guo Renzhang and the others. In sum, until Bandit Zhang is removed from office and the disturbances in Hunan resolved, there is no alternative but to put this fund temporarily under the care of the Hunan gentry, where it must not be touched. When social order is restored in Hunan, let the use of the money be decided according to the will of the people of the whole province. If, during this time, any shameless person should attempt to do otherwise, he shall be regarded as a public enemy. All our people of Hunan must be conscious of defending our-

---

7. This is a reference to Zhang Jingyao and his brothers Jingshun, Jingyu, and Jingtang. The given names of the brothers (Yao, Shun, Yu, and Tang) are those of the legendary sage kings of Chinese antiquity. There was also an adopted son Jizhong; all were made officers in Zhang Jingyao's army.

8. Guo Renzhang, *zi* Baosheng, was from Xiangtan, Hunan. While circuit intendant of Shanxi, he had been dismissed on grounds of corruption. He was an influential member of the Hunan gentry who had good connections with those in government and was once head of the Hunan Mining Bureau.

9. This Association was set up by Guo Renzhang and others in Beijing to protect Zhang Jingyao and his position as governor of Hunan. It became known as the Protect-Zhang Clique (Bao Zhang tuan). It was made up mostly of landlords in the pay of Zhang, and Anfu clique politicians.

selves; relax our grip in the slightest and all is lost. Pray be vigilant! Respectfully submitted, representatives of the citizens of Hunan: Luo Zonghan,[10] Mao Zedong, Peng Huang, Zhang Huai,[11] He Shuheng,[12] Kuang Rixiu;[13] representatives of the teaching faculty and staff: Luo Jiaoduo,[14] Zhang Jingyun, Yang Yufu, Jiang Yuhuan, Xiong Mengfei;[15] representatives of the students: Liu Min, Gao Biao, Xiong Kexian, Li Simi, Ouyang Jiaoru, Li Si'an, Peng Xianze, Gao Yeru, Li Zhenpian,[16] Li Qihan,[17] Li Guojun, Li Gongjia, Huang Ying, Hu Weiyin, Li Caiju, Wang Guolin, He Yuanpei, Zhang Xinmin, Chen Zonghan, Liu Zuozhou, Chen Chuncui,[18] Mao Douwen, Yi Xun, Yi Kexun, Yi Jieyi, Liao Ruixiang, Liang Guoqian, Miao Kunshan, Jiang Zhuru,[19] Xiong Keqi, Xiong Zhuowu, Wei Xianlie, Li Zonglie, Qiu Weiqin, Lin Yunyuan, Xu Qingyu, Zhang Shusheng, Fu Diliang, Zhong Xiu, Xu Ying, Cao Yangli, Wu Junchen, Chen Shiquan, Peng Guangqiu.

---

10. Luo Zonghan (1896–1927), also known as Zhiyu, was born in Anhua, Hunan. He was a student of Hunan First Normal School, and an active participant in the New People's Study Society.

11. Zhang Huai (1896–), also known as Boling, was a native of Changsha. He was a student of Hunan First Normal School and an early member of the New People's Study Society. In early 1920 he went to Beijing as a member of the expel Zhang Jingyao delegation, and worked as a reporter for the People's News Agency. In May 1920 he went to France on the work-study program.

12. He Shuheng, also known as He Zhanggu. For details, see note to the text of February 19, 1920.

13. A native of Hunan, Kuang Rixiu was a student at Beijing Normal University at the time of the May Fourth movement, and a participant in the movement. He joined the New People's Study Society and was active in the struggle to oust Zhang Jingyao.

14. Luo Jiaoduo was a member of the urban gentry and leader of a "common man's educational movement" in Changsha in the early 1920s. In October 1921 he established a free school devoted to middle school extension using provincial funds.

15. Xiong Mengfei (1895-?), also known as Ren'an, was born in Ningxiang, Hunan. He was an active member of the New People's Study Society. He was arrested as a counterrevolutionary in 1949, and died soon afterward.

16. Li Zhenpien, also known as Chengde, a native of Hunan, was a student of the Hunan-Yale Medical School. He later went to America to study.

17. Li Qihan (1898–1927), also known as Li Junhan and Li Sen, was born in Hunan, and was a member of the New People's Study Society.

18. Chen Chuncui (1896–1951), also known as Tianmin and Shouzhen, was born in Jiangxi, and was a member of the New People's Study Society.

19. Jiang Zhuru (1899–1967), also known as Jixu, Weiwan, and Qingpu, was born in Xiangtan, Hunan. He was a classmate of Mao's at First Normal School, and a member of the New People's Study Society.

Appeal to the Central Government in Beijing by Hunanese Citizens in All Walks of Life Accusing Zhang Jingyao of Ten Major Crimes

(January 19, 1920)

Chen Shaoxiu and other citizens from all circles in Hunan accuse Zhang Jingyao of ten major crimes and urge the Central Government in Beijing to dismiss him immediately from office. Their appeal reads as follows:

As the disaster in Hunan is now extreme, and the people are suffering miserably, we appeal urgently and sincerely to the Central Government to dismiss the governor of Hunan from office and punish him, so as to maintain the law and rescue the people from calamity. In recent years, Hunan has constantly met with catastrophes. Slaughtered and robbed by the former governor, Tang Xiangming,[1] the people of Hunan have long lived in tragic circumstances. The mutiny at Lingning brought war throughout the province.[2] Since Zhang Jingyao came in April 1918, the people of Hunan have further sunk into disaster. Here we present to you the facts about Governor Zhang's crimes and hope the central government will be able to perceive the misery that the people of Hunan have suffered. Beginning in May 1918, the entire town of Yuling, amounting to more than ten thousand houses, was burned down. The conflagration also spread to the outskirts and continued for ten days. In Zhuzhou alone, several thousand shops were ransacked at the same time. During the battle of Huangtu Hill in You *xian*, so many women were raped and died that their bodies covered the hill, while tens of thousands were massacred.[3] Even the most remote villages could not escape being ransacked by Zhang's troops. Unable to return home, people are forced to live in exile. The dead cannot be buried, while the living have no place to stay. With the greater part of the buildings burned down, and nine out of ten dwellings

1. On Tang Xiangming, see the note to Mao's letter of July 18, 1916.

2. The Lingning garrison under the command of Liu Jianfan declared the independence of Hunan on September 18, 1919, and at this time severed all relations with the Duan Qirui government.

3. Huangtu Hill is situated 45 kilometers north of the capital of You *xian*, on the border of Liling *xian*, on the north–south route. Because of this location, Huangtu Hill became a stronghold for both armies, of the north and the south, and fierce fighting resulted there.

empty, conditions in Yuzhou and Baoqing[4] are too horrible to contemplate. One might think that this calamity was caused by war and that the devastated areas were too remote for Zhang to control. But things are just the same in Changsha, where Zhang's headquarters are located. Robberies by Zhang's soldiers occur every day, and his younger brother Zhang Jingtang is frequently seen to seize goods from shops without paying a single copper cash. The contingents sent by Zhang to the nearby countryside often arrest innocent people at will and then extort money from their families and relatives. The price to redeem one person is from one thousand to several thousand *yuan.* There is plenty of evidence of such cases. The disorders have ruined the livelihood of the Hunan people, but now they are again heavily exploited by Zhang and are forced to sell wives and children to pay the excessive taxes and levies. There is not even a single day of peace as Zhang's soldiers go out every day in groups to ransack households with the excuse of searching for bandits. As a result, peasants cannot farm, nor are merchants able to take care of their business. Letting soldiers tyrannize the people and bring calamity to them is Zhang's first crime. There used to be the Bank of Hunan, which issued bank notes in the province. On his arrival, Governor Zhang abolished the Bank of Hunan and replaced it with a bank of his own, the Yuxiang Bank,[5] to absorb currency. His brother Jingtang[6] has also set up a bank named the Rixin Bank to monopolize the financial market. By purchasing copper coins in Hunan and selling them in Wuhan, he has made huge profits. Moreover, invalidating over 40 million *yuan* in Bank of Hunan notes, Zhang issued "Benefit the People"[7] lottery tickets and ordered them to be distributed throughout the province to absorb Bank of Hunan notes as well as other currency. When the outcome of the lottery was declared, however, few who got the winning numbers were given the prizes. In this way, as savings are taken away and the bank notes become invalidated, people have nothing left and the finan-

---

4. In the spring of 1918, during the war between the north and the south, the towns of Yuzhou and Baoqing were set on fire by troops, and two to three thousand residents were killed in their sleep.

5. The Yuxiang Bank was set up by Zhang Jingyao in August 1918. It was organized without any real assets, and Zhang's deputy Xu Kechang was made supervisor; it was obviously a means by which Zhang could accumulate private wealth.

6. Zhang Jingtang, fourth younger brother of Zhang Jingyao who, along with two other brothers (Jingshun, Jingyu), was made an officer in Zhang Jingyao's army. Jingtang was known as the "Fourth General" and was the most infamous of them all for tyrannical rule, abuse of power and venality, as well as being showy and flamboyant.

7. In November 1918 Zhang Jingyao ordered the Bank of Hunan Stock Department to issue two million lottery tickets to distribute amongst the people at a cost of five *yuan* each. According to an article in the *Dagongbao*, the aim of the tickets was to recall bank notes, as during the year too many had been issued, their value had dropped, and the price of many goods had risen. They were called "*Huimin*" as they were supposedly designed to "benefit the people" in this way. Many people complained, but Zhang enforced a rigid apportionment policy, causing widespread discontent.

cial resources of Hunan are exhausted. This is Zhang's second crime. After illegally leasing the Shuikoushan Lead Mine to foreigners,[8] Governor Zhang has again handed over the lead-smelting factory to American businessmen as pledge for 1.4 million *yuan.* In addition, despite the strong protest from the people throughout Hunan, Zhang has leased all mines in Hunan to the British merchant Grant for 30 million *yuan*[9] and sold the Hunan Textile Factory to a Tianjin merchant at the price of 1.5 million *yuan.* The reclaimed paddies owned by the Bank of Hunan were also sold by him for 200,000 *yuan.* Both the national and private enterprises in Hunan have now gone into bankruptcy and can never be recovered. These acts are Zhang's third crime. Hunan used to be known for its strict ban on opium-smoking and the opium trade, and there had been no opium-smoking and no opium-growing throughout the province since the founding of the Republic. However, that good practice is gone because Governor Zhang is an opium addict himself, and most of the officers and soldiers in his army are also addicted to opium. Zhang recently has even ordered people to grow opium. Under his order, there must be 40 *mu* of opium per 100 *mu* of land, and Zhang levies 20 *yuan* on every *mu* of opium. In Changsha *xian* alone, 40,000 packets of opium seeds have been planted. Not long ago, Zhang brought 45 sacks of poppy seeds from Liaoning, but they were confiscated at the Zhanyutao Railway Station in Wuchang on the way to Hunan. The case was brought to court, people all over the country were outraged, and even foreigners lodged protests. Nevertheless, Governor Zhang used his troops to seize the seeds. If the situation continues, it will not only make Hunan an opium-addicted province, but also cause diplomatic disputes, ruin the image of our country abroad, and make China a laughingstock all over the world. This is Zhang's fourth crime. Governor Zhang has drastically cut the budget for education since he came to Hunan. He withheld the fund set up in the term of former Governor Tan as the annual award for meritorious primary school teachers, and then paid only 40 to 60 percent of the money, and even completely stopped payment from January 1919. When teachers of various schools went on strike last October to protest against withholding funds for education, Zhang spread rumors at will to slander the teachers, ordered soldiers to beat students, and drove educational personnel out of office, thus causing a boycott of classes throughout the schools of Hunan. In addition, he has used schools as barracks for his army since he came to Hunan. As school buildings have been destroyed and facilities damaged, students now cannot go to school or have classes. This is Zhang's fifth crime. Governor Zhang's soldiers

8. The Shuikoushan mine was the largest mine under provincial government ownership in 1918. In December 1919 Zhao's Beijing representative signed a draft contract with the American Pacific Enterprise Co. for transfer of the mines to joint ownership in return for American investment. A protest in Beijing blocked the deal. For further details, see the text dated December 27, 1919.

9. For further details see the text of December 27, 1919.

often commit crimes. But once they are caught, Zhang always frames innocent citizens to protect his soldiers. This notorious practice has been frequently exposed by the press. Last July, Wu Canhuang, a Hunanese, returned to Changsha from Shanghai with his friend Cheng Peng and lived in Chuanshan School. Because Wu was a member of the Shanghai National Assembly, Zhang had his adopted son Zhang Jizhong[10] lead soldiers to break into the school at midnight and to bayonet Wu and Cheng to death.[11] Assassinating citizens and deliberately trampling on the law is Zhang's sixth crime. The *Dagongbao* in Changsha and the *Hunan Gazette*[12] have been closed twice by Zhang because they supported public opinion.The *Xiang River Review*, a journal of academic research published by the United Students' Association, was likewise shut down. Various weekly school journals were also banned. The people of Hunan feel bitterly angered but dare not speak out because freedom of speech has been completely swept into the dust. This is Zhang's seventh crime. There is evidence in the form of a telegram issued by the ministry concerned that Governor Zhang appropriated several thousand bags of salt, which were confiscated by the Beijing–Hankou Railway. Furthermore, on every bag of salt sold in Hunan, a one-yuan tax is levied, in addition to the three-yuan handling and shipping fee. As a result, the price of salt has risen sharply, and average people cannot afford to buy salt for cooking. Violating the laws governing the sale of salt and defying the authority of the central government constitute Zhang's eighth crime. Governor Zhang frequently extorts money from the merchants and gentry in Changsha and in many other *xian* to pay for his army. The figure is often as high as several million *yuan*. In Xiangxiang *xian* alone, he has extorted 5 million piculs of rice for his troops. He secretly transported to Tianjin 100 million piculs of rice taken from the people of Hunan to sell to Japan, but was repeatedly obstructed by the gentry of Hunan. There are documents to prove all of this. Zhang has seized the ship *Huasheng* [Prosperous China] from the China Merchants' Steam Navigation Company. Claiming to be a "meritorious official" himself, he has renamed the ship *Xunhua* [Meritorious China] and put it under his ownership. As for land tax in the various *xian*, 20 to 50 *fen* have been added for each *yuan* collected. In some cases, the levy has even been doubled. The people's livelihood in rural areas has

---

10. Zhang Jizhong, original name Mao Sizhong, was the adopted son of Zhang Jingyao. At this time he was a troop commander in Zhang Jiangyao's army.

11. Wu Canhuang, a Hunanese from Pingjiang, was executive secretary of the Shanghai National Assembly and director of the China Industry Association. Cheng Peng, from Anhui Province, was a special representative of the Industry Association. They were in Hunan to organize a similar Assembly, and to make preparations for setting up a Hunan branch of the Industry Association. Zhang Jingyao feigned sympathy for their cause, but on the night of August 16 they were killed in the circumstances described by Mao.

12. This should read *Hunan Daily* (Hunan ribao), as the *Hunan Gazette* (Hunan gongbao) ceased publication in 1916 after the death of Yuan Shikai.

been extremely meager since the war, and the produce of the land is insufficient to maintain their livelihood. Nevertheless, regardless of the misery of the people, Governor Zhang grabs the spoils without taking part in the robbery. This is his ninth crime. Governor Zhang has controlled only about 20 of the more than 70 *xian* in Hunan, but he falsely claimed to rule them all and forged votes accordingly to reelect the Provincial Parliament. The election has been repeatedly denounced by the people of Hunan in telegrams. Also, the Provincial Council on Education was originally an unofficial[13] organization, but after this reelection, Governor Zhang had the officials run it on his behalf, thus creating a *fait accompli*. He has also dismissed the former president of the Hunan Agricultural Association.[14] Falsifying public opinion and sabotaging social organizations to serve his own interests constitute Zhang's tenth crime. The aforementioned facts are only a brief account of Zhang's ten crimes. The details are reported in *A Brief Account of Calamity in Hunan*, *A Brief Record of War Disasters in Liling*, *A Brief Record of War Disasters in Baoqing*, and the monthly *Hunan*,[15] as well as other sources. Evidence of Zhang's crimes is also recorded in many previous appeals and telegrams from the Hunan United Reconstruction Association of the gentry, and by student representatives. We hold that Governor Zhang is the source of all the disasters in Hunan and is guilty of the most heinous crimes. Because of the calamities brought by him, the people of Hunan have suffered beyond description. As long as he stays in Hunan, the people will live in an endless abyss of misery. If the central government still considers Hunan part of the Republic of China and the people of Hunan as Chinese citizens, it ought to remove the tyrant in order to save the people. It definitely has this responsibility. We hereby sincerely urge the president and the cabinet to take into consideration this and our previous earnest appeals, to dismiss Governor Zhang Jingyao of Hunan promptly, to transfer him back to Beijing, and to punish him to the full extent of the law. It is our strong hope that you can appoint an honest and capable official to replace him, so as to satisfy the people's demands and their urgent needs.

Respectfully submitted to the president and the premier[16] by citizens from all circles of Hunan:

Chen Shaoxiu, Peng Huang, Mao Zedong, Zhang Huai, Luo Zonghan,[17] Yang

---

13. *Minli*, literally "set up by the people," as opposed to *shengli* (set up by the province).

14. On December 28, 1919, the Association was banned by Zhang, who thought it might serve as a node for agitation during the anti-Zhang student strikes of the time.

15. This last publication was created in July 1919 in Shanghai by members of Hunan literary circles and the Hunan United Reconstruction Association. Its main aims were to expose the crimes of Zhang Jingyao, oppose warlord rule, and spread democratic thought.

16. At this time the president was Xu Shichang, and the premier was Jin Yunpeng.

17. See the note to the text of January 18, 1920.

Shuda,[18] Luo Jiaoduo, Wu Xiaoshan, Zhu Jianfan,[19] Zhou Junnan, Li Fengchi, Zeng Yisheng, Luo Zan, and many others whose names are omitted here.

18. Yang Shuda was a leading New Culture advocate in Changsha and was one of two (the other being Luo Zhaotong) elected to represent the teachers in petitions to the premier during the January 28, 1920, demonstrations against Governor Zhang in Beijing.

19. See the note to the text of July 21, 1919, "The Founding and Progress of the 'Strengthen Learning Society.' "

Petition by Teachers in Hunan for Dismissing and Punishing Zhang Jingyao

(January 19, 1920)

Luo Jiaoduo and other representatives of the teachers in the schools in the provincial capital of Hunan presented a petition to Xu Shichang. The text reads:

> We solemnly ask that you dismiss and punish the governor of the province for the devastation he has brought to education in the province, so that education may be improved and the human capital of our country may be nourished. Please give the matter your immediate attention:

We believe that there is no more urgent task for our country today than the pursuit of strength, and the foundation of the pursuit of strength is education. Since the inauguration of our president, he has issued one order after another to promote education. Those who are local government officials should follow the spirit of these orders and execute them fully, so as to live up to the expectation of educating talent and making the country prosperous. But Zhang Jingyao, governor of Hunan, has blatantly ignored these orders. Since Governor Zhang arrived in Hunan, his daily preoccupation has been with running all types of businesses to compete with ordinary people for personal gain. He has imposed all kinds of levies and taxes to rob people of their wealth. He has imported opium in the greedy search for more revenue. He has let his soldiers pillage and plunder, ravaging the lives of ordinary people. The sacred constitution of the state and the clear orders of the government are viewed as matters of utter insignificance in the eyes of Governor Zhang. All his crimes are well known, and we assume the government, too, knows a great deal about them. Jiaoduo and the others who are studying and teaching know of Governor Zhang's destruction of education in the greatest detail, and feel all of these crimes most acutely. We request permission to set them out one by one for our president. First, embezzlement of appropriations for education. Hunan previously appropriated over 800,000 *yuan* for education. Since Governor Zhang's arrival in Hunan, he has drastically cut it by half — to something over 400,000 *yuan*. At first, the people of Hunan thought that because of the military emergency at that time and extreme financial difficulties Governor Zhang was forced to cut appropriations for education. Cutting expenses was, however, only a pretext. In reality, he just grabbed the money to line his own pockets. After April 1918, the funds for each school were first cut by 20 to 30 percent. After September, they were again cut to 60 percent of the original allocation. Moreover, after these repeated reductions, Governor Zhang did not disburse the amount in silver dollars, but in paper notes issued by the Bank of Hunan valued at 6,000 copper cash per silver dollar. At the same time, those who wanted to exchange the paper notes issued by the Bank of Hunan for silver dollars at the Yuxiang Bank owned by Governor Zhang had to pay an exchange rate of 10,000 to 15,000 coppers for one silver dollar. The rate later went to more than 30,000 copper cash for one silver dollar. By January 1919, funds for education had become even scarcer. By February, the real value of the paper notes issued by the Bank of Hunan declined to less than 20 percent of their face value. Three days after the education appropriations were disbursed, Governor Zhang suddenly ordered that paper notes be abolished. Every school that had already received its allocation had the equivalent of nothing. During March and April, only 40 percent of the education funds were disbursed. The disbursement of the education funds for May and June was repeatedly delayed, and eventually canceled altogether. By November, the teachers of all the schools in the provincial capital collectively resigned because of the hardships in making ends meet. Only then did Governor Zhang ask the banks to disburse the education funds, but the actual amount was no more than 50 percent. There has been no news whatsoever since July. Notifications for collecting each month's funds are issued several months later. After the notices are issued, the financial officer of each school has to make dozens of trips before he actually gets the money. Most of the time, it is because the appointments are not kept, or conflicting appointments are made. There were often incidents of conflict between the two sides. Regardless of what percentage of the allocation is actually disbursed, however, Governor Zhang has ordered that schools must sign a receipt for the full allocation before they get any money. At this moment, when the financial situation is extremely difficult, Governor Zhang, as an important local official, should demonstrate integrity and selflessness in order to bring respect to the government and win popular confidence. Since Governor Zhang has disbursed education funds in reduced amounts, the receipts should be made out only for the reduced amounts. While the amounts of money he has disbursed have been less than the allocation, his reimbursement accounts are submitted for the full amount. No ordinary man or woman with a modicum of self-respect would stoop to such acts. But Governor Zhang, as the highest military and civil official of the province, has actually gone so far as to engage in such acts of fraud, thereby making fools of the educators of Hunan, deceiving the central government, and misleading our president. What monstrous crimes! This is one reason why he should be dismissed and punished. Another is that he has seized school buildings and furniture. The buildings of many schools in Changsha, such as First Normal School, First Middle School, Category A Agricultural College, Category A Technical College, Category B Technical College, Changjun Middle School, Guangyi Middle School, Miaogaofeng Middle School, Fuchu Middle School, Lianxi Middle

School, Changsha Normal School and its affiliated primary school, First Higher Primary School of Changsha, Chuyi Primary School, as well as those of the Council on Education have all been occupied by Zhang's troops. They have used the boards from doors and windows as firewood for cooking. Classrooms and auditoriums have been turned into kitchens and stables. The books and instruments that had been acquired in the twenty years since the end of the Qing dynasty have been completely destroyed. The machines and boilers that are the very life of the technical colleges have been carried off to be used in munitions factories. The total amount of these losses is at least one million *yuan.* At this moment, when the task of educating the talented is extremely urgent, more instructional equipment should be acquired. While we are worrying about where to get it, how can the existing equipment be allowed to be wilfully wrecked? The president issued an explicit order last fall banning troops from occupying schools. But Governor Zhang has ignored this order. Even if the cause of education for the people of Hunan is not worth worrying about, what about the explicit order from our president? This is the second reason why he should be dismissed and punished. Then there is defaming the character of educators. In April last year, a proposal to dismiss Governor Zhang was made at the Shanghai Peace Conference.[1] Afraid that his position was insecure, Zhang made the then chief of the Reclamation Bureau, Xu Qingtai, and the former magistrate of Changsha, Ji Bingyuan, call a meeting of all school principals and, in exchange for disbursement of allocated education funds, ordered them to sign their names to a telegram petitioning that Zhang remain in office. The school principals all considered that it was properly the duty of the government to disburse these funds, but Governor Zhang resorted to political deception and played base tricks. Because they did not want to be defiled by this, the principal of the Special Technical College, Bin Bucheng, the principal of the Special Business School, Tang Song, the principal of First Women's Normal School, Ma Jinxi, the principal of Category A Technical School, Cai Xiang, and the principal of First Normal School, Wang Fengchang, all slipped away to Shanghai and Hankou, to escape his rude threats. Thus, Governor Zhang's grudge against the educators deepened. In other private schools, men like Chen Runlin, the president of Chuyi School, who was also the head of the Council on Education, were threatened by troops because they opposed the election of a provincial assembly. Xu Teli, the superintendent of the orphanage, was falsely accused of being in league with bandits because he denounced the harassment by Governor Zhang's special police [*qingxiangdui*]. A warrant for his arrest was issued, forcing him to flee in

1. The Shanghai Peace Conference was a meeting between representatives of the Beijing government and of the Guangzhou military government, which took place from February to May 1919 in Shanghai. No agreements were achieved, though the Conference retained a shadowy existence until 1920. The resolution demanding that Zhang be replaced was put forward by the Guangzhou delegates on April 9.

fear into exile elsewhere. In November, the teachers of all the schools in the provincial capital collectively resigned because they had not been paid for six months and could not pay their living expenses. Instead of offering assistance, Governor Zhang issued a public order scolding them for a lack of discernment, and accusing them of having ulterior motives. These teachers are hired by the school principal and have a contract to teach. When the employer is unable to fulfill the terms of the contract, the employee is certainly entitled to resign. How can Governor Zhang, as the top local government official, not know this? His deliberate insults and abuses heaped upon talented educators are not only humiliating for the educators of Hunan, but insulting to educators throughout the country. On December 2 last year, the students in all the schools in the provincial capital of Changsha, aroused by the Fujian warning,[2] and in accordance with the resolution of the Hunan Association for Chinese-made Goods, went to the Council on Education to burn bad[3] merchandise. Governor Zhang, however, dispatched his brother, Zhang Jingtang, the chief of staff, to command soldiers to surround the students. He cursed the students, calling them bandits, and forcibly arrested five of their representatives, taking their pictures and threatening to shoot them. He repeatedly ordered his troops to charge the students. At that time, the business manager of Changjun Middle School, Liu Dingan, stepped forward to intervene on behalf of the students. Zhang Jingtang slapped him in the face and ordered his troops to force Liu to his knees. The students, who had arrived proclaiming their genuine patriotism, returned after being subjected to extreme insults. Their pent-up anger led to the tragic collective exodus from the schools on December 8. Relying on the use of force, Governor Zhang wilfully insulted and abused both teachers and students. This is the third reason for dismissing and punishing him. Another reason is the illegal reappointment of the Council on Education. The Hunan Council on Education is an academic institution for us educators to study the schools. The procedure for reappointment has always been managed autonomously by the staff and members of the Council. This is the method used in all provinces, and Hunan is no exception. But in retaliation for the previous opposition by the provincial Council on Education to the provincial assembly elections, Governor Zhang appointed Jiang Daoying and Wang Bingkun to make preparations for reappointment. Governor Zhang ignored a telegram of protest from the educators from all *xian* and districts and from the National Council on Education. His intention was to turn a local public organization into his obedient lackey, totally rejecting higher orders and in violation of the will of the people. This is the fourth reason for dismissing and punishing him. What has been described here is only a brief summary of his ill deeds. There are all kinds of other incidents too numerous to be related here. In the city of

2. The reference is to a report of the wounding of Chinese students by Japanese in Fuzhou, which aroused widespread protests.

3. I.e., Japanese.

Changsha today, except for a few religious schools, silence has descended upon every place of learning. Tens of thousands of youth are out of school at the same time. If this situation is allowed to continue, all Hunan will be turned permanently into a barbarian outpost. Even if the people of Hunan are not worth worrying about, what of our president's clear edict on the promotion of education? Jiaoduo and the other [signatories] have been teaching in Hunan for more than a decade and have never meddled in politics. But today, because Governor Zhang, relying on illegal military force, is destroying education, matters have reached such a point that we are forced to come to Beijing to beseech our president to uphold the law and to dismiss and punish, to the fullest extent of the law, the governor of Hunan, Zhang Jingyao. We also request that the education appropriations he has embezzled be accounted for in full and that he be ordered to turn them over. We likewise request that an explicit order be promulgated to set aside the education appropriations for Hunan, so that in the future top military and civil officials in Hunan may never take a penny out for other purposes, education will be respected, and the foundation of our country will be developed. We anxiously await your instructions!

Respectfully submitted to
the president (and to the Ministry of Education)
by representatives of teachers and staff of all schools in the provincial capital of Changsha:
Luo Jiaoduo, Yang Shuda, Zhu Jianfan, Luo Zonghan, Zhang Huai, Mao Zedong, and others

January 19, 1920

An Obituary Notice Mourning Mr. Yang Changji

(January 22, 1920)

To Whom It May Concern:

Mr. Yang Huaizhong of Hunan died of illness at the German Hospital in Beijing at 5 A.M. on January 17. Mr. Yang possessed a high moral character and was dedicated to learning. His colleagues, on hearing of his death, all felt a great loss. In his earlier days, Mr. Yang studied at Kobun Academy and the Higher Teachers' College of Tokyo, Japan. Later, he studied at the University of Scotland, Great Britain [*sic*].[1] Upon graduation, he went to Berlin to investigate education, and stayed there too for over a year.[2] In the winter of 1911, when the revolution broke out, Mr. Yang returned from abroad to Changsha, where he took up teaching positions at the Higher Normal School and First Normal School. His dignity and diligence in teaching year after year won great admiration from his students. More than seven years passed.[3] In 1918 Changsha was occupied by troops and even the normal schools became barracks for the soldiers. Education was literally destroyed, and nothing much could be done there. Hence, Mr. Yang came to Beijing and became a professor of ethics at the national university. Besides doing research and teaching, he also translated books and wrote surveys.[4] Because of his mental overexertion, he became ill. At first, it was a gastric ailment, then it was overall swelling. Thus, he had to convalesce in the Western Hills. Summer and fall having gone by, beginning from this past winter, his illness steadily worsened, and he was then admitted to the German Hospital for treatment. The doctors said overall deterioration was found in his internal organs and it would not be easy to treat him. Alas, Mr. Yang's illness eventually proved incurable. Academic work in our country is far from being fully developed, and accomplished scholars are as scarce as the stars at

1. In fact, Yang Changji studied at the University of Aberdeen in Scotland; there is, of course, no "University of Scotland."

2. According to a note by Yang himself, he spent only nine months in Germany. He graduated from Aberdeen University in 1912.

3. He actually returned to China in the spring of 1913 and went to Beijing in the summer of 1918. He taught for the intervening period of five years in Changsha.

4. For two translations by Yang, see below the text dated October 22, 1920.

dawn. Mr. Yang assuredly dedicated his whole life to his studies. Heaven did not grant him a longer life, and he was not able to achieve even one percent of his objectives. Indeed, this is a severe blow both to education and to his personal friends. Mr. Yang sought neither material gain nor worldly fame for himself, and from his income accumulated only a few *mu* of poor land, relying for his livelihood on salaries. His survivors have no means of support. Since he had served in education for almost ten years, we, basing ourselves on the principle of honoring teachers and respecting scholars, hereby propose to establish a memorial fund to assure the livelihood of his family. The funds collected could either constitute their savings or be used as capital for a business, so that his orphans[5] may have something to live on. We sincerely hope that you, gentlemen and former friends of Mr. Yang's, will give generously toward this fund.

Yours sincerely,

Liang Huanyi, Hu Mai, Liu Liwei, Li Jinxi, Liang Huankui,[6] Fang Biao, Xue Dake, Zhu Jianfan, Zhang Shizhao, Li Mu, Liao Mingjin, Chen Runlin, Cai Yuanpei, Chen Jie,[7] Zhang Jiguang, Chen Hengke,[8] Fan Yuanlian,[9] Li Tang,[10] Fan Zhihuan,

---

5. The reference is to Yang Changji's widow, his son, Yang Kaizhi, and his daughter (and Mao's future wife), Yang Kaihui.

6. Liang Huankui was a Hunanese mining industrialist and educator. In 1893, while teaching at the Zhengwen Academy in Changsha, he became influenced by the reform movement. In 1905 he established a commercial school in Changsha to train students in new technology and science. Later, he formed (with Yang Du) the Huachang Antimony Refining Company which held a monopoly on production of pure antimony in Hunan.

7. Chen Jie (1878–1933), *zi* Qingcun or Cansan, better known as Chen Jiongming, was a native of Guangdong, who graduated from the Guangdong College of Law and Government in 1908. In 1909, he moved to Shanghai, joined the Tongmenghui, and participated in the revolutionary movement. He was active in various anti-Yuan campaigns, and later became known in the field of education. In 1919 he started the newspaper *Minsheng bao* (Voice of the People) in Zhangzhou; he was considered at that time as very progressive.

8. Chen Hengke (1876–1923), *zi* Shizeng, *hao* Huaitang, was a respected traditional Chinese painter who had received his education in Japan and taught both in Jiangsu and in Hunan.

9. Fan Yuanlian (1876–1927), *zi* Jingsheng, a native of Hunan, was a graduate of the School of Current Affairs who later studied in Japan. He was an intellectual and fellow revolutionary of Cai Yuanpei, head of Qinghua University in Beijing for a time, and minister of education and internal affairs in the Beijing government from 1917. Fan was very active in the movement to oust Zhang Jingyao at this time. In 1922 he was appointed head of Beijing Normal University.

10. Li Tang (1884–), *zi* Dang, was born in Hunan. He graduated from the University

Tao Lügong,[11] Yang Du,[12] Fan Rui, Xiang Ruizhi, Hu Yuantan,[13] Zhou Dalie, Luo Chao, Wang Zhiqun, Mao Zedong, Xiong Congxu

Contributions to the memorial fund can be sent to:

Mr. Li Tang (Hunanese), 16 Daziying, Jiajia Lane, Xuanwai, or c/o Mr. Hu Yanyuan, 3 Shenpizi Lane, 18–1/2 Xikouzhong, Xuannei

---

of Berlin in finance and served as professor at Beijing University from 1914 to 1923.

11. Tao Menghe (1887–1960), *zi* Lügong, was from Tianjin. He graduated in sociology from the University of London, was editor of the Commercial Press for a time, and a contributor to *New Youth.* In 1922 he was one of the founders of the influential liberal magazine *Nuli zhoubao* (Endeavour Weekly), edited by Hu Shi. He was a professor at Beijing University from 1914 to 1927, and acting dean in Cai Yuanpei's absence.

12. Yang Du (1875–1931), *zi* Xizi, a Hunanese, was an early advocate of constitutional monarchy for China. He was Yuan Shikai's representative during the 1911 revolution, and in 1915 he was the principal architect of Yuan's attempt to restore the monarchy. After Yuan's death, he underwent a period of eclipse, but in his last years, he became active in leftist causes.

13. Hu Yuantan (1872–1940), *zi* Zijing, *hao* Nai'an, was born in Hunan. Hu was a well-known educator imbued with Confucian precepts who had been influenced by Fukuzawa Yukichi while a student in Japan. In 1903 he returned to Changsha and founded the Mingde Schools, comprising initially a normal school and a middle school. In 1912 Mingde College in Beijing was founded, but this closed in 1915 as a result of financial difficulties.

Petition to Mr. Jin

(January 28, 1920)

The Honorable Premier Jin:[1]

Since Zhang Jingyao entered Hunan, he has been engaged in arson and murder; he has let his soldiers loot and plunder; he has forced people to grow opium; he has destroyed education, extorted money from merchants, illegally increased the salt tax, stolen and sold mineral products, appropriated public rice stores, assassinated citizens, promoted sorcery, stifled public opinion, forced people to donate food to his army, smuggled salt, stopped honoring paper money, forced people to buy lottery tickets, auctioned off textile mills, ravaged the countryside, sold off public assets, smuggled weapons, illegally raised land taxes, manipulated finances, and illegally created his own Council on Education, Provincial Assembly, and Provincial Agricultural Association. All his crimes have been repeatedly exposed by various sources, and petitions for his dismissal and punishment are pending. The people of Hunan have been forced into misery, and their very survival is in great peril. Aroused by the popular fury, we, the representatives of the people of Hunan, have come to Beijing and presented one petition after another. After more than a month of waiting, we have not heard of any decision. We are deeply troubled and puzzled. Today, we can wait no longer. We sincerely request that our premier, as soon as possible, publicly dismiss Governor Zhang and appoint a worthy and able successor. We are most urgently awaiting your decision.

1. Jin Yunpeng.

Letter to Tao Yi[1]

(February 19, 1920)

Dear Miss Siyong,

(Opening passage deleted)

I feel we should organize a noble, pure, valiant, and dedicated society of comrades. We comrades, in the preparatory stage, should have a goal of "outward expansion." I have a number of thoughts about this question. Many people talk about reform, but it seems to me to be only a vague goal. To what extent should we reform (i.e., what is the ultimate goal)? How shall we reach this goal? Where do we ourselves, or other comrades, start? Very few have studied these questions in detail. Individually, perhaps, yes; but, as a group, together, little has been done. An individual may have plans, such as "I will study it this way," "I will prepare myself this way," "I will destroy such and such," "I will build such and such," but most of these plans will lead to error. The reason for their failure is that these plans are built purely on the imagination of one individual. Such imaginings, though deemed good by that person, will often not work once they are put into practice in society. This is a drawback. There is a second drawback. The means thought out by one individual, sound as they may be, are only known to him, and study, preparation, and application are limited to that individual. This phenomenon of "individual fighting," of "sporadic struggle," "exerts a lot of effort, yet yields little results"; it is "least economical." To overcome this drawback, there is one way, which is "group discussions." There are two points in group discussion: (1) to discuss our common goals, and (2) to discuss the methods we can jointly employ. After goals and methods have been fully discussed, we must then further discuss how to put the methods into practice. Only after

1. Tao Yi (1896–1930), *zi* Siyong, born in Xiangtan, Hunan Province, was Mao's first sweetheart. Yang Changji regarded her as one of the best women students at Hunan Normal School, and in 1919 she was one of the first female members of the New People's Study Society. She was active in the Hunan self-government movement and helped Mao organize the Cultural Book Society. In 1920 she was working at Zhounan Girls' School. She and Mao soon developed ideological differences (she later rejected communism) and parted on friendly terms. Tao Yi went to Shanghai, where she founded the Lida School and remained until her death. The opening passage, which has been deleted on the only existing copy of this letter, was presumably of a personal character, but Mao nevertheless addresses her politely as "Xiansheng," which we have rendered in this case as "Miss," rather than "Mr."

such group discussions can we have common study (in the academic realm), common preparations, common destruction, and common construction in the future. Only then will we be able to see concrete results. "Sporadic fighting" is doomed to fail and is least effective. Discussing together and advancing together means that we will have "united forces," "allied armies," and that we will have a guarantee of victory. We have to guard ourselves against "sporadic fighting." We have to organize united forces to fight together.

The above problem is a great problem. There is yet another problem which is also serious. It is "the proper placement of people for studying abroad or working." If we want to achieve a certain objective (reform), we have to pay attention to proper methods. One of them is how to place people properly. Especially during the present "shortage of talents," we have to be economical about talents. Otherwise, talents will be redundant, piled up, or wasted. Some comrades in Paris are trying very hard to convince others to join them there. If they attract more people from the general public to Paris, that is fine. But if they attract more comrades there, it will inevitably lead to some errors. We comrades should be scattered all over the world to conduct investigations. Some of us should go to every corner of the globe; we should not all be in one place. The best way is to have one or several comrades open up a certain area. We should open up all "fronts." We should send people to act as our vanguard in all directions.

The several dozens of us got to know one another rather late. And it has not been too long either since we met. (The New People's Study Society was founded only in April 1918.) We haven't had time yet to study these problems thoroughly (or, rather, we have not even studied them yet). I, for example, have been quite ignorant, have had little to contribute, and have seldom studied these problems before. But during my recent visit to several places, I observed various situations, got to meet some people, thought over some things, and feel that these problems are very much worth studying. Quite a few people in various places outside our circle are like me, and have never studied them. They, too, have been sleeping inside a drum. What a shame! You are a very enlightened and purposeful person. What do you think about all these things? I expect that you have perhaps thought them over long before I did.

What I have said so far is still rather vague. Let's be more specific.

The members of The New People's Study Society and those of the Dawn Study Society[2] should hold frequent group discussions regarding our common goals and the means to achieve them. Each member's plans for studying abroad

---

2. The Dawn Study Society was an independent study society established in January 1920 by mostly female Hunanese students who did not go to France on the work-study program, yet wanted to continue to study new ideas and raise their awareness. The majority of members were students of Zhounan Girls' School and Hunan First Girls' Normal School. One of the aims of the society was to raise the status of women. The society established links with similar groups, including the New People's Study Society and the Young China Association.

or for work should be properly coordinated so that he has a specific responsibility and his activity will be a conscious and organized one. There should be a plan as to where each should be sent: how he opens up a new front at a certain place; how he attracts or wins over new comrades; how he creates his new life. The same will apply to you, to Wei, Zhou, and Lao,[3] to the other comrades in Changsha and those who have already gone abroad, and to myself in the future.

What I have set out above are only some general ideas. Now I will jot down a few more random thoughts.

Fellow-member Zhang Guoji[4] has set his heart on going to Southeast Asia. I'm in favor of this. Xiao Zizhang[5] and more than ten others in Shanghai are getting ready to go to France, and this is also very good! Peng Huang[6] and some others are organizing a work-study mutual-aid group in Shanghai,[7] which is also an excellent thing!

Peng Huang and I do not want to go to France; rather, we desire to go to Russia. He Shuheng[8] wants to study in France. I exhorted him saying that he

---

3. Wei is Wei Bi; Zhou is Zhou Dunxiang; and Lao is Lao Junzhan. For detailed notes on these three, see the note to text of November 25, 1920.

4. Zhang Guoji (1893–), also known as Yisheng, was from Yiyang, Hunan Province. Zhang was a classmate of Mao at Hunan First Normal School, and from 1919 a member of the New People's Study Society. In February 1920 he went to Singapore to teach at the Daonan School and the Overseas Chinese High School. On returning to China, he joined the Chinese Communist Party in 1927 and worked in the education office of the Wuchang Peasant Movement Training Institute.

5. On the early years of Xiao Zizhang, also known as Xiao Zhifan, Xiao San, or "Emi Siao" (because of his admiration for Rousseau's *Emile*), see the note to Mao's letter of August 3, 1915, to his elder brother, Xiao Zisheng. He was one of the inaugural members of the New People's Study Society, present at its first meeting in April 1918, and in May 1920 went to France under the work-study program, returning to China later that year. He joined the Chinese Communist Party in 1922 and went to Russia to study in 1923, returning to China in 1924.

6. As indicated in the note to the text of July 30, 1919, Peng Huang was a close friend of Mao from an early date. During the May Fourth movement, he was a student leader in Hunan, becoming chairman of the Department of Criticism and Discussion of the Hunan United Students' Association. He was a student at the Commercial Vocational School where the association was located. In September 1919 he was one of the expel-Zhang delegation sent to Shanghai to spread anti-Zhang propaganda. He worked with Mao and others to organize a number of groups, such as the the Association for Promoting Reform in Hunan, the Frugal Study Society, the Cultural Book Society, and the Russia Studies Society.

7. See below, pp. 498–500, the "Fund-Raising Notice . . . " of this society.

8. He Shuheng (1870–1935), school name He Zhanhu, also known as He Zhanggu or Laowu, was born in Ningxiang, Hunan. He studied at the local Yunshan Primary School and in 1913 joined First Normal School, where in 1917 he was one of Mao's teachers in the training department. He was one of the original thirteen founding members of the New People's Study Society in April 1918, and the oldest. He was active with Mao in petitioning for the ousting of Governor Zhang and was a member of the Cultural Book Society. He was chosen, together with Mao, from the Hunan Marxist group to attend the First Congress of the Chinese Communist Party in Shanghai in July 1921.

should not necessarily go to France, and that it would be better to go to Russia instead. As for my own plans, I will go to Shanghai within one week. Once order has been restored in Hunan,[9] I will go back to Changsha and form a "Free Study Society" (or it might be simply called a Self-Study University), hoping that within one or two years I will be able to master the outline of all fields of study, ancient and modern, Chinese and foreign, so that I may be equipped to study abroad (otherwise, I could not conduct investigations there). Then I will form a work-study team to go to Russia. As for women going to Russia, there should not be any problem. I'm sure they will be particularly welcomed by the Russian women comrades. To form a "Work-Study Society for Women Students to go to Russia," following the precedent of the same for France,[10] is also in no way impossible. On this matter (going to Russia to study) I'm consulting Mr. Li Dazhao and others. I have been told that Professor Tang Shoujun[11] of Fudan University, Shanghai (former principal of the Commercial College) is also interested in going. I am so filled with joy and hope by this that I want to tell you especially! I believe you said earlier that Yang Runyu[12] has also joined our society. Recently I have read some back issues of *Dagongbao* and have come across some of her writings, which are excellent. What has she been doing for a living lately? Could you please let me know when you have a moment? Today I went to the Women's Work-Study Group.[13] There were eight people, including four newcomers from Rice Field.[14] Among the eight, six were from Hunan, one from Korea, and one from Soviet Russia. Quite interesting! But what will their future achievements be? It depends on their abilities and their moral force. Perhaps in the end they will fail (the men's group can be said to have failed already). Within Beijing Girls' Higher Normal School, there is a spontaneous and lively spirit among the students, but the teachers and staff are rather unenlightened. I have received

9. I.e., once the "disorder" or unrest resulting from Zhang Jingyao's misrule and the popular movement to expel him has come to an end.

10. The "Hunan Women's Society for Work and Study in France" was formed by Xiang Jingyu, Cai Chang, and others in Changsha in December 1919. They aimed to use their experience in France to revitalize education in China on their return. The society was to be responsible for raising funds to send women to France, and for promoting the movement in Hunan.

11. Tang Song. See the relevant note to the text of July 21, 1919, on the "Strengthen Learning Society."

12. Yang Runyu (1899–), born in Changsha, was a graduate of Hunan First Girls' Normal School. She was an activist in the women's movement in Changsha, and in February 1920 she became a member of the New People's Study Society.

13. This is the Beijing Women's Work-Study Mutual Aid Group formed in early 1920. Most of its members were students at the various women's schools in Beijing.

14. The Girls' Normal School in Changsha was known as Old Ricefield (Daotian) Normal School.

a letter from Li Yichun[15] saying that she will teach at Zhounan. I don't know whether she has arrived yet or not. I'll write you later.

Mao Zedong
Beijing, February 1920

15. Li Yichun (1899–1984), from Changsha, was a graduate of Changsha Zhounan Girls' School. She joined the Chinese Communist Party in 1925.

The New Campaign of Hunan Representatives to Expel Zhang

(People's News Agency dispatch, February 28, 1920)

In the attempt to expel Zhang Jingyao, the Hunan Petition Delegation has been in Beijing for over two months now, during which time they have submitted their petition to the government no fewer than ten times and have also requested an interview no fewer than ten times, yet the government has still not made any response. Their last mass petition gained no more than a promise that someone would be sent to conduct a secret investigation. These representatives realize that the central government alone can hardly be expected to punish Zhang at this time. In addition to making energetic efforts to influence the various offices that command actual power in Hengyang, Chenzhou, Guangxi, and Guangdong, they are also contacting all those forces that are connected in one way or another with these offices to help out. Because a delegation was to be sent to Baoding to ask Cao Kun,[1] inspector general of the four provinces of Hunan, Sichuan, Jiangxi, and Guangdong, to exercise his authority as inspector general to give as much support as possible, representatives Luo Zonghan, Xiong Kexian, Liu Ying, and others, went earlier to Baoding and got in touch with every important person under Cao, all of whom expressed their strong desire to be of help. On the seventeenth, the inspector general's headquarters sent an aide to the place where the representatives were staying to arrange a time for a meeting with the secretary-general and the chief aide-de-camp. On the afternoon of the eighteenth, the representatives went to the inspector general's headquarters and enumerated the facts regarding the disasters that Zhang had caused to Hunan. When they came to the more tragic and painful events, everyone present was moved. Mr. Wang, the secretary-general, said, "The crimes that Governor Zhang has committed in Hunan and the other things you have related in your petition or told us personally have been known to us, and in even greater detail. They have long been decried in the Chinese and foreign press, so they are also widely and thoroughly known

1. Regarding Cao Kun, see the note to Mao's letter of July 18, 1916. As indicated there, Cao was a leader of the Zhili clique. Since Zhang Jingyao was a protégé of Duan Qirui of the rival Anfu clique, it was hoped that Cao's sympathies would lie with the delegation to oust Governor Zhang. In fact the Hunanese were successful in gaining the support of Cao Kun's principal subordinate, the commander in chief of his best troops, Wu Peifu. Cao had recently been given the resounding ancient title of "high commissioner *(jinglueshi)* of the four provinces" by Duan Qirui, in a futile effort to conciliate him.

to the public. Inspector General Cao has expressed his profound sympathy with the request you have made." The representatives submitted again to Mr. Cao materials such as *A Brief Account of Calamity in Hunan*, *A Brief Record of War Disasters in Liling*, *A Brief Record of War Disasters in Baoqing*, and the monthly *Hunan*, as well as the *History of the Crimes of Zhang Jingyao* published by the citizens of Huoqiu and Yingshang *xian* in Anhui Province. What will be done cannot be anticipated at this time; we shall have to wait and see what happens.

A Fund-Raising Notice for the Shanghai Work-Study Mutual Aid Society

(March 5, 1920)[1]

In Chinese society today, educated people cannot do manual labor, and laborers cannot get education. Because those who are educated do not toil, education has almost become something that creates hooligans. Because the laborers are not educated, an occupation has almost become something that creates slaves.

The current Chinese educational system does not allow students to earn a living while going to school; and once one starts working, he cannot go back to school. If you cannot work during the time you study, knowledge becomes formalistic and mechanical; if you cannot go to school when you are working, knowledge is neither continuing nor progressive.

Thus, education and occupation clash with each other, and living and study clash with each other. How then can they be considered rational education and proper living? In order to find a method for combining education and occupation, learning and livelihood, we are establishing this mutual aid society so that all young Shanghai men and women imbued with the new thought can shake off the various economic and ideological fetters placed on them by the old society and the old family system. In their stead, there will emerge a new life and a new organization, to carry out the method of part-work, part-study, and of mutual aid. This is our only purpose as the initiators of this project.

But at this preparatory stage, we need 1,000 *yuan* for expenses. If you agree with our purpose and are willing to help ordinary young people, we would greatly appreciate it if you could show your support in economic terms!

SUMMARY REGULATIONS OF THE SHANGHAI WORK-STUDY MUTUAL AID SOCIETY

1. Purpose — This society has as its purpose part-work and part-study to provide mutual help and assistance.
2. Membership — All those who volunteer to join us need three members' recommendations, and need to be approved by the entire body of the society in order to be admitted as members.

1. This notice is dated March 7 in the *Wengao*; it was in fact published in the Shanghai *Shenbao* on the fifth, as indicated here.

3. Service — Every member must work six hours every day. If the living expenses cannot be covered by this, the number of hours worked may be increased temporarily after discussion by the members.
4. Privileges — Members' daily needs for clothing, food, lodging, and tuition, as well as medical and book costs are provided by the society, but books will be owned by the collective.
5. Kinds of Work — These can be classified for the time being under four headings:
   (a) A restaurant for ordinary people;
   (b) A laundry;
   (c) A lithographic printing shop;
   (d) Selling goods and books and magazines.
6. Work — All income will be held in common by the society.
7. Facilities — A reading room and a club will be set up.
8. Organization — Several officers will be elected to discuss important business of the society. Among them, there will be a chief accountant in charge of the finances of the society as a whole; several business accountants in charge of the finances of each section; several officers in charge of general affairs, responsible for purchases and sales and various matters of each section. The officers are to be elected once a month.
9. Regulations — If any member is found to be lazy at work, aside from private admonitions, the officers may call a general meeting and reprimand him as a body. If he still makes no effort to perform his duties after three admonitions, he will be asked to leave the society.
10. Leaving the Society — Members are free to leave the society upon submitting a statement of reasons.
11. Number of Members — This is temporarily limited to forty, but when funds allow, we will consider increasing the number.
12. Supplementary Articles — These summary regulations may be added to or changed by a joint decision of the members.

The society will be established in Xujiahui. As for the allocation to the work teams and their organization, detailed regulations will be made after it gets started.

Initiators: Chen Duxiu, Wang Guangqi,[2] Wang Mengzou, Jiang Jihuan,[3] Tang

---

2. Wang Guangqi (1892–1936) was an intellectual reformer who studied in Japan. He was one of the initiators of the Young China Association in Beijing in 1918 as well as of the Work-Study Mutual Aid Society.

3. Jiang Jihuan (1879–1935), *hao* Yonghong, from Changsha, had earlier been a member of the provincial assembly and supporter of Tan Yankai and served as magistrate of his native Changsha *xian.* Subsequently, he became heavily involved in May Fourth

Song, Zong Baihua, Chen Zishou, Chen Bao'e,[4] Zuo Shunsheng,[5] Kang Baiqing,[6] Zhang Guotao,[7] Tu Kaiyu,[8] Kong Zhaoshou,[9] Deng Shibing, Liu Qingyang,[10] Mao Zedong, Zhang Boling, Peng Huang, Xiao Zizhang, Li Si'an,[11] Cheng Shengrui, Zeng Yisheng, Cao Yangli, Chen Xu, Zhou Jiguang, Qi Tiechen

---

activities in Changsha. He was prominent in the movement to expel Zhang Jingyao, was a member of and contributor to the Cultural Book Society, and was elected secretary-general of the Russia Studies Society. In 1920 he was head of the Hunan Department of Finance.

4. Chen Bao'e, also known as Chen Jianxiao, was an intellectual who, as a student in 1919, was one of the radical founding members and elected administrators of the Beijing University Student Union.

5. Zuo Shunsheng (1893–1969), also called Xuexun, was a native of Changsha. He was active in the Nanjing-Shanghai branch of the Young China Association in 1919–1920 and served as editor of the Association's journal, *Shaonian Zhongguo* (Young China). In 1920 he was working at the Zhonghua Publishing House.

6. Born in Sichuan, Kang was a student of Beijing University in 1920. He was an important New Tide Society member.

7. Zhang Guotao (1897–1979), *zi* Teli, was a native of Pingxiang *xian* in Jiangxi. A student at Beijing University from 1916 to 1919, he played a leading role in the May Fourth demonstrations. He had come to Shanghai at the end of 1919 as a representative of the Beijing Students' Federation. During the period from October to December 1919, he had participated in an experiment in collective living called the Morning Garden, of anarchist inspiration, which shared many of the characteristics of the Shanghai Work-Study Mutual Aid Society. At the First Congress of the Chinese Communist Party in July 1921, he was elected a member of the Central Committee, and from that time forward he was a major figure in the Party leadership. In 1935 he came into open conflict with Mao Zedong, and after three years of rivalry, he left Yan'an in 1938 for territory controlled by the Guomindang, and renounced communism.

8. Born in Changsha, Tu Kaiyu was head of the Singapore Overseas Chinese Middle School in 1920.

9. Kong Zhaoshou was a former principal of Hunan First Normal School and also taught at Mingde School for a time.

10. Liu Qingyang (1894–1977), of the Hui nationality, was a native of Tianjin. She was a student leader of the May Fourth movement in Tianjin, as well as of the women's movement, and was an active member of the Tianjin Awareness Society. She joined the New People's Study Society and went to France in 1920 under the work-study program.

11. For a detailed note on Li Si'an, see Mao's letter to her dated November 25, 1920.

Letter to Li Jinxi

(March 12, 1920)

Mr. Shaoxi:

Enclosed please find two copies of the "Conditions for the Reconstruction of Hunan."[1] There are quite a few points in it that need to be seriously reconsidered. I, your younger brother, do not really understand just how we should reform our province of Hunan in the future. Moreover, since it is a province within China, it would not be easy for Hunan to establish its independence, unless the whole situation changes in future, and our status becomes like that of an American or German state. Judging from China's present overall situation, anyone with the slightest degree of awareness ought to start, as you, sir, have said, with "radical solutions." It is best to ignore the fluctuations of the current situation and let them play themselves out. Such begging for chewed-up meat from a tiger's mouth never leads to very great benefits, even though we may be assured that "it can be done." This time, however, we are already on the tiger's back, and if we are not even able to accomplish the "second best"—which is actually "the best" in China's current situation—then we should be ashamed of ourselves.

As you, sir, are a person who thoroughly understands Hunanese affairs, I respectfully ask you carefully to consider each point in the proposal, adding or deleting as appropriate, and to let me have your instructions. I can then take the revised version with me to Shanghai and act accordingly. I eagerly await your reply.

Your humble fellow-villager
Mao Zedong

1. Mao's precise role in the drafting of this proposal, signed by Peng Huang, is not known. The copy which he enclosed with the present letter does, however, bear markings in Mao's own hand, as explained in the notes to the next document.

Conditions for the Reconstruction Of Hunan (for Discussion)[1]

(March 12, 1920)

I. Military Affairs

A. Abolish the position of "**military governor**,"[2] set up a "**commissioner of military affairs**" located in Yueyang.

B. Station the army, with **a division** as the largest unit, respectively in Yueyang, Changde, and Hengyang.

Public order in the provincial capital is to be maintained by police, subordinate to the provincial governor, and troops are absolutely not to be stationed there. Public order in each *xian* is to be maintained by the police subordinate to the *xian* magistrates. Abolish the garrison forces and the title of "defense commissioner."

C. Total military expenditure must not exceed <u>one-twelfth</u> of the total provincial revenue.

II. Finance

A. **The Bank**[3] is to be run by the people. The issuance of <u>paper money, and the reserve fund, are to be placed under the supervision of the Provincial Assembly.</u> The ratio between the reserve fund and the paper money issued is to be <u>determined by the Assembly.</u>

B. Introduce <u>an inheritance tax, income tax, and tax on business</u>. Reduce the salt tax. Abolish all exorbitant taxes imposed in the last two years.

C. Hunan No. 1 Textile Mill will be run by the people.

III. Expenditure on Education

A. Restore the amount of expenditure on education to the level of <u>1913</u>, and increase it later to meet the needs of the times.

B. Determine the sources.

---

1. This document constitutes the enclosure to Mao's letter of the same date to Li Jinxi.

2. Words which Mao emphasized by placing a dot next to the characters are set in bold. Other passages he marked with a wavy line, meaning that, as indicated in his postscript to this text, he had doubts about the point in question. These are underlined here.

3. The later version of this proposal, appended to the text of April 1, 1920, makes plain that the reference here is to the Bank of Hunan.

C. Authority for managing these resources is to be vested in an "**Office for Managing Educational Expenditure**" to be organized and set up by all provincial public schools.

IV. Self-Rule

A. Restore and reestablish *xian*, township, and *xiang* organs of self-government.

B. Set up and recognize *xian*, township, and *xiang* trade unions.

C. Set up and recognize *xian*, township, and *xiang* peasants' associations.

V. Fully protect the people's freedom of assembly, association, speech, and the press.

VI. Help accelerate the construction of the Hunan segment of the Guangdong-Wuhan rail line.

Proposed by: Association for Promoting Reform in Hunan
Address: Peng Huang, National Association of All Circles, Yongleli, Baxianqiao, French Concession, Shanghai

The underlining indicates passages regarding which I have doubts; tomorrow or the day after I will come in the evening to your honorable residence to seek your instruction.[4]

4. This postscript, intended for Li Jinxi, has been added in Mao's handwriting to the lithographed text of the document.

Letter to Zhou Shizhao[1]

(March 14, 1920)

Dear Elder Brother Dunyuan:

I have received a letter from Mr. Zhang Wenliang,[2] and am grieved to learn that your mother has passed away as a result of illness. This is a painful trial in human life. For people like us, who are always away from home and are therefore unable to take care of our parents, such an occurrence especially causes sorrow: "If I would return your kindness, it is like great Heaven, illimitable."[3] In this respect, you and I share very similar circumstances.

Some time ago I received the favor of a long letter you sent me. I am ashamed to say that I lost it before I had finished reading it. Nevertheless, I have a basic idea what the gist of it was. I imagine that since you are staying home at present, you must be in the midst of preparing a plan for future action. I do hope that my plan will be completely in line with yours, so that we can synchronize our actions. I feel that you might truly come to love me, and be my benefactor. If we could harmonize our plans and actions, it would be excellent.

I am very eager to discuss my thoughts with you. I am going to jot them down here; I may have already talked to you about some of them.

In my opinion, there is really no reason why one has to pursue knowledge at a "prescribed place." Too many people are infatuated with the two words "going abroad." There are no fewer than tens of thousands, or even hundreds of thousands, of Chinese who have been abroad. Only very few of them are really good.

---

1. Zhou Shizhao (1897–1976), *zi* Dunyuan, alternative names Duiyuan and Dongyuan, a native of Hunan, was a fellow student of Mao's at First Normal School. After graduation in 1919, he taught at Changsha Xiuye School. He was a member of the New People's Study Society and participated in the summer of 1920 in setting up the Cultural Book Society.

2. Zhang Wenliang, born in Xiangtan, Hunan, was at this time studying at Xiuye School in Changsha. He was an early member of the New People's Study Society and has left detailed notes of meetings with Mao in the autumn of 1920, in the prelude to the establishment of the Socialist Youth League. According to Li Rui, in the end Zhang did not join the revolution, but became "mentally deranged" (Li Jui, *Early Mao*, p. 164 and note 10, p. 338).

3. Lines from the *Book of Poetry*, II, V, IX, 4 (Legge, Vol. IV, p. 352). The poem as a whole deals with the theme of a son who deplores his hard fate in being prevented from rendering the last services to his parents.

As for the majority, they are still "muddled," still "unable to make head or tail of it." This provides concrete proof. I have consulted Hu Shizhi[4] and Li Shaoxi[5] about this, and they both agree with me. Hu Shizhi even wrote an essay entitled "Reasons for Not Going Abroad for Education." Therefore, I am thinking of staying in China at least for the time being, in order to study the essentials of the various disciplines. I feel that doing research in China for a time offers the following advantages:

1. It takes much less time to read translations than to read the originals; therefore one can learn more in less time.
2. World civilization can be divided into two currents, Eastern and Western. Oriental civilization constitutes one half of world civilization. Furthermore, Eastern civilization can be said to be Chinese civilization. It seems that we should begin by studying the essentials of ancient and modern Chinese systems and schools of thought. Only thus will we be equipped with a useful frame of reference when we then go to study in the West.
3. If we want to contribute our bit to the world today, we naturally cannot do so outside this domain of "China." It seems that we cannot do without on-site investigation and research on conditions in this domain. If we postpone this task until we come back from studying abroad, we might face difficulties because of occurrences in our lives and the pressure of earning a living. It is better to do it now, to save us from the difficulties just mentioned and also because it would provide us with the experience we could rely on to provide a standard of comparison when we eventually do go to the West to investigate.

To be honest, I still do not have a relatively clear concept of all the various ideologies and doctrines. I plan to form a lucid concept of each of them by studying translations and newspaper and magazine articles by contemporary discerning people, distilling the essence of theories, Chinese and foreign, ancient and modern. If there were time to edit the excerpts to make a book, that would be even better. Therefore I attach special importance to the first of the above three points.

I have dealt with this issue from the point of view of the "individual," and from the perspective of "knowledge." Now I am going to speak of it from the perspective of "the group," and of "action."

We cannot detach ourselves from the life of society, and we all want to achieve something in the future. Well then, it is necessary for us to start now doing some preparatory work in cooperation with people of similar aspirations. Although many people have overlooked this, it is a very important issue, in my opinion. We ought to do it, not carelessly and haphazardly, but purposefully and

4. Hu Shi.
5. Li Jinxi.

in an organized fashion. This is the only economical way to produce relatively great results within a relatively short period of time (i.e., within a single lifetime). I intend (1) to unite the comrades, and (2) to establish, within economical and feasible limits, the basic foundation that will be needed in the future. I feel that we should pay particular attention to these two methods at present.

As for the two aspects discussed above (the individual and the group), the first must be considered as primary, and the second as subordinate. The first aspect should take up most of one's time, and the second a smaller portion of it. The total should not take more than three years (at most); the locale is set in Changsha.

For these reasons, I do not agree with your suggestions about working in Paris, or in Southeast Asia, or in Beijing. I do, however, agree with you completely in your proposal about "Here in Changsha."

I think we need to create a new kind of life in Changsha. We could enlist comrades to join together, rent a house, and establish a Self-Study University (Mr. Hu Shizhi coined this term). In this university, we would practice a communist life. Possible channels through which we can raise funds to defray living expenses are:

1. Teaching. (Six to ten hours a week per person)
2. Writing for publication. (Essays or newspaper articles)
3. Editing books. (Edit one or several books of which we can sell the manuscripts)
4. Manual labor. (This item is mainly to avoid unnecessary expenditure, for example, by doing cooking and laundry ourselves)

All proceeds will be held entirely in common. Those who earn more will help those who earn less; the goal is subsistence. I think that if we two decided to act, we could reasonably expect He Shuheng[6] and Zou Panqing[7] to participate. This kind of organization could also be called a "Work-Study Mutual Aid Society." Crucial to this organization would be the establishment of an "Academic Symposium," which would have to meet no less than two or three times a week to discuss academic questions.

The above are my plans if we decide to stay in China for the time being to do research, instead of going abroad to study. I am not, however, absolutely opposed to studying abroad. On the contrary, I advocate a policy of studying abroad in a big way. I think the only correct solution is for each of us to "go abroad" once, just to satisfy our craving for it.

I consider Russia to be the number one civilized country in the world. I think that two or three years hence we should organize a delegation to visit Russia.

6. On He Shuheng, see note 8 to the text of February 19, 1920.
7. On Zou Yunzhen, *zi* Panqing, see note 24 to Mao's annotations on Paulsen.

That is for a later date, and it is best not to mention it now.

It would be difficult to publish a magazine, in my opinion. If the Self-Study University proves to be a success, and we get some results through self-education, we can consider publishing a magazine (most people here talk about re-establishing *Xiang River Review*). I will save the discussion of the routine work of the committee for when we meet. I won't go into details here. Please drop me a note when you get a chance.

Your younger brother,

Zedong
March 14, 1920
99 Beichang Street
Beijing

The Inside Story of the Hunan Peace Preservation Association

(March 25, 1920)

To Newspapers, Social Organizations, and Fellow Hunanese Everywhere:

Guilty of the most heinous crimes, Zhang Jingyao has long been accused and condemned by the people of Hunan. With one voice, citizens throughout China have also denounced him in speech and in writing. It is our strong common desire to drive him away as far as possible and to get rid of him, the sooner the better. Now, however, an organization calling itself the Beijing Branch of the "Hunan Peace Preservation Association" has published and distributed pamphlets to defend Zhang. Mixing up black with white, they urge people to act with caution and not defame Zhang's reputation. But the fact is self-evident: during the past three years, the people of Hunan have continuously suffered many privations and can scarcely survive. Numerous men have died, leaving their families without anyone to care for them. Countless women have committed suicide, and their bodies have been left unburied in the open. Zhang Jingyao is the source of all these disasters. As long as he stays in Hunan, there will never be any hope for us. Therefore, in order to save Hunan, we must first of all drive Zhang away. Only by getting rid of him can we restore normality in Hunan. If what the Association declares is true, then we would ask, how do they propose to solve the problems of Hunan as long as Zhang is in the province? As they cannot offer any kind of solution, it is clear that they are nothing but hypocrites, and all they want is to serve Zhang's interests. In fact, the Association has been set up by Guo Renzhang[1] and others. Guo is a vile character whose notorious history is well known throughout the country. Bribed by Zhang this time, Guo gathered a few followers to set up the Association. Their sole purpose is to betray the people of Hunan and protect Zhang for the sake of money. Ashamed of Guo's behavior, Hunanese residing in the capital all condemn Guo and his followers as being a "Clique of Zhang Protectors" and a "Party of Traitors Selling Out the Province." We representatives here believe it is our unshakable duty to drive Zhang out of Hunan and to eliminate traitors such as Guo. Therefore, we have decided to speak out to expose the lies and rumors spread by Guo, so as not to allow them to confuse people and mislead the public. We are confident that the

1. On Guo Renzhang, see note 8 to the text of January 18, 1920.

true colors of the tyrant and traitors will soon be revealed. With truth and justice on our side, we can surely succeed in uniting people around us and defeating the pro-Zhang traitorous clique.

Representatives of the citizens of Hunan: Mao Zedong, Luo Zonghan, Peng Huang, Chen Shaoxiu, Zhang Huai, Luo Jiaoduo, Yang Shuda, Zhang Weiyi, He Shuheng, Cai Renlong, Xiong Mengfei, Jiang Yuhuan, Li Simi, Liu Min, Gao Biao, Zhang Yaoluan, Chen Chuncui, Liu Zuozhou, Zhang Xinmin, Chen Shiquan, He Yuanpei, Li Si'an, Wang Guolin, Peng Xianze, Peng Yili, Wu Junchen, Jiang Zhuru, Xu Ying, Liu Dingfu, Ouyang Jiaoru, Li Qihan, Fu Diliang, Zhang Shusheng, Xu Qingyu, Hu Weiyin, Peng Guangqiu, Zhu Houzheng, Wang Qufei, Mao Douwen, Huang Ying, Yi Xun, Zhong Xiu, Cao Yangli, Gao Yeyu, and Li Zhenpian.

Declaration on the Occasion of the Founding of the Association for Promoting Reform in Hunan

(April 1, 1920)[1]

Since he arrived in Hunan, Zhang Jingyao has gone to extremes in plundering, looting, raping, and killing. The people of Hunan have endured heavy sufferings, which can scarcely be described. As a result of many days of effort on all sides, the present movement to drive Zhang out of Hunan has gained the sympathy of the people both in the south and in the north who advocate justice and humanity. By now we can begin to hope that Zhang will be driven out of Hunan. We must not, however, become overly optimistic. Why? First of all, when one Zhang Jingyao is gone, a hundred Zhang Jingyaos may want to come. By then we may be too tired of the difficulties and hardships of driving them out of Hunan, so that we "chop and change," have a "brave beginning but a weak ending,"[2] or settle for "a change in form but not in essence." Would that not show how shortsighted we are? Since Hunan became part of the Republic, it has been invaded by troops three times.[3] It has endured the most terrible sufferings and made particularly great sacrifices. If we want to trace the origin of the sufferings, it is none other than the evil system of the "military governorship." This is the root of the calamity. As long as the military governorship is not abolished, the turmoil in Hunan cannot be stopped. It simply doesn't matter whether those in authority are linked to the south or to the north, or whether the people in power are good or bad. If today's methods continue to prevail, today's customs cannot be changed, and there is no hope of maintaining public order in Hunan. This has long been the hard and invariable fact. If even such a great sacrifice as this is still not enough to arouse the consciousness of the Hunanese, then their minds have truly become deathly still. With such apathy, it is very difficult to survive in a world full of surging new tides. Moreover, the efforts to solve the problems in China today are constrained by various kinds of special forces, and there is no chance for a comprehensive solution to succeed. The practical approach is for

1. According to the editors of the *Wengao*, this document was drafted in final form on April 1, 1920, but openly published only on June 14 of the same year.

2. Literally, "a tiger's head and a snake's tail."

3. Between 1913 and 1920 Hunan was ruled by the Beiyang warlords Tang Xiangming, Fu Liangzuo, and Zhang Jingyao.

the masses to take the initiative in one local area. In our humble opinion, if we want to build an ideal Hunan, we must start with "fundamental reform," but we should first put forward some minimum demands and suggest some conditions which fit the situation in order to appeal to the public opinion of Hunanese living both inside and outside the province. We should also eradicate all the selfish opinions and selfish interests. With such a program, we can direct the mass movement in a reasonable and continuous way and carry it through to the end. Some people regard Hunan as the Switzerland of the East. We can indeed look at Switzerland as a model for our "ideal Hunan." From now on, if our 30 million people thoroughly reform themselves and strive to march forward, there should be no reason why we cannot bring this about one day. The world situation clearly tells us that the tide of change is already sweeping through wild Siberia, and Korea, which has lost its national existence, also wants self-determination. This is a general trend, and no one can resist it. Now look at this area of rivers and lakes, which extends south from the great lake,[4] and north from Cangwu.[5] This area is rich in natural and human resources. It is exactly the right stage on which to act out our self-rule and self-determination. In addition, its proud sons, who are young and talented and have attracted the world's increasing respect, can be relied on to improve themselves. As for the affairs of Hunan, we suggest that the first step is to "get rid of Zhang"; the second step is to consider "how to carry out reconstruction after Zhang is gone." Now we list our recommendations for military affairs, finance, education, self-rule, the rights and freedom of the people, and transportation. On each of these major topics, we invite comments and suggestions from Hunanese everywhere. The spirit of these recommendations lies in the two major proposals for "overthrowing military force" and "implementing people's rule." We should abolish the military governorship and cut the size of the army in order to achieve the goal of "overthrowing military force." We should establish banks run by the people, make education independent, promote self-rule, guarantee the people's rights and freedoms, and facilitate transportation in order to achieve the goal of "implementing the self-rule of the people." We must disregard all obstacles, maintain our faith, and strive forward. The realization of civil rights and human rights in every country in the world has come only after active struggles and movements. We can make greater progress. Hunan is a part of China, and the reform of Hunan is one part of the reform of China. Its impact, direct or indirect, is indeed great. We earnestly hope that people all over the country will show their support and sympathy for us, helping us fulfill our wish and giving us encouragement. Organized by our comrades, this association takes as its sole aim the promotion of reform in Hunan. The methods of promotion include putting forward opinions and advocating ideas for the masses of the people. As for

4. Lake Dongting, on the northern boundary of Hunan.
5. A locality in Guangxi, not far south of the Hunanese border.

actual political activity, we hope that certain talented and knowledgeable people will get involved in it. We ourselves, however, do not wish to take part in it. At this moment of the founding of the Association, we hereby issue this declaration. The headquarters of the Association is located at 29 South Minhou Lane, Hatong Road, Shanghai.

Conditions for the Reconstruction of Hunan (for discussion)[6]

I. Military affairs

A. Abolish the military governorship.

B. The largest unit in the army is to be one division; these will be stationed respectively in Yueyang, Changde, Hengyang, Baoqing, and Hongjiang. Public order in the provincial capital will be maintained by the police under the jurisdiction of the provincial governor, and troops must absolutely not be stationed there. Public order in each *xian* will be maintained by the police under the jurisdiction of the *xian* magistrate. The garrison forces and the title of defense commissioner are to be abolished.

C. Total military expenditure must not exceed one-twelfth of the total provincial revenue.

II. Finance

A. The Bank of Hunan is to be run by the people. The Bank will be supervised by the Provincial Assembly as regards the issuance of paper currency and setting the amount of the reserve fund. The ratio between the reserve fund held by the bank and the volume of the paper currency issued is set by the Provincial Assembly, which will also have the authority to review the bank's accounts at any time.

B. An inheritance tax and an income tax will be introduced, and the tax on salt reduced. All the exorbitant taxes imposed during the past three years will be abolished.

C. Hunan No. 1 Textile Mill will be run by the people.

III. Education

A. The education fund is to be independent. The amount is set at one million *yuan*, and should subsequently be increased as appropriate. The source of the education fund must be determined. Authority for maintaining the education fund is exercised by the "Office for Managing Educational Expenditure" to be organized and established by all the provincial public schools.

B. A policy of universal compulsory education is to be adopted, and within a period of no more than fifteen years, compulsory education shall be fully established in the seventy-five *xian*.

6. It will be seen that this is a slightly revised version of the document which Mao had drafted on March 12, 1920, and sent to Li Jinxi on the same date.

IV. Self-Rule

A. Preparations will be made to establish genuine organs of popular self-government in the smallest subdivisions of various *xian.*

B. Trade unions shall be established and recognized in the *xian,* towns, and villages.

C. Peasant associations shall be established and recognized in the *xian,* towns, and villages.

V. Transportation

A. Efforts will be made to complete the Hunan segment of the Guangdong–Wuhan railway within the shortest possible period of time.

B. Roads shall be built between all the important cities and towns and the villages of the whole province.

VI. The people's freedom of "assembly," "association," "speech," and "publication" will be fully guaranteed.

Proposed by: The Association for Promoting Reform in Hunan

The Hunan People Are Fighting Hard to Get Rid of Zhang Jingyao

(April 27, 1920)

The Hunan Relief Association and the Union of All Circles of Hunanese Residing in Shanghai sent telegrams yesterday strongly protesting the provision of the peace agreement that would not remove Military Governor Zhang from office. They read as follows:

> Telegram to Commander-General *(zongcai)* Lu[1] in Nanning and Commander-General Tang[2] in Yunnan

We are extremely shocked to read the recent newspaper reports concerning the conditions of the peace negotiations between the south and north. Going back to the reopening of the peace conference, eight conditions were proposed, upon which subsequent negotiations were supposed to be based, with the statement that mutual compromises too were supposed to be resolved in accordance with the law, even if it meant rejecting the Shanghai meeting. Should a private peace distort the arguments for justice, any hope for peace will be a long way off. We are already trembling in fear of the dangers that lie ahead. Failure to remove Military Governor Zhang from office is totally incompatible with the fourth condition. All the calamities that Zhang Jingyao has brought to Hunan are monstrous crimes too numerous to count. The Hunan people have been waiting urgently a long time for just a single chance to save themselves. Desperately hoping for peace they have suffered and awaited a settlement. But now, on the contrary, the arch-criminal is to be allowed to continue to ravage the province of

1. Lu Rongting (1856–1927), *zi* Ganxing, a native of Guangxi, began life as a bandit, and then became an officer in the imperial army. After 1911, he first supported Yuan Shikai and then turned against him. In August, 1917, he supported Sun Yatsen in the establishment of a military government in Guangzhou; in the spring of 1918, he joined in the reorganization of this regime under a board of seven directors, including himself, presided over by Cen Chunxuan (see the note on Cen below). At the time of this telegram Cen and Lu seemed in full control of the area, but by October 1920 their forces had been defeated by Chen Jiongming, acting on behalf of Sun Yatsen, and Lu's political career soon came to an end.

2. Tang Jiyao (1881–1927), *zi* Xuangeng, a native of Yunnan, supported Sun Yatsen and Cai E during the "second revolution" of 1913. In August 1917, he was elected, together with Lu Rongting, as one of the two military commanders of Sun's government in Guangzhou, but remained in Yunnan, where he had established a power base.

Hunan. The whole province is to be sacrificed in exchange for the personal power and interests of a few individuals. The Hunan people would rather die than accept this settlement. Even if there are only three families left, they will resolve to fight to the end. We earnestly urge you to defend the constitution and save the country in a spirit of rescuing people from disaster. We hope you will take control of the whole situation and rescue the Hunan people from misery. Otherwise, if the confidence of the people is lost, everything will break up. Can disaster in Hunan be good for the southwest? We relate this to you with tears in our eyes, hoping you will examine it closely.

Telegram to Commander-General Cen[3] of the Guangzhou Military Government

It has recently been reported that the Beijing government has informally suggested to you and to Commander-General Lu conditions for the peace negotiations, which include an item about not touching Zhang in Hunan. We are very shocked to read this. Although the rumors are piecemeal and as yet unconfirmed, there is much talk in the streets of private backroom deals among important persons of the north and south. Rotten things produce worms, and suspicions are inevitable. Ever since Hunan first rose in revolt, the sacrifice of life and property by the Hunan people has been much greater than in Fujian and Shaanxi. And the calamities that Zhang Jingyao has brought to Hunan are many times worse than what Li[4] has done in Fujian or Chen[5] has done in Shaanxi. Now, in all the talk about peace, the governorship is listed in a special article according to which the Hunan military governor is to be allowed to retain his position. If this were to be true, it would indeed be turning a deaf ear to the many years of suffering and the appeals of the Hunan people. Deals made just in the interests of important personages can be called the unenlightened use of power, disregarding right and wrong. Who could trust them? The northern court[6] has long ignored the suffering and misery of the people, who can hardly be blamed for rashly proposing that the governorship cannot be privately conferred by the northern court. A wise person

3. Cen Chunxuan (1861–1933), *zi* Yunjie, a native of Guangxi, served in many high positions under the empire, including that of governor-general of Guangdong and Guangxi. A long-time rival of Yuan Shikai, whose efforts at monarchical restoration he opposed, he served, beginning in August 1917, as a codirector of the régime set up by Sun Yatsen in Guangzhou. In 1918, he replaced Sun as the head of this military government, and remained in control of it until he was himself ousted in October 1920, and retired from politics.

4. Li Houji (1870–1942), *zi* Peizhi, from Jiangsu province, was military governor of Fujian province at this time. He had strong ties with Duan Qirui, and was ousted in the late summer of 1922.

5. Chen Shufan. See note 2 to the text of January 4, 1920.

6. The document here uses the term *ting,* which formerly designated the imperial court, obviously with the aim of suggesting that the northern warlord government is behaving like the old regime.

ought to realize that by cheating the province of Hunan he is striking a terrible blow against upholding the law. A humane person ought to take pity on them. Moreover, Hunan is the gateway to the southwest. If it is known that a lawless military man and traitorous villain like Zhang Jingyao is entrenched there, then Sichuan, Yunnan, Guangxi, and Guangdong are all in danger. How can someone who cannot save himself talk of saving the nation? At this time, the people of Hunan still regard you, sir, as a leader who upholds the law, a man of principle and humanity who would not abandon Hunan. We ask you to support strongly the demands of the masses for driving Zhang out, and not to overturn the preconditions already established for the peace conference, and to get rid of the evil in Hunan. This will be a relief for the nation, in addition to fulfilling the hopes of 30 million people throughout Hunan. And the future and the interests of the entire southwest and of the nation depend on it. We send this telegram in fear and trembling, and await your response.

Public Letter to Representatives Zhang Xingyan[7] and Peng Jingren

Recent newspaper reports say that the northern government has unofficially proposed conditions and made contact with the southwest. Although the reports are piecemeal, and perhaps without basis, on the outside there is much talk of all kinds of dark deals that are especially frightening. An examination of these conditions shows that apart from the distribution of loans and of the power and position of various important persons they do not address at all the suffering of the people or the urgent need to save the nation. What is especially shocking is that even though the military governor of Hunan, Zhang Jingyao, who has brought about terrible disasters, and the people of Hunan, who have been trying to drive him out, cannot possibly coexist, nevertheless these conditions, as with Chen in Shaanxi and Li in Fujian, maintain the status quo. What crime have our people committed that they should be subjected to his poison forever? Peace will be impossible until the suffering of Hunan is ended. Before this peace conference began there was a special investigation that finally settled on the eight conditions as the essential items, but now these have been totally ignored. In the interests of just two or three individuals from the south, 30 million people are to be sacrificed in exchange. The Hunan people would rather die than accept this. You gentlemen have an obligation to your native place, so please look into this. You too have fought to expel Zhang, and made it the first condition for the peace negotiations. Please hold on to your original idea and carry out this goal. Otherwise, we Hunanese will be indifferent to life and death, the whole situation will deteriorate, and then you gentlemen will not be able to face the people of Hunan. Written in haste and in tears, without choosing our words.

7. Zhang Shizhao. For a detailed note, see the text of July 14, 1919, "The Arrest and Rescue of Chen Duxiu."

The Hunan People Denounce Zhang Jingyao for Sabotaging the Peace

(June 5, 1920)

To All Newspaper Offices and All Groups, for Public Information:

We have just received an admirable telegram sent by the general headquarters of Hunan forwarded through Guangzhou, which says that Division Commander Wu has withdrawn his garrison and the three parties have reached an agreement. When any Hunan troops go to get food and supplies, the same procedures are to be followed as previously agreed on, and they should not be stopped. However, when our army sent some men to purchase rice the other day, they came under heavy fire from Zhang Jingyao's relief troops when passing the defense line. A total of thirteen of our soldiers were killed or wounded. Driven beyond forbearance, our troops were forced to take appropriate defensive actions. Such an incident of fighting against each other is a sabotage of the peace, for which Zhang Jingyao must be held responsible. We hope that you can tell the whole country to expect the public trial of Zhang Jingyao, who is infamous both in China and abroad for bringing calamity to Hunan. He must now be held responsible for the premeditated provocations that have upset the whole situation. We urge you to stand for justice and root out oppression. This is a matter of great urgency, and we anxiously await your response. Respectfully,

Union of Hunanese of All Circles Residing in Shanghai

Letter to Li Jinxi

(June 7, 1920)

Dear Mr. Shaoxi:

After I left Beijing, I spent some time on the way visiting Tianjin, Jinan, Taishan, Qufu, and Nanjing, and did not reach Shanghai until twenty-five days later.[1] I am now staying at 29 South Minhou Lane, Hatong Road. There are four us living here.[2] Since we were really unsure of the Work-Study Society,[3] we have decided to cancel our sponsorship of it and instead to set up a separate self-study society to work half-time and study half-time. All of my housemates want to go to Russia, and I have also decided to go. For the moment, I will study on my own, and go when the road to Russia opens up in a year and a half or two. I would like to find a Russian with whom to study the Russian language, but I have not found one yet. I have always had an intense hatred for school, so I have decided never to go to school again. It is not at all impossible to study freely, so long as you have discipline and proper methods. Foreign languages are truly doors which we must open. I am now studying a little English every day. If I can keep at it, I will be able to gain some small benefit. I do not intend to concentrate on any specific subject as yet. I would like to use the X-ray method, reading cursorily in every field. I am inclined to feel that I do not have enough general knowledge, so it is hard to concentrate on attacking one subject. By accumulating general knowledge and organizing it, it will be easier to reach depths. [Herbert] Spencer hated to be confined by national boundaries, and I feel that the boundaries between fields of study are also very harmful. I admire you and the late Mr. Huaizhong[4] the most, for you have both read widely. Unfortunately, I am too emotional and

---

1. Mao left Beijing on April 11 and arrived in Shanghai on May 5, 1920.

2. This address is the present-day No.63 Anyi Road, Shanghai, where Mao lived when he was involved with the Association for Promoting Reform in Hunan, and in organizing the campaign against Zhang Jingyao. The other three people staying there were Li Fengchi, Li Si'an, and Chen Shunong. Mao also helped with editorial work for *Tianwen* (The Tianwen Weekly), founded in February 1920, the organ of the Hunan Student Delegation for the Expulsion of Zhang Jingyao in Shanghai.

3. The Shanghai Work-Study Mutual Aid Society, for which Mao had signed, only three months earlier, the fund-raising notice dated March 5, 1920, which appears above.

4. Yang Changji, *zi* Huaizhong, Mao's teacher and (by this time) posthumous father-in-law. See in particular the notes to the "Classroom Notes" of 1913, and to the tribute to Yang dated January 22, 1920.

have the weakness of being vehement. I cannot calm my mind down, and I have difficulty in persevering. It is also very hard for me to change. This is truly a most regrettable circumstance! I would very much like to study philology, linguistics, and Buddhism, but I have neither the books nor the leisure to study them, so I slack off and procrastinate, and am reduced to saying: "If I fail to study today, there is always tomorrow." If you come across any books in these two fields, linguistics and philology, and Buddhism, I hope you will send me the titles. If you have any extra printed materials, please send them on to me too. Since I have gathered some books, I should set aside a certain time and really devote it to this. Recently I have been concentrating on the study of three subjects only: English, philosophy, and newspapers. For philosophy, I have started from the "three great contemporary philosophers,"[5] and will gradually learn about the other schools of thought. In English I am reading one short lesson from the simplest primer each day. As for newspapers, I read them very carefully every day and clip the good materials. Since I am still at a child's level in foreign languages and cannot read any original works, I plan to use the tool I already possess, Chinese, during the next two or three years before I go abroad, to read current newspapers, magazines, series of books, and all the translations. Thus I will seek to learn about the outline and main themes of Eastern and world thought and scholarship, to lay a foundation for studying abroad. The latest trend everywhere in China has been putting out series of books. Quite apart from their motivations and contents, this has a certain value for a person like myself who is "hungry and thirsty for knowledge." Is it really possible for the Association of Scholars Resident in Beijing[6] to publish a journal? It is very hard for such a mixed group to work together. We had better find something else concrete, fresh, and enthusiastic, which will more easily yield results and arouse more interest. I think that in human society, no matter whether it be a movement or a theory, it has to fulfill these three conditions — to be concrete, fresh, and enthusiastic. Without them, it is only a vassal, not a great nation; it only copies but does not create; it is only reformist and not revolutionary. I have been wanting to write an article entitled "Concreteness, Freshness, and Enthusiasm, and New Movements," but have not had the time or opportunity to gather my thoughts, so I am afraid I will not be able to write it after all. You, sir, know how to arrange your daily life: when to "go to the office," when to "go home," when to "work," and when to "study." You arrange everything so perfectly, and this is truly not easy. I am so driven by emotions that it is hard for me to live a disciplined life. When I

5. Mao is referring to Henri Bergson, Bertrand Russell, and John Dewey.

6. The Association of Hunanese Scholars Resident in Beijing was established in the spring of 1920. The head of the Association was Fan Yuanlian, and Mao was one of those in charge of editorial work. The main task of the Association was to hold an academic gathering each Sunday to which an important speaker would be invited. A monthly publication was planned, but never appeared. The Association ceased its activities in the fall of 1920.

consider you, sir, it seems to me that you are living far above, in the heavens. I imagine it is very hot in Beijing now. It is also getting warmer in Shanghai. I will write more later. My respectful compliments.

Mao Zedong
June 7, 1920

The Hunan People Are Fighting for Their Moral Character

(June 9, 1920)

The purpose of the Hunan people's movement to expel Zhang was explained in detail one day by "a Hunanese." But as I understand it, there are also two further points. One is that if Zhang wanted to grow opium and had just openly forced the people to grow opium, it might not have been regarded as a crime. But he did not do that. He hung up signs everywhere banning opium even while Yu Zhaotong, the Changsha *xian* magistrate, summoned more than 100 heads of organizations from all over Changsha *xian* last July to a secret meeting in the *xian* office to announce the general's[1] instructions and distributed 40,000 packets of opium seeds. After the meeting, these leaders made this secret public. The other point concerns the teachers' wages. They actually received only 70 percent of their wages, but had to write on the receipt that they had received 100 percent. The teachers were so angry that they sent a representative to the capital with the evidence to file a suit. When this representative arrived at Xinyangzhou, however, he was grabbed by detectives who had rushed to get there the same night. These two things are more than enough to arouse the bitter hatred of the Hunan people. In sum, after murder and arson, to cheat people so blatantly is quite unbearable. When the movement to expel Zhang began, all kinds of people, both young and old, joined in, precisely because of these many kinds of severe provocation. Thus the Hunan people reject Zhang precisely because Zhang's moral character is incompatible with that of the Hunan people. The people of Hunan reject Zhang precisely because they are "fighting for their moral character." This is just like Mr. Cai Songpo[2] swearing in Yunnan, "I am fighting for my moral character."

---

1. I.e., Zhang Jingyao.

2. For a note on Cai E, referred to here by his *zi* Songpo, a revolutionary hero in Mao's eyes because he led the struggle against Yuan Shikai in 1915, see the text of July 25, 1916.

The People of Hunan Must Take Another Step Forward

(June 11, 1920)

The newspapers report that the southern army has taken Changsha. Thus the negative aspect of the movement of the Hunanese to drive Zhang out is actually coming to an end. The people of Hunan should take another step forward and work for a "movement to abolish the military governorship." How to abolish the military governorship and how to establish rule by the people are really the big issues to which the Hunan people should give their active attention from now on.

The idea of abolishing the military governorship has been suggested for several years, but the military governorship has still not been abolished. It is certain that the theories of abolishing the military governorship by Lu Yongxiang[1] and by Tang Jiyao[2] will have little actual impact. But now there is a good chance to abolish the military governorship in Hunan if Zhang Jingyao is indeed gone. (1) The Hunan people's expulsion of Zhang was their own decision, and it is not tied to any of the dark forces. If they are really awakened to the need to abolish the military governorship, they can simply kick it out themselves. (2) Both the Hunan and western Hunan armies have been imposing grain levies for seven or eight years. Although they have now taken Changsha, it has long since become a barren rocky field.[3] On the other hand, the Bank of Hunan has suffered a loss of 50 to 60 million. Both the government finances and the general economy are bankrupt, so there is no alternative but to disband the army. After the army is dissolved, the military governor will have no military to govern. It would be best

---

1. Lu Yongxiang (1867–1933), *zi* Zijia, from Shandong Province, was a graduate of the Beiyang Military Academy who worked his way up through the ranks to become a commander of the Beiyang Army under Yuan Shikai. He was appointed military governor of Zhejiang in August 1919. On April 23, 1920, he sent a telegram in favor of abolishing the military governorship and appealed to the Beijing government that this be carried out in Zhejiang.

2. Tang Jiyao, military governor of Yunnan, also sent a telegram to the Beijing government to this effect on April 27, 1920.

3. The metaphor of a rocky field *(shitian)*, meaning a useless conquest, is taken from the *Zuo zhuan*, XII, XI (Legge, Vol. V, pp. 825–26). Remonstrating with the ruler of Wu, who was bent on attacking the neighboring state of Qi, an adviser declared, "You may get your will with Ts'e [Qi], but that is like getting a stony field, which can be of no use."

simply to abolish it. (3) Tan Yankai has already had a taste of the military governorship before. His involvement in the movement to expel Zhang this time is basically just to expiate his crimes by doing a good deed. He should be willing to get rid of this skeleton of the military governorship. The Hunan people have had the courage to expel Tang Xiangming, Fu Liangzuo,[4] and Zhang Jingyao. Why not pluck up a little courage and abolish the military governorship? The Hunan people have always been somewhat stubborn, rebellious, and destructive. It is a pity that they so lack any talent for being constructive. It will really be a great shame if this time they again throw away a good opportunity. As far as I can see, there is absolutely no hope for fully establishing people's rule in China within the next twenty years. Twenty years will be simply a period of preparation. The preparations will take place only with the peoples of one province after another putting in order and solving their own problems (such as abolishing the military governorship, disarming, and developing education, industry, and commerce). If the Hunan people can take the lead now, then Shaanxi, Fujian, Sichuan, and Anhui provinces, having similar conditions, will follow, and then some ten to twenty years later, they may join together in providing a general solution to the problems of the whole country. I wish that the Hunan people would look at the overall situation of the world and reflect on the sufferings they have endured in the past eight or nine years, and make a determined effort to act in this way.

---

4. Fu Liangzuo (1873–1924), *zi* Qingjie, a Hunanese, graduated in 1904 from the Japanese Military Officers' Academy and rose in rank to general in Yuan Shikai's Beiyang Army. When Yuan became president of the Republic, Fu was made chief of the Military Affairs Bureau. A close follower of Duan Qirui and supporter of his plans to unify China by military means, Fu Liangzuo was appointed governor of Hunan in August 1917, taking up the post in September. He was an unpopular leader, being a subordinate of Premier Duan and a prominent member of the Anfu clique, and was forced to resign from the position and flee from Changsha on November 14, 1917.

The Self-Rule of the People of Hunan

(June 18, 1920)[1]

Now that Zhang Jingyao has gone, I have the feeling that a situation in which "there is no Zhang Jingyao, but there are difficulties in the way of self-rule for the people of Hunan" will frequently be repeated in the future. Can we go along with such situations in which there is no Zhang Jingyao, but there are difficulties in the way of self-rule for the people of Hunan? Whether they be Hunanese or not, all those who resolve to place obstacles in the way of the self-rule of the whole Hunanese people are naturally the deadly enemies of Hunan.

The turmoil in China has been going on continuously for eight to nine years. The turmoil itself is not surprising. What is most surprising is that the turmoil has been going on for a long time without the slightest result. Society is so corrupt, and our people is so decadent, that unless tremendous efforts are made to get at the root of the situation, it is impossible to talk about overthrowing and sweeping away [the old order]. The responsibility for making such efforts rests with the people of the whole country, not with a few bureaucrats, politicians, and military men. The latter care only about their personal desires, not the public interest; they are imperious and not sincere; they sell out their country and are not patriotic; they bring harm and not benefit to the people.[2] It is all because these men are trying to seek their personal gain that the great turmoil has continued for eight or nine successive years. The extremely corrupt [Beijing] government and the professional prostitutes of the Anfu clique have established their hold on the country, and delight in doing evil. They have sold out all our

1. A text similar to this appeared on May 16, 1920, in *Tianwen*, under the title: "Declaration of the Hunan People's Association for Self-Rule." It did not include the opening paragraph of this piece, and was preceded by the following notice: "For the consideration of citizens of the whole country, all newspaper offices, all groups reflecting public opinion, the soldiers, civilians, and officials of all provinces, the representatives from Hunan in the upper and lower houses of the parliament of the Military Government in Guangzhou, Mr. Tan Yankai in Bingzhou, Mr. Wu Peifu in Hengzhou, Mr. Xiong Xiling, Mr. Fan Yuanlian and Mr. Guo Zongxi in Tianjin, Mr. Zhang Shizhao, Mr. Peng Yunyi, and Mr. Xu Fosu of the Peace Council in Shanghai, and all fellow Hunanese in Beijing, Tianjin, Shanghai, Nanjing, Hankou, and Japan." There were also some other variants. As usual, we follow the Chinese text in the *Wengao*, but significant differences are noted below.

2. Here the May 16 version adds: "they recognize classes, and not equality."

railways, mines, forests, and trading ports; they beg Japan[3] for guns, funds, and officers to train their troops, and slaughter the people, doing battle with the urban population and the students.[4] As for the Province of Hunan, the turmoil has been created by a few military men. But the people of Hunan have kept their mouths shut, their tongues tied, their hands clasped, and their legs locked. They are half dead and half alive. They did not speak out when they should have, and they did not resist when they should have. Having first shown their own weakness, how can they blame others for taking advantage of them and taking violent actions against them? Today, we have suddenly come to realize that Hunan belongs, now and in the future, to those engaged in proper and legitimate business in the territory of Hunan. Hunanese affairs should be decided by all the people of Hunan themselves. Whoever supports such self-rule is the friend of the Hunanese people, and whoever obstructs it is their enemy. It is the sole desire and responsibility of the people of Hunan to regain our freedom, and we cannot but urge our fellow countrymen, and people of ideals and integrity all over the country, to make a tremendous show of sympathy.

---

3. The May 16 text has "from their Japanese father."
4. Here the May 16 version contains the following additional passage:

> Our Hunan has been plunged into an abyss of suffering. The 30 million Hunanese have been massacred, raped, imprisoned, insulted, exploited, and plundered; no one knows how many of them have died. Zhang Jingyao, who was merely a petty Anhui brigand, has invaded Hunan with his military forces and is waging war against the citizens and the students. He has allowed his evil brothers and adopted son to run wild in Changsha, regarding murder and torture as everyday occurrences. Every day that Zhang Jingyao is still alive is a day when we Hunanese cannot live. If we consider carefully how the people of Hunan came to undergo such suffering, it is true that it definitely began with the warlords, but our people also share responsibility in bringing this about.

Reply to Zeng Yi from the Association for Promoting Reform in Hunan

(June 23, 1920)

Your Excellency Mr. Zeng Yi:[1]

We have carefully read your kind letter and greatly appreciate your honest and straightforward words. If the situation in Hunan is utterly disastrous, it is entirely because the majority of the people are unable to achieve self-consciousness, to stand up, and to speak out. The people of Hunan do not say what is on their minds, and they do not put forward their opinions, so the military men from the north and the south[2] have taken advantage of this to bully and humiliate the Hunan people. They have forcibly occupied Hunan as their own territory and pocketed the wealth of the people. We shall not talk about the past. From now on, the essential things for us to do are, in negative terms, to abolish the military governorship and cut the military forces, and on the positive side, to build people's rule. From our observation of the current situation, there is no hope for fully establishing people's rule in China within the next twenty years. During this period, Hunan had best protect its own boundaries and implement its own self-rule, making Hunan a haven of peace[3] without bothering about the other provinces or the central government. Thus it can place itself in a position similar to that of one of the states on the North American continent a hundred years ago. We should run our own education, promote our own industry, and construct our own railways and motor roads. By bringing into full play the spirit of the people of Hunan, we can create a Hunanese civilization within the territory of Hunan. We would do so not because we want to become a small tribe, but because this

---

1. Zeng Yi (1879–1953), *zi* Songqiao, original name Zeng Wei, was born in Hanshou, Hunan. He studied in Japan and there joined the Tongmenghui in 1906. In 1913 he was arrested for his journalistic activities; after another brief period in Japan in 1914, he edited the Shanghai *Zhonghua xinbao* (New China) from 1915 to 1919. At the end of 1919 he became professor of Chinese at Nanjing Hehai Engineering College. He visited Changsha in 1920. This letter, drafted by Mao on behalf of the Association for Promoting Reform in Hunan, was first published on June 28, 1920, in the Shanghai *Shenbao* and *Guomin ribao*.

2. I.e., the Beiyang warlords and the warlords from the Southwest.

3. Literally, "a peach-blossom spring," from the peaceful arcadia first described by the poet Tao Qian. (See endnote 22 to Mao's commentary on Paulsen.)

area of Hunan is the only place where we can exert our efforts. For the past four thousand years, Chinese politics has always opted for grand outlines of large-scale projects with big methods. The result has been a country outwardly strong but inwardly weak; solid at the top but hollow at the bottom; high-sounding on the surface but senseless and corrupt underneath. Since the founding of the Republic, famous people and great men have talked loudly about the constitution, the parliament, the presidential system, and the cabinet system. But the more noisily they talk, the bigger mess they make. Why? Because they try to build on sand, and the edifice collapses even before it is completed. We want to narrow the scope and talk about self-rule and self-government in Hunan. We boldly assert that Hunan belongs to the Hunanese people. Neither Lu Rongting nor Tang Jiyao nor Duan Qirui[4] is Hunanese, and they have no proper or legitimate business in the territory of Hunan and should not be allowed to deal with the affairs of Hunan. If we want to talk about unalterable principles, this is an unalterable principle. Hunan is a big country which extends to the Five Ridges in the south, and reaches Lake Dongting in the north. It is well watered and fertile, and talented people abound there. Hunan can supply food, clothing, and housing for itself. It can also exchange its tea, rice, and minerals for silver dollars and other necessities of daily life. Among men and in the heavens, Hunan is great and impressive. It is like Switzerland in the West or Japan in the East. Although it may sound a bit exaggerated to say so, it will definitely not be difficult to reach this goal if our 30 million people all work hard together. To construct a high building without first constructing a foundation has been the mistake of the Chinese for the past four thousand years. To plow the land of others without working on their own land has been the mistake of the Hunanese in the recent past. When we propose "self-determination for the people of Hunan," we do not mean tribalism or separatism. What we mean is that the Hunanese should themselves assume responsibility for creating a civilization on the territory of Hunan. This is a responsibility that they dare not and cannot deny. Those who oppose the creation of a Hunan civilization are the warlords, the high commissioner of

4. Duan Qirui (1865–1936), *zi* Zhiquan, a native of Anhui, graduated from the Beiyang Military Academy in 1887; after a period of study in Germany he returned to China to teach at the Weihaiwei military school. He became one of Yuan Shikai's chief military aides and commander of a number of Beiyang Army divisions in the early 1900s. When Yuan became president of the Republic, Duan was appointed minister of war. After Yuan's death much power passed to Duan, who acted as premier in 1916–17 during the presidencies of Li Yuanhong and Feng Guozhang. With the powerful Beiyang military clique as a power base, he began a serious campaign to unify China militarily. He dismissed Tan Yankai from the Hunan governorship in August 1917 and appointed one of his own subordinates, Fu Liangzuo, to the post. Duan's fourth and final term as premier in 1918 was marked by agreements with Japan which aroused public opposition. Factionalism within the Beiyang clique, and the resulting split into Zhili and Anfu groups, led to his resignation as premier in October 1918, though Duan remained the dominant figure in Beijing until the summer of 1920.

Hunan, Guangdong, and Guangxi,[5] the high commissioner of Hunan and Hubei,[6] the National Protection Army,[7] the Pacification Army,[8] and the Southern Expeditionary Army.[9] Enemies of this kind must all leave the territory of Hunan and never be allowed to enter Hunan again to oppress the Hunanese people. Thus the people of Hunan will be able freely and naturally to develop their own nature and create their own civilization. This is the essence of what we mean by self-determination of the Hunanese people.

The gist of your letter is: "self-rule for the Hunanese, abolishing the military governorship and abolishing the army, staying above the power struggle among the parties from the south and the north, and making Hunan a buffer zone." We absolutely agree with these excellent ideas. As for the proposal that "no single soldier be stationed in Hunan," it is noble in purpose and unassailable. Nevertheless, this Association suggests that all the garrison corps and the office of defense commissioner be abolished, but that a well-disciplined division of the regular army be maintained temporarily, while you believe that the garrison corps will be needed in place of the regular army to keep order locally. Although the differences in their names may not mean much, their roles are totally different. First, the garrison corps are the friends of the local bandits. Without the garrison corps, the bandits will get no weapons; without the local bandits, the garrison corps will have no opportunity to go out on campaigns, and will not get higher campaign pay or plunder from the villages nearby. The regular army is comparatively well disciplined, and is feared by the bandits. Second, whereas it only requires the addition of one army division at most to do the job, at least seven to eight headquarters and three to four defense commissioner's offices will be needed if the garrison corps are to be placed all over Hunan. This will greatly increase the number of troops. Third, self-determination for Hunan definitely does not mean nonresistance[10] when invaders come; nor does it mean that people will tolerate the use of violence against them. Should violence recur, formal resistance will be indispensable. Self-determination for the Hunan people is like

5. I.e., Lu Rongting.

6. I.e., Wang Zhanyuan.

7. The Huguojun, or National Protection Army, was originally founded in Yunnan in December 1915 by Cai E, Li Dazhao, Tang Jiyao, and others in opposition to Yuan Shikai's plans to restore the monarchy. One of Cai's officers was none other than Zhu De, later commander in chief of the Red Army.

8. The Jingguojun, or Pacification Army, was organized in 1917 in Yunnan, Shaanxi, and other provinces. In September 1917, when Sun Yatsen organized a government in Guangzhou based on the Hufajun (Law-Protecting Army), Tang Jiyao, the Yunnan military governor, sent him a telegram approving this idea. Other provinces followed, but by 1921 the Pacification Army had begun to disintegrate.

9. This was an army organized in 1918 by the Beijing government as an expeditionary force which would move south to unify China.

10. Here Mao refers, more literally, to "self-determinationism" *(zijuezhuyi)* and "nonresistancism" *(wudikangzhuyi)*.

the Monroe Doctrine. Hunan belongs to the Hunanese people. The people of Hunan have no right to intervene in the affairs of other provinces. By the same token, the people of other provinces have no right to intervene in the affairs of Hunan, and if there is intervention, it will be resisted. Therefore, the establishment of a division of the regular army addresses the issue of manpower, of bandits, and also of resisting violence if necessary. This is the third argument. Alas for Hunan! After Yu Xiong founded the state [of Chu],[11] Hunan began to emerge. Zeng Guofan and Zuo Zongtang[12] were our predecessors. Huang and Cai[13] were model compatriots. Since then Hunan has been in constant decline. Now Guangxi and Guangdong want to take the southern part of it. Yunnan and Guizhou want to take the western part of it. The northern warlords want to take the northern part of it. Yueyang has been under the control of the troops of the northern warlords for six years. Changsha has been frequently trampled on by the troops of Tang, Fu, and Zhang.[14] Whoever has seen this situation must weep for the people of Hunan. Although the Hunanese are dying, they are not all dead. When oppressed to the utmost, they might close their eyes, but the negative force of sabotage and destruction still lies in their character, as is shown in the movement to drive Tang Xiangming, Fu Liangzuo, and Zhang Jingyao out of Hunan. From now on, what we need to pay attention to is positive construction. It is of immediate importance to observe the whole situation around the world, to establish the institutions of self-rule, to spread culture, and to reform education. A population of 30 million people is equal to the population of Japan when the Meiji Restoration was being carried out. Geographically, Hunan is in a much better position than Switzerland. [Our people are] numerous, but inadequate; [our land is] large, but inadequate. We do not have the knowledge, abilities, and training that the Japanese or the Swiss have. We have often plucked up our courage with empty programs and we are usually good at destroying things passively and unconsciously. Thus neither a glorious country such as Switzerland, nor a wealthy state such as Japan, is to be found in the Yangzi River valley. Your excellency is also a Hunanese, and your letter shows that you share our feelings about the province. All of us are just common people, and our views regarding

11. During the Spring and Autumn period, the kingdom of Chu, which encompassed present-day Hunan as part of a much wider territory, emerged as the largest and most powerful state in the South. Yu Xiong was its earliest known ruler.

12. Zuo Zongtang (1812–1885), *zi* Jigao, *hao* Laoliang, a native of Hunan, was a military leader and statesman of the late Qing and a promoter of Westernization. Though he held many important official posts, Mao is obviously thinking here of his collaboration with Zeng Guofan in crushing the Taipings. Subsequently, he himself led the campaign in 1876–78 for the recovery of Xinjiang from Muslim rebels.

13. Huang Xing, one of the two fathers of the 1911 revolution, and Cai E, both frequently mentioned above.

14. In the text which appears in the Tokyo edition (*Bujuan,* Vol. 1), these names are amplified as follows: "Tang Xiangming—the butcher, Fu Liangzuo—the tyrant, and Zhang Jingyao—the beast."

the conditions for transforming the affairs of Hunan can be found in the published manifesto of our Association. The first principle is self-determination. The second is people's rule. Tan Zu'an,[15] Zhao Yanwu,[16] and other officers and soldiers who were in the movement to drive Zhang Jingyao out of Hunan worked hard and performed a valuable service and have become heroes among our compatriots. In future, we hope they will pay attention to the following points: First, defend self-rule and do not open the door to dangerous tigers. Any tiger that has already got in, or may get in hereafter, must be officially rejected and expelled. Second, to defend the people's rule they must think of themselves as members of the common people, and get rid of the bad habits of the soldiers, the bureaucrats, and the gentry. From now on, their actions must be guided by the public opinion of the 30 million common people. Most important of all is to abolish the military governorship and to cut the size of the army. Money must not be wasted, and efforts must be made to expand education. Our 30 million people must all have freedom of speech, publication, assembly, and association. These are our greatest hopes. Your letter has already appeared in the Shanghai papers. The great turmoil has just begun to be contained, and everyone among the 30 million should speak out, each putting forward his own views independently arrived at, and share the responsibility for reform. We would gladly welcome any further instruction you might be kind enough to grant us.

Association for Promoting Reform in Hunan

June 23

29 South Minhou Lane, Hatong Road, Shanghai

---

15. Tan Yankai. For details on his and Zhao's role in the movement to oust Zhang Jingyao, see the text of October 5–6, 1920.

16. Zhao Hengti (1880–1971), *zi* Yiwu, *hao* Yanwu, was from Hengshan, Hunan. He studied at the Japanese Officers' Academy in Tokyo and after the establishment of the Republic worked under Governor Tan Yankai in Hunan. After the expulsion of Zhang Jingyao and another brief period of rule by Tan Yankai, Zhao became governor of Hunan in November 1920. As governor he was an active promoter of the federal reform movement, and by granting a provincial constitution and establishing a new government on January 1, 1922, he made Hunan the spearhead of the movement for decentralization in China. In March 1926, he was forced to resign his office to his subordinate Tang Shengzhi, backed by the Guomindang, in the context of the Northern Expedition.

Letter to Hu Shi[1]

(July 9, 1920)

Mr. Shizhi:

Has the letter I sent from Shanghai[2] reached you? I got back to Hunan the day before yesterday. With the departure of Zhang, there is an entirely new atmosphere in Hunan, and education is in a rather flourishing state. In future, there will be many points on which Hunan will need to ask your help once again. When the time comes, we can discuss it in detail, but for the moment I won't burden you further. With respectful best wishes.

1. This missive was, in fact, written on a postcard.
2. Nothing is known of this letter, which does not appear to have survived.

General Regulations of the Xiangtan Society for the Promotion of Education[1]

(July 27, 1920)

Article 1: The name of this Society is the Xiangtan Society for the Promotion of Education.

Article 2: The purpose of this Society is to promote education in Xiangtan.

Article 3: The office of this Society is located at No. 4, Yihuihou Street.

Article 4: The tasks of this Society are:

1. Making suggestions regarding educational administration.
2. Conducting basic studies on the organization of the *xian* Council on Education.
3. Conducting studies on the regulation, expansion, and allocation of the educational budget of the whole district.
4. Conducting studies of concrete plans for universal education.
5. Conducting studies regarding temporary incidents which may occur in education in the *xian*.
6. Conducting studies on the theory of education and on the dissemination of the New Culture.
7. All the results of the studies conducted by this Society will be published in the journal of the society, or as separate pamphlets.

Article 5: All those who agree with the purpose of this Society, and are capable of serving the cause of education, may become members of the Society on the recommendation of two members.

Article 6: Any member who has acted contrary to the purpose of this Society, or damaged the reputation of this Society, will be deprived of his membership by a two-thirds vote at a meeting where over half of the total members are present.

---

1. No author's name is given on this text, but according to a report published in the Hunan *Dagongbao* on July 26, 1920, Long Yi, Wu Yuzhen, Ma Wenyi, and Mao Zedong were chosen to draft these regulations at the founding meeting of the Society, held on July 25.

Article 7: The detailed rules as to how meetings should be conducted will be laid down separately.

Article 8: This Society will have eight[2] officers. Their responsibilities will be as follows:

1. A general manager to take charge of all the Society's affairs.
2. Two recording secretaries to be in charge of records and documents.
3. A business officer to be in charge of revenue and expenditures, and accounting.
4. Four liaison officers to take charge of dealings with the outside world.
5. When a journal or any other publication is being edited, several members may be temporarily appointed editors by the officers.

Article 9: Every member of the Society shall pay dues of one silver dollar. When the Society publishes journals, or funds are required for other special expenses, the officers may call special membership meetings to raise funds.

Article 10: The present General Regulations are not adapted to every circumstance and may be modified, added to, or cut with the approval of two-thirds of the members.

---

2. In the regulations as published in *Dagongbao* on July 28, 1920, this number appears as six, and the number of business officers is given as two. A name list of the officers of the society, which appeared in the same issue of the newspaper, makes plain, however, that the correct figures are respectively eight and one, and the editors of the *Wengao* have corrected the text of the regulations accordingly. Mao was one of the two "recording secretaries."

The Founding of the Cultural Book Society[1]

(July 31, 1920)

People of other provinces find it very strange to see the Hunanese propagate the New Culture in Hunan. Some people with no eyes in their heads have even added the epithet "impossible"[2] to "the Hunanese." As a matter of fact, the people of Hunan and the New Culture are poles apart. Strictly speaking, the New Culture has nothing to do with the people of Hunan as a whole. If you say that this is a baseless assertion, then let us ask, how many of the 30 million Hunanese have ever had any schooling? Of the ones who have had some education, how many are functionally literate, and understand the whys and wherefores of things? And of those who are literate and understand things, how many know what the New Culture is? We have to understand that having read or heard a few new terms does not mean that I have mastered a field of learning, much less the New Culture. It is even more impossible to say that Hunan already has the New Culture. Indeed, if we really face the facts, not only Hunan, but the whole of China, still does not have the New Culture. Similarly, the whole world does not yet have the New Culture. A tiny blossom of New Culture has appeared in Russia, on the shores of the Arctic Ocean. For several years, fierce winds and heavy rains have been testing it, and we still do not know whether it will develop successfully or not. Gentlemen, if we know that there is as yet no real New Culture in the whole world, this fact imposes a responsibility on us. What is that responsibility? "How can we bring about a New Culture in the world, and how can we launch it from this Hunan in which we live, where there is no New Culture near at hand?" Is this not the shared responsibility of all the people of Hunan? We fellow members of the Cultural Book Society are willing to do our

1. The Cultural Book Society, founded in July 1920, was formally established on August 2, and the bookstore opened for business on September 9, 1920. By March 1921 a total of seven branch stores had opened. The Society was closed down in 1927 by the Guomindang. The text of this statement was written by Mao. When it was first published in the *Dagongbao* of July 31, 1920, it was preceded by the following editorial note, which is not by Mao: "Comrades in journalistic and educational circles in the provincial capital have recently founded a Cultural Book Society as a headquarters for disseminating new publications. This is indeed an indispensible event for the present New Culture movement. We hasten to record below the reasons for its emergence."

2. *Liaobude,* a common expression which (as noted above in another context) can mean either "terrific" or "fantastic," or on the other hand "terrible" or "awful." Here the sense would appear to be something like impossible, absurd, or hopeless.

best to fulfill our small share of this common task. It is for this reason that we have founded this Cultural Book Society. (Besides the bookstore, we also urgently need to set up research, editorial, and printing societies.) We are firmly persuaded that the absence of New Culture stems from the absence of new thought, that the absence of new thought results from the absence of new research, and that new research is impossible without new materials. At present, the minds of the Hunanese are even more famished than their bellies. Young people in particular are crying for nourishment. The Cultural Book Society wishes to introduce, through the fastest and easiest channels, all kinds of new Chinese and foreign books, newspapers, and magazines, which will serve as the source materials for new research by the young, and by the Hunanese people as a whole. Perhaps, as a result, new thought and New Culture will emerge. We devoutly pray this will be the case, and are filled with hope.

The Cultural Book Society was initiated by a few of us who understand and trust each other completely. The capital invested, no matter who the investor, can never be withdrawn, and there will never be any dividends. This Book Society will forever be jointly owned by the investors. If it does well, if the capital reaches hundreds of millions, we will not consider it a source of private gains. If it fails, and not a penny is left from the venture, we will not blame one another. We will be content to know that on this earth, in the city of Changsha, there was once a "collectively owned" Book Society.

Declaration of the Xiangtan Society for the Promotion of Education

(July 31, 1920)

By their proposals put forward in common, the members of the Xiangtan Society for the Promotion of Education[1] seek to promote education in our city. We jointly resolve to issue the following declaration:

It has been nearly twenty years since our city opened its first school. The achievements were quite good during the reigns of the Guangxu and Xuantong emperors.[2] Progress was especially rapid at the beginning of the Republic. Although the content remained imperfect, a basic framework was built. In recent years, the European tide has flowed to the East, and new schools of thought have emerged daily. Scholars all over the country have been enthusiastically responding to the new trends and engaging in reforms. The educational community of our city alone is neither able to meet the needs of the times and seek innovation nor capable of restoring its original spirit and maintaining the status quo. Half of the schools have closed; knowledge-hungry youth have nowhere to turn. Tuition is rising every year, but money is ill-spent. The fundamental cause is that those who are in charge of education do not keep abreast of world trends, remain ignorant of their own shortcomings, and lack a sense of responsibility and an inspiring spirit. This is the cause of the problem. Education is an instrument for promoting the progress of society; an educator is a person who utilizes this instrument. That is why the theories and methods of education must progress constantly in order to promote the advancement of society. And the thinking of educators must progress constantly in order to be able to absorb and utilize these progressive theories and methods and promote the progress of society. As world intellectual trends are changing constantly, the New Culture movement in our country has emerged. The reform of literature and the liberation of thinking are rapidly sweeping the country. Dr. Dewey of America has come to the East.[3] His new theory of education is well worth studying. Our *xian*, however, remains

1. This Society was formally established on July 27, 1920, and Mao was elected a recording secretary. (See, above, the regulations adopted on that date.). The first business meeting was held on July 30, and the decision was taken to have Mao draft this declaration, which appeared in *Dagongbao* on August 3 and 4, 1920.

2. The Guangxu era lasted from 1875 to 1908, and the Xuantong era from 1909 to 1911.

3. John Dewey lectured in China from 1919 to 1921, visiting Changsha in October 1920.

isolated, closed-off, and ignorant of the situation outside. Those in charge are conservative, ill-informed, confused, and ignorant. If it cannot respond to the new intellectual trends, education loses its effectiveness. We look toward the future with profound anxiety! The decadent state of education in our city is known far and wide. It is an undeniable fact that many abnormalities do indeed exist. Those in charge of education have neither a definite policy nor a concrete plan. Furthermore, they have neither the will to get things done nor the determination to seek improvement. Consequently the educational community lacks the spirit that can inspire others, and the public gradually comes to distrust the schools. If we do not act urgently and jointly to seek remedies, the situation will get worse and worse, leading education in the entire city into complete bankruptcy. Motivated by their respect for their native place, the members of this association, in the search for a plan to promote education, want to work together with colleagues in the educational community throughout the *xian* to review trends in the outside world, to examine our internal deficiencies, to take responsibility, and to arouse a new spirit. As to how to plan for education throughout the *xian*, and how to implement it, how to expunge what is old and decayed, and how to bring in new knowledge, how to allocate funds properly and employ the right people and avoid mistakes, how to break down and bridge the non-problematic boundaries between the old and the new, and how to resolve and change previous personality disputes — all these issues will be dealt with in consultation and according to the truth. All these critically important issues can be solved only by uniting the people and moving forward courageously. Although our strength is small, sincerity is our sword. All our proposals will be made in the public interest, and never on the basis of personal preferences or emotional reactions. We shall always adopt an open-minded attitude toward all views and treat each other sincerely. Those with similar interests will be inducted as comrades. Today is the beginning. Be it so declared.

Business Regulations

(1920)

(I) This Society's[1] business falls under the following three headings: (1) Books; (2) Magazines; (3) Daily newspapers.

(II) (Omitted)

(III) The price of the books, newspapers, and magazines we carry will be no higher than that of the original publishers, and may be lower, as long as we manage to cover the shipping and handling costs.

(IV) Book Society transactions are in silver dollars.

(V) Purchases are in cash only. Credit may be given only to those who have good credit and are backed by a credit guarantor. Purchases made on credit have to be paid in full within a month.

(VI) Outstanding accounts will be closed on the last day of each month, bills will be delivered the first day of the following month, and someone will be sent to collect payment on the third. Bills are to be settled every month. No exceptions will be made for anyone.

(VII) Any schools or organizations in other *xian* that are willing to act as agents for the distribution of our Society's books and periodicals may come in (or write to us) for the Distribution Guidelines and sign an agreement to be a distributor. In order to promote the use of teaching materials in colloquial Chinese, anyone in another *xian* who wants to conduct primary school teaching using textbooks in colloquial Chinese may ask us to place orders for him. We will order immediately as requested and will pack and mail the order free of charge.

---

1. I.e., the Cultural Book Society.

General Regulations for Branch Offices

(1920)

According to Article 5 of the Outline of the Organization of the Cultural Book Society, "This Society will establish its general office in the provincial capital and will have branches in every *xian*." In order to disseminate our new publications in every *xian* throughout the province, we encourage comrades in all *xian* to establish branch stores in the *xian* capitals and market towns (wherever there is a post office) to sell the new publications carried by this Book Society. The branch stores will attach their local place-names to that of the Cultural Book Society (for example, Pingjiang Cultural Book Society, Liuxi Cultural Book Society). Procedures will be as indicated below:

(I) Discounts. Branch stores will receive the full discounts offered to the Cultural Book Society by the original publishers' outlets.

(II) Shipping costs. To be assumed by the branch stores.

(III) Handling fee. To be assumed by the branch stores (handling fee of 4 cents on each *yuan*).

(IV) Payment. Purchases shall be prepaid before they will be shipped. In special cases, a request may be made by a person this Book Society fully trusts to act as guarantor to the Book Society, to pay one-half the purchase price before delivery, accounts to be settled in full each month.

(V) Book orders. The branch stores will investigate and determine what kinds of books, papers, and magazines are needed in their localities, and then select the books, magazines, and newspapers they need from the Book Society catalog. Branch store orders will be mailed out the same day that they are received at the Book Society.

(VI) Newspaper subscriptions. The branch stores may sell subscriptions to the Shanghai *Minguo ribao* (Republican Daily) and *Shishi xinbao* (China Times), the Beijing *Chenbao* (Morning Post), and the Hunan *Tongsubao* (Popular Daily). For ten or more copies of one newspaper, the Book Society will arrange with the newspaper publisher to have the newspapers shipped directly to the branch store.

(VII) Book returns. The branch offices are entitled to return, within one and a half months, books and magazines that have been received but cannot be sold. However, soiled or damaged books are not returnable; nor are magazines and newspapers. Branch stores are responsible for the cost of shipping returned books.

For the Attention of Branch Offices

(1920)

(I) This Society[1] is established by the joint efforts of comrades. Investments will not be returned, nor will dividends or interest be paid, but the Society shall forever be jointly owned by the investors. All branch offices should be organized according to this procedure, in order to ensure a firm foundation. Setting up a branch store may cost 50 *yuan* for fewer books, or 100 *yuan* for more books.

(II) If it is difficult to set up an independent branch store, it might be best to affiliate with a school or other public institution (like the Education Society, the Education Promotion Association, etc.). For branch stores organized by just three or so comrades, they can operate in their homes. In the beginning, small stores are more suitable. Methods of operation should be realistic, with expectations for gradual growth. The thing to be most avoided is a lot of empty noise. If expenses are too large and accounts are not settled, the situation will become untenable.

(III) Branch office sales may best be promoted by the methods of publicity and persuasion.

(IV) Each branch office shall make a sales report to the Book Society every six months. The Book Society will collect and edit these materials as a "Report on Book Society Activities," and send it to all branches, so they can make comparisons which will prompt them to make further progress.

1. I.e., the Cultural Book Society.

Outline of the Organization of the Cultural Book Society

(August 25, 1920)

1) This Society takes as its main task the supply and sale of all kinds of worthwhile books, newspapers, and magazines, both Chinese and foreign. In selling books, newspapers, and magazines, we shall seek to make them both inexpensive and rapidly available, so that all sorts of worthwhile new publications may circulate throughout the province, and everyone will have the opportunity to read them. As for books published outside the province, our society has entered into special agreements with various bookstores and publishers, so that every time a new title is published, it will be sent to Hunan with the utmost speed and can quickly be read. As regards worthwhile newspapers, we will subscribe to those for which there is a relatively large number of readers in our Society, and act as sales agents. In the case of worthwhile periodicals, we will enter subscriptions with the various publishers, and act as distributors.

2) No limit will be placed on the amount of capital to be invested in the Society. When the initial promoters have subscribed the amount necessary to begin operations, we will begin on a small scale and gradually expand. Eventually, the whole of the Society's assets will be owned in common by all investors. Anyone at all who agrees with the purpose of the Society can invest one *yuan* or more at any time, but the capital invested by each individual must be recognized as the common property of the Society as a whole. Funds once invested will no longer be the property of the individual concerned; they can never at any time be withdrawn, nor will the investor ever be entitled to interest.

3) A council of the Society will be organized by the investors and will appoint a manager, vested with full powers to run all the Society's affairs. In order to run the Society's affairs, the manager may employ such assistants as are necessary. The manager and his assistants should receive suitable amounts for living expenses and as compensation for their work, such amounts to be determined by the council.

4) The manager will be required to balance the accounts separately every day, and again every month. Every six months, there must be an audit, which must be reported to the council. The council will meet every half year (in March and September) to examine the state of operations as reported by the manager and discuss progress.

5) This Society will establish its general office in the provincial capital and

will have branches in every *xian.* Branches will be established as soon as they have sufficient funds for operation.

6) The Society will set up a reading room on its premises, in which books and periodicals will be displayed and made available for the masses to read. Such reading rooms should also be established in the branches whenever there are sufficient funds available.

7) The business activities of this Society shall be public knowledge, and every month a report on operations will be made available. In normal circumstances, anyone who would like to know the situation of the Society can visit the office, or send a written inquiry at any time, and will receive a full reply.

8) Detailed regulations regarding the council, and the operation of the Society, will be formulated separately.

The Fundamental Issue in the Problem of Hunanese Reconstruction: The Republic of Hunan

(September 3, 1920)

After resting in the tranquillity of the countryside, where three weeks passed almost without my noticing it, I arrived in the provincial capital[1] on September 1. Leafing through *Dagongbao*, with its cover printed in red, I have found so many comments very much to my liking that in my delight I am anxious to write down some of my own reflections.

I oppose the "Great Republic of China," and advocate a "Republic of Hunan." What are the reasons?

Broadly speaking, there has hitherto been a fallacious argument to the effect that "only great states[2] will be able to struggle for existence in the world of the future." The baneful influence of such views has served to expand imperialism, to repress weak minorities in the mother countries, and in the struggle for colonies overseas to turn semicivilized or uncivilized nations into utter slaves, depriving them of the right to survive and develop, and forcing them into unconditional obedience and submission to its power. The most notorious examples are England, America, Germany, France, Russia, and Austria. Fortunately, all of them achieved a success that was not really a success. There is another country, namely, China, which did not even achieve a success such as that. What China has obtained is the annihilation of the Manchus and the reduction of the

1. Changsha.

2. In the numerous articles on Hunanese autonomy which begin with this one, Mao uses several terms for state, including the single characters *guo* and *bang*, and the compound *guojia*. All of them evoke in some degree both the state as a political entity, and the country more loosely defined. Because it is important to make as clear and unambiguous as possible in English whether Mao is talking about regional autonomy, or about Hunan as a state in the full sense of the word, we have adopted in this series of texts uniform translations of the terms just mentioned. *Guo* has been rendered as "country," and *bang* as "state." (That is not the case in this volume as a whole, where *guo* has been translated sometimes as "state," sometimes as "country," depending on the context.) *Guojia*, which is the term appearing here, points strongly to the state machine, and is therefore also translated "state."

Mongols, Huis, and Tibetans to their last gasp; turmoil in the eighteen provinces; the emergence of three governments[3] and three parliaments;[4] more than twenty "kings" in the shape of military governors, viceroys, and commanders in chief. Its people are dying of murder and rape every day. Its wealth is being looted. Its foreign debt is as high as a mountain. Though China claims to be a Republic, there are very few citizens who really know what a republic is. Out of the total population of 400 million, at least 390 million people are not able to write letters or read newspapers. There is not a single railway line in the whole country which we can call our own. China cannot run a postal service, sail foreign-style ships, or handle the salt trade. Many of the eighteen provinces, such as Hunan, Sichuan, Guangdong, Fujian, Zhejiang, and Hubei, have become conquered provinces, repeatedly trampled on by others, the victims of tremendous damage. Whose fault is all this? It is, I have no hesitation in saying, the fault of the imperialist countries, the fault of the big countries, and the fault of the fallacy that "only great states are able to struggle for existence in the world." In the final analysis, it is the fault of the people.

Now we know that most of the big countries of the world have fallen apart. Russia's flag has turned red, and it has truly become an internationalist world for the common people. Germany has been dyed half red. Poland has won its independence, and so have Czechoslovakia and Hungary. The Jews, the Arabs, and the Armenians have all reestablished their own countries. Ireland desperately wants to divorce itself from England, as Korea does from Japan. Even in the far eastern region of Siberia, which lies to our northeast, three governments have been set up. A storm of change is rising throughout the entire world; the call for "the self-determination of nations" echoes to the heavens, smashing the illusion about big countries. People know these are merely lies used by the ambitious to deceive them. They are determined to overthrow imperialism and never let it abuse them again. Throughout the world, there are a great many people who have already awakened.

What about China? China has also awakened (except for the politicians, bureaucrats, and warlords). Having experienced nine years of a false republic and the turmoil of civil war, people have been forced not only to wake up, but to realize that for the time being there is no hope for nationwide general reconstruction. The best method is, as a general thing, not to attempt nationwide reconstruction, but instead to promote separation; to encourage each province to work

---

3. The "three governments" are: the 1912 Beijing warlord government in Beijing; the 1916 Military Government established by the National Protection Army in Guangdong; and the 1917 southern opposition government set up by Sun Yatsen in Guangzhou, with the support of the Law-Protecting Army.

4. The "three parliaments" are: the August 1916 parliament convened in Beijing under Li Yuanhong; the August 1917 Extraordinary Parliament convened by Sun Yatsen in Guangzhou; and the August 1918 New Parliament (also known as the Anfu Parliament) convened by Duan Qirui in Beijing.

toward its own separate reconstruction, and to carry out "self-determination by the people of each province." With twenty-two existing provinces, three special areas, and two frontier regions,[5] making twenty-seven regions in all, it would be better to divide China into twenty-seven countries.

What about Hunan? As for this Hunan of ours, every one of its 30 million people must wake up right now. There is no other way for the people of Hunan. The only method for us is to pursue self-determination and self-government and create a "Republic of Hunan" on the territory of Hunan. I have thought it over time and again, and I have come to realize that only by doing so can we save Hunan, save China, and stand hand in hand with all the liberated nations of the earth. If the people of Hunan themselves lack the determination and courage to build Hunan into a country, then in the end there will be no hope for Hunan.

As regards the reconstruction of Hunan, I believe that this is a fundamental issue. I have these few ideas and would like to make them known, in the hope that my 30 million fellow citizens will share my concern and join me in a discussion of this most significant great question. What I have written here today is merely a beginning. I will have more to say about it in the days to come.

---

5. The "three special areas" are Rehe, Chaha'er, and Suiyuan. The "two frontier regions" are Mongolia and Tibet.

Break Down the Foundationless Big China and Build Up Many Chinas Starting with Hunan

(September 5, 1920)

It can well be argued that there is no China because the big China that has existed for four thousand years has no foundation. Even if we say there is a China, it is only China in form, not in reality, because it has no foundation. In my letter of reply to Zeng Yi[1] on behalf of the Association for Promoting Reform in Hunan, I said, "For the past four thousand years, Chinese politics has always opted for grand outlines of large-scale projects with big methods. The result has been a country outwardly strong but inwardly weak; solid at the top but hollow at the bottom; high-sounding on the surface but senseless and corrupt underneath. Since the founding of the Republic, famous people and great men have talked loudly about the constitution, the parliament, the presidential system, and the cabinet system. But the more noisily they talk, the bigger mess they make. Why? Because they try to build on sand, and the edifice collapses even before it is completed." This is sad but true. Nothing can stand without a foundation. Political organization depends on a foundation of social organization. Without social organization, there can be no political organization, or if there is, it will be hollow and false. The foundation of a big country is its small localities. Without first constructing small localities, there is no way to build a big country. A forced attempt at construction simply will not work. It is the individual citizens who comprise the foundation of the citizenry as a whole. If the individual citizens are not healthy and sound, one cannot expect the citizenry as a whole to be healthy and sound. One theory has been that political organizations can reform social organizations, that the state can promote development in the local areas, and that group forces can transform the individual. But this is possible only in a certain environment under certain conditions. For example, Lenin depended on millions of party members to start an unprecedented course of popular revolution that made a clean sweep of the reactionary parties and washed away the upper and middle classes. He had the ideology (Bolshevism), and the opportunity (the defeat of Russia). He was prepared, and had a truly reliable mass party that rose up at the first call and carried out orders as smoothly as

1. See above, Mao's letter dated June 23, 1920.

flowing water. The class of toiling peasants, constituting some 80 to 90 percent of the whole population, also responded immediately. Here lay the reasons for the success of the Russian Revolution. I would give my support if there were a thorough and general revolution in China, but this is not possible (I will not go into the reasons right now). Therefore, in the case of China, we cannot start with the whole, but must start with its parts. My teacher Mr. Yang Huaizhong once said: "It is better to make plans not for the whole but for the part; not at the top but at the bottom; not for oneself but for others." Planning for the whole, at the top, for oneself, is the old method that has been used in China for four thousand years right down to the present day. The result is that "there is no China." Thus today the only way is to "break down the foundationless big China and build many small Chinas."

I suggest that the original twenty-seven local regions, which include the twenty-two provinces, three special districts, and two protectorates, be reconstructed by the people as twenty-seven countries. This will require the self-consciousness of the people in all these provinces and localities. We cannot be certain whether or not the people in all the provinces and local areas will in the end be self-conscious, so we can only focus on our own province of Hunan. Hunanese! We must awaken! Big organizations are ultimately hopeless; small organizations offer boundless hope! The people of Hunan are truly capable and talented. Let us dare to build a Republic of Hunan that shines like the rising sun. Break down the foundationless big China and build up many small Chinas "starting with Hunan."

Absolutely Support the "Hunan Monroe Doctrine"

(September 6, 1920)

Several people have put forward a Hunan Monroe Doctrine,[1] saying, "If put before the people in a general referendum, it would certainly win support by a great majority. . . ." Nevertheless, between a "great majority" and the "whole," there is still the difference of that small minority. Although this small minority is only a small minority, it seems clear to me that sometimes it has a great deal of influence. According to the interpretation of those who propose it, the Hunan Monroe Doctrine contains three principles, "diligently minding our own business," "absolutely not meddling in the affairs of others," and "absolutely not allowing others to meddle in our own affairs," all of which are in line with what the great majority of the people think. I expect that this great majority of the people must include: 1) the peasants who cultivate the land; 2) the workers who work; 3) merchants engaged in trade; 4) students who are serious about their studies; and 5) other people, young and old, who mind their own business. These people all believe that they "should mind their own business," that in the past (forty years ago), the Hunan people liked to meddle in the affairs of others, doing such things as trampling on the area south of the Yangzi River, trampling on Fujian and Zhejiang, trampling on Hubei, Shaanxi, Gansu, and Xinjiang. This was a violation of the principle of "absolutely not meddling in the affairs of others." It is because of this that all of a sudden everyone despised the Hunan people, and that Hunan has been overrun three times within nine years, and has suffered the terrible disaster of having "others meddle in our own affairs." (Take a look at Zhang Jian's[2] open telegram in which he says that, because the Hunan people have trampled on the area south of the Yangzi River, on Jiangsu, Zhejiang, and other areas, they are now suffering the natural retribution. Although there is no inevitable correlation in what he said, it is certainly true that no one can escape the law that the bully will be bullied.) If we want to turn disaster into a good thing, we must first abide by the second principle of "not

1. "The 'Hunan Monroe Doctrine' " was the title of an article by Long Jiangong, the editor-in-chief of the *Dagongbao*, which appeared on September 5, 1920.

2. For more on Zhang Jian, see note to the text "What Kind of Talk Is This?" of July 14, 1919, p. 355.

meddling in the affairs of the others," for only then can the third principle of "others not meddling in our own affairs" be realized.

Even though the peasants, workers, merchants, students, and all those, young and old, who mind their own business, compose the great majority, and would cast their votes in favor of the "Hunan Monroe Doctrine," there is a small minority of people who are neither peasants, workers, merchants, nor students, nor among those young and old who mind their own business, who would cast their votes to "oppose the Hunan Monroe Doctrine." Some people may say that the votes of the minority cannot change the decision made by the majority, so the majority wins and the minority loses. However, I still have some doubts. I want to know to which of the two parties the people supervising the ballot boxes belong, the majority party or the minority party? If the former, of course, there is no problem. But if it is the latter, then the result of the vote will inevitably be that "the original proposal is defeated" and its opposite, the vote for "Hunan aggressionism" is passed by a large majority. Experience shows that this assumption is true over 99 percent of the time. That is why I say that "although it is only a small minority, sometimes it has a great deal of influence."

The clamor to "support Guangdong"[3] does not come from the peasants, workers, merchants, or students, or from those, young and old, who mind their own business. It does not come from the great majority of the people, but rather from a small minority of people who have no occupation, who are neither peasants, nor workers, nor merchants, nor students, nor those young and old who mind their own business. Seriously, if they really want to support Guangdong, I suggest they hold a general referendum. In order to prevent the bad practices described above from occurring, I suggest that the ballot boxes be put into the hands of our "great majority." I make such a proposal because I absolutely support the Hunan Monroe Doctrine.

3. This is a reference to a telegram which was sent by Tan Yankai on September 6, 1920, on the question of Guangdong–Guangxi relations, and the proposal that "Guangdong people rule Guangdong."

Hunan Is Burdened by China: Proof from History and from the Present Situation

(September 6–7, 1920)

Ever since there has been a China, there has also been a Hunan. In ancient times, Hunan was a land of the Man.[1] Under the Zhou Dynasty, it became the state[2] of Chu; under the Han, it was the kingdom of Changsha; under the Tang Dynasty, it became a commandery; under the Song, it was the Southern Circuit of Jing-Hu; under the Yuan Dynasty, it finally became a province, and has remained so through the Ming and Qing Dynasties down to the present day. In such a long period of four thousand years, the human race as a whole has been evolving, but what has evolved in Hunan? During the Spring and Autumn period, Jing-Chu rose to prominence, so that it could almost compete with the larger states in the Central Plains.[3] At that time, the various states existed side by side, with no central government over them, and each was able to develop in its own way. Although those in power in these states were ambitious and heroic princes and ministers, obsessed with rivalry and invasion that had nothing to do with ordinary people, and their glorious achievements were fleeting, like sound and lightning, they were able to develop some of their states' particular qualities. This was infinitely superior to being slaves under the dark and all-embracing rule of a despot. The center of what was called Jing-Chu was not, however, in Hunan, but in Hubei. This piece of land bordering the Xiao and Xiang rivers, compared with the Yangzi and Han rivers, was what a junior clerk is to a high official. Thus Hunan was not of much account in the China of that time. The kingdom of Changsha was simply a small, weak, pitiful state, without independence or self-government. Under the commandery, and the Southern Circuit of Jing-Hu, the Hunanese were, quite simply, ruled like slaves. During the Five Dynasties Pe-

1. The name Man was used generically in ancient times for the national minorities of the South. Its primary meaning has come to be "barbarous" or "savage," but here Mao probably intended simply to underscore the fact that Hunan was part of a region not yet entirely Sinified.

2. When *guo* stands for a particular named entity, as in this sentence, we have translated it not as "country," but in accordance with common usage. Thus, *Chu guo* is rendered as "the state of Chu," and *Changsha guo* as "the kingdom of Changsha."

3. Jing was the original name of Chu. The kingdom of Chu, as indicated in the note to Mao's letter of June 23, 1920, was the largest state in the South during the Spring and Autumn period.

riod, Hunan was turned into a separate state by Ma Yin.[4] Its poverty and weakness are too well known to require comment. As for the period when Hunan was a province, it was just an official residence serving the emperor during his tours. Thus the whole of Hunan was enslaved by a single king. During the long dark night from the Yuan and Ming through the Qing dynasties, Hunan experienced nothing but the worst suffering and pain. From this we can see that, during four thousand years of history, the people of Hunan have never been able to stand up or speak out. The history of Hunan is simply a history of darkness. The civilization of Hunan is simply a civilization of grayness. This is the result of Hunan's having been burdened by China for the past four thousand years, and having been unable to develop naturally in its own way.

In China's Reform Movement, it was Hunan that came first. In 1897 and 1898, Hunanese were dynamic and full of vigor. In the study of the new thought, in the building of new education, and in leaders like Tan Sitong and Xiong Xiling,[5] Hunan was unsurpassed in the whole country. Before long, however, Xiong was driven out and Tan was executed. The moribund Qing government used its official forces against Hunan, the vigorous new impulses were quickly suppressed, and soon the cause of reform was dead. This is another result of Hunan having been burdened by China and having been unable to develop naturally in its own way.

Hunan produced Huang Keqiang,[6] and thus China had a practising revolutionary. But during the uprising of 1904, Pingjiang and Liling were lost, while Huang Keqiang went into hiding. Ma Fuyi[7] had also been one of the leaders, and the Qing court used naked force to humiliate the people of Hunan. Thus Hunan was not able to carry out revolution before 1911, and to overthrow the Manchu Qing Dynasty before the 1911 Revolution, breaking the shackles of slavery. This

4. Ma Yin (852–930), *zi* Shuangtu, a native of present-day Hebei, after serving as governor of Hunan, was named king of the Chu state by the emperor of the posterior Tang dynasty, during the epoch of the Five Dynasties. His kingdom included Hunan and some of the surrounding areas.

5. On Xiong Xiling, see the note to "An Overall Account of the Hunan United Students' Association" of August 4, 1919. After abandoning the premiership in 1914, Xiong had played only a limited role in politics, though he participated in the Shanghai peace converence of 1919. During the Hunan provincial independence movement, he again attracted attention when he drafted an outline self-government law for Hunan, published in the *Dagongbao* at the end of August 1920. It provided that the provincial and *xian* assemblies, the Council on Education, and the Chamber of Commerce should nominate three candidates for the governorship, of whom the president in Beijing would appoint one.

6. Huang Xing, with Sun Yatsen one of the two principal revolutionary leaders prior to 1911. For a full note, see Mao's letter of March 1917 to Miyazaki Tōten.

7. Ma Fuyi (1866–1905) a Hunanese, was a leader of the secret society known as the Gelaohui (Society of Brothers and Elders, or Elder Brother Society), which played a key role in this uprising. In 1905 Huang Xing returned from Japan with firearms to be used in an uprising planned by Ma. The shipment of firearms was discovered, and Ma was captured and executed.

is again the result of Hunan having been burdened by China and having been unable to develop naturally in its own way.

When the Republic was established, those in favor of centralization prevailed over those in favor of separation. Bandit Yuan[8] controlled state power, and butcher Tang[9] came to Hunan. Thus Hunan was conquered for the first time. After the people of Hunan had driven out Tang, Duan Qirui in the North also wanted to realize his pipedream of unifying the country by military means. Fu Liangzuo,[10] a Hunanese relying on support from the North, was appointed governor of Hunan. Thus Hunan was subjugated for the second time. Then the people of Hunan rose again to drive out Fu. When the rebel troops arrived in Yueyang, however, they encountered a more powerful enemy. Zhang Jingyao proceeded to capture Changsha and Baoqing, and Hunan was conquered for the third time. Today, thanks to the Hunanese forces for self-determination, they have arisen to drive out Zhang and to restore the integrity of Hunan. In nine years, Hunan has been subjugated three times, and has been frequently trampled underfoot by the military forces of the northerners, who under the false pretense of unifying the country under the central government, actually ravaged the local areas in Hunan. Don't these recent events constitute an even greater instance of Hunan having been burdened by China, and having been unable to develop naturally in its own way?

If Hunan had not been burdened by China, and had been able to develop naturally in its own way, how could it have been like today's Hunan? Controlled by a big organization, a small organization has to get permission for everything from the central authorities, and has to obey other people's orders about everything. This has produced the evil consequences we see today. Without delving into the distant past, if the people of Hunan could have become independent and self-governing earlier, if they had not been restrained by the central government in 1897–1898, when Hunan led the entire country in the spirit of reform, would they not have created a new Hunan long ago? Secondly, when the 1911 Revolution broke out, Hunan was the first to respond, and Hunan came to be governed by the Hunanese. This continued for two years. Had it not been for the dominance of the so-called central government, and if the people could have been awakened and could have exerted their best efforts in creation and reconstruction, and if Hunan had not suffered the calamity of being thrice subjugated, wouldn't the people of Hunan have been able to build a new Hunan earlier? I have thought this over again and again, and I conclude that if we were not able to build a new Hunan in the past, it was not only because the people in Hunan were weak, but because there were no opportunities as well. Then what about now? The opportunity has come. It has really come, because all of China is now in a

8. Yuan Shikai.

9. Tang Xiangming. (See the note to text of January 17, 1920.)

10. On Fu Liangzuo, see the note to the text of June 11, 1920.

state of anarchy and great turmoil. I expect this situation to continue for at least seven or eight years. Later, China is going to be extremely divided and extremely rotten. The military men will run amok even more savagely, and politics will be even more corrupt. Out of all this, however, a new situation is bound to come. What is this new situation? It is a situation under which there is a change from monopolistic control over the local areas by the military men and bureaucrats to provincial self-government by the people of each province. Since they have suffered so much under the dictatorial and monopolistic rule of military men and bureaucrats, the people in every province will stand up to fight for freedom. It is inevitable that there will be self-government by the people of Hunan, by the people of Guangdong, by the people of Sichuan, and even by the people of Zhili and Fengtian. Within ten to twenty years, "there will arise a new blue-turbaned army,"[11] and that will lead to thoroughgoing general revolution.

Hunanese! Our mission is indeed great, and our opportunities are indeed excellent. We must strive with all our might, first toward the goal of establishing a Republic of Hunan, and then, by realizing our new ideals, creating a new life, and creating a new world in this region at the confluence of the Xiao and the Xiang rivers, to give an example for the other twenty-seven small Chinas to follow. Hunanese! We must all strive together!

---

11. The clause in quotation marks is taken word for word from the biography of Xiang Yu in the *Records of the Historian,* Vol. 7 (p. 207 of the Yangs' translation). It is there attributed to the young men of Dongyang *xian,* who had killed their magistrate at the beginning of the period of uprisings which led to the overthrow of the Qin dynasty and the establishment of the Han, and proceeded to urge his secretary Chen Ying to proclaim himself king, and to establish such a force.

Statutes of the Russia Studies Society

(September 23, 1920)

The Russia Studies Society, organized by Hunanese, held a meeting on the sixteenth of this month and elected its official staff members: Jiang Yonghong[1] as secretary-general, Mao Zedong as secretary, and Peng Huang as treasurer, and asked Peng to live at the office of the Society to take care of all administrative affairs. Mr. Jiang Yonghong made a voluntary donation of one hundred *yuan.* Other members of the Society also made their respective donations. A meeting will be held sometime in the future to raise funds to cover special expenses for sending observers to Russia and for a publication series. Since Beijing has sent several letters saying that arrangements have already been made for a Russian representative to come to Beijing, given the fact that there are many people in Hunan who would like to go to Russia, they have requested that one person first be sent to Beijing. It was decided that Mr. Zhang Peizong would be sent to Beijing to accompany the Beijing delegation to Russia. Two letters of introduction were prepared, one to introduce him to people in Beijing and the other to people in Russia. Mr. Zhang has decided to depart for the north on the seventeenth. Everyone thinks that it is very necessary to study the academic spirit and the affairs of Russia. The blind opposition to this on the part of those whose brains are atrophied will be to no avail. Finally, four items were decided upon:

1. Individual research: members are to collect materials individually.
2. Research seminars: every Saturday and Sunday afternoon the members are free to come to the Society office to participate in group discussions; twice a year, in the spring and autumn, a conference will be held; when scholars specializing on Russia come to Hunan they will be invited to ad hoc seminars as guest speakers.
3. The Society shall collect as many books, newspapers, and magazines related to Russian studies as possible, for all to read.
4. Research results obtained from the above three items, together with other special translated works, shall be compiled into a Russia publication series.

Also, because many of the people who have come to the Society office recently to discuss their desire to visit Russia have requested that a Russian class

1. Jiang Jihuan. For details see note 3 to the text of March 5, 1920.

be started following the model of the French class, preparations are being made. Mr. Guo Kaidi offered to assume responsibility for setting up a class at the Chuanshan Study Society, and said that it would be possible to hire Russians in Shanghai to come to Hunan as teachers.

The Statutes of the Society are recorded as follows:

Article I

The main purpose of the Russia Studies Society is to study everything related to Russia. Membership is open to anyone who is recommended by three members of the Society.

Article II

The activities of the Society shall be as follows:

1. Conduct research on everything related to Russia and compile the research results into a publication series on Russia;
2. Send people to Russia to conduct field studies;
3. Promote a work-study program in Russia.

Article III

The expenses of the Society shall come from voluntary contributions by its members.

Article IV

The Society shall have three staff members with the following functions:

1. One secretary-general, in charge of the overall activities of the Society, who represents the Society in outside contacts.
2. One secretary, responsible for note-taking and other paperwork.
3. One treasurer, to manage the accounts of the society.

Article V

The address for correspondence with the Society shall be 56 Chaozong Street, Changsha, the provincial capital.

It Is Time to Launch a "Hunan Self-Government Movement"

(September 26, 1920)

In any matter whatsoever, if there is a "theory" but no "movement" to carry it through, the aim of this theory cannot be realized. Hunan self-government should encourage and promote such theories as "the necessity for self-government," "now is the best opportunity for planning Hunan self-government," and "Hunan and the Hunanese people do indeed have the ingredients and the capacity for independence and self-government" in order to arouse the interest and courage of those Hunanese who are as yet unenlightened. But if these are not followed up with a real movement, then Hunan self-government will remain just a pretty thing on paper, or a nice-sounding phrase on our lips, and will never become a reality. In theory, moreover, a great many people, after undergoing direct experience with more than their share of misery, have already understood. Thus the only thing lacking now is a real movement, and what is most urgent at present is precisely this real movement.

I believe that there are two kinds of real movements: one is the kind of movement that works from the inside to engage in concrete construction; the other is the kind of movement that is set up on the outside to push things forward. Both are important, but the second kind of movement is especially important right now and in the immediate future. It can probably be said that the success or failure of Hunan self-government, and whether it is good or bad, depend on this kind of movement.

I also feel that the Hunan self-government movement should start from the "people." Even if Hunan self-government really happens this time, but it comes not from the "people," but from outside the "people," then I venture to say that this kind of self-government will not last long. Even though it may have the external form, when it is opened up it will be seen to be without content, or its content will definitely be rotten, false, hollow, or withered.

Now is definitely the time to launch the "Hunan self-government movement." We do not necessarily have to engage in a concrete movement to establish it, but we certainly must not fail to engage in a movement that promotes it. We need not avoid doing it just because our numbers are few. Even though our numbers are few, if we are sincere we will have an effect. Nothing ever succeeds right at the beginning, or is met with sympathy and support right from the start. Rather, everything grows from near to far, from few to many, from small to large. If there are some who say that the Hunanese people are still unenlightened, and communications are not convenient, so it would be hard for self-government to work well, I don't think that people generally will believe such nonsense.

Clearing Up the Doubt

(September 27, 1920)

There is currently a certain doubt in the minds of some people about something they should not "doubt." They say: "The problem of self-rule for Hunan is too big and involves too many complicated details. People like me who know nothing about politics and the law are really afraid to open our mouths. But in my heart I have always felt that this issue is very important. It is just that, not having studied politics and the law, I am always somewhat afraid to open my mouth." This view still regards politics as something that belongs to a special class, and it regards politics as a special vocation only for those who have crammed their minds with the study of politics and the law, and who cloak themselves in long gowns. This is altogether erroneous. In the Spring and Autumn period, when Zichan ruled the state of Zheng, the people of the state of Zheng often gathered in the village schools to discuss government and politics.[1] Had all these people of the state of Zheng studied politics and the law? The laborers of Italy, Britain, France, and the United States keep saying that they will "take over and replace the existing government." Have these laborers all studied politics and the law? In Russia, all politics is controlled by the Russian workers and peasants. Have the Russian workers and peasants all studied politics and the law? Following the Great War, both politics and the law have changed greatly. The politics and laws of the past are no longer of the slightest use. From now on, politics and the law will not be found in the minds of those gentlemen who wear long gowns, but in the minds of the workers and peasants, who can do whatever they want to do politically and write the laws any way they like. Only those who have an occupation will be allowed to discuss politics and the law and to deal with politics and the law. Those who have no occupation will simply have no say in politics and legal matters. So those people who do have occupations must definitely discuss and deal with politics and the law. If you do not discuss politics and the law, politics and the law will come daily to discuss you; if you do not deal with politics and the law, they will come daily to deal with you. Is self-rule for Hunan an issue that we can evade under the pretext of having no knowledge of politics and the law? Self-rule for Hunan is just a very simple and ordinary matter that is

1. Gongsun Qiao (581–521 B.C.), *zi* Zichan, served as prime minister of his native state of Zheng. When he had ruled for three years, it was said that "doors were not locked at night and lost articles were not picked up on the highway." Confucius described him as a benevolent man, and the people of Zheng wept at his death.

not at all abstruse or mysterious. There is no reason at all why it should be based on a certain body of law codes or a certain doctrine. It simply means cutting loose from all the creeping vines by which the central government and other provinces have intervened in and controlled Hunan in the past, and returning control of all matters within the territory of Hunan to the Hunan people themselves. That's all there is to it. What's so abstruse or mysterious about this? I read an article by a Mr. Cao in one of the newspapers, the gist of which was: "Although Xiong Xiling has political experience, he has no knowledge of the law, so his draft document for self-rule is terrible."[2] Whether Xiong's draft is really terrible or not is another matter. What I cannot agree with is that only those who have a knowledge of the law can write a self-rule draft. "Law studies" are derived from the "laws." And the "laws" in turn emerge from the "facts." We are simply going to create the reality of Hunan self-rule, and there is no reason why there cannot be a law of self-rule even if we have never seen one before (formerly the English constitution was not a written one). Of course, we may want to make a law of self-rule for the sake of ornamental show or for the sake of holding up an idol to scare off the central government, to scare off other provinces, and to frighten away anyone with wild ambitions in this province, too. And this law of self-rule can be made and discussed by the majority of the people. And it will be good only if it is drafted by and discussed by the majority of the people. If that minority of aloof politicians who have no occupations were entrusted with drawing up and discussing a law of self-rule, it would certainly be bad. Are you a Hunanese? Provided only that you have reached the age of fifteen (this is the age of adulthood that I adopt) and provided also that you are not mentally ill, you always have the right to speak out, whether you be peasant, worker, merchant, student, teacher, soldier, policeman, beggar, or woman. Furthermore, you certainly should speak out, and you certainly can speak out. As soon as you rid yourself of that little bit of self-doubt that really should not exist, you will immediately discover your great talent and your heavy responsibility. As soon as this talent is discovered in the depths of your heart, this responsibility will fall immediately upon your shoulders.

2. The reference is obviously to the draft law published at the end of August 1920. (See, above, the note to "Hunan Is Burdened by China" of September 6–7, 1920.)

More on the "Promotion Movement"

(September 28, 1920)

The day before yesterday I talked about why a promotion movement is important, but did not fully explore its significance. The fact that Hunan self-government will not happen all by itself is well understood and needs no further explanation. It would also be a great mistake, however, to think that self-government could be realized if a small number of officials or "gentry" would just make up their minds that they wanted to carry it out. We should also consider whether anything at all can be accomplished by a minority of people. In the politics of any country, if there is no confrontation between the party in power and the opposition party, or between the laboring society and the political society, or if, although an opposition party and a laboring society exist, their strength is inadequate to stand up to the party in power or to the political society, then nine times out of ten the politics of that country will not be well conducted. When anything is in its initial stage of development, and when it is moreover an extremely important thing, if there is not a goodly number of persons engaged in a movement to promote it, supervising it from the side and criticizing it from the rear, can this thing be done successfully and well?

"Hunanese Rule of Hunan" Versus "Hunanese Self-Rule"

(September 30, 1920)

"Hunanese rule of Hunan" is the opposite of "non-Hunanese rule of Hunan," such as having someone from Hubei or Anhui rule Hunan. This is, however, still rule by bureaucrats, not by the people. If the purpose of driving out Tang and Zhang were just to get rid of a non-Hunanese, this would once again be merely a change in form, leading once again to Hunanese rule of Hunan. Well then, Zhang Zuolin[1] in Fengtian, the two Caos[2] in Zhili, Zhao Ti[3] in Henan, Chen Shufan in Shaanxi, Ni Cichong[4] in Anhui, Lu Rongting in Guangxi, Tang Jiyao in Yunnan — all these are natives of their respective provinces. This is indeed "Fengtianese rule of Fengtian," "Zhilian rule of Zhili," "Henanese rule of Henan," "Shaanxian rule of Shaanxi," and "Anhuian rule of Anhui." How is this really any different from the "non-Hunanese rule of Hunan" by Tang Xiangming or Zhang Jingyao, or the "non-Hubeian rule of Hubei" by Wang Zhanyuan, or the "non-Fujianese rule of Fujian" by Li Houji,[5] or the "non-Guangdongese rule of Guangdong" by Mo Rongxin?[6] Furthermore, it was with this excuse of having a "Hunanese rule Hunan" that Duan Qirui sent Fu Liangzuo to Hunan. We, therefore, must completely oppose the idea of having a "Hunanese rule Hunan" because it contains many evil intentions. It sets up a few special persons as the rulers, and the common ordinary people become the ruled. The rulers are made masters, and those they rule are made slaves. Such rulers are just like Yu and Tang, Wen and Wu,[7] and we oppose them all. Should we not oppose even more strongly the Fu

1. Zhang Zuolin (1875–1928), *zi* Yuting, from Liaoning Province, was leader of the Beiyang clique of warlords. At this time he was military governor of Fengtian and inspector-general of the three Northeastern provinces.

2. Cao Kun and Cao Rui. Cao Rui, *zi* Jianting, was Cao Kun's younger brother, his close supporter, and a Tianjin government official.

3. Zhao Ti (1871–1933), *zi* Zhouren, from Henan Province, was allied with the Anfu and Zhili warlord cliques and at this time was military governor of Henan.

4. Ni Sichong (1868–1924), *zi* Danchen, was actually a former governor of Anhui Province, having just been removed from his post after the Anfu clique's defeat.

5. Wang Zhanyuan was from Shandong Province, and Li Houji was from Jiangsu Province.

6. Mo Rongxin (1853–1930), *zi* Richu, was born in Guangxi Province.

7. I.e., the kings and emperors of old: Yu, founder of the Xia dynasty; Tang, founder

Liangzuos of the past and the countless Fu Liangzuos of the future? The idea that we propose and welcome is "Hunanese self-rule." Not only are we unwilling to be ruled by someone from another province; we do not want to be ruled by a few privileged persons from our own native province either. We advocate the establishment of total self-rule in the villages, total self-rule in the *xian*, and total self-rule for the province. Village mayors are to be elected by the people, *xian* magistrates are to be elected by the people, and the provincial governor is to be elected by the people. Only when we ourselves elect from among our peers reliable people to perform public functions can it be called "Hunanese self-rule." There are always some people who want to confuse "Hunanese rule of Hunan" with "Hunanese self-rule." It seems to me that this slight difference had best be clarified.

---

of the Shang dynasty; King Wen (posthumous title of Duke Zhou) and his son, King Wu, founder of the Zhou dynasty.

"Complete Self-Rule" and "Semi-Self-Rule"

(October 3, 1920)

Those of us who advocate the establishment of a "country of Hunan" do not necessarily want to change literally the word "province" in Hunan Province into the word "country." We just want to achieve "complete self-rule," and will not be satisfied with mere "semi-self-rule." A "country" has the essential elements of land, people, and sovereignty, of which the most essential is sovereignty. The people of Hunan do not have complete sovereignty to deal with their own affairs themselves, but have long been invaded and occupied by the central government or other provinces which have done them more harm than good. The Hunanese are not insensate; they should certainly have some feelings and should stand up for independence, precisely at this time. Mr. Liu Chunren[1] suggests that a federal state[2] be created. I want to ask: how can we talk about a federation now when there are no states at all in China? For the time being, we can only work hard to create states and forget about a federation. Both Germany and the United States had states before they joined together in federations. Once states are created, federation will be simply the natural result. I have doubts about an overall organization to run China within twenty years, so I not only oppose Wu Ziyu's[3] national congress, I also oppose Liang Qichao's national constitutional referendum, and at the same time, I oppose even more strongly the north–south peace negotiations. I believe that our minimum demand should be the separate existence of north and south, which may then lead to self-rule in each individual province. Among all the provinces, Hunan and Guangdong are in the best position to capitalize on the revolutionary spirit, overthrow everything, and create the Hunan desired by the Hunanese (a new and ideal Hunan) and the Guangdong desired by the people of Guangdong (a new and ideal Guangdong), thus setting

1. Liu Chunren's identity is unknown; his article, calling for a federation, appeared in the *Dagongbao* on September 29–30, 1920.

2. *Lianbang*, literally "united states" or "federal state." The following sentence, which uses the word *lian* (united or federated) on its own, might be rendered, " . . . how can we talk about federation now when there are no states [*bang*] in China [to federate]?"

3. Wu Peifu (1874–1939), *zi* Ziyu, a native of Shandong Province, was a trusted subordinate of Cao Kun. Like Cao, he was a member of the Zhili faction of warlords, hostile to Duan Qirui, whose policies he had been criticizing since 1918. In June 1920, after Duan had dismissed him from his command for insubordination, he sent an open telegram stating his opposition to the Anfu clique's monopolizing the North-South Peace Conference, and proposed convening a national congress.

up models of self-rule. Being in such a good position, it would be painful and exasperating if they were to be deceived by a toothless measure like "semi-self-rule." That would truly be an injustice and a shame. I think that the Hunan people definitely have a number of endearing qualities; they are hard-working, energetic, courageous, and have a spirit of unity. But they really lack ideals. Because the Hunan people lack ideals, they cannot improve their lives. They can only follow along after others; they are not able to transcend their environment, and themselves achieve what they would like to achieve. I have an extremely lengthy theory on the question of a "country of Hunan," but because I have been otherwise occupied, I have not been able to write it down. Later on, I shall write it out and offer it to my compatriots. I have presented here just the general idea, in reply to the doubts of Mr. Liu and other friends.

Proposal That the "Hunan Revolutionary Government" Convene a "Hunan People's Constitutional Convention" to Enact a "Hunan Constitution" in Order to Build a "New Hunan"

(October 5–6, 1920)

Proposed by: Long Jiangong, Yang Jisun, Zhang Shen'an, Wang Yiseng, Cheng Sen, Cheng Yizhong, Kuang Rixiu, Zhu Jianfan, Tao Yi, Ma Xuchang, Luo Jiaoduo, Wei Junming, Liu Yujie, Mao Zedong, Wu Dayou, Guo Kaidi, He Shuheng, Wang Zongxun, Peng Huang, Tang Yaozhang, Li Xichun, et al., a total of 377 persons (too many to be listed).

We are convinced that now is the time to launch a Hunan people's "self-government movement." The present offers an extremely good opportunity, an opportunity such as occurs once in a thousand years. If we let this opportunity pass, it will be very difficult subsequently to find such an opportunity again.

The question of "whether or not Hunan should be self-governing" is by now no longer subject to dispute. Today the proposition that "Hunan should be self-governing" would probably be approved by each and every Hunanese save those who are wholly without conscience. Thus, "whether or not Hunan should be self-governing" is no longer a question, and the only question is, "How can Hunan self-government be realized?"

As regards the drafting of a basic law for Hunan self-government, during the past month some people have been suggesting that it be done by the provincial government. Others have proposed that the law be drafted by the provincial assembly, and still others that the provincial government and the provincial assembly draft it jointly. Some have advocated that it be drafted by the provincial government and the provincial assembly, together with the provincial Council on Education, the provincial Agricultural Association, the provincial Labor Union, the provincial Chamber of Commerce, the Hunan Law Association, the Hunan United Students' Association, the Hunan Journalists' Federation, and so on. Some have suggested that ideas devised by individuals and put forward in drafts should be combined, with the endorsement of others, to form a kind of draft proposal by several people.

We do not agree with any of the above several proposals, for the following reasons:

1) The basic law for Hunan self-government will be the Hunan constitution. To propose at this time a constitution for Hunan is to refuse to recognize the Provisional Constitution of the Republic of China[1] and the various laws and ordinances deriving from the Provisional Constitution. The provincial government, the provincial assembly, the provincial Council on Education, the provincial Agricultural Association, the provincial Labor Union, the provincial Chamber of Commerce, the Hunan Law Association, and so on, are all organs established in accordance with the former Provisional Constitution or other laws and ordinances; they "may have" only the power to oppose the Hunan constitution, they "may not have" the power to propose or draft a Hunan constitution. Furthermore, they "should" only use their power to oppose a Hunan constitution, but "should not" use their power to propose or draft a Hunan constitution. It is for this reason that the first four proposals listed above will not stand up theoretically.

2) That individuals should formulate views and put forward drafts is in itself a very good idea, which would avoid the difficulties of the first four proposals, and is also based on the strongest grounds. Nevertheless, we cannot agree with it. First, the times at present are not such as will allow us to sit down for a relaxed discussion. If one individual put forward his ideas in a draft, 30 million people could put forward as many as 30 million drafts, and by the time the waters had cleared, who knows when a Hunan constitution would emerge? Who knows when we could build a new Hunan? Second, at present the people's level is extremely low, and in the past there have been no strong people's organizations or parties. Consequently, even if a draft were proposed by the people, if there were a discrepancy between the ideas of the people and the ideas of the present government, what power would the people have to stand up against the government?

3) The above five proposals speak only of producing a draft, and are wholly unconcerned with what comes before and after the draft. This is truly laughable. We are convinced that the first step is to launch the initiative; the second step is to compose a draft, and also to adopt it and promulgate it; the third step is to put it into practice. Formally speaking, these three steps are systematically and coherently related. In reality, they are three separate items, and should certainly not be mixed up. Of the above five suggestions, apart from the one for drafts proposed by individuals, which is fairly reasonable, the four remaining ones are all unclear about procedural relations. On what grounds can it be said that a draft is

1. I.e., the so-called "New Constitution" *(Xin yuefa)* promulgated on May 1, 1914, by Yuan Shikai, to replace that of 1912, following his repudiation of the "Temple of Heaven" draft. (See the note to Mao's letter of July 25, 1916, to Xiao Zisheng.)

supposed to appear suddenly when there has been no attempt to find a basis for launching the initiative? We feel that in times as urgent as these, there are two points which must not be neglected: (1) in theory, it must be convincing, and (2) in practice it must be carried out. We are persuaded that the first four suggestions are not theoretically convincing, and that the last suggestion cannot in reality be carried out. Thus we do not endorse any of them.

What, then, do we propose? Our proposal is:

> "That the Hunan revolutionary government convene a Hunan People's Constitutional Convention, and enact a Hunan Constitution, in order to build a New Hunan."

We feel that this proposal is both theoretically convincing and feasible in practice. Let us now explain this in detail below:

I. The Hunan Revolutionary Government

The present government of Hunan, organized and led by Mr. Tan Yankai, is actually a revolutionary government, as explained below: (1) Mr. Tan's action in leading troops to overthrow Zhang Jingyao, the official appointed by the Northern government, was quite obviously a revolutionary action directed against Zhang Jingyao and the Northern government. (2) Mr. Tan has issued a circular telegram proclaiming that this expulsion of Zhang was an act of self-determination on the part of the Hunanese, having nothing to do with the overall situation in the Southwest, and the head and commander in chief of the Southwest government, Mr. Cen Chunxuan, sent a telegram to the Northern government informing them that the Southwest had in no way ordered Tan Yankai's attack on Zhang Jingyao. This expulsion of Zhang was purely a matter of Hunanese self-determination. It is true that before expelling Zhang Mr. Tan did indeed have a relationship of subordination with the Southwest government, but since the day on which he set out to expel Zhang, any such relationship has been broken off, and he has been acting entirely in accordance with his own free will. Thus, his actions have been entirely revolutionary actions. (3) On September 13, at his general headquarters, Mr. Tan convened a Hunan self-government conference, thus carrying out an even more manifestly revolutionary act. Disregarding the Southwest government, Mr. Tan used a revolutionary army to overthrow the official appointed by the North, proceeded to establish a revolutionary government in Changsha, and then convened, within the revolutionary government, a self-government conference forbidden by the Provisional Constitution. In itself, this was right and proper, but if it had not been the act of a revolutionary government, it would have been rejected as illegal and traitorous. Why so? Would it not have been an illegal and traitorous act for a nonrevolutionary government to convene a self-government conference forbidden by the Provisional Constitution? (The Provisional Constitution does not stipulate that the provincial officials can change the local organizations at will.)

For the above reasons, there is no longer any doubt that the present government of Hunan is not the former so-called provincial government, but is indeed a revolutionary government. Hitherto in Hunan, local individuals and organizations either have not opposed this revolutionary government (that is, have not said that it should not have made revolution and expelled Zhang), or on the contrary have supported the actions of this revolutionary government, such as convening the Hunan self-government conference (since the general headquarters self-government conference, no one has raised objections; what the papers have all without exception opposed is having the old provincial government or the old provincial assembly monopolize the "drafting"). Thus, the position, both of individuals and of organizations, in terms of the Provisional Constitution of the Republic of China, and of all laws based on the Provisional Constitution, has been utterly destroyed.

We have argued above in terms of theory. If we now speak in terms of reality, the Hunanese people have all truly participated in this movement to expel Zhang. They have not just passively "not raised objections" or "given their approval." All those who, each and every one, on his own initiative, have become members of the revolutionary army, or thought to themselves that they wanted to propose a self-government bill, have already unanimously proclaimed that they have cast off the former laws.

II. The Hunan People's Constitutional Convention

This is a question of terminology. There are those who suggest "Hunan National [*guomin*] Assembly" or "Hunan National Constitutional Convention," but we feel that until Hunan has decided and formally declared its establishment as a country, the use of the term citizen [*guomin*][2] can be objected to on the grounds that either it can be confused with "citizen of China," or that it "has no basis." There are those who propose a "Hunan Self-Government Conference," but in our opinion the self-government law that Hunan needs now is similar to the American state constitutions or the constitutions of the German states. China today is split into many fragments, and no one knows when a constitution for the whole country will come into being. In fact, there will probably first have to be separate constitutions for each province, and only then can there be an overall constitution for the whole country. This is just like the route from division to unity taken by

2. The Chinese expression *guomin* means literally "people of the country" and on its own is usually translated "citizen." As an adjective, however, it commonly takes the meaning "national," as in Guomindang (Nationalist Party). Both renderings are used here, according to the context.

America and Germany.[3] We believe that at present in Hunan, the use of the term "constitution" is most appropriate, and the organ that is to give birth to the constitution should be called the "Hunan People's Constitutional Convention."

III. The Convening of the Hunan People's Constitutional Convention by the Hunan Revolutionary Government

In most cases, when revolutions arise in a country or locality (apart from the emergence under the old autocractic political system of new kings and emperors who decided everything and did not allow the people to participate), a constitutional convention has been convened by the revolutionary government. This has been true of the most recent examples, such as that of the [Provisional] Constitutional Assembly (the National Council) convened in 1910 [*sic*][4] by the military government of the Republic of China, the constitutional convention called in 1917 by the Russian Kerensky government, the All-Russian Congress of Workers' and Peasants' Soviets convened in 1918 by the Russian government of Lenin, and the German constitutional convention called in 1919 by the Ebert government. The reason for this is that when the old government has already fallen, and the old system has been basically overthrown, the revolutionary government becomes the only central power, so there is no institution other than the revolutionary government that can convoke a constitutional convention. If you say that it should be proposed by the people, the head of the revolutionary government is one of the people. Since the leader of the revolutionary government, along with his staff and all the other members of his party, have already become a great force, the fact that it is they who convene the constitutional convention is really an inevitable process that is not at all unreasonable. We feel that for Hunan today, in the presence of this fleeting opportunity, the Hunan revolutionary government should convene a people's constitutional convention, and cut the Gordian knot. This will not lead to further complications, but can in reality be done. We hope soon to see before us a constitutional convention, so that Hunan self-government may soon be realized. Here there is another point to which we should pay close attention, namely, the "method of election" used in calling together "representatives to the people's constitutional convention." These methods for convening the convention are laid down in the name of the Hunan revolutionary government, but in reality they must involve, at the very minimum, the residents of the provincial capital, and by custom (not by law), they must take account of the views of various bodies such as the old provincial

3. Mao and his co-authors are plainly thinking in this passage of the process of establishment of the German empire as carried out by Bismarck, and not of the Weimar Republic, which had barely come into existence at the time of writing.

4. In fact, the Provisional National Council *(linshi canyiyuan)* met from January 1912 to April 1913 to frame the Provisional Constitution *(linshi yuefa).*

assembly, the provincial Council on Education, the provincial Chamber of Commerce, the provincial Agricultural Association, the provincial Labor Union, the United Students' Association, the Teachers' Federation, the Journalists' Federation, the Law Association, and so on. They must also, at the very least, fulfill the following two conditions: (1) direct, equal, and universal suffrage, and (2) one delegate to be selected from among every 50,000 persons.

IV. The Adoption of a Hunan Constitution by the Hunan People's Constitutional Convention

This includes three steps: (1) drafting, (2) passing, and (3) promulgating. It is only in this context that the recently much-disputed question of drafting can properly be considered. We recognize only the right of the revolutionary government to convene a constitutional convention. We definitely do not recognize it as having the right to draft the constitution. The drafting of the constitution is, of course, the affair of the constitutional convention. The procedure is as follows. Once the delegates of the people from the whole province have been brought together in the provincial capital by the Hunan revolutionary government, they will constitute themselves into the convention. First, they will appoint a suitable number of persons to put together a draft constitution for Hunan. Next, they will adopt a resolution on the draft constitution, thus turning it into a formal constitution. Then, in the name of all the delegates to the Hunan constitutional convention, they will promulgate this final constitution.

Here there arises a question: after the constitution is enacted by the convention, should it be presented to the people of the entire province to be ratified in a general referendum, and only then be promulgated? Concerning this point, there are arguments on both sides. The arguments to the effect that this "should be" done are: (1) That if it is possible to get 30 million people to cast their individual votes expressing their opinion for or against a Hunan constitution, this constitution will be more closely linked to our 30 million people, and that will have great educational significance; and (2) that a Hunan constitution which has been passed by the constitutional convention, and then approved in a general referendum of all the people, will have very deep roots that cannot easily be shaken by some unexpected maneuver to destroy it by the wild ambition of someone from the central government or from other provinces or from our own province. These are two highly important reasons with which we at first fundamentally agreed. The reason we now take the position that this "should not be" done relates entirely to practical questions. We feel that the Hunan constitution should be fully ratified and promulgated within six months at the latest. If we were to have a general referendum, this could scarcely be accomplished in eight or even ten months, and we are afraid the opportunity might be lost. If everyone feels that delaying promulgation slightly is not so important, that this opportunity will definitely not be lost, and that there is no danger that the establishment of a self-government constitution could be basically undermined and never carried out, then we would undoubtedly agree with holding a general referendum of all the people.

V. Building a New Hunan

Once the Hunan Self-Government Constitution has been promulgated, the official Hunan assembly and Hunan government, as well as seventy-five *xian* assemblies and *xian* governments, and the smallest district organs of self-rule at the town and village level, will be created in accordance with the constitution. With this, the construction of a new Hunan will be complete.

This is the end of our proposal. We have made it because this is indeed a matter of the widest implications. Since the expulsion of Zhang, things have been put off, the falling leaves warn of winter, and the time grows late. There is talk of self-government every day, but day after day nothing gets done. The government vacillates and is at a loss; the masses are anxious but silent. If, having driven out Zhang, we still cannot establish self-government, then Zhang's expulsion will have been entirely in vain! Since we have some views on the subject, it is certainly our duty to put them forward for everyone's consideration. But this is simply a proposal "to convene a constitutional convention." As for the questions of how we should afterward go about convening it, how the constitution should be enacted, and how, once it has been enacted, construction should be carried out, these are all extremely serious questions. Unless many dedicated people devote all their efforts to a real movement, [these stages] can certainly not be carried to completion. We feel that today the people of Hunan, following the "movement to expel Zhang," should all arise in an extremely broad and universal "movement for Hunan self-government." Hunanese have always had a good deal of courage; the expulsion of Zhang, the expulsion of Fu, and the expulsion of Tang are the most recent evidence of this. Henceforth, the Hunanese people should change their negative and destructive spirit and come focus their attention on positive construction. We also feel that this time, proposals for Hunanese self-government should advocate "full self-government" and not "semi-self-government." We definitely should not concern ourselves with the center,[5] or with the various provinces. The Hunanese people know only that there is a Hunan on this earth, and that within Hunan, there must be self-government. They must definitely not allow their courage to be deflated by worrying about what lies ahead or what comes afterward, or discard "complete self-government" for that half-hearted "semi-self-government." The Hunan people must fight for freedom, with no pity for those who would dare to obstruct Hunanese self-rule.

5. I.e., with the central government.

Appeal to the 300,000 Citizens[1] *of Changsha in Favor of Self-Rule for Hunan*

(October 7, 1920)

Self-rule for Hunan is the single most important matter at present, a matter of life and death, of honor and disgrace for the Hunan people. I urge the Hunan people, I urge my 30 million beloved fellow Hunanese: when your parents die, don't be in a hurry to bury them. Let us all come and build this sea wall of self-rule before we do anything else. A tempest and a tide are coming. This tempest and tide have swept over us many times in the past, and now they are coming to sweep us again. Our sea wall has not been completed, indeed has not yet been begun! Does everyone realize how dangerous this is?

The 30 million people, however, are too scattered. Our road is long and those endowed with consciousness are few. It would be too late to wait for thirty million people to wake up and build this sea wall. Therefore, the responsibility has inevitably fallen on the shoulders of our 300,000 citizens of Changsha. If the citizens of Changsha do not rise up immediately in a self-rule movement, there will never be any hope for self-rule in Hunan. Citizens of Changsha! Although your 30 million fellow Hunanese are not aware that they have placed this responsibility on your shoulders, they have already silently done so. If you succeed, 30 million people will benefit. If you fail, 30 million people will suffer. You must know that your responsibility is not light.

The political and social reforms of the Western countries all started with movements of the citizens. Not only did the great transformations in Russia, Germany, and other countries which have shocked the world recently originate with the citizens, even in the Middle Ages it was the citizens of the free cities alone who wrested the status of "freemen" from the autocrats. The power of the citizens is truly great! The citizens are truly the proudest people under Heaven!

Citizens! Arise. The creation of Hunan's future golden age depends wholly on today.

1. *Shimin,* literally "townspeople," appears to be used here as the conscious equivalent of the original meaning of "citizens" as burghers or "city dwellers." Compare the last paragraph of this article with the article of October 10, 1920, "Petition for the Hunan Self-Government Movement."

Essentials of the Organic Law of the Hunan People's Constitutional Convention

(October 8, 1920)

1. The Hunan People's Constitutional Convention shall be composed of representatives elected by the people of each *xian* in Hunan.

2. The number of representatives to be elected from each *xian* shall be allotted according to the size of the *xian*: eight for a big *xian*, six for a medium-sized *xian*, and four for a small *xian*.

3. The provincial assembly shall specially appoint its own representatives, the number of which shall be the same as that of a big *xian*.

4. The representatives shall convene and run their meetings themselves.

5. The time limit allowed for the representatives to write the constitution shall be three months.

6. Representatives shall be given travel expenses to and from the convention, to be paid from public funds on the basis of the distance of the journey.

7. The representatives shall receive no salary. They shall be given one *yuan* for expenses for each session attended.

Essentials of the Electoral Law of the Hunan People's Constitutional Convention

(October 8, 1920)

1. The method of direct election shall be used.

2. The system of universal suffrage shall be adopted without restrictions on either voters or candidates regarding their property or tax status, gender, or profession.

3. People who belong to any one of the following categories shall not have the right to vote or to stand for election: (a) minors (adulthood is defined as eighteen years of age); (b) people who are mentally ill; (c) opium addicts or traffickers.

4. Anyone currently working as a government official or in the military, on being elected as a representative to this convention, shall be relieved of his or her government or military duties.

5. The registered voter ballot method shall be adopted.

6. The voters shall go to vote in person.

7. The date of the election shall be decided by the revolutionary government and shall be on the same day for all *xian.*

8. The time limit for holding the elections shall not exceed two months at most.

Yesterday's General Meeting on Proposing the Convocation of a People's Constitutional Convention

(October 9, 1920)

At nine o'clock yesterday morning, the sponsors of the resolution "For a Hunan People's Constitutional Convention to Be Convened by the Hunan Revolutionary Government" used the conference hall of the provincial Council on Education to hold a general meeting to discuss procedures and important points of the electoral law and organizational law. Many people attended the meeting. First, Mr. Long Jiangong reported on the general purpose of the meeting. He said that the majority of the people present at the meeting had already signed their names and there were only a few who had yet to sign. As most already understood the general purpose, only a simple explanation was needed. The initial sponsors of the resolution were Mr. Mao Zedong, Mr. Peng Huang, and three others. Now that more than four hundred people had agreed to support this resolution, it was necessary to discuss the issue of how to present it to the government on the one hand, and to society on the other. The most important issue at the moment was to recognize that the revolutionary government must convene a people's constitutional convention. But the revolutionary government must be given the concrete means. Therefore, several provisions covering the main points of the electoral and organizational laws had to be drafted and presented to the conferees for a vote, so that the whole matter could proceed. Then, the issue was again raised of whether to send representatives to petition and consult with the revolutionary government, or whether it should be a petition of the whole, to be decided by a general referendum. But our primary overall purpose was to go ahead step-by-step, and to move step-by-step toward a conclusion. It was hoped that everybody would express his view on the above issues. Next, Mr. Mao Zedong was elected chairman by acclamation. He remarked that the most important item on the agenda for the day was to draft procedures, and to vote on the important items of the electoral and organizational laws. He also said that the proposal on Hunan self-government as originally initiated by the Hunan government would have created a constitution formulated by the provincial government and provincial assembly alone. This would in reality have been monopolistic and theoretically indefensible, so the provincial assembly, which was aware of these difficulties, backed down. Nevertheless, both the government and the people generally agree on the issue of self-government for Hunan. Therefore, we have proposed this resolution as being both realistically workable and theoretically defensible. It should preferably be acted upon quickly and without delay. Today we ask all those present at the meeting to comment on the procedures.

Petition for the Hunan Self-Government Movement

(October 10, 1920)

The Subject of Our Petition:

We venture to recall that it has already been nine years since it was written into the constitution[1] that the sovereignty of the Republic of China belongs to its people as a whole. During these nine years, although under the constitution the citizens[2] should have enjoyed all kinds of liberties and rights, in reality they have been entirely stripped of these by a few bureaucrats and warlords. The reason for this is that the fundamental supreme laws of the country have not yet been established, nor has local self-government been carried through. Hunan Province has been plagued year after year by incessant coups, bringing disaster and chaos in their wake. No matter whether Hunan was governed by a Hunanese, or by someone from another province, the only difference was whether bureaucratic rule was better or worse. It had nothing to do with government by the people. Therefore, faced with the repeated disasters brought on us by the soldiers, the citizens had no choice but to endure the pain and suffering, with no means of deliverance. Now that good fortune has brought stability to Hunan, the people are yearning for good government. The blessings of a golden age, the hope for a happy land of government by the people, and the expectations of people both in China and abroad have come together. The citizens know only too well the tribulations of the past and the difficulties of the future. After careful collective deliberation, we venture to assert that great prosperity will not be brought to Hunan unless local self-government is instituted immediately, and that self-government cannot be perfected unless a people's constitutional convention is called immediately. In this regard, we the citizens believe that the organizational and electoral laws of the people's constitutional convention are especially important. Basically, there are six key points in these laws: (1) that delegates to the constitu-

1. The reference here is, of course, to the Provisional Constitution of 1912, providing for a parliamentary system, not to Yuan Shikai's presidential-style "New Constitution" of 1914 as in the text dated October 5–6, 1920.

2. *Shimindeng,* literally "townspeople and others." The use of this expression confirms that, as suggested in the note to the text dated October 7, 1920, Mao and his fellow authors are thinking of the urban population as the key element among the citizenry.

tional convention be elected by the *xian* on the basis of their size; (2) that there be a three-month time-limit on the duration of the constitution-making process; (3) that the method of direct election be used; (4) that the method of election by universal suffrage be used; (5) that delegates not be allowed to hold an administrative or military office at the same time; and (6) that the duration of the electoral process be no more than two months at most. The resulting people's constitutional convention, to be organized on the basis of the above six points, will certainly be able to put together the ideas of the majority and draw up an excellent constitution, which will increase the happiness of the people of Hunan and be a model for the whole country. Moreover, our province is now in a special position; we should exercise our revolutionary spirit, cut off all the old fetters, and practice complete self-determination and self-government in one province, Hunan. We will not depend on the central government or other provinces; we will eradicate the old habits and create a new state.[3] With respect to the spirit of government which should prevail from now on, it is appropriate to adopt democracy and socialism, in order to solve particularly difficult political and economic problems, and avoid another tragedy of a bloody revolution in the future. Furthermore, in light of the situation in Hunan today, we should adopt a Hunan Monroe Doctrine. The people of Hunan will be completely self-governing; they will not interfere in the affairs of other provinces, nor will they be subject to interference from other provinces.

We, the citizens, present these views, which are shared by the vast majority, to the commander in chief.[4] We respectfully request that they be adopted and put into practice. Submitted to:

Hunan Commander in Chief Tan[5]

From: all the citizens of the provincial capital of Hunan.

---

3. The term used here is not *guojia*, which could refer merely to a state apparatus, but *bang*, which definitely means a separate political entity.
4. I.e., to the military governor.
5. Tan Yankai. See note 9 to Mao's letter of July 25, 1916, to Xiao Zisheng.

Oppose Unification

(October 10, 1920)

By now it is quite clear that Chinese affairs cannot be run well by unification. China is not totally without people who are concerned about national affairs, nor are these people who are concerned about national affairs totally without knowledge and ability. The reason that things have not been managed well is that China is very large and seriously lacks a foundation and grass-roots organizations. Buildings constructed upon islets of sand will collapse even before they are completed. The twenty-four dynasties of China may be regarded as twenty-four buildings built on islets of sand, every one of which collapsed precisely because not one of them had a foundation. The four-thousand-year-old China is merely an empty frame. All the activities of its many politicians and all the scholarship of its many scholars have been just sketches painted on this empty frame. Every dynasty had a few dozen or a hundred or so years of peace that was based on one condition alone, massive killings and bloodshed. As the population declined and the killings ceased, peace came, but it had no genuine foundation. Thus, our ancient and civilized country with its four thousand years of history has never really been a country at all. The country is merely an empty frame with absolutely nothing inside. It might be said that there were people, but the people were scattered. It is a pity that "a sheet of loose sand" does indeed describe them![1] The Chinese people have lived and died for four thousand years, but what have they done? They are totally disorganized; there is no organized society to be seen, nor is there any local organization. Would it make much difference whether or not there were Chinese people within this piece of territory, China? Does it matter much to the human race that there are Chinese? The ultimate cause of this misfortune lies in the two characters *Zhongguo*,[2] and the unification of this China. The only remedy now is to dismantle China and oppose unification.

The Chinese do not have scientific minds. They do not know the relationship between analysis and synthesis, that big organisms are necessarily composed of small cells, and that an organization necessarily consists of individual members.

---

1. This characterization of the Chinese is commonly identified with Sun Yatsen, and Mao's quotation marks no doubt implied a reference to him. The best-known source is in the opening passage of the lectures on the *Three People's Principles,* delivered in their present form only in 1924, but the metaphor had already been used earlier by Sun.

2. *Zhongguo,* the Chinese name for China, means, of course, "the central country," and it is this notion which Mao is attacking.

Most Chinese have a kind of empty vanity for wearing big hats. When something happens, they just stare straight ahead, seeing only generalities. They do not feel comfortable unless they can put on a big hat. The present peace talks are like this. Some people carry "peace talks" in both hands and run around from north to south and from south to north. They frown when there is no hope and laugh when there is a glimmer of hope. I am utterly opposed to the peace talks. I believe that the peace talks represent an extremely great danger. My reasons involve neither Duan Qirui's argument for unification, nor the legal theories of Zhang Taiyan[3] and Sun Hongyi.[4] I just believe that the only means to build a genuine China in the future is to break up the present phony China. At the very least, the South and the North should not be unified again, and it would be better yet if each province enjoyed self-determination and self-rule.

Many people already realize that self-determination and self-rule in each province is the only way to rebuild a genuine China. This is an unexpected outcome of the war between the North and the South. Although only a few provinces, Hunan, Guangdong, Jiangsu, and Hubei, have taken the initiative, the trend will inevitably become a torrent in which all the provinces of the country will join. This will be an extremely gratifying phenomenon. There are two issues to be discussed now: One concerns the internal matter of self-rule in each province, i.e., how to promote the establishment of provincial self-rule. The other concerns the external matter of provincial self-rule, i.e., how to reduce the effect of the obstacles to provincial self-rule or prevent their development.

With regard to the former issue, I have two points to make. (1) The use of military force to drive away the old forces, as in the two provinces of Hunan and Guangdong, should be considered a form of revolution. The revolutionary governments of the two provinces should convene "people's constitutional conventions" in each of the two provinces to draft a "Hunan constitution" and a "Guangdong constitution." Then, a new Hunan and a new Guangdong should be set up in accordance with their constitutions. The people of these two provinces must work the hardest. Their constitutions should adopt a spirit of thorough reform based on the criterion of developing the special characteristics of the two respective provinces as fully as possible. (2) Provinces such as Hubei and Jiangsu cannot take revolutionary action. They will have to begin with a Hubeian

3. Taiyan is the *hao* of Zhang Binglin. (See the detailed note to Mao's letter of December 9, 1916.) A noted classical scholar and veteran revolutionary, Zhang had adopted a relatively conservative position at the time of the May Fourth movement. In 1920, however, he promoted federalism and the idea that each province should draw up its own formal constitution and not recognize the Provisional Constitution of the Beijing government.

4. Sun Hongyi (1870–1936), *zi* Bolan, born in Tianjin, was a former aide to Yuan Shikai, and cabinet minister in the Duan Qirui government. He was heavily involved in the organization of the committee to discuss the constitution and believed in "local government by the local people."

ruling Hubei and a Jiangsuan ruling Jiangsu (as governors). When military power returns to the natives of their respective provinces, then they can proceed to organize local self-rule. The above two methods may be adapted according to the particular situations. The former method may be set up as a model of self-rule for all provinces that in actuality will have the characteristics of a "country" and may implement a form of "full self-rule," and therefore is the most promising method. As for the latter method, although for the time being it can realize only "semi-self-rule," this form of self-rule may then be used as the basis for instituting a movement to abolish the military governorship. As soon as the military governorship is abolished, full self-rule will quickly follow. Although this method may be a little more peaceful and not as exciting, it is also fine to adopt this method as an adaptation to the circumstances.

Regarding how to remove the obstacle to provincial self-rule, it is my opinion that the obstacle is not the military governor, but the demand by many people for "unification." I believe that, at the very least, the North and the South should be independent of each other. This is crucial to promoting provincial self-rule. If unification is realized, a new national assembly will be formed to draft a constitution, and provincial self-rule will be more or less restricted by this constitution (even though the central government will never be run properly), as has happened to Hunan and Guangdong, and the provinces will certainly not be able to give full play to their own special characteristics. In addition, talented people will head for the central government, and the localities will inevitably lament the lack of talent. Yet a bigger disadvantage is the fact that if a central government is established, the attention of the whole country will be focused on the central government again, and the old Chinese malady of looking up and not down, of dealing in empty abstractions rather than with concrete realities, will show itself again. And provincial self-rule will again be considered a trivial issue. I feel that the present political situation in China resembles that at the end of the Qing dynasty. In the light of this, we Chinese should not expect it to improve, but rather to get worse and worse. I think that at present the situation has not reached the worst extreme, that we cannot use our strength to accelerate its deterioration, but should not do anything to alleviate the deterioration. It is better for us to ignore it. We should not mention the peace talks again, or support the argument of resolving national affairs by a national assembly. If we do support a national assembly, we should promote Mr. Zhang Dongsun's[5] idea of using the national assembly to solve the affairs of the provinces.

Mr. Hu Shi has proposed not talking about politics for twenty years. Now, I propose not talking about the politics of the central government for twenty years. The people of every province should focus all their attention on their respec-

---

5. Zhang Dongsun (1886–1973), *zi* Shengxin, was at this time working as a journalist in Shanghai. He later became one of China's foremost philosophers, particularly well known for his teaching of Western philosophy.

tive provinces and adopt a provincial Monroe Doctrine, namely, that every province close its doors and ignore what happens outside its doors. National Day[6] celebrates the Republic of China, and I frankly do not like it. I deliberately take the opportunity of the special occasion offered by this celebration of National Day to express some of my views opposing unification, in the hope that a kind of "provincial day celebration" may take place.

6. October 10 was proclaimed National Day by the Beijing government's provisional parliament in September 1912 to commemorate the uprising on that date in 1911 which led to the founding of the Republic of China.

First Business Report of the Cultural Book Society

Report on Circumstances During the Preparatory and Interim Business Periods

(October 22, 1920)

According to Article 7 of the "Outline of the Organization of the Cultural Book Society," "The business activities of this Society shall be public knowledge, and every month a report on operations will be made available." There follows a report of all the circumstances of the preparatory and interim period business activities of the Society.

(I) Circumstances of the Founding and of the Preparatory Stage

The Society was founded in July of this year. The founders feel that it is necessary to study the new thought tides of the world, that such study requires good materials, and that it is essential to have organs to introduce new publications. Thus they gathered together to make plans to found a bookstore. On August 2, the inaugural meeting was held, making use of premises at Chuyi School. An eight-article Organizational Outline was discussed and passed, and Messrs. Yi Lirong, Peng Huang, and Mao Zedong were appointed to the preparatory committee, with the task of preparing for setting up the Book Society, and of drafting regulations for the board of directors and for business activities. The "preparation and start-up" stage may be dealt with under the following three headings:

1. Accomodation. We first considered finding a suitable location on Changzhi Street, or at the Council on Education, but there was not enough time to find one there, so we first rented from the Hunan-Yale Medical School[1] a portion of No. 56 Chaozong Street, the former location of Hunan-Yale. With references from Mr. Zhao Yunwen,[2] a founder, a lease was signed on August 20.

---

1. On the Xiang-Ya or Hunan-Yale Medical School, see the note to the text of May 29, 1918.

2. Zhao Yunwen, also known as Hongjun, was well known in Hunan cultural and education circles. At this time he was in charge of the general affairs of the Xiang-Ya Medical School.

2. Capital. The Society is a public organization. All investments become public property, and no interest will be paid, so funding sources will necessarily be limited to those who are in sympathy with the principles of our Society and know us well. From the inaugural meeting of August 2 through the first board of directors meeting on October 22, the investors have included Jiang Jihuan, Zuo Xueqian,[3] Zhu Jiao, Yang Jisun, Fang Weixia, Yi Peiji, Wang Bangmo, Mao Zedong, Zhu Jianfan, Kuang Rixiu, Xiong Mengfei, He Shuheng, Wu Yuzhen, Yi Lirong, Lin Yunyuan, Zhou Shizhao, Tao Yi, Chen Shunong, Guo Kaidi, Peng Huang, Zhou Yunzhen, Zhao Yunwen, Pan Shicen, Xiong Chuxiong, Liu Yujie, and others, twenty-seven persons[4] in all, who have given a total of 519 *yuan*.

3. Business Transactions with Agencies Outside of Hunan. Besides a number of magazine companies, formal publications trade agreements have been signed by the Book Society with Taidong Book Company, Yadong Library, Zhonghua Book Company, Qunyi Bookstore, *China Times*, and New Youth Press in Shanghai, the Beijing University Press, New Tide Press, Scholarly Lectures Society, and *Morning Post* in Beijing, and the Liqun Bookstore in Wuchang, eleven in all. Thanks to credit references from Messrs. Li Shicen,[5] Zuo Shunsheng, Chen Duxiu, Zhao Nangong, Li Dazhao, and Yun Daiying,[6] the publishing companies waived the security deposit. But most of the first purchases had to be paid in cash, and besides, in order to establish a good credit rating, we did not want to buy on credit. Consequently, we had little circulating capital, and turnover was slow. Negotiations back and forth took a full month's time. By September 9, books, papers, and magazines were arriving one after the other, and we opened for business on that day. Of the three members of the preparatory committee, Mr. Yi Lirong was appointed acting manager, with full charge of everything. It was also decided that Mr. Luo Zonghan should be general representative of the Book Society in Beijing, and Mr. Mao Fei general representative in Shanghai.

---

3. Zuo Xueqian (1876–1951), *zi* Yizhai, a native of Changsha, was prominent in Hunan politics in the early days of the Republic. He was active in the movement to oust Zhang Jingyao and in the democracy movement in Hunan. At this time he was head of the Hunan Chamber of Commerce.

4. Except for Jiang Jihuan and Zuo Xueqian, they were all from cultural and education circles in Hunan, and twelve were members of the New People's Study Society.

5. Li Shicen (1892–1934), original name Bangfan, was born in Liling, Hunan Province. He had studied in Japan and worked as an editor and university professor on his return. At this time he was an editor at the Shanghai Commercial Press.

6. Yun Daiying (1895–1931), born in Hubei Province, organized the Mutual Aid Society in 1918 and had been very active in the May Fourth movement. He was one of the prime organizers of the Chinese Socialist Youth Corps in 1920, and joined the Chinese Communist Party in 1921.

(II) Brief Statistics of Books, Newspapers, and Magazines Sold[7]

The Society deals in books, magazines, and newspapers. We have 164 different titles of books, 45 different magazines, and 3 newspapers.[8] The following are brief statistics of the major books, newspapers, and magazines sold in the one month and twelve days (from September 9 to October 20) of the interim business period:

Russell, *Political Ideals* .... 30 copies
On Women[9] .... 20 copies
[Ernst] Haeckel, *Monism*[10] .... 20 copies
Darwin, *Origin of Species* .... 10 copies
Russell, *Principles of Social Reconstruction* .... 25 copies
Observations During Six Weeks of Travel in Russia .... 10 copies
The Coming of Age of Love .... 5 copies
Five Major Lectures by Dewey .... 5 copies
History of Western Ethics[11] .... 5 copies
Survey of Philosophy .... 8 copies
Basic Problems in Ethics[12] .... 5 copies
The Thought of Kropotkin .... 30 copies
Studies of the New Russia[13] .... 30 copies
The Worker-Peasant Government and China[14] .... 30 copies

---

7. The enumeration of books which follows, like the longer list in the "Cultural Book Society Announcement" of November 10, 1920, was apparently compiled in haste. Some titles are accurate and complete, but other entries may be only approximations for purposes of identification, and the books are listed in no particular order. An important document for clarifying these matters is a much fuller list of books sold by the Cultural Book Society, including names of authors or translators, and the prices charged, which has been reprinted in *Xinmin xuehui ziliao* (Materials on the New People's Study Society) (Beijing: Renmin chubanshe, 1980), pp. 262–72. This has not been attributed to Mao, and is therefore not reproduced here, but information from this source has been incorporated into the notes in some cases.

8. The master list referred to in note 7 includes 161 titles of books, 50 periodicals, and 4 newspapers.

9. According to the master list of books sold by the Cultural Book Society, the author of the work was Feng Fei.

10. This work, originally published in 1899 as *Die Welträtsel*, based its "monistic" view of the world on Darwin. It enjoyed a considerable vogue in China at this time, and Mao evoked the name of Haeckel in conversations with German visitors toward the end of his life.

11. In the Cultural Book Society announcement of November 10, 1920, and in the master list, Yang Changji is shown as the author of this book. In fact, Yang had translated it from the Japanese of Yoshida Seichi (1872–1945), a prolific writer on ethics.

12. This book, though Yang Changji is given as the author in the November announcement and the master list, was also a translation and not an original work.

13. According to the master list, the author was Shao Piaoping.

14. According to the master list, the author is Zhang Mingfei.

A Newly Punctuated *Water Margin* .... 30 copies
Hu Shi, *A Book of Experiments*[15] .... 40 copies
Hu Shi, *Short Stories*[16] .... 30 copies
On the Scientific Method .... 30 copies
Superstition and the Mind[17] .... 20 copies
New Youth, Vol. VIII, No. 1 .... 165 copies
Vol. VIII, No. 2 .... 155 copies
Xinchao [New Tide], Vol. II, No. 4 .... 25 copies
Gaizao [Reconstruction], Vol III, No. 1 .... 30 copies
Xin jiaoyu [New Education], Vol. III, No.1 .... 20 copies
Minduo [The People's Tocsin], Vol. II, No. 1 .... 35 copies
Shaonian Zhongguo [Young China], Vol. II, No. 1 .... 10 copies
Vol. II, No. 2 .... 20 copies
Vol. II, No. 3 .... 20 copies
Shaonian shijie [Young World], Vol. I, Numbers 7, 8, 9, each ..... 15 copies
Laodongjie [Labor World] , Nos. 1–9, each .... 130 copies
Xin shenghuo [New Life], Nos. 39 and 40, each .... 150 copies
Jiating yanjiu [Studies of the Family],[18] No. 1 .... 40 copies
Chenbao [Morning Post], First sales .... 12 copies
Now .... 42 copies
Shishi xinbao [China Times], First sales .... 28 copies
Now .... 65 copies

(III) Expenses and Profit
(A) Expenses

Start-up equipment and miscellaneous items .... 24 *yuan*
Rent .... 8 *yuan*
Food .... 22 *yuan*
Postage .... 25 *yuan*
Printing .... 13 *yuan*
Paper .... 9 *yuan*

Total .... 101 *yuan*

(B) Income .... 136 *yuan*
(C) Income minus expenses equals net profit .... 35 *yuan*

(Note) The acting manager, one salesman, two delivery persons, one cook-and-errand person receive no wages.

---

15. This was a volume of Hu's new poetry in the vernacular.
16. According to the master list, this was a volume of stories translated by Hu Shi.
17. According to the master list, the author was Chen Daqi.
18. This may or may not be the same as the *Kexue jiating yanjiu* (Scientific Studies of the Family) in the other list.

The above is a brief account of the circumstances of the preparatory and interim business periods. As soon as an official manager is elected at the first business meeting, he will be in full charge. This report covers the period from the inaugural meeting on August 2 through October 20.

For public perusal.

October 22, 1920

Cultural Book Society
Preparatory Committee
Yi Lirong
Peng Huang
Mao Zedong

Notice from the Cultural Book Society

(November 1, 1920)

For the attention of all education representatives and of all students:

Our society has been organized jointly by a group of comrades. Its sole function is to introduce all kinds of new publications. At present, in order to spread such publications to every *xian* in the entire province, and to make it possible for a large number of people to have the opportunity to read them, we propose to establish in every *xian* a branch office, or a liaison station. If any of you gentlemen are interested in assuming this responsibility, please be so good as to come to the Society's offices at 56 Chaozong Street to discuss the matter. (We can also be contacted by mail.)

Cultural Book Society Announcement to All Who Are Eager to Learn

(November 10, 1920)

(I) The Book Society is publicly owned by the community. Its purpose is to sell new publications.

(II) Our selling prices for books, newspapers, and magazines will be no higher than the original publishers' prices. Some will be lower in price than the original publishers' prices, with charges only to cover shipping and handling costs.

(III) Our inventory of publications includes:

(1) Book titles—164
(2) Magazines—45
(3) Daily newspapers—3

(IV) Important books we carry are: Russell, *Political Ideals*; Russell, *Principles of Social Reconstruction*; Introduction to Marx's *Capital*; *Five Major Lectures by Dewey*; Haeckel's *Monism*;[1] Darwin, *Origin of Species*; *History of Socialism*;[2] *On Women*; *Observations During Six Weeks of Travel in Russia*; *The Coming of Age of Love*; *On the Scientific Method*; *Superstition and the Mind*; *A Short History of European Political Thought*;[3] *Life of Tolstoy*; Hu Shi, *Outline of the History of Chinese Philosophy*; *A History of European Literature*;[4] *An Outline of Psychology*;[5] *Survey of Indian Philosophy*;[6] *A Critical Account of the League of Nations*; *Anthropology*;[7] *The Persian Question*; *Scientific Socialism*; *Problems of Reform in the Countries of Europe and America*; *Psychology of Revolution*; *Creative Evolution*; *Modern Thought*;[8] Plato, *The Republic*; *On the*

1. Annotations to this and other titles which appear in the list appended to the "Business Report" of October 22, 1920, are not repeated here.

2. This was undoubtedly Kirkupp's *History of Socialism*, which was, Mao told Edgar Snow, one of the three books which built up in him a faith in Marxism in 1920. (The others were the *Communist Manifesto* and a work by Kautsky.)

3. According to the master list of books sold by the Cultural Book Society, cited in note 7 to the "First Business Report," the author of this work was Gao Yihan.

4. According to the master list, the author of this work was Zhou Zuoren. Zhou was the younger brother of Lu Xun (pseudonym of Zhou Shuren). His work has been relatively neglected until recently, because of his collaboration with the Japanese after 1937.

5. According to the master list, this work was by Chen Daqi.

6. According to the master list, this book was by Liang Shuming.

7. According to the master list, the author of this work was Chen Yinghuang.

8. According to the master list, the author of this book was Guo Yaogen.

Chinese Population; *On the New Ethics*; *The World of Biology*;[9] Sun Yatsen, *The Doctrine of Sun Yatsen*;[10] *A Treatise on Science*;[11] *Critique of Contemporary Thought Tides*; *On the History of Modern Economic Thought*; *Modern Sociology*; Hu Shi, *Short Stories*; Wu Zhihui, *Random Talk about Things Old and New*; A Newly Punctuated *Water Margin*; *Three Leaves Anthology*;[12] *Fiction of Famous Russian Writers*; *The Thought of Kropotkin*; *Studies of the New Russia*; Wu Zhihui, *Talks With Guests at the New Moon Temple*; *The Worker-Peasant Government and China*; *A Discourse on Spiritual Phenomena*;[13] *Pragmatism*;[14] Dewey, *Trends in Modern Education*; Dewey, *On the Development of Democracy in America*; *Modern Psychology*;[15] *Astronomy*; *Western Modernist Painting*; *The New Zoology*;[16] *Society and Ethics*[17]; *Society and Education*;[18] Cai Yuanpei, *Principles of Ethics*;[19] Cai Yuanpei, *The History of Chinese Ethics*; *Marriage and Posterity*; Yang Huaizhong, *History of Western Ethics*; Yang Huaizhong, *Basic Problems in Ethics*; *Journalism*;[20] *Survey of Philosophy*; *Drops of Water*, translated by Zhou Zuoren.[21]

---

9. According to the master list, this work was produced by the Shangzhi ("Emphasize the Will") Study Society.

10. *Sunwen xueshuo,* completed in 1918 and subsequently retitled *Xinli jianxue* (Psychological Reconstruction), was the second of Sun's three works on reconstruction. An English translation appears in his *Memoirs of a Chinese Revolutionary*.

11. According to the master list, this work was produced by the Chinese Science Society.

12. According to the master list, this was the work of three authors: Tian Shouchang, Zong Baihua, and Guo Moruo.

13. According to the master list, this work was by Chen Daqi.

14. The master list includes two books with this title, one by Hu Shi, and another translated by Fang Dongmei, with no indication of the author.

15. The master list gives the author as Chen Daqi.

16. This title appears here as *Dongde xin jiaoshou*, which might be rendered as "New Teachings on Motion," but is not good Chinese, and does not really mean anything. The editors of the *Wengao* acknowledge as much by adding a note reading "Like this in the original document." (See p. 542, note 2.) The master list of books sold by the Cultural Book Society contains the item *Dongwu xin jiaoshou* (New Teachings about Animals, or The New Zoology), and there can be little doubt that *dongde* (of motion), both here and in the Second Report of the Society, dated April 1921, which will appear in Volume II of this edition, is a misprint for *dongwu* (animal). We have therefore made the necessary emendation.

17. This book was by Kang Baozhong.

18. According to the master list, the author of this book was Tao Lügong.

19. The reference is in fact to Paulsen's book, translated by Cai Yuanpei under this title.

20. According to the master list, the author of this book was Xu Baohuang.

21. This is a collection of twenty-one stories translated and edited by Zhou Zuoren. The first nine are by Russian writers, including Tolstoy and Chekhov. The title is taken from a passage in the preface to Nietsche's *Also Sprach Zarathustra*, which reads: "Ich liebe alle Die, welche wie schwere Tropfen sind, einzeln fallend aus der dunklen Wolke, die über den Menschen hängt; sie verkündigen, dass der Blitz kommt, und gehn als Verkündiger zu Grunde."

(V) The more important magazines: *New Youth*, *Xin Jiaoyu*, *Zhonghua jiaoyujie* [Chinese Education Circles], *Xin chao*, *Gaizao*, *Shaonian Zhongguo*, *Shaonian shijie*, *Xin shenghuo*, *Laodongjie*, *Laodongzhe* [The Workers], *Laodong chao* [Labor Tides], *Fendou* [Struggle], *Minduo*, *Kexue jiating yanjiu* [Scientific Studies of the Family], *Yinyue zazhi* [Music Magazine].

(VI) The more important newspapers: *Shishi xinbao*, *Chenbao*.

If you would like to purchase books, newspapers, or magazines mentioned above, please contact our Book Society at 56 Chaozong Street in the provincial capital.

A Respectful Notice from the Cultural Book Society to the Gentleman Who Has Bought This Book

(November 1920)

The fact that you, sir, have purchased this book will undoubtedly have a great deal of influence on the progress of your thought, and on that we wish to congratulate you. If, after you have read this book, your unslakeable thirst for knowledge inclines you to buy a few more books to peruse, we invite you, sir, either to come once more to our society to purchase them, or to do so by correspondence. We are prepared to welcome you!

The items which our society has for sale have undergone a rigorous process of selection. They consist exclusively of comparatively valuable new publications. (We want nothing to do with stale and outdated thought.) We have books (124 titles), newspapers (4 titles), and periodicals (50 titles, including 33 monthlies, 2 semimonthlies, 2 quarterlies, and 13 weeklies). Our goal is that the thought of everyone in Hunan should progress as yours has done, so as to bring about the emergence of a new culture. Our method is most sincerely and earnestly to carry on the work of introducing new books and periodicals, with the aim of spreading them throughout Hunan Province.

We are profoundly mortified that our abilities are too meager to shoulder the great responsibility of propagating culture, and we hope that superior men of goodwill from all walks of life will grant us their assistance. If you, sir, can help us by taking the trouble to introduce us by word of mouth, we shall be extremely grateful. Our society has printed a large number of book lists; if you or your friends would like to see them, it suffices to write, and they will be sent immediately, postage paid. The manager of our society, Mr. Yi Lirong, is responsible for all our activities and is present at the society every day. Whenever anyone at all writes to ask about books, newspapers, periodicals, book lists, or other matters, he will receive an immediate answer from Mr. Yi personally.

We wish you, sir, continued good health.

Colleagues of the Cultural Book Society
56 Chaozong Street, Changsha

The Budget for Girls' Education and the Budget for Boys' Education

(November 19, 1920)

This year's educational budget, including regular expenses of 1,040,000 *yuan*, and incidental expenses of over 1,110,000 *yuan*, totals over 2,150,000 *yuan*. The portion pertaining to girls' education is itemized below:

First Girls' Normal School	33,024 *yuan*
Second Girls' Normal School	30,705 *yuan*
Third Girls' Normal School	22,764 *yuan*
Provisional Girls' Middle School	10,000 *yuan*
Total	96,493 *yuan*

The total budget for girls' education is less than 100,000 *yuan*, a mere one twenty-second of the total educational budget. Men and women have the same obligations to pay taxes, but when it comes to their rights to education, the women only get one twenty-second of what the men do. Ah, men! How hard-hearted you are!

In the whole of Hunan Province with its fifteen million women, there is not even one girls' middle school! How utterly shameful! The 1921 educational budget listed, for the first time in history, the allocation for a "Provisional Girls' Middle School" (6,000 *yuan* for regular expenses and 4,000 *yuan* for incidental expenses). I have been told that some legislators are even contemplating canceling it. I am amazed that women have been degraded to such an extent.

Zhang Wenliang's Record of Mao Zedong's Comments on the Issue of Establishing the League[1]

(November 21, 1920)

Met Mao (at the Popular Education Office).[2] He said he was about to go to Liling in a few days to investigate education there. He also talked about the Youth League, saying that emphasis should now be given to looking for real comrades, and that it was better to go slowly, and not advance too hastily.

---

1. This is an entry from Zhang Wenliang's diary. The league in question was the Socialist Youth League, later to be redesignated the Communist Youth League. At this time Zhang Wenliang was studying at First Normal School and had very close contact with Mao.

2. At this time He Shuheng was head of the Popular Education Office. He invited Xie Juezai and others to supervise its publication, the *Hunan Tongsubao* (Hunan Popular News) , and Mao very often went to the office to assist with editorial work.

Letter to Xiang Jingyu [1]

(November 25, 1920)

Dear Elder Sister Jingyu,

I received your letter some time ago, but could not reply earlier. Please forgive me! When I visited Shanghai last winter, you forcefully presented to me your views on Hunanese affairs. For one year now, I, together with Yinbo and others, have also tried our best indirectly, but to no avail. Education here being backward and the people not enlightened, a majority of the Hunanese are still dreaming. The so-called intellectuals have neither ideals nor plans. I, together with Yinbo and the others, advocate that Hunan set itself up as an independent country; it must cut itself away from those unprogressive northern provinces as well as the southern provinces which have very different situations, break down the hollow and disorganized great China, and embrace all the other peoples endowed with self-awareness in the world. But those who understand this are few indeed. When the issue of autonomy first emerged, the atmosphere was very negative. But since the idea of "building a new Hunan based on a Hunanese constitution to be drawn up by a Hunan People's Constitutional Convention called by the Hunan revolutionary government" has been put forward, there has been a new excitement in the air. The majority of the people, however, are still baffled or even alarmed by this seemingly bizarre idea. In the last few months, I have seen through the Hunanese: muddle-headed with neither ideals nor long-term plans. In political circles, they are lethargic and extremely corrupt, and we can say that there is absolutely no hope for political reform. We can only disregard all this, carve out a new path, and create a new environment. Education is my profession, and I have made up my mind to stay in Hunan for two years. But working will

1. Xiang Jingyu (1895–1928), also known as Junxian, was born in Xupu, Hunan Province. Xiang was one of the earliest female members of the New People's Study Society. In December 1919 she went to France on the work-study program, where she and Cai Hesen concluded a "union based on love," which Mao regarded as a model. (See his letter of November 26, 1920, to Luo Xuezan.) She was active in mobilizing women to join in the work-study in France movement. On returning to China in 1922 she joined the Chinese Communist Party, was present at all Party congresses, was the first head of the Women's Department of the Party's Central Committee and secretary of the Women's Council. She went to Moscow to study in 1925. On May 1, 1928, in Wuhan she was shot by the Nationalist army.

deprive me of the opportunity to study. What a great sacrifice! There is extremely little progress in girls' education in Hunan (the same goes for boys' education). I hope you can persuade a large number of women comrades to go abroad. Each extra person you can lure there will be one person saved. Wishing you progress! My best regards to Aunt Jianhao[2] and Sister Xianxi![3]

Your younger brother,

Zedong

November 25, 1920

2. "Aunt Jianhao" was Ge Jianhao (1865–1943), born Lanying, in Xiangxiang, Hunan. She was the mother of Cai Hesen and Cai Chang and would have been around fifty-five at this time, deserving of the status of "aunt." She enrolled in Hunan Women's Teachers College at forty-nine *sui*, and after graduation founded First Women's Vocational School in her native Xiangxiang *xian*. She was the oldest to go to France at the end of 1919 on the work-study program, together with Cai Hesen, Cai Chang, and Xiang Jingyu. In 1924, after her return to China, she became head of Changsha Popular Women's Vocational School.

3. "Sister Xianxi" was Cai Chang (1900–1990), also known as Xianxi, a native of Xiangxiang, Hunan, and the younger sister of Cai Hesen. In 1920 she became a member of the New People's Study Society, and she was an active organizer of the Socialist Youth Corps during her stay in France under the work-study program. In 1923 she joined the Chinese Communist Party and held posts in the Central Committee's Women's Department and the Women's Council. After 1949, she became one of the most important women's leaders in the Chinese Communist Party.

Letter to Ouyang Ze[1]

(November 25, 1920)

Dear Elder Brother Yusheng,

I approve of all your four points about a common spirit. I also agree absolutely that there shouldn't be any provincial boundaries when admitting new members. Needless to say, there should not be any national boundaries either. I said in Beijing that there should be such boundaries because, at present, the New People's Study Society does not yet have a firm foundation. Emphasis should now be given to contacts and mutual encouragement among the comrades. Emphasizing moral support, we should strive to edify and understand each other so that we can be as close as blood brothers and sisters. Only then can we advance toward establishing ties with other comrades throughout China, and even with those from all over the world, to seek together to solve all kinds of problems confronted by the human race. My humble opinion is that it is very important to have a solid foundation. I have seen quite a few groups fail. They were like stores run by inexperienced entrepreneurs; before the merchandise has been adequately stocked, the shop sign has gone up, and advertisements have gone out all over the place. Inevitably, they collapsed. The consensus of the Bansong Park conference[2] was that the Society should adopt a "latent attitude." With this I agree 120 percent. You and the other Changsha comrades are also among those who agree. I think this is a positive phenomenon within the New People's Study Society. Any endeavor that is to flourish and endure must build its foundation on this "latent attitude."

I received your letter in Shanghai and have shown it to Peng [Huang], Zhou, Lao, and Wei.[3] I returned to Hunan in July but have been too busy to reply.

---

1. Ouyang Ze (1897–1924), *hao* Yusheng, also known as Yushan, was born in Yiyang, Hunan Province. He was an early member of the New People's Study Society who went to France on the work-study program in autumn 1920. His letter addressed to Mao, Peng Huang, and others was written from France on May 22, 1920.

2. On this meeting, see the note to Mao's letter of the same date to Zhang Guoji, which appears below.

3. Zhou Dunxiang (1898–1980), also known as Zhunru, was born in Changsha. Miss Zhou was a student of Hunan Zhounan Girls' School and a member of the New People's Study Society. She then studied at Nanjing Teachers' College continuation school. In 1921 she went to Singapore to teach at Southeast Asian Girls' Middle School (Nanyang Nuzhong). Lao Junzhan (1900–1976), also known as Jiru and Qirong, was also born in

Please forgive me! I trust everything is well with you. I forgot whether you are in Fontainebleau or Montargis. Please let me know in your next letter. Because of my recent overwork, I have come to Pingxiang to relax. This letter, therefore, is written during my stay here. Words cannot completely express my feelings.

Your brother,
Zedong
November 25, 1920
On a trip to Pingxiang

Changsha. She was a student of Zhounan Girls' School, and a member of the New People's Study Society. In 1920 she went to France under the work-study program, returning in 1927. Wei Bi (1897–1969), also known as Yunchang and Yun'an, was born in Changsha. She was a student of Zhounan Girls' School and a member of the New People's Study Society. In 1920 she went to France under the work-study program, returning to China in 1927. All three of these young women, like Peng Huang, were participants in the Bansong Park conference.

Letter to Luo Aojie[1]

(November 25, 1920)

Dear Elder Brother Zhanglong,

I hope you have already received the letter I sent you yesterday. Rereading your letter of July 25, I realize that I did not really respond to any of your questions in my previous letter. I am truly sorry! My responses are broadly as follows. Although I am not opposed to piecemeal solutions, I'm not in favor of the kind of solution that "treats the head when the head aches and treats the foot when the foot hurts," without any guiding principles. When I suggested that the Hunanese should pay no attention to outside affairs but only concentrate on putting their own province in order, I meant two things: (1) China is so vast. Each province differs greatly from the others in sentiments, interests, and the level of popular wisdom. One simply does not know where to begin to put things right. Both Kang [Youwei] and Liang [Qichao]'s reform, and Sun [Yatsen] and Huang [Xing]'s revolution (although each had its own merits which deserve separate discussion) tried to work things out solely from within this big organization, but both failed. The urgent task, then, is to change course and start from the smaller organization, on the provincial level. The Hunanese should make their province the leader of the whole country. Once each smaller provincial organization is sound, there is no reason to fear that the overall national organization will not be sound as well. (2) Hunan's geography and the nature of its people have great potential. If they are mixed up in the nationwide organization, their particular strengths will be undermined, and they will be restrained from further progress. Granted independence and autonomy, Hunan can draw up a rather progressive method (i.e., a Hunanese constitution). Internally, the rivers and mountains of Hunan will shine with stately splendor; externally, we shall join hands with the enlightened peoples of the world to work together toward great global reform. Other provinces throughout the country may then be stimulated to progress. Therefore, I advocate directly that Hunan should be an independent state, completely autonomous, neither suffering the slightest interference by outside forces, nor burdened by an ineffectual "China." This is actually a necessary step toward a total solution, not like those solutions that some people call piecemeal solutions, which are, in

1. On Luo Zhanglong, born Luo Aojie, see the note to Mao's poem dedicated to him written in the spring of 1918.

fact, halfhearted. Since I did not spell out this idea completely in my last letter, I want to add this here.

Indeed, it is important to have what you call "good and powerful morale." The bad atmosphere in China has penetrated all too deeply, and is all too thick. We really must create a powerful new atmosphere, for only thus can we change it around. To create such an atmosphere naturally requires a group of hardworking and resolute "people," but even more than that, it requires an "ism" that everyone holds in common. Without an ism, the atmosphere cannot be created. I think our Study Society should not merely be a gathering of people, bound by sentiment; it must become a group of people bound together by an ism. An ism is like a banner; only when it is raised will the people have something to hope for and know in what direction to go. What do you think?

The *Report on the Society's Affairs* only records the official business of the Society; it does not carry commentaries or essays. I have not begun editing it yet. It is probably sufficient to publish it quarterly. As for the correspondence of members, it will be published in a separate collection, which will be a special forum for members to debate and discuss various issues.[2] If you have any items of such correspondence, either old or new, please send them to me.

The *Xiang River [Review]* has not come out yet. The reason is that I have been very busy, and also that I fear I could not do it well. I am still debating whether to publish it or not.

My work at the primary school attached [to First Normal School] in the south of the city this term, plus some other responsibilities, have left me with very little time for self-cultivation. Reading your words, "Time has quickly gone by and cannot be retrieved," and "my thoughts and learning have gradually ossified," etc., made me shiver.[3] When I first returned to Hunan, I was determined to spend one hour reading newspapers and two hours reading books every day, but have not been able to practice this. After this busy winter, I definitely hope to fulfill this requirement in the new year. I have some plans about the sequence in which I should pursue my studies, which I will tell you later.

Speaking of education in Hunan, truly it makes me want to cry, but no tears come to my eyes.[4] I have only two hopes for education in Hunan: (1) I hope that every single one of the evil educators still living will die off. This, of course, cannot be realized. (2) I hope that the students themselves will have self-determination. This is my only hope. No wonder it is said, "Hunan students are quite naive" (Shen Zhongjiu's words[5]). No one has ever fed them with any thoughts,

2. See below, the announcement regarding this publication.
3. These words were written by Luo in his letter to Mao of July 25, 1920.
4. An idiom conveying a feeling of helplessness.
5. Shen Zhongjiu was a teacher at First Normal School.

nor has it ever occurred to them that they could develop their own. Why would they be anything other than naive? Please write often.

Your younger brother,

Zedong

November 25, 1920

Letter to Li Si'an[1]

(November 25, 1920)

Dear Sister Qinwen,

I received your letter in August. Later I got another long letter and some printed matter you had sent from Singapore. Thank you very much for your kindness. I have been too busy to reply, but I trust that you will forgive me. *Xiang River [Review]* has not yet come out. Hunan needs some resolute people who will devote themselves to practical reforms. Do not think that the job can be done simply by a few articles. Although the truly eminent persons are not yet firmly established, less eminent persons (the politicians) are very well fortified in their positions. I think that the best way to deal with them is to ignore them. Instead, we need to think of other ways, create other conditions, and make long-term preparations and precise plans. Once we have developed real strength, results will naturally manifest themselves. We do not need to strive for temporary superiority over them. Do you agree? Although I imagine you are busy, I urge you to spend some time reading new books and newspapers. I also hope that you will be able to continue your self-examination and become aware of your own shortcomings. You asked me to pass on your last letter to Jixu.[2] I have already done so. Please tell me how you are doing when you have time.

Your younger brother,

Zedong

November 25

1. Li Si'an (1892–1969), also known as Qinwen, was born in Changsha. Miss Li was a student of the Hunan Canye Training Institute and an early member of the New People's Study Society. At this time she was in Singapore teaching at the Qingcheng Women's School. On returning to China in 1925, she joined the Chinese Communist Party and took up a post as head of the Women's Department of the Hunan Federation of Trade Unions. Her letter to Mao was written from Singapore on August 19, 1920.

2. Jiang Zhuru. See note to text of December 18, 1919.

Letter To Zhang Guoji[1]

(November 25, 1920)

Dear Yisheng,

I have received two successive letters from you,[2] but have not replied for a long time. I am very sorry for that! I basically agree with you on all the six points you mention concerning the operation of the Society: (1) The need to publish reports on the Society. We have already decided to issue two new publications, one containing the correspondence among members, and the other reports on the Society's affairs. (2) The desirability of seriousness in the admission of new members. (3) No applicant should be discriminated against on the basis of sex or age. The consensus of my consultation in Shanghai this last summer with Kunfu, Zanzhou, Zizhang, Yinbo, Wangcheng, Yun'an, Dunxiang, Jiru, and Yusheng at Bansong Park[3] and a similar one later with fellow members here in Changsha, was that each new member should be required to have the following three qualities: (a) to be pure, (b) to be sincere, and (c) to have a desire to make progress. He or she will also need five personal references. Upon approval by the review committee, his or her membership will be solemnly announced to all members of the Society. This is precisely in agreement with your proposition. (The comrades in Southeast Asia must, of course, be contacted.) (4) The need for a headquarters for the Society. This is also urgent. We will have to find a proper office for the Society in Changsha in the near future. The acquisition of periodicals and books will be helpful for members to do research. Changsha, Paris, and Southeast Asia should each have their own supplies, and the costs should be defrayed by the local members. (5) Fund-raising. I think as long as the members

---

1. For a note on Zhang Guoji, see Mao's letter of February 19, 1920, to Tao Yi.

2. The first, concerning the New People's Study Society, was written on May 23, 1920, and the second, about the Southeast Asia News Agency, on September 19, 1920.

3. Kunfu was a Hunanese, Xiong Guangchu; Zanzhou was Chen Shaoxiu; Zizhang was Xiao Zhifan; Yinbo was Peng Huang; Wangcheng was Liu Mingyan; Yun'an was Wei Bi; Dunxiang was Zhou Dunxiang; Jiru was Lao Junzhan; Yusheng was Ouyang Ze. They were among the twelve participants in the conference of New People's Study Society members held in Bansong Park in Shanghai on May 8, 1920, just before the Hunanese work-study students set sail for France on May 11. (These students were Kunpu, Zanzhou, Zizhang, Wangcheng, Yusheng, and Zhang Huai.) On this occasion, Mao's formulation of the goals of the society, "To transform China and the world," was adopted and Mao was made responsible for activities in Changsha.

pay their annual dues, we should have enough to cover the day-to-day expenses. The only additional expenses will be the printing of the correspondence and of the reports. But these will not be too costly and can be defrayed by the members at the time. The membership directory is included in the report on the Society's affairs. We should be able to put out one issue by the end of this year. The organization of the Southeast Asia News Agency is of utmost importance. But I have a different opinion on Hunanese going to Southeast Asia, namely that those Hunanese who go there should follow the example of Mr. Li Shizeng[4] and others in sending students to France to learn cosmopolitanism, but not colonialism. Cosmopolitanism seeks to benefit not only oneself but also others. In essence, it is an ism to benefit everyone. Colonial policy, however, seeks only to benefit oneself and not to benefit others. In essence, it is a policy for benefiting oneself at the expense of others. With cosmopolitanism, there is no place that one does not feel at ease, as can be seen from the case of Li Shizeng and others. With colonialism, there is no place one can hide for shame, as illustrated by the Japanese. Southeast Asian civilization is parochial; therefore, those Hunanese who go there should take upon themselves the responsibility of developing its civilization. If all of you can initiate a new culture movement there, to introduce the new culture recently generated within China, the inhabitants of Southeast Asia (not only the overseas Chinese) will be greatly benefited. Also, a nation-building movement needs to be launched immediately in Southeast Asia. If there are noble-minded people who are willing to give themselves to this cause in order to save tens of thousands of helpless people from untold miseries and enable them to ascend to a place of repose, is there any greater undertaking than this? I think we need to get a great number of members to live in Southeast Asia to engage in educational and cultural movements. Once there are some results, they should then organize overseas Chinese, as well as the natives, from all sectors and all walks of life, to launch nation building. Worldwide universal harmony [*datong*] must be built on the foundation of national self-determination. If the Southeast Asian peoples attain that, it will be one of the preliminary steps toward building universal harmony. Please write when you have time.

Your younger brother,

Zedong

November 25, 1920

---

4. Li Shizeng, also known as Li Yuying, from Hebei Province, had been one of the founders of the *Xin shiji* (New Century) anarchist group in Paris in 1907. He played a more conservative role in political and academic affairs under the Guomindang beginning in the late 1920s, but at this time, as a leader of the returned students from France with a strong interest in education, he understandably appeared to Mao in a positive light.

Letter to Luo Xuezan [1]

(November 26, 1920)

Dear Rongxi,

Ever since I received your letter, I have read it over and over. Rereading it today, I was especially moved. I agree with every word you say. I have decided on a method for pursuing my studies which for the moment I need not explain; the essential point is that I shall do what you say. Your resolve to make determined efforts is admirable. Your present circumstances are quite good and are conducive to careful observation and profound reflection. I have learned that you have left school and are now working in a factory. Thus you will be able to find out how a factory is run in the West; besides, you can experience what Tolstoy said, "To earn your living through labor is true happiness!" Now I want very much to do manual work. In Shanghai, Mr. Li Shengxie[2] urged me to work in a factory, and my heart was somewhat moved [in this direction]. Now I think it is extremely miserable to lead a life in which you use only your brain and your mouth. I think I would really like to devote a period of time just to doing manual work. Mr. Li Shengxie was a student at First Normal School when he began working as a blacksmith at the Jiangnan Shipbuilding Factory. It only took him a couple of months to get quite familiar with his new trade. From earning nothing at all, he gradually progressed to a monthly salary of 12 *yuan*. His current address is 2 Yuyang Street, in the French Concession of Shanghai, and he is helping Mr. Chen Zhongpu[3] and others to organize the mechanics' union.[4] You can correspond with him. Qimin[5] is at Zhounan Girls' School on Tai'an Street. Dunyuan is working at *Tongsubao*[6] [Popular News] on Liwen Avenue. Educa-

1. On Luo Xuezan, also known as Luo Rongxi, see the note to Mao's letter to him dated August 11, 1918.

2. Li Shengxie (1897–1951), *zi* Yinxia, also known as Li Zhong, a Hunanese, was Mao's classmate at First Normal School. Around the time of the founding of the Chinese Communist Party he was involved in the workers' movement in Shanghai.

3. Chen Duxiu.

4. I.e., the Shanghai Mechanics' Union.

5. Qimin is the alternative name for Chen Shunong (1898–1970), a native of Changsha, Hunan. A graduate of Hunan First Normal School, he was a member of the New People's Study Society, and at this time was teaching at Zhounan Girls' School.

6. *Tongsubao* was the official newspaper of the Hunan Popular Education Office, publishing government announcements and official speeches. In September 1920, He

tion in Xiangtan is extremely decadent. Some of us who are currently staying in Hunan have organized the "Xiangtan Society for Promoting Education,"[7] but it has produced no great effect. The Association of Xiangtan Students of First Normal School[8] also plans to do something about it. I have not forwarded your letter there, but will do so a little later. The articles you sent on your journey have all appeared in the *Hunan Daily*, hence there is no need for me to forward those to them. I have already answered your letter once, and have now added a few recent thoughts of mine.

Your younger brother,

Zedong

November 26, 1920

Shuheng was appointed director of the Education Office, and became editor of the newspaper. He turned the newspaper into an advocate of the new culture movement, working closely with Mao and other members of the New People's Study Society, who offered editorial suggestions. It soon came under attack from more conservative elements of the bureaucracy. In May 1921, He Shuheng was dismissed from his post as Director and editor, and all members of the New People's Study Society on the staff then resigned. Zhou Shizhao quoted Mao as saying that the "*Tongsubao* was very well run that year." The paper was forced to close on June 15, 1921.

7. See the texts regarding this society dated July 27 and July 31, 1920.

8. This was an Association established by Mao, Luo Xuezan, and others in September 1917.

Letter to Luo Xuezan

(November 26, 1920)

Dear Rongxi,

Each and every one of the arguments put forward in your letter of July 14 is extremely penetrating. Physical health is indeed a big problem. You maintained that the reasons why Chinese scholars have paid for their studies with their lives are to be found in the extremely bad environment created by their families, society, and the schools. This is an objective reason, and you are assuredly correct. There is also, however, a subjective reason, which is psychological inertia. Once studying becomes a habit, one will go on studying without a rest. According to the principles of hygiene, for each hour of brain work, one needs to rest for fifteen minutes. I, however, often do not stop for three or four hours at a stretch, or even go on into the night. It is not because I love to do so and am not tired; in fact, I am really tired, and yet I do not stop. I do not think the laborers in China are physically weak, only the intellectuals are. To correct this, socially, we need to create a good environment, and individually, we need to form a habit of combining work and study, or at least of combining study and play. My life is really too tiring. When Mr. Huaizhong[1] was alive, he frequently urged me to take it easy and get more rest, but I would not credit his words. Now I have decided that for every two months of living in the city, I will spend one week in the countryside. This trip to Pingxiang is for the purpose of a rest. Henceforth, I plan to take a trip somewhere every two months.

You were able to explain the four types of error most thoroughly.[2] If only I could print 400 million copies of your words and distribute them to every person in China, all would be well. Sentiment is a very important part of human life, but we should not make judgments based on sentiment. To generalize from a part to the whole is a misapprehension of space. To generalize from one moment to eternity is a misunderstanding of time. To generalize from the subjective to the objective is a misunderstanding of both sentiment and space. All four are logical

1. Mao's former ethics teacher, Yang Changji, *zi* Huaizhong, who had died in January 1920. (See the obituary notice signed by Mao in this volume.)

2. In a letter of July 14, 1920, Luo Xuezan had defined four types of error: judging things on the basis of sentiment rather than of reality, considering only a part rather than the whole, failing to consider changes over time, and judging according to one's subjective beliefs.

errors. The intense arguments I have often got into recently with my friends all fall into these four categories. I am confident that my errors in the last three categories are few, but I am unable to avoid those of sentiment. The only area in which I cannot avoid making mistakes is that of sentiment. But I do not mean the same kind to which you refer. Mine tends to be personal. I often feel that, as regards certain people who address themselves to the public,[3] if I don't admire them, or if I find out that there are some shortcomings in their characters, I am disinclined to believe their arguments. I recognize that to dismiss someone's argument because of his personality is one of my shortcomings. I must strive to correct this from now on. I often make mistakes of the last three types, especially when I am talking excitedly and enthusiastically, even though I know I am wrong. This is called offending wilfully (sometimes in writing, too).

I hear that the "Work-Study Promotion Association" has been renamed "Work-Study World Association,"[4] but I do not know the details. Please write me about the organization, progress, administration, and so on. I have not received your correspondence yet. As far as exchanging newspapers, I can deal with this. Please continue to send me your articles. (Mail to Changsha Cultural Book Society, to my attention.)

The marriage system based on capitalism is absolutely undesirable. In theory, it offers legal protection to that most unreasonable thing, rape, while forbidding that most reasonable thing, free love. In practice, innumerable men and women around the world voice their discontent about this institution. I think the problem is that although many people have spoken out in opposition to the marriage system, no one has yet taken any action. The reason they do not act is quite simply "fear." So when I heard of the "union of Xiang and Cai,"[5] I rejoiced. Xiang and Cai have already smashed this "fear," and have carried out the rejec-

---

3. Mao refers here to *yanlunjie*, literally "discussion circles." It appears that he has in mind both those who write for the public, such as journalists, and those politicians and political activists who engage in public speaking — in other words, all those who seek to shape public opinion.

4. In February 1920 Li Fuchun, Li Weihan, and others formed the Work-Study Promotion Association in Paris. Most of its members were Hunanese members of the New People's Study Society in Paris on the work-study program. In August 1920 the name was changed to the Work-Study World Association. It ceased activities in June 1922 after the founding of the Chinese Youth Communist Party in Europe.

5. Cai Hesen went to France in 1919 on the work-study program. He returned to China in 1921, joined the Chinese Communist Party, and served as editor of its organ *Xiangdao zhoubao* (The Guide Weekly) in 1922. He remained in active correspondence with Mao during his stay in France, and urged on Mao the necessity of following the Russian model of proletarian dictatorship. At the same time, he and Xiang Jingyu took the lead in flouting social conventions. Mao alludes here to Cai's letter of May 28, 1920, stating that Cai and Xiang had concluded "a kind of union based on love" to give outward expression to their long-standing relationship. For the relevant passage, see *Xinmin xuehui ziliao,* p. 127.

tion of marriage. I think we should regard Xiang and Cai as our leaders and organize an "Alliance for the rejection of marriage." Those who have marriage contracts should break them (I am opposed to humanism). Those who do not have marriage contracts should not enter into them.

Once the alliance is formed, the members will immediately become the army of the alliance. At first, we can take a passive stance, "defending" outwardly against our enemies who oppose us. Inwardly, we should strive to straighten out the internal order, so that all members hold fast to the vow of "abolishing marriage." Later, we can turn to an active stance, beginning to carry out "propaganda" directed at the world, and to "attack" the enemies who oppose us, so that the whole human race will be liberated from the marriage system and all of them will become members of our alliance. This may sound like a joke, but actually the "miseries of the family" you bitterly regret cannot be eliminated without implementing such comical measures. Even if no one agrees with my method, my own "alliance of one" has already been concluded. I think that all those men and women who live under the marriage system are nothing but a "rape brigade." I have long since proclaimed that I would not join this rape brigade. If you don't agree with me, please put into writing your opposing views. Wishing you progress!

Your younger brother,

Zedong

November 26, 1920

Letter to Xiao Zizhang

(November 1920)[1]

Dear Brother Zizhang,

I have received all the letters and photos you sent me along the way. Thank you very much for your kindness. I haven't sent you even a single letter in reply. I apologize profoundly! Since the conclusion of the "Bansong Park Conference," resolutions have been taken to Europe by you and Zanzhou,[2] and the "Montargis Conference" records have been brought back to Asia by you and Zisheng.[3] Moreover, Zisheng himself has returned to China, and I will be able to see him in no time. How happy I am! I trust you are well and are still at the school. I hope that you will devote yourself to one field of study in France, selecting at least one field suited to your own nature and mastering it really thoroughly. I have felt recently that just relying on general knowledge is inadequate. I am angry with myself because I have not specialized in any one field. In the last two years, I have been distracted by many things and have not been able to work hard on my studies. I truly feel sharp regret at this and hope that you can give me some advice. The two publications put out by the Society are *Collected Correspondence of Members* and *Report on the Affairs of the Society*. At least three collections of correspondence will be issued this year. Please try to collect the manuscripts of new and old correspondence among Society members in France and mail them to me at the "Changsha Cultural Book Society," as material for the fourth and fifth issues. Thank you very much. (Please tell all the friends to use the Changsha Cultural Book Society as the mailing address from now on.)

Your younger brother,
Zedong

---

1. The original of this letter is undated. As noted by the editors of the *Wengao*, it must have been written in November because of Mao's allusion to the fact that he was engaged in editing the correspondence of the New People's Study Society. Xiao's letter to which he is replying was dated June 22, 1920.

2. Chen Shaoxiu.

3. Xiao Zisheng went to France in 1919 on the work-study program. He was delegated to return to China in the winter of 1920 immediately after the Montargis Conference to report on conditions in Europe to New People's Study Society members at home. He met with Mao in March 1921 in Changsha. In early 1923 he went to France again, returning in late 1924. For details of his early life, and relationship with Mao, see the note to the "Letter to a Friend" of July 1915.

Comments in Response to the Letter from Yi Lirong[1] to Mao Zedong and Peng Huang

(November 1920)

Lirong couldn't be more sincere and to the point when emphasizing the necessity for preparations in his discussion of the methods by which we should carry out our affairs. My point of view has been spelled out concretely in my letters to Sister Tao Siyong[2] and Brother Zhou Dunyuan,[3] and on my way back to Hunan I also talked to Lirong face-to-face several times.[4] As I see it, last year's movement to expel Zhang, and this year's autonomy movement were not, from the perspective of our members, political movements we deliberately chose to carry out. The reasons why we engaged in these two movements were simply, in the first case, to protest against this most unbearable despot, Zhang Jingyao. In the case of the autonomy movement, we simply hoped to establish a method (the Hunan constitution) for creating a better environment in Hunan, in which we might carry out some concrete preparatory work. When you come right down to it, both movements are only expedient measures in response to the current situation and definitely do not represent our basic views. Our proposals go way beyond these movements. At this point, just as Lirong said, "preparation" is important, but what about the "method" of preparation? This remains to be studied. Last year in Beijing, Chen Zanzhou was skeptical about "expelling Zhang." He said that since we believe in cosmopolitanism and fundamental

1. Yi Lirong (1898–), alternative names Runsan, Runsheng, and Yunshan, was a member of the New People's Study Society and a close friend of Mao's. Born in 1898 in Xiangtan, Hunan, Yi was a student at the Vocational Training School. He was one of the organizers of the Hunan Students' Association and was very active in the movement to oust Zhang Jingyao. He was one of the committee of three elected in the summer of 1920 to organize the Cultural Book Society, and at this time was first manager of the society's store. He also worked at Hunan Self-Study University, and was principal of Xiangjiang Middle School during this period. His letter to Mao and Peng Huang was written on June 30, 1920.

2. See above, Mao's letter of February 1920 to Tao Yi (Tao Siyong).

3. Zhou Shizhao, *zi* Dunyuan. For a detailed note see Mao's letter to him dated March 14, 1920.

4. In July 1920 Mao met Yi Lirong in Wuhan on his return from Shanghai, and they traveled back to Hunan by train together.

reform, we should not concern ourselves with small problems and petty affairs and should not "expel Zhang." There is naturally some truth in his words, but I hold a somewhat different view. The movement to "expel Zhang," the autonomy movement, and so on are also means to achieve a fundamental transformation, means that are most economical and most effective in dealing with our "present circumstances." But this is true on one condition, namely, that we always keep ourselves in a "supportive" role from beginning to end (i.e., from the outbreak of these movements to their conclusion). To put it bluntly, we must absolutely not jump on the political stage to grasp control. I think we members of the New People's Study Society should pursue the following ways to forge ahead:

1. Those who are abroad should do one of two things. Either they may pursue specialized fields of study so that there will be more scholars with a solid foundation, as Luo Rongxi and Xiao Zisheng propose to do. Or they should become active in planning and organizing for fundamental reforms, to establish a basis for reform, such as the Communist Party proposed by Cai Hesen.

2. Those who have not gone abroad can also be divided into two groups. Those who are currently studying in our province or elsewhere in the country should naturally take studying and acquiring skills as their main task. Those who are involved in social movements can initiate and carry out various valuable social movements and social undertakings from various directions. They may also devote some effort on the side to helping along those political movements deemed most efficient and most effective, such as "the autonomy movement," the "movement for universal suffrage," and so on. But on no account allow yourselves to be contaminated by old social habits; above all, do not forget our basic common ideals and plans. It is, of course, very important to unite the comrades, as suggested by Lirong. But our union is one of mutual aid. We should be open and frank with one another, we should have common goals, and we must never let any true comrade who shares our views feel that he does not fit in.

Zedong

Announcement of the Publication of the Collected Correspondence of Members of the New People's Study Society *(Volume 1)*

(November 1920)

Dear members:

This society has two publications, *Collected Correspondence of Members* and *Report on the Activities of the Society*. In addition to the semiannual *Report on the Activities of the Society*, the *Collected Correspondence of Members* provides a forum for our members to air and exchange views with each other. Any letters between our members, whether new or old, long or short, if they can be made public, are requested. Please mail to the Society either the original or an accurate duplicate so that a selection can be made for publication in the *Correspondence* after Volume 4. Letters that are not selected for publication will be returned. Those that are to be published may also be returned upon request. Please address your letters to Mr. Mao Zedong, Cultural Book Society, Chaozong Street, Changsha.

New People's Study Society

The Purpose and Procedures for the Publication of the Collected Correspondence of Members of the New People's Study Society *(Volume 1)*

(November 1920)

The pieces collected in Volume 1 are mostly old letters of the past year or two, yet they are quite important to the Society, as most of them pertain to promoting and developing group enterprises. With regard to the campaign for study in France, only Mr. Cai's[1] letter to all members of the Society is printed in this volume. As for the letters written by other members to Mr. Cai, he is expected to send the more important ones to us for selection and publication. *Collected Correspondence* is being printed to bring together fellow members who have a common purpose, to encourage discussion and study of ways to find one's place in and transform the world. It will be published irregularly, most likely once every two months. It is proper for the members to be perfectly open about their personal feelings and about the activities of the Society. However, ostentatious ranting is not appropriate. Therefore, other than one copy of the *Collected Correspondence* for each member, only a few dozen additional copies have been printed to be made available to comrades outside the Society who would like to read them. Because the Society has a tight budget, everyone, whether a member or a nonmember, is expected to pay a small fee to cover the printing costs. For those letters in the collection that discuss particular problems it is sincerely hoped that when they come out our members will further criticize and discuss them, so that the *Collected Correspondence* may become a forum for the membership, and each issue may become richer, more profound, and more progressive than the previous one. This would be truly excellent.

1. Cai Hesen.

On the Readers Club by Colleagues of the Cultural Book Society

(November 1920)

Recently a number of people have advocated a "Readers Club." This strikes us as an excellent idea. It has three advantages: (1) When one person buys a book, he pays one *yuan* just to read a one *yuan* book. If five or even ten people organize a readers club to buy books, every member can read 10 *yuan* worth of books for one *yuan*. For a very small financial outlay, the return in learning is great. (2) In the Chinese "closed-door research method," each individual hides behind his closed doors to study, never exchanging opinions, never criticizing others, never correcting his own work. This is really a very bad habit. It would be better to invite some compatible friends to set up a small readers club and study together. For instance, after finishing this book you, dear reader, are bound to have many comments, or questions, or new ideas, that you would like to expound or discuss. This little readers club would provide you an opportunity to speak out and debate. (3) Everyone wants to read the newspapers. This is a good way to become a "scholar who knows everything in the world without leaving his doorway."[1] There are many students today who do not read the newspapers because the schools cannot afford to buy many newspapers, and there are too few copies of the ones they do get. It would be wonderful if each class could set up its own readers club. If every person put in just a few dimes per month, the sum total would be quite significant. In addition to purchasing books, they could subscribe to at least one newspaper, maybe several. And so, they could instantly become all-knowing "scholars" without leaving their rooms. Wouldn't that be excellent? If you, sir, think these advantages are worth considering, why don't you organize a "readers club" yourself? If you want newly published books, papers, or magazines on the new thought, our Book Society has them all. We are looking forward to your orders.

1. This is a common popular saying expressing respect for the capacities of the literati.

Preface to Collected Correspondence of Members of the New People's Study Society *(Volume 2)*

(November 30, 1920)

This Volume 2 of *Collected Correspondence of Members of the New People's Study Society* is a collection of twenty-eight letters of members of the Society. The most important are the following: one on planning for women's development, and another that discusses the problems of women in their work-study program in France and the problem of communication among women, both by Xiang Jingyu; one by Ouyang Ze on the common spirit of the New People's Study Society; one by Mao Zedong maintaining that the New People's Study Society should adopt an attitude of latent potentiality; one by Xiao Zizhang reporting on the life of our members, both male and female, in France; one by Yi Lirong maintaining that we must be prepared before we act; one by Luo Aojie urging the Society to oppose the vulgar and strive for the highest values; one by Mao Zedong on Hunan self-rule and his suggestion that the Society members should seek a common ideology; one by Zhang Guoji on the activities of the Society, and another, also by him, giving an account of the Hunanese in Southeast Asia; one by Mao Zedong discussing the attitude that the Hunanese should adopt in going to Southeast Asia, in which he urges the members to go to Southeast Asia and work for culture and nation-building there; one by Zhang Guoji telling an unusual story from Southeast Asia; one by Luo Xuezan hoping that fellow members will pay attention to physical education, dispel four types of myths and solve family problems; one by Mao Zedong proposing to organize an alliance to reject marriage. The above-mentioned letters are beneficial either to cultivating healthy minds and bodies, or to the discussion of academic problems, or to progress in the Society's activities. Furthermore, they can all make the collective life of the membership more interesting. The rest of the letters, some of which discuss directions to take, while some talk about concrete methods, and others are reports on individual situations, are presented here as a representative sample of the whole.

Editor, November 30, 1920

Bibliographic Note

In this volume, Mao mentions the writings of several hundred individuals from Chinese history and literature. For most of them, the references in the notes give only the title, and on occasion the volume or *juan* number of the work in question, so as to enable those with a knowledge of Chinese to locate the relevant passages. To have listed here all these names and titles alone would have taken an inordinate amount of space, and would have been of limited utility. We therefore include below only those works in Chinese for which a specific edition is cited in the notes, as well as items in Western languages, and translations of Chinese texts. For the convenience of the reader, we have repeated here the short titles for certain works, which are given on the first appearance of each entry in the notes.

Analects, in Legge, Vol. I.

Book of Poetry, in Legge, Vol. IV.

Book of Historical Documents, in Legge, Vol. III.

Brockdorff-Rantzau, Ulrich Karl Christian, Graf von, *Dokumente und Gedanken um Versailles*. Berlin: Verlag für Kulturpolitik, 1925.

Cao Xueqin, *Honglou meng* (Dream of the Red Chamber) tr. David Hawkes, under the alternative title *The Story of the Stone*. Penguin: Harmondsworth, 1973–1980.

Couvreur, Séraphin, *Mémoires sur les bienséances et les cérémonies*. (Translation of the *Liji* or Book of Rites) Paris: Cathasia, 1950.

Couvreur, Séraphin, *Les quatre livres*. Paris: Cathasia, n.d.

Creel, H.G., *Chinese Thought from Confucius to Mao Tse-tung*. London: Eyre and Spottiswoode, 1954.

Day, M. Henri, *Máo Zédōng 1917–1927. Documents*. Stockholm: University of Stockholm, 1975 (Skriftserien för Orientaliska Studier no. 14).

Doctrine of the Mean, in Legge, Vol. I.

Duyvendak, J.J.L. *The Book of Lord Shang* (translation of *Shangjun shu*). London: Arthur Probsthain, 1928.

Er Cheng ji (Collected Writings of the Two Chengs). (Beijing: Zhonghua shuju, 1981.)

Esherick, Joseph, *Reform and Revolution in China. The 1911 Revolution in Hunan and Hubei*. Berkeley: University of California Press, 1976.

Feuerwerker, Albert, *China's Early Industrialization. Sheng Hsuan-huai 1844–1916 and Mandarin Enterprise*. Cambridge, Mass.: Harvard University Press, 1958.

Fukuzawa Yukichi, *An Outline of a Theory of Civilization*. (Tokyo: Sophia University, 1973), translated by David A. Dilworth and G. Cameron Hurst.

Graham, Angus (tr.), *The Book of Lieh-tzu*. London: John Murray, 1960.

Graham, Angus, *Chuang-tzu. The Seven Inner Chapters and Other Writings from the Book Chuang-tzu*. London: Allen & Unwin, 1981. (Short title: Angus Graham, *Chuang-tzu.)*

Great Learning, in Legge, Vol. I.

Han Yu, *Changli xiansheng shi jizhu* (Poems of Han Yu collected and annotated), ed. Gu Sili. Reprinted Taibei: Xuesheng shuju [1967].

Han Yu, *Changli Xiansheng ji* (Collected Works of Han Yu). (Short title: Han Yu, *Collected Works.*) (All page references are to the *Hanfenlou* edition published by the Commercial Press.)

Hsüeh Chün-tu, *Huang Hsing and the Chinese Revolution.* Stanford: Stanford University Press, 1961.

Legge, *The Chinese Classics.* Vol. I, *Confucian Analects, The Great Learning, The Doctrine of the Mean.* Vol. II, *The Works of Mencius.* Vol. III, *The Shoo King [shujing] or the Book of Historical Documents.* Vol. IV, *The She King [shijing] or the Book of Poetry.* Vol. V, *The Ch'un Ts'ew [chunqiu] with the Tso Chuen [Zuo zhuan].* Hong Kong: Hong Kong University Press, 1960.

Li Yu-ning (ed.), *Shang Yang's Reforms and State Control in China.* White Plains, N.Y.: M.E. Sharpe, 1977.

Li Jui [Li Rui], *The Early Revolutionary Activities of Comrade Mao Tse-tung.* Tr. Anthony W. Sariti. White Plains: M.E. Sharpe, 1977. (Short title: Li Jui, *Early Mao.*)

Mao Zedong ji (Collected Writings of Mao Zedong), ed. Takeuchi Minoru. 10 vols. Tokyo: Hokubōsha, 1970–1972; second edition, Tokyo: Sōsōsha, 1983.

Mao Zedong ji. Bujuan (Supplement to the Collected Writings of Mao Zedong), ed. Takeuchi Minoru. 10 vols. Tokyo: Sōsōsha, 1983–1986.

Mao Zedong zaoqi wengao, 1912.6–1920.11 (Draft Writings by Mao Zedong for the Early Period, June 1912-November 1920), ed. Department for Research on Party Literature of the Central Committee of the Chinese Communist Party and Editorial Group for *Mao Zedong zaoqi wengao* of the Hunan Provincial Party Committee of the Chinese Communist Party. Changsha: Hunan Chubanshe, 1991.

Mao Zedong, *Selected Works of Mao Tse-tung,* Vols. I-IV. Peking: Foreign languages Press, 1960–1965.

Mao Zedong shici duilian jizhu (Annotated Edition of Mao Zedong's Poems and Couplets). Changsha: Hunan wenyi chubanshe, 1991 (Short title: Mao Zedong, *Poems and Couplets*).

McDonald, Angus. W., *The Urban Origins of Rural Revolution. Elites and the Masses in Hunan Province, China, 1911–1927.* Berkeley: University of California Press, 1978.

Mencius, in Legge, Vol. II.

Nishi Moroo, *Shixue zhizhen* (Guide to Practical Studies). Tokyo: Huabei yishuju, 28th year of Guangxu [1902].

Paulsen, Friedrich, *System der Ethik.* 2 vols. Stuttgart and Berlin: J.G. Cotta'sche Buchhandlung Nachfolger, various editions. The translation by Frank Thilly (Friedrich Paulsen, *A System of Ethics.* New York and Chicago: Charles Scribner's Sons, 1899) was made from the third German edition. The Japanese translation, by Kanie Yoshimaru and others *(Rinrigaku taikei.* Tokyo: Hakubunkan, 37th year of the Meiji Era [1904]), was made from the original German, but like Thilly's English version, omitted Book IV, on the state and forms of social life. Cai Yuanpei, in his Chinese version *(Lunlixue yuanli.* Shanghai: Commercial Press, 1909), translated, as indicated in note 22 to the Introduction to this volume, only Book II.

Shiji (Records of the Historian). Extracts, tr. Yang Hsien-yi and Gladys Yang. Hong Kong: The Commercial Press, 1974. (Short title: *Records of the Historian.*)

Siao-yu, *Mao Tse-tung and I Were Beggars.* Syracuse: Syracuse University Press, 1959.

Snow, Edgar, *Red Star over China.* London: Gollancz, 1937.

Sun Yatsen, *San Min Chu I.* The Three Principles of the People. (Tr. Frank W. Price.) Shanghai: China Committee, Institute of Pacific Relations, 1927.

Temperley, H.W.V., *A History of the Peace Conference of Paris.* London: Henry Frowde and Hodder and Stoughton, 1920.

von Zach, Erwin, *Die chinesische Anthologie*. Cambridge: Mass.: Harvard University Press, 1958.

von Zach, Erwin, *Han Yus poetische Werke*. Cambridge, Mass.: Harvard University Press, 1952.

Wieger Léon, *Les péres du systéme taoïste*. Paris: Cathasia, 1950. (A translation of the *Laozi, Liezi,* and *Zhuangzi.)*

Yang Changji wenji (Collected writings of Yang Changji). Changsha: Hunan Jiaoyu Chubanshe, 1983.

Zuo zhuan, in Legge, Vol. V.

Index

About the Editor

Stuart R. Schram was born in Excelsior, Minnesota, in 1924. After graduating from the University of Minnesota in physics, he took his Ph.D. in political science at Columbia University. From 1954 to 1967, he conducted research at the Fondation Nationale des Sciences Politiques in Paris, and from 1968 until 1989, he was Professor of Politics with reference to China at the School of Oriental and African Studies, University of London. Since 1989, he has worked at the Fairbank Center, Harvard University, on the edition of Mao Zedong's pre-1949 writings of which this is the first volume.

His research has dealt with Leninist theories and their application in Asia, Chinese history and politics in the twentieth century, and the influence of the Chinese tradition on the theory and practice of the state in China. His works include *Mao Tse-tung* (1967), *The Political Thought of Mao Tse-tung* (1969), *Marxism and Asia* (in collaboration with Hélène Carrère d'Encausse) (1969), *Ideology and Policy in China since the Third Plenum, 1978–1984* (1984), and *The Thought of Mao Tse-tung* (1989). He has also edited a volume entitled *Foundations and Limits of State Power in China* (1987). *Mao Tse-tung* and *The Thought of Mao Tse-tung* have been translated into Chinese and published in Beijing.